OVERLAND WEST

The Story of the
Oregon and California Trails

VOLUME I

1812–1848

"Pilgrims of the Plains," by Alfred R. Waud, *Harper's Weekly,* December 23, 1871.

SO RUGGED

and

MOUNTAINOUS

Blazing the Trails to

Oregon and California

1812–1848

WILL BAGLEY

UNIVERSITY OF OKLAHOMA PRESS ❀ NORMAN

ALSO BY WILL BAGLEY

A Road from El Dorado: The 1848 Trail Journal of Ephraim Green

Frontiersman: Abner Blackburn's Narrative

West from Fort Bridger: The Pioneering of Immigrant Trails across Utah, 1846–1850 (with Harold Schindler)

This Is the Place: A Crossroads of Utah's Past (with Pat Bagley)

The Pioneer Camp of the Saints: The 1846 and 1847 Mormon Trail Journals of Thomas Bullock

Scoundrel's Tale: The Samuel Brannan Papers

Army of Israel: Mormon Battalion Narratives (with David L. Bigler)

Blood of the Prophets: Brigham Young and the Massacre at Mountain Meadows

Always a Cowboy: Judge Wilson McCarthy and the Rescue of the Denver & Rio Grande Western Railroad

Innocent Blood: Essential Narratives of the Mountain Meadows Massacre (with David L. Bigler)

Library of Congress Cataloging-in-Publication Data

Bagley, Will, 1950–
    Overland West : blazing the trails to Oregon and California, 1812–1848 / Will Bagley.
       p. cm.
    Includes bibliographical references and index.
    ISBN 978-0-8061-4103-9 (v. 1 : hardcover : alk. paper)—ISBN 978-0-87062-381-3 (v. 1 : special edition : alk. paper). 1. Oregon National Historic Trail—History. 2. California National Historic Trail—History. 3. West (U.S.)—Description and travel. 4. Frontier and pioneer life—Oregon National Historic Trail. 5. Frontier and pioneer life—California National Historic Trail. 6. West (U.S.)—History—To 1848. 7. West (U.S.)—History—1848–1860. 8. Overland journeys to the Pacific. I. Title.
    F597.B15 2010
    978'.02—dc22

2009028667

1 2 3 4 5 6 7 8 9 10

For
Gregory M. Franzwa

I did not invite the Americans to come. To be frank, I greatly regretted their coming, but they did come, covered with the dust of travel, worn out by fatigue, hardships and dangers incident to a very long and perilous journey. They came without food or raiment. I fed and clothed them. The Bible tells me that if my enemy is hungry, I must feed him, if naked, I must clothe him, but these destitute men and helpless women and children were not my enemies, and I am sure that God does not want me to do more for my enemies than these.

John McLoughlin, quoted in
Robert Cummings Johnson, *John McLoughlin: Father of Oregon,* 252

When I wrote you last April from the state of "Messuri" we were then about to start out on a long, tedious, & perilous journey. . . . I may as well tell you before hand that if I should mention but a few of the curiosities, that I have seen it will appear almost as bad to you as "Gulliver's Travels." But I will write nothing but the truth.

Robert Caufield to "Dear brother and sister,"
1 April 1848, Oregon Historical Society

The migration of a large body of men, women, and children across the Continent to Oregon was, in the year 1843, strictly an experiment not only in respect to the numbers, but to the outfit of the migrating party. Before that date two or three missionaries had performed the journey on horseback, driving a few cows with them. Three or four wagons drawn by oxen had reached Fort Hall, on Snake river, but it was the honest opinion of most of those who had traveled the route down Snake river that no large number of cattle could be subsisted on its scanty pasturage, or wagons taken over a route so rugged and mountainous.

Jesse Applegate, "A Day with the Cow Column in 1843,"
Overland Monthly (August 1868), 127

CONTENTS

Illustrations

MAPS

PREFACE

All peoples have a myth, and as Americans we love our legends but often loathe our history. Many of us prefer to view our past more as a heroic parable than as a complicated and contentious record of the human experience. Few epochs in the history of the United States have achieved a status as legendary as the creation of a continental nation from a few struggling Spanish, French, English, and Dutch colonies on the borderlands of today's Southwest and along a narrow strip of the Atlantic seaboard. The story of the overland trails that brought more than a half million new settlers to the American West between 1840 and 1870 is central to this beloved tradition.[1] Like all legends, it is a powerful mix of fact and fable.

During much of the twentieth century, movies and popular histories cast the achievements of covered-wagon families as pageant celebrating the triumph of civilization over savagery. This heroic epic dramatized the sacrifices of the noble pioneers, but it ignored the grim toll overland emigration took on the people who already called the region their native home. The traditional story ignored the wider and less comforting consequences of this swift, violent, and transformative saga. As historian Elliott West observed, the myth of the pioneers is as out of place on the historic trails as an ox would be in an opera house. If we accord such a fable "the forged authority of history," West observed, "the stories we write and call history will be woefully incomplete, hopelessly simplistic, and shamefully neglectful of others who were there."[2]

The truth about our nation's expansion is powerful enough. "This great migration across the American continent-ocean had no equal in modern times," wrote

---

[1] John D. Unruh estimated that 253,397 people traveled overland to the Far West between 1840 and 1860. Merrill J. Mattes revised his "most defensible" 1978 estimate of 350,000 travelers using the Platte River Road between 1841 and 1866 to 500,000; in 1994, Mattes raised the number to 525,000. See Mattes, "Potholes in the Great Platte River Road," 10.

[2] West, "American Pathways," 28–29, 31.

historian Daniel J. Boorstin, quoting Bayard Taylor's observation that the cavalcade to the West more than matched "the great military expeditions of the Middle Ages in magnitude, peril, and adventure."[3] The saga of the Oregon and California Trails is Homeric in its dimensions and significance. It is the story of a remarkable transformation—for when the era began, every acre of land between the Kansas River and the Pacific Crest belonged to Indian peoples. When it ended three decades later, they owned almost none of it. Even the men and women who saw it all and made it happen—those who built the cities, towns, farms, ranches, mines, and railroads and created the modern West—could hardly believe what they had witnessed with their own eyes, for they had seen a new world created and another utterly devastated. The overland trails were the engine that drove this astonishing change, and the purpose of this work is to explain why and how it happened.

I am a public historian. Ten years ago, I contracted with Superintendent Jere Krakow of the National Park Service's Long Distance Trails Office to conduct a historic resource study to support the planning, development, and protection of the congressionally created Oregon and California National Historic Trails. The project's purpose was to survey the historic record of the two trails, create a new body of research materials, and synthesize the information into a comprehensive narrative of the trails. The study generated four public documents, which will (I hope) be available on the National Trails System's website: a historic resource study, "'The Change Time Has Wrought': The Legacy of the Oregon and California Trails"; a social history, "'A Long, Rugged, and Weary Road': Life on the Oregon and California Trails"; a chronological narrative, "'The Long and Arduous Journey': The Story of the Oregon and California Trails, 1840 to 1870"; and a bibliography.

So for many years I have been engaged in a great adventure: seeking out the journals, recollections, histories, government documents, maps, photographs and works of art, newspapers and periodicals, folk songs, films, physical remnants, and lost trails that constitute the historic record of the Oregon and California National Historic Trails. While this was a dream job, it was intimidating and disheartening, since the more I grasped the size and complexity of these records, the less I could ever hope to master them all. The best a hardworking chronicler can do with such an immense story is to contribute to the understanding of a great historic legacy and hope to create a work that will inspire and assist future storytellers and scholars seeking to create new perspectives on this significant period.

---

[3] Boorstin, *The Americans*, 57.

To bring this story to a wider audience, I have extensively rewritten these studies into a four-volume work, *Overland West: The Story of the Oregon and California Trails.*[4] This volume, *So Rugged and Mountainous: Blazing the Trails to Oregon and California, 1812–1848,* tells the story of the men, women, and children who first traveled the trails from the Missouri to the Pacific and opened all the major elements of the northern overland wagon roads in eight short years. Subsequent volumes cover the California gold rush and the creation of the mining West, the revolutionary changes and growing conflict along the trails that marked the 1850s, and the war for the "Medicine Road" during the 1860s, when America's last free and independent Indians rose up to defend their homelands.

Some of America's best writers have told this tale. Francis Parkman, Abigail Scott Duniway, Alonzo Delano, Horace Greeley, Mark Twain, and Joaquin Miller wrote lively eyewitness reports about the trail. Novelists and historians as diverse and talented as Washington Irving, Hubert Howe Bancroft, Frances Fuller Victor, Josiah Royce, Jack London, Bernard DeVoto, Henry Nash Smith, Frederick Merk, Charles L. Camp, Irene Paden, George R. Stewart, A. B. Guthrie, Jay Monaghan, Dale L. Morgan, Fawn Brodie, Vardis Fisher, Thomas Berger, David Dary, James Welch, Wallace Stegner, and Alvin M. Josephy have told all or part of this story—and they have told it very well. My hope is to recast this old tale in a new and more complete fashion. In this spirit, this study draws on more than five hundred overland narratives unknown to scholars before 1988. The book devotes more attention to forgotten figures, such as Richard Grant, James Sinclair, Samuel J. Hensley, Levi Scott, and Narcissa Vasquez, who made great contributions to trail history, than to more celebrated characters such as Narcissa Whitman, Jim Bridger, and Jesse Applegate. Wherever possible, I have used the voices of overlooked men and women to bring a fresh perspective to these pages.

At the same time, I realize that no historian should ignore the classic stories or their tellers. The chronicles of the Donner party disaster and the tragedy of the Sager children have endured so long not only because they tell us much about what it means to be an American but because they are compelling sagas that speak to the heart of the human condition.

Early on I realized how difficult it would be to write a comprehensive history of three decades of overland travel. John Unruh's 1979 masterwork, *The Plains Across: The Overland Emigrants and the Trans-Mississippi West, 1840–1860,* remains the definitive social history: it brilliantly set the standard against which all subsequent

---

[4] The series will encompass a century, from 1812 to 1912. I based these dates on Robert Stuart's discovery on South Pass in 1812 and on the last evidence of wagons using the Lander Cutoff of the Oregon Trail in 1914.

work on the subject must be judged, including this one. Recognizing this, I have used *The Plains Across* as the baseline, hoping to supplement Unruh's masterpiece with the results of three decades of subsequent research and writing.

Overland West deals with both the Oregon Trail and the California Road, which share much history and geography. It quotes people who used the Mormon Trail, since daily life was much the same for everyone who crossed the plains. But each trail was also a distinct entity. This study traces the development of the overland wagon roads and tracks the organic evolution of these trails, each of which took on an identity all its own: the characters of the modern states they helped create reflect many of the social and economic distinctions that set the three trails apart.

The opening of a wagon road to the Far West began a transformation far greater than anyone in America could imagine. One of this story's challenges is that it has a cast not of thousands, but a cast of more than five hundred thousand—the men, women, and children who made their way to Oregon and California with wagons, carts, or mule trains between 1840 and 1870. Each had their story, and their ordeals and triumphs. From the moment the first wagon train set out for the West Coast in 1841, overland travelers often recognized that the trek would be the most significant event of their lives: many understood they were part of an enterprise that would change the course of American history and our nation's life. A few wrote letters from the trail or kept journals, and some later recorded what they recalled of their experiences. These narratives fall into three categories: "starkly contemporary records," such as diaries and letters; "travel narratives written and published soon after the event"; and "the often richly-colored reminiscences which look back down the years," Dale L. Morgan concluded.[5] Naturally, the contemporary record captures the experience most accurately, while those trail veterans who lived into the twentieth century achieved the status of honored pioneers, and they often transformed their youthful adventures to match the legend and the triumphal celebration of America's conquest of the West.

A more realistic understanding of this history developed with the centennial of the California gold rush. Over the next six decades Americans gained a deeper appreciation of the era as many of us realized that this was not a simple chronicle of inevitable progress but one of both triumph and tragedy. The settlement of the American West over three decades was an overwhelming achievement, especially in light of the sacrifices that made it possible. Yet the pioneers' victory came at the

---

[5] Morgan, *In Pursuit of the Golden Dream*, vii. Mattes, *Platte River Road Narratives*, 9, distinguished between diaries and journals, but this study uses the terms interchangeably.

cost of the freedom of the West's original inhabitants and led to the destruction of resources upon which their lives depended. It is a hard story: as a brilliant young scholar observed, "The violent transformation of Indian lands and lives" characterized American expansionism, just as violence drove the "rapid accumulation of new resources, territories, and subject peoples" that the trails made possible.[6] This is a story of the growing conflict and a bitter conquest whose consequences still haunt the American West.

This complex, compelling, and controversial tale encompasses national expansion and Manifest Destiny, the development and destruction of natural resources, and peaceful encounters and violent clashes between peoples and cultures in a struggle to determine who would control America's future. It raises this question: whose story is it and how should it properly be told? Traditionally, the pioneers and their descendants made the story their own and told it as a chronicle of heroism, triumph, and sacrifice; the perspectives of the first Spanish and French settlers and the native peoples they displaced were long ignored. With little regard for justice or the facts, they made the Indian Nations of the Great Plains, Rocky Mountains, Great Basin, Oregon, and California the villains of the pioneer era.

Deborah A. Miranda recently described how she reclaimed her native identity, and from that day on vowed to let that voice speak, which led her to argue "with my children's teachers over school curricula such as 'The Oregon Trail' unit and Columbus Day celebrations." Her book told Jane Waite's story of how Anapao, her third-grade son, was assigned to write a diary imagining his family had traveled the Oregon Trail. "I know we couldn't have been, plus we weren't allowed there anyway," he said.[7] The traditional presentation of trail history justifies these views, since the central role of Native peoples is so often marginalized.

The failure, however, lies not in our history but in how we have taught and told that history. A more encompassing perspective must show that without the cooperation and support of dozens of tribes, overland emigration would have been impossible. It was not Marcus Whitman who led the first American wagons over the Blue Mountains, but Stickus, a Cayuse leader respected by Anglos and Indians alike. A party of Wyandotte Indians from present-day Kansas joined the rush for California in 1849, and members of one tribe made up such a large a part of a company from today's Oklahoma that they left their name on the Cherokee Trail, the road they blazed from the Arkansas River to Fort Bridger that became a key component of the California Trail. Native peoples dominate this story from

---

[6] Blackhawk, *Violence over the Land,* 9.
[7] Seale and Slapin, *A Broken Flute,* 1, 13.

its beginning to its end: an Indian family accompanied the Bidwell-Bartleson party—the very first wagon train—from Fort Laramie to Green River in 1841, and when Lakota warriors attacked the corralled wagons of the Lamoreaux-Lajeunesse train near the ruins of Fort Caspar in 1868, Lamoreaux's pregnant wife confronted them and demanded that they stop shooting at her children: "I am Woman Dress, sister of your chief, Gall," she shouted. "Beware lest you harm me! I have my children here. Go away or you will rue it!"[8] Such stories place Indians in their rightful place at the center of trail history, not on its margins.

Overland West seeks to tell an American story that includes all the peoples— Indians, whites, blacks, Hispanics, Polynesians, and Asians; male and female, young and old—whose lives the road across the plains transformed. As such, it is not a legend with heroes or villains, culprits or victims; it is a story of people who struggled to do the best they could for themselves and their families in a time and place marked by hardship, peril, and rapid change. The history of America's overland wagon roads to Oregon and California is a dramatic record of sacrifice and suffering, endurance and failure, death and survival, and the small victories and great defeats that marked the lives of the people who followed these trails to new lives in the West: it is not only a great American epic but an enduring tribute to the human spirit.

---

[8] Guenther, "Pioneers Extraordinaire," 9–10.

Editorial Procedures

For published trail narratives, this study attempts to cite the most easily accessible source, so the reader will find repeated references to comprehensive compilations of primary documents such as Kenneth L. Holmes's *Covered Wagon Women,* Doyce Nunis's *The Bidwell Bartleson Party,* and Dale L. Morgan's *Overland in 1846.* When quoting from handwritten documents, I have tried to represent the primary records in a readable format. With the following exceptions, quotations preserve the grammar, spelling, and style of the originals. I have capitalized the first letters of sentences and personal names and added periods to the ends of sentences and other punctuation where needed for clarity. Commas employed in the place of periods are converted to periods. When the case used in a manuscript is ambiguous, I followed standard capitalization. I have made little use of ellipses and occasionally omit intervening text from quotations when two separate statements are divided by attribution, such as "so-and-so said." Occasionally I resequenced sections of quotations divided by attribution to improve the narrative flow. Where I have worked from the original sources, I have done my best to produce transcriptions that are as accurate as possible, but this arduous task does not encourage any claim to infallibility.

I have only used "*sic*" when the item in question is especially significant and could be easily mistaken for a typo. I have corrected a few obvious transcription errors. Brackets enclose added letters, missing words, and conjectural readings. I placed interlined insertions in their logical location in the text. The abbreviations A.M. and P.M. are set in small capitals. I have italicized underlined text and omitted crossed-out text. Cost equivalents were made using inflation calculators available on the internet.

The selected bibliography contains a complete listing of all the abbreviations, primary sources (including interviews), secondary sources (including books, articles, government documents, theses and dissertations), and maps referenced in the footnotes and full publication information about them. I have italicized book titles and put article, website, thesis, and dissertation titles in quotation marks. Manuscript citations appear in plain text without quotation marks. Footnote citations are as short as possible, using only author, title, date, and/or page number. Where available, newspaper citations are to page/column: for example, 2/3.

To identify geographic locations, I use the toponyms contemporary with the events described and have avoided using later names until they were given. For example, I use "Truckee Lake" and "Truckee Pass" for the years before 1847 instead of "Donner Lake" and "Donner Pass." *So Rugged and Mountainous* gives preference to documents created by people who went west before 1849, but for elements of the trail experience that did not change significantly from decade to decade, I have included later sources. After delving into these narratives for more than a quarter century, I find my admiration for the simple eloquence of these voices from the dust knows no bounds: wherever possible I have tried to let these people tell their own stories.

SO RUGGED

and

MOUNTAINOUS

Blazing the Trails to
Oregon and California
1812–1848

PROLOGUE

Bald eagles circled high above the painted canvas tops of the first wagons to cross the Missouri River on their way to the Far West. These keen-eyed raptors had watched a thousand generations of humans—their only natural predators—move along the waterways below as they made their seasonal rounds. The two-legged travelers often carried valuable goods—turquoise, watertight baskets, pottery, fur, buffalo robes, salt, dried fish, seeds, and feathers—that spread to trading centers as far away as the Mandan and Hidatsa villages far up the Missouri, the ancient pueblos on the Pecos, and The Dalles on the Columbia. Other goods reached sites such as South Pass in the Shoshone and Absaroka lands, where the peoples of the Northwest and the Great Basin bartered with traders from the Great Plains. Over time this transcontinental enterprise expanded to include new traders and their treasures, such as the Spaniards who brought guns and horses to the Rio Grande. Many of the Native peoples honored the eagle, whose feathers ranked high among the prized goods in this vast trade network. Their expeditions regularly crossed the continent, but even with an eagle's keen eyes, before 1840 the paths worn by human feet, dog travois, and horses' hooves were scarcely visible west of the Missouri River.

John James Audubon saw bald eagles nesting near Independence, Missouri, in 1843. To this day the state provides a home to hundreds of nesting pairs. Like the Indians, the light-skinned newcomers crossing the river that year recognized the eagle as a potent symbol. When the first American settlers set out for the Pacific, they carried gold coins bearing the eagle's image. In their tradition, too, the eagle signified freedom and power. After seeing one of his nation's emblems, a traveler at Scotts Bluff in 1846 opened his family bible to a familiar passage in Job: "Doth the eagle mount up at they command, and make her nest on high? She dwelleth and abideth on the rock, upon the crag of the rock, and the strong place. From thence she seeketh the prey, and her eyes behold afar off."[1]

---

[1] Thornton, *Oregon and California in 1848,* 230, quoting Job 39:27.

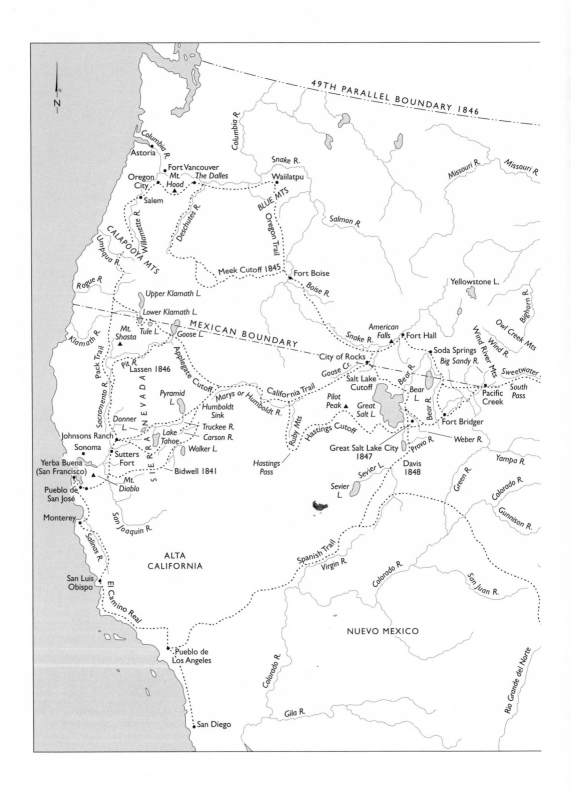

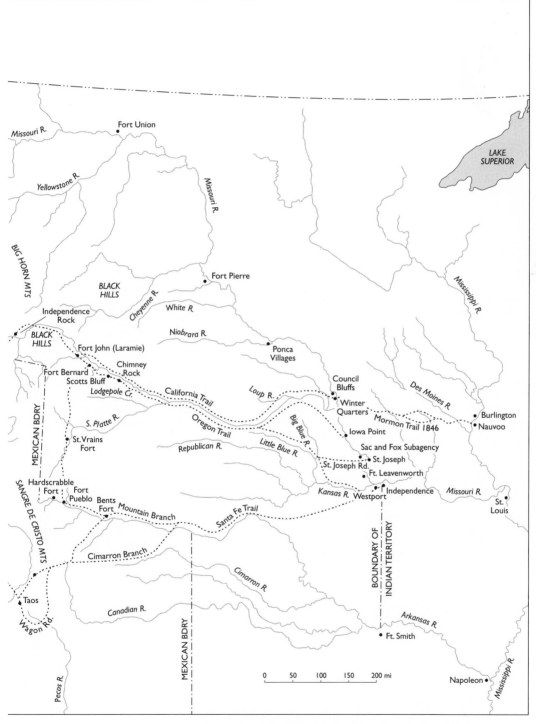

The Oregon and California Trails, 1848. Based on map from
Dale L. Morgan, ed., in *Overland in 1846: Diaries and Letters of the
California-Oregon Trail*, vol. 2. Georgetown, Calif.: The Talisman
Press, 1963. Courtesy Talisman Press Collection, California
State Library.

From on high, eagles had watched human hunters move across the landscape for millennia, their paths dictated by river courses. Three great river systems— the Missouri, the Platte, and the Arkansas—flow from the eastern slopes of the Rocky Mountains. As Europeans explored westward, all three rivers played key roles, but the central location and flat terrain of the Platte River Valley and its tributaries created a natural highway. The shallow but swift river did not lend itself to navigation by canoe or keelboat, but once fur hunters followed the well-worn paths up both its banks, they found that the North Platte and its alpine tributary, the Sweetwater, led to the portal of the Rocky Mountains at South Pass. They called it the best natural road in the world, and for decades the trail up the Platte was the only practical corridor over the Continental Divide for traders and travelers bound for the rivers of the West—the Green, the Bear, the Snake, the Humboldt, the Sacramento, the Columbia, and the Willamette.

There never was a single trail to Oregon or California. From the Missouri River, emigrants left "jumping off" points at Independence, Westport, Fort Leavenworth, or Council Bluffs along the old fur caravan roads soon known as the Oregon Trail. The several routes became a single cord approaching South Pass, but the rope began to unravel again beyond the divide at the Parting of the Ways. Travelers had to make the first of many hard choices between a difficult shortcut or a longer, safer route. West from Fort Bridger, guides and government explorers were constantly seeking better ways through the deserts of the Great Basin and across the palisades of the Sierra Nevada. Conditions changed with the seasons, and the trails evolved dynamically, for the weather could transform a good route into a bad one in a single afternoon.

Eagles nesting along the Missouri saw more signs of human presence in 1840 than their ancestors had over decades. Towns had grown up at the edge of the Great Plains, and barges and steamboats dodged the sandbars and sawyers of the Big Muddy. These raw settlements served as supply depots for traders and trappers heading west in search of furs and fortunes, scientists sent to chart unknown lands, visionaries with elaborate schemes for personal or national aggrandizement, and missionaries eager to carry the word of their god to the continent's Native peoples. Some of this traffic went south on the well-established Santa Fe Trail to New Mexico, but most settlers headed to the Far West were bound for the Oregon Country. The first of them followed a faint trace that crossed broad prairies to the natural road up the Platte River.

Eagles are lazy and opportunistic: they migrate only when they get hungry, such as when freezing rivers make such an unprofitable expenditure of energy absolutely necessary. Though no single eagle ever followed the trail west to

Oregon or California, the majestic raptors soared above the entire route from a unique and lofty vantage point. Since those traces followed rivers whenever possible, eagles in fact overlooked almost every mile of the way: five of the eleven largest bald eagle wintering grounds in the United States can be found along the Oregon and California Trails in Kansas, Nebraska, Wyoming, Utah, and Idaho. For three decades they watched over America moving west.

From high above the square at Independence, an eagle could follow a faint trace south along a ridge to the ford of Missouri's Big Blue River. The trail to Oregon shared the path to New Mexico as far as New Santa Fe, a settlement on the border of Indian Country; beyond that imaginary line, Native tribes ruled every foot of ground to the Sierra and Cascade ranges. To the west lay several campsites named for their trees—Lone Elm, at the head of Cedar Creek; Elm Grove, some two miles away; and Sapling Grove, on the direct route from the new settlement at Westport. The road soon divided, and the newer, less-traveled trace to Oregon left the venerable Santa Fe Trail and turned north to cross the Wakarusa River, pass by the Blue Mound, and ford Shunganunga Creek: traders and missionaries followed this trail to the Kansas River and on to the Rocky Mountains. Later travelers simply headed west from Westport—present-day Kansas City—to the Santa Fe Trail and the Shawnee Mission, and from the mission on up the Kansas River.

Ferries later crossed the Kansas west of present-day Topeka at spots scattered over twenty miles. The trail followed the Big Blue River and forded it near Alcove Spring, where it turned to ascend the valley of the Little Blue River as it ambled from the northwest. Travelers later called the scenery beautiful and delightful, and both eagles and emigrants appreciated that the stream was filled with fish. As the trail wound west and north, woods gave way to open prairies, and soon the only trees clung to watercourses. Some twenty-five miles from the ford, an Indian trail came in from the Missouri, where the Americans now had a military post at Fort Leavenworth.

Ten miles on, the trace crossed the 40th parallel, and a little farther north what would become the Kansas-Nebraska border. Graves and stagecoach stations later dotted the low and increasingly arid sandhills, but in 1840 only the streams, springs, and bluffs along Rock Creek, the Little Sandy, and the Big Sandy marked the broad valley of the Little Blue. (The Narrows, where the vale contracted, later became notorious as an ambush site.) Not far from where the trail left the stream a single massive cottonwood, one of several legendary "Lone Trees" along the trail, stood until the wind toppled it in 1865.

The ridge that divided the waters of the Kansas River from those of the Platte marked a change of vegetation: trees vanished and cacti flourished on the sandy sides of the grass-covered northern hills. To the north, the meandering Platte glistened silver as it wandered down its broad valley. The Otoe Tribe is said to have called the river *Nebrathka,* meaning "flat water," and early travelers dubbed the hills that bordered its valley "the Coast of the Nebraska." These hundred-foot bluffs were ten to fifteen miles apart, and in the spring, the river was as much as two miles wide. Except on its islands, there was not a single stick of timber to be seen on what appeared to be one interminable prairie. Some scientists now blame the lack of trees on prairie fires and the arid climate, but the vast herds of bison that swept through the central plains every summer may have played a more important role. Sandhill cranes, great herons, and the longbilled curlew shared the river valley with wolves, elk, antelope, and prairie dogs. White alkaline and soda flats glistened in low spots between the sandhills, but the compacted black soil of the long, flat valley made a natural road.

Flying at a speed of thirty miles per hour, an eagle from the Missouri could reach the Platte River with a long day's flight, but it would take land-bound emigrants almost a month. Here the traces from Missouri began to parallel an eighty-mile trail on the north side of the river from Council Bluffs, where the sandbars of the wide and troublesome Loup River made it difficult to cross at its mouth and forced wagons to ascend the tributary to better fords. This northern route was the shortest and most direct approach to the head of Grand Island, a wooded seventy-mile-long sandbar that divided the shallow, mile-wide Platte River. As on the road from Independence, by 1840 fur-trade carts and missionary wagons had already etched its course into the wide bottomlands.

French explorers first described the Missouri's largest tributary and immediately recognized it as a natural highway across the central plains. They sometimes called it La Rivière au Cerf—Deer River—but it generally came to be known by the less poetic name the French gave it—La Rivière-Plate. The great Platte River was "full of low sleepy islands, and bounded on either side by rich bottom lands, often a mile [or] two in breadth, but little higher than the stream itself, and apparently quite as level," Warren Ferris wrote after seeing it in 1830: "Beyond the bottoms a rolling sandy prairie stretches its lazy level, but scantily covered with a coarse short grass, and eve[ry] now and then in barren spots as nude as an antique statue destitute of the seemliness of a fig leaf."[2]

"The Missouri Territory is a vast wilderness, consisting of immense plains, destitute of wood and of water, except on the edges of streams that are found near the turbid La Platte," John B. Wyeth wrote after his trip up the river in 1832. The foul and muddy river and the "scarcity of water in the dry and comfortless plains"

---

[2] Ferris, *Life in the Rocky Mountains,* 98–99.

intimidated him.[3] Traveling with Wyeth, John Ball thought "the river riley, broad and rapid, [with] no falls, but a sufficient descent in the country to give a rapid current—from a half to a whole mile wide and very shallow. It gives its full share of the mud of the Missouri—some timber on its islands and on its shores, bottoms broad and rich bounded by broken bluffs and all the country beyond rolling." West of Grand Island, the river wandered through a vast ocean of land—Ball called it "this prairie sea"—under a more expansive sky than anyone from east of the Mississippi had ever seen.[4]

Few changes would mark an eagle's westward flight toward an unbroken horizon, for only O'Fallons Bluff could be considered a landmark, and Plum Creek was the only sizable stream that flowed into the Platte from the south. Thirty-five miles west of Grand Island, even this little branch looked "more like a pool of water than a running stream," one sojourner commented in 1845.[5] From Plum Creek, a morning's flight would take an eagle up the meandering river to the beginning of the arid West at the 100th meridian. Fifty miles farther on the Platte divided. Not far up the northern fork, a small creek cut a gash some two or three hundred feet deep into the red sandstone at Ash Hollow, which sheltered the first large trees for three hundred miles.

Here the wagon trace came up from the South Fork, and soon the massive landforms of the Wildcat Hills rose above the flat western horizon. Rivers such as the Niobrara and the Arkansas provided other ways to cross the Great Plains, but as Samuel B. Crockett soon observed, "some of the greatest wonders in God's creation" adorned the North Platte.[6] Built of volcanic ash, Brule clay, and Arickaree sandstone, wind and time had carved these hills into "monuments of great dimensions." Travelers named them after courthouses, jails, mansions, chimneys, and ruins, where "nature in her solitude cuts to mock the puny works of man."[7]

These landmarks—most notably Courthouse Rock and Chimney Rock—ended at the vast stone fortress of Scotts Bluff, where golden eagles from the west joined their bald cousins to form a convocation. In 1846, perhaps in front of one of these precipices, J. Quinn Thornton watched a very large eagle soar above her nest as she "gracefully and majestically circled upward," trying to induce her eaglets to take to the wing. Her fledglings declined to leave the safety of "their lofty rock-built nest," and their angry mother tossed the nest, eaglets and all, down the face of the cliff. "In a moment, she was below them with outspread wings, as though

---

[3] Wyeth, *Oregon,* 29.
[4] Ball, *Autobiography,* 69.
[5] Field, Crossing the Plains, 31 May 1845, Oregon Historical Society.
[6] Crockett to "Dear Friends," 16 February 1845, Oregon Historical Society.
[7] Anonymous, Diary, 18 June 1849, in John T. Mason Diaries, Beinecke Library.

she intended to break their fall," but now the young birds discovered their wings. "They began to rise, at first, slowly and rather heavily. Soon the parent bird led the way, describing gradually enlarging circles as she ascended, while her young ones followed, and appeared every moment to rise with more ease and grace," Thornton rhapsodized. "Upward they continued to ascend into the vast expanse above; and upward still the noble birds arose, until the eaglets became mere specks upon the sky, and then disappeared, and soon the parent bird herself was lost in heaven's pure depth of blue."[8]

From the bluff's summit, Laramie Peak, the first outcropping of the Rocky Mountains, loomed above the western horizon, and eagles soared above Horse Creek. Not far upriver, during the summer in 1840 Mexican masons replaced the rotting timber stockade of the American Fur Company's post on the Laramie River with an adobe citadel—perhaps they gave their name to Mexican Hill, where the trail west of the fort pitched down off a bench to return to river. Beyond a large hot spring known as "the washtub," the trace left the narrow canyon of the North Platte to wind through the Black Hills, above the swallows' nests in the soft limestone precipice at Register Cliff, which was already etched with the names of traders and adventurers. Three miles beyond the cliff, the tracks of fur-caravan carts were carving deep ruts in a chalky hill. The trace climbed up and down the ridges dividing creeks called Bitter, Cottonwood, Horseshoe, Middle Bear, Elkhorn, La Bonte—where the various routes came together—Wagonhound, Bed Tick, Sand, and the red gorge of La Prele Creek, spanned by Ayres Natural Bridge, and finally Boxelder. The trail returned to the river at the broad meadows at the mouth of Deer Creek, a grassy oasis shaded by cottonwood, ash, chokecherry, and willow trees.

At present-day Casper, the North Platte turned south toward the Red Buttes. The primitive wagon trace left the river at Bessemer Bend and headed west into the badlands, passing over Emigrant Gap and by the Poison Spring, Poison Spider Creek, and the spiny ridge of Rock Avenue—the Devils Backbone—to Willow Spring, the first decent water in twenty dusty miles. Over the next mile the trail climbed to the top of Prospect Hill, named for the sweeping view that spread out toward the sunset.

The Sweetwater Valley was filled with wonders, from baking-soda playas called alkali lakes to Independence Rock, "a tremendous castle of solid rock rising out of the level plane."[9] Looking as if it had been "cemented together with cast iron," this massive granite turtle covered more than twenty-seven acres not far from

[8] Thornton, *Oregon and California in 1848*, 230–31.
[9] Crockett, "Diary of Samuel Black Crockett," 15 August 1844.

where the trail struck the meandering Sweetwater. More than a mile in circumference, the rock is 700 feet wide, 1,900 feet long, and rises 136 feet above the rolling prairie—as tall as a twelve-story building. It was already covered with names when the first emigrant wagon train passed by. To the west lay "some of the wildest, rugged rocky mountains, thrown into all shapes and forms that the imagination can picture."[10]

The trail made nine crossings of the Sweetwater River as the stream wandered like a green snake through its tan-and-gray valley. Five miles beyond the great rock, the Sweetwater cut through the Rattlesnake Hills to form Devils Gate, a 370-foot-deep and 1500-foot-long granite gorge that narrows to a mere 50 feet. Split Rock or Gunsite Rock, the Old Castle, and the subterranean beds of frozen water buried under peat bogs at Ice Slough marked the trace as the towering Wind River Range came into sight. At Rocky Ridge the trail ascended the backbone of North America to the stream's ninth and last crossing. The Sweetwater flowed through South Pass to within a quarter mile of the Continental Divide to create a singular gateway: without such a gap, few wagons ever would have crossed the Rocky Mountains. Just beyond the pass, at the cottonwoods surrounding what was soon renowned as Pacific Springs, eagles roosted just inside the eastern border of the Oregon Country.

West of South Pass, the trail unraveled like a frayed rope. Different traces headed for the widely separated sites where the fur trade rendezvous—a combination trade fair, brawl, drunken blowout, and liars' festival—had been held every summer for fifteen years. Beyond the Dry, Little, and Big Sandy rivers, trappers credited old Caleb Greenwood with discovering a fifty-mile-long waterless passage across the desert to Green River. It would remain a favorite route, but the earliest wagon roads stayed close to the Big Sandy and followed its southerly course to Green River and Blacks Fork, where in 1842 James Bridger and Louis Vasquez established a ramshackle outpost in the shadow of the Uintah Mountains.

The dry and the drier routes reunited on Bear River and followed it north until the stream outflanked the Wasatch Range at the thermal wonderland fur trappers called Beer Springs at present-day Soda Springs, Idaho. Paul Darst described one iron oxide–coated red mound as the "devils gass pipe," for its effusions would "kill birds or any other insect or animal."[11] Other springs cast up geysers or howled like steamboats. A faint trace led north over the hills from Sheep Rock at Soda Point, where Bear River turned south to the Great Salt Lake. The road left the

---

[10] Boardman, "The Journal," 27 July 1843, 105.
[11] Darst, Crossing Plains in 1847, University of Oregon.

The engravings Charles Fenn made from twenty-three-year-old artist Frederick Piercy's sketches are some of the most evocative images ever created of the wagon road across the plains. Here Piercy captured what Independence Rock looked like when he passed in 1853. From *Route from Liverpool to Great Salt Lake Valley*, author's collection.

Great Basin before crossing the Portneuf River, which emptied into the Snake River. Here some of the last wagon tracks on the trace from the Missouri reached Fort Hall, the Hudson's Bay Company stronghold.

No wagon ever traveled beyond Fort Hall before 1836, and the Company's skilled veterans thought no one could take a wagon over such broken terrain. The annual pack trains from Oregon that supplied the post followed Indian trails along the Snake River. Everywhere in the West water is the key to survival, and even on the Snake, one of the region's great rivers, wingless creatures often could not reach the bottom of its steep, lava-walled canyon. One traveler found much of the river was "enclosed by a perpendicular ledge of rocks & the thirsty animals were obliged to toil for miles together in the heat and dust with the sound of water in their ears & neither man [n]or beast able to get a drop."[12] This did not worry the eagles that soared over American Falls, and the river's many trout provided them with ample prey.

From the south, the Raft River and Goose Creek flow into the Snake: in a few years the California Trail would follow these streams back to the rim of the Great Basin and on to the Humboldt River and California. Near the mouth of Rock Creek, the Snake tumbled 212 feet over the Shoshone and Twin Falls, which could be heard some five miles away on the trail. The river again boiled into whitewater at Kanaka Rapids, named for the Hawaiians killed nearby in 1820. Just above the Indian fishing stations, the Lost River burst from the north bank of the Snake at the end of its 150-mile subterranean journey to Thousand Springs. Migrating Chinook salmon, whose runs choked the lower river from spring to fall, could not ascend beyond the cascades at Salmon Falls, and so both sites became important fishing spots for Shoshonean peoples.

Near present-day Glenns Ferry, islands divided the river into an ideal ford. Here the trails split: one continued up the south side; the second crossed the river and headed inland, seeking the springs and streams that usually made it the better choice. The perilously dry South Alternate hugged the river's shore as it passed the Bruneau River and Castle Butte through what two travelers soon called "the most rugged desert and dreary country, between the western borders of the United States and the shores of the Pacific." The trace that crossed to the Snake's north shore wound past hot springs named after a nearby rock called Teapot Dome and connected with an Indian trail leading east to Horse Heaven, the Camas Prairie. After a dreary traverse of arid country, the trail came to Bonneville Point, a spot overlooking the woods along the Rivière Boisée with its "mingled grandeur and beauty of mountain

---

[12] Coon, "Journal of a Journey over the Rocky Mountains," 8 August 1852, in Holmes, *Covered Wagon Women,* 5:198.

and plain, of bright running streams and vast grassy meadows waving to the breeze" that Captain Bonneville had called "the most enchanting" country in the Far West.[13] From the cottonwoods surrounding Fort Boise, the trading post at the river's mouth, eagles watched sojourners cross the wide river as best they could.[14]

Flying north along the Snake River to its confluence with the Columbia River, an eagle would pass near the mission station at Lapwai just east of present-day Lewiston, Idaho. But the trader's pack trail took a more direct line to the Columbia, crossing the Malheur River at what is now Vale, Oregon. Twenty-two miles of bone-dry country brought the trace to Birch Creek and—two miles on—to Farewell Bend, where travelers caught their last glimpse of the Snake before it rushed into Hells Canyon.

The trail twisted its way up the narrow canyon of Burnt River to the valley of the Powder River, on whose bank a tall but doomed lone pine had stood for generations. Ahead loomed the Blue Mountains, where the country assumed a new beauty as the pack trail descended a steep hill into the Grande Ronde, a circular valley that was tinted blue when the camas flowers bloomed and sheltered thousands of the Cayuse Nation's horses. The trace climbed through the thick forests of ponderosa and lodgepole pine, western larch, Engelmann spruce, and grand fir shrouding the Blue Mountains, past Lee's Encampment and Emigrant Springs, over 4,193-foot Deadman Pass, and down to Emigrant Hill and its expansive view of the Umatilla Valley.

To the northwest lay Fort Walla Walla, where the Hudson's Bay Company had supplied outbound fur caravans for decades. In 1840 a faint trail and another day's travel led to an Indian mission at Waiilatpu. Later, the trail would continue down the Umatilla River, which it crossed for the last time at present-day Echo, to begin a long trek over a rolling, dusty, treeless prairie to Well Spring, Willow Creek, Four Mile Canyon, and the John Day River. Near the Deschutes River ford, travelers got their first glimpse of the Columbia River. Twenty miles more brought the trail to the Methodist mission at The Dalles, where the Oregon Trail reached its practical end, for just to the west lay the rapids that began at Celilo Falls and the precipice of Mount Hood, which raised a formidable obstacle to wagon travel that would take years to surmount. Most early sojourners risked the rapids in the Columbia River to reach the Willamette Valley, the prize they had crossed the West to win.

None of the traces that led to Oregon in 1840 was a road in the modern sense. Overland travelers followed a series of Indian trails, continually choosing between

---

[13] Irving, *The Rocky Mountains*, 103.

[14] Johnson and Winter, *Route across the Rocky Mountains*, 31.

one pathway and another. Lacking an eagle's high vantage and broad vision, earthbound humans could only hope the choices they made would lead to their destination and not to desert wastelands or frozen mountain passes where they would perish of thirst, exposure, or starvation. To an eagle soaring ten thousand feet above, the movements of these obsessive creatures must have seemed chaotic and inexplicable. Yet through trial and error, and sheer dogged persistence, in less than a decade these intrepid pioneers created a complex network of practical trails a wagon could follow from the Missouri River to the Pacific Ocean. In less than a dozen years, they had forged what De Smet called "the broadest, longest and most beautiful road in the whole world."[15]

An eagle could have flown from the Missouri River to the Willamette in six days. The same journey would take those who blazed the wagon roads to the Pacific six long months.

---

[15] De Smet, *Life, Letters and Travels,* 671–72.

CHAPTER 1

We Had to Travel
through an Indian Country

When Joel Walker's two wagons—carrying the first American family that crossed the plains to settle in the Far West—set out in 1840, they did not enter an uninhabited wilderness: they entered Indian Country. The family "met a large number of Snake Indians" at Independence Rock, Walker recalled, and traveled with them for about two weeks.[1] "From the time we crossed the Missouri River we had to travel through an Indian Country to the Pacific Ocean," wrote 1847 Oregon emigrant David Shelton.[2] In addition to the dozens of tribes that lived along the route, the West was already home to hundreds of men of European, African, and Polynesian descent. Different nations asserted their sovereignty over the western half of North America, but their power existed mostly on paper.

From the Continental Divide to the Pacific, Mexico held title to a vast territory south of the 42nd parallel, but it controlled only a narrow strip of California's coast and the old settlements in New Mexico. North of the parallel, the United States and Great Britain both claimed the Pacific Northwest up to Russian Alaska, but Indian Nations and a corporation, the Hudson's Bay Company, ruled the land. Thomas Jefferson had engineered the purchase of the French claim to "full Sovereignty" over the Louisiana Territory in 1802, but he also promised to execute all treaties and agreements between France "and the tribes and nations of Indians until by mutual consent of the United States and the said tribes or nations other Suitable articles Shall have been agreed upon."[3]

---

[1] Walker, *A Pioneer of Pioneers,* 18.

[2] Shelton, Autobiographical Sketch, Allen Library.

[3] "Treaty between the United States of America and the French Republic," *The Connecticut Courant,* 2 November 1803.

Congress created "Indian Country" west of the Missouri River in 1834, but the tribes who lived there had not ceded one square yard of earth to the federal government. "You know as well as we, that every foot of what you proudly call America, not very long ago belonged to the red man," Shoshone leader Washakie once reminded the governor of Wyoming Territory.[4] All the lands between the Missouri and the Pacific Crest—the Great Plains, the High Plains, the Rocky Mountains, the Snake River drainage, and the Great Basin—were under the firm control of Native peoples. Many Indian nations held conflicting claims to the same "particular district of country," as the treaties put it, but the post traders and white fur hunters living in the West had no legal title to the ground they lived on: they were as landless as medieval serfs.

Far from being a static, unchanging, and idyllic Eden in 1840, the American West had experienced sweeping changes for centuries. Before 1700 C.E., tribes such as the Absaroka, Lakota, Pawnee, Cheyenne, and Arapaho had hunted and raised corn on the Great Lakes and along the Missouri and Mississippi rivers. Like the overland emigrants who followed them, unrelenting forces drove Indian nations farther west as displaced eastern tribes armed with the magic of powder and steel fled an advancing invasion from across the sea.

Long before the tribes of the American West actually encountered whites, the European discovery of what it called the New World had profound impacts on the continent's Native population. Word of the arrival of hairy white-skinned men raced across the continent. Many Indians could greet the first white men in their land as the Comanche Ten Bears welcomed an emissary from Washington: "I heard of your coming when you were many sleeps away."[5] Spreading from one people to another over ancient trade routes, European technologies, goods, animals, and deadly diseases reached the tribes well in advance of the mercenaries, merchants, and missionaries who brought these wonders to the New World. Less tangible, but just as consequential for the Indian peoples, were their encounters with the strangers' radically different belief systems.

The first Americans to settle on the Pacific Coast also brought with them a tradition of seizing Native lands extending back to the first English adventurers to reach Virginia. The drama that played out over the next four decades between Indians and emigrants echoed historic themes, events, and philosophies that had already embroiled North America for centuries. The peoples of the Far West could have learned from the words of Mahican John Quinney, who spoke at a

---

[4] Washakie, "A Protest to Governor John W. Hoyt of the Wyoming Territory, 1878," in Hebard, *Washakie*, 212–13.

[5] Ten Bears, "Speech at the Medicine Lodge Indian Council," in Moquin and Doren, *Great Documents in American Indian History*, 208.

Fourth of July celebration in New York in 1854: "Smallpox, measles and firewater have done the work of annihilation. Divisions and feuds were insidiously promoted between the several bands. They were induced to thin each others ranks without just cause; and subsequently were defeated and disorganized."[6]

The Work of Annihilation:
Old World Diseases and Technology in the New World

From the moment Columbus arrived, European diseases devastated Native populations who had no resistance to plagues such as smallpox and measles. Spanish explorer Bruno Heceta introduced smallpox to Oregon in 1775, and new epidemics swept through the Pacific Northwest in 1781 and 1830. A large population survived the first onslaught—in the 1850s an old trapper told Lieutenant Lawrence Kip he had often seen a thousand canoes pulled up on the beach at Fort Astoria. The introduction of the horse to the Cayuse and Nez Perce helped them thrive, but even before overland emigration began, John McLoughlin estimated that 90 percent of the Indian population west of The Dalles had been swept away.[7] For some groups, the destruction was total, or nearly so. For most, the new diseases decimated families, bands, and tribes, taking the fathers who hunted game, the mothers who gathered or tended plants, and the children who would have been the next generation.

Tribes devastated by the new diseases suffered more than the loss of key individuals and families: the enormous death toll left the survivors disoriented and easy prey for a cynical strategy of divide and conquer. Encounters with nineteenth-century technology and its obvious advantages undercut the spiritual foundations of Indian society, increasing the dislocation already tearing at the tribes. Steel, firearms, textiles, mirrors, and books fueled their desire to somehow master the white man's medicine.

Traditional leaders and healers found themselves unable to vanquish these new plagues. In many tribes, the recognition that their medicine was powerless against these deadly incursions instigated a profound debate about what course the people should follow. Traditionalists held that the fault lay not with their gods but with the people who had forsworn ancient ways or had forgotten the rituals needed to maintain harmony in the universe. Young warriors argued that only force could stop the deadly invaders; others hoped to negotiate with the newcomers. As time passed with no respite, many began to suggest that acquiring the

---

[6] John Quinney, "Fourth of July Address at Reidsville, New York, 1854," in ibid., 169.

[7] Lawrence, *The Indian Council in the Valley of the Walla-Walla, 1855,* 1; and Parker, *Journal of an Exploring Tour,* 178.

white man's magic and the ability to decode the books in which it was recorded was a matter of urgent necessity.

America's Native peoples quickly recognized the advantages of European technology and acquired it eagerly. The white man's goods may have been unfamiliar, but the trading networks that distributed them throughout western North American were ancient. For centuries Pacific Coast dentalium shells had moved far inland from one tribe to another. Southwestern turquoise made its way north, west, and east, and skillfully crafted baskets and pottery were appreciated in villages far from the peoples who made them. Traders brought salt to those who had none in their lands, and buffalo hunters exchanged fine robes and meat with tribes that raised squash, beans, and maize.

With the goods came new or better ways of performing familiar tasks. Neighboring peoples shared, adopted, and adapted more effective methods of chipping a flint blade or trapping game. Initially the Indians had no reason to suspect that the goods and technologies Europeans brought would differ in significant ways from those that preceded them. "We did not know there were other people besides the Indian until about one hundred winters ago, when some men with white faces came to our country," Chief Joseph of the Nez Perce said of his people's first encounter with French traders. "They brought many things with them to trade for furs and skins. They brought tobacco, which was new to us. They brought guns with flint stones on them, which frightened our women and children. Our people could not talk with these white-faced men, but they used signs which all people understand."[8]

Different peoples had differing interests, but alcohol and firearms were the most popular items in the Indian trade, followed by metal tools and utensils, glass or metal beads, mirrors, and woven fabrics. The trinket trade enriched cagey white traders, but firearms could alter the balance of power, giving those who first acquired them immediate superiority over their enemies. Yet single-shot weapons were unreliable at best, and traditional snares or bows and arrows were often more effective for hunting. "It is unlikely that the gun swept like a wave across the plains, nor did the native peoples everywhere accept it immediately as an unmitigated boon," Preston Holder noted. "The bow lasted alongside the gun for many decades."[9] Cumbersome and erratic muskets made better weapons for defense than for offense, and the more accurate and effective repeating rifles and revolvers that could give a tribe a manifest advantage against its enemies were late arrivals. Still, as more and more nations acquired these weapons, guns became essential

[8] Chief Joseph, "The Fate of the Nez Percés," *North American Review,* April 1879, in Moquin and Doren, *Great Documents in American Indian History,* 238.

[9] Holder, *The Hoe and the Horse on the Plains,* 115.

for survival. When the German immigrant adventurer Frederick A. Wislizenus visited Fort Hall in 1839, most of the tribes still relied on bows and arrows, but through trade many of them had obtained firearms, "the use of which they have well learned."[10]

THE FOUR-FOOTS

Life on the Great Plains is completely dependent on water. Grass, the green engine that ultimately powers both animals and people, depends on the generosity of the heavens, and when the clouds are miserly, life retreats in both range and numbers. The notion that there is an "average" yearly rainfall in the American West is an illusion, since the arid West is dominated by extremes—it either rains like hell or it does not rain at all. Cycles of flooding downpours and devastating drought follow one another randomly, and rainfall varies so dramatically from year to year that the mathematical average of precipitation is meaningless. Over the broad sweep of history, drought has been the recurring reality, and during the five thousand years before the birth of Christ, aridity was the defining feature of the plains and the life it supported—for example, during the driest years at the beginning of the cycle, the better adapted *Bison bison* replaced the huge *Bison antiquus,* whose horns could span six feet. Dry years extended the short-grass and mixed-grass prairies that fed the bison, but wet years produced the tall grasses that later fueled oxen and mules. When one of the wettest periods in the central plains' history ended about 1220 C.E., more Indians were living there than ever before or since, but during the thirteenth century cultures across the West withered and sometimes disappeared in an extended drought. The decades before 1840, however, were once again blessed with ample rainfall and its result, bountiful grass.[11]

Perhaps nothing sparked a greater transformation in Native culture than the introduction of the horse, a living engine that could transform the most immense resource on the Great Plains—grass—into a power Indians could harness to travel, hunt, trade, and make war. "All flesh is grass," an American military officer observed on the Platte River in 1845, quoting Isaiah.[12] The horse made a man more than a match for the fiercest bison—and for traditional adversaries who had not yet acquired the new technology. But if the animals expanded a tribe's

---

[10] Wislizenus, *A Journey to the Rocky Mountains,* 151. In 1912 the Missouri Historical Society, which Wislizenus helped establish, published this translation of the 1840 German edition, which appeared in Saint Louis.

[11] West, *Contested Plains,* 21, 25–28, 31, 231. West uses the example of the Woodland peoples, but the displacement of ancient cultures in the Great Basin with the arrival of the Shoshoneans is another. He notes, too, that not all experts agree that there were centuries-long "megadroughts."

[12] Isaiah 40:6, in Cooke, *Scenes and Adventures,* 4 June 1845, 298.

range, power, and capacity to transport goods, they also provoked conflict, since horses required a vast territory to produce enough grass to support the mounts. "The wealth of an Indian consists chiefly in horses," Wislizenus reported, and he assumed that "all stealing is permissible among the Indians, but horse-stealing is honorable."[13]

The arrival of the horse sparked dynamic changes from the Missouri to the Pacific. Adopting the equestrian lifestyle often upset traditional alliances and embittered existing rivalries. Newly armed and mounted enemies posed the greatest threat to farmers settled in permanent villages, since these peoples could not simply evade armed marauders. By 1840 the struggle to command the resources that provided food, fuel, shelter, and clothing, complicated by the introduction of the gun and the horse, made most of the Native West contested ground.[14]

The Utmost Good Faith Shall Always Be Observed: American Indian Policy

Like smallpox, guns, and horses, European political systems and philosophies touched the Far West long before most tribes had seen a white face. Each of the nations that explored and repopulated the North American continent developed policies designed to govern their relations with the Native inhabitants of the lands they "discovered." The young American government, drawing on these precedents and a history of Enlightenment thought on the status of Indians, soon began to articulate an idealistic policy. "The utmost good faith shall always be observed toward the Indians; their lands and property shall never be taken from them without their consent," pledged the 1787 Northwest Ordinance, the first legislation of an independent United States to deal with Indians, "and in their property, rights, and liberty, they never shall be invaded or disturbed unless in just and lawful wars authorized by the Congress."[15]

Following European precedent, the new nation held that the "right of discovery" superseded the rights of aboriginal title. According to Enlightenment philosophers, under both moral law and the "laws of nature," individuals who cultivated the land had a privileged position because the human race could not survive without their efforts. Swiss political theorist Emmerich de Vattel held that hunting and gathering alone, which might have been adequate to meet the needs of the people "in the first ages of the world," could no longer sustain a rapidly growing

---

[13] Wislizenus, *A Journey to the Rocky Mountains*, 154.
[14] Elliot West developed these ideas in *The Way to the West* and *Contested Plains*.
[15] Article 3, Northwest Ordinance.

population. Peoples that "inhabit fertile countries but disdain to cultivate their lands," choosing instead to "live by plunder," deserved to be exterminated "as savage and pernicious beasts."[16] The concept that those who tilled the land should own it brought a beneficial revolution to the lives of European serfs, but it was fraught with peril for American Indians—even those who were themselves horticulturalists. But before American citizens could legally take Indian lands for cultivation, federal law required negotiating treaties with the Indian inhabitants to extinguish their aboriginal title.

Congress quickly asserted its right to "regulate commerce with foreign nations, and among the several states, and with the Indian tribes." In 1831, the State of Georgia challenged federal jurisdiction over Indians. As the Supreme Court ruled, "the acts of our government plainly recognize the Cherokee nation as a state, and the courts are bound by those acts." The justices held that "the Indians are acknowledged to have an unquestionable, and, heretofore, unquestioned right to the lands they occupy, until that right shall be extinguished by a voluntary cession to our government." The Court defined the tribes as domestic dependent nations—that is, as nations with full control of their internal affairs but limited external sovereignty. The federal government had a "trust responsibility" to act as a guardian for the tribes. The law recognized "that their territory was separated from that of any State within whose chartered limits they might reside; that within their boundary, they possessed rights with which no State could interfere; and that the whole power of regulating the intercourse with them, was vested in the United States."[17]

The government specifically addressed the fate of the Indians in the Far West. When the United States acquired the Louisiana Purchase, the treaty of cession included the "promise to execute such treaties and articles as may have been agreed between Spain and the tribes and nations of Indians" until by mutual consent they came to an accord. The 1848 Treaty of Guadalupe Hidalgo with Mexico (which the Gadsden Purchase treaties of 1853–54 conveniently abrogated) provided that "the sacredness of this obligation shall never be lost sight of by the said government when providing for the removal of the Indians from any portion of the said territories, or for its being settled by citizens of the United States; but, on the contrary, special care shall be taken not to place its Indian occupants under the necessity of seeking new homes."[18]

---

[16] Vattel, *The Law of Nations*, 92. Vattel's 1758 *Le droit des gens* profoundly influenced how Franklin, Washington, and Jefferson viewed Indian rights; his writings were also consistently cited in key Indian cases heard by the Supreme Court.

[17] Spicer, *A Short History of the Indians of the United States*, 185–89, 190–93.

[18] Adams et al., *Report on Trust Responsibilities and the Federal Indian Relationship*, 91–92.

You Must Move a Little Farther:
The Displacement of the Eastern Tribes

Americans have always been a people on the move, and this was as true before 1492 as it was after. For millennia America's Indian nations had migrated over thousands of miles in response to weather, disease, war, and perhaps simple wanderlust, but 1840 found many tribes settled on lands that had been their homes for only a few decades.

With the Proclamation of 1763, King George III created an official border between the British colonies and Indian "Hunting Grounds" at the crest of the Appalachians, which the British hoped would reduce violence on the empire's frontier. Rather than ensure peaceful relations, the crown's attempt to limit American expansion destroyed the speculative fortunes of men such as George Washington, Patrick Henry, and Thomas Jefferson, and helped provoke a revolution. Yet for generations the goal of separating Indians from new settlers was never far from the minds of North American policymakers. Some believed separation would protect the Indians and enable them to make a gradual transition to a new way of life that mirrored that of their white neighbors. Others saw it simply as a pragmatic way to minimize what became known as "the Indian problem," though with more justice it could have been called "the voracious settler problem."

Laws defining a permanent settlement frontier, like the ubiquitous clauses in Indian treaties guaranteeing tribal land possession as long as the sun shone or the grass grew or the rivers ran, had durations far shorter than their framers envisioned. Within a few years non-Indian expansion, a changing political climate, and new laws and policies erased the imaginary lines that designated "Indian land in perpetuity." Government policy consistently undercut Indian land tenure in favor of the interests of white settlers, whose phenomenal birthrate, together with successive waves of European immigration, fueled an insatiable hunger for land.

President James Monroe informed Congress in 1825 that the removal of Indian tribes from the lands they occupied within the several states and territories "within our own acknowledged boundaries, is of very high importance to our Union, and may be accomplished on conditions, and in a manner, to promote the interest and happiness of those tribes." As Andrew Jackson observed in 1829, the Indian nations of the Northeast, "by persuasion and force," had "been made to retire from river to river and from mountain to mountain, until some of the tribes have become extinct and others have left but remnants to preserve for awhile their once terrible names." The newly elected Great White Father called for the removal of all the Indian tribes east of the Mississippi to the West.[19] While

---

[19] Schoolcraft, *History of the Indian Tribes of the United States,* 407, 429–30.

Jackson may not have made the famous taunt ascribed to him after the Supreme Court rejected his Indian removal policies—"Justice Marshall has made his decision, now let him enforce it"—the legend reflects his longstanding disregard for the nation's Indian policy, Indian law, and Indian rights.

"When the white man first came to these shores, the Muscogees gave him land, and kindled him a fire to make him comfortable," recalled Speckled Snake, a Cherokee, responding to Jackson's process of dispossession in 1830. "But when the white man had warmed himself before the Indians' fire, and filled himself with the Indians' hominy, he became very large; he stopped not for the mountain tops, and his feet covered the plains and the valleys. His hands grasped the eastern and the western sea." He became the Indian peoples' great father and loved his red children, but said, "You must move on a little farther, lest I should, by accident, tread on you." The great father still loved his red children, "and he soon made them another talk. He said much; but it all meant nothing, but 'move on a little farther; you are too near to me.' I have heard a great many talks from our great father, and they all begun and ended the same."[20]

The Indian Removal Act of 1830 made forced relocation the official American policy, sending between 46,000 and 70,000 eastern Indians (many of whom, ironically, were already farmers) "west of the river Mississippi." Although the legislation was primarily directed at the Five Civilized Tribes of the South—the Cherokee, Chickasaw, Choctaw, Creek, and Seminole nations—it was also used to push the last surviving bands out of Indiana and Illinois, precipitating the Black Hawk War of 1832. Thus Indian peoples, not white pioneers, became the first westward-bound emigrants to reach the trans-Mississippi West in significant numbers.

Congress defined yet another permanent Indian frontier in the Indian Trade and Intercourse Act of 1834, this one west of the Mississippi and comprising the states of Louisiana and Missouri, and the territory of Arkansas. All Indian lands not covered by a ratified treaty became "Indian Country."[21] Most Americans, who considered the region a worthless desert, saw no good reason why the tribes should not own it until the end of time. That other Indian peoples already occupied and used these lands proved no impediment to the relocation of eastern Indians there. Progressive thinkers, such as Isaac McCoy of Missouri, envisioned that these Indian lands might eventually gain statehood.[22] Others anticipated that the Indians would vanish either through inevitable decline or through assimilation, but most cared little what happened to them, so long as they no longer posed a

---

[20] Moquin and Doren, *Great Documents in American Indian History,* 149.
[21] Beckham, Buan, and Lewis, "Federal-Indian Relationships," in *The First Oregonians,* 39–41.
[22] Thrapp, *Encyclopedia of Frontier Biography,* 894.

threat to the settlement of the fertile river valleys of the Mississippi. Only six years later, the first white settlers crossed this "inviolable" boundary.

If the introduction of the horse and the gun generated struggles for land, the westward movement of displaced peoples compounded the problem. By 1840 many of the oldest inhabitants of Indian Country—the Pawnee, Omaha, Otoe, Osage, Ponca, and Kanza (also Caw or Kaw) Nations—had made treaties with the federal government, often ceding lands in what is now Kansas that the government then assigned to tribes newly exiled from their homes in the East. Emigrants who crossed Indian Country in the 1840s met many tribes that had only recently moved into the lands they occupied. Major cultural changes, new technologies, and increasing competition for land and resources had already disrupted the ancient relationships among the tribes that lived along the frontier, but the influx of displaced eastern nations imperiled their already precarious position.

What Mockery to Confound Justice with Law: Implementing Indian Policy

"Oh, what mockery to confound justice with law!" Mahican John Quinney exclaimed in 1854 during his impassioned Fourth of July oration. "Will you look steadily at the intrigues, bargains, corruptions and log rollings of your present legislatures, and see any trace of justice?"[23] Long before 1840 the drive for expansion had trumped the noble rhetoric of the Northwest Ordinance. Laws could be changed or allowed to languish. Most Americans disagreed with the lofty philosophical goals originally outlined for the young republic's Indian policy, concurring instead with General Andrew Jackson, who wrote to the Great White Father in 1817 that he had "long viewed treaties with the Indians as an absurdity not to be reconciled with the practices of our government."[24]

Even the best-intentioned of Indian policies had to be implemented by hundreds of individual emissaries, many far from the center of government at Washington and vulnerable to pressure from those who wanted Indian lands and resources. And not all of those who entered federal service were of the highest caliber. "I don't want any more such men sent out there, who are so poor that when they come out there their first thoughts are how they can fill their own pockets," Ogallala leader Red Cloud later complained. He also had little use for the other kind of men the Great Father sent—"men who drank and quarreled, men who were so bad that he could not keep them at home, and so he sent them out there."[25]

---

[23] Moquin and Doren, *Great Documents in American Indian History,* 169.

[24] Spicer, *A Short History of the Indians of the United States,* 228.

[25] Red Cloud, "Speech at Cooper Union, New York, July 16, 1870," in Moquin and Doren, *Great Documents in American Indian History,* 213.

"How shall we know when to believe, being so often deceived by the white people?" Seneca leader Sagu-yu-what-hah, known as Red Jacket, said in 1805.[26] Western Indians soon learned the bitter lessons that had been taught to Powhatan, Metacomet, Pontiac, Tecumseh, and Osceola. They were initially hopeful and trusting of the new government, but forty years of conflict had revealed the harsh reality underlying American policy toward the Native peoples of the West.

Indians are ubiquitous in overland narratives, but they are at best a shadowy presence. As Ohio Buckeyes, British aristocrats, "pukes" from Missouri, German peasants, French-Canadian trappers, Yankee farmers, Mormon refugees, and slave-owning southerners met Native peoples along the trails, the potential for misunderstanding, mistaken assumptions, deadly ignorance, and a resulting disaster was immense. No generalizations about cultural assumptions can adequately portray the views of all Indian peoples, but an awareness of the broad diversity of characters and cultures that collided on the road to the West is essential to understanding what took place. Too often, overland emigrants believed that an Indian was an Indian, which meant that for their purposes Indians became interchangeable. If one Indian committed a crime, the Americans might exact revenge on the next Indians they met on the trail; many tribes enforced similar codes by simply killing the nearest white man to avenge a tribal member's death. When it came time to acquire land titles, the letter of the law could be observed by finding any Indian who could be induced to sign away land, and the treaty makers rarely inquired with any diligence whether the Indian who put his X on the line even lived in the land he was signing away, let alone had any authority among his own people to do so.

The dozens of Indian cultures across the Far West differed in myriad ways. Each had expectations as distinct as their languages about the nature of honorable and polite behavior, truth telling, the meaning of gift giving, the form of a legally binding agreement, and the reparations required to redress an injury or grievance. As different as their customs might be, tribes often shared attitudes toward land ownership, religion, and governance that were distinct from Anglo-European concepts. Among some Native peoples, an individual might hold or inherit the right to hunt, fish, or cultivate a particular tract of land or maintain an irrigation ditch, but no tribe regarded the earth as something any person could possess in the American sense. The prairies, mountains, valleys, and rivers, and every animal, bird, fish, and plant, belonged collectively to The People. No single Indian had the authority to sell, trade, lease, or give away any part of The People's resources on his or her own. In most cases, bands reached decisions by consensus.

---

[26] "Red Jacket's Reply to a Missionary," in Spicer, *A Short History of the Indians of the United States,* 264.

About 1852, Red Iron, a Sisseton, complained when his people were not included in Minnesota treaty negotiations. "This was not according to our customs," he said, "for among the Dakotas chiefs and braves go to council together."[27]

Native belief systems varied greatly, but all found proselytizing or forcing others to adopt their belief systems an alien concept. Missionary schools and federal agencies, by contrast, actively sought to convert Indians into "civilized" Christians and farmers. Trails expert Morris Werner has identified twenty-seven separate Methodist, Baptist, Presbyterian, Catholic, and Moravian missions that ministered to the Delaware, Iowa, Sac and Fox, Kanza, Kickapoo, Miami, Osage, Ottawa, Pottawatomie, Shawnee, Stockbridge (Mohegan), Wea, and Wyandot tribes in Kansas.[28] The Shawnee Mission, established in October 1839 to serve the Delaware and Shawnee peoples, eventually worked with the Kanza, Munsee, Ottawa, Chippewa, Otoe, Osage, Cherokee, Peoria, Kickapoo, Pottawatomie, Wea, Gros Ventres, Omaha, and Wyandot tribes. This proliferation of denominations, all claiming to represent the "one true God," was confusing. "You say there is but one way to worship and serve the Great Spirit. If there is but one religion, why do you white people differ so much about it?" Red Jacket asked a missionary in 1805. "We never quarrel about religion," he added, saying that if the man's preaching made the local whites more honest and less disposed to cheat Indians, his people would reconsider what the preacher had to say.[29]

As western travel increased, communication became increasingly problematic. Individuals from many cultures had long used Chief Joseph's "signs which all people understand" to parley or determine how many pelts to trade for a knife. A man might make a model of the surrounding country out of sand, as the Absarokas did to show Jedediah Smith's men how to find South Pass, or draw a simple map, as the illiterate Jim Bridger often did to show someone where the trail headed. Merchants usually learned at least a few key phrases to converse with their customers, and men who married into the tribes often became quite fluent in one or more Native languages. This met the needs of trappers and traders, but when missionaries seeking converts, settlers claiming land, and fortune hunters prospecting for minerals took to the trails, they no longer sufficed. What signs could have conveyed the meaning of alien concepts like recorded land titles, constitutional authority, state and federal jurisdiction, or the unprecedented idea that these newcomers expected the people to abandon their beliefs, customs,

---

[27] Moquin and Doren, *Great Documents in American Indian History,* 164.

[28] Werner, "Indian Missions in Kansas," Kansas Heritage, retrieved 14 December 2006 from http://www.ku.edu/heritage/werner/mission.html. Morris Werner has received little recognition, but he has done pioneering work in trails history.

[29] Spicer, *A Short History of the Indians of the United States,* 262–65.

dress, and ways of life, as well as their homelands? Big Eagle, a Santee Dakota, expressed the Indian position simply: "If the Indians had tried to make the whites live like them, the whites would have resisted, and it was the same way with many Indians."[30]

ROUGH AND DARING: THE PLAINS INDIANS

Overland travelers usually failed to identify the peoples they met with a particular tribe or nation. Those who did most often mentioned the Pawnees, Sioux, or Shoshones. The tribes wagon trains typically encountered on the Great Plains—the Kanzas, Pawnees, Lakotas, Cheyennes, Arapahos, and Absarokas— had generations of experience dealing with whites, and only the Pawnees and the Absarokas had troubled relations with emigrants during the 1840s. But as a perceptive military officer observed in 1845, the government seemed poised "to break all the last and most binding pledges of their country's faith" to the Plains Indians, who now constituted "the congregated remnants of many defenceless tribes of Indians, who own every acre of its arable land."[31]

The Kanzas were the first Indian nation early plains travelers encountered. Explorer Jacques Marquette's map of 1673 first referred to the *Tadje unikacinga*— the Wind People—as the "Kansa." A Dhegiha-Siouan people, they were relatives of the Osages, Omahas, and Poncas, and once may have been mound builders. The tribe ceded all their lands in the state of Missouri and much of their twenty-million-acre domain in modern-day Kansas to the United States in 1825 in exchange for a reservation and a twenty-year annuity of $3,500, receiving a strip of land thirty miles wide starting sixty miles up the Kansas River, west of what is now Topeka.[32] The tribe raised corn and hunted buffalo, and they were almost continually at war with the Pawnees. John Ball described one of their villages in 1832: "They dug holes in the dry ground some five or six feet deep and then built a roof of split plank, [and] so made quite a warm winter house."[33] William Johnson ran a mission for the Methodist Episcopal Church among them, but he had accomplished little by his death in 1842.

Fur traders left a colorful if often inaccurate record of how the Kanzas appeared to passing travelers. "The unusual sight of a train of wagons caused quite a sensation" when Captain Benjamin Bonneville's expedition rolled through in 1832; in fact, the experience would not have been as exceptional for the Indians as the cap-

[30] Moquin and Doren, *Great Documents in American Indian History*, 173.
[31] Cooke, *Scenes and Adventures*, 26 May 1845, 288.
[32] Unrau, *The Kaw People*, 1–5, 42.
[33] "Kansas River," in Ball, *Autobiography*, 66.

tain's chronicler thought, since Santa Fe Trail traders had hauled freight through Kanza homelands for almost a decade. Still, the tribe "thronged about the caravan, examining everything minutely, and asking a thousand questions: exhibiting a degree of excitability, and a lively curiosity" about the white man's latest technology.[34] Wislizenus found both sexes "adorn themselves with all possible ornaments of beads, coral, brassware, feathers, ribbons, gaudy rags," creating an appearance that terrified many whites, but the people who visited his camp were very peaceable. They brought hides (especially tanned deer hides) to barter for knives and other trifles or money, but Wislizenus discovered what they wanted most was flour and bacon: already, "they were starved out."[35]

The Pawnees consisted of four autonomous Caddoan tribes—the *Chaui* (or Grand), *Pitahauerat* (or Tappage), *Kitkehahki* (or Republican), and *Skidi* (or Wolf). United States treaty commissioners identified them as the "Grand Pawnees, Pawnee Loups, Pawnee Republicans, and Pawnee Tappaye, residing on the Platte and the Loup fork." The Chauis had been wintering on the Arkansas at least since Coronado spoke to a Pawnee leader there in 1541. They numbered some 10,000 when the United States acquired Louisiana, but their population had declined to 6,233 by 1840, when they lived in six riverside agricultural villages in today's Nebraska and Kansas, from which they launched semiannual bison hunts. They built sophisticated (and warm) earth lodges and raised corn, beans, squash, and pumpkins, but as settlers began heading for Oregon, they were hard pressed by smallpox, missionaries, and their Siouan neighbors—the Lakota, Cheyenne, Omaha, and Kanza. American agents wanted to concentrate them in one large village on the Loup, but their leaders protested that this would put them at the mercy of their tribal enemies. These fears were justified: during 1841 their rivals, including the Kanza but most especially the Lakota, raided and slaughtered the people in their scattered camps while their warriors were away.[36]

Traditional Pawnee ways intimidated most early travelers, but not all descriptions of this "rough and daring tribe" were negative.[37] Narcissa Whitman met a large band of Pawnees on her way west in 1836. "They seemed to be very much surprised and pleased to see white females; many of them had never seen any before," she wrote. "They are a noble Indian—large, athletic forms, dignified countenances, bespeaking an immortal existence within."[38] Peter Burnett observed a few Pawnee warriors on the Blue River returning from a buffalo hunt.

[34] Irving, *The Rocky Mountains,* 11.

[35] Wislizenus, *A Journey to the Rocky Mountains,* 33–34.

[36] Tyson, *The Pawnee People,* 2, 56–58.

[37] Robinson, A Brief Review of the Life of Isaac Constant, 1852.

[38] Hunsaker, *Seeing the Elephant,* 40.

"They had quantities of dried buffalo-meat, of which they generously gave us a good supply. They were fine-looking Indians, who did not shave their heads, but cut their hair short like white men."[39]

The Lakota people, almost universally known as the Sioux, a name given them by their enemies, were the most powerful tribe emigrants encountered along the Platte River. The Ogallala, Brule (Burnt Legs), Teton, Santee, Blackfoot, Hunkpapa, Miniconjou, and Two Kettle bands made up the tribe: emigrants most often met the Ogallala, Brule, and Miniconjou.[40] The Lakota consistently impressed travelers, and fur-trade chronicles described their proud and colorful appearance. "We discovered several objects on the brow of a neighboring bluff, which at first we took to be antelopes, but were soon undeceived, for they speedily transformed and multiplied themselves into several hundreds of Indians, who came rushing like a torrent down upon us," Warren Ferris wrote after an incident in 1830. The panicked mountaineers prepared to fight, but the visitors "made signs of friendship, and gave us to understand that they were Sioux." The warriors gathered in a semicircle and broke out four American flags. "Many of them had on long scarlet coats, trimmed with gold and silver lace, leggins and mocasins richly, though fantastically ornamented, and gay caps of feathers," Ferris recalled. "Some wore painted buffalo robes, and all presented a lively, dashing appearance. They were, without exception, all finely mounted; and all armed—some with swords, shields, and lances, others with bows and arrows, and a few with guns."[41]

Nine years later Wislizenus encountered a camp of several thousand Brules, Tetons, and Ogallalas, plus some Cheyennes and Arapahos whom he assumed were Sioux. His guide, "Black" Harris, gave the Indians small presents, especially tobacco, and fed them sweetened mush, which they liked so much they took the leftovers with them. (What the German traveler failed to understand was that it was "considered an insult by an Indian for a Stranger whether White man or Indian to return any part of the food which is set before him to eat," as Osborne Russell observed. An Indian visitor offered more than he could eat would take the remainder with him to avoid giving offense.) The Lakotas "appeared in gala attire, decked as far as possible with ornaments and bright rags, and with their faces freshly painted." One of them wore a red British uniform, and a second group carried two colored flags embroidered with a star and a rooster whose bearers had their faces painted red and black.[42]

---

[39] Burnett, *Recollections and Opinions of an Old Pioneer*, 17 June 1843, 106.

[40] The other Lakota bands occasionally came in contact with the trails, except for the Hunkpapa, who lived well to the north.

[41] Ferris, *Life in the Rocky Mountains*, 101–102.

[42] Wislizenus, *A Journey to the Rocky Mountains*, 55–56; and Russell, *Journal of a Trapper*, 79.

Despite their consistent friendliness to emigrants, the Lakotas called their American visitors *Wasichu,* meaning "one who takes the fat" or simply greedy, indicating they were not entirely charmed by the new visitors to their homeland. Unlike their American contemporaries, Lakota parents never beat their children, and after wagons began passing through their lands, they used stories of the Wasichu to frighten their children into obedience.[43]

The Bird People, popularly called the Crows but known to themselves as the Absarokas, were a Siouan people who ranged from the Big Horn and Powder rivers to the Rocky Mountains. Bitter enmity separated them from their northern neighbors, the Blackfeet, while the Teton Sioux pressed them from the east and the Shoshones fought them to the west. Missionary Jason Lee estimated they numbered about four hundred lodges and four thousand souls in 1834, but Osborne Russell, who knew them better, believed the ravages of war and smallpox had "reduced their numbers to about 2,000, of which upwards of 1200 [sic] are females." Unlike many of their neighbors, they had "a great aversion to distilled spirits of any kind terming it the 'White mans fool water' and say if a Crow drink it he ceases to be a Crow."[44] The Absarokas were continually at war with their Native enemies, and "the battle-ground of these three nations is about the headwaters of the Platte, Green, and Snake rivers" near South Pass, explorer Charles Wilkes reported. The Crows, his informants said, were "much the most shrewd and intelligent of the Indian tribes."[45] They frequently raided wagon trains for horses, and emigrants feared and respected them.

Horse raiding was an intrinsic rite of passage for young warriors among the Plains Indians. "They have stole most all the horses from all the companies," complained Amanda Esrey Rhoads after Pawnees struck her train in 1846. She considered it useless for anyone to take more than two horses on the journey, since raiders would run off any animal not closely guarded.[46] Otherwise, Indians seldom troubled wagon trains during the first years of overland travel. Their weapons of choice indicate they were not even armed to make such attacks. They relied on bows and arrows (which could be fired much more rapidly than a firearm) to hunt buffalo and preferred shotguns to rifles.[47] Their limited range made arrows and shotguns poor offensive weapons against better-armed whites.

---

[43] Tate, "From Cooperation to Conflict," 21; and Hassrick, *The Sioux,* 276, 288. Variant spellings include *Waisichu* and *Waischu.*

[44] Lee to the *Christian Advocate,* 1 July 1834, in Anderson, *The Rocky Mountain Journals,* 31; and Russell, "The Crow Indians," *Journal of a Trapper,* 145–49.

[45] Wilkes, *Narrative of the United States Exploring Expedition,* 4:471–74.

[46] Rhoads to "Dear Parents," Fort Laramie, 15 June 1846, Bancroft Library.

[47] Field, Crossing the Plains, 20 June 1845, Oregon Historical Society. The firearms Shoshones liked best, Field said, were "smooth-bores with single triggers and flint locks; they prefer a shot-gun to a rifle."

As he traveled up the South Platte in 1843, Peter Burnett "saw several Indians, who kept at a distance, and never manifested any disposition to molest us in any way. They saw we were mere travelers through their country, and would only destroy a small amount of their game." Burnett thought the grand appearance of the long line of wagons, teams, cattle, and men impressed the Indians with the emigrants' power. The tribes Burnett saw were not nearly as naïve or intimidated as he supposed: long experience had taught them that the whites made better allies and trading partners than they did enemies.[48]

Brave, Robust, Active, and Shrewd: Shoshonean Peoples

"I will now cross the Rocky Mts by way of the south pass," Thomas "Broken-Hand" Fitzpatrick wrote in 1846 as he described the land "lying between the Columbia river on the north and the Colorado on the south, all of which belongs to the Shoshonee or Snake Nation." Fitzpatrick identified the Utes, Paiutes, Bannocks, and "all the numerous small tribes in the great desert west of the Salt Lake" as Shoshonean peoples. The Comanches were their relatives, he realized, for he "found their language exactly the same."[49]

As tribal historian Brigham D. Madsen observed, about two thousand Eastern Shoshones lived "astride the Oregon Trail" between the Sweetwater and Bear rivers. After a leadership crisis in the early 1840s, an astute leader known as Washakie guided the tribe until his death in 1900. Some 1,600 Northern Shoshones lived along the trail around Fort Hall and at the salmon fisheries on the lower Snake River, while a similar number of Northwestern Shoshone thrived in the valleys of northern Utah.[50]

They usually introduced themselves as "Sho-sho-nee" or some variant, but travelers almost always called them Snakes. It was perhaps an epithet their enemies invented because they used snake heads painted on sticks to terrify their foes, or perhaps because a snakelike motion signified Shoshone in sign language. Even after living among them for nine years and learning more of their language than any white man ever had, Osborne Russell "never saw one of the nation who could give me either the derivation or definition of the word Sho sho nie." Like most tribal names, it probably meant "The People."

The Shoshones were "kind and hospitable to whites thankful for favors indignant at injuries and but little addicted to theft," wrote Russell, who, like most mountaineers had excellent relations with the tribe. "I have found it to be a general fea-

---

[48] Burnett, *Recollections and Opinions of an Old Pioneer*, 113.
[49] Fitzpatrick to Abert, 5 February 1846, in Abert Family Papers, Missouri Historical Society.
[50] Madsen, "Shoshoni Indians," in Powell, *Utah History Encyclopedia*, 497.

ture of their character to divide the last morsel of food with the hungry stranger." Russell estimated their population at five to six thousand, evenly divided between those who lived in large villages and hunted bison and the small detached bands made up of two to ten families that subsisted on roots, fish, seeds, and berries. The buffalo hunters lived in spacious buffalo-skin lodges and were "well armed with fusees and well supplied with horses." Their government was a democracy with elements of meritocracy, since "deeds of valor promotes the Chief to the highest points attainable from which he is at any time liable to fall for misdemeanor in office."[51] Other whites had mixed feelings about the Eastern Shoshones. Warren Ferris thought they were "brave, robust, active and shrewd, but suspicious, treacherous, jealous and malicious" and the greatest rascals in the Rockies.[52]

Travelers showed much less sympathy for the Shoshones' desert-dwelling cousins. Emigrants used the epithet "Diggers" to refer to the Great Basin tribes—the Western Shoshones, Goshutes, Bannocks, and Northern Paiutes. The adaptations these peoples made to their harsh environment, including digging for the roots and insects that made up part of their diet, led to their name, and their customs appalled overlanders. "Those 'Root Digging Indians' run principally naked," wrote Robert Caufield after his party lost five horses to them on the Snake River in 1847. "Some are partly covered with rabbit skins & some have a few willows sewed together to cover their nakedness."[53] Joseph Williams "heard the mountain men tell of the miserable state of the Indian root-diggers. Numbers of them would be found dead from pure starvation, having no guns to kill game with, and poor shelters to live in, and no clothing except some few skins." They struck the reverend as a vivid example of the depravity of heathens in their natural state: "These creatures, when traveling in a hurry, will leave their lame and blind to perish in the wilderness," he charged.[54]

The bands now known as the Goshutes and Western Shoshones numbered almost ten-thousand souls in 1840, by far the largest component of the Shoshone nation. They roamed the deserts west of the Great Salt Lake in "as many as eleven major bands distributed from the present Utah-Nevada border to Winnemucca on the west," Brigham Madsen noted. They were notorious for using quartz or obsidian-tipped arrows poisoned with rattlesnake venom mixed with antelope liver to cripple passing travelers' livestock.[55]

---

[51] Russell, "The Snake Indians," *Journal of a Trapper*, 143–45.

[52] Powell, *Utah History Encyclopedia*, 497; and Ferris, *Life in the Rocky Mountains*, 385–87.

[53] Robert Caufield to John Caufield, 1 April 1848, Oregon Historical Society.

[54] Williams, *Narrative of a Tour*, 53.

[55] Russell, *Journal of a Trapper*, 143–44.

The *Banakwut,* a name the Shoshones may have given them meaning "people from below," were generally called Bonacks, Bonarks, or Panocs in overland sources. The nation was closely related to the *Numa*—the Northern Paiutes—and more distantly to the Shoshones. The Bannocks ranged from the Humboldt River in the south to the Salmon and Beaverhead rivers in the north, where they gave their name to Bannack, Montana's first capital. They controlled much of the trail along the Snake, where they became "the scourge of western roads from Fort Bridger on the east to Humboldt Sink and Fort Boise in the west." They occasionally made war against the Shoshones, but the Cayuse people were their particular enemies. Missionary Mary Walker found the Bannocks she met on Snake River "more savage than any we have seen in their appearance." Although trappers regarded them "as a treacherous and dangerous race," Thomas J. Farnham considered the Bannocks to be a fierce, warlike, and athletic people.[56]

"The set called diggers or chochoukos are misserable objects nearly altogether naked and starving the greater part of the year, different Kinds of roots with crickets and nuts are the principal part of their food," Richard Grant reported.[57] White observers almost always spoke contemptuously of "that branch of the great Snake tribe called Shoshokoes, or Root Diggers," the relatively sympathetic Washington Irving reported. "They are, in general, very poor; destitute of most of the comforts of life, and extremely indolent; but a mild, inoffensive race." Based on reports from Benjamin Bonneville's encounters with bands living near Oregon's Powder River, Irving described the complicated game enclosures they built to trap antelope. "The Shoshokoes do not appear to be destitute of ingenuity. They manufacture good ropes, and even a tolerably fine thread" used to make perfectly watertight baskets. These masters of survival ground seeds they collected into a flour that made a "very palatable paste or gruel." The Shoshokoes dried fish for winter or to trade, "giving a large quantity in exchange for an awl, a knife, or a fish-hook. Others were in the most abject state of want and starvation."[58]

John C. Frémont ranked the Great Basin's Indians with "the lower animal creation," but he at least noticed they were "constantly occupied in struggling to support existence." He considered the "unusually gay savages" he met at Salmon Falls to be poor people, but they were "still a joyous, talkative race, who grow fat and become poor with the salmon." Frémont also found Northern Paiutes at Pyramid Lake who "were very fat, and appeared to live an easy and happy life."[59] Ironically,

[56] Madsen, *The Bannock of Idaho,* 7–8, 18, 63–64; and Wilkes, *Narrative of the United States Exploring Expedition,* 4:471–74.

[57] Grant to Simpson, 15 March 1844, HBC Archives, D.5/1, fo. 427.

[58] Irving, *The Rocky Mountains,* 173–74.

[59] Spence and Jackson, *The Expeditions of John Charles Frémont,* 1:487, 530–31, 609.

when a Numa band first met him, his blue eyes and beard convinced them he was
half man and half owl, and their leader Winnemucca believed Frémont was actually the white man's devil.[60]

The "poor miserable wretches" west of Salt Lake, Thomas Fitzpatrick predicted in 1846, would soon become extinct.[61] Despite wars and atrocities against
them that persisted until the end of overland emigration, the Great Basin tribes
would do what they had always done—survive. They were well aware of what had
happened to them: "The white people took everything away from the Indian," a
Northern Paiute tradition recalled, "because they were snakes . . . That's why they
took everything and told the Indians to go way out in the mountains and live."[62]

First Encounters: A Snake of Dust

While the Indians who lived in the Missouri basin had long experience with
European traders and adventurers, in the remote reaches of the Great Basin, the
situation was entirely different. The first known outsiders to visit the Humboldt
River did not arrive until the mid-1820s, and the traditions of some tribes indicate the first whites they encountered came in wagon trains.

The westernmost of these Indians, the Wa She Shu or Washoes, may have
been the first to encounter Europeans. They ranged throughout the central Sierra
Nevada and along the rivers that drained its eastern slopes. Between fifteen hundred and three thousand Washoes shared the far western valleys of the Great
Basin from Honey Lake to Carson Valley with their more powerful neighbors,
the Northern Paiutes.[63] The life-sustaining water of *Daowaga,* the Washoe name
for Lake Tahoe and the source of its modern name, was the center of the Washoe
world. They believed the waters of the sacred lake breathed life into the land and
its inhabitants—the plants, animals, fish, birds, and people. No records survive
describing Spanish and Mexican expeditions into the Sierra, but the Washoe have
preserved traditions and use Spanish words, indicating they had met and fought
white men before the emigrants arrived.[64]

The tribe subsisted on pine nuts, acorns, deer, rabbits, trout, and other plants
and game. In addition to bows, they used long nets "perhaps 30 to 40 feet long,

---

[60] Inter-tribal Council of Nevada, *Numa,* 20.

[61] Fitzpatrick to Abert, 5 February 1846, in Abert Family Papers, Missouri Historical Society. Fitzpatrick passed
on rumors that the Western Shoshone and Northern Paiutes had "been known in many cases to eat their own off-
spring. This occurs from desperate necessity."

[62] "White Men are Snakes," in Ramsey, *Numa,* 258.

[63] Downs, *The Two Worlds of the Washo,* 4; Kroeber, *Handbook of the Indians of California,* 570–71.

[64] Amy James, Reno-Sparks Indian Colony, interview with Jo Ann Nevers, 23 October 1975, in Nevers, *Wa She
Shu,* 5, 38.

kept upright in the ground by slight sticks at intervals" to hunt rabbits and birds. They showed John C. Frémont the first part of their route over the Sierra, and even in the dead of winter he watched them "skimming along like birds" over the highest peaks on circular snowshoes about a foot in diameter. While lost in the mountains in February 1844, the explorer found them comfortably camped in deep snow, living on "an abundant supply of pine-nuts" six thousand feet above sea level. While his own party nearly starved to death, the Washoes thrived on this simple food, which formed "their great winter sustenance—a portion being always at hand, shut up in the natural storehouse of the cones."[65] The Washoe preserved intriguing traditions about their first experiences with explorers and wagon trains. They closely observed the behavior of these strange-looking out-landers and their extraordinary animals. One band caught a stray ox, and having studied how the whites used the animal they "packed the ox and led it for a time, then they experimented with riding the beast. Finally they tired of the novelty and butchered the ox and feasted on its flesh." Later, Washoes kept a party of starving emigrants under surveillance at Donner Lake and occasionally left them gifts of food.[66]

"No doubt we are the first whites they have seen," Peter Skene Ogden wrote after encountering Northern Paiutes in southern Oregon in 1828, "and [they] sup-pose we have come with no good intentions towards them." As Joseph Walker's subsequent slaughter of Paiutes in 1834 indicates, it was a fair assumption. The first contacts between American fur traders and Great Basin Natives gave both Western Shoshones and Northern Paiutes good reasons to be wary of whites— although when Ogden's Hudson's Bay brigade encountered "upwards of 200 Indi-ans marching on our camp" on the Humboldt River in 1829 and concluded it was a war party from their dress and drums, the Canadians avoided killing any of them.[67] Curiosity was a powerful factor when Great Basin Indians first met whites, but violence would be a constant reality in relations between the two peoples for the next three decades.

Despite the bloody encounters that preceded and followed it, the first recorded meeting between overland emigrants and an Indian in today's Nevada was a happy event. In mid-September 1841, the Bidwell-Bartleson party's castoff goods and abandoned wagons made one ancient Western Shoshone the richest and most technologically advanced inhabitant of his land.[68] Most other first encounters left bitter memories. "When the whites first came to Nevada there were a great many

---

[65] Spence and Jackson, *The Expeditions of John Charles Frémont,* 29 January 1844, 1:621.

[66] Downs, *The Two Worlds of the Washo,* 73.

[67] Ogden, *Peter Skene Ogden's Snake Country Journals,* 4 November 1828 and 28 May 1829.

[68] Bidwell, 15–16 September 1841, in Nunis, *The Bidwell-Bartleson Party,* 44.

Indians living here, but many were killed off by soldiers and pioneers," Western Shoshone Josie Carson recalled. "The Indians escaped by hiding under sage-
brushes during the night, because during the daylight the whites found them and
killed them."[69] Tribal tradition tells that Shoshones did not initiate the violence:
"Whites started the fighting between Indians and whites as the whitemen used
to attack the Indian women and they never let the Indians alone," Te-Moak tribal
chair Hugh Stevens remembered. "When the whitemen first came the Indians
used to hide when they seen them coming."[70]

The passage of the first wagons through the Great Basin dramatically altered
the lives of the peoples who had lived there for centuries. Sometime during the
early 1840s, a young father and his family surveyed the Humboldt River from a
cave high on the side of *Wongoguttah,* a peak near what is now Battle Mountain,
Nevada. This Newe family, as the Western Shoshones call themselves, "saw a
cloud of dust—a snake of dust. They had never seen anything like it before, nothing they knew could make that much dust," Lois Whitney, the man's great-great-
granddaughter, recalled. "I believe he watched it for several days [as it] stopped
and started again in the morning." The father, being very curious, wanted to
know what it was, but to be safe he hid his family in the cave and covered it over
with rocks and brush. He told them, "If I don't return by this time you will know
I have met my demise," and they should join the main band. "You go to them to
let them know what is happening here," he said.

But the father returned and told his family what he had learned after he slipped
up as close to the wagon train as he dared. "He could see fires and around the fire
people were doing things, like dancing. It was the first time he saw a human with
hair on the face, with a beard. They made strange noises, not threatening. They
were dancing and they had musical instruments he had never seen before, vio-
lins. So he watched them from a distance at night, crouched near the sagebrush."
These strange people had huge, unknown animals and houses that moved. The
next morning the father was amused, for the strangers had made strange prints in
the dirt, he said. "When they left, the trail left by the wagons was like a snake."
Lois Whitney said. "That's all I remember."[71]

Visionary Northern Paiutes had foreseen the coming of the whites. A shaman
now remembered only as Cap John's father dreamed that two men "with white
skin and white eyes, with hair on their faces, leading two strange creatures with

[69] Josie Carson, 18 December 1974 interview with June Tom, in Crum et al., *Newe,* 25.
[70] Hugh Stevens, 24 October 1974 interview with June Tom, in ibid., 25.
[71] Whitney interview, 9 January 2002, Elko, Nevada. According to Whitney, "This story was told to me by my
mother. My mother's name was Elizabeth Jackson Brady. The story was told to her by her grandmother's father,
which would have been my great-great-grandfather."

big ears and wall eyes" surprised two young women who were fanning chaff to make meal: they screamed, threw down their *yattahs,* and ran away. After the dream came true, a Paiute hunting party met two men near the Forty-mile Desert and "knowing it was not right for men to be so different from themselves, stoned them to death." They cut up their big jack rabbits for meat and each took a piece of the men's clothing. The people fought so much over the clothing that it had to be cut into small pieces and divided among the band. "Everybody had something now," Annie Lowry recalled, "and nobody had anything."[72]

"I was a very small child when the first white people came into our country. They came like a lion, yes, like a roaring lion, and have continued so ever since, and I have never forgotten their first coming," wrote Sarah Winnemucca. She was born as Thocmetony—Shell Flower—in about 1844, and her grandfather Truckee told her how the first mother and first father had two sets of children. "One girl and one boy were dark and the others were white," he said, but the children fought. "Why are you so cruel to each other?" their father asked. "Go across the mighty ocean and do not seek each other's lives." Truckee had once camped near Humboldt Lake, where someone in his band spotted a party traveling east from California. When he learned the white strangers had hair on their faces, he jumped up, clasped his hands, and cried, "My white brothers—my long-looked for white brothers have come at last!" These people must, he thought "be our white brothers, and I want to welcome them. I want to love them as I love all of you."

Winnemucca, Thocmetony's father, was more skeptical than Truckee: "I fear we will suffer greatly by their coming to our country; they come for no good to us, although my father said they were our brothers, but they do not seem to think we are like them." Winnemucca described a dream he had for three nights running: "I looked North and South and East and West, and saw nothing but dust, and I heard a great weeping. I saw women crying, and I also saw my men shot down by the white people. They were killing my people with something that made a great noise like thunder and lightning, and I saw the blood streaming from the mouths of my men that lay all around me," he said. "I saw it as if it was real. Oh, my dear children! You may think it is only a dream,—nevertheless, I feel that it will come to pass.[73]

Winnemucca's prophetic dream soon proved more accurate than Truckee's peaceful legend. "While we were in the mountains hiding, the people that my grandfather called our white brothers came along to where our winter supplies were. They set everything we had left on fire," Thocmetony recalled. "This whole

---

[72] Scott, *Karnee,* 4–5.
[73] Hopkins, *Life among the Piutes,* 5–7, 14. Hopkins's book shows the influence of her editor, Mrs. Horace Mann. Most historians believe Truckee and Winnemucca were about the same age.

band of white people perished in the mountains, for it was too late to cross them. We could have saved them, only my people were afraid of them. We never knew who they were, or where they came from. So, poor things, they must have suffered fearfully, for they all starved there."[74]

A QUIET, CIVIL PEOPLE, BUT PROUD AND HAUGHTY:
OREGON'S INDIANS

When the first missionaries arrived in Oregon in the 1830s, its Native peoples had been in contact with Europeans since at least 1774. Even before that, Old World diseases had a devastating impact on their cultures: direct contact increased the toll. Meriwether Lewis and William Clark estimated the population of the lower Columbia at eight thousand, but diseases, notably epidemics of smallpox and malaria, became established in the lower Columbia after 1830 and dramatically reduced the Chinook population on the Pacific and in the Willamette Valley. "The Indians of the Columbia were once a numerous and powerful people; the shore of the river, for scores of miles, was lined with their villages," wrote naturalist John Kirk Townsend. When he visited in 1834, only ruins marked these formerly prosperous sites. "The depopulation here has been truly fearful," he observed. "A gentleman told me, that only four years ago, as he wandered near what had formerly been a thickly peopled village, he counted no less than sixteen dead, men and women, lying unburied and festering in the sun in front of their habitations."[75]

Oregon's diverse Native population is generally sorted into four geographic groups: those who lived along the coast and in the interior valleys, and the tribes living east of the Cascades on the Columbia Plateau or south of the Crooked and Burnt rivers in the Great Basin. Travelers on the Oregon Trail met the Paiutes and Bannocks who lived from the Upper Snake River to the Powder River Valley; the Nez Perces, Cayuses, Umatillas, Walla Wallas, and Wascos of the plateau who ranged from the Blue Mountains to The Dalles; and the Upper Chinook Celilos, Multnomahs, and Clackamas who lived from Celilo Falls to the Willamette River.

By the time emigrants began arriving, the Native population of the Willamette Valley was already overwhelmed. "The Indians of this valley consists of 4 or 5 small tribes, perfectly inoffensive, they haven't the courage to collar a hen generally," Clarborne Campbell Walker wrote in 1845. "They are hired to work by

---

[74] Ibid., 12–13. Sarah Winnemucca's evocation of the Donner party, which had re-entered American consciousness with the publication of McGlashan's *History of the Donner Party* four years before *Life among the Piutes* appeared, is suspect. However, 1846 overlander Joseph Aram recalled that after Paiutes killed five of his company's oxen, "To get even with them we set fire to their houses and returned to camp."

[75] Townsend, *Across the Rockies*, 222–23.

the whites and they generally work well for Indians. They are diminishing very fast by veneral [*sic*] disease."[76] The tribes of the plateau and Great Basin survived the arrival of traders and missionaries with their cultures intact, largely because their far-ranging seasonal rounds helped spare them from the plagues brought in by seaborne traders that had reduced the coastal population by some 90 percent.

The policies of the Hudson's Bay Company produced mixed results for Oregon's Indians. Its posts provided access to useful European technology, but the fur trade disrupted traditional economies and put the tribes at the mercy of the Company's often-ruthless servants, sometimes with fatal results. "The life of an Indian was never yet by a trapper put in competition with a beaver's skin," wrote early Indian-rights advocate Herbert Beaver, who served as a chaplain in Oregon from 1836 to 1838 and claimed contact with twelve tribes living within a ninety-mile radius of Fort Vancouver. Beaver reported "several most atrocious outrages" and alleged that an HBC party killed an Indian, probably mortally wounded another, and threw a child into a fire after a quarrel over a missing knife that later turned up in the possession of a Company man. If whites had always treated the Indian properly, Beaver concluded, they would never have resorted to acts of violence to drive whites from their country, but "constant ill-usage" had taught the tribes to regard them as their natural enemy.[77]

The horse had transformed the lives of the Columbia Plateau tribes, who had previously made their living along the Columbia and its tributaries in the Blue Mountains. The animals thrived in the rich grasslands between the Cascade Range and the Blue Mountains, and horses enabled the tribes to extend venture eastward to hunt bison. The dignity, sophistication, and magnificent horses of eastern Oregon's Native peoples impressed the first Americans to visit the country. Joseph Williams met To-a-yah-nu, a young Walla Walla leader whose English name was Elijah Hedding, the "son of one of the chiefs, who could talk some English, had obtained religion, and was my interpreter." After Williams preached to the tribe, Elijah "exhorted them some himself" and "they seemed to be much affected, and were very friendly." As his party left the Umatilla River, Williams "passed some of the prettiest gangs and bands of horses I ever saw in my life, belonging to the Indians. Some of the Indians own four or five hundred head."[78] The Americans who followed Williams would bring death to Elijah Hedding and as hard a fate to the Indians' horses.

[76] Clarborne Campbell Walker to "Dear Brother, Sister and Friends," [December?] 1845, Purvine Family Records.

[77] Beaver, "Indian Conditions in 1836–38," 338.

[78] Williams, *Narrative of a Tour,* 4, 17 May 1842, 47–48.

Much Fabulous Talk about the Indian Character:
White Perceptions of Native Peoples

"There has been much fabulous talk about the Indian character," wrote Frederick A. Wislizenus, the perceptive German who marched up the Platte River and over the Rockies to Fort Hall in 1839 and left an insightful record of the Native peoples he encountered. "Some pose them as Roman heroes and unspoiled sons of Nature; others as cowards and the scum of humanity. The truth is between these extremes," he observed.[79]

The expectations emigrants brought with them inevitably colored their descriptions of their encounters with the dozens of tribes that lived along the trail. Many had heard or read popular accounts of Indian life, most of which were wildly inaccurate, before they headed west. Travelers often set out with elaborate theories about Indians, with some believing they were descendents of Israel's lost tribes or that they were either doomed to extinction or destined for conversion and redemption. A few, perhaps, had attended artist George Catlin's 1839 traveling show, which included more than five hundred images of Indians from forty-eight tribes he had sketched while traveling up the Missouri and through the heartland. In addition to the paintings, the production featured a Crow teepee, Indian dancers (or non-Indian actors performing supposed Indian dances), and archery demonstrations. A handful might have seen Alfred Jacob Miller's romantic paintings of his trip to the Rockies that recorded the last days of the fur trade; these were exhibited in New York in 1839, giving the country its first accurate visual glimpse of the Rocky Mountain West.[80]

A few may have attended *Metamora,* winner of America's first playwriting contest in 1828, which required that the principal character be "an aboriginal of this country." The wave of "stage Indians" that followed *Metamora*'s success became, in the words of one critic, "a perfect nuisance."[81] Many more Americans had seen or heard about these depictions of Indians second- or third-hand; others formed their ideas of Indians from the noble warriors and fearsome savages who populated advertisements, calendars, labels, and cheap pictorial reproductions. American popular culture, especially the phenomenally popular novels of James Fenimore Cooper, informed the expectations and fears of the vast majority of overland travelers who had never met an Indian. Too often, those assumptions were based on ignorance, expediency, apprehension, and prejudice.

Indigenous peoples living in the most remote corners of the West who might never have seen a white face before wagons rolled across their lands had already

[79] Wislizenus, *A Journey to the Rocky Mountains,* 150.
[80] Goetzmann and Goetzmann, *The West of the Imagination,* 26, 58–68.
[81] Bird, *Dressing in Feathers,* 13.

experienced generations of changes wrought by the intrusion of the first Spanish fortune hunters into the borderlands in 1540. Along the Missouri frontier,
emigrants encountered Indians whose lives had been dramatically altered by the
advance of the Americans. "Westport was full of Indians," Francis Parkman wrote
after his visit in 1846, "whose little shaggy ponies were tied by dozens along the
houses and fences. Sacs and Foxes, with shaved heads and painted faces, Sha-
wanoes and Delawares, fluttering in calico frocks and turbans, Wyandots dressed
like white men, and a few wretched Kanzas wrapped in old blankets, were stroll-
ing about the streets, or lounging in and out of the shops and houses."[82]

However knowledgeable they might have felt about Indian ways when they
set out on the trail, most emigrants knew virtually nothing about the nature of
the peoples they would encounter—not their languages, their social and governmental structures, their economies, their beliefs, or even what they called
themselves. Often the travelers supplied their want of information with convenient assumptions. If they needed an Indian to handle negotiations, many simply
chose one who proved compliant and designated him a "chief." They identified all
Indian groups as "tribes"—ignoring the wide variety in organizational structures
among these varied cultures. Many used names for the peoples they met without
knowing that the word they chose might derive from a derogatory term used by
the group's enemies or from simple linguistic confusion. As missionary Samuel
Parker observed, the Flatheads did not have flat heads, and the Nez Perces did not
pierce their noses. "That those names have been given by white men, is evident,
since they do not call each other by the names," he noted.[83] Ironically, these
names persist, but each nation typically called itself *The People*.

In 1840 the tribes beyond the plains were essentially unknown to most Americans. Shoshonean peoples—the Ute, Shoshone, Paiute, and Bannock—ruled the
Great Basin and the central Rockies. Although these tribes had long-established
ties with New Mexico, only a few veterans of the Rocky Mountain fur trade knew
anything about them. The Shoshones, Flatheads, Blackfeet, Nez Perces, Umatillas,
Cayuses, and Wascos had encountered Lewis and Clark, but the Klamath, Modoc,
Shasta, Washoe, Maidu, and Miwok peoples of Oregon and Alta California could not
have been more mysterious had they lived on the moon. Many early explorers had
only the dimmest understanding of these cultures; their reports were riddled with
mistakes and misunderstandings, and emigrants would carry on the tradition.

So the Indians of the Far West were a mystery to most of the sojourners who
would soon crowd the trails to Oregon and California. But before the first Amer-

---

[82] Parkman, *The California and Oregon Trail*, 12–13.
[83] Parker, *Journal of an Exploring Tour beyond the Rocky Mountains*, 76.

ican family had taken a wagon across the plains, Frederick Wislizenus predicted that the ultimate destiny of the "wild tribes" could be "foretold almost to a certainty" from what had already happened to Indians in the established states. "The waves of civilization will draw nearer and nearer from the East and from the West, till they cover the sandy plains, and cast their spray on the feet of the Rockies," he prophesied. "The few fierce tribes who may have maintained themselves until that time in the mountains, may offer some resistance to the progress of the waves, but the swelling flood will rise higher and higher, till at last they are buried beneath it."[84] As the young American nation embarked on the conquest and settlement of its western provinces, the stage was set for confrontation, violence, suffering, and tragedy, and one of the most rapid, dramatic, and sweeping transformations in human history.

---

[84] Wislizenus, *A Journey to the Rocky Mountains,* 160.

CHAPTER 2

DIFFICULTIES
WHICH NEVER OCCURRED
TO THEIR MINDS

Fur Traders, Adventurers, and Visionaries

Westward movement looms large in American history: even the North American continent has been sliding west over an ancient seafloor for most of the past 200 million years.[1] Yet "westering" was a concept that had no fixed geographic destination. In the early nineteenth century, most American settlers migrating west were bound for the fertile land immediately beyond the Appalachian Mountains. Confiscating and occupying Indian lands in the Ohio and Mississippi river valleys consumed most of the young republic's limited military power and accommodated the country's swelling population for decades. Those with an urge to venture beyond the settled frontier generally headed toward Mexico's northern provinces—to trade in Santa Fe or to settle and conquer Texas. Until the 1830s, the Rocky Mountains and the northern plains remained terra incognita, a vast unmapped territory known largely through myth and rumor.

Yet even before Lewis and Clark returned from the Pacific in 1806, fur traders were pushing up the Missouri River and following Indian trails across mountain passes, filling in the blank space on early maps representing unknown country. The exploration of vast reaches of the American West fell to the practitioners of the fur trade, the single enterprise whose rewards outweighed the risks of a venture as fraught with peril as penetrating the Rocky Mountains. The great stone spine of the continent long remained a geographic mystery, but by the late 1830s the "mountaineers," as they were known among themselves, had ranged the Far West and explored most of the traces that later became overland wagon roads. In the process, they rapidly obliterated the animals that provided their livelihood.

---

[1] Meldahl, *Hard Road West*, 110.

The heroic era of the Rocky Mountain fur trade flourished from the first ren-dezvous of 1825 to the last in 1840, barely fifteen years. With the virtual extermi-nation of the beaver, it appeared that since the region lacked any known source of wealth other than furs, Americans might well abandon the Rocky Mountains and Oregon to the Indians and the British, as they had done during the War of 1812. A quarter century later, the only Americans interested enough in Oregon to risk their lives going there were missionaries possessed by visions of bringing salvation to the savage Indians or obsessed promoters of national destiny and themselves. Yet the glories of the fur trade, the march of Christianity, and national expan-sion proved to be only parts of a much larger drama of international intrigue that had followed the fall of Napoléon. In the end, a handful of extraordinarily com-mon people—fewer than ten thousand—would determine the outcome of the struggle to control the West Coast of North America.

Thomas Jefferson reportedly said it would take a hundred generations for Americans to settle the lands of the Louisiana Purchase, and the best experts expected it would take at least a generation, if not more, to blaze a single-season wagon road to Oregon. The uncoordinated efforts of fur hunters, government explorers, and missionaries did the job in a little more than a dozen years. By the end of 1838, six American women had accomplished what had long been con-sidered impossible: between summer and fall, they had traveled by wagon and horseback from the Missouri to the Columbia River.

THE GREAT AMERICAN DESERT: EARLY EXPLORATION

The origins of the trails that connected the United States to the Pacific Coast extend far back in the continent's recorded history—"as far back as one has the will to go," the great trail historian Dale L. Morgan observed.[2] The first known expedition up the Platte River, the broad valley that led to South Pass and made overland wagon travel possible, began in 1739. Brothers Pierre-Antoine and Paul Mallet and six Canadians set out from the Illinois Country to open a trade route to Santa Fe. They became the first—and for many decades the only—Europeans known to have ascended the Platte River Valley to the Rocky Mountains. Like most of the early adventurers who followed them, the Mallets took the river's south fork and turned south along the Front Range to reach the passes leading to the Spanish colony of Nuevo Mexico.

The Mallet brothers followed hunting and trade routes that were already millen-nia old. The contribution American Indians made to overland trails was enormous.

---

[2] Morgan, *Overland in 1846*, 14.

Like many nomadic peoples, most of the tribes who ruled the lands on the way to Oregon or California had inviolable traditions of friendship and hospitality toward strangers, and their thirst for European technology inclined them to welcome Americans passing through as appreciated visitors and trading partners.[3] Native trading routes spanned the continent in a complex web, but no single Indian trail ran from the Missouri to the Pacific, and their proud cultures appeared to pose as great a challenge to American settlement as the alien and imposing geography of the plains, mountains, and deserts of the Far West.

Alexander Mackenzie became the first European to reach the Pacific Ocean from the United States or Canada in 1793, and American explorers, fur traders, and settlers later found that generations of French-Canadians had beaten them to the West Coast. After Lewis and Clark's Corps of Discovery discovered nothing of any apparent practical value except fur-bearing animals, the American government did surprisingly little to explore its western territory for almost four decades. Its few attempts did little to change the perception that the West was a hazardous land whose rewards did not match its risks. Spanish authorities arrested members of Lieutenant Zebulon Pike's expedition in 1807, and the army lost 160 men to scurvy and exposure in 1819 trying to establish two posts near Council Bluffs. The Long expedition in 1820 explored the headwaters of the South Platte, Arkansas, and Red rivers but failed to expand America's geographic knowledge significantly. Its greatest contribution to overland trails, historian Richard Dillon observed, was to create a potent myth that convinced "both Government and people that the way west was blocked by the Great American Desert."[4]

Indians had laid down complicated networks of hunting, trade, and war trails across the Great Plains and the Rockies long before the first wagons headed west. Traveling with one of the last fur-trade caravans in 1839, Frederick Wislizenus "crossed the so-called 'Pawnee trails,' a broad road made by the Pawnees" and observed that the marks of their "prairie buggies"—the travois poles on which Indians "put their lodges, camp equipage, children, and sometimes their dogs"—made their roads easily recognizable.[5] The topographical challenge confronting the mountain men was to link these hundreds of trails into a road that went from the Missouri frontier over plains, mountains, and deserts to the beaver dams of the West. The mountaineers did not blaze many trails. Instead, they learned to pick the best route to get them where they wanted to go from a dozen existing Indian traces. The journals of fur-seeking explorers like Jedediah Smith and

---

[3] Tate, "From Cooperation to Conflict," 21; and *Indians and Emigrants.*

[4] Dillon, "Stephen Long's Great American Desert," 93.

[5] Wislizenus, *A Journey to the Rocky Mountains,* 40. The correspondent of the *Missouri Republican* at the Fort Laramie treaty conference used the term "prairie buggies" on 5 October 1851.

James Clyman often spoke of their debt to the Indians, both for the trails themselves and for the aid and advice the tribes gave them.[6]

THE BOSTONS AND KING GEORGE'S MEN

Besides hoping to find the mythical Northwest Passage, Thomas Jefferson initially conceived of the Corps of Discovery as a way to make inroads into the lucrative British fur trade in North America.[7] When Lewis and Clark descended the Missouri in 1806, they met Americans heading up the river, independent adventurers who were determined to break the monopoly of well-established English fur corporations such as the North West and the Hudson's Bay companies. By the next year, Manuel Lisa had built the first American fort in present-day Montana. Andrew Henry, Lisa's partner in the Missouri Fur Company, established trading posts at Three Forks and Fort Henry near present-day St. Anthony, Idaho, dispatching three parties in 1811 to explore the country.

On his way to becoming America's first millionaire, John Jacob Astor launched the American Fur Company to capitalize on the commerce of the Great Lakes. He founded the Pacific Fur Company in 1810 to capture the Oregon trade, reflecting his determination to dominate the fur business in North America. He dispatched a maritime expedition that established Astoria, an outpost at the mouth of the Columbia, in March 1811. At the same time, Astor's partner, Wilson Price Hunt, left his winter camp south of Council Bluffs to lead a party up the Missouri and overland to Oregon. Hunt's men, mostly French-Canadian veterans of Astor's Great Lakes operations, crossed the Rocky Mountains at or near Union Pass. At the recently abandoned Fort Henry in October 1811, Hunt divided his company and unwisely traded his horses for canoes, in which he hoped to descend the Snake River. The voyage soon ended in disaster at Cauldron Linn, "the Devil's Scuttle Hole." Hunt again divided his party and set out on a long hard march down the river to Oregon, during which his men had to eat their moccasins. Hunt reached the Umatilla River on 8 January 1812, and six weeks later his bedraggled company arrived at Fort Astoria, a month behind the men he had left at Fort Henry and three months ahead of the party Ramsey Crooks and John Day led down the opposite side of the Snake.[8]

The destruction of its supply ship *Tonquin,* blown up after Indians seized it, and war with Britain doomed the Pacific Fur Company. Upon learning of the *Tonquin*'s fate, in June 1812 Hunt sent Robert Stuart east to ask Astor to send another ship. The return journey of the Astorians to the United States had enduring

---

[6] Korns and Morgan, *West from Fort Bridger,* 1–2.
[7] Worsham, "Jefferson Looks Westward," 254–59.
[8] Chittenden, *The American Fur Trade in the Far West,* 1:182–94.

consequences, for Stuart made the first known crossing of the Rockies via the South Pass corridor, a breakthrough in geographic knowledge with immense political and financial implications. Stuart's discovery was little noted at the time, but from the mouth of the Columbia to the Kansas River the returning Astorians explored most of what became the Oregon Trail. Astor's partners sold Fort Astoria to the North West Company in October 1813, just in time to avoid its capture by the British Navy, but the deal effectively ended American influence in Oregon for two decades.[9]

Most of the Americans who first visited the Pacific Northwest were Yankee seafarers, known to the Oregon tribes as "Bostons." Their rivals, Great Britain's "King George's men," effectively shut down the American fur trade during the War of 1812. For the young republic, the loss was unfortunate, since the two great British commercial powers in North America, the North West Company and the Hudson's Bay Company, were locked in a bitter trade war. Relative peace came when the Hudson's Bay Company absorbed its rival, creating what Henry Nash Smith called a "mercantilist colossus." Parliament issued a license in 1821 to the Company, whose crimson banner displayed the initials "HBC," which wags said stood for "Here Before Christ," and extended the firm's exclusive right to control the Indian trade from the drainage of Hudson's Bay to the Oregon Country. In evaluating its prospects west of the Rockies, the combined corporation considered abandoning its profitless posts in New Caledonia (roughly two-thirds of what is now British Columbia, one of the richest fur countries in the world) and the Department of Columbia.[10] Instead, in 1824 the Company sent Dr. John McLoughlin west to manage its Oregon interests. The relentless and talented George Simpson, the corporation's new chief executive, followed him to determine if the region was worth the effort.[11]

At Rivière la Biche, the hard-driving Simpson overtook McLoughlin, who was traveling with his wife and two youngest children in Red River carts. The six-foot-four-inch McLoughlin stood ten inches taller than the average white male of his time, and towered above his diminutive boss. The doctor's shock of shoulder-length hair had reportedly turned white after a canoe capsized on Lake Superior, drowning all aboard except the redoubtable Scotsman. Simpson, noting McLoughlin's Herculean size, commented, "He was such a figure as I should not like to meet in a dark Night" in a rough London neighborhood, while the doctor's

[9] Ronda, *Astoria and Empire*, 288–91.

[10] New Caledonia was the original British name for today's Pacific Northwest: the modern spelling "Oregon" first appeared in Jonathan Carver's 1778 *Travels through the Interior Part of North America*. William Cullen Bryant's 1817 poem, "Thanatopsis" ("in the continuous woods/Where rolls the Oregon"), gave it American connotations. For the word's probable origin, see Goddard and Love, "Oregon, the Beautiful," 238–59.

[11] MacKay, *The Honourable Company*, 158, 183–84, 187.

beard "would do honor to the chin of a Grizzly Bear."[12] As historian Malcolm Clark Jr. observed, time would prove that McLoughlin "was a great man, which handicapped him, and a good man, which handicapped him more."[13] The balding Simpson and the lion-maned giant became titans in the struggle to control the Pacific Northwest.

His 1824 visit convinced Simpson that under Chief Factor Archibald McDonald, the Columbia Department had been "neglected, shamefully mismanaged and a scene of the most wasteful extravagance and the most unfortunate dissension," but he was sure he and McLoughlin could make it pay. More importantly, he recognized the Columbia River's strategic significance, and the "Little Emperor" devised a strategy to keep its most valuable provinces in British hands forever. He abandoned the "large pile of buildings" at Fort George (the renamed Fort Astoria), and moved the district's headquarters up the Columbia and across the river from its confluence with the Willamette. He named it Fort Vancouver after the distinguished navigator to recall "our claim to the Soil and Trade with his discovery of the River and Coast on behalf of Gt. Britain."[14] Simpson insisted on putting the post on the heights of Mill Plain, but after two years without floods McLoughlin moved the fort to its permanent location closer to the Columbia.

Simpson dispatched former Nor'Wester Peter Skene Ogden to lead an expedition with orders to destroy all the fur-bearing resources in the "Snake Country"— roughly the area that is now Idaho and western Montana. Ogden extended his assignment into the Great Basin, which was legally Mexican territory. "If the region could be converted into a fur desert," ran Simpson's ruthless but compelling logic, "it would be difficult for the Americans either to reach or maintain themselves on the Columbia."[15]

ENTERPRISING YOUNG MEN: REVOLUTION IN THE FUR TRADE

In Saint Louis on 13 February 1822, frontier politician and entrepreneur William Ashley announced in the *Missouri Gazette* that he was seeking one hundred "Enterprising Young Men." This simple help-wanted ad signaled America's re-entry into the fur trade. Some of the men he recruited—Jedediah Smith, Hugh Glass, Hiram Scott, Mike Fink, Etienne Provost, and William Sublette—would become American legends. Other Ashley men, notably James P. Beckwourth,

---

[12] Simpson, *Fur Trade and Empire*, 26 September 1824, 23.

[13] Clark, *Eden Seekers*, 28.

[14] MacKay, *The Honourable Company*, 190–93. Vancouver had actually sailed past the Columbia and learned of its existence from the river's true discoverer, Robert Gray of the American ship *Columbia*.

[15] Morgan, *Jedediah Smith*, 131–32.

James Bridger, James Clyman, Thomas "Broken Hand" Fitzpatrick, and Moses "Black" Harris, would ensure the success of American overland emigration by blazing trails and leading wagon trains. Collectively they comprised a collection of characters that road-builder F. W. Lander considered "the best explorers in the world—the old beaver-trappers and hunters of the fur companies."[16]

Disaster forced General Ashley to revolutionize the American fur trade between 1823 and 1825. Traditionally, the fur business had always relied on rivers for transportation. Along them companies established trading posts, served by *engagés,* boatmen and hunters who worked for set periods at fixed salaries. In the last days of the British North West Company, Donald Mackenzie tried a new approach—leading brigades of veteran trappers into the Snake Country and packing in supplies to sell at annual trading fairs. This experiment proved successful, but none of Mackenzie's successors could keep it going.[17]

On the first of June 1823, Arikara warriors ambushed and killed one-sixth of Ashley's brigade in present-day South Dakota. After the mountaineers and American troops punished the Indians, in desperation Ashley sent Jedediah Smith and a dozen men west that fall on horseback. They wintered with the Absarokas, and then Smith, Fitzpatrick, Clyman, Sublette, and the others set out to find the Seeds-kee-dee, the Green River. In early 1824 they rediscovered South Pass and then fanned out through the area that is now Wyoming, Idaho, and Utah, trapping a fortune in beaver. Thomas Fitzpatrick returned to Saint Louis that fall and persuaded Ashley to send supplies to his men at a designated spot in the Rocky Mountains the following summer. Thus, out of necessity, Ashley adapted Mackenzie's brigade system to his purposes, creating the rendezvous and the free trapper, celebrated in history as the mountain man. Pack-train caravans replaced keelboats as the lifeline of the American fur trade, and the roving annual rendezvous supplanted trading posts as the collecting point for furs.

Meanwhile, Jedediah Smith traveled north to observe the Hudson's Bay Company operations. Sir George Simpson learned much from "our American visitant." Flattering reports of the Oregon Country had drawn notice in Missouri and raised speculation about its agricultural prospects, but on his arduous treks Smith and his men had "discovered difficulties which never occurred to their minds, and which are likely to deter his Countrymen from attempting that enterprize." In their geographic ignorance, Americans believed settlers could cross the central Rockies and "embark on large Rafts & Batteaux and glide down current about 800 or 1000 Miles at their ease to this 'Land of Promise,'" Simpson

---

[16] Lander, *Maps and Reports of the Fort Kearney, South Pass, and Honey Lake Wagon Road,* 8.
[17] Dodds, "Fur Trade," in Lamar, *The New Encyclopedia of the American West,* 415.

wrote. Like Smith, they would learn that Oregon was protected by "Mountains which even Hunters cannot attempt to pass, beyond which, is a Sandy desert of about 200 miles, likewise impassable, and from thence a rugged barren country of great extent, without Animals, where Smith and his party were nearly starved to Death." Settlers could never even think of trying the Snake River route. "So that I am of opinion, we have little to apprehend from Settlers in this quarter, and from Indian Traders nothing," Simpson concluded. Unless "the all grasping policy of the American Government" committed part of its national wealth to expansion, he was convinced the Hudson's Bay Company had nothing to fear from the Yankees—an uncommon misjudgment for the dynamic young executive.[18]

The times justified Simpson's assumptions: Oregon seemed excessively remote even to the most enthusiastic promoters of the West, and the difficulty of founding settlements in the Rocky Mountains appeared overwhelming. "I see no object which would induce any civilized man to locate himself in that Region, except those in pursuit of furs," William Ashley wrote in February 1828. There was much rich land around the Great Salt Lake, but it was "so divided by rough mountains that no Settlement could be made upon them sufficiently dense & Extensive to defend them against the depredations of the numerous tribes of Indians that inhabit that Country," a problem he considered "insurmountable."[19]

Yet American mountaineers had already proven that, as Joshua Pilcher observed, "The man must know but little of the American people who supposes they can be stopped by any thing in the shape of mountains, deserts, seas, or rivers."[20] Topography and risk did not deter the traders, fur hunters, and Indians who gathered at the annual rendezvous to swap furs for provisions, powder, alcohol, and goods from the states. Most fur men allied themselves with one or more tribes, married into them, and adopted local customs. "The white trappers, or hunters," John B. Wyeth wrote after traveling with them in 1832, "are a sort of half Indians in their manners and habits."[21]

"There is quite a number of men from the States throughout the Mountain Wilderness; They tell me there is more real pleasure in one year in the mountains than a whole Lifetime in a Settled Country," Richard Martin May wrote after meeting Joseph R. Walker in 1848. "There is no political strife no Religious Contention no domestic Broils no agricultural pursuits to tire and weary the Limbs. Though Last [but] not Least No Law nor Lawyers to Pettifog among them to mar their Peace and Sow discord among them." May added, "Their duties are confined

[18] Simpson, *Part of Dispatch from George Simpson . . . March 1, 1829*, 66–67.
[19] Ashley to Bates, 20 February 1828, in Morgan, *The West of William Ashley*, 179.
[20] Pilcher to Eaton, ca. December 1830, in Jackson, *British Establishments on the Columbia*, 7.
[21] Wyeth, *Oregon*, 63.

to the horse and gun and when they become Tired of one place they remove to another." Indian wives, not mountaineers, did all the heavy lifting, according to May, whose romanticized view ignored the miserable and dangerous work required to trap beaver in winter streams, as well as the risk and exploitation that characterized the business.[22] Still, something about the mountaineer's life, even with all its perils, led many of them to forswear civilization.[23]

These men touched off a brief golden age of exploration. In 1826 and 1827, Jedediah Smith led two parties down the Wasatch Front and across the Mojave Desert to southern California. He was seeking the Buenaventura, the mythical river that legend said originated near Great Salt Lake, cut through the Sierra Nevada, and flowed to the Pacific. On his return to the mountains in 1827, Smith used Ebbetts Pass and the west fork of the Walker River to make the first known crossing of the Sierra Nevada. His travels indicated that the Buenaventura was a wishful fantasy. He traversed the Great Basin too far south to strike the Humboldt River, which Peter Skene Ogden discovered and named the Unknown River in November 1828 on one of his Snake Country Expeditions.[24] For the next twenty years the river was best known as Marys River, perhaps in tribute to the Native wife of one of Ogden's *engagés* or to his own companion.[25]

William Ashley abandoned the wagon he took west from Fort Atkinson in fall 1824, but in 1827 William Sublette hauled the first wheeled vehicle—a four-pounder cannon—over South Pass.[26] Sublette—whose contemporaries considered him "one of the most active, intrepid, and renowned leaders" in the business—again showed what was possible when he took ten wagons and two buggies to the Wind River Mountains in 1830, stopping just short of the Continental Divide. That was as far as his firm "wished the wagons to go," but they "could easily have crossed the Rocky Mountains, it being what is called the *Southern Pass,* had it been desirable for them to do so," Sublette and his partners, Jedediah Smith and David Jackson, told Congress. "This is the first time that wagons ever went to the Rocky mountains; and the ease and safety with which it was done prove the facility of communicating over land with the Pacific ocean," they

---

[22] May, *The Schreek of Wagons,* 26 July 1848, 70–71.

[23] Richard J. Fehrman, "The Mountain Men—A Statistical View," in Hafen, *The Mountain Men,* 10:13. The 292 men studied in Hafen's collection had an average life expectancy of sixty-four years, but as Hafen observed, so little was known about most of the men who died in the trade "that no biographical sketches could be written." Ibid., 10:14.

[24] Morgan, *Jedediah Smith,* 210–14; and Smith, *The Southwest Expedition,* 170–9[2] Hostile Indians forced him to turn back, but Smith initially tried to cross the mountains by the American River, "which would have brought him down into the basin of the Humboldt River," Morgan observed; "he would have stumbled on the natural route across the Great Basin."

[25] Morgan, *The Humboldt,* 5, 45–46.

[26] Morgan, *The West of William Ashley,* 100, 166, 261n42.

prophesied. "The route from the *Southern Pass,* where the wagons stopped, to the Great Falls of the Columbia, being easier and better than on this side of the mountains, with grass enough, for the horses and mules; but a scarcity of game for the support of the men."[27]

Congress periodically expressed its desire to assert the American claim to the Oregon Country, but the U.S. Army essentially did nothing to explore the Rocky Mountains until 1842.[28] Captain Benjamin L. E. Bonneville had to take leave from the army to participate in the fur trade, and exactly what he was up to has always been something of a mystery. Known documents offer evidence both to counter and confirm the suspicion that he was a government agent, but it seems most probable that Captain Bonneville used private capital to bring his twenty wagons across South Pass in 1832. "He went all the way to the mountains," wrote John Ball, who passed Bonneville's wagons on the Blue River, "but with much difficulty."[29] The captain was unable to find the rendezvous at Pierres Hole and instead built Fort Bonneville at the mouth of Horse Creek on the Green River in what is now western Wyoming. Although the site was so unpromising that mountaineers called it "Fort Nonsense," it did lure six of the last eight rendezvous to the neighborhood.

Searching for the Buenaventura: Joseph R. Walker

Seeking to recoup some of the fortune he was losing in the fur business, Bonneville dispatched Joseph R. Walker to California to find, he hoped, a virgin country with an untapped beaver population. His party of mountaineers organized on Green River—ostensibly to trap on the waters of the Sierra Nevada, recalled William Craig, who accompanied the expedition. "In fact," Craig said, "the object was to steal horses from the Spaniards residing in California."[30] Bonneville may have dispatched the expedition at least in part to gather information about the Mexican province: he had at least secured a visa in Walker's name during a visit to Washington.[31]

Despite Jedediah Smith's exploration of the Great Basin, Walker hoped he might discover the legendary Buenaventura and follow its water-level passage through the Sierra Nevada. His portentous venture across the Great Basin had immense influence on the ultimate course of western trails, for he and his men were the first

---

[27] Morgan, *Jedediah Smith,* 343, 346.

[28] Goetzmann, *Army Exploration in the American West,* 22.

[29] Ball, *Autobiography,* 66.

[30] Beall, "Recollections of Wm. Craig," *Lewiston Morning Tribune,* 3 March 1918, 8.

[31] Utley, *A Life Wild and Perilous,* 122.

Americans to follow Ogden's Unknown River as it cut its way through the basin-and-range country of present-day Nevada. Bonneville called it "this most disgraceful expedition" after Walker's men killed some forty Indians near the Big Meadows, marring with violence the Northern Paiutes' first encounter with Americans.[32]

"Mr. Walker was a man well calculated to undertake a business of this kind," an old colleague said of the leader of the first journey by United States citizens down the Humboldt River and on to California. "He was well hardened to the hardships of the wilderness—understood the character of the Indians very well—was kind and affable to his men, but at the same time at liberty to command without giving offence," wrote Zenas Leonard, "and to explore unknown regions was his chief delight."[33]

Walker left the rendezvous in July or August 1833 with forty of Bonneville's men and perhaps twenty free trappers "to steer through an unknown country, towards the Pacific." They laid in sixty pounds of buffalo meat per man and crossed the "extensive & barren plains" on the west side of the Great Salt Lake to the headwaters of the Humboldt, which the Americans called the Barren River. The expedition spent weeks among the "abject and forlorn tribe of Shuckers, or more generally termed, Diggers and Root eaters." Most of them had never seen a white man, and none of them had ever seen an American. Ogden and the Western Shoshones had already hunted out the beaver, but the Indians stole the party's traps, to the great annoyance of some of the men, who "were for taking vengeance before we left the country—but this was not the disposition of Captain Walker." The malcontents killed several Indians, Zenas Leonard remembered, but "the Captain found it out, and immediately took measures for its effectual suppression."[34]

Despite the harshness of the country, Leonard said as they descended the river, they "found that the trails of the Indians began to look as if their numbers were increasing," and upon reaching Humboldt Lake they saw smoke rising from the tall meadow grass in every direction. They had stumbled into a large camp of Indians, probably Northern Paiutes gathered for a harvest festival. "The Indians issued from their hiding places in the grass, to the number, as near as I could guess, of 8 or 900," Leonard wrote. The estimate was probably high, but the Americans "readily guessed that these Indians were in arms to revenge the death of those which our men had killed up the river; & if they could succeed in getting any advantage over us, we had no expectation that they would give us any quarter." The large assembly

---

[32] Todd, "Benjamin L. E. Bonneville," in Hafen, *The Mountain Men,* 5:48–55.

[33] Leonard, *Narrative of the Adventures of Zenas Leonard,* 104–105.

[34] The following sections are based on Zenas Leonard's *Narrative of the Adventures of Zenas Leonard,* 104–54, the only primary account; Dale Morgan's *The Humboldt,* 46–61; and Ardis Walker's sketch in Hafen, *The Mountain Men,* 5:365–70.

of Paiutes that "marched straight towards us, dancing and singing in the greatest glee" probably had none of the dark intentions the trappers feared. But the Americans resolved to defend themselves as best they could.

In the ensuing confrontation, Walker ordered a charge, "saying that there was nothing equal to a good start in such a case." Thirty-two armed men fired on the Indians, leaving thirty-nine dead on the field, and "the remainder were overwhelmed with dismay," Leonard wrote, "running into the high grass in every direction, howling in the most lamentable manner." Walker ordered his men to shoot the wounded. "The severity with which we dealt with these Indians may be revolting to the heart of the philanthropist," Leonard admitted, justifying the cruelty with the circumstances: "the country we were in was swarming with hostile savages, sufficiently numerous to devour us. Our object was to strike a decisive blow. This we did—even to a greater extent than we had intended."

Walker's men crossed the Forty-mile Desert to reach the Carson River with their supplies running low, sometimes seeing hundreds of Indians and killing more of them. In October the expedition set out to cross the Sierra using the east fork the river that now bears Walker's name. The trappers soon consumed all their jerked meat, and their scouts found no signs of game and no practical way to cross the mountains. "No one was acquainted with the country, nor no person knew how wide the summit of this mountain was," wrote Zenas Leonard. "We had travelled for five days since we arrived at what we supposed to be the summit—were now still surrounded with snow and rugged peaks—the vigour of every man almost exhausted." The expedition's poor horses were starving, while the men themselves survived on the tough flesh of the starved animals, insects, and juniper berries—"gin berries," as they called them. The terrain was daunting and exhausting: "Our course was very rough & tiresome," Leonard recalled, "having to encounter one hill of snow and one ledge of rocks after another." After spending more than two weeks struggling over this "cold and famished region of snow," they probably surmounted the range around today's Tioga Pass. Walker's men did not discover Yosemite Valley, but they became the second party known to cross the mountains and the first to do so from the east.[35]

The Americans took refuge in the Mexican settlements during the winter. Seeking an easier pass the next spring, they followed the range south until they discovered what is still known as Walker Pass in May 1834. "Walker's party got away with five or six hundred head of the Spaniards horses and they drove them through what is now known as Walker's basin and Walker's pass of the Sierra

---

[35] Joseph R. Walker did, however, claim he discovered Yosemite. See Dale Morgan's sketch of Walker in Anderson, *The Rocky Mountain Journals,* 379.

Nevada mountains," William Craig said years later.[36] The expedition saw great numbers of Indians until they reached the site of their confrontation in the fall, which they dubbed Battle Lakes. They now found twice as many Indians, all "a good deal aggravated." Leonard insisted the trappers tried to conciliate the Paiutes, but finally the mountaineers "fell on the Indians in the wildest and most ferocious manner we could," killing fourteen and wounding many more as they rode them down. The Americans were not molested again, Leonard claimed, but for the next forty years the trappers' violence haunted Paiute relations with outsiders.

"There is a large number of water courses descending from this mountain on either side," Zenas Leonard had noted while lost in the Sierra, "but in no place is there a river course through the mountain."[37] John C. Frémont found Joseph Walker to be "animated with the spirit of exploratory enterprise," and Walker told Frémont that as he traveled across the Great Basin in 1833, "day after day he was searching for the Buenaventura, thinking that he had found it with every new stream." At last, like Frémont, Walker "abandoned all idea of its existence," but the impossible legend of the Buenaventura would die hard.[38]

A GREAT MAJORITY OF SCOUNDRELS: NATHANIEL J. WYETH

Massachusetts ice mogul Nathaniel J. Wyeth fell victim to the same siren song of making a fortune in furs that had lured Bonneville to the Rockies. Wyeth had made a fortune shipping New England ice to the tropics, but he was now looking for new challenges. He briefly joined Hall Jackson Kelley's American Society for Encouraging the Settlement of the Oregon Territory in 1831. A visionary promoter, Kelley had read everything he could find about voyages of exploration "until he had heated his mind to a degree little short of the valorous Knight of La Mancha," John B. Wyeth sourly observed, and Kelley believed every word he read. The enthusiast had never been to the territory, "or seen the Rocky Mountains, or a prairie-dog, or a drove of buffaloes": his knowledge of Oregon came exclusively from books and guesswork maps.[39] Kelley promoted various Oregon schemes for years, but his fanaticism undercut his ability to realize his dreams and convinced many people he was mad.[40]

Wyeth, in contrast, was an eminently practical businessman who believed

---

[36] Beall, "Recollections of Wm. Craig," *Lewiston Morning Tribune*, 3 March 1918, 8.

[37] Leonard, *Narrative of the Adventures of Zenas Leonard*, 213, 215.

[38] Spence and Jackson, *The Expeditions of John Charles Frémont*, 29 January 1844, 1:622.

[39] Wyeth, *Oregon*, 82–83.

[40] Kelley made a disastrous trip to the West in 1832 but soon returned home to dedicate another twenty-five years to promoting Oregon.

another fortune in salted salmon and furs awaited him in the West. He sent supplies to Oregon in the brig *Sultana* in 1832, organized a company of adventurers, and followed William Sublette's caravan to the rendezvous at Pierres Hole. From there, Milton Sublette guided him to Fort Walla Walla on the Columbia. John Ball, Oregon's first overland emigrant farmer and schoolteacher, came west with Wyeth's expedition, but he gave up after one season and returned home. The hard trip and the unfortunate loss of the *Sultana* should have discouraged Wyeth from further ventures in the fur trade, but, still seeing bright prospects in the Oregon Country, he proposed to trap the region south of the Columbia for the Hudson's Bay Company. He also investigated farming and salmon packing, both of which proved more challenging than he imagined.

After meeting the "great majority of Scoundrels" employed in the fur trade at the 1833 rendezvous, Wyeth won the Rocky Mountain Fur Company's contract to supply the next year's trade fair. He returned to Boston and founded the Columbia River Fishing and Trading Company, believing that he could deliver supplies to the Rocky Mountains by ship from Boston and New York for less than overland caravans from Saint Louis. He planned to pay for it all with salted salmon and pocket the profits. Ruthless frontier competition, however, dashed his dreams. He lost the race to the rendezvous, and the Rocky Mountain Fur Company disbanded without buying the supplies it had ordered. Wyeth felt the partners, notably William Sublette, Thomas Fitzpatrick, and Jim Bridger, had double-crossed him. "Gentlemen," he reportedly told them, "I will roll a stone into your garden that you will never be able to get out."[41]

To roll this stone, he and a formidable band of mountaineers built a trading station on the Snake River plain not far from the mouth of the Portneuf River, near present-day Pocatello. They "commenced the Fort which was a stockade 80 ft. square built of Cotton wood trees set on end sunk 2½ feet in the ground and standing about 15 feet above with two bastions 8 Fort square at the opposite angles," Osborne Russell wrote. Wyeth's men completed the fort on 4 August 1834, and the next day at sunrise they unfurled the stars and stripes.[42] Wyeth and his men "drank a bale of liquor and named it Fort Hall" in honor of his oldest partner, Henry Hall.[43]

Such an incursion into the Snake Country did not go unnoticed: Wyeth's project inspired the Hudson's Bay Company to build Fort Boise at the mouth of the Boise River. Hemmed in by competition, Wyeth sold Fort Hall to the Company,

---

[41] Victor, *The River of the West,* 164.

[42] Russell, *Journal of a Trapper,* July, August 1834, 5.

[43] Wyeth, *The Journals of Captain Nathaniel J. Wyeth's Expeditions,* 6 August 1834, 77.

returned to his prosperous ice business, and never went west again, though he did add informed support to proposals for American settlement of Oregon. Meanwhile, Fort Hall became "the trade center of a hungry land."[44]

Wyeth had rolled a larger stone than his trading post into the mountaineer's garden, for his second caravan brought a lank, morose Methodist evangelist named Jason Lee west in 1834. On his way home two years later, Wyeth met Eliza Spalding and Narcissa Whitman, wives of American missionaries bound for Oregon. "The two ladies were gazed upon with wonder and astonishment by the rude Savages," noted Osborne Russell, "they being the first white women ever seen by these Indians and the first that had ever penetrated into these wild and rocky regions."[45] Their arrival was a sure sign that the Far West was changing.

"The American Fur Co. have made a poor collection of furs this year," missionary Asahel Munger wrote at the next-to-last rendezvous in 1839. Having virtually exterminated beaver in the central Rockies, American companies folded their operations one by one. While Hudson's Bay Company agent Francis Ermatinger guided Munger and his companions to Fort Hall, two of the missionary's own hired hands stole two of his horses. "The men are most of them out of business and know not what to do," the missionary noted, and such raids became increasingly common along the evolving trail. As this incident suggests, the white men who had made the Rocky Mountains their home would soon find new ways to profit from life in the West.[46]

From Fort Vancouver in late 1839, James Douglas warned George Simpson of "an approaching change in Mountain affairs" that had ominous implications for British interests. Simpson's fur desert policy had brilliantly defeated the free trappers, but it had utterly failed to keep Yankees out of Oregon. Fifteen American mountaineers had already settled in the Willamette Valley. Worse yet, the people of the United States were now "much attracted to this country by the overcharged pictures of its fertility and commercial importance." The valley's missionary stations pumped out frequent optimistic reports, encouraging more evangelists to join those already on their way "to bewilder our poor Indians, already perplexed beyond measure, by the number and variety of their instructors." Douglas predicted that "the tide of emigration will soon flow into this quarter either with or without the sanction of government."[47]

---

[44] Minto, "Reminiscences of Experiences on the Oregon Trail in 1844," 215.

[45] Russell, *Journal of a Trapper,* 1 July 1836, 41.

[46] Munger, *Diary of Asahel Munger and Wife,* 5 and 9 July 1839.

[47] McLoughlin, *The Letters of John McLoughlin from Fort Vancouver, 1839–44,* 225–27.

TO DO THEM GOOD:
MISSIONARIES, VISIONARIES, AND THE ROAD TO OREGON

How the tribes of the Northwest learned about Christianity is shrouded in competing Catholic and Protestant legends. The Nez Perces and Flatheads apparently learned of Catholicism from far-ranging Iroquois converts who settled among them.[48] George Simpson directed Chief Trader Alexander Ross at Spokane House to send two Indian boys to the Episcopalian mission at Red River in 1825 to receive a Christian education. Ross selected the sons of two prominent local leaders; the boys became known as Spokan Garry and Kootenai Pelly. Their fathers did not give them up easily: "We have given you our hearts—our children are our hearts," Illim-Spokanee told Ross, "but bring them back again before they become white men."

Anglican missionaries taught the boys to read and write. Garry returned to his people in 1829, speaking fluent English with a Scottish burr, writing a very fair hand, and afire with Anglicanism, his teachers having instilled in him an enduring dislike of Catholicism. He held regular Sunday services and told his people tales of the Book that was the heart of the white man's magic. The next year he and Pelly returned to Red River with five more young Indians. Kootenai Pelly died on Easter morning in 1831, leaving Garry to bring news of his death back to Oregon and carry on with the white man's "book of heaven" and the Book of Common Prayer.

Like tens of thousands of Indians who would later go to school far from home, Garry learned his education was a mixed blessing: for the rest of his life he was caught between two worlds. He returned with a burning devotion to his faith, established a school, and had some success sharing his passion for his new religion with his people. In contrast, the Catholic missionaries who arrived over the next decade made not a single convert among the Spokanes. Still Garry had to endure ridicule from those of his own people who preferred the old ways, condescension from white professionals who undercut his authority, and the curiosity of the "Bostons" who were soon streaming into Oregon and had never seen an educated Indian. Eventually he abandoned his school and gave up dressing in white man's clothes.[49]

In early October 1831, Flathead tribal elder Man-of-the-Morning and three Nez Perce emissaries met with Indian Superintendent William Clark. They had come on a strange mission: through sign language, Clark understood that they had made the long trek to Saint Louis to find someone to teach their people about the powerful book that described the white man's medicine. Quite naturally, the veteran explorer interpreted their inquiry as a request for a minister who could explain the Bible to them. In truth, neither party could comprehend the other's

---

[48] Lavender, *Westward Vision*, 313.

[49] Thrapp, *Encyclopedia of Frontier Biography*, 1348; and Jessett, *Chief Spokan Garry*, 24, 30–44.

worldview. To the Indians, medicine "was the art of theurgy, the art of control-ling the powers of nature, seen and unseen," and the power of white medicine was self-evident. To Clark, medicine meant religion. He assured his visitors that such an emissary would come to them in due time. Only one of the men, Rabbit-Skin-Leggings, survived to return to his disappointed people with "no wizard of the Book and no more than a vague promise that one would follow."[50] The Catho-lic bishop of Saint Louis described the visit for a French journal, and in March 1833 the Methodist *Christian Advocate* issued the call, "Let the Church awake from her slumbers and go forth in her strength to the salvation of these wandering sons of our native forests."[51]

This call opened a new chapter in the history of the Oregon Country. On 15 September 1834, Jason Lee, his nephew David, and their small party arrived at Fort Vancouver. After leaving Nathaniel Wyeth at the rendezvous on Hams Fork, the first American missionaries traveled to Oregon with Thomas McKay's Bay Company brigade. The Methodist Mission Board had sent Lee, a strapping thirty-year-old Yankee lumberjack who had only recently entered the ministry, to establish a mission among the Flatheads. The rendezvous had convinced Lee that the wilderness was not safe for evangelists, so he brushed off the Salish del-egation that had come to meet him.

Happily accepting John McLoughlin's warning that maintaining a mission in the Flathead country would be difficult as well as dangerous, Lee moved sixty miles south into the Willamette Valley. He built a station at Mission Bottom, where disease had virtually eliminated the Native population. Lee took in a few surviving children, but many of them died. He quickly concluded "that the Indi-ans are a scattered, periled, and deserted race" who without God's help would soon "be blotted out from under Heaven."[52] Developing the mission farm and dealing with internal conflict consumed Lee's time until he turned his attention to secular enterprises. "I fear the world, and speculation, has too much influence over these missionaries," the Reverend Joseph Williams observed in 1842.[53]

The Flathead and Nez Perce tribes were still without the missionaries they had requested, and with the encouragement of Samuel Parker, a fifty-four-year-old Congregational pastor, the American Board of Commissioners for Foreign Mis-sions (the ABCFM, an alliance of the Congregational, Presbyterian, and Dutch Reform churches) somewhat reluctantly answered the call. Parker went to Mis-souri too late to join the fur-trade caravan in 1834, but next spring he set out

[50] Clark, *Eden Seekers*, 68–72.

[51] White, *Plains and Rockies, 1800–1865*, 264–70.

[52] Clark, *Eden Seekers*, 84–88, 95.

[53] Williams, *Narrative of a Tour*, 36.

for Oregon with a new recruit, Dr. Marcus Whitman, who at rendezvous won
the respect of mountaineers and Indians alike when he extracted a three-inch
iron arrowhead from Jim Bridger's back with "great self-possession and perseverance."[54] Whitman returned east that fall to recruit volunteers while Parker stayed
to locate sites for missions. They planned to reunite at the next summer's rendezvous. Parker visited the Nez Perce homeland in present-day Idaho and wintered
at Fort Vancouver. Worn out by his explorations, Parker decided to return home
by sea and sent letters for Whitman east with the Nez Perces.

PILLAR OF FIRE: THE WHITMANS

In September 1836 a Hudson's Bay Company bateau brought several surprising
visitors down the Columbia to Fort Vancouver, "the New York of the Pacific."
Missionaries Henry Spalding and Marcus Whitman arrived with their wives,
Eliza Hart Spalding and Narcissa Prentiss Whitman, the first American women
to cross South Pass.[55] "It is astonishing how [well we] get along with our wagons
where there are no roads," Narcissa Whitman wrote from Fort Laramie. "I may
say [it is] easier traveling here than on any turnpike in the States."[56] The natural
roadway ended west of Laramie, and it had been an arduous honeymoon for the
Whitmans, who had arranged their marriage to support their missionary work.
The ABCFM would not send single women on missions, so Narcissa Prentiss had
agreed that if the doctor could find a suitable mission station for the devout spin-
ster, the couple would marry.[57] Now, not only had the Protestant envoys demonstrated that women could cross the continent to Oregon, they had even driven a
wagon to Bear River and a cart to Fort Boise.

When she set out for Oregon at age twenty-eight, Narcissa Whitman was "viva-
cious, attractive, gregarious, idealistic, and sentimentally religious," a charming,
insightful letter writer and diarist, and a skilled outdoorswoman with an impressive soprano voice.[58] She was also resilient. The missionaries joined the "moving
village" that accompanied Thomas Fitzpatrick's fur-trade caravan to rendezvous.
The evangelists believed they traveled under the protection of heaven. "Surely the
children of Israel could not have been more sensible of the pillar of fire by night
than we have been of that hand that has led us thus safely on," Narcissa wrote.[59]

---

[54] Parker, *Journal of an Exploring Tour,* 63; and Thompson, *Whitman Mission National Historic Site.*

[55] Lavender, *Westward Vision,* 302–303. The New York metaphor is Narcissa Whitman's.

[56] Drury, *Marcus and Narcissa Whitman,* 1:185.

[57] As noted, three distinct churches financed the ABCFM stations, but they are here referred to as Presbyterian
missions to distinguish them from the Methodist efforts.

[58] Drury, *Marcus and Narcissa Whitman,* 1:97.

[59] Lavender, *Westward Vision,* 271, 290–91, 300–302; and Drury, *First White Women over the Rockies,* 1:81.

From the rendezvous, the missionaries followed a Hudson's Bay party to Fort Hall and the Columbia, with Marcus Whitman resolutely driving a wagon and then a cart farther west than any vehicle had ever gone before. At first, his wife thought it was not worth the trouble. "One of the axle trees of the waggon broke today. Was a little rejoyced, for we were in hopes they would leave it & have no more trouble with it," she wrote on Bear River, but her rejoicing was in vain. The men made a cart of the back wheels, lashing the front wheels to the contraption, "intending to take it through in some shape or other," Narcissa wrote. "They are so resolute & untiring in their efforts they will probably succeed." She developed an increasing appreciation for the cart even as the obstacles barring its way grew worse. "The hills are so steep [and] rocky that Husband thought it best to lighten the waggon as much as possible & take nothing but the wheels, leaving the box with my trunk," Narcissa Whitman reported at Salmon Falls. "Poor little trunk!" (She was quickly learning that "the custom of the country is to possess nothing & then you will lose nothing while traveling.") "Perhaps you will wonder why we have left the wagon, having taken it so near[ly] through," Narcissa wrote when they finally abandoned the cart. Their animals were failing, she explained, and the Blue Mountains were said to be impassable. She had become attached to the vehicle, saying that if they could not trade for one at Vancouver, they would send for it. "We have been to so much labour in getting it thus far," she observed. "It is a useful article in this country."[60]

Marcus Whitman may have failed to bring a wagon to the Columbia River in 1836, but the trek had instilled in him a burning desire to prove it could be done. The party crossed the Blues, taking a direct route that was impassible for wagons and different than the future Oregon Trail. They inspected a projected mission site at Waiilatpu, "the place of the rye grass," and descended the Walla Walla and Columbia to Fort Vancouver. After meeting with John McLoughlin, who saluted Narcissa as the first white woman to cross the Rocky Mountains (he apparently forgot to mention Eliza Spalding), the Whitmans followed a Hudson's Bay brigade upriver to their new home.

The Presbyterians set about their primary task, establishing missions. The Whitmans went to work among the Cayuses at Waiilatpu and the Spaldings settled with the Nez Perces at Lapwai, some 110 miles to the east, in what is now Idaho. The evangelists began their work with the noblest intentions and high expectations. Upon first meeting a Nez Perce delegation, Spalding "told them we had left our friends and home, and come many hundred miles to live with them, to teach them how good white men live, to teach them about God and to do them good." By 1839

---

[60] Whitman, *My Journal,* 28 July, 7, 12, 22 August 1836, 17–18, 25, 27–29, 30, 32.

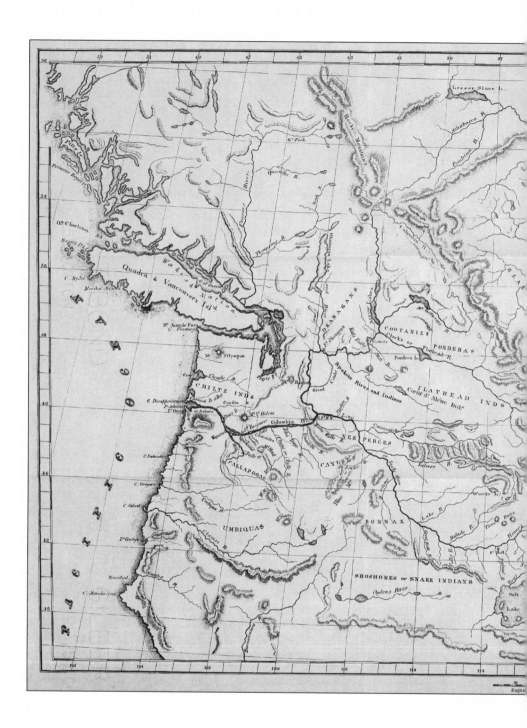

64

This 1838 map from Samuel Parker's *Journal of an Exploring Tour beyond the Rocky Mountains* shows
the general location of Indian nations and the mythical Buenaventura River. From *Journal of an
Exploring Tour beyond the Rocky Mountains, Under the Direction of the A.B.C.F.M. Containing a Description of the Geography, Geology, Climate, Productions of the Country, and the Numbers, Manners and Customs
of the Natives: With a Map of Oregon Territory.* Ithaca, N.Y.: Mack, Andrus, and Woodruff, for the
author, 1838. Reprint, Minneapolis: Ross & Haines, 1967.

Spalding was printing books in the Nez Perce and Spokan languages, the first books published in the Pacific Northwest. Cushing and Myra Fairbanks Eells and Elkanah and Mary Richardson Walker arrived at Waiilatpu in August 1838 and established a mission at Tshimakain, about twenty-five miles northwest of Spokane.[61]

Meanwhile, the competition—Jason Lee's mission in the Willamette Valley—had not been asleep. Eventually the Methodist-Episcopalians established missions at The Dalles, the Clatsop Plains, Fort Nisqually, the Falls of the Willamette, and Chemeketa. Reinforcements arrived via Cape Horn in 1837: among the notable arrivals was Dr. Elijah White, his wife, and two children. Contention already plagued the mission, and the officious and conniving Dr. White did nothing to improve matters. His flattery made him popular with women, but men considered him an effeminate and insincere sycophant. H. H. Bancroft, who relied on White as a key source for his history of Oregon, had a low opinion of the doctor. The longer White dwelt on the coast, "the more he became smooth and slippery like glass," his history observed.[62] Within six months, the new arrivals had blamed Lee for luring them to Oregon and expressed their dissatisfaction in a petition to the mission board, probably written by White. To respond to these complaints and appeal for more support, Lee set out overland in March 1838 for the states, carrying the first petition from Oregon settlers asking Congress to take possession of the country.

Jason Lee's promotional lectures attracted various adventurers, including Thomas J. Farnham, one of two members of the "Oregon Dragoons" of Peoria, Illinois, who actually traveled to Oregon in 1839. Like many later American freebooters, Farnham arrived broke and lacking even clothes, which McLoughlin graciously provided for him from Hudson's Bay Company stores. He spent most of his brief stay in Oregon on an isolated Tualatin Valley farm. A born troublemaker and ingrate, Farnham allied himself with White and cosigned another petition to Congress, this time evoking the dark threat of a ruthless British monopoly dominating and exploiting an American territory.

Lee's remarkable celebrity in the East restored his confidence and stirred interest in Oregon. Impressed with his enthusiasm if not his leadership abilities, the mission board endorsed Lee's expansionist plans. He won the support of the powerful Cushing family of Massachusetts, whose political and mercantile interests in the Cushing & Company of Newburyport both supported and profited from the growing colony in Oregon. As Congressman Caleb Cushing began lobbying for American control of Oregon, his family's ships set sail for the Pacific Northwest.

---

[61] Spalding to Leavitt, 11 July 1836, White, *Plains and Rockies,* 297.

[62] Bancroft, *History of Oregon,* 1:155. His talented staff, in this case Frances Fuller Victor, produced most of Bancroft's histories.

Lee's success was partly the result of a technological revolution that was quickly transforming how Americans viewed their republic. Before the invention of the steamboat, the railroad, and the telegraph, a continental nation was impossible, since it would take most of a representative's two-year term to travel from the Pacific to the Atlantic. Thomas Jefferson believed independent "sister Republics" would fill North America, and in 1836 the Texas Revolution indicated the process was underway. This changed, however, with the explosion of railroad building in the 1830s and Samuel F. B. Morse's demonstration of his new invention, the telegraph, in 1838. "Electricity and steam had annihilated space and time as limitations on God's will," observed historian Frederick Merk.[63] Suddenly, a continental nation bound by steel rails and telegraph wires was possible. Freebooters continued to chatter about forming a separate nation on the Pacific as long as Mexico controlled California and the Hudson's Bay Company dominated Oregon, but once an American president set his sights on the Pacific, their dreams were doomed.

Ironically, the "Great Reinforcement" of 1840 that Lee enlisted was his undoing. He had brought back fifty-one missionaries aboard the ship *Lausanne,* along with materials to build grist mills and sawmills, but Lee's recruits proved no less quarrelsome than their predecessors. The mission had never been able to introduce more than a handful of Indians to the glories of civilization, and the situation did not improve as the effort increased. Successive waves of devastating diseases had demoralized the survivors of the Willamette Valley's Native population, and they had little interest in Christianity.

Lee turned his attention to political enterprises, engaging in a conscious effort to counteract everything John McLoughlin did. He moved his Willamette headquarters ten miles south from its malaria-infested, constantly flooded bottoms at Chemeketa, later renamed Salem, and set about building an Indian labor school: of the first class of five, two died and one ran away. Lee's vendetta with McLoughlin led him to send missionaries to establish a station at Nisqually at the southern end of Puget Sound, a spot almost entirely lacking in Indians but whose location challenged the Hudson's Bay Company's hegemony north of the Columbia. Lee's missionaries, however, proved unequal to the task of wilderness empire building. Reverend Joseph Williams, a fellow Methodist, visited Lee's mission early in 1842 and found "a great deal of business on hand which seems a hindrance to the work of religion." Williams was "very sorry to see some of them so high-minded, and doing so little in the cause of God. I fear they have lost the spirit to speculation."[64]

---

[63] Merk, *Manifest Destiny and Mission in American History,* 51.

[64] Williams, *Narrative of a Tour,* 39, 43.

Superintendent Lee became embroiled in another vendetta upon his return to Oregon when he asked to examine the financial records of Elijah White, who had managed the mission during Lee's absence. Ultimately, a church court tried White on charges of peculation and sexual improprieties and voted to expel him. In September 1840, White departed for New York with his family aboard the *Lausanne,* vowing vengeance.

To Settle Points:
Britain, France, Mexico, and the Geopolitics of 1840

On the Weber River near today's Mountain Green, Utah, Peter Skene Ogden's Snake Country brigade had a run in with Johnson Gardner's American trappers in May 1825. The two outfits debated who had trapping rights, even though both were trespassing in Mexico and neither had any legal claim to the furs they were harvesting. Ironically, the only legitimate trappers in the area were with Etienne Provost, who had a license from the governor of New Mexico, but Provost declined to join the debate.[65] After two tense days, Gardner, one of the hardest characters in the rough business of the American fur trade, lured away Ogden's Iroquois trappers and essentially stole the British company's furs.[66]

The confrontation on Weber River reflected the chaotic state of international affairs that made the destiny of the West Coast of North America an open question in 1840. Two imperial European powers, Russia and Britain, had established trading empires in Alaska and Oregon, while France had dreams of its own. Based on the discoveries of Captain James Cook of the Royal Navy in 1778 and American merchant seaman Robert Gray in 1791, Britain and the United States asserted sovereignty over the Oregon Country under the joint occupancy agreement negotiated in 1818. Russia had claimed all the land north of the Columbia River in 1810, but by 1825 the empire abandoned its territorial ambitions south of 54°40', although it maintained a significant commercial presence, including an outpost eighty miles north of the San Francisco Bay.

Spain first settled Alta California in 1769 after reports of Russian fur-trade ventures in the North Pacific. The Russian-American Company established Rossiya, now known as Fort Ross, in 1812, much to the discomfort of local Spanish authorities. Initially built to exploit the rich sea otter trade, the settlement became a supply station for Alaska after rapacious hunting depleted the otters. Czar Alexander closed Alaskan waters to foreign vessels in 1821 and claimed that

---

[65] Eldredge and Gowans, "The Fur Trade in Utah," in Powell, *Utah History Encyclopedia,* 210.
[66] Haynes, "Johnson Gardner," in Hafen, *The Mountain Men,* 2:157–59.

the territory of the Russian American Company extended south to the fifty-first parallel, which both Britain and the United States considered part of Oregon. Within a year, President James Monroe threatened Russia with armed reprisals if it attempted to establish colonies on territories the United States claimed in the Pacific Northwest.[67]

By 1840 Spain, France, and Russia had tacitly accepted the Oregon claims of the United States and the United Kingdom. The Hudson's Bay Company reigned supreme and had positioned British interests to acquire control of the Oregon Country. Yet American optimism could already conjure up a different future. Would "the federal government ever succeed in civilizing the thousands of savages now roaming over these plains" to permit "her hardy freeborn population" to build their homes, towns, and cities, "and say here shall the arts and sciences of civilization take root and flourish?" asked fur hunter Zenas Leonard in 1839. He answered yes, but American xenophobia could easily envision a vast conspiracy to deprive the republic of its rightful dominion. "The Spaniards are making inroads on the South—the Russians are encroaching with impunity along the sea shore to the North," wrote Leonard, capturing his countrymen's fears. Farther north, the British were pushing their stations into what men like Leonard considered the very heart of American territory, and to them they looked more like military forts built to resist invasion than trading stations. "Our government should be vigilant," Leonard insisted. "She should assert her claim by taking possession of the whole territory as soon as possible."[68]

Yankee sea captains had long profited from trade and smuggling in Mexican California, but beyond the presence of a few itinerant fur hunters and missionaries, the United States had few people and no settlements worthy of the name west of the Rockies to buttress its territorial claims to Oregon. Spain had bequeathed Mexico a vast territory, Alta California, whose borders reached east to the Rocky Mountains and north to the 42nd parallel. But Mexico's control did not extend beyond a string of small ranchos and settlements on the California coast that terminated just north of San Francisco Bay. Mexico's shaky authority in its frontier province, compounded by its inept and corrupt administration, suggested that if the local Californios, as these distinctly independent people were known, did not assert their independence first, the country would ultimately fall prey to European or American territorial ambitions.

The United States had its own growing interest in Oregon and the ports of California. As early as 1839, Thomas Farnham heard that an American adventurer

---

[67] Owens, "Frontiersman for the Tsar," 3–21, summarizes Russian ventures in North America.

[68] Leonard, *Narrative of the Adventures of Zenas Leonard,* 155.

was westbound "with the lofty intention of conquering California." Farnham, who historian Henry Wagner suggested made his trip to Oregon and California as an agent of the American government, later made that "lofty intention" his own.[69]

Having failed to establish a profitable agricultural settlement in northern California that could supply their posts in Alaska, the Russians decided to withdraw. Early in 1839, the Hudson's Bay Company agreed to supply the Russian American Company's Alaskan settlements with wheat, peas, barley, butter, beef, and ham. The deal promised to yield a small profit, but the British company's motive was not financial: the contract reflected its desire to keep its Yankee competitors at bay. American commercial enterprises in the Rocky Mountains had virtually ended by 1840, but the only two real contenders for control of the Oregon Country were still the United States and the British Empire. No one knew how this complex political contest would sort itself out. Andrew Colvile, one of the governors of the Hudson's Bay Company, thought the conflict between British and American interests could only be resolved "by a war—I fear it must end in that before the two countries will negociate [*sic*] in a way to settle points."[70]

PEOPLE FROM ALL PARTS OF THE WORLD: THE WEST IN THE 1840S

As Francis Parkman approached the Missouri frontier in 1846, he saw "signs of the great western movement that was then taking place": he felt the parties of emigrants he met represented "that race of restless and intrepid pioneers whose axes and rifles have opened a path from the Alleghenies to the western prairies." As a Boston patrician and an unabashed chauvinist, he also saw "some thirty or forty dark slavish-looking Spaniards, gazing stupidly out from beneath their broad hats," a band of Indians "belonging to a remote Mexican tribe," and "French hunters from the mountains with their long hair and buckskin dresses." Parkman later saw Pierre D. Papin's boats stranded on the Platte River—the prominent French-American trader was reclining on a pack of furs—and the young writer thought he was "a rough-looking fellow." But the appearance of the multinational workers manning the flatboats was equally singular: "The crews were a wild looking set," Parkman wrote, referring to the buckskin-clad French and American traders who had their "hair glued up" in Indian fashion, while "the oarsmen were Spaniards."[71]

[69] Farnham, *Travels in the Great Western Prairies,* 61; and Wagner and Camp, *The Plains and the Rockies,* 126. Rumors about Farnham's status as a spy may originate in a January 1843 Senate speech on whether the British government was making illegal land grants in Oregon to the Hudson's Bay Company. James Morehead said the American minister in London received information from Farnham, and the president asked whether "the intelligence contained in Mr. Farnham's letter" was well founded. See Morehead, "Speech," *Appendix to the Congressional Globe* 27, no. 3 (1843): 229.

[70] Galbraith, "Early History of the Puget's Sound Agricultural Company," 242–43.

[71] Parkman, *The Journals of Francis Parkman,* 4 June 1846, 2:434.

The characters they met along the Missouri gave overland travelers a sample of what lay ahead. Since its founding in 1827, Independence had been a major outfitting point for fur hunters bound to the Rocky Mountains and entrepreneurs preparing to haul calico, buttons, buckles, paper, knives, needles, and thread down the Santa Fe Trail to trade for wool, silver, and mules. A stroller on the courthouse square on any spring evening in the 1840s might encounter silver-adorned Mexican traders in spurs and sombreros, English nobles bound for a safari on the Great Plains, black stevedores, Indians from tribes as far away as Mexico or Oregon, Protestant and Catholic clerics, fur-trade magnates from old French-American families, and mountaineers on a spree. Five years later, westbound emigrants from virtually every state in the Union and most of the countries of Europe joined the crowd.

The origins of those living at the trails' destinations were even more varied. "We have a mixed community here, people from all parts of the world, English, Americans, French, half-breeds, Quartroons, and Sandwich Islanders," Clarborne Walker wrote after reaching the Willamette Valley in 1845.[72] The diversity he found in Oregon was characteristic of the small communities of Indians and trappers that were scattered along of the entire trail during the 1840s. "Here is a mixture of people," Joseph Williams observed at Fort Laramie in 1841, "some white, some half breeds, some French."[73] This assortment of humanity represented an intriguing set of nations and peoples. Beginning with tribes that had been driven from homes as far away as the Chesapeake Bay, overlanders encountered dozens of Indian nations. They ranged from "the most warlike and formidable tribes" of the Great Plains and the Rockies to the "poor miserable wretches" who inhabited the Great Basin.[74] They all had strikingly different languages, traditions, and feelings toward whites.

In addition to the peoples who had called the West home since time immemorial, emigrants met a variety of newcomers from other cultures. The Indians, French-Canadians, Polynesians, and American mountaineers "gone native" struck travelers as barbaric savages whose wild appearance alone was enough to arouse suspicion if not absolute terror. At Fort Vancouver in 1845, Samuel Hancock found a number of "Kanakas," as Hawaiians were known, working alongside French-Canadians for the Hudson's Bay Company "at very low wages."[75]

To the south, John Bidwell discovered that the native Californians held the handful of Americans living in the province in distinct disfavor. All the foreigners—

---

[72] Walker to "Dear Brother, Sister and Friends," 1845, Purvine Family Records.

[73] Williams, *Narrative of a Tour,* 28.

[74] Fitzpatrick to Abert, 5 February 1846, in Abert Family Papers, Missouri Historical Society.

[75] Hancock, *The Narrative of Samuel Hancock,* 38.

"and all were foreigners except Indians and Mexicans"—did not number more than one hundred; "nor was the character of all of them the most prepossessing." Many were Rocky Mountain fur trade veterans who had not seen civilization for decades: the mountaineers who found their way to California from Mexico or Oregon were "men who would let their beards grow down to their knees, and wear buckskin garments made and fringed like those of the Indians, and who considered it a compliment to be told 'I took ye for an Injin.'" Others had come to steal four or five hundred horses in a single raid on the sprawling Spanish ranches and returned to stay. But the majority of recent arrivals were sailors who had deserted their ships. The Americans he met in Mexican California, Bidwell admitted, "were not generally a class calculated to gain much favor with the people."[76]

On the trek up the Platte River, emigrants continually encountered the people who had been the first white residents of the Great Plains: the French. The trappers, traders, and "French Indians" were generally descended from French and Spanish families, who were the earliest European settlers of the Mississippi Valley, or from French-Canadians. By 1840 most of them were American citizens, having been born in Missouri or Illinois after the Louisiana Purchase. They had been in the country so long they were at ease with the peoples they lived among. Whites in Indian Country adopted Native customs from necessity and convenience, but as John Ball observed, "The Canadian Frenchman seems to adopt their life as readily as though raised in that way, and others the same after a little time."[77] Parkman wrote that the fur company at Fort Laramie ran a tyrannical monopoly that employed multitudes of hunters, trappers, and traders, who were mostly French "and both from their breed and their mode of life, utterly careless of tomorrow."[78]

Historian Hiram Chittenden calculated that of the five thousand men engaged in the American fur trade, four thousand were of French origin, and they subsequently dominated trade along the trails in similar proportion.[79] "I believe that ¾ of the trappers, hunters, and traders in this region are French men," observed Forty-niner Edward C. Harrow. "The women do the work and ride and drive the loose horses, over the necks and shoulders of which they sling their young children, after the same fashion that a dragoon does his shoulder pistols."[80]

Washington Irving compared the French creoles of Louisiana with "the trapper of the old American stock, from Kentucky, Tennessee, and others of the western States": not surprisingly, in his estimation the Americans came out on top. The French trapper, Irving claimed, was "a lighter, softer, more self-indulgent kind of

[76] Nunis, *The Bidwell-Bartleson Party,* 103.
[77] Ball, *Autobiography,* 80.
[78] Parkman to "My Dear Father," Fort Laramie, 28 June 1846, *Letters of Francis Parkman,* 46.
[79] Lecompte, *French Fur Traders and Voyageurs in the American West,* 11.
[80] Harrow, *The Gold Rush Overland Journal,* 33–34.

man. He must have his Indian wife, his lodge, and his petty conveniences. He is gay and thoughtless, takes little heed of landmarks, depends upon his leaders and companions to think for the common weal, and, if left to himself, is easily perplexed and lost." The American trapper was never at a loss in the wilderness; he was fearless, and immune to privation. "I consider one American," a veteran trader told Irving, "equal to three Canadians in point of sagacity, aptness at resources, self-dependence, and fearlessness of spirit."[81] Recalling that French trappers outnumbered their American counterparts by 4 to 1 puts such comments in perspective.

Americans of French origin played an enormous role in the exploration of the Far West. Most of the men who went overland to Astoria with Wilson Price Hunt in 1811 were French-Canadian veterans of John Jacob Astor's Great Lakes operations. Two of the seven men who found South Pass in 1812 were French: François LeClaire, a mixed-blood; and André Valée, a Canadian voyageur.[82] A few famous American mountaineers accompanied John C. Frémont's expeditions, but they were principally manned by "Creole and Canadian French": of the thirty-two men he listed as members of his second expedition, all but seven had French or Spanish surnames.[83] Howard Stansbury carried on the tradition by enlisting one of Frémont's men, Auguste Archambault, as his expedition's guide when his topographical engineers surveyed the Great Salt Lake in 1849. The *St. Louis Weekly Reveille* reported the expedition employed twelve Frenchmen as hunters.[84]

The influence of French traders was evident everywhere along the trails, down to place names they left on the land's rivers, valleys, and mountains and ultimately its cities and towns. They included creeks such as La Bonte, Richeau, Sybille, and La Prele; rivers named Laramie, Fontenelle, Boise, Malad, Malheur, Duchesne, Provo, and Cache La Poudre; and places such as Bellevue, Coeur d'Alene, Grande Ronde, Cache Valley, Montpelier, Rickreall, Pend d'Oreille, Gillette, Grand Coulee, LeCompton, Marquette, Pierres Hole, the Tetons, Lebec, and French Camp. An "old Canadian Frenchman," who had been in the mountains eighteen years, explained the origin of one name to James Field. "He said one of the first trading parties to this part of the country, in crossing the stream at a time when it was swollen by a freshet, got 17 pounds of sugar drowned in it, and so christened it Sweetwater."[85]

Just as emigrants usually lumped together the members of any tribe they met under the general heading Indians, they usually referred to anyone speaking French as a Frenchman. "The emigrants felt a violent prejudice against the

---

[81] Irving, *The Rocky Mountains*, 10–11.

[82] Crooks, "Who Discovered the South Pass?" 51.

[83] Spence and Jackson, *The Expeditions of John Charles Frémont*, 1:426–29.

[84] "Death on the Plains," *St. Louis Weekly Reveille*, 2 June 1849.

[85] Field, Crossing the Plains, 12 July 1845, Oregon Historical Society. Others attributed the name to the excellent quality of the river's water.

French Indians, as they called the trappers and traders," observed Francis Parkman. "They thought, and with some justice, that these men bore them no good
will. Many of them were firmly persuaded that the French were instigating the
Indians to attack and cut them off."[86] Such rumors persisted for years: "The indians are every day commiting some depredation or other, they steal and rob from
every train and those dirty french put them up to it," Amelia Hadley complained
in 1851. "I think if congress knew how bad they were they would protect the emigration. As I have said it is cruel, for them to hold out inducements for people to
settle Oregon and leave them unprotected and to fight theyr [sic] way as best they
can."[87] As the demand for trading posts and ferries exploded in the late 1840s,
however, it was French traders who provided most of these services.

"Noticed a number of half-breeds among the young Indians, and am told it is the
regular custom of the traders to keep Indian wives at the fort," James Field wrote
at Fort Laramie. "They say it is necessary for their personal safety, as they are then
considered one of the tribe."[88] Thousands of mixed-blood French plainsmen participated in white enterprises, but an even larger number probably stayed with their
mothers' tribes and were often indistinguishable from their compatriots.

A few observers tried to explain the nature of the "French Indians." After crossing Robidoux Pass at Scotts Bluff in May 1849, William Kelly "saw a man running
across the plain to meet us, who we first thought was an Indian, but as he came
up proved to be a French trapper, clad in a buckskin suit, with a fine rifle on his
shoulder." The son of a French fur trader from the Red River, the man spoke tolerable English. His father had brought him to the plains while he was still a boy, and
he stayed in the country after his father's death and "married the daughter of an
Indian chief, in whose society he forgot every feeling or desire to visit the crowded
thoroughfares of the world." He secured "the main staples of existence with his
gun, and obtaining the few superfluities he desires at the fort, in exchange for
the skins of the game he kills." Kelly marveled that most of the men who came
to Indian Country as trappers or tourists acquired a taste for Native life: he saw
innumerable instances of men of independent fortune who had "forsaken the con-
ventionalities of polished society for the simple, unsophisticated association of
those children of nature, demonstrating the inherent tendency of man to the natural in preference to the artificial, wherever freewill is left a loose rein."[89]

Emigrants did not have a much higher regard for Anglo-Saxon mountaineers,
including even James Bridger, than they did their French-American colleagues.

---

[86] Parkman, *The California and Oregon Trail*, 134.
[87] Hadley, "Journal of Travails to Oregon," in Holmes, *Covered Wagon Women*, 3:87.
[88] Field, Crossing the Plains, 20 June 1845, Oregon Historical Society.
[89] Kelly, *An Excursion to California*, 153–54.

Edwin Bryant estimated that the white population of the Rocky Mountains in 1846 was five hundred to one thousand men, scattered among the Indians or living like nomads around the trading posts. He expressed the common prejudice against white men who had married Indian women. "Adventure, romance, avarice, misanthropy, and sometimes social outlawry, have their influence in enticing or driving these persons into this savage wilderness," he concluded. They rarely returned to civilization except to visit. "Many of them have Indian wives and large families. Polygamy is not uncommon. They conform to savage customs, and from their superior intelligence have much influence over the Indians, and frequently direct their movements and policy in war and peace."[90]

Another major factor helped define the West and the lives of its inhabitants in 1840: the bison. Peoples living as far from the Great Plains as the Nez Perces relied on the great beasts. The North American bison had once ranged from Pennsylvania to Florida, west to Oregon and California, and from Mexico north to the Yukon. Not long before overland emigration began, the range of *Bison bison* extended from the valleys of the Great Salt Lake and the Snake River to the Missouri. Weather and predators exterminated them west of the Sierra Nevada and the Cascade Range, while hunting and farming had the same effect east of the Missouri River. During the 1830s or early 1840s, the bison disappeared from the Salt Lake Valley and the Snake River plain shortly after the arrival of firearms, or perhaps following a devastating winter storm.[91] The diminishing range of the great beasts was a harbinger of changes to come.

By 1840 few Americans had ever seen a bison, whose range was now reduced to the plains between the Missouri River and the Rocky Mountains. But veterans of the fur trade knew them well. "Oh, there they were, thousands and thousands of them! Far as the eye could reach the prairie was literally covered, and not only covered but crowded with them," recalled trapper Warren Ferris when he described his first encounter with a herd on the Platte River in 1830. "It was a gallant show; a vast expanse of moving, plunging, rolling, rushing life—a literal sea of dark forms, with still pools, sweeping currents, and heaving billows, and all the grades of movement from calm repose to wild agitation. The air was filled with dust and bellowings, the prairie was alive with animation," Ferris wrote. "I never realized before the majesty and power of the mighty tides of life that heave and surge in all great gatherings of human or brute creation."[92]

---

[90] Bryant, *What I Saw in California,* 3 July 1846, 120.

[91] Lupo, "The Historical Occurrence and Demise of Bison in Northern Utah," 168–80. Forty-niner Jonathan Manlove saw "plenty of old horns and bones along the road, but no fresh ones" on the Humboldt. Indians told him an 1838 sleet storm had "covered the ground for two weeks and the buffaloes had all starved." Manlove, An Overland Trip, California State Library.

[92] Ferris, *Life in the Rocky Mountains,* 100.

THE PARCHED AND TRACKLESS WASTE: THE CHALLENGE

"No one, at this late day, can form an idea of the difficulties and hardships attending travel across the Continent," pioneer John Henry Brown remembered forty-one years after he made the arduous trek to California in 1845.[93] Twenty years after his journey in 1841, John Bidwell recalled how he had "crossed the parched and trackless waste which then separated the Atlantic from the Pacific slope of the continent."[94] Like the thousands of Americans who made the journey, Bidwell and Brown stressed the physical test the trip posed. But beyond the pain the trail afflicted on flesh and bones, the challenges facing emigrants hoping to take wagons from the Missouri River to the Pacific in the 1840s were technological, logistical, and psychological. Animal-powered wagons were bulky and slow, and they usually lacked even such simple features as effective brakes, and no one was sure if draft animals could endure the rigors of the trip. Logistically, the only places emigrants could even hope to resupply in 1840 were at three ramshackle outposts on the Laramie and Snake rivers. Yet the image of a wide and hostile wilderness perhaps made the mental test the most difficult of all: westbound Americans left behind their families and their social and political traditions, for the journey would not only put thousands of miles between such sojourners and the ones they loved and the world they knew, it also placed them on the far side of a vast and uncertain temporal divide.

"A tide of immigration appears to be moving this way rapidly," Narcissa Whitman wrote in May 1840, noting that there were already fourteen American women in Oregon. "We are emphatically situated on the highway between the States and the Columbia River, and are a resting place for the weary travelers, consequently a greater burden rests upon us than upon any of our associates—to be always ready."[95] Over the next seven years, Whitman would see the number of weary travelers increase from a dozen or so a year to thousands. But as the first wagon trains began assembling on the Missouri frontier, the geographic problem alone was daunting. Of all the many challenges a traveler encountered on the road to the Pacific, none surpassed crossing the mountain barricade the Cascade Range and the Sierra Nevada created at its end, and the Cascades offered even fewer prospects for a viable wagon road than did the Sierra Nevada with its east-flowing rivers. All in all, the obstacles to wagon travel in 1840 led the best experts on the American West to predict that no one would cross these vast distances in a wagon for decades—if such a feat could ever be accomplished at all.

---

[93] Brown, *Reminiscences and Incidents*, 12.

[94] Bidwell, *Addresses, Reminiscences, etc.*, 49.

[95] Drury, *Marcus and Narcissa Whitman*, 224–25; and Ruby and Brown, *The Cayuse Indians*, 70. Waiilatpu is about seven miles west of today's Walla Walla, Washington.

CHAPTER 3

THE STERN FACTS OF GEOGRAPHY

Americans Head West, 1840 and 1841

Fur-trade carts and missionary wagons had left a trail up the Platte River Valley in their wake, but it was still a mere scratch across the face of the prairie. Caravans had beaten out the broad Santa Fe road, a perceptive observer noted in 1839, whereas the nascent Oregon Trail was only "a narrow wagon road, established by former journeys to the Rocky Mountains, but often so indistinctly traced, that our leader at times lost it, and simply followed the general direction." A year later, Father Pierre-Jean De Smet described traveling over immense plains, destitute of trees or shrubs, "where our voyageurs lowered and raised the carts by means of ropes," so even the level highroad up the Platte Valley plain posed substantial challenges to early travelers. According to Frederick Wislizenus, beyond Fort Laramie it was even worse: "The road was growing daily more difficult. Steep ascents and deep clefts and ravines often made it necessary to lower the carts with ropes and pull them up again, or else make a wide circuit."[1]

At least a wagon trace followed the Platte River and its North Fork by 1840, but as yet no one had ever taken anything with wheels across the Great Basin or the Blue Mountains, let alone over the Cascades or the Sierra Nevada. Veteran traders such as Richard Grant of the Hudson's Bay Company believed no one could reach the Pacific coast in a wagon. Yet between 1841 and 1848, Americans used the knowledge of experienced frontiersmen, trial and error, and dogged persistence to open a complex network of practical wagon roads from the Missouri River to Oregon and California. Within a decade, these intrepid pioneers had forged what De Smet called "the broadest, longest and most beautiful road in the whole world" from the United States to the Pacific Ocean.[2]

As trails to the Pacific developed during the 1840s, what historian Dale L. Morgan called "the stern facts of geography" dictated the course they must follow.[3]

---

[1] Wislizenus, *A Journey to the Rocky Mountains*, 31, 72; and De Smet, *Life, Letters and Travels*, 201.
[2] Ibid., 671–72.
[3] Korns and Morgan, *West from Fort Bridger*, 2.

West of Missouri, the great overland historian Merrill Mattes observed, "the various routes and trails were all simply components of one big natural and providential travel corridor, the Platte River valley."[4] Beyond the Great Plains two geographic obstructions—the canyons of the Colorado River and the Great Salt Lake and its surrounding deserts—posed barriers to overland travel that appeared insurmountable. But the third great obstacle, the Rocky Mountains, had a natural gateway that some thought God had wrought, for the Platte River system led emigrants up a natural road to South Pass, the only easy crossing of the Continental Divide south of Marias Pass, which no white man would describe until 1889. Hundreds of miles of barren deserts lay west of the pass, and should travelers survive these wastelands, they struck the Sierra Nevada or the Cascades, the western rampart of the cordillera stretching from Mexico to Canada that guarded the back door to the Pacific Slope. No natural features in eastern North America could compare to the snowcapped mountains, volcanoes, basins and ranges, deep gorges, and desolate tracts that nature seemed to have raised as battlements to bar the rest of the continent from the Pacific.

As emigrants soon learned, neither game nor outposts focused on the Indian trade provided reliable sources for provisions. Despite the common perception that trading stations were stocked with everything needed for a western journey, the only three commercial operations on the trail in 1841 were enterprises clustered around Fort John on the Laramie River and the HBC posts at Fort Hall and Fort Boise. They each dealt in Indian trade goods and only stocked enough supplies to feed the workers, and sometimes they lacked even that. Flour sold at Fort Hall in 1841 for one dollar a pint—about twenty of today's dollars—if it was available at all.[5] "There is little or nothing to be had in the way of provisions at the forts on the way," Jesse Looney observed in 1843.[6] Most overlanders who ran out of food would find no place to buy supplies to carry them to Oregon or California.

Americans raised in New England or the Mississippi Valley were psychologically unprepared for the arid West. In an age without photographs, travelers entered a landscape unlike anything they had ever seen or could even imagine back home. Western terrain was more alien to overlanders than the surface of Mars would be to citizens of the twenty-first century. Besides fantastic geological formations, emigrants encountered wonders such as mirages, geysers, perpetually snowcapped mountains (not to mention mid-summer blizzards), mummified carrion, grizzly bears, and other phenomena completely outside their experience. English even lacked a vocabulary to describe the landscape—for example, it had

---

[4] Mattes, *Platte River Road Narratives*, xi.
[5] Williams, *Narrative of a Tour*, 33.
[6] Looney to Bond, 27 October 1843, Oregon Historical Society.

After the army renamed it Fort Laramie in 1849, Frederick Piercy sketched what remained of the American Fur Company's Fort John in 1853. To the right is "Old Bedlam," now the oldest surviving structure at this critical frontier outpost. The army demolished the ruins of Fort John during the Civil War. From *Route from Liverpool to Great Salt Lake Valley,* author's collection.

no word equivalent to the Spanish *cañon*. "This word, pronounced canyon, was originally used by Mexicans and Spaniards, to denote a narrow gorge, or defile in a mountain, where the sides are walls of rock, nearly or quite perpendicular, and of great height," one guidebook author patiently explained.[7]

When George Simpson concluded in 1829 that the Hudson's Bay Company in Oregon had little to fear from the Americans, he was convinced settlers could never bring wagons down the Snake River.[8] Yet Americans had the will, and where there were willing Americans, there was a way. Almost obsessively, fur traders and missionaries drove wagons deeper into the Far West. After Benjamin Bonneville led the first twenty wagons over South Pass in 1832, fur-trade caravans routinely transported goods to the mountains in wagons and carts, and four years later Marcus Whitman drove a wagon to Bear River and a cart—"this symbol of civilization"—as far as Fort Boise.[9] Yet even such bold ventures as the fur trade were dying, and it seemed entirely possible that the Panic of 1837 and the subsequent depression had taken the wind out of America's expansionist sails.

RIVER, VOLCANO, AND EDEN:
THE COLUMBIA, CASCADES, AND WILLAMETTE VALLEY

In the Western Hemisphere, the Columbia River is the largest watercourse flowing into the Pacific: in some years its volume is larger than the Mississippi. A handful of French-Canadians, Britons, and a very few Americans had made a few "quite unimportant settlements" along its banks by 1839, but in all the distance between the Columbia and the Missouri, no plow had cut the earth and no settler had built a cabin.[10] The Great Plains and the Rocky Mountains were the domain of Native peoples and mountain men, and they seemed destined to remain that way. Considering the distance and difficulties that stood between Oregon and the United States, it is hardly surprising that the governors of the Hudson's Bay Company felt little threat from Americans until it was too late.

The volcanic peaks of the Cascade Range raised such an imposing barrier that even the resourceful servants of the Hudson's Bay Company never found a reliable road over the mountains—instead, they relied on the one natural passage between the peaks, the Columbia River. The Company used the great river of the West as the final link in the chain of rivers, streams, mountain passes, and prairie trails its *voyageurs* used to connect the Great Lakes to the Pacific Ocean across Prince

---

[7] Wadsworth, *National Wagon Road Guide,* 50.
[8] Sullivan, *The Travels of Jedediah Smith,* 149–50.
[9] Korns and Morgan, *West from Fort Bridger,* 4.
[10] Wislizenus, *Journey to the Rocky Mountains,* 19; and Drury, *Marcus and Narcissa Whitman,* 223.

Ruperts Land, the vast territory that encompassed all the rivers flowing east to Hudson's Bay. The Columbia was a key waterway, but low water periodically transformed the narrows at The Dalles into treacherous rapids and waterfalls.

Towering above this bottleneck, Mount Hood dominated the landscape for one hundred miles. Below the volcano's glaciers, dense forests of huge evergreens—hemlock and fir, spruce and cedar—stood like so many pickets, while a thick undergrowth of ferns, laurels, and briars choked its steep sides. Only a few ancient and narrow footpaths crossed the peak's deep canyons, rockslides, and precipitous cliffs. There seemed no possible way to take a wagon over this eighty-mile barrier.

But beyond the mountains lay Eden: the Willamette Valley.

Rolling from its headwaters in the Calapooya Mountains and the Cascades, the Willamette River meandered north for a hundred miles through a broad valley of virgin prairies and forests sheltered by the Coastal Range. North of the Santiam River, a broad savanna spread from the Waldo Hills east to the Eola Hills until the river tumbled over Willamette Falls, creating a bar to navigation and the natural mill site that became Oregon City. The valley's black soil supported lush grasslands broken by stands of timber. At the head of this vale, conical buttes jutted up hundreds of feet above a sea of grass, and dozens of tributaries swelled the river as it rolled to the Columbia.

Six miles above the Willamette's confluence with the Columbia stood Fort Vancouver, the center of civilization in the Pacific Northwest. By 1832 the post "was quite an extensive stockade enclosure, on a prairie, some little back from the river, with the store houses, the houses for the Governor and gentlemen, as partners and clerks were called, and quite a garden," John Ball reported.[11] Its split-pine palisade stood eighteen feet high, measured about 638 feet by 318 feet, and enclosed thirty-six buildings, including a bastion, mansion, and jail. North of Mexico, the fort was the most imposing establishment on the Pacific Coast.[12]

Only a handful of people lived in the Willamette Country in 1840—perhaps two thousand scattered survivors of the Calapooya, Clackamas, and Molalla peoples—all that was left of the valley's original twenty or perhaps thirty thousand original inhabitants, plus retired engagés of the Hudson's Bay Company, refugees from the dying Rocky Mountain fur trade, and a few Methodist missionaries tending to their dwindling flock—altogether only a few hundred white souls. But the first American family to arrive overland from the United States that fall was only the vanguard of a restless people seeking the earthly paradise that always seemed to be waiting twenty—or two thousand—miles to the West.[13]

---

[11] Ball, *Autobiography*, 90–91.

[12] Hussey, *Fort Vancouver Historic Structures Report*, chapter 1.

[13] O'Donnell, *An Arrow in the Earth*, 40–42.

The First Train of Emigrants, 1840

When Narcissa Whitman predicted in early May 1840 that a tide of immigration appeared to be moving rapidly toward the mission at Waiilatpu, she commented on the transformation of her world. So far, that tide was a mere trickle of missionaries, farmers, or entrepreneurs who had come to Oregon intending to settle or found great enterprises but had soon decamped. Whitman sensed that a revolution was underway: "A great change has taken place even since we first entered the country," she wrote, and she had no reason to believe it would stop.[14]

Andrew Drips led the American Fur Company caravan out of Westport at the end of April 1840 to what proved to be the last rendezvous of the fur trade. Two legendary trappers, Jim Bridger and Henry Fraeb, accompanied the outfit, which included two wagons hauling three "self-supporting" Protestant missionary families—Alvin Smith, Harvey Clarke, Philo B. Littlejohn, and their wives—and two wagons belonging to Joel Walker, a veteran of the Santa Fe trade and older brother of the renowned Joseph R. Walker. Walker, his wife Mary, and their four children, John, Joe, Newton, and Isabella, were true pioneers. As he remembered years later, "this party formed the first train of emigrants to Oregon." Walker had come to Missouri planning to start in the spring to California with the forty people who had agreed to accompany him. "When the time for starting arrived," he recalled, "there was not one of them ready except myself and family."[15]

A black-robed Catholic missionary joined Drips's train. Pierre-Jean De Smet had immigrated to the United States from Belgium in 1821, and two years later he became one of the founders of the Missouri Province of the Society of Jesus. He had worked with American Indians ever since, establishing Saint Joseph's Mission to the Pottawatomie tribe at Council Bluffs in 1838: he served them well by arranging a peace with the Yankton Sioux during the summer of 1839. The next spring De Smet answered the longstanding call to send missionaries to the Salish tribes in the Oregon Country.

Almost forty years old and standing not much more than five-and-a-half feet tall, as a youth De Smet's stocky build was so solid he had won the nickname Samson. His sandy hair fell to his shoulders, framing a round, clean-shaven face set off with blue eyes that reflected his natural buoyancy and good humor. He had "a nose with which a Greek or Roman would not find much fault," and "a mouth of ordinary size, which hardly ever opens save to laugh or to make others laugh; it makes people love the good Lord in that manner." His frank expression contributed to making him an extraordinarily attractive man. Father De Smet always wore the

---

[14] Whitman to "Dear Mother," 2 May 1840, in Drury, *Marcus and Narcissa Whitman*, 1:468.
[15] Walker, *A Pioneer of Pioneers*, 12, 17.

cassock and crucifix of a Jesuit priest, an American general later observed, which won him his Indian names, Blackgown and Black Robe.[16] He "was a heavy set, fine looking man," Joel Walker recalled. "I became well acquainted with him and liked him," as did almost everyone who met the charming priest over the next three decades.[17]

"Nothing particularly worth noticing occurred during this journey," De Smet wrote of the trek to Green River. There he met a Salish convert, Pierre Gaucher, and an escort of nine warriors that had battled the Blackfeet all the way from Pierres Hole to the rendezvous to fetch him. Amidst the last great blowout of the Rocky Mountain fur trade, De Smet celebrated the first Mass in the mountains and hired a guide, Jean-Baptiste De Velder, a fellow Belgian and former grenadier in Napoléon's army who had spent fourteen years as a trapper. The Indian escort led the priest to the camp of a thousand Flatheads, Pend d'Oreilles, and Nez Perces at the foot of the Tetons. De Smet passed the rest of the summer with the tribes on their summer buffalo hunt. He set out from the headwaters of the Missouri in late August 1840 and floated down the Gallatin and Yellowstone rivers to return to Saint Louis on New Year's Day, at the end of an arduous 4,300-mile odyssey. The priest immediately left for Philadelphia to raise money to finance his return in the spring to establish a permanent mission in the Rockies.[18]

Robert Newell, a ten-year veteran of the fur trade, had improvised surgical skills learned during his apprenticeship as a saddlemaker that won so much respect from his fellow mountaineers that they called him "Doc." Newell remembered he found "no beaver and everything dull" at the rendezvous.[19] Bill Craig, who had trapped with Joel's brother Joseph, guided the Walkers and several trapper families west to Fort Hall.

Unaware of the difficulties that stood in their way, Walker had intended to take his family to California, but at the fort he changed his mind and decided to go to Oregon with the Hudson's Bay pack train that was hauling the year's returns to Fort Vancouver. That fall, Joel Walker brought the first American family over the trail to come to Oregon as settlers, not as missionaries.[20]

---

[16] Killoren, "Come, Blackrobe," 59; and De Smet, Life, Letters and Travels, 13, 111, 1585.

[17] Walker, A Pioneer of Pioneers, 18. De Smet is not without his critics. He spent very little time with Indians, had no regard for Native culture or beliefs, was not successful in his missionary efforts, and represented the interests of the United States government and the American Fur Company—not Indian interests, George E. Tinker observed. In 1864 an Indian agent said the priest was "a good simple minded old man but completely under the Company's control." Information about how positively Indians responded to him is based almost entirely on his own fundraising letters. See Tinker, Missionary Conquest, 69–70, 73, 81. But De Smet was the only white man "for whom I have ever seen the Indians evince a real affection," Gen. David Stanley wrote in 1864. See De Smet, Life, Letters and Travels, 1585.

[18] Carriker, Father John Peter De Smet, 31–43.

[19] Newell, "Memorandum of Robert Newells Travels in the Teritory of Missourie," in Hafen, The Mountain Men, 8:272.

[20] Walker, A Pioneer of Pioneers, 12, 18. Walker's wife gave birth in January 1841.

The missionaries sold their wagons to Doc Newell at the rendezvous, and he agreed to guide them to Oregon if they would hire his brother-in-law, Joe Meek, and a few other destitute fur trappers as teamsters and road builders. (Meek took along his Indian wife and daughter, Helen Mar.) Newell said, "Come, we are done with this life in the mountains—done with wading in beaver-dams, and freezing or starving alternately—done with Indian trading and Indian fighting," Meek recalled. "The fur trade is dead in the Rocky Mountains, and it is no place for us now, if ever it was."[21]

According to Newell, his party of nine men and three women reached Fort Hall at the end of September. "I concluded to hitch up and try the much-dreaded job of bringing a wagon to Oregon," he recalled. Newell, Craig, and Meek set out with their families for the Columbia with the missionaries and three wagons, including one Joel Walker had abandoned. The men quickly realized that breaking trail through sagebrush "which was in many places higher than the mules' backs, was no joke," and they "finally threw away our wagon-beds and were quite sorry we had undertaken the job." With some difficulty, they got their charges to Fort Walla Walla. "Thare I left one waggon and the other I had took down in a boat to vancouver," Newell recorded, even though he had actually stripped the vehicles of their boxes and brought only their running gear to the Columbia. As Asa Lovejoy explained, "they cut the wagon in two, and used a pair of wheels." By Christmas Newell had settled in the Willamette Valley. Next spring he proudly noted in his memorandum book, "I likewise brought 2 american cows with me. This is to be remembered that I Robert Newell was the first who brought waggons across the rocky mountains."[22] He had also brought Oregon its "first real emigrants, who were neither fur-traders nor missionaries, but true frontiersmen—border-men."[23]

Newell's achievement was a tribute to his determination, but his trek and his carts did not a wagon road make.

OUR IGNORANCE OF THE ROUTE WAS COMPLETE:
THE PIONEERS OF 1841

Some seventy adventurers assembled early in May 1841 on the edge of Indian Country around Westport, Missouri, a frontier town a few miles west of Independence. Located at the mouth of the Kansas River where the Missouri makes its great bend to the east, Westport, which was later absorbed by Kansas City, would always

---

[21] Victor, *The River of the West*, 264.

[22] Marshall, *Acquisition of Oregon*, 85–86; and Newell, "Memorandum," 8:273. A letter from Newell quoted in Marshall says the party left Fort Hall on 5 August 1840. For the most complete account of this venture, see Tobie, *No Man like Joe*, 83–88.

[23] Victor, *The River of the West*, 26.

be an important "jumping-off point" for westbound Americans. The odd gathering of missionaries, sportsmen, veteran and would-be mountaineers, and families now known as the Bidwell-Bartleson party marked "the inception of the emigration across the plains," Josiah Belden proudly remembered. "This party opened the road, so to speak, [this] was the beginning." The venture started "as an exploring expedition to find their own way out there, and see what the country was," he continued. "This expedition should have the credit of starting the emigration to California. Those who joined it were really pioneers, for there was no emigration before; there was nothing known of the road, or how to get there." It was, as Belden observed, "something of a perilous undertaking, and it was the beginning of the whole settlement of the country."[24]

The party's adventures reveal how little the American public knew about the Far West in 1841. None of the land west of the Continental Divide was sovereign American soil: the United States shared Oregon with Great Britain, and Mexico's borders if not her rule encompassed everything west of the Rocky Mountains and south of the 42nd parallel. No one was sure if South Pass was in Mexico or the United States. Much of the public's image of the Far West was simply fantastic lore derived from trappers' tales. Washington Irving's *Astoria* and *The Rocky Mountains,* published in 1836 and 1837, contained a wealth of accurate information, but general knowledge of western geography was largely anecdotal and sometimes entirely mythical. Oregon already had a host of promoters, but like Hall Jackson Kelley, most of them had fallen in love with the country without ever having seen it.

The most reliable information about the American West derived from Lewis and Clark, and much of the fascination Americans had for Oregon can be traced directly to Nicholas Biddle's publication of their journals in 1814.[25] "My father's reading of Lewis and Clark's journals was the cause of our crossing the plains," Andrew Jackson Chambers recalled.[26] One Oregon pioneer family claims their ancestors first heard of Oregon from Robert Frazier, a veteran of the Corps of Discovery, who often visited their home in Missouri "and related his adventures of 30 years before. He had kept a journal and read it—along with his personal recollections" to the family. "He described western Oregon Territory as 'Eden on earth' with prairie and timber alternating as far as the eye could see. He insisted that for grandeur, beauty and fertility, the land had no equal."[27]

---

[24] Josiah Belden, "Historical Statement," in Nunis, *The Bidwell-Bartleson Party,* 128.

[25] See, for example, William Shaw in Rumer, *The Wagon Trains of '44,* 54; Case, "Reminiscences," 270; and Shaw, *El Dorado,* 53–54.

[26] Chambers, *Recollections,* 5.

[27] McBride, "Dr. James McBride—Uncle Jim—Circuit Riding Oregon Preacher." The Frazier journal McBride described has disappeared.

When J. A. Cornwall thought about what inspired his family to trek to Oregon in 1846, he credited "especially the thrilling narrative of the expedition of Colonels Lewis and Clark."[28] Thomas Shadden decided to go west after first being burned out and then flooded out when a waterspout dropped out of the sky on his Tennessee farm, but he also credited the advice of a friend "who had made a study of Lewis & Clarke's explorations, and Irving's Bonneville, and never ceased to speak of the greatness and wonders of Oregon."[29]

Many future pioneers had long family traditions of following the sun to new homes. "When a man moved out West," John Bidwell recalled, "as soon as he was fairly settled he wanted to move again." Bidwell had frontier wanderlust in his bones, for his father had migrated from New York to Canada to Pennsylvania and on to Ohio. By the time he was twenty, Bidwell had followed his desire to see the great prairies of the West to the Missouri River, settling only miles from Fort Leavenworth. While Bidwell was visiting Saint Louis, a neighbor jumped his claim: since he was still a minor, he could not contest the outrage in court. Late in 1840 Bidwell met fur trader Antoine Robidoux (or perhaps his brother, Louis), who had recently returned from California. The mountaineer's description of the country was so superlative "that I resolved if possible to see that wonderful land," Bidwell remembered.[30]

Bidwell was not the only man on the frontier excited by the prospects of California. Harvard graduate John Marsh had wandered into the province in 1836 and established a ranch at the foot of Mount Diablo. Marsh's letters to old friends awakened "a great desire to see the country." When Marsh's letters, which included a vague description of a possible route, appeared in newspapers such as *The Western Atlas,* California fever began to spread.[31]

The result was the formation of the Western Emigration Society at a rally in Independence on 1 February 1841.[32] During the winter, Bidwell organized a similar meeting at Weston, Missouri, to let the public hear Robidoux tell of the wonders of California. He described a land "of perpetual spring and boundless fertility, and laid stress on the thousands of wild horses and cattle. He told about oranges." When asked if there was any fever or ague in the country—a preeminent concern of frontier folk looking to escape from the pestiferous malarial bottoms of the Missouri country—Robidoux said only one man had ever had a chill there, and people had walked eighteen miles to see him shake. His descriptions made California

---

[28] Cornwall, "The Cornwall Family Coming to the Oregon Country," *Oregon Statesman,* 12 July 1941, Typescript, Nevada Historical Society, 2.

[29] Shadden, in Evans, "Thomas J. Shadden," in *History of the Pacific Northwest.*

[30] John Bidwell, in Nunis, *The Bidwell-Bartleson Party,* 100–101, 121n7.

[31] Ibid., 8–9.

[32] Barnett, "The First Overland Letter to California," 30n15.

"seem like a Paradise." In response to the Society's efforts, within a month some five hundred people had signed a pledge to purchase a suitable outfit and meet in May "armed and equipped to cross the Rocky Mountains to California."[33]

Of those who signed the California pledge, only John Bidwell arrived at Sapling Grove on the specified date. Local merchants had denounced the plan as "the most unheard-of, foolish, wild-goose chase that ever entered into the brain of man for five hundred people to pull up stakes, leave that beautiful country, and go away out to a region that we knew nothing of."[34] Others who were eager to learn about trading prospects told John Marsh that doubts had "arisen as to the practicability of the route for waggons and families" and indicated that those who did go went only "for the purpose of exploring the country and returning to the United States."[35] In addition, attorney-adventurer Thomas Jefferson Farnham, who had stopped briefly in California on his return from Oregon, wrote a widely printed letter that painted the Mexican province as dangerous and hostile to Americans. (Farnham was at work on a book so bigoted that historian David Weber credited him with being largely "responsible for the spread of racist opinions about Mexicans."[36])

"Our ignorance of the route was complete," recalled John Bidwell. "We knew that California lay west, and that was the extent of our knowledge." The party actually had Marsh's letter and a few old maps, but such sources were no more useful than the chart belonging to Elam Brown, Bidwell's landlord, which showed two big rivers flowing to the Pacific from a large source near the Great Salt Lake. The legend of the Buenaventura died hard: Brown advised Bidwell to take tools to build canoes, "so that if we found the country so rough that we could not get along with our wagons we could descend those rivers to the Pacific." On the Kansas River the company elected John Bidwell secretary and John Bartleson captain of the train, "but no one knew where to go, not even the captain."[37]

The first man chosen to lead a wagon train received mixed reviews. Bidwell later complained that Bartleson was not the best candidate but let his comrades know that if he was not elected captain he and his several wagons would not go. Bidwell, a teetotaler who went on to be the Prohibitionist Party's presidential

---

[33] John Bidwell, in Nunis, *The Bidwell-Bartleson Party*, 101.

[34] Ibid., 103.

[35] Barnett, "The First Overland Letter to California," 21.

[36] Churchill, *Adventurers and Prophets*, 224n10.

[37] John Bidwell, in Nunis, *The Bidwell-Bartleson Party*, 102–104. Brown's map was badly outdated; by 1840 most cartographers were aware that Jedediah Smith's explorations had demonstrated the mythical nature of Rio Buenaventura. The 1837 "Map of the Territory West of the Rocky Mountains" in Irving's *The Rocky Mountains*, based on information from Captain Bonneville, gave a fair approximation of the course of "Mary or Ogden's River" and its termination east of the "California Mountains." See Wheat, *Mapping the Transmississippi West*, 2:157–59.

candidate in 1892, was unhappy that Bartleson had brought whiskey to trade with the mountaineers, and he criticized his lack of judgment. History would show that leading a wagon train was not calculated to win even the most talented captain many friends, and Bidwell may have been unfair. Father Nicholas Point considered Bartleson the most remarkable of the Americans in the company. Already "somewhat advanced in years," he was "calm in temperament but enterprising in character," Point observed. The tolerance Bartleson exhibited to all party members produced "the most perfect concord."[38]

Bidwell thought there was not $100 cash in the whole party, but whatever the emigrants lacked in money, knowledge, and numbers, they made up for in determination and luck. These naïve sojourners' good fortune became apparent when they joined forces with a band of Catholic missionaries on its way to minister to the Flathead nation "with an old Rocky Mountaineer" as their guide. Having secured approval to establish a permanent mission to the Salish peoples, the indefatigable Father De Smet printed a few thousand pamphlets that helped him raise $1,100 dollars in New Orleans to underwrite several beneficent projects and found a Jesuit mission in the Rockies. His companions included two other priests, Gregory Mengarini and Nicholas Point; three Jesuit brothers, William Claessens, Charles Huet, and Joseph Specht; and an Alsatian carpenter. Although the English Reformation had bequeathed a legacy of anti-Catholicism to nineteenth-century American Protestants, De Smet's character won over all who met him. "He was genial, of fine presence, and one of the saintliest men I have ever known," recalled John Bidwell. "I cannot wonder that the Indians were made to believe him divinely protected. He was a man of great kindness and great affability under all circumstances; nothing seemed to disturb his temper."[39]

The missionaries had engaged the services of a legendary mountaineer, Thomas Fitzpatrick, whose knowledge of the Far West and its peoples was virtually unsurpassed. Born in Ireland, Fitzpatrick had been engaged in the fur trade since 1823, was among those who rediscovered South Pass, and knew the Platte River Road as well as any man alive. Having guided missionary Marcus Whitman west in 1836, he was on his way to becoming the most renowned wagon-train pilot of all time. Joseph Williams, a Protestant minister who joined the emigrants near the Vermillion River, considered Fitzpatrick "a wicked, worldly man" who strongly opposed sending missionaries to the Indians, but Williams found himself in the midst of "an ignorant and hard-hearted people" and conceded that their guide had some intelligence.[40]

---

[38] Nunis, *The Bidwell-Bartleson Party*, 104, 114, 227.
[39] Ibid., 104–105, 240.
[40] Williams, *Narrative of a Tour*, 26.

While De Smet and his companions waited at Soldier Creek for stragglers, they met with the grand chief of the Kanzas, who assigned two warriors to guard the party for three days and nights. "We continued our journey to the number of seventy souls, fifty of whom were capable of managing a rifle," De Smet wrote on 19 May, "a force more than sufficient to undertake with prudence the long march we had to make."[41]

The band that assembled on the Kansas prairie that May was, as De Smet wrote, "an extraordinary mixture of different nations"—his eleven Catholic companions alone represented eight European states. The sojourners, Father Point recalled, "were a composite of all ages, languages and denominations." Doyce Nunis, the leading authority on the venture, concluded that the Bidwell-Bartleson party set out with seventy-seven total members. The company included six Jesuits; an Iroquois scout named Ignace Hatchiorauquasha (aka John Grey); bank embezzler Paul Geddes (aka Talbot Green); European immigrants Charles M. Weber, John L. Schwartz, William Belty, and (apparently) Charles Flügge and Henry Lyons Brolaski; future California Trail promoters Joseph Ballinger Chiles, Charles Hopper, and James P. Springer; and Josiah Belden, Elias Barnett, and Grove C. Cook, who would all play a role in California's subsequent history; English adventurer W. G. "Lord" Romaine; mountaineers Jim Baker, William Mast, and one Piga; and three brothers and their wives from the Kelsey clan. At least fifteen were women and children, including the extraordinary Nancy A. Kelsey, the seventeen-year-old wife of Benjamin Kelsey and mother of a six-month-old daughter named Ann.[42] In addition, Martha Williams Reed remembered that her parents, Richard and Lizzie Huckaby Williams, set out with six children, including an infant girl.[43]

THE MOST WONDERFUL AND MOST USELESS PLATTE RIVER

From Westport, the Bidwell-Bartleson party followed the Kansas, Big Blue, and Little Blue rivers to reach the valley of the Platte near the head of Grand Island, over what became the classic route of the Oregon-California Trail. At first the trace crossed rolling prairie country not unlike that in Missouri and Iowa. Nicholas Point described the terrain's "endless undulations which bear a perfect resemblance to those of the sea when it is agitated by a storm."[44] The beauty of

---

[41] De Smet, in Nunis, *The Bidwell-Bartleson Party,* 208, 209.

[42] Ibid., 196, 208, 209, 227, 247–55. Nunis only accounted for one of the Williamses' six children, but his total appears to be close to the mark.

[43] Reed, "Old California Pioneer Passes Away."

[44] Nunis, *The Bidwell-Bartleson Party,* 228.

the rich black land, laced with tree-lined streams and covered in a lush carpet of springtime flowers and grass, won the praise of many travelers. Joseph Williams hailed "these beautiful plains" that seemed "almost to have no end." As the wagons reached the Platte, the rolling prairie gave way to the flat expanse of the river valley, and the land became less familiar to most sojourners. "We traveled through the most level plains I ever saw in my life," Williams commented. "Here is such a scenery of beauty as is seldom witnessed."[45]

The Platte was, as one wag observed, "a thousand miles long and six inches deep."[46] Pierre-Jean De Smet thought it might be "the most wonderful and most useless of the rivers of North America" after his first trip up its valley. "It is 2,000 yards in width from one bank to the other, and its depth is seldom more than two to six feet," he observed. Its bottom was quicksand, De Smet reported, and it flowed 1,030 miles from the headwaters of its north fork in the Colorado Rockies before emptying into the Missouri some eight hundred miles north of Saint Louis.[47] Occasional groves of cottonwoods had stood along the bottomlands in the early 1830s, but now "wood was very scarce,—and hard to be got" along the river, as Joseph Williams reported.[48] Two years later John Boardman said the lower Platte was "destitute of timber."[49]

The fur-trade trace up the Platte was not yet a wagon road. "We had a great deal of work to do in digging down banks to cross ravines," Nicholas Dawson recalled. Here the trail entered country that appeared starkly barren and alien to Americans raised in the verdant, forested east. Pierre De Smet attributed the lack of trees, "so much at variance with what is seen in other parts of North America," to two principal causes: the custom of the plains tribes to burn the prairie in the fall to improve spring pastures; and the poor nature of the soil. The passage of huge buffalo herds contributed to the lack of vegetation, "which renders a journey through the Far West extremely long and tedious." Trees stood so thickly on the river's islands "that they have the appearance of a labyrinth of groves floating on the waters." Nicholas Point ascribed the scarcity of timber to the increasing aridity. "This connection between trees and water was so obvious," he wrote, "that our pack animals, after only a week on the plains, would, especially after a long march, become excited and double their speed at the sight of trees in the distance."[50]

---

[45] Williams, *Narrative of a Tour*, 25–26.

[46] This aphorism has been attributed to early explorers, mountain men, and pioneers, but it seems to have originated with Henry Cabot Lodge's observation that William Jennings Bryan's speeches resembled "the Platte River of his native West, three thousand miles long, and six inches deep."

[47] De Smet, *Life, Letters and Travels*, 203. De Smet derived the "most useless" quotation from Irving's *Astoria*, 154.

[48] Williams, *Narrative of a Tour*, 1 June 1841, 27.

[49] Boardman, "The Journal," 24 June 1843, 101.

[50] Nunis, *The Bidwell-Bartleson Party*, 148, 211, 214, 228.

The travelers met members of the Kanza, Pawnee, Shawnee, Delaware, Absaroka, Cheyenne, Lakota, and Arapaho tribes. "We had no trouble with the Indians," Martha Williams Reed remembered. "This was before they got to molesting
the settlers."[51] Although their appearance often panicked emigrants, for years the
Indians seldom threatened the lives of the whites they met, and even an unarmed
man traveling alone could cross hundreds of miles of Indian Country without
losing his life. Property was another matter, for the Plains tribes considered raiding—especially seizing horses—a noble endeavor, as Nicholas Dawson learned
from hard experience. Despite Thomas Fitzpatrick's warnings, Dawson's curiosity and a herd of antelope lured him out of sight of the party's wagons. A "whoop"
alerted him to danger, he remembered, but "in an instant I was surrounded by
Indians." The band relieved Dawson of his mule, weapons, and clothes. He caught
up with the wagons and wanted to avenge his misfortune, but Fitzpatrick's "forc-
ible language" persuaded him to avoid violence. Fitzpatrick managed to retrieve
all of Dawson's property except his pistol, but after the encounter, the young man
remembered, "I was called 'Cheyenne' Dawson."[52]

West of Grand Island, the scenery of "the Prairie Ocean" may have seemed dull
and monotonous, but the native wildlife—antelope, elk, wolves, and bison—was
spectacular. The emigrants encountered fur-laden wagons and bullboats, a craft
made by stretching buffalo hide and sinews over a frame of willow branches. The
wagons were filled with "rusty mountaineers" bound for the settlements whose
oxen "looked as though they received a thousand lashes every day of their existence," while the men "looked as though they never had seen razor, water, soap,
or brush." Buffalo especially intrigued overlanders, but even in 1841 some predicted the demise of the huge herds. John Bidwell described the immense piles
of buffalo bones scattered everywhere that made the Platte River Valley appear
to be "but one complete slaughter yard." Even though he later recalled that the
innumerable buffalo posed a great danger, Bidwell noted that it was only a few
years since the bison had abandoned the frontiers of Missouri, and the animals
were now retreating to the Rocky Mountains. He expected that if the buffalo
continued to decline as they had during the previous decades, "they will ere long
become totally extinct."[53]

The wild weather was dramatically different from anything in the travelers'
experience. Tornadoes and hailstones surprised them especially—it seemed "that

---

[51] Reed, "Old California Pioneer Passes Away."

[52] Nunis, *The Bidwell-Bartleson Party*, 147–48. Martha Williams Reed recalled Dawson's encounter: "Some Indians
caught one of our company away from the train, took his coat and hat then followed him into camp. The captain of
our company got them all off to themselves, the emigrants gave them their supper and they gave us no trouble."

[53] Nunis, *The Bidwell-Bartleson Party*, 30–32, 81, 210.

all the winds had been let loose from the four corners of the compass." In early June the party saw "a sublime sight. A spiral abyss seemed to be suddenly formed in the air" and "the noise we heard was like that of a tempest," De Smet wrote. The emigrants watched as a twister crossed the Platte and formed a water column that appeared to be a mile in height. "We saw a lofty waterspout, towering like a huge column to support the arch of the sky," John Bidwell recorded. "It moved off with the swiftness of the wind and was soon lost among the clouds." Hailstones larger than turkey eggs then pummeled the train, while violent winds uprooted trees and scattered their boughs in the twinkling of an eye. "But," as the priest noted, "what is violent does not last."[54]

Some fifty miles upstream from Grand Island, a perceptible change marked the imaginary line of the 100th meridian. Here the dew stopped forming and the humidity that still is a constant fact of life in the eastern half of the continent gave way to the skin-cracking aridity that defines much of the West. The sandhills along the Platte made hard pulling for teams, and the murky river's shifting quicksand made it as muddy as the Missouri: "I verily believe," John E. Murphy wrote, "there is sand enough of the very best quality on the Platte to plaster the globe."[55]

A hundred miles west of Grand Island a range of hills divided the Platte into north and south forks. Here the trail left the muddy, wandering giant, forded the South Platte, and crossed to the North Platte, a lively mountain stream. Some fur company caravans forded the South Fork about eight miles above the confluence at the modern town of North Platte, Nebraska, but later wagon trains used three main fords, beginning with the Lower Crossing located near O'Fallons Bluff about two miles southwest of present-day Sutherland. The Middle Crossing was some thirty-two miles to the west at Ogallala: the trail then followed the South Platte for a dozen miles to the Upper Crossing, located four miles west of what is now Brule. Known as the California Crossing during the gold rush, it led to California Hill, a quick but steep climb to a dry open plain where travelers often saw bands of wild horses.[56] The roads from the Lower Crossing converged on the ridge's top and then followed it to "a wild rocky glen called Ash Hollow."[57] Here the road descended into the hollow on a gradual grade, but those coming from the Middle and Upper Crossings faced a steep descent to the North Platte down the sharp pitch of Windlass Hill.[58]

[54] Ibid., 214; and Bidwell, Journal, 5 June 1841.

[55] Murphy to Mr. Smith, 9 June 1852, in *Monmouth Atlas,* 16 July 1852, Henderson Collection.

[56] Wyeth, *The Correspondence and Journals,* 23, 27 May 1834; Wyeth, *Oregon,* 66; and Mattes, *The Great Platte River Road,* 265.

[57] Field, Crossing the Plains, 8 June 1845, Oregon Historical Society.

[58] Thanks to Todd Berens, Greg Franzwa, and Kay Threlkeld for helping sort out these routes. There is no evidence anyone ever used a windlass to lower wagons down "Windlass Hill" into Ash Hollow.

The Bidwell-Bartleson train spent the ninth of June crossing the shallow but swift South Platte at the Lower Crossing, which was about half a mile wide with a sandy bottom.[59] "We got across with some difficulty, but not much danger," Joseph Williams wrote. "Some places the wagons nearly swam."[60] According to Father Mengarini, the last wagon *did* swim. Just before the priest's horse foundered in the quicksand, he saw a wagon topple over near the far shore. Mengarini could not swim but clung to his horse until the animal pulled up on the bank. He "turned to look at the wagon and saw it abandoned and floating down the stream. No lives were lost."[61]

The party climbed over the twenty-mile bench to the North Platte and came to Ash Hollow, a small ash grove of some twenty-five trees, one of the only wooded sites between Grand Island and Fort Laramie. The next morning, a Sunday, an accident claimed the life of the unfortunate but all too well named George Shotwell. "The poor fellow had incautiously taken his gun by the muzzle to draw it from his wagon, the piece accidentally discharged, the bullet pierced his liver, and in two hours he was dead," Gregory Mengarini recalled.[62] It was the first—but far from the last—death by accidental gunshot on the trails.

West of Ash Hollow, the spectacular and strange formations and monumental bluffs of the Wildcat Hills rose like castles along the North Fork's south bank, while Ancient Bluff Ruins loomed above the north shore. Laid down some thirty million years ago, these eroded remnants of Brule clay are interspersed with volcanic ash beneath a hard cap of Arickaree Sandstone. Unlike anything early sojourners had ever seen before, these colorful hills were "strangely worn into many fantastic shapes" and reminded them of ancient temples, courthouses, and citadels.[63]

Tall sandy hills lined the banks of the North Platte, and the aridity of the high plains became increasingly apparent, for as John Ball had noted, "We saw not a spring or crossed a stream in traveling hundreds of miles up the North Platte."[64] Even before reaching Court House Rock, the party could see the inverted funnel of Chimney Rock, "a striking landmark in this prairie sea." Nathaniel Wyeth said the Indians called it the Elk Prick. The Chimney could be "seen towering like a huge column at a distance of 30 miles," John Bidwell wrote, and Father De Smet considered it the Platte's most remarkable landmark. Sojourners loved to speculate on the

[59] Mattes, *The Great Platte River Road*, 265.

[60] Williams, *Narrative of a Tour*, 28. Williams thought the ford was one-quarter mile wide, but Bidwell estimated its width at two-thirds of a mile.

[61] Nunis, *The Bidwell-Bartleson Party*, 223.

[62] Ibid., 32, 33, 222. For one of many emigrants who died performing the same operation, see Burrows, "Crossing the Plains," 12–13.

[63] Ball, *Autobiography*, 69.

[64] Ibid.

cause of "the wonderful formation of this curious ornament." Even in 1841 De Smet accurately foresaw that erosion would gradually reduce the height of the Chimney's tower, and he encouraged scientists to study it before a large cleft split the rock and left nothing but its memory.[65]

The trail now climbed through "a gap in a range of high hills called Scott's Bluff," named for the spot where two mountaineers had abandoned their sick brigade leader, Hiram Scott. They "reported him dead and buried," James Field later wrote, "but his body was afterward discovered at a different spot from where they reported him buried, and other circumstances made it apparent he had died of starvation and want."[66] James John thought the Bluff had a splendid appearance, while the landmark's "beautifully grand and picturesque" formation impressed John Bidwell with its "lofty spires, towering edifices, spacious domes and in fine all the beautiful mansions of cities." From the summit of Scotts Bluff, a sharp-eyed observer could see Laramie Peak, rising to an elevation of 10,274 feet. Many considered it their first view of the Rocky Mountains. Bidwell called it Black Hill Mountain, for it loomed "like a dark cloud in the western horizon" for days as the trail wound around the arching bow of the North Platte.[67]

Sixty miles west of the bluffs three trading posts stood near the mouth of the Laramie River, "a big, rapid, turbulent tributary" of the North Platte. Fort William was a ramshackle timber stockade established in 1834 on the North Platte about half a mile above its confluence with the Laramie River. The post was "made of cottonwood logs, about fifteen feet high, hewed off, and wedged closely together," Wislizenus reported in 1839, when only five men garrisoned the post—four Frenchmen and a German. (Asahel Munger counted ten men, but only one could speak a little English.) Fort William was by no means a military post, Wislizenus pointed out, but simply "a safe point for storing their goods, from which barter may be carried on with the Indians."[68]

Nearby stood Fort Lupton, better known as Fort Platte, a rival operation built of adobe and owned by Lancaster P. Lupton, a West Point graduate who left the dragoons to pursue the fur trade in 1836. To keep up with the competition, the American Fur Company abandoned Fort William's rotting stockade and built a new adobe citadel on a low bluff about two miles up the Laramie River. When the Bidwell-Bartleson party camped between the forts on 22 June 1841, a Mexican construction crew was building the new stronghold. "We passed an old fort

---

[65] Nunis, *The Bidwell-Bartleson Party*, 33, 212–13. One of the last assaults on Chimney Rock took place in 1995, when summer lightning blasted fifteen feet of rock from its spire.

[66] Field, *Crossing the Plains*, 15 June 1845, Oregon Historical Society.

[67] Nunis, *The Bidwell-Bartleson Party*, 33–34, 166.

[68] Ball, *Autobiography*, 71; Wislizenus, *A Journey to the Rocky Mountains*, 67–68; and Munger, *Diary of Asahel Munger and Wife*, 14 June 1839.

John Bidwell,
the "Prince of California Pioneers,"
as he appeared in 1850, nine years after he crossed
the plains to California. Author's collection.

below the mouth of the Larrimee River;" Joseph Williams wrote, "and crossing that river, we went up to a new fort that they were building, called Fort Johns."[69]

Whatever their official names, the posts were universally called Fort Laramie. Joseph Williams thought the residents appeared healthier than at any other place in the country. Someone said they had not heard a sermon for twelve years, and he tried to preach twice, with, he admitted, little effect. "Here is plenty of talk about their damnation," Williams observed, "but none about their salvation."[70] Large camps of visiting Lakotas or Cheyennes surrounded the post almost continually, and an Indian family joined the wagon train at the fort. Father Point sketched them as the "Native family wanting to follow us everywhere," but they accompanied the emigrants only as far as Green River. Mountaineers at the fort warned the Bidwell-Bartleson party they would now cross "a country pretty badly infested by the Crow and Blackfeet Indians," whose hostility to whites was notorious.[71]

"After we left Laramie we came to the Black Hills, the worst of all traveling— hilly, sandy and full of wild sage—'tis death on a wagon," John Boardman complained after crossing the trail in 1843.[72] Above Fort Laramie, the North Platte flowed through a canyon that funneled early travelers into the Black Hills, the sprawling range clad in a dark growth of Rocky Mountain juniper that runs from the Dakotas into Wyoming. Early travelers kept to the south side of the river, where the trail divided into river, bluff, and mountain routes. About fourteen miles from the fort, near the Warm Spring, the several trails crossed red sandstone valleys decorated with odd formations such as window rocks, natural bridges, and pyramids of red stone. Bidwell described crossing bluegrass meadows and rivulets "affording as good water as ever run," past "an immense quarry of beautiful white alabaster" as the party marched through the Black Hills among plenty of bison.

The wagons left the North Platte River behind after fording it near what is now Casper, Wyoming. The trail became a mountainous track passing poisoned springs and the Avenue of Rocks, also known as the Devils Backbone, which formed a jagged stone obstacle course for wagons. On the Fourth of July, the emigrants followed Fitzpatrick "over hills and dales, scorched with heat [and] came to a small copse of red willows, from which issued excellent springs of water," soon known as Willow Springs.[73] The next day they climbed Prospect Hill, whose summit offered a panoramic view of the valley of the Sweetwater,

---

[69] Williams, *Narrative of a Tour*, 28. In 1847 both William Clayton and James Smithies gave the distance between the ruins of Fort Platte and Fort John as two miles.

[70] Ibid., 28–29.

[71] Nunis, *The Bidwell-Bartleson Party*, 130, and drawing no. 15, following page 230.

[72] Boardman to Wells, 17 July 1844, *Quarterly of the Oregon Historical Society*, 274–76.

[73] Nunis, *The Bidwell-Bartleson Party*, 35.

the loveliest tributary of the Platte, and that evening the company camped at the turtle-like dome of Independence Rock.

Climbing imperceptibly, the valley of the Sweetwater stretched for almost one hundred fifty miles from the river's confluence with the North Platte to its head-waters at the very foot of the Continental Divide. A chain of formations adorn the Sweetwater Valley: Devils Gate, where the river slices through the Rattle-snake Mountains, Split Rock, the Old Castle, Names Cliff and Names Rock, and Ice Slough, along with wonders such as alkali lakes, beds of saleratus—baking soda—and ice springs hidden beneath the sod. The greatest trail landmark of them all stood next to the first crossing of the Sweetwater. De Smet celebrated "the famous Rock Independence" as the "Great Register of the Desert" for the hundreds of names already carved and painted on its sides.[74]

After three days' traveling up the river valley, the peaks of the Wind River Range "were dimly seen through the misty clouds that obscured the western horizon," John Bidwell wrote. Rumor had it that the range included a peak that the Hudson's Bay Company had measured "geometrically and barometrically" and found to be 25,000 feet in elevation: the tallest mountain in the Wind River Range, Gannett Peak, actually tops out at 13,804 feet, but the range does seem to disappear into the sky. The party camped "in full view of thousands of buffalo," killed twenty of them, and began to dry a supply of meat they hoped would last them to California. Bartleson stopped to trade with a band of Shoshones, and the party found that on some nights it was hard to keep warm. In the middle of sum-mer banks of snow still lingered not far from the trail, a sight that never failed to astonish settlers used to the sultry summers of the Mississippi Valley.[75]

The broad corridor of South Pass crosses a ridge so unimposing that many way-farers failed to notice they had left the waters of the Mississippi and reached the headwaters of the Colorado until they saw the waters of Pacific Springs flowing west. On 18 July, Fitzpatrick led the party "toward the heights of the Far West, ascending, sometimes clambering, until we reached the summit, from which we discovered another world," De Smet wrote, "the immense Oregon Territory."[76]

RAKING AND SCRAPING: WEST FROM SOUTH PASS

The strands of all the trails to Oregon and California came together on the road to South Pass. West of the divide, three faint traces penetrated one hundred miles of sagebrush desert watered only by the Dry, Little, and Big Sandy rivers. In

---

[74] De Smet to de la Croix, 4 February 1841, in De Smet, *Life, Letters and Travels,* 214.

[75] Wislizenus, *A Journey to the Rocky Mountains,* 80; Nunis, *The Bidwell-Bartleson Party,* 36, 244.

[76] Ibid., 36, 216.

addition to the trapper's road to the rendezvous sites at Horse Creek, fur traders had worked out two routes to Green River that crossed this arid, broken land, including a roundabout but well-watered trail to Blacks Fork of Green River and a second difficult shortcut that offered a direct course but not a drop of water for more than forty miles. The dry alternative, first known as the Greenwood Cutoff and later as the Sublette, headed directly west to Green River. It was about fifty miles—or three days' travel—shorter, but the suffering it inflicted on livestock made it a dangerous bargain.

This web of traces baffled the party. "This morning John Gray and Romaine were sent on to Green River to see if there were any trappers at the rendezvous," John Bidwell wrote at Independence Rock. They returned with the news that for the first time in fifteen years, no rendezvous would take place. Game was getting scarce, so the party marched over the extremely dry and dusty country, stopping wherever they could find feed for teams "already much jaded for want of grass." Near the Big Sandy, Fitzpatrick or Bartleson misread the trail and "the caravan for three days wandered at random," De Smet noted sourly. At last they reached the Green, where Gray had met Henry Fraeb's band of some twenty mountaineers, who postponed their buffalo hunt to trade with the emigrants. Before setting off, the party disposed of two wagons—Joseph Chiles sold his. James Baker joined Fraeb's brigade to launch his legendary career in the West, and half a dozen men set off on a hunting excursion before returning to the states.[77]

Rocky Mountain society did not impress Joseph Williams: he thought Fraeb's "wicked, swearing company of men" was "mostly composed of half breeds, French, and Dutch and all sorts of people collected together in the mountains." Then again, he did not think much more highly of his own companions. "On the Sabbath we have nothing but swearing and fishing," he complained.[78] The subsequent death of Fraeb and several of his men in an Indian fight on the Little Snake River was another sure sign of the emigrant party's very good fortune, but the abstemious Bidwell concluded it was not the Sioux but the whiskey Bartleson had sold to the trappers that caused their demise.[79]

Years later, Martha Williams Reed told of traveling to Fort Hall with her parents and six siblings. On Green River, twelve-year-old Martha assumed responsibilities far beyond her age. "Mother and sister were both sick and I had to do the cooking and take care of my baby sister," she recalled. The Williams family became one of the first to learn a hard fact of overland travel: food often ran out long before the trail did. "There wasn't much to cook, as we were very short of

[77] Ibid., 345–37, 217.

[78] Williams, *Narrative of a Tour*, 23, 25 July 1841, 30–31.

[79] Nunis, *The Bidwell-Bartleson Party*, 109.

rations. Father only had one wagon so couldn't haul enough provisions." One man (probably Chiles) had supplies to sell, "but he sold them so high and Father hadn't much money, so he couldn't afford to buy much, and as a result we went hungry a good deal of the time."[80]

Breaking new trail, the wagons "forced their way raking and scraping" through barren hills covered only with sagebrush standing several feet tall. "Horseback riders also had the clothes torn off them." The journey was now more difficult, with more mountains and fewer valleys, Nicholas Dawson recalled. On steep mountainsides, "sideling" trails required the men to use ropes to keep their wagons from tipping over.[81] A wagon broke down on Hams Fork, and the party crossed the weirdly sculptured hills to Blacks Fork in hot, sultry weather, even though they could see snow on the towering Uinta Mountains.[82] As August began they spent two days seeking a practical way over the high divide separating the Green and Bear rivers, working out a difficult route into the Great Basin.

The Bear flowed through "a wide and beautiful valley, surrounded by lofty mountains and often intersected by inaccessible rocks," De Smet wrote. The emigrants followed the river north, keeping to its banks except when cliffs and canyons barred the way. "The bluffs were exceedingly high, and no person could ever believe that wagons ever passed these huge eminences of nature, did he not witness it with his own eyes," John Bidwell journalized. The scenery was grand. From one summit a sunset spread across the sky, illuminating "a most beautiful landscape": the rugged peaks on the western horizon, a small alpine lake, as "the river meandered proudly through the valley among willows and scattering cottonwoods, till it disappeared among the hills in the shades of the evening."[83] Wandering along the Wasatch Range, the Bear at last found a break in the mountains at a thermal hotspot packed with natural wonders. Here the company of mountaineers, missionaries, and migrants parted ways.

THE SODA FOUNTAIN: SODA SPRINGS

Westbound travelers followed the Bear River to its northernmost bend at "one of the most notable spots in the whole mountain country—the Beer Spring, so well known to every mountain traveler," Wislizenus wrote.[84] Now called Soda Springs, its marvels included small geysers, fissures spewing poisonous gases, and hot, cold, and carbonated springs. "We found the waters a luxury indeed, as good

---

[80] Reed, "Old California Pioneer Passes Away."
[81] Nunis, *The Bidwell-Bartleson Party,* 148–49.
[82] Williams, *Narrative of a Tour,* 28, 30 July 1841.
[83] Nunis, *The Bidwell-Bartleson Party,* 38, 216.
[84] Wislizenus, *A Journey to the Rocky Mountains,* 98.

soda as I ever drank, boiling up out of the earth," Asahel Munger wrote in 1839. "The water is clear and has a smart taste like small beer, though it has more of the sting to it than any beer I ever drank. I drank freely of it. It had a very good effect."[85] To this day, soft drinks do not sell well in the town: residents prefer to make their own superior carbonated beverages using the local waters.

Father Nicholas Point considered Soda Springs the most beautiful campsite on the journey and thought its "limpid springs, refreshing fruits, game in great abundance, the most varied and picturesque views, all seemed to invite travelers to make this their winter quarters." John Bidwell called this "great curiosity" the Soda Fountain. Within three or four miles there were no fewer than one hundred springs, "some bursting out on top of the ground, others along the banks of the river, . . . and some even in the bottom of the river," he wrote.[86] Joseph Williams thought the place might once have been a great volcano. Many springs boiled like a pot of water, but only one of them was hot, while another shot up a three-foot column of water every fifteen seconds and had a vent that made a noise like a steamboat, though not as loud. The soda-impregnated water deposited red sediment wherever it gushed from the earth that petrified into "large mounds of porous rock, some of which are no less than fifty feet high." The hollow ground echoed as they rode their horses over it.

Here the party that had journeyed together from the Missouri River broke apart. The Jesuit missionaries met their Salish guides, and De Smet "with his little company, left us, and turned to the right to go to the Flat Head tribes, where he had a mission," the Reverend Williams reported. It is a tribute to De Smet's charm that even Williams felt sorry to part company with the genial Jesuit. The sojourners "had lived together for three months amidst the same perils" and seemed almost countrymen, Father Mengarini recalled. "Farewells were sad. Many prejudices had disappeared during the journey."[87]

Almost all the emigrants had initially set out for Mexican territory, but now they divided over whether to go to Oregon or Alta California, especially since they were losing Thomas Fitzpatrick, their veteran guide. Thirty-two discouraged members of the company "decided not to venture without path or guide into the unknown and trackless region toward California," Bidwell recalled. They chose instead to follow the missionaries north to Fort Hall and "thence find their way down Snake and Columbia rivers into Oregon" on the established pack trail, while the rest set off down Bear River to look for California.[88]

[85] Munger, *Diary of Asahel Munger and Wife*, 16 July 1839.
[86] Nunis, *The Bidwell-Bartleson Party*, 39, 235.
[87] Williams, *Narrative of a Tour*, 31; and Nunis, *The Bidwell-Bartleson Party*, 235.
[88] Ibid., 110.

Martha Williams Reed told of traveling to Fort Hall with her parents and six siblings. At Fort Laramie a man calling himself Cochran (who was actually Richard Phelan) joined the train, and near Green River, Father De Smet had married Phelan to Nancy Kelsey's sister, Betsey Grey. Somewhere on the trail Cochran/Phelan persuaded Richard Williams to give up the notion of going to California and head to Oregon instead—Phelan told Williams he could never get his family to California alive. At Soda Springs, "Cochran and his wife and little girl started back to Missouri on horseback," Martha remembered. "We heard afterwards that the little girl died three days before they got there and they carried the body for three days."[89]

"This day we parted with some of our company," wrote Oregon-bound Joseph Williams. "There was some division and strife among us about going; some who set out for California changed their minds to go to the Columbia." At Sheep Rock, where the Bear River turned south at Soda Point to flow to the Great Salt Lake, the Californians went south and the Oregonians headed north. Bidwell wrote, "The two companies, after bidding each other a parting farewell, started and were soon out of sight."[90]

SUCH A DREADFUL JOURNEY: THE TRAIL TO OREGON, 1841

Turning north, the faint trace that led to Fort Hall left the Bear and crossed rough terrain to escape the Great Basin, reaching the Snake River between the Blackfoot and Portneuf rivers. As they cut out a road, the little Oregon company could not get their wagons down a stream and had to retrace their steps to the previous night's campground.[91] Fort Hall, the Hudson's Bay Company's southernmost outpost, stood in a meadow next to the Snake. The stronghold was originally "made of hewed logs, with roofs covered with mud brick chimneys and fireplaces also being built of the same; no windows, except a square hole in the roof, and in the bastion a few port holes large enough for guns only. The buildings were all enclosed in a strong log wall," Narcissa Whitman wrote in 1836.[92]

By the time Frederick Wislizenus saw the post in 1840, the Hudson's Bay Company had replaced Wyeth's pickets with a twelve-foot-high wall of partly baked brick. (John Boardman later called them "squaw cakes of mud baked in the sun": he considered the whole operation inferior to Fort Laramie.) "The fort lies hard by the river, and is built in a square of about eighty by eighty feet, suggestive of barracks,"

[89] Reed, "Fallbrook's Prima Donna," *The Fallbrook Enterprise,* 26 September 1913, Fallbrook Museum, 1–3.

[90] Williams, *Narrative of a Tour,* 11 August 1841, 32; and Nunis, *The Bidwell-Bartleson Party,* 39.

[91] Williams, *Narrative of a Tour,* 32.

[92] Whitman, *My Journal,* 4 August 1836, 22.

This engraving of a wagon train pushing west in all its glory—drooling oxen, sheep, dogs, mounted outriders, ox-drivers, and a woman with shovel or broom—is a classic image of life on the overland trail. Author's collection.

Wislizenus wrote. He found many horses, six cows, and a small cannon in the court-yard—perhaps the gun Ashley had brought across South Pass in 1826, or maybe the first wheeled vehicle to traverse the Blue Mountains. "The whole garrison consisted of six men," he noted, "among them two Sandwich Islanders and a German."[93]

At the fort—"a beautiful place, in a handsome part of the country," Joseph Williams said—the party purchased a few provisions, paying a dollar for a pint of flour. The emigrants had reached the drainage of the Columbia River, but a series of waterfalls, rapids, whirlpools, and deep canyons prevented them from simply floating down to the Pacific. Fort Hall's retiring commander, Francis Ermatinger, "one of the most liberal, free-hearted men in this country," agreed to let the emigrants accompany the pack train taking the post's annual "returns" to Fort Vancouver. The Williams family joined Ermatinger's men, trading their wagons and ox teams for horses. "We rode half of them and had packs on the others," Martha Williams remembered.[94]

The pack trail to Oregon followed the left bank of the Snake River to American Falls across a broad, dry, sage-covered plain, as the river surged through "broken chasms, boiling through narrow channels, or pitching in beautiful cascades over ridges of basaltic columns."[95] Desolate country stretched for miles on both sides of the Snake, land so barren that for three hundred miles Marcus Whitman could not "recollect a single fertile spot to the amount of an acre on the River for the whole distance."[96] Reverend Williams admired the scenery at American Falls and the bounty of Salmon Falls, where a large band of Shoshones lived in grass-and-willow lodges and caught thousands of the red fish. Here Williams became the first overland emigrant to apply the derogatory term "Diggers" to the skilled survivalists whose diet of roots and grubs appalled white Americans.[97]

Sometimes nightfall forced the travelers to make a dry camp on the rim of the river's precipitous canyon, within sight but out of reach of the waters of the torrential river. The river could be difficult or impossible to access from the dismal country of its barren plateau, so thirsty sojourners could often hear the cascading water without being able to drink it. John Kirk Townsend gave two reasons why wayfarers along the Snake suffered from extreme thirst: the aridity, compounded by the intense heat of the sun on the open and exposed plains, and the dust. "The air feels like the breath of a sirocco, the tongue becomes parched and horny, and

---

[93] Boardman, "The Journal," 11 September 1843, 111; and Wislizenus, *A Journey to the Rocky Mountains,* 106. Sandwich Islanders were Hawaiians.

[94] Reed, "Fallbrook's Prima Donna," 2.

[95] Irving, *The Rocky Mountains,* 170.

[96] Whitman to Greene, 5 September 1836, in Hulbert and Hulbert, *Marcus Whitman, Crusader,* 1:215.

[97] Williams, *Narrative of a Tour,* 32–33.

the mouth, nose, and eyes are incessantly assailed by the fine pulverized lava, which rises from the ground with the least breath of air," he wrote after trekking down the river in 1834.[98]

"We traveled over some tremendous bad roads," Preacher Williams continued. They crossed the deep and treacherous Snake at what is now Glenns Ferry, where the river was "divided by two islands into three branches," as Narcissa Whitman observed after fording the river in 1836. The party forged ahead, reaching Fort Boise on the first of September; there Williams "could scarcely sleep for the Indians, who sung all night in a very curious manner. This is their practice when they are gambling," he wrote. "The salmon also kept a great noise, jumping and splashing about in the water." Here the party once again crossed the Snake and set out for Fort Walla Walla "over hills and rough roads" that Williams called very dangerous.[99]

After leaving the Malheur River, the pack train made a long dry trek to Birch Creek and Farewell Bend, where the trail at last left the Snake before the river vanished into Hells Canyon. The Willamette Valley, the goal of the Americans, was still two mountain ranges, several long desert crossings, and four hundred miles away. The trail ascended the aptly named Burnt River and crossed Virtue Flats to find relief in the Powder River Valley, which early on was noted for its Lone Pine, a solitary tree that towered above the empty plain. Lightning flashed, thunder roared, and rain poured down on Abigail Smith as her missionary party entered the valley in August 1840. "I was about to say what will become of us when the Lone tree presented its self to my eye which encouraged me much. Truely we had found a blessed guide," she wrote. As night fell, it stopped raining and a pale moon lighted her seven companions to the tree, which she described as "a large pine tree standing entirely a lone. Its top reaches very high." The Powder River flowed nearby through deep grass, providing an ideal spot to spend the Sabbath. "I felt to thank God for giving us such a tree," Smith wrote. With its abundant grass, wood, and water, the countryside at Powder River was an oasis after the stark deserts of eastern Oregon.

Like the tens of thousands of Oregon emigrants who followed him, Williams praised the "pleasant plain" at Powder River and the beautiful springs on the spurs of the Blue Mountains. The trail then climbed over Ladd Hill to the Grande Ronde Valley, a beautiful, fertile prairie in the shadow of the Blue Mountains. "We stayed on the Grand Round, a beautiful plain, about twenty miles long and ten miles broad. It is well calculated for farming, and well watered," Williams

---

[98] Townsend, *Narrative of a Journey,* 7 August 1834, 112–13.

[99] Williams, *Narrative of a Tour,* 34; and Drury, *First White Women over the Rockies,* 1:85. A flood at Glenns Ferry created a third island in the late 1800s, which led to its being called Three Island Crossing.

wrote. "Here we pass some beautiful pines, spruce and fir trees." After crossing the Blue Mountains, the emigrants reached the Umatilla River where Williams found "a variety of fruits, black haws and brown cherries; and trees like the balm of Gilead, with pods and gum on them."[100]

"We were short of provisions most all the time and went hungry lots of time until we got to Dr. Whitman's," Martha Williams Reed remembered. "There we got some wheat and ground it on a hand mill, and I think some pickled pork. They had tomatoes there, but we didn't eat tomatoes then." The mission left a lasting impression on the young girl: "Dr. Whitman and his wife had been there with the Indians for several years and had them civilized. We could hear them say their prayers at night and morning and evening. They had learned them to do all kinds of work the same as white people."[101]

The Presbyterian missionaries at Waiilatpu impressed the Reverend Williams as kind, friendly people, but he was especially pleased they had "all kinds of green vegetables which they gave to us very freely." Marcus Whitman held a Sunday meeting with his Native congregation and Williams preached to them. From Waiilatpu, the Americans took a very dangerous road to The Dalles, where the Columbia River "contracted to not more than twenty yards wide." Here Williams found the Methodist mission, where Jason Lee's brother Daniel treated the emigrants well and gave them free supplies. "I was often invited to eat with them," Williams recalled after his four days at the mission, "but not to sleep in the house."

With Mount Hood towering to the southwest, the emigrants encountered the mountain wall that would stop wagons on the eastern slope of the Cascades for the next five years. After resting for three days, Williams set out with four men and Samuel Kelsey's family to cross the Cascades, passing through "the thickest woods I ever saw in my life," with undergrowth so dense it was like night at noon. "The high hills, logs, and mud-holes made travel very difficult, and even dangerous. There was a woman and three children in company with us, while we lay out two nights in the rain." he wrote. Williams arrived at the "the beautiful plains of Willamette" and the small settlement at the river's falls on 9 October 1841.[102]

Whitman had sent an Indian guide to lead Richard Williams's family to The Dalles, where "another Indian piloted us on to Willamette Falls, what is Oregon City now," Martha recalled. There Williams tried to persuade a missionary—probably Alvan Waller or storekeeper George Abernathy—to let him have some flour, but was refused. The next day the family received some potatoes "and we

---

[100] Williams, *Narrative of a Tour,* 34.
[101] Reed, "Fallbrook's Prima Donna," 1–3.
[102] Williams, *Narrative of a Tour,* 34–35.

really enjoyed the potatoes." That same day an "old man" named Moore—no doubt Robert Moore, a veteran of the Peoria Party—came down the river in a canoe and "told Father to put his family in the canoe and take them across to the other side and we could share what he had, and we did."[103] Williams and his son-in-law, Zade Kelsey, claimed a farm where Hillsboro now stands, "built log houses and split shakes to cover them," and set about the hard work of settling a new country. The missionaries may have refused to help the family, but Williams visited Fort Vancouver and the Hudson's Bay Company "agreed to furnish him provisions until he could raise wheat to pay for them," his daughter recalled. "We lived on boiled wheat lots of the time."[104]

"The emigrants were twenty-four in number—two families, with small children, from Missouri," Narcissa Whitman wrote after meeting the first large party of overland emigrants to reach Oregon. "This company was much larger when they started. About thirty went another route, to California."[105] Mrs. Whitman was very pleased to see a mother like Mrs. Williams "with so many children around her, having come so far—such a dreadful journey."[106] And as Martha Williams Reed proudly wrote of her youthful adventures, "I was the first white girl to cross the planes to Oregon."[107]

No Roads and No Pilot, Except the Setting Sun: The Bidwell-Bartleson Trail to California

At Soda Springs the California-bound members of the Bidwell-Bartleson party "parted company with the crowd that was going to Oregon, which crowd included Fitzpatrick and the priests." As Nancy Kelsey recalled, after their wagons turned south down Bear River, the emigrants "had no roads and no pilot, except the setting sun." Hoping to find a substitute for the irreplaceable Fitzpatrick, the emigrants sent several men to Fort Hall to recruit a guide who could show them the way to California.[108]

Fort Hall produced no pilot or even anyone who knew the trail to California. The fort's residents did, however, provide an accurate if vague and intimidating

---

[103] Robert Moore set out with the Peoria Party in 1839 and was almost sixty years old when he arrived in Oregon in 1840. He settled west of the falls and established a farm he named "Robin's Nest," where he died in 1857. See Bancroft, *History of Oregon,* 1:237n29.

[104] Reed, "Fallbrook's Prima Donna," 3.

[105] Whitman to "My Dear Jane," 1 October 1841, in Marshall, *Acquisition of Oregon,* 303.

[106] Drury, *Marcus and Narcissa Whitman,* 1:425.

[107] Reed, "Fallbrook's Prima Donna," 3. For another version of Reed's story, see "Old California Pioneer Passes Away." Larry Cenotto of the Amador County Archives discovered this previously unknown account of the 1841 Oregon contingent of the Bidwell-Bartleson party.

[108] Nunis, *The Bidwell-Bartleson Party,* 149, 235; and Nancy (Roberts) Kelsey's Own Story, Mattes Library.

description of the difficulties facing travelers trying to surmount the natural barriers of the Great Basin. The scouts "brought the information that we must strike
out west of Salt Lake—being careful not to go too far south, lest we should get
into a waterless country without grass," John Bidwell recalled. "They also said we
must be careful not to go too far north, lest we should get into a broken country
and steep cañons, and wander about, as trapping parties had been known to do,
and become bewildered and perish."[109]

The party's predicament reveals only one of the challenges to blazing a road to
California. Hindsight suggests the Raft River route Joseph R. Walker had used
to return from California in 1834 offered the easiest way for wagons to penetrate
the Great Basin and reach the Humboldt River Valley. But what appears inescap-
able from the perspective of the present was unknowable in 1841. From Soda
Springs, the emigrants worked out a route to the Humboldt that no subsequent
wagon party ever followed, even though it was described in John Bidwell's journal, which inadvertently became the first published overland guide to California.
In its game of geographic blindman's buff, the Bidwell-Bartleson wagons came
very close to defining a trail that could have become the main road to California.
The train moved west from Great Salt Lake along the general line that the first
Transcontinental Railroad later followed, but their scouts missed the railroad's
route through Emigrant Canyon, which would have taken them directly to their
objective, the headwaters of the Humboldt River. Had they found this passage,
other wagons might have followed them down the Bear River.

The depleted Bidwell-Bartleson party set out for California with thirty-four
members, including Nancy Kelsey and her infant daughter. "It was considered
almost rash for a woman to venture on so perilous a journey, but Mrs. Kelsey
said, 'Where my husband goes I can go. I can better endure the hardships of the
journey than the anxieties for an absent husband.' So she was received in the company," Joseph Chiles fondly recalled. "Her cheerful nature and kind heart brought
many a ray of sunshine through the clouds that gathered round a company [of]
so many weary travelers." Chiles's tribute reveals how valuable her presence was
in the first organized wagon train and suggests the importance of subsequent
contributions of women to overland travel. "She bore the fatigues of the journey
with so much heroism, patience, and kindness that there still exists a warmth in
every heart for the mother and her child that were always forming silvery linings
for every dark cloud that assailed them," Chiles wrote.[110]

The train started with nine wagons (including, apparently, a cart belonging to
the Kelseys). At Pilot Peak on the present-day Nevada-Utah border, the emigrants

---

[109] Nunis, *The Bidwell-Bartleson Party,* 111.

[110] Ibid., 142–43, 247–55.

fell in with what later became the western section of the Hastings Cutoff, but the snow on the peak made it clear that the slow progress of the lumbering vehicles was a threat to their survival. By mid-September, the party abandoned the last of their wagons south of what is now Oasis, Nevada. As the men rigged up packsaddles, an ancient Indian, probably a Western Shoshone, came down from the mountains to the camp. By signs, the man indicated the Great Spirit had told him where he would find "some strange people, who would give him a great many things." Nicholas Dawson recalled they left behind "the happiest, richest, most religious man I ever saw."[111]

Driving their surviving oxen along as pack animals and reserve food supply, the company descended the Humboldt River and approached the Sierra Nevada via the Walker River. The Washoe tribe's Mill Creek band later told John C. Frémont that twelve white men had gone up the river "and crossed to the other waters."[112] "We hired two Indians for guides to take us across the mountains, but the scoundrels led us into the very worst part of the mountains and then ran away in the night and left us there," Josiah Belden complained to his sister the next winter. "We could see nothing but mountains upon mountains as far as the eye could reach." It seemed there was no way to get over them. At the crest of the Sierra, Charles Hopper said, "If California lies beyond those mountains we shall never be able to reach it."[113]

The desperate sojourners scattered "to find the best way to descend the mountains. I was left with my babe alone, and as I sat there on my horse and listened to the sighing and moaning of the winds through the pines, it seemed the loneliest spot in the world," Nancy Kelsey recalled fifty-five years later. An old man with the party (probably George Hanshaw) became so exhausted that his companions had to threaten to shoot him if he did not keep going.[114] They toiled slowly up and down the mountains for twenty-two days, Josiah Belden reported, and at last reached the Central Valley "almost worn down with hunger and fatigue."[115]

By an astonishing combination of luck, grit, and desperate courage, most of the emigrants reached John Marsh's rancho on 4 November 1841, six weeks after abandoning their wagons. "An event which will probably be regarded as of some importance in the future history of California, was the arrival in Nov. last year of an exploring party, from the United States," Marsh reported. "This consisted of thirty-one men, and one woman and child from Independence a town on the

---

[111] Ibid., 44, 151.

[112] Spence and Jackson, *The Expeditions of John Charles Frémont*, 29 January 1844, 1:621.

[113] Nunis, *The Bidwell-Bartleson Party*, 52, 138–39. For the likely and possible routes the party used to cross the Sierra Nevada, see Gillis and Magliari, *John Bidwell and California*, 36.

[114] Kelsey, Nancy Kelsey's Own Story, Mattes Library, 4–5.

[115] "Letter of Josiah Belden," in Nunis, *The Bidwell-Bartleson Party*, 139.

Nancy Roberts Kelsey was seventeen years old when she, her husband, Ben, and her infant child headed west in 1841 with the first wagon train to attempt to reach California. Along the way, John Bidwell heard her exclaim, "I wish to the Lord I had never got married!" Ben never lost his wanderlust, and his family followed him to Oregon and Texas before returning to settle in California, where he died in 1889. Nancy homesteaded in the Sierra Madre Mountains in northwest Santa Barbara County. She died at her mountain cabin on 10 August 1896. Courtesy Society of California Pioneers and Utah State Historical Society.

western frontier of Missouri." Remarkably, everyone who had left the Oregon Trail at Soda Springs made it to California. "If any proof were wanting of the unprecedented energy and enterprise of the people of our western frontier," Marsh observed, "I think this would be sufficient."[116]

Martha Williams Reed remembered that Ben and Nancy Kelsey and their child made the trek to California. "They had many hardships, got out of food and had to kill their oxen and eat them, and leave their wagons and come on foot all the way; they all but starved," she wrote. Reed then observed the simple fact that made this teenage mother an icon in overland history: "Mrs. Kelsey was the first white woman to come across the planes (direct) to California."[117] Tragically, after all she had endured, Nancy Kelsey gave birth to a son at Sutters Fort early in 1842, but the child, Samuel Kelsey, lived only eight days.[118]

THE SOUTHERN ROUTE

The Bidwell-Bartleson party is widely celebrated in overland lore, but the twenty-five Americans who reached the San Gabriel Mission in southern California from New Mexico at the same time are virtually forgotten. The Dominguez-Escalante expedition of 1776 had failed to find an overland trail that would link Spain's colonies in New Mexico with those on the Pacific Coast, and the Spanish Empire always relied on separate kings' highways running north and south to communicate with its frontier provinces. After Mexico achieved independence, traders from Santa Fe opened what was called the Old Spanish Trail, a pack-train route that connected Santa Fe with Los Angeles in 1829. No one ever drove a wagon over the precipitous desert trace, but until 1848 it supported a lively commerce in horses, mules, blankets, and slaves.

Apparently inspired by the Western Emigration Society, frontiersmen William Workman and John Rowland organized a party in Missouri and headed west in 1841 over the well-established Santa Fe Trail. The emigrants left Abiquiú with pack animals in September with veteran trapper Benjamin D. Wilson (who more accurately called it "the Old Mexican Trail") and the annual trade caravan bound for Los Angeles. "They drove a flock of sheep for food; [and] met with no adventures and few hardships." Workman and William Gordon brought their

---

116 Ibid., vi.

117 Reed, "Fallbrook's Prima Donna," 2. As Dale Morgan observed, the first American women to reach California overland first went to Oregon. They were Mary Walker and her sister Martha Young, who arrived at Sutters Fort with Joel Walker on 22 October 1841. Morgan, *Overland in 1846*, 14–15. Nancy Kelsey crossed the border of the modern state about three days earlier.

118 Roy M. Sylar reported this in his notes to Nancy (Roberts) Kelsey's Own Story of Her Life, Typescript, NFTC Manuscripts, Mattes Library, 7.

wives and children along, and three Mexican families migrated to California with
them. About half the members of the party became permanent settlers.[119]

The Workman-Rowland party's November arrival meant they "narrowly
missed the distinction of being the first party of American emigrants to enter
California by an overland route," historian Harlan Hague observed.[120] They have
generally been ignored in the annals of the California Trail, which by long practice has been exclusively identified with the northern road. Nonetheless, they
demonstrated that emigrants could reach the Pacific by at least one alternate
route that started at Santa Fe. Almost no settlers subsequently used the Spanish
Trail, but tens of thousands of Americans, particularly Southerners, would find
their way to the Pacific via roads that led through New Mexico.

THE NORTHWEST TRAIL

As the Bidwell-Bartleson party wandered across the Great Basin, James Sinclair of the Hudson's Bay Company was leading twenty-two families from the
Red River to the Pacific Northwest. Three years earlier, John McLoughlin had
warned that American emigration might seriously imperil the Company's interests in Oregon. Counter-migration by British subjects, the doctor suggested, "to
be settled north of the river seems to offer possibilities to encourage the gradual
emigration of settlers from the Red River Colony to the Columbia River."[121]

The Hudson's Bay Company belatedly recognized the threat American settlers posed to its control of Oregon. Governor-in-Chief George Simpson's chance
encounter with missionary Jason Lee at New York late in 1839 led him to believe
that two hundred Americans would set out for the Pacific Northwest the next
summer, an illusion spurred on by Missouri Senator Lewis Linn's aggressive Oregon resolutions of December 1839. Initially the Hudson's Bay Company hoped to
attract yeomen from Great Britain, specifically Scots farmers spurred on by poverty, but the Company's scheme emphasized its centralized control, "since free
settlement was hostile to the interests of the fur trade." British farmers ignored
the Company's enticements to settle in Oregon, so Simpson cast about for a more
immediate solution. He found it in central Canada's Red River country, whose
restive population appeared primed to accept promises of new homes in Oregon.
In 1841 Simpson moved to win the contest with the United States.[122]

---

[119] Bancroft, *History of California*, 4:276–78; and Rowland, *John Rowland and William Workman*, 46–50.

[120] Hague, *The Road to California*, 197.

[121] Lent, *West of the Mountains*, 100.

[122] Galbraith, "Early History of the Puget's Sound Agricultural Company," 248–52. As Galbraith noted, this
strategy "would siphon off population from a settlement which was becoming an increasing object of concern as a
menace to the fur trade of Rupert's Land."

Implementing Simpson's policy of colonizing Oregon to protect the fur trade, the Honourable Company planned to start a regular annual migration that would populate its holdings north of the Columbia with people loyal to the British crown. History proved that Puget Sound, with the best harbors on the Pacific Coast north of San Francisco, was a prize worth contesting. The Company charter prevented it from owning land, so the leading officers in the Columbia District set up the Puget's Sound Agricultural Company to manage the new colony.[123]

The Hudson's Bay Company had immense advantages. First, it was tightly organized, highly capitalized, and firmly established not only in the Pacific Northwest but in all of western Canada. A fleet of HBC ships connected its outposts to England, while a complex network of well-run forts and a sophisticated courier system linked Fort Vancouver with both Hudson's Bay and the Great Lakes. The Company had firm alliances with the First Nations and employed hundreds of veteran frontiersmen, many of them skilled leaders and business managers. While Americans bound for the West had only speculative opportunities awaiting them, the Company could offer prospective settlers a subsidy and a contract. By almost any measure, it appeared all British interests needed to win a battle for Oregon was the will to do so. Historians have paid scant attention to the undertaking, but Sinclair's trek had immense implications. The contrast between the two approaches reveals much about the nature of migration to the West Coast and helps explain why the chaotic and disorganized American ventures on the Oregon Trail had surprising advantages over the plans of the greatest monopoly in North America.

Late in 1839, Sir George Simpson sent instructions to Red River to encourage "steady respectable half breed and other settlers" to migrate to Oregon. A few prospective tenants had already located on the Puget's Sound Agricultural Company's farms, but most of them drifted off to take up better lands south on the Tualatin Plains, west of today's Portland. Simpson directed the Chief Factor at Red River in September 1840 to recruit as many as fifty families for the western venture. Eventually, the Company hoped to settle fifteen to twenty families on farms north of the Columbia every year.[124] The corporation set about "facilitating such migration by making advances and affording passages to persons" so disposed.[125]

The Company offered supplies for the trip and promised to provide its Oregon settlers with one hundred acres of cleared land, homes and farm buildings, provisions for the first year, Indian herdsmen and as much livestock as they could manage, agricultural implements, and even capital. What it could not offer the

---

[123] Ibid.; and Ficken, "The 'Real' Oregon Trail," 5.

[124] Galbraith, "Early History of the Puget's Sound Agricultural Company," 252–53.

[125] McLoughlin, *The Letters of John McLoughlin from Fort Vancouver, 1839–44*, 17n1.

colonists were land titles. The Canadian emigrants had only the assurance that they would own the land they worked "on halves" after they had paid their debts to the Hudson's Bay Company and the boundary question was finally settled. Until then, they would be little more than glorified sharecroppers.[126]

The corporation could not have found a better man to lead the Red River emigration than James Sinclair. Son of a Scots chief factor and a Métis—French and Indian—mother, he was born about 1806 at Oxford House, a post his father had founded in northern Canada. After attending Edinburgh University, Sinclair joined the Company at Red River for a year's service. He then ventured into free trade, which often involved illegal dealings with Americans, and each summer he accompanied the Métis on their buffalo hunt.

Sinclair and his 120 followers, including 77 children, left Fort Garry near present-day Winnipeg on 3 June 1841, some twenty-eight days ahead of George Simpson, who had been knighted earlier that year and was preparing to cross the Canadian Rockies as part of an ambitious "Overland Journey round the World" that would take him across Siberia to Saint Petersburg. Sinclair's party of fifty Red River carts, sixty horses, seven oxen, and two milk cows followed the Assiniboine River before striking northwest to Fort Carlton.[127] Unlike American overlanders in 1841, the Canadians could count on a string of well-supplied posts such as Brandon House and Forts Ellice, Pitt, Edmonton, and Colvile for supplies and protection during their journey. At Fort Carlton they struck the North Saskatchewan River, which they followed to Fort Edmonton, some nine hundred miles from Red River.[128]

Racing over the plains at a pace that killed more than two hundred horses as he crossed nineteen hundred miles in forty-seven days, George Simpson overtook Sinclair's party at Frenchmans Butte. The "Little Emperor" found the cavalcade "all healthy and happy; living with the greatest abundance and enjoying the journey with great relish." He saw one woman of about seventy-five years who was following her son west. "Each family had two or three carts, together with bands of horses, cattle and dogs. The men and lads traveled in the saddle, while the vehicles, which were covered with awnings to protect against the sun and rain, carried the women and young children," Simpson reported. "As they marched in single file, their cavalcade extended above a mile in length." Several women had given birth along the way, so there were more members in the party than when they started.[129]

---

[126] Lent, *West of the Mountains*, 102–103.

[127] Ficken, "The 'Real' Oregon Trail," 5.

[128] Gibson, *The Lifeline of the Oregon Country*, 30; and Lent, *West of the Mountains*, 125–26. Sinclair had a touchy personal connection with Simpson, who had fathered an illegitimate child with Sinclair's sister.

[129] Simpson, *Overland Journey round the World*, 62.

The officious Simpson ordered Sinclair to follow the traditional Athabaska Trail across the Continental Divide to the Boat Encampment on the Columbia, while the governor general himself set out to discover a new pass across the Rockies. Sinclair, however, had similar ambitions. He simply disregarded his orders and hired a Cree guide named Mackipictoon—Bras Croché or Broken Arm—whose travels, some said, had once taken him to a private audience with President Andrew Jackson. He knew a better pass than his rival Peechee, Simpson's chosen pathfinder.

Sinclair's party left Edmonton House in mid-August to open a new trail over the mountains. The emigrants abandoned their carts east of the Rockies at the deserted Mountain House. Mackipictoon took them south to Devils Gap and the Bow River on a pack-train trail that led to an almost imperceptible crossing of the Great Divide and down to the Kootenay River in the Columbia River drainage. The party then crossed several more ranges before Sinclair's people reached the Columbia at Fort Colvile. From here the emigrants headed overland to Fort Walla Walla, arriving on 4 October 1841. That night the fort caught fire and burned to the ground. The emigrants helped rescue the post's livestock and property, and their "opportune presence" saved many of its trade goods. After putting out the fire, they boarded bateaux for the final descent of the Columbia to Fort Vancouver.[130]

"Thus we see Oregon fast filling up," missionary Mary Walker wrote after meeting James Sinclair.[131] In a remarkable feat of frontier leadership, he had delivered an overland party that matched the numbers of the entire 1841 American emigration to Oregon by land and sea. The trail he blazed across Whiteman and Red Rock passes was by no means a wagon road, but even the circuitous traditional Athabaska Trail was comparatively better than the rough road to Oregon from Missouri. Sinclair had discovered a way across the northern Rockies that was "much simpler and easier to follow than anyone might have expected," a passage with only one two-day desert crossing.[132] He had shown the Hudson's Bay Company what was possible, but it was an opportunity the huge monopoly let pass. Traders, not farmers, selected the sites of its farms at Cowlitz and Nisqually, whose dark glens and gravelly soils could in no way compare with the fertile, open prairies of the Willamette Valley.

Simpson was visiting Alaska when the Red River emigrants arrived at Fort Vancouver, so Chief Factor John McLoughlin delayed sending them north until his return. McLoughlin had been among the original proponents of British colonization

---

[130] This summary is from Lent, *West of the Mountains,* 128–53; and Evans, *History of the Pacific Northwest,* 1:229–30.

[131] Drury, *Marcus and Narcissa Whitman,* 1:426.

[132] Lent, *West of the Mountains,* 81, 141.

of the Northwest, but he was aware of the problems with the chosen settlements. McLoughlin alerted the Company's board to his concerns, and he was reluctant to send the new arrivals to sites with such poor prospects. On his return Simpson delegated responsibility for the emigrants to McLoughlin, who was too busy to deal with their problems immediately. The fort's managers assigned the settlers tasks they considered demeaning, and the delay encouraged them to listen to the Company's American critics. McLoughlin eventually sent most of the families to Nisqually, while Simpson ordered Sinclair to return to Red River to lead another party west. Thirteen families spent the winter at Fort Nisqually, but the colonists complained that the Company failed to comply with their contract.[133]

By 1843 every one of the Red River families had decamped from Nisqually to Cowlitz or south to the fairer fields of the Willamette Valley. The Hudson's Bay Company reverted to its old conviction that settlement meant the death of the fur trade. Waiting at Red River for instructions early in 1843, James Sinclair was told to abandon further operations. Their plan had been "completely frustrated by the migration of these people from the Cowlitz and Nisqually to the Wallamet," the company's directors informed him, so they did not think it "advisable to burden the fur trade with the expense of translating any more to the same quarter."[134] The Company's 1839 decision "to checkmate the Americans by British coloni- zation," historian John S. Galbraith concluded, was "an experiment which was never really attempted."[135]

The apparent advantages of a subsidized emigration system over a disorganized and unrestricted popular movement vanished in the contest to win the Pacific Northwest. The narrow interests of the Hudson's Bay monopoly dictated restric- tive policies that doomed its efforts to populate its vast holdings with pliable dependents. In contrast, a spirit of enterprise and individual initiative constantly drove the chaotic American migration to seek out better ways to the West; the promise of free land and financial independence, however illusory, soon swelled the movement from a trickle to a flood.

Governor Simpson commissioned James Sinclair to lead another cart train overland from Red River in 1854, hoping to revive the Company's trading posts in the land it had once ruled. Sinclair's brother-in-law, John V. Campbell, pub- lished an account of the trek sixty-two years later.[136] Simpson offered Sinclair command at Fort Walla Walla, now a ghost of its former self, but Sinclair wanted to open his own post since "a great deal of ready cash might be picked up" from

---

[133] Ibid., 101–102, 155–58; Galbraith, "Early History," 255; and Evans, *History of the Pacific Northwest*, 1:230.

[134] McLoughlin, *The Letters of John McLoughlin from Fort Vancouver, 1839–44*, 77n2–78.

[135] Galbraith, "Early History of the Puget's Sound Agricultural Company," 258; and Lent, *West of the Mountains*, 163.

[136] Campbell, "The Sinclair Party," 187–201.

emigrants on their way to an American territory that now extended all the way to the 49th parallel. Ironically, James Sinclair died on the Columbia River in 1856 fighting to save a party of American settlers besieged by Indians.[137]

Masterly Inactivity:
The Arrangement with the Messrs. Benson

As American families began heading west, their government showed little public interest in assisting them. Secretary of War Joel Poinsett urged Congress to authorize three military posts along the trail to Oregon in 1840. The next year his successor suggested establishing of a string of forts from Council Bluffs to the Pacific, and in his first annual message as president, John Tyler called on Congress to fund a similar chain of military stations to support the fur trade and cultivate "friendly relations with savage tribes." These posts would insure "the means of safe intercourse between the American settlements at the mouth of the Columbia River and those on this side of the Rocky Mountains." Tyler wanted this done with as little delay as possible, but it would be years before Congress did anything to encourage western migration.[138] Restless citizens pushed west anyway, while private business interests, often backed by powerful if hidden political connections, rushed in to fill the void. The tremendous influence of these mercantile operations on western migration provided President Tyler with a quiet way to achieve his policy goals through the confidential use of commercial enterprises.

Representative Caleb Cushing of Massachusetts sponsored the petition to extend the blessings of American democracy to the Pacific that Jason Lee carried east in 1838 for his fellow Oregonians. Cushing's family was deeply invested in the Northwest trade, and with Missouri Senator Lewis Linn, he presented legislation in 1839 to establish military posts in Oregon, which clearly violated the joint-occupancy treaty with Britain. The bills went nowhere, but Congress directed the departments of War and State to investigate the matter, which produced a long and widely distributed government report incorporating the expansionist views of Cushing and Linn. Cushing published a long article in January 1840 in the influential *North American Review,* calling the Hudson's Bay Company's dominance of the region a "foul blot on our national honor" that must soon "be wiped out, if there is one spark of true patriotic feeling left in the breasts of Congress and the Federal Administration."[139] The Cushing and Company brig *Mary-*

---

[137] Lent, *West of the Mountains,* ix, 231.

[138] Tate, "Civilization's Guardian," 3; and Tyler, Annual Message to Congress, 7 December 1841, in Richardson, *A Compilation of the Messages and Papers of the Presidents,* 4:87.

[139] Lavender, *Westward Vision,* 330.

land arrived at the Willamette in June 1840 to seine for salmon and left behind
George LeBreton, a family political operative whose 1844 murder obscured his
significant role in organizing Oregon's provisional government in 1843.[140]

As Americans and Canadians set out for the West Coast early in 1841, the
American government appeared to be firmly committed to an Oregon policy
that John C. Calhoun later dubbed "masterly inactivity."[141] In truth, shortly after
John Tyler assumed the presidency on the death of William Henry Harrison,
Secretary of State Daniel Webster presented the new chief executive and his cabinet with a memorial from New York merchants Alfred G. and Arthur W. Benson. The brothers had excellent political connections: A. G. Benson was an old
acquaintance of Webster, and in May 1842 Caleb Cushing recommended Benson
to Webster as a "despatch bearer to England."[142] Tyler later explained that the
Benson brothers wanted the supply contract for the Navy's Pacific Squadron, and
in 1841 A. G. Benson and Co. contracted with the Navy Department "in further-
ance of a national policy" with the support of the administration "to establish a
line of transport ships to the Oregon Territory, conveying fifty passengers by
each trip without charge." In return, this arrangement gave the Bensons "the
benefit of transporting all government supplies to the Pacific at the rate of $3 per
barrel freight"—fifty cents more than the going rate.

This early covert operation was secret: "a confidential letter" from the secretary of the navy and a written statement that Tyler put on file authorized the
arrangement. This very quiet but "highly acceptable" proposition represented the
first federal financial support of American migration to the Pacific Coast, for the
Bensons agreed "to convey, passage free, all the emigrants that might offer, of
both sexes, (not exceeding fifty at each shipment,) to the Oregon territory, as
permanent settlers." During an investigation of the Bensons' naval lumber con-
tracts in 1845, Tyler explained that the "prominent inducement" for the deal was
the free transportation to Oregon for Americans "male and female—the latter
the more important." He believed the contract had been faithfully fulfilled.[143]
Tyler felt that "considerations of state policy" justified taking "this clandestine
and unprecedented arrangement for the use of a non-state actor as the government's 'chosen instrument'" without congressional approval. Historian Edward
P. Crapol concluded he did so to "help secure an American foothold in Oregon

---

[140] Clark, *Eden Seekers*, 141.

[141] Merk, *The Oregon Question*, 218.

[142] Webster, *Correspondence*, 9 May 1842, 5:464; and 6:65n4; 6:344n1.

[143] "Report to the Committee on Naval Affairs," 3 March 1851, Senate Report 319 (31-2): 1–3. For Tyler's 26
February 1845 letter recounting the Oregon arrangement, see "Letter from the Secretary of the Navy," 3 March
1845, House Report 161 (28-2): 21–22.

without unduly alerting the British government to his administration's ambitions in the Pacific Northwest."[144] Meanwhile, Congress and the army did nothing to encourage emigration to Oregon.

Or almost nothing. Quietly and methodically, the U.S. Army Corps of Topographical Engineers had extended its survey of America's frontiers westward. "We are still lamentably ignorant of the geography and resources of our country," Secretary of War Poinsett complained in 1838. To remedy the situation, Poinsett created the corps and assigned command to Colonel John J. Abert, who recruited astronomer and cartographer Joseph Nicollet to conduct the engineers' first scientific venture, an expedition to the upper Mississippi. Over the next three years, Poinsett proposed extending "our researches over the Rocky Mountains to the shores of the Pacific Ocean" to survey and map the country accurately.[145]

Nicollet was preparing in 1842 to lead an ambitious expedition to map the Kansas River and the Platte River system to the head of the Sweetwater when he fell ill; his subsequent death "caused untold damage to the potential scientific achievements of the corps." Command of the expedition fell to Nicollet's protégé, Lieutenant John C. Frémont, son-in-law of Missouri's powerful senator Thomas Hart Benton. Abert's orders to Frémont omitted any mention of South Pass, perhaps believing it lay in Mexico, whose borders the corps did not intend to violate. Benton lobbied Colonel Abert to extend Frémont's orders to include "the great pass through the Rocky Mountains, called the South West Pass," believing it would "be a thorough fare for nations to the end of time." Abert's orders to Frémont remained unchanged, but he gave him unofficial permission to extend the survey should time permit.[146]

So it was that in spring 1842 the handsome and well-connected young lieutenant set out on the first of three topographical surveys that would make John C. Frémont the world's most famous explorer and spur America's explosive expansion into the Far West.

---

[144] Crapol, "John Tyler and the Pursuit of National Destiny."

[145] Volpe, "The Origins of the Fremont Expeditions." In 1843 John C. Frémont named Lake Abert, a saline sink in southeastern Oregon, after his patron.

[146] Spence and Jackson, *The Expeditions of John Charles Frémont,* 1:122; and Volpe, "The Origins of the Fremont Expeditions."

CHAPTER 4

Jumping Off

Preparations, Provisions, and Partings

The venturesome few who crossed the plains before 1849 and survived to great age were celebrated as pioneers—and deserved the honor. This odd collection of farm families, freebooters, fanatics, and fugitives embarked on a venture fraught with uncertainty and peril, and most responded to its immense hardship with character and grit. The men and women who launched what became an immensely significant national enterprise were a singular lot, but if they had realized the nature of the challenge, most of them would have stayed home. Yet by the end of 1848, some twenty thousand Americans had packed up, left their homes, families, and civilization behind, and headed west to make a new life in Oregon, California, or the Rocky Mountains.

Today it is almost impossible to appreciate how alien the western landscape appeared to people raised east of the Mississippi River. Popular artwork depicting the frontier and its inhabitants bore little resemblance to the real West. The treeless expanse of the Great Plains and the seemingly endless prairies, mountains, and deserts that lay between the Missouri River and the Pacific Coast were unlike anything early-nineteenth-century Americans had experienced. The region's distant horizons and essential vastness defied imagining. "Oh the mountains such mountains, such mountains as I never saw," wrote Mary Stone Smith. "Surely this is a world of wonders; no one can form any idea of this scenery from description."[1]

Despite its exotic and unfamiliar character, prairie travelers often commented on the splendor of the new lands and marveled at phenomena such as mirages that astonished them with their "stupendous grandeur and sublime magnificence," Edwin Bryant wrote. "But it is in vain to attempt a description of these singular and extraordinary phenomena. Neither prose or poetry, nor the pencil of the artist, can adequately portray their beauties."[2] The scenery beyond Green River

---

[1] Smith, Diary, 11 and 26 July 1854, Western Historical Manuscript Collection.
[2] Bryant, *What I Saw in California*, 174–75.

dazzled Wilson Blain in 1848. "We beheld the whole country spread out beneath the eye as far as the eye could reach. The elevated grandeur, the wild confusion and utter desolation filled the soul with thoughts too big for utterance. Here were the sources of mighty rivers and here the Creator's power is displayed on the most magnificent scale."[3]

Upon reaching the arid high plains, the very atmosphere was transformed as emigrants escaped the universal humidity of the Midwest. If the comments found in their journals are any indication, the "everlasting snow" they saw atop the Rocky Mountains in the middle of summer astonished them all. After encountering the Rockies, which made the Appalachians look like foothills, sojourners crossing the Cascades and Sierra Nevada found trees whose primeval proportions defied belief. Settlers arriving in Oregon in 1847 could have witnessed the volcanic eruption of Mount Saint Helens—a natural wonder totally unknown in the states.

At the trail's end, Peter Burnett concluded that Oregon was one of the loveliest spots on earth. "The scenery of her mountains and valleys is simply magnificent. Her snow-clad mountains, her giant forests, her clear skies in summer, and her green and blooming valleys, constitute a combination of the beautiful that can not be excelled," he wrote.[4] Sometimes a spectacular landscape helped mitigate the difficulty of the trek: "Hot & dusty, worn out, scenery grand," Harriet Talcott Buckingham said simply.[5]

Throughout the 1840s, overland emigration was not a universally admired undertaking, and few who embarked on such a risky venture as trekking to the Pacific had any notion of what awaited them on the trail. "Singular as it may seem," Edwin Bryant observed, there were many sojourners who went west with him in 1846 who had "no just conceptions of the extent and labor of the journey before them."[6] On 11 June 1844, the *Missouri Republican* called the movement a "miserable infatuation" and denounced Oregon as "the very worst speculation a man in this country can get at." Oregon was "mountainous and rugged; its plains are dry and barren; nothing but rain in winter, nothing but sun in summer; very few fertile valleys, and those of very limited extent, and no navigable rivers to compare with the great water courses of the Mississippi Valley. This," the influential journal concluded, "is Oregon."[7]

Newspaper editors from New York to New Orleans ridiculed those who chose to undertake the "madness and folly" of a journey to the Pacific. Leaving behind

---

[3] Blain to Kerr, *The Preacher*, 22 August 1849, 130, Oregon Historical Society.
[4] Burnett, *Recollections and Opinions of an Old Pioneer*, 141.
[5] Buckingham, "Crossing the Plains," 21 August 1851, in Holmes, *Covered Wagon Women*, 3:47.
[6] Bryant, *What I Saw in California*, 24 May 1846, 57.
[7] Watkins, "Notes of the Early History of the Nebraska Country," 127.

fertile lands and a stable government to strike out across the wilderness had "an aspect of insanity," Horace Greeley wrote in New York. "There is probably not one among them whose outward circumstances will be improved by this perilous pilgrimage." Tempting women and children to cross "this thousand miles of precipice and volcanic sterility to Oregon" was "palpable homicide," he charged.[8] Greeley may have later advised, "Go west, young man, go west," but in 1843 he strongly encouraged everyone to stay home.[9]

On the Stretch for Something New: Why Go West?

Ever since Daniel Boone crossed the Appalachian Mountains in 1769, "the West" has held the promise of freedom and opportunity for generations of Americans. "My family were old pioneering stock, and always, when the region began filling up with settlers, we moved further west to a new country," James Newton Angel recalled, eighty-six years after he came to California as a barefoot boy in 1847. "For years we never stayed in any one locality long enough to take root, but we had to pull up stakes and strike out for some place far removed from settlement that promised better range or farming conditions." Angel thought his grandfather had followed Boone to the dark and bloody ground of Kentucky, where his father was born in 1816. His people were always looking for a bigger, better farm, and "there is always a fascination about the country beyond the horizon or on the far side of the blue ranges," he said. If they had stayed in any of the places they had passed through, "we would have been far better off financially than we are today," Angel concluded.[10]

Footloose and restless folk like the Angels were easily persuaded that a better life awaited them somewhere in the West, and throughout the 1840s promoters worked hard to create an idyllic picture of the prospects for greater fortune and better health open to all those who made the long journey to Oregon or California. Many students of western migration have concluded that free land drew people to Oregon, whereas the siren song of quick riches beckoned them to California, "the El Dorado of the 19th century."[11] But the passions that fired both overland migrations were not so simple.

What made Americans go west in the 1840s? Farms were to be had for the taking in Oregon, but there was no shortage of cheap and fertile soil in the Midwest

---

[8] *New-York Daily Tribune,* 19 July and 18 December 1843, in Unruh, *The Plains Across,* 38–39.

[9] As historian David White noted, Greeley stole the "go west" phrase from journalist Frank Soulé.

[10] Angel, Memoir of 1847, Mattes Library.

[11] *The Polynesian,* 27 June 1846, 22/3. References to El Dorado predated the 1848 gold discovery. See Lippincott to Bub, 6 February 1847, Bancroft Library.

long after people began migrating to the Pacific, and unlike land in Oregon, farms in the United States came with legal land titles. Until 1846 the political fate of the western edge of North America was still unsettled. The prospect of wealth was always compelling, but the dangers of a long journey to the West Coast made it an unlikely gamble. Despite much hallowed mythology, few people were willing to take that risk before the gold rush began. The impression that large numbers of Americans lined up at the border of Indian Country is an illusion: before gold opened the floodgates in 1849, the annual migration to California and Oregon averaged fewer than sixteen hundred souls. Throughout most of its existence, the road across the plains was not the most popular route to the Pacific: only about one-third of the travelers bound for the West Coast between 1849 and 1860 came by way of South Pass.[12]

Americans chose to abandon their homes in the East and brave the ordeals of the overland trails for reasons as varied as the "honest looking open harted people" themselves.[13] One 1846 traveler noted that his companions all "agreed in the one general object—that of bettering their condition," but their individual hopes and dreams "were as various as can well be imagined."[14] So were the emigrants themselves. Americans of all sorts crossed the plains—rich and poor, black and white, young and old. "Our party consisted of thirty wagons, 300 head of cattle and a lot of hands made up from Mexico, Ireland, England, Wales, France and Germany," wrote Joseph P. Hamelin, Jr., in 1857. "I took three ladies, purely out of charity."[15] Before its story ended, the most famous of all California wagon trains, the Donner party, included Mexican and French frontiersmen; Miwok Indians; Irish, English, Belgian, and German emigrants; infants and elders; and Catholics, Protestants, Mormons, and perhaps an Austrian Jew.

Some thought the entire undertaking was irresponsible. After meeting the 1845 trains, army officer Philip St. George Cooke suspected "the wantoness of discontent,—a diseased appetite for excitement and change" and "a restless habit of vagrancy" drove the early overlanders, not magnanimous or patriotic motives.[16] "We are anxious to get over into California, and then we will want something else," Belinda Cooley Pickett observed on the road to the City of Rocks. "I believe that human beings are bound never to feel satisfied."[17] Others went west simply

---

[12] Unruh, *The Plains Across*, 119, 401. Other routes included traversing the American Southwest, rounding Cape Horn, or crossing Mexico or Central America. Unruh estimated almost a quarter million people had crossed Panama and Nicaragua by 1860. Ibid.

[13] Clyman, *James Clyman, Frontiersman*, 224.

[14] Thornton, *Oregon and California in 1848*, 1:26.

[15] Hamelin, Journal, 5 June 1857, Beinecke Library, 149–50.

[16] Cooke, *Scenes and Adventures in the Army*, 12 June 1845, 331.

[17] Pickett, Covered Wagon Days, 23 July 1853, Mattes Library.

seeking adventure. "Like a great many boys who have picked [up] novels I have read of the life of mountaineers. I was very conscious to make a trip across the plains so that I could Kill buffalo, etc., deer etc., and have a good time," recalled Antonio B. Rabbeson. "That was about all of my motive—a young fellows idea of adventure."[18]

Some wanted to see what had seldom been seen before. "My greatest pleasure in travelling through the country is derived from the knowledge that it has seldom been traversed, or at least never been described by any hackneyed tourist, that everything I see or look upon has been seen by me before it has become common by the vulgar gaze or description of others," Dr. Joseph Middleton observed, even as he endured temperatures approaching 110° on the Black Rock Desert.[19] Some travelers left home seeking pleasure or profit, missionary Nicholas Point concluded, but "still others, of the age of the prodigal son, only to relieve their families of their unfortunate presence."[20]

Patriotism became increasingly prominent as a motive in recollections. "My husband [was] fired with patriotism to help keep the country from British rule, and I was possessed with a spirit of adventure and a desire to see what was new and strange," Miriam Thompson Tuller recalled, remembering the reasons she and her first husband went to Oregon in 1845. "Well, I allow that the United States has the best right to that country," John Minto recalled his father-in-law saying about Oregon, "and I am going to help make that right good."[21]

Observers came to similarly diverse conclusions about why people exchanged a settled life for such an unknown future. "Many were in pursuit of health. Some were actuated by a mere love of change; many more by a spirit of enterprise and adventure; and a few, I believe, knew not why they were on the road," Jessy Quinn Thornton recalled. He also noted that many were looking for a better climate or fleeing "pecuniary embarrassments"—and even as prominent a figure as Peter Burnett went to Oregon hoping to pay off his debts.[22] "My object in leaving home where I have spent so much of my life [was] to improve my fortunes in a new and richer country," wrote James D. Cauthorn.[23]

Gabriel Brown took his six daughters—the "Belles of Oregon"—west in 1842 seeking better prospects for finding a husband.[24] "I have often perplexed myself

---

[18] Rabbeson, Growth of Towns, Bancroft Library.

[19] Middleton, 27 September 1849, Diary, Beinecke Library, 138.

[20] Nunis, *The Bidwell-Bartleson Party,* 227.

[21] Minto, "Reminiscences of Experiences on the Oregon Trail in 1844," 130.

[22] Thornton, *Oregon and California in 1848,* 15 [16] May 1846, 1:26.

[23] Cauthorn, Diary 1865, University of Oregon Library, 1. Cauthorn had another reason: "to find a country free from the disturbing and embarrassing effects of dreadful civil war."

[24] Thornton, "Occasional Address," 36; and Tompkins, "The Law of the Land," 85.

to divine the various motives that give impulse to this strange migration," Francis Parkman confessed at Westport in 1846. He could not determine if it was "an insane hope of a better condition in life, or a desire of shaking off restraints of law and society, or mere restlessness," but he was certain that multitudes who went west bitterly repented making the journey, "and after they have reached the land of promise are happy enough to escape from it."[25] Most of the emigrants came from Missouri, he observed at Fort Laramie. "The bad climate seems to have been the motive that has induced many of them to set out."[26]

Many people sought to escape the diseases that were endemic among Mississippi River Valley residents, such as misunderstood afflictions like "ague"—malaria. "Generally the first question which a Missourian asked about a country was whether there was any fever and ague," recalled John Bidwell.[27] Nancy Kelsey told her daughter she went west "because of Mr. Kelsey's health and adventurous disposition."[28] The floods that produced the "Great Overflow" of 1844 caused a "General Sickness," and the suffering of his family convinced John Craig to take a trip to the Pacific Ocean "for the benefit of my health and to See if I could find a health[y] country to remove my family."[29] His father left Missouri in 1846, A. H. Garrison recalled, because "he could not think of staying in that sickly country another summer."[30] The continual suffering caused by Illinois's undrained swamps, Joseph Henry Brown remembered, "determined my grandfather and parents to emigrate to Oregon."[31]

The "cure" could be surprisingly effective. "Many persons within my knowledge," Willard H. Rees wrote from Oregon in 1846, "would have long since fell Victims to Disease had they not by migrating thither found relief in the fresh and balmy atmosphere of this most Excelent Clime."[32] Ironically, some of the diseases emigrants sought to escape, such as malaria, were established in Oregon and California before 1841, and not all experts agreed with those who praised the health of the West. "I beg leave to differ from a great many, regarding the health of this territory," Dr. William Standley wrote from Oregon in 1853. "I take it as an unhealthy place; at any rate there are a great many pale faces here. Fever, ague, and typhoid fever are common."[33]

---

[25] Parkman, *The California and Oregon Trail,* 15.

[26] Parkman, *The Journals of Francis Parkman,* 17 June 1846, 442.

[27] Nunis, *The Bidwell-Bartleson Party,* 102.

[28] Kelsey, Nancy Kelsey's Own Story, Mattes Library.

[29] Craig to Boosinger, 4 October 1847, in Morgan, *Overland in 1846,* 133–34.

[30] Garrison, Reminiscences of A. H. Garrison, Oregon Historical Society.

[31] Brown, Recollection of 1847, Bancroft Library.

[32] Rees to "Mother," Oregon City, 20 March 1846, NFTC Manuscripts, Mattes Library.

[33] Standley, Letter, 30 January 1853, Western Historical Manuscript Collection.

John Minto's future father-in-law, Robert Wilson Morrison, was a respected pioneer of Andrew County, Missouri. At a farewell dinner before he set out for Oregon, a local judge asked, "Well, Wilson, why are you going, anyhow?" Morrison, who was naturally slow of speech, hesitated and then said, "I am not satisfied here. There is little we raise that pays shipment to market; a little hemp and a little tobacco." Unless a man owned slaves, which he refused to do, "he has no chance, he cannot compete with the man that does," Morrison said. "I'm going to Oregon, where there'll be no slaves, and we'll all start even."[34]

Whatever the reasons people gave for going west, the main purpose was to find a more secure future, historian Doyce Nunis concluded.[35] From the beginning to the end of the trail era, Americans consistently said they went west seeking a better life and better economic opportunities for their families. "I am willing to go," Tamsen Donner wrote from Independence in May 1846, "& have no doubt it will be an advantage to our children & to us."[36]

No scholar has provided a more compelling explanation of what drew Americans west than the great frontiersman James Clyman, who pondered the question on the trail in 1846. He concluded that such irrational risk taking was simply part of American culture: "It is remarkable . . . and strange that so many of all kinds and classes of People should sell out comfortable homes in Missouri and Elsewhere pack up and start across such an emmence Barren waste to settle in some new Place of which they have at most so uncertain information but this is the character of my countrymen." Contemplating a lonely trailside grave, Clyman wrote, "all ages and all sects are found to undertake this long tedious and even dangerous Journy for some unknown object never to be realized even by those most fortunate—and why? Because the human mind can never be satisfied [or] at rest [but must be] allways on the stretch for something new."[37]

Clyman may well have been correct that it was in the American character always to be seeking "something new," just as it was to be continually on a quest for a better life. Yet perhaps the question defies a final answer. "It may be asked why did such men peril everything—burning their ships behind them, exposing their helpless families to the possibilities of massacre and starvation, braving death—and for what purpose?" wondered 1843 emigrant James Nesmith. "I am not quite certain that any rational answer will ever be given to that question."[38]

---

[34] Minto, "Reminiscences of Experiences on the Oregon Trail in 1844," 130.

[35] Nunis, *The Bidwell-Bartleson Party*, 2–3.

[36] Donner to Eliza Poor, 11 May 1846, in Morgan, *Overland in 1846*, 527.

[37] Clyman, *James Clyman, Frontiersman*, 224, 226, 228. Punctuation added.

[38] Nesmith, "The Occasional Address," 52.

MEN OF FINE INTELLIGENCE OR
SCUM AND REFUSE—WHO WENT WEST?

"It was men of the character and disposition to face such dangers accompanied by their heroic wives, mothers and sisters, who severed all connecting them with home and civilization," 1843 Oregon pioneer David Arthur recalled in 1889, "and struck out boldly upon a trackless desert, known to be inhabited by howling wolves and merciless savages, surrounded by dangers, seen and unseen."[39] When T. T. Geer celebrated his pioneer ancestors in 1912, they "were all of the stuff out of which real men and women are made." They "conquered the desert, met the savage Indians without fear, mocked at the roadless mountains, swam the fordless rivers, used 'buffalo chips' for fuel, went hungry much of the time at the last end of the trip, and finally reached the promised land destitute, most of them, many of them sick, but all of them brave and hopeful."[40]

This heroic view of the settlers of Oregon and California as model yeomen is still widely honored, and the historic record shows it is not without foundation. Even before the emigration left Missouri in May 1843, the press had painted the undertaking as the latest valiant venture of a noble people. *The Liberty Banner* said it consisted of "a number of citizens of inestimable value to any community— men of fine intelligence and vigorous and intrepid character; admirably calculated to lay the firm foundation of a future Empire."[41] Certainly, by any standard, those who crossed the wagon roads of the West were an extraordinary collection of men and women.

But contemporary comments challenge the mythic image of the noble pioneer and reveal that their ranks included a sizeable contingent of ne'er-do-wells and outright scoundrels. When Francis Parkman passed through Independence, he saw a multitude of healthy children and a number of his "very sober-looking countrymen" among the emigrants who thronged the streets, but he also found "some of the vilest outcasts in the country."[42] A former resident of California told Edwin Bryant "there was not a man in the country, now that he had left it, who was not as thoroughly steeped in villany as the most hardened graduate of the penitentiary."[43] Men often went west to escape debt, the law, or family responsibilities. Yet what sets apart the pioneers of the 1840s was that they were generally very ordinary people who undertook an extraordinary task. Many of them were impatient and curious. "Emigrants are generally too impatient, and over-drive

---

[39] Arthur, "Arthur's Prairie First Furrow Plowed in Clackamas County," *Sunday Oregonian,* 1889.

[40] Geer, *Fifty Years in Oregon,* 131.

[41] *St. Louis Daily Missouri Republican,* 27 May 1843, citing *The Liberty Banner,* in Boardman, "The Journal," 99n2.

[42] Parkman, *The California and Oregon Trail,* 15.

[43] Bryant, *What I Saw in California,* 27 June 1846, 114.

their teams, and cattle," William Ide noted. "They often neglect the concerns of the present, in consequence of great anticipations of the future—they long to see what the next elevation hides from their view."[44]

Few old residents of the West in the 1840s considered the "hordes of Yankee immigrants" to be model citizens. Governor Pío Pico allegedly complained, "Already have the wagons of that perfidious people scaled the almost inaccessible summits of the Sierra Nevada, crossed the entire continent and penetrated the fruitful valley of Sacramento."[45] Richard Grant formed a very low opinion of the Americans who passed Fort Hall and insisted he was very cautious in his dealings with them, for he was "too well acquainted with the disposition & nature of these Animals" to engage in altercations with them.[46]

Other Hudson's Bay Company officers painted an even less flattering picture of the first Americans to reach Oregon. Many settlers arrived "destitute both of clothing, and even the necessaries of life, and are not in general what may be called enlightened Citizens, but in most cases, the scum and refuse of the back States," John Kennedy reported early in 1844. Despite his low opinion of their character, Kennedy noted, "Many of them came across with wagons; how they managed to get thro or over the mountains with their clumsy machines, is the wonder and talk of this side of the mountains." Ominously for British interests, he expected a larger emigration in 1845, "and a greater still will succeed the following years."[47]

At the same time, John Work complained, "The Gentlemen at Vancouver must have their hands full with those swarms of Americans pressing in upon them. I hear a batch of lawyers have arrived (there were parsons and doctors enough before)."[48] James Douglas wrote, "No people can be more prejudiced and national than the Americans in this country, a fact so evident to my mind, that I am more suspicious of their designs, than of the wild natives of the forest."[49] Alex Anderson reported "a fearful influx of Americans into the Columbia during the last year—in all about fifteen hundred souls, counting from the child in arms to the huge Missisipi Yahoo." At Fort Hall "they invaded poor Mr. Grant like a cloud of locusts, flour and other luxuries stood at a premium." But Grant "reaped a handsome profit from his caravan load of Customers."[50]

Overlanders often failed to impress educated Americans. "It is not easy to calculate the depravity of many of the emigrants to this country," American mission-

[44] Ide, "From Our Oregon Correspondent," 25 June 1845, *Sangamo Journal*, 4 September 1845.

[45] Gaston, *The Centennial History of Oregon*, xiv.

[46] Grant to Simpson, 4 January 1849, D.5/24, HBC Archives, 227.

[47] Kennedy to Simpson, 25 February 1844, D.5/10, HBC Archives, 291.

[48] Work to Simpson, 20 February 1844, D.5/10, HBC Archives, 259.

[49] Douglas to Simpson, 4 April 1845, D.13/5, HBC Archives, 391.

[50] Anderson to Simpson, 13 February 1844, D.5/10, HBC Archives, 222.

ary George Gary conceded.[51] "For the most part, they were the rudest and most ignorant of the frontier population; they knew absolutely nothing of the country and its inhabitants," commented Francis Parkman. He described the emigrants he met at Fort Laramie in 1846 as a "crowd of broad-brimmed hats, thin visages, and staring eyes. . . . Tall awkward men, in brown homespun; women with cadaverous faces and long lank figures" whose curiosity in exploring the fort made them appear to be "devoid of any sense of delicacy or propriety, they seemed resolved to search every mystery to the bottom."[52]

Some of the roughhewn emigrants who answered Commodore Robert Stockton's call for volunteers to fight the Mexican War in California failed to impress even Ordinary Seaman Joseph T. Downey of U.S.S. *Portsmouth,* who was no snob. "Such a mass was never seen before by mortal man. They were literally the rag tag and bobtail of all Creation. Here they came, some with coats and some no coats—some with deer skin trowsers and some with awful looking things in the shape of trowsers, some with moccasins, some with Boots, some with shoes, and a great majority with no covering to their feet," Downey recalled. "In one thing they were uniform: they had good rifles and shocking Bad Hats."[53]

Yet from the very beginning, overland emigration was largely a family affair, which brought a stabilizing force to the West. Women and children made up almost a quarter of the Bidwell-Bartleson party when it left Missouri, while Lansford Hastings reported that only half the 1842 Oregon migration consisted of armed men.[54] Wagon companies were often composed of several large families linked to each other by blood and marriage, interconnections that often go unrecognized. Yet the more closely any particular company is examined, the key role extended families played in organizing wagon trains becomes more apparent.[55] The gold rush would temporarily transform the migration into a largely male affair, but during the 1850s and 1860s women and children outnumbered men by a sizeable majority in many, if not most, trains.

The great migration of 1843 "consisted of people from all the States and Territories, and nearly all nationalities," James Nesmith recalled. "The most however, from Arkansas, Illinois, Missouri and Iowa."[56] Emigrants came from everywhere,

---

[51] Gary, Diary, 5 May 1846, in Morgan, *Overland in 1846,* 64.

[52] Parkman, *The California and Oregon Trail,* 133, 135.

[53] Downey, *The Cruise of the* Portsmouth, *1845–1847,* 154.

[54] Nunis, *The Bidwell-Bartleson Party,* 253; and Hastings, *The Emigrants' Guide,* 5.

[55] For example, see Kristin Johnson's work on the Donner party; the analysis of the parties that built the Free Emigrant Road in Menefee, Menefee, and Tiller, "Cutoff Fever," part 3, "The Migration for the West Forms, 1853"; and Martha Williams Reed's revelations on the family connections in the Bidwell-Bartleson party in chapter 3. Even companies like the Donners and the 1857 Fancher party that took final shape west of South Pass retained their complex family ties.

[56] Nesmith, "The Occasional Address," 346.

but by far the greatest number hailed from Missouri, perhaps due to its location on the edge of the frontier. The state's residents had gone as far west as Americans could go in 1840 without leaving their country, and most of them were following family traditions of westering that were generations old. Such folk found the call of new frontiers irresistible. The available statistics suggest that Missourians made up about half of those who went west in wagons, while the majority of the rest came from other midwestern states, notably Illinois, Iowa, Michigan, and Wisconsin.[57] A number came from border states like Kentucky and some from Tennessee, but many southerners chose to go west using the trails through Santa Fe. Overland trains sometimes included a surprising number of Europeans, especially British and German travelers. "The party consisting of Americans, French, Germans and Irish are now divided into groups," noted R. S. Poor in 1857, "none seeming to sympathize with the others."[58]

Age failed to deter many from making the trip across the plains. Sarah Keyes was seventy years old when she died near Alcove Springs in May 1846. From Independence, the *Missouri Republican* described "a venerable man, 72 years of age, who has been a sea captain," and was "now going to bury his bones upon the shores of the Pacific"—probably John Brown, who was actually seventy-seven but managed to ride horseback all the way to Oregon.[59] Among the most astonishing emigrants was Mary Ann Harlan Smith's grandmother, "an old lady, between eighty and ninety years of age and blind," who survived the Hastings Cutoff in 1846.[60] Malinda Thompson, "aged *eighty-one* years, [and] who frequently travelled on foot from one to two miles at a time, while in the mountains," arrived in California in 1854 in more robust health than when she started.[61] At Green River Ferry, Mary C. Fish saw the grave of "E. Hall of Missouri who died June 1852 aged 69 years."[62] Alexander Hamilton Willard, who had first seen the Pacific with Lewis and Clark in 1805, was seventy-four years old when he arrived in California by covered wagon in 1852. Someone there took Willard's picture, the only known photograph of a member of the expedition.[63]

Peter Burnett helped put the character of the men (almost no one said anything about the qualities of the women) with whom he traveled to Oregon in perspective. "Some were idle, worthless young men, too lazy to work at home, and too genteel to steal; while some others were gamblers, and others were reputed thieves," he

---

[57] Unruh, *The Plains Across*, 405.

[58] Poor, Journal 1857, American Heritage Center, 1–2.

[59] Morgan, *Overland in 1846*, 530.

[60] Smith, "Recollection of a Pioneer Mother," 29.

[61] "A Veteran Emigrant," *Alta California*, 24 August 1854, 2/3.

[62] Fish, Diary, 20 July 1860, OCTA Manuscripts, Mattes Library.

[63] Clarke, *The Men of the Lewis and Clark Expedition*, 56.

remembered. "But when they arrived in Oregon they were compelled to work or starve. It was a dire necessity. There were there no able relatives or indulgent friends upon whom the idle could quarter themselves, and there was little or nothing for the rogues to steal." Frontier conditions imposed a standard of virtue on even the most recalcitrant "Missisipi Yahoo": as an old American proverb noted, in the new and remote settlements it was root, hog, or die. "I never saw so fine a population, as a whole community, as I saw in Oregon most of the time while I was there," Burnett concluded. "They were all honest, because there was nothing to steal; they were all sober, because there was no liquor to drink; there were no misers, because there was no money to hoard; and they were all industrious, because it was work or starve."[64]

WAGONS AND WAYBILLS: OUTFITTING FOR THE TRAIL

Preparing a family to move west was a complicated and expensive proposition that often required a large investment in supplies, wagons, and livestock. Contemporaneous writers estimated a family could make an overland passage for between $100 and $200 per person (between $2,200 and $4,500 in today's money), but John Unruh concluded that conservatively, the cost of a family's fully outfitted wagon would be $1,500, an amount equal to about $33,000 today. The truly determined could make the trip for much less, and single men often worked their way across the plains as teamsters.[65] ("Two Irishmen passed us with nothing in the world but a milk cow apiece and a small sack of crackers. They left St. Joseph May 8th and are now out-traveleing ox-teams," wrote William Renfro Rothwell. "Hurrah for the Irish!"[66]) Once the gold rush began, commercial operators charged between $200 to $300 for the trip, about the cost of a voyage around Cape Horn.

The challenge of merely preparing for the trek was daunting, since emigrants essentially had to arrange for a four- to six-month camping trip that required crossing some two thousand miles of increasingly rugged terrain. They had to be ready to provide for all their needs and meet any emergency, since before 1847 the handful of ramshackle trading posts seldom had enough supplies to trade, even at the highest prices. Some travelers had access to a doctor, but even the most skilled medical practitioners had little to offer beyond alcohol, laudanum, and psychological comfort. The first overlanders had no one to rely on for safety but themselves, for until after the Mexican-American War, beyond Fort Leavenworth there was not a single American soldier stationed north of Texas.

---

[64] Burnett, *Recollections and Opinions of an Old Pioneer*, 181.

[65] Unruh, *The Plains Across*, 407–408. Faragher, *Women and Men on the Overland Trail*, 21–22, estimated an outfit cost between $70 and $150.

[66] Rothwell, Notes of a Journey to California in 1850, Beinecke Library, 127–28.

No emigrant wagon—except, perhaps, those of the Death Valley Forty-nin-ers—ever followed a trail that was not already known to Indians and mountain-eers. The mountain men "fell heir to trails already age-old," Dale Morgan noted, and "their accomplishment consisted in learning to distinguish from among the multiplicity of Indian trails the one that would best serve a given need."[67] Hooves and paws cut game trails into the plains, mountains, and deserts, and later san-dals, moccasins, and travois turned these traces into trading routes. Blazing the Oregon and California trails involved simply connecting these ancient routes to create a road to the Pacific.

Like the water barrel, another myth created by movies and television, the role of wagon-train guides (or in the lore, scouts) was more romance than reality. "You need no pilot," Lilburn Boggs reported from his experience in 1846, "the road is large and plain."[68] Nathaniel Ford agreed that pilots were unnecessary, but he thought "a person that has traveled through with wagons would be useful to a company on account of [knowing] the watering places, &c."[69] Some of the most famous veterans of the fur trade—Thomas Fitzpatrick, Joseph R. Walker, Moses Harris, James P. Beckwourth, Joe Meek, Kit Carson, Caleb Greenwood, and James Clyman—blazed many of the most significant sections of the Oregon and California Trails while guiding trains. They played an essential role in the army exploration and mapping of the West, but the use of mountain men as guides was short-lived. As Richard White pointed out, once topographical engineers such as John C. Frémont had codified and published their observations, the moun-taineers had used up "their intellectual capital—their knowledge of the West."[70] It was part of the sad fate of the legendary mountain men. "These trappers have made a thousand fortunes for eastern men," John Gunnison observed in 1852, "and by their improvidence have nothing for themselves."[71]

Early overlanders often tried to convert their experience into cash with limited success and sometimes with disastrous results. "Persons who cross the mountains for the purpose of guiding the emigrants merely for the very trifling salaries," Lansford W. Hastings admitted, "have not time, while acting as guides, to ex-amine the extensive country through which they pass."[72] Experienced hands who

[67] Korns and Morgan, *West from Fort Bridger*, 2.

[68] Boggs, "Route to the Pacific," *St. Louis Weekly Reveille*, 22 May 1848.

[69] Ford, "Letter from Oregon," 6 April 1845, in Clyman, *James Clyman, Frontiersman*, 271.

[70] White, *It's Your Misfortune and None of My Own*, 122.

[71] Gunnison, *The Mormons*, 151.

[72] "Paisano," *California Star*, 27 February 1847. Josiah Royce identified Paisano as Hastings.

later volunteered as guides for friends and family usually proved more effective, providing practical advice and useful warnings.

Guidebooks ranging from the very useful to the totally worthless became available almost as soon as wagons headed west. The first such guide was Philip Leget Edwards's *Sketch of the Oregon Territory: or, Emigrants' Guide.* Like John Bidwell's account at the Bancroft Library of his 1841 overland journey, only one known copy has survived. Based on references in overland journals, any number of guidebooks simply disappeared.[73] Edwards's guide was originally a letter to Dr. T. M. Bacon and may not have been intended for publication, but it appeared at Liberty, Missouri, as a twenty-page pamphlet in 1842.[74] No title page exists for George McKinstry's single surviving copy of Bidwell's letter-journal. It was probably issued at Independence or Weston, Missouri, between 1843 and 1845, perhaps with the title *A Journey to California,* but as Doyce Nunis observed, "there is no way of ascertaining for certain the printer, place of publication, and year."[75]

The Reverend Joseph Williams's 1843 *Narrative of a Tour from the State of Indiana to the Oregon Territory in the Years 1841–2* was the first guidebook published by its author. As Williams hoped, the narrative of his adventures with the Bidwell-Bartleson party was indeed "of great interest to those who may contemplate emigrating" to Oregon, but the book contained little of the specific information about preparations, distances, campgrounds, and the availability of wood and water that came to characterize the best trail guides.

The most influential book ever written on overland emigration first appeared as a government document in 1843. John C. Frémont's *Report of the Exploring Expedition to the Rocky Mountains* described his 1842 expedition to South Pass, while an updated 1845 edition covering Frémont's second expedition added "*and to Oregon and North California in the years 1843–'44*" to the title. Written with the help of Jessie Frémont, the reports sold tens of thousands of copies and helped make her husband a national hero.[76] They proved so popular with the public "that they have even stolen it out of the library."[77] They had limited value as practical guidebooks, but they inspired many Americans to head west and reassured them along the way.

The most infamous and controversial example of the genre, *The Emigrants' Guide, to Oregon and California* by Lansford W. Hastings, appeared early in 1845, in

---

[73] Dawson, "The Only Known Copies of Emigrant Guides," 165–66. The only copy of Edwards's *Sketch* is at the Beinecke Library.

[74] Camp, "Colonel Philip Leget Edwards and His Influence," 73.

[75] Wagner and Camp, *The Plains and the Rockies,* 130–33; and Nunis, *The Bidwell-Bartleson Party,* 7. Nunis reviewed everything known about Bidwell's guide in his introduction.

[76] Frémont's detractors charged that Jessie Frémont wrote the narratives, but her prose style did not match that of her husband's reports. See Chaffin, *Pathfinder,* 143–44.

[77] Orson Hyde to Joseph Smith, 26 April 1844, in Roberts, *History of the Church,* 6:375.

time for William Findley to carry his copy to Oregon.[78] Hastings provided little information about the trail itself—for example, all he said about the arduous trek down the Snake River was that it "proceeded with much less difficulty than we had anticipated." His unfortunate claims about the California Trail, which did not exist when he went to Oregon in 1842, made his guidebook an easy target for criticism. Bancroft generously credited the verbose Hastings with some writing ability but called the volume worthless and said its information about wagon routes could "hardly be said to have been of any value." To make his point, he quoted Hastings's claim that "wagons can be as readily taken from Fort Hall to the bay of St. Francisco, as they can, from the States to Fort Hall." Hastings's comments on native Californians, Bancroft wrote, "displayed nothing but inexcusable ignorance and bitter prejudice." In fairness, the book's chapter on equipment, supplies, and teams provided useful advice, and despite its critics, the guide was reprinted under various titles in 1847, 1849, and 1857 with virtually no alterations. This might be due to the good practical advice found in the book, but more probably it reflects the demand for any publication offering advice about the trail and the general disregard of copyright laws in the mid-nineteenth century.[79]

The quality of overland guides rose dramatically in 1846 with the publication of Overton Johnson and William Winter's *Route across the Rocky Mountains,* Rufus B. Sage's *Scenes in the Rocky Mountains,* and John M. Shively's *The Road to Oregon and California.* These were the first guidebooks to offer practical data about the physical trail, a feature shared by Joel Palmer's *Journal of Travels over the Rocky Mountains to the Mouth of the Columbia River.* The 1846 emigration also produced T. H. Jefferson's extraordinary *Map of the Emigrant Road from Independence, Mo., to St. Francisco, California,* which appeared in New York in 1849 and provided a mile-by-mile description and the first commercial map of the California Trail and Hastings Cutoff.[80]

The best guides provided a "waybill"—a list of campsites, trading posts, landmarks, river crossings, and the distances between them—along with advice on what to take, the best routes, and how to deal with Indians. Perhaps the most useful was William Clayton's *The Latter-Day Saints' Emigrants' Guide,* issued in Saint Louis in

---

[78] Findley, Overland Journey to Oregon and a Return Trip, 1845–1847, Beinecke Library, 38.

[79] Hastings, *The Emigrants' Guide,* 20, 137, 143–52; and Bancroft, *History of California,* 3:734, 3:778, 4:397–98. Thomas F. Andrews has argued that the book was unfairly maligned. See Andrews, "The Controversial Hastings Overland Guide," 21–34.

[80] Korns and Morgan, *West from Fort Bridger,* 187–195. Little new information has appeared on this mysterious character since 1950, but Benjamin S. Lippincott formed a bachelor's mess in William Russell's company, including "Jefferson with whom [he] left New York." He wrote, "after three days journey we kicked Jefferson out of the company which I never regretted afterward, although at the time inclined to stay with him." See Lippincott to John L. Stephens, 6 February 1847, Bancroft Library. Historian Rush Spedden made a compelling argument that the cartographer was the son of Thomas Jefferson and Sally Hemings. See "Who Was T. H. Jefferson?"

1848. Relying on an odometer designed and built by members of Brigham Young's 1847 pioneer company, Clayton's guide ended at Great Salt Lake City, but it provided the first reliable information on distances.[81] Edwin Patterson praised it as "the best road book I ever saw."[82] Widely plagiarized and pirated, the book won the admiration of fellow guidebook authors. Philip Platt and Nelson Slater, whose excellent *Travelers' Guide* provided distances to California derived from Platt's 1850 journey with his "Roadometer," considered Clayton's guide "very good for the road to which it applies," while in his 1852 overland guide, Hosea B. Horn complained that all the guidebooks he had consulted "proved worthless, save one—that of Mr. Clayton."[83]

A LIGHT STRONG WAGON

A covered wagon provided westbound families with shelter from the elements and a way to transport their property and provisions. "The wagon was plainly a community vehicle," historian Daniel J. Boorstin observed: "everything about it required traveling in groups."[84] Farm families often assembled the basic outfit of teams, wagons, and supplies from equipment they already owned, could make, or purchase from their neighbors. Those wealthy enough set out with several wagons, but many people had to fit all the food, clothing, bedding, cooking utensils, weapons, tools, and personal treasures needed to start a new life into a single wagon that could haul little more than a ton. This posed a daunting challenge, since families had to decide how much food they would need and which of their accumulated family heirlooms they could not leave behind.[85]

Despite popular legends, few early emigrants used Conestoga wagons, which were heavy freight wagons built to a design developed in Pennsylvania.[86] A few "swayback" or "crooked" wagon owners adapted the curved sides and bottom style for use on the trail, but most emigrants used "straight wagons" that were basically boxes. Ordinary farm wagons made ideal prairie schooners, since they were small, simple, light, and highly adaptable to trail conditions. Emigrants could sleep in or under them, and at trail's end they provided a temporary shelter or could be

---

[81] Despite claims that Clayton and his friends invented the odometer, such devices had existed since ancient times. T. H. Jefferson apparently used an odometer in 1846 to create his *Map of the Emigrant Road.*

[82] Patterson, Diary and Letters, 4 June 1850, Mattes Library.

[83] Horn, *Hosea B. Horn's Overland Guide,* Preface; and Platt and Slater, *Travelers' Guide,* xvi.

[84] Boorstin, *The Americans,* 56.

[85] The classic study of wagons is Nick Eggenhofer's *Wagons, Mules and Men,* while the best contemporary work is Mark L. Gardner's *Wagons for the Santa Fe Trade.* Capps's "Wheels in the West " and Davis's "Where Have All the Wagons Gone?" provide excellent overviews of historic and surviving overland wagons.

[86] The persistence of the Conestoga myth in popular culture is remarkable. "World of Wonder," a Sunday comics feature, illustrated its "Heading West" installment on 31 March 2002 with an image of six Conestogas with oxen hitched to the wrong end of the wagons. A 2004 article in *True West* claimed "most of the freight and people traveling westward until 1850 did so in a Conestoga wagon." See Bommersbach, "Hitching Your Wagon to a Star," 41.

sold, often at a profit. "In preparing for the journey across the mountains, you cannot be too particular in the choice of a wagon—it should be strong in every part and yet should not be too heavy," Jesse Looney cautioned in 1843. "The large size, two horse Yankee wagons are the most suitable wagons I have seen for the trip. You should have nothing but your clothing, bedding and provisions—flour and bacon. Goods are cheaper here than in the states. Put as much loading as one yoke of cattle can draw handily, and then put on three good yoke of cattle and take an extra yoke for a change in case of lameness or sore necks, and you can come through without difficulty."[87]

"No heavy wagons," Bruno Schmölder warned in the guidebook he wrote for German emigrants after crossing the plains in 1843. "These ruin their teams, while light vehicles meet all demands."[88] Most emigrants used wagons that could carry between two and three thousand pounds of cargo, but almost every sort of wheeled vehicle imaginable—from wheelbarrows to massive freight wagons—made the trip. Simplicity was much preferred to size, and the quality of the materials used to build the vehicle was important, since green wood proved disastrous in the arid West. "Buy a light strong wagon, made of the best seasoned materials," advised J. M. Shively, "for, if the timbers be not well seasoned, your wagon will fall to pieces when you get to the dry, arid plains of the mountains."[89] (Studebaker Brothers Manufacturing made the first kiln-dried lumber in the United States to meet an 1857 government contract for wagons.[90]) "Bring wagons made of the best materials and thoroughly seasoned and then have some black-smith's tongs and harness for setting tires," wrote William Porter. "You can get tires cut and set at Laramie but you will frequently have occasion to set them on the road."[91]

Advice to prairie travelers was not always consistent, and some early trail experts recommended large wagons. "Good and substantial wagons should always be selected," Lansford Hastings wrote, and however "firm and staunch" they appeared, a competent mechanic should invariably closely examine and repair them.[92] Writing from Fort Laramie in 1845, William Ide advocated using a "strong two horse waggon capable of bearing three thousand pounds on common roads, wide track, block tongue, coupled twenty inches back of the forward axle, body 13 to 18 feet long, straight; bed 14 to 16 inches high in the clear."[93] Merchant James Maxey of Independence told James Frazier Reed to take one that

[87] Looney to Bond, 27 October 1843, Oregon Historical Society.
[88] Schmölder, *Der Führer für Auswanderer nach Californien,* typescript translation, Huntington Library.
[89] Shively, "The Shively Guide," in Morgan, *Overland in 1846,* 735.
[90] Davis, "Where Have All the Wagons Gone?" Part 1, 36.
[91] Porter to "Dear Father, Mother, Brothers and Sisters," 24 June 1848.
[92] Hastings, *The Emigrants' Guide,* 145–46.
[93] Ide, "From Our Oregon Correspondent," 25 June 1845, *Sangamo Journal,* 4 September 1845.

"will beare about 6 thousand pounds."[94] (As Reed's subsequent travels with the Donner party demonstrated, this was not good advice.)

"An ordinary two-horse wagon, with eighteen-hundred weight, good double cover, and three yoke of light, active cattle are the best outfit a man can have," Captain Medorem Crawford advised twenty-one years after his first trip to Oregon: wagons should only be loaded to half their capacity, and each person should take at least 250 pounds of provisions, consisting of flour, bacon, sugar, coffee, tea, rice, and dried fruit. "Each man should be armed, and keep his gun convenient," but not capped. Crawford advised leaving personal possessions behind; emigrants should take "nothing but what was actually required on the journey."[95]

Trail veterans consistently warned not to overload the wagons. "No useless trumpery should be taken," wrote Joel Palmer.[96] "You should not start with a pound of any thing that can be done without," Samuel Crockett advised in 1845, "for it is much better to throw away an unnecessary article than to haul it."[97] Few emigrants were able to estimate their practical requirements accurately, but if family treasures were not left behind at the beginning of the journey, almost inevitably they joined the piles of abandoned furniture, tools, stoves, tinware, crockery, clothing, saddles, carpets, and even firearms that lined the trail from its start to its end. The "roads about the mountains are literally covered with such articles," Peter Lassen reported from South Pass in 1848: he cautioned there was "no danger in the world to be feared from any cause but overloading."[98]

On a two-thousand-mile journey that could last six months, a wagon had to perform a range of duties. With a properly waterproofed cover and well-organized contents, it provided shelter from wild prairie storms and a bedroom. A well-constructed box at the endgate could serve as both a kitchen and dining table. Since it was easily disassembled, the wagon box could be separated from its cover and running gear and be hauled over otherwise impassible obstacles or serve as a ferryboat. Caulking the bed of a wagon created an amphibious vehicle that was fairly effective at fording rivers.

Wagons were jammed with tools, provisions, and household goods, so many travelers slept in tents. William Martin advised that each mess should have a tent big enough to accommodate five to eight persons.[99] William B. Ide recommended one made of "stout Osnaburg," a heavy, coarse cotton fabric similar to canvas that orig-

---

[94] Morgan, *Overland in 1846*, 474.

[95] Crawford, "To Emigrants."

[96] Palmer, "Necessary Outfits," *Journal of Travels*, 258.

[97] Crockett to "Dear Friends," 16 February 1845.

[98] Lassen, "From the Emigrants," 16 July 1848, *The Brunswicker*, 9 September 1848, 1/2. Courtesy of Wendell Huffman.

[99] Martin to "Mr. Editor," 5 January 1846, "Oregon Out-Fit," *St. Joseph Gazette*, 23 January 1846, 3/1.

Nick Eggenhofer's sketch of a "prairie wagon" captures the simplicity of the basic wagon design most Americans relied upon to head west. From the artist's *Wagons, Mules and Men: How the Frontier Moved West*. Courtesy Evelyn E. Herman.

The typical overland wagon was built of wood and canvas, as shown in this Katie Hoefelmeier illustration. A small amount of iron (shown in black) re-enforced critical elements of the running gear and rimmed the wheels. Author's collection.

inated in the German town Osnabrück. William Porter felt that a good tent was essential and suggested using poles and pins made of iron or buckhorns.[100] In contrast, J. M. Shively wrote, "Take no tents with you, nor any thing of weight that can be dispensed with."[101]

How Wagons Worked

The light farm wagons typically used in the 1840s appear to be primitive vehicles consisting of a large rectangular box mounted on two axles and four wheels, with square or rounded "bows" stapled to its sides to support a linen or canvas cover. A wagon had to be light to burden its teams as little as possible but strong enough to stand up to two thousand miles or more of pounding over rocky roads. Durability was more important than weight, so emigrants preferred vehicles built of tough, well-seasoned hardwoods such as oak, ash, hickory, maple, and Osage orange, with iron used for tires, tongue joints, and axle skeins where strength and resilience were essential.[102]

---

[100] Johnson, "William B. Ide Describes Palace Car in 1845," *Crossroads* 6, no. 4 (Fall 1995): 7–8; and Porter to "Dear Father, Mother, Brothers and Sisters," 24 June 1848.

[101] Shively, "The Shively Guide," in Morgan, *Overland in 1846, 735.*

[102] Stewart, "The Prairie Schooner Got Them There"; and Susan Badger Doyle, "Wagons," background paper provided to author.

A wagon, however, was a surprisingly complex machine. It consisted of three basic elements: the box with its bows and cover, the front running gear, and the rear running gear. The box or bed came in many sizes, usually built of oak and either made of simple planks or a frame with panels. A light wagon box was nine to twelve feet long, a bit less than four feet wide, and had sideboards about two feet high with a hinged endgate to provide access to its contents. Joel Palmer advised building storage boxes as tall as the sideboards to create "a smooth surface to sleep upon." Fancier versions came with side extensions that sat on top of the box and extended its width and depth. Palmer called such a design a "Mormon fashioned wagon bed" and thought it was "the best. They are usually made straight, with sideboards about 16 inches wide, and a projection outward of about four inches on each side, and then another side board of ten or twelve inches; in this last, set the bows for covers, which should always be double."[103] The box was often painted: Catharine Scott Coburn recalled her family's five wagons were "gorgeous in green and yellow paint."[104]

Hickory, renowned for its toughness and flexibility, was the preferred wood for bows, which provided a frame to support the wagon's cover. The bows were made from soaked strips of hickory, which were bent into U shapes and dried. "Every wagon should be furnished with substantial bows and double osnaburg covers," Randolph Marcy advised, "to protect its contents from the sun and weather."[105] The wagon top was generally made of linen, canvas, or a type of denim known as "cotton drilling," waterproofed with several coats of linseed oil or paint. The cover was stretched over the bent-hickory hoops, while a ridgepole or stringer connected the tops of the bows and stabilized the frame. William Ide advised using osnaburg "drawn on as tight as may be, and sized and painted with 3 coats of oil paint."[106]

Flaps at the front and back, secured with a "puckering string," created a small room of wood and canvas. "The wagon should be covered with an untarred, thick covering that rests on strongly made arches. The side-walls should have their corners properly taken off, so that water flowing from the roof will be drawn to the outside," Bruno Schmölder recommended. "It is also advisable to cover the wagon bed on the inside, likewise to keep off the water. In a wagon prepared in this manner one is as safe as in a house."[107]

Later artwork typically pictured overland wagons with spotless white covers, but fabrics such as osnaburg had a natural yellow tinge that deepened when treated with linseed oil, and wagons that did have white covers often had been painted. Other covers were painted green and blue, and Americans could not

---

[103] Palmer, "Necessary Outfits," *Journal of Travels,* 257.

[104] Scott, Recollections, *Morning Oregonian,* 17 June 1890, in Holmes, *Covered Wagon Women,* 5:27.

[105] Marcy, *The Prairie Traveler,* 27.

[106] Ide, "From Our Oregon Correspondent," 25 June 1845, *Sangamo Journal,* 4 September 1845.

[107] Schmölder, *Der Führer für Auswanderer nach Californien,* typescript translation, Huntington Library, 1. I have reworded the translation.

resist customizing their prairie schooners. "Our wagon covers were painted to make them water-proof, and each had its driver's name painted on it," recalled Jacob Wright Harlan.[108] "Most of the emigrant wagons had the names of the owners, place where they were from and where they were bound, marked in large letters on the outside of the cover," Nancy Hunt remembered.[109] After his family abandoned the trail, John K. Stockton recalled that their wagon covers "were made into sheets, and were used for many years by the family."[110] What these sheets lacked in comfort, they apparently made up for in durability.

The wagon bed rested on two beams known as bolsters. Wooden cleats at the front and rear secured the wagon box to them, allowing the box to be easily removed. The bolsters rested on top of the axles and were part of the front and rear running gear that consisted of the bolsters, axletrees, wheels, and hounds. The axles began as hand-hewn oak or hickory beams about five feet long and ended in iron-sheathed tapered clouts or spindles that fit into a wheel's gum-wood hubs. A linchpin pierced the clouts to hold the wheels in place. Iron axles appeared in America in the early 1830s, but they were brittle and prone to fracture and so were seldom used on the early overland trails.

Wooden wheels made of a hub, fourteen to sixteen spokes, and rims called felloes were mounted on each spindle. "The wheels and their related axle spindles contained the greater part of wagon art," historian and curator Richard M. Davis observed.[111] Rear wheels measured four to five feet in diameter; front wheels had fewer spokes and, to expedite turning, were usually 20 to 30 percent smaller than the back wheels. They came sheathed in an iron tire that had been heated until cherry red, slipped over the rim, and cooled in a stream of water that shrank the metal and tightened the entire assembly. This treatment gave the wheel an arched concavity known as "dish," which reduced stress from the axle. Joel Palmer said the tires should be at least 1¾ inches wide, "two inches, however, is the most common width," but three inches was even better.[112] "If the wheel had been made correctly and the tire had the proper draft," Arizona wagonwright Fred Ronstadt recalled, "the completed wheel would have the correct dish and ring like a bell."[113]

The rear running gear's bolster rested on the axletree, with the wishbone-shaped hounds (or hawns) pinned or loosely mortised between the rear bolster and axletree. To provide a counterbalance, the back hounds extended a short dis-

---

[108] Harlan, *California '46 to '88*, 25; and Brown, Recollection of 1847, Bancroft Library.

[109] Hunt, "By Ox-Team to California," 322.

[110] Stockton, "The Trail of the Covered Wagon," 1852.

[111] Davis, "Where Have All the Wagons Gone?" part 1, 17, 38.

[112] Palmer, "Necessary Outfits," *Journal of Travels*, 257.

[113] Sherman and Ronstadt, "Wagon Making in Southern Arizona," 14. Fred Ronstadt was also a gifted musician and grandfather of a famous singing star.

tance behind the axle, while the two front wings linked to the coupling pole or reach, which connected the front and rear running gears. Several reachpin holes pierced the coupling pole, and the placement of the pins determined the length of the gears so they could accommodate different-sized wagon boxes. The reach slipped into the front running gear between a two-part bolster, the upper box bolster and the lower "sand beam." A foot-long kingpin ran through both front bolsters, the reachpin hole, and the axletree. The box bolster was pinned to the wagon box but not bound to the axletree, which let the front gears pivot on a kingpin so the front wheels could turn independently of the wagon box.

The two front hounds came together about three feet in front of the axletree at the "jaws of the hounds": they sometimes connected to a more complicated assembly called the inner hounds. The jaws held the wagon tongue, which extended forward about fifteen feet and acted as the wagon's power train, connecting the wagon to its engines, the ox, horse, or mule teams. The wings of the front hounds extended back from the bolster and connected to a cross arm near the center of the wagon that helped balance the weight of the tongue. Prairie travelers preferred a drop to a fixed tongue, since a drop tongue could be raised and lowered on a bar known as a queenpin. The drop tongue worked better with oxen and in rough country—plus, on a treeless plain, it could serve as a makeshift gallows.

The running gear was the most important and complex element of the wagon, but it needed to be both light and strong—contradictory requirements that generally favored lightness. Tongues, axles, and the iron-rimmed wooden wheels were fragile and prone to breaking, so most trading posts and even wagon trains had a blacksmith to handle such problems. Lansford Hastings advised that "every wagon should be supplied with extra axletrees, chains, hammers, and the like," but abandoned wagons often provided spare parts.[114] All wagons had a tar bucket to hold some sort of lubricant to reduce the constant friction between the hubs and spindles. William Porter advised bringing "rosin and tallow to grease wagons. Black lead will do but is very inconvenient to haul. It will black everything."[115] The grease spread everywhere: "There is nothing you can do to prevent it," one modern-day overlander testified, "and nothing will wash it out!"[116]

Advancements in wagon technology, such as iron axles, springs, and brakes, had been made years before the great western migrations began, but few of these innovations found their way west during the first two decades of overland travel. Brakes, or "rubbers," appeared on Conestoga wagons about 1825, but were little used on the trails until the Civil War. Early emigrant wagons seldom had brakes:

---

[114] Stewart, *The California Trail,* 108–16; Kimball, *Heber C. Kimball,* 130–31; and Hastings, *The Emigrants' Guide,* 146.

[115] Porter to "Dear Father, Mother, Brothers and Sisters," 24 June 1848.

[116] Kay Threlkeld to author, 1 June 2004.

to slow them down on steep descents, their drivers "rough locked" the wheels with chains that prevented the wheels from turning, and occasionally they tied a fallen tree to the back of the wagon to create drag. Sometimes they slipped metal "shoes" under the wheels to reduce wear on the locked wheels.[117]

Riding in an ox wagon was such an uncomfortable experience that it proved more exhausting than walking. An Englishman patented an elliptical spring in 1805 as an antidote to the continual jolting, but "spring wagons"—which, much like modern automobiles, had leaf-spring suspension systems—only appeared on the trail after the gold rush. During the 1860s spring-mounted seats came into fashion, but until then, teamsters usually rode a wheelhorse while ox-drivers walked on the left (or near) side of their teams.[118]

A large oak barrel hanging from the side of an emigrant wagon is a standard feature of modern trail pictures, but such an "ox-killing monstrosity" would have been useless and impractical during most of an overland journey and dangerous if not impossible to haul across a desert.[119] Contemporaneous images often show a small box attached to a wagon side, and sometimes they reveal a small barrel slung underneath the back of the wagon box.[120] Even empty oaken barrels were heavy, and hanging a barrel filled with dozens of gallons of water weighing hundreds of pounds from the side of a wagon would have thrown it seriously off balance. Filling a large barrel required considerable effort, and one traveler even found it "a caution to keep our kegs supplied" for dry spells.[121]

The earliest pioneers had little concept of the arid West and often had no containers to carry water when they reached the long dry stretches west of South Pass. An empty flour barrel sometimes provided a solution, but such weighty objects were usually abandoned long before they were needed to haul water. Experience taught travelers to carry small containers. Lilburn Boggs advised having "a good five gallon water keg to each wagon, iron hooped and painted" and a few buckets for hauling water.[122] "To prepare for crossing the deserts," Margaret Frink wrote, "we also had two India-rubber bottles holding up to five gallons each, for carrying water."[123]

Despite the wealth of advice, by the time the first wagons reached Oregon and California, many emigrants were close to starvation and had abandoned virtually all of their precious possessions along the trail. As the trickle of emigration swelled to a

[117] Capps, "Wheels in the West," 9.
[118] Davis, "Where Have All the Wagons Gone?" part 1, 17–19.
[119] Stewart, *The California Trail,* 119.
[120] Stenhouse, *The Rocky Mountain Saints,* 251.
[121] Anonymous, 8 August 1849, in Mason Diaries, Beinecke Library.
[122] Boggs, "Route to the Pacific," *St. Louis Weekly Reveille,* 22 May 1848.
[123] Frink, "Adventures of a Party of Gold Seekers," in Holmes, *Covered Wagon Women,* 2:62.

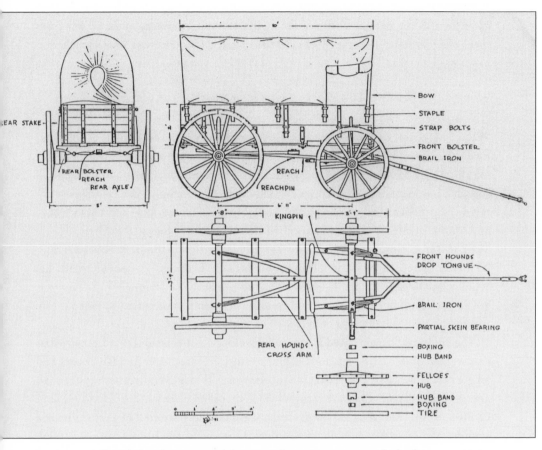

A typical emigrant wagon's box, running gears, tongue, and wheels.
Researched and drawn by Richard M. Davis.

flood, the problem got worse. "It is perfectly incredible that men with the least degree of common sense would ever have thought of starting on *such* a journey with *such* cattle and wagons," Wilson Blain wrote in 1848, seeking to explain the ruined wagons abandoned by luckless emigrants he found at nearly every campsite. "In some cases the wagons would break where they could not be mended and must be left; in other cases the cattle were not sufficient for their task, and the wagon must be left from sheer inability to get it along."[124] On the road west, experience was a hard teacher.

MUCH MORE CONVENIENT ABOUT TRAVELING: CARRIAGES AND CARTS

Wagons were not the only vehicles used to cross the plains. Nineveh Ford recalled fording the Snake River in a "strong carriage" with the assistance of Marcus Whitman in 1843. Several Mormon apostles used them during their 1847 trek, and Joseph Chiles took a carriage on his 1848 trip to California.[125] But carriages were not very practical for crossing thousands of miles on a rough and rocky road, and no one seems to have taken one all the way to Oregon or California before 1849. A Mr. Crump overturned his carriage coming off the Bear River Divide, "and although its top was most thoroughly broken in pieces, yet providentially his top was not broken at all," J. Quinn Thornton marveled. "I am glad the buggy is gone," Delia Thompson Brown wrote after her party traded theirs, "for no one wanted to ride in it after the novelty of having it was gone."[126]

The Métis of Canada's Red River had developed a specialized cart by 1803 that was well adapted to the demands of the western frontier. The Red River cart had a light box, a wooden axle, two enormous wheels that helped in crossing streams, and occasionally "a white covering to protect the articles within." A single line of three to five mules usually powered the carts, and they could easily outpace a wagon. As Alfred Jacob Miller's wonderful images of the fur trade reveal, such carts were widely used in the caravans that supplied the annual rendezvous, and they remained popular and widely used throughout the West: Francis Parkman's French-Canadian guides harnessed their mules to a "small French cart, of the sort very appropriately called a 'mule-killer' beyond the frontiers." These carts could transport as much as one-half ton of cargo—one expert calculated they could carry ten times as much as a packhorse.[127]

---

[124] Blain to Kerr, *The Preacher*, 22 August 1849, 130, Oregon Historical Society.

[125] Ford, The Pioneer Road Makers, Bancroft Library, 7; and Smith, "A Journal of Scenes and Incidents," California State Library, 138.

[126] Thornton, *Oregon and California in 1848*, 1:151; and Brown, Diary, 7 July 1860, Nevada Historical Society.

[127] Vrooman, "The Métis Red River Cart," 8–20; Lamar, *The New Encyclopedia of the American West*, 952; and Parkman, *The California and Oregon Trail*, 21.

Although not often noted in trail histories, references to carts appear in a surprising number of sources. The fur caravan Narcissa Whitman accompanied in
1836 included a cart drawn by two mules.[128] The American Fur Company train
Joel Walker traveled with in 1840 had thirty carts.[129] Pierre-Jean De Smet's
Canadian teamsters used Red River carts instead of wagons. They hitched a line
of mules to each cart and added additional animals to climb steep hills. "Sometimes a cart would go over, breaking everything to pieces," John Bidwell recalled,
"and at such times Father De Smet would be just the same—beaming with good
humor." The carts were easily upset, Bidwell recalled, "but aside from that were
much more convenient about traveling than our wagons."[130] Emigrants often
made carts out of their wagons, and a wagon's adjustable reach lent itself easily
to such a conversion. On the Snake River in 1844, the Shaws, Catherine Sager
Pringle's guardians, lay by to convert her family's wagon into a cart to ease the
burden on its team. "Into this was loaded what was necessary," Pringle recalled—
and at the end of the trail, few vehicles of any sort contained anything that was
not absolutely essential.[131]

Mules or Oxen Are Preferable to Horses: Teams

What was the best way to cross the plains? As long as wagons headed west, emigrants debated whether oxen, horses, or mules made the best team. "There has
been much discussion regarding the relative merits of mules and oxen for prairie
traveling," Captain Randolph B. Marcy wrote in 1859, "and the question is yet far
from being settled." Marcy himself preferred mules for journeys not exceeding
one thousand miles and felt they traveled faster and endured heat much better
than oxen, which like dogs cannot sweat and must cool themselves through their
mouths. But for long marches or over rough, sandy, or muddy roads, Marcy felt
young oxen outperformed mules. Oxen were used as saddle animals in Africa.
If all else failed, he concluded, "a saddle-ox might be found serviceable." No one
seems to have tried Marcy's experiment.[132]

"The kind of animals used should depend on the kind of company you have on
the plains." Families should travel "with a respectable sized train for safety and

---

[128] Whitman, 28 July 1836, in Drury, *First White Women over the Rockies*, 1:51. Citing Gray's *Oregon*, 133, Peter
Burnett said Whitman "had taken a wagon as far as Fort Boise, by making a cart on two of the wheels, and placing the
axletree and the other two wheels in his cart." See Burnett, *Recollections and Opinions of an Old Pioneer*, 116

[129] Walker, *A Pioneer of Pioneers*, 11.

[130] Nunis, *The Bidwell-Bartleson Party*, 80, 105.

[131] Pringle, Across the Plains in 1844, Oregon Historical Society.

[132] Marcy, *The Prairie Traveler*, 27–28.

if there are enough of mule teams to secure safety for the women and children then I would prefer mules and if not you would be compelled to travel with ox teams," Daniel Kilgore wrote. "Oxen will be the cheapest and the safest all things considered but mules are much the speediest," he concluded. "But either mules or oxen are preferable to horses."[133]

Kilgore's low opinion of horses as long-distance draft animals was widely held. "Mules and oxen should be used for teams," wrote trail veteran Medorem Crawford. "Horses will not do to depend upon for service."[134] Many emigrants brought riding horses that survived the trip fairly well, but Andrew Murphy explained the problem with using horses to haul wagons: "Some of the party exchanged their large horses which they had brought from the states, for Indian ponies. Horses that had been raised on grain can not stand the trip."[135] When compelled to haul heavy loads, American horses faltered early in the journey. "Some horse teams look badly," Forty-niner Alphonse Day recorded near the Platte River ford. "Oxen from 5 to 7 years old look better generally than younger [animals]."[136]

There was an exception to the rule, however: "The Indian horses are the most hardy animals of the kind I have ever seen," Edwin Bryant wrote at Fort Laramie. "Many of the breeds higher up in the Rocky Mountains have powers of endurance nearly equal to the Mexican mule; an animal which I regard as superior to any other on the continent of America for long, toilsome, and difficult journeys."[137]

Mules fared better than farm-raised horses on a diet of native grass, but oxen thrived on the prairie pastures and better endured the deprivations of a desert crossing. As he watched his "faithful oxen dying inch by inch, every day becoming weaker, and some of them giving out" on the road to Oregon, Peter Burnett observed that once an ox wore out, "there is no hope of saving him. It requires immense hardship, however, to bring him to that point." The ox was the noblest of draft animals, he concluded, and had more "genuine hardihood and pluck" than a mule or horse. An ox would "climb rocky hills, cross muddy streams, and plunge into swamps and thickets for pasture. He will seek his food in places where other animals will not go." Oxen were so resilient that they would often fall dead under the yoke before they would give up. Overlanders were greatly attached to their oxen, for their lives depended on them.[138] Oxen were cheaper than horses or mules, easier to manage, more reliable, and, as one early Oregonian noted, if it became necessary, they were much better to eat. Joel Palmer stated the case

---

[133] Kilgore to Bradley, 28 February 1859, California State Library.
[134] Crawford, "To Emigrants," Broadside, 1863, Clackamas County Historical Society.
[135] Murphy, Diary, 9 June 1849, Western Historical Manuscript Collection.
[136] Day, Journal of the Trip to California, 1 June 1849, BYU Library.
[137] Bryant, *What I Saw in California,* 109.
[138] Burnett, *Recollections and Opinions of an Old Pioneer,* 99–100.

quite simply in 1847: "Oxen stand the trip much better, and are not so liable to be stolen by the Indians, and are much less trouble."[139]

The ox is not a special breed of animal. Oxen are bulls of the genus *Bos* that are castrated when four years old or older, as contrasted to steers, which are castrated when young. "Of course," recalled one old freighter, "they were not oxen until they were broke to work"—a task that modern expert Dixon Ford reports takes about forty hours, whereas training a man to drive an ox team properly could take hundreds of hours.[140] Oxen were less likely to panic than horses or mules, but when motivated, it was "astonishing with what speed a team of four yoke of oxen can run," Joseph Henry Brown recalled.[141] Indians seldom stole oxen on the plains, but when old oxen got among a bison herd they soon became "as wild as the wildest buffalo," remembered John Bidwell, "and if ever recovered it was because they could not run so fast as the buffaloes or one's horse."[142] As Joseph Williams observed, the two species "seemed to form an attachment to each other."[143]

Ox teams had many advantages. Expensive harnesses, singletrees, a double-tree, and stay chains tied to the front axletree connected a wagon to its horse and mule teams, but a simple wooden yoke coupled an ox team to a wagon. Two oxen yoked together were counted as one team, or yoke. The physical yoke that bound these matched pairs of oxen to the wagon tongue was a single piece of hewn wood, usually seasoned ash, black gum, pine, sassafras, yellow poplar, or hard maple, shaped and finished with a drawshave or bowie knife, and preferably fitted to its team. An auger drilled four holes through the yoke, and two "hickory bows were inserted in the holes and fastened on the upper surface of the yoke with a wooden key—a peg put through a small hole in the bow," an Iowa pioneer remembered. Soaked hickory saplings about forty-five inches long were bent into U shapes to make ox-bows, which were then tied securely and left to dry and set. The bow fit snuggly under an ox's neck and connected it to the yoke, which it shared with its mate. An iron bolt or staple ran through the center of the yoke and held two rings, one smaller than the other, through which passed chains or ropes that connected the first yoke to the wooden tongue: all the ox power that drove a wagon used this connection. One ring secured the yoke to the tongue, and ox drivers fastened log chains or ropes to the center bolt and tied them to the wagon hounds. "No pioneer teamster ever began operations without providing himself with one or more log chains," one veteran recalled.[144]

---

[139] Conroy and Barney, *The Oxen Handbook*, 2; and Palmer, "Necessary Outfits," *Journal of Travels*, 257.

[140] Riley, *Recollections*, 15.

[141] Brown, Recollection of 1847, Bancroft Library.

[142] Bidwell, "The First Emigrant Train," in Nunis, *The Bidwell-Bartleson Party*, 106.

[143] Williams, *Narrative of a Tour*, 7 June 1841, 28.

[144] Bonebright-Closz, *Founding of Newcastle Now Webster City, Iowa*, 205–206.

It generally took multiple teams to power a wagon. The team closest to the wagon were the wheelers, or tongue cattle, usually the largest, most powerful animals in a hitch, while the leaders, or pointers, led the assembled team. Chains or ropes connected the wheelers' yoke to the tongue. Ropes or more typically chains connected the yokes of additional teams to the wagon tongue, sometimes through a metal device called an evener. Trained oxen worked in pairs and could be spotted by the wear on their horns from striking the staple. Teamsters used these marks to match teammates and tell on which side of the yoke each ox belonged.

Yoking up teams of oxen and hitching them to a wagon was a scientific operation. "Each man will first take his wheel yoke, take out one bow, put the yoke on your shoulder and the bow in your right hand," James Francis Riley wrote, recalling how one wagonmaster taught a crew of thirty-six greenhorns the finer points of ox driving, which began with catching a team. Occasionally untrained teams or a stubborn "yoke turner" would fight being hitched up, rolling around until the bows were over instead of under its neck. To prevent this, teamsters would tie the bushes of a team's tails together, which prevented the animals from "turning the yoke." Sometimes yokes would be carved to accommodate a specific team. "Now, when you get your wheelers yoked up take them out and put them on the tongue of your wagon," the wagonmaster advised his young apprentices.[145]

Despite modern misrepresentations, a teamster walked alongside his oxen and did not control them from the wagon box, since the yoke had no reins and oxen did not wear bridles. The driver always led the team from the animal's left, and an experienced drover could issue commands simply through body movements. But most drovers used a stick, whip, or goad to reinforce five basic commands: gee (go right), haw (go left), get up, back up, and whoa. Constant practice refined a teamster's ability to communicate with his teams.

Always prodding the animals from the same side reduced the likelihood they would mistake the sting of the whip for something like an insect bite. "Ox teams should be carefully drove so that each yoke in the team does its whole duty if not your team will soon give out, die and go to naught," advised Daniel Kilgore. "The driver must walk the whole time and give his undivided attention to his team."[146] Not everyone followed Kilgore's advice, and some drovers apparently let oxen find their own way. Peter Burnett recalled drivers who went to sleep sitting in the front of their wagons: the oxen often would stop until their masters awakened. Burnett and his wife took turns driving and sleeping during the day.[147]

[145] Riley, *Recollections,* 17, 21.
[146] Kilgore to Bradley, 28 February 1859, California State Library.
[147] Burnett, *Recollections and Opinions of an Old Pioneer,* 108.

Not only oxen and steers served as draft animals. "I once saw a small cow yoked beside a large ox, and driven about six hundred miles attached to a loaded wagon, and she performed her part equally well with the ox," Randolph Marcy recalled. "It has been by no means an unusual thing for emigrant travelers to work cows in their teams."[148] After Indians stole his family's lead ox in 1847, James Newton Angel's father "had to break in two cows, and when well broken, they made the best leaders in the whole wagon train and carried us the rest of the distance into California. At night, after grazing, they were milked, and they supplied us with milk, cream, and butter throughout our journey."[149] Many emigrants took along cows strictly to provide milk—Narcissa Whitman started out with four.

Crossing the plains convinced Bruno Schmölder that oxen were the best animals for the journey, and he felt cows did very well. "But both sexes are more serviceable to the purposes of the emigrant than mules. Besides they are easier to keep—there is little fear of their losing their way or foundering—they cost less at the beginning of the journey, and at the end are worth at least quadruple." Anyone who crossed the plains would "grow fond of the animals long before the end of the journey. Their patience, their tameness and their steadfast goodwill, compels attachment from everyone," this German pioneer wrote. "Another advantage is that there is almost no work harnessing them, while this is not the case with horses and mules."[150]

Mules had their own fervent devotees, for they were intelligent, hardy, and fast—at least under most conditions. Edwin Bryant considered the Mexican pack mule superior to any other beast for long, toilsome, and difficult journeys.[151] "On the frontier a mule is better than any watch-dog," Jacob Wright Harlan recalled after being awakened by the snorting of his company's mules one night in 1846. "If an Indian, or a bear, or wolf approaches one's camp, the mule is sure to give the alarm."[152] Mules had an unerring instinct about whether to trust dangerous spots on treacherous ground: "My mules know whether they are safe long before I do," P. Dexter Tiffany observed at the Green River ford, "& I can not whip or spur him on to one which is dangerous."[153]

But mules had problems. They did not fare well at river crossings, and Nineveh Ford recalled the fate of an Englishman with a family in his care who tried to ford

---

[148] Marcy, *The Prairie Traveler*, 30.

[149] Angel, Memoir of 1847, NFTC Manuscripts, Mattes Library, 2.

[150] Schmölder, *Der Führer für Auswanderer nach Californien*, typescript translation, Huntington Library, 1. I have reworded the translation.

[151] Bryant, *What I Saw in California*, 23, 28 June 1846, 109, 115.

[152] Harlan, *California '46 to '88*, 46.

[153] Tiffany, Journal, 25 July 1849, Mattes Library, 91.

the Snake River near American Falls in 1843. "He was riding a mule and went over that shallows and into the deep water and drowned he and his mule."[154] John Bratt noted in 1862, "Mules are great cowards in water, they prefer drowning to swimming."[155] Randolph Marcy disagreed: he thought mules were good swimmers unless they got water in their ears, in which case they drowned.[156] For men not used to working with animals, they could be dangerous. "We have been busy all fore noon which I assure you is no fun," Henry Wertz wrote home. "Young Oberlin was hooking up his mules the other day while in the act one of his mules got to acting up and like to kill him. He fell some how or other and the mules jumped on his breast." They could also kill: "Some other young man from Kentucky was kicked by one last week and died in a day or two."[157]

Many, if not most, of the mules offered for sale on the Missouri frontier were unbroken animals from New Mexico, and these young and wild mules caused considerable havoc. For greenhorns, domesticating a mule proved a formidable challenge. "A wild, unbroken mule is the most desperate animal that I have ever seen," Kimball Webster observed. "We tried in vain to break our mules by putting large packs of sand on their backs and leading them about, but it availed very little, as the second trial was as bad as the first; and they were nearly as wild and vicious when we started on our journey as they were when they were first packed." Webster and his companions worked from early morning until five o'clock in the evening to pack their animals for the first time, but managed to get them loaded by noon the next day. "It took as many men to pack a mule as could stand around it, and we were obliged to choke many of them, before we could get the saddle upon their backs," Webster wrote. "They would kick, bite and strike with their fore feet, making it very dangerous to go about them. Several of our company were quite badly disabled by working with them, so that they were unable to assist in packing."[158] Such obstinacy had a price, P. Dexter Tiffany observed, for "one contrary mule will detain a whole team with several men for several hours rearing & pitching, breaking harness, getting tangled & doing every thing else."[159]

"A horse is an animal that may have some 'sense,'" wrote journalist Kirk Anderson, "but we are altogether skeptical about mules." He saw a young mule kick a man fifteen feet, and he thought the animals should be disposed of in a fashion similar to the "hard Boston crackers" used as food on the trail. "'Adobe' crackers for breakfast

---

[154] Ford, The Pioneer Road Makers, Bancroft Library, 7–8.
[155] Cited in Mattes, The Great Platte River Road, 269.
[156] Marcy, The Prairie Traveler, 102.
[157] Wertz to Honored Parents, 7 April 1850, Beinecke Library.
[158] Webster, The Gold Seekers of '49, 35–37.
[159] Tiffany, Diary and Letters, 10 May 1849, Mattes Library, 14.

should be well soaked in water all night and then thrown away the next morning," he advised, "and a vicious mule should be bridled, saddled and—then shot."[160]

Draft animals, even oxen, were almost always shod and provided ample work for blacksmiths along the trail. "Your *work cattle* will need shoes of leather or iron or rawhide many days before you reach Fort Laramie—& worse afterwards," advised George W. Davis.[161] An ox shoe consisted of two J-shaped iron bands nailed to each side of an animal's cloven hoof. Shoeing an ox took skills not required to shoe a horse or mule, which could be done by simply lifting the animal's legs one at a time. An ox could not maintain its balance on three legs, and so it had to be thrown on its side to perform the operation.

To do so, the men shoeing the ox tied a rope to cut off blood to its back legs. When the legs went numb, the animal could be knocked over with a simple push. They then tied ropes to its legs and stretched them out, using a snubbing post to tighten the lines and several stout men to hold the animal still. Others reportedly used a more complicated technique. "To shoe the cattle a trench the length of the animal and the width and depth of the shovel was dug," Lydia Milner Waters recalled. "The animal was then thrown and rolled over so that its back bone lay in the trench and all four of its legs were up in the air. In this position it was helpless and the shoes were nailed on readily."[162] Waters's account is suspect, however, since an ox left on its back for very long will suffocate. Why overland travelers would go to the trouble of digging a trench is puzzling, and if they did, the ox's head must have been left out of the hole, since it had to first raise its head to get back up.

When Benjamin Franklin Owen reached Pacific Springs in 1853, he found two businesses: a small trading post "& an Ox Shoeing device. There the Ox was swung up bodily without consulting his wishes, giving the Stalwart Blacksmith all the advantages."[163] However it was done, shoeing an ox was a dangerous business for both man and beast. "Some of the men had their oxen thrown & shod by a man with whom we happened to camp at noon," noted John Melvin Graham. "One of the oxen broke off one of his horns while down."[164] During a recent wagon train recreation, a toppled ox threw its head and broke one of its handler's ankles.[165]

Wealthy prairie travelers hired teamsters to drive their wagons and manage the stock. "Be careful to get an industrious, careful hand to drive your team and one that will not leave his post at any time," William Porter advised.[166] Most drovers

[160] "Mule Emetic," *Valley Tan*, 6 November 1858, 2/2.

[161] Davis to Walter Watkins, 6 December 1850, Beinecke Library.

[162] Waters, "Account of a Trip," 64.

[163] Owen, My Trip across the Plains, 8 July 1853, Lane County Historical Society.

[164] Graham, Diary, 23 May 1860, Mattes Library.

[165] Correspondence with Candy Moulton and Terry Del Bene, February 2004.

[166] Porter to "Dear Father, Mother, Brothers and Sisters," 24 June 1848.

were new to the profession, simply being young men seeking to work their way across the plains, like Grove Cook of the Bidwell-Bartleson party, who "begged to be allowed to pay his way by driving our wagon, as he could furnish nothing," Nicholas "Cheyenne" Dawson recalled. (Dawson bought an interest in one of John Bartleson's wagons and set out with only seventy-five cents—"and I still had that left when I reached California.")[167] Later, many teamsters were trail veterans. At Kanesville, Iowa, in April 1851, Samuel James hired three teamsters, "all choice hands," who agreed to work for their board. One of them, Alanson Pomeroy, had gone to Oregon in 1842 when he was about twelve years old, "and came back overland with Captain Palmer & 16 others packing on horses & mules."[168] As overland freighting grew, so did the disrepute of professional teamsters, who became notorious for their colorful language and vile oaths. One 1844 driver, Charles Smith, claimed "no man could get all the pull out of an ox without swearing at him."[169]

"When a person starts with a *good* wagon and sufficient team, it is rare, indeed, that such [a] person does not get through safely," wrote Wilson Blain. Still, the length of the trip was a trial for even the best animals. "I call four yokes of good strong oxen a sufficient team for one wagon. We had three yokes to a wagon and succeeded in getting through, but the cattle were perfectly exhausted," Blain reported.[170] Ultimately, the success of any journey west depended on how well a traveler managed his animals—how heavily a wagon was loaded, how a wagon driver managed his teams, and how effectively a packer loaded and paced his mules. Pulling a heavy load day after day wore out the best animals. David Campbell recalled that his 1846 company split up because "some of the men wanted to rush through while others favored the more sensible plan of traveling without too much haste." Those who pushed their stock too hard "soon found that their cattle could not stand it, for by the time they had reached the Platte River their cattle were tender-footed and gave out." Although they traded for new animals at Fort Laramie, before the 1846 emigration got to Fort Hall the hard drivers had fallen behind those who set a reasonable pace.[171] Modern expert Dixon Ford is convinced abusive masters pushing their teams beyond their natural endurance caused most fatalities among oxen: he has never found an account of a woman working an ox to death.[172]

[167] Nunis, *The Bidwell-Bartleson Party,* 146–47.

[168] James to Thomas H. Foxwell, 27 April 1851, James Family Papers, Allen Library.

[169] Nichols, "Across the Plains in 1844," chapter 2.

[170] Blain to Kerr, *The Preacher,* 22 August 1849, 130, Oregon Historical Society.

[171] Campbell, "Pioneer of 1846," *Porterville Recorder,* 11, 12, and 13 August 1910.

[172] Author's conversation notes with Dixon Ford, 12 May 2007.

Overlanders often formed deep bonds with their draft animals, sometimes showing a remarkable degree of empathy for these beasts of burden. They gave their oxen names such as Tip and Tyler; Duke and Brandy; Tom and Jerry; Cherry and Star; Merry, Flory, and Reddy; Bully and Turk; and Pride and Beauty.[173] Almost eighty years after he crossed the plains in 1852, James Meikle Sharp could recall each "personal name" given to his family's six yoke of oxen: Bill and Berry, leaders; Broad and Darby; Buck and Bright; Joe and Lion; Sam and Pomp; and Jack and Charley.[174]

"I must pay tribute to our wheel oxen, Dick and Berry, who drew the family wagon all the way across the plains. They were gentle, kind, patient and reliable," recalled Mary Medley Ackley. "I loved them and my heart often ached for them when they tried to hold back the wagon on a steep hill."[175] A man in her party rode "a little black mule that is very intelligent & a pet with him," Harriet Buckingham reported.[176] An exceedingly cold rain affected his mules very badly, Alexander Nixon wrote. "Indeed they look the very object of pity and despair appears to be depicted on their care worn but interesting faces. I feel like I could almost take some of them into my tent and Share with them my blue blanket."[177]

Profoundly aware that their own survival depended on their teams, migrants recorded their deaths with great emotion. "Our whole dependence is on our stock," one 1849 southern-route diarist noted. "If they give out we are left in the wilderness among the savages with no way of escape from ruin."[178] James Abbey and two friends stayed behind their train one morning with a sick ox. "We watched the faithful animal and ministered to him all the remedies in our possession, but he died. It seemed like parting with an old friend. He had shared with us all the vicissitudes of this toilsome journey, and now to see him expire was truly painful."[179] B. F. Nichols called oxen poor dumb brutes, but he thought they "should have been decently buried at death and a monument erected over their graves reciting their patient and silent suffering and their faithful service to the cause of emigration to the far West."[180]

[173] Knight, "Iowa to the Columbia River," 14 April 1853, Holmes, *Covered Wagon Women,* 6:38; Rockefellow, The Story of My Life, Southern Oregon Historical Society; Fosdick, Across the Plains in '61, Beinecke Library; Lieuallen, The Journal of 1864, End of the Oregon Trail Interpretive Center; and Porter, "Iowa to Oregon, 1864," in Holmes, *Covered Wagon Women,* 9:16, 26, 30.

[174] Sharp, *Brief Account of the Experiences,* 3.

[175] Ackley, *Crossing the Plains,* in Levy, *They Saw the Elephant,* 20.

[176] Buckingham, "Crossing the Plains," in Holmes, *Covered Wagon Women,* 3:18.

[177] Nixon, Diary of an Overland Journey, 30 May 1849, 13.

[178] Stevens, Trip of Capt. Archibald Sampson RoBards, 27 June 1849, Western Historical Manuscript Collection.

[179] Abbey, *California. A Trip across the Plains,* 10 August 1850, 56.

[180] Nichols, "Across the Plains in 1844," chapter 9.

THE LONG WAY AROUND: THE PECULIARITIES OF WAGON ROADS

The very word "pioneer" derives from the military, where it described units sent ahead to prepare the way for an army. The first trains to use the Oregon and California trails literally had to pioneer a road: they had to bridge rivers, excavate approaches to river crossings that could not be bridged, clear away rocks and boulders, fell trees and cut through thickets, and break trail through sagebrush— a brutal task that often left a team's bloody forelegs stripped to the bone. In the early years of overland travel, changing weather conditions often swamped last year's trail so that the basic pioneering work had to be done all over again. This made the earliest journeys immensely more difficult than those who came after thousands of men and women and their loyal animals had helped transform a trail into a national road.

"The character of terrain has been the first and often the final consideration in the making of any trail," observed Dale L. Morgan, the dean of overland historians. The way a wagon and its teams coped with different obstacles was the second major factor that defined these roads, and this meant that an overland trail had entirely different requirements than a modern highway.[181] The need for wood, grass, and water—"the great staples of an overland journey"—dictated the course a wagon trail followed. Wood could be dispensed with when necessary, but grass and water were essential to the survival of a train's draft animals, and so to the survival of the emigrants themselves.[182]

These unbending realities, along with an ox's natural inclination to seek the easiest way between and through virgin sagebrush, meant wagon roads seldom followed a direct course or even approximated the shortest distance between two points. It explains why wagon roads looked more like sine waves than straight lines, sometimes becoming what a frustrated James Frazier Reed called "a perfect snake trail." Wagon traces followed ridges and rivers—"where water ran, ordinarily, there would a trail go also, through mountains or around them. A gap in a mountain range, whether or not low enough to allow passage of a stream, would exert an equal compulsion." Such trails were worked out at the cost of "laborious trial and painful error," Morgan noted. "They wander off to one side or the other of our relentlessly engineered modern highways, for grass, wood, and water are no longer, as they once were, controlling factors in the location of a road, and motorists are content to take the long way around rather than traverse a steep divide which wagons routinely challenged."[183]

---

[181] Korns and Morgan, *West from Fort Bridger*, 1–2.

[182] "The Little Blue Eighteen Years Ago," Waterville, Kansas, *Telegraph*, 14 January 1870.

[183] Korns and Morgan, *West from Fort Bridger*, 1.

Except in difficult terrain, wagon trains seldom kept to a single narrow track, and wagons never traveled in single-file lines if they had an opportunity to spread out to avoid dust. Some of the trail's better physical traces show that wagons often traveled five or six abreast and in many places these tracks spread out over hundreds of feet. In addition, these roads were constantly evolving as travelers found shorter and easier routes. "The roads from St. Joseph to the agency are very hilly and crooked," William Porter noted in 1848. "Here are several branches to the road any of which will be right. Keep the best which lies on the dividing ridge."[184] Given the obstacles that stood in their way—swamps, rivers, gullies and gulches, sand dunes that buried wheels and tormented teams, oceans of sage-brush that could stand taller than a man's head, and hills and mountainsides that sometimes led to sheer cliffs—it is hardly surprising that wagons followed the path of least resistance. In broken country, they sought the ridges and dry high ground that avoided ravines, streams, and mudholes—"there being no road and the mud being so deep it was necessary to keep on the highest ground so that we could go at all; so by keeping on the dividing ridges between the streams we were enabled to reach the trail," Thomas Shaw recalled after the deluge at the start of the 1844 emigration.[185]

While he traced the divide that separated the waters of the Nemaha and Kansas rivers, Lewis Beers outlined the logic of traveling along ridges: "The object is to shun the streams and deep crevices that would have to be crossed if [the road] ran nearer either. There is scarcely a place on the road that you cannot see streams and timbers on each side of you. In the distance but far below you there are many places you can see the heads of creeks," each of which would require crossing on a lower route.[186] "We passed from a hill to the side of a bluff, upon a high, narrow ridge of just sufficient width upon the top for the wagon road, the sides descending very steep each way," James Field wrote on the Snake River in 1845. "Just as the wagons were upon this a gale of wind in advance of a thunder shower struck us, and blew with such violence directly across the track that it seemed as if wagons, teams and all would be blown away."[187]

Inevitably the ridges descended to watercourses that could be crossed or followed, and again, terrain dictated where a wagon or rider would go. The unfortunate teams that followed James Hudspeth down the Weber River in 1846 had to wade in the stream to get by the narrows at the mouth of the canyon. Wagons and animals went "directly down the foaming riverbed, full of great boulders,"

[184] Porter, Oregon Trail Diary, 7 May 1848.
[185] Shaw, "Reminiscence of 1844," *Oregon Statesman,* 12 June 1885.
[186] Beers, Diary, 7 May 1852, cited in Lewin and Taylor, *The St. Joe Road,* 22.
[187] Field, Crossing the Plains, 14 August 1845, Oregon Historical Society.

Heinrich Lienhard wrote. "We had to be very careful lest we lose our footing on the slippery rocks under the water and ourselves be swept down the rapid, foaming torrent" (The ordeal destroyed the last of Lienhard's three pairs of boots).[188] As Edward M. Kern rode down the Humboldt River in 1845, "the high, rocky ridges that bound the bottom came so close to the banks of the river, we were obliged to pass in the water," which played hob with an animal's hooves.[189]

Just as their massive herds dominated the Great Plains, the bison even affected the physical nature of the Platte River road. Wagons faced on odd challenge in buffalo country: the deep ruts the animals cut across the trail. With their tendency to travel in single file when going to the Platte to water, the bison created trench-like paths that proved hazardous for passing wagons. "They invariably travel the same routes over and over again, until they make a path some ten inches deep and twelve inches wide," Peter Burnett recalled. These paths often resulted in broken axles. His train had been warned of the danger, Burnett recalled, and each wagon carried an extra axle.[190]

A singular fact about wagon roads—and a surprise to people accustomed to engineered roads—was that when confronted with hills or mountains, they went straight up and over rather than around, and seldom used switchbacks to surmount a steep hill. This was especially effective for ox-teams, which could climb grades steeper than those that would defeat the most powerful locomotive. When teams were not enough, enterprising travelers used ropes and tackles to haul wagons over passes. Descending a steep slope with locked wheels and a fallen tree dragging behind a wagon, however, was much more difficult and dangerous than climbing one. Near City of Rocks, Leander V. Loomis captured the awe this "wild uninhabited yet majestic and beautiful Land" inspired among those who wandered "up and down along the paths which nature had formed in some places leaving walls on either side some 300 feet high, almost perpendicular, [which] causes man to Gase with astonishment, and wonder, at natures doings."[191]

THE MYSTERIES OF PACKING: OVERLAND TRAVEL WITHOUT WAGONS

Wagons had great advantages for families moving west: they provided a home on wheels that offered shelter and a way to transport a few personal possessions and enough provisions to ward off hunger. A wagon afforded refuge from extreme weather, and it could haul a person debilitated by accident or disease. Wagons

---

[188] Lienhard, "The Lienhard Journal," 6 August 1846.
[189] Kern, "Journal of Mr. Edward M. Kern of an Exploration," 11 November 1845.
[190] Burnett, *Recollections and Opinions of an Old Pioneer,* 108.
[191] Loomis, *Journal of the Birmingham Emigrating Company,* 7 July 1850, 77–78.

gave men and women alike a sense of security, but many guidebooks advised single men to have nothing to do with wagons or teams, for packing on horseback or in mule trains was quicker and cheaper than wagon travel. "If I were to come to this country again, I would not come with wagons, but would pack animals, either mules or horses—mules are rather better than horses generally for packing, but the latter for riding," John Bidwell advised not long after reaching California. "This journey with packed animals could be performed in three months, provided the company have a pilot (and surely no other company than ours ever started without one)." J. M. Shively estimated that with a saddle horse and pack mule to change every day, a man could make the trip in seventy or eighty days, while wagons could not hope to take less than four months.[192] Like many early guidebook authors, Shively was being overly optimistic, but in 1845 Elijah White and three companions crossed from Oregon to Independence in ninety days.[193]

"Packing is an art, and something that only an experienced mountaineer can do well so as to save his animal and keep his pack from falling off," Bidwell recalled.[194] After Jacob Snyder and his friends abandoned their wagon at Fort Bridger in 1845, Snyder expressed his appreciation for the kind attention and assistance of Joseph Walker and Louis Vasquez in initiating them into the mysteries of packing, a "mode of travel being entirely novel to us."[195] Although free trappers had long relied on pack trains to supply them and haul their furs out of the mountains, no one knew the art of packing better than Mexicans. "They understand the habits, disposition, and powers of the mule perfectly, and will get more work out of him than any other men I have ever seen," trail veteran Randolph Marcy reported.[196]

Frederick Wislizenus described the usual way to pack a mule in 1839: "The baggage is divided into two equal parts, each part firmly bound up, and hung by loops on either side of the yoke-shaped pack saddle." A "lash rope" made of stout buffalo leather was wound around the body of the animal, "and then in diamond shaped turns as firmly as possible around the pack." Wislizenus's baggage weighed 150 to 200 pounds, "a quite ordinary load for a mule," but he quickly found that like most novices he had to repack repeatedly until he had mastered the art.[197]

Twenty years later, Captain Marcy advised making up two packs of equal weight and bulk to keep the saddle from swaying and chafing the animal's back.

[192] Shively, "The Shively Guide," in Morgan, *Overland in 1846*, 734; and Nunis, *The Bidwell-Bartleson Party*, 67.

[193] White, "Overland Mail from Oregon," *Independence Express*, 17 November 1845, in *Times and Seasons*, 1 December 1845, 1,045.

[194] Bidwell, "The First Emigrant Train," in Nunis, *The Bidwell-Bartleson Party*, 112–13.

[195] Snyder, "Diary While Crossing the Plains," 28 July 1845, 243.

[196] Marcy, *The Prairie Traveler*, 98.

[197] Wislizenus, *A Journey to the Rocky Mountains*, 28.

"Packing"—driving mules loaded with the bare essentials for an overland trek—proved to be the cheapest, quickest, and most dangerous way for a young man to cross the plains. Here Nick Eggenhofer pictured a packer whose goggles mark him as a veteran of the trail. From the artist's *Wagons, Mules and Men: How the Frontier Moved West.* Courtesy Evelyn E. Herman.

After saddling the animal, two men standing on opposite sides of the mule each took a pack and threw it over the pommel and cantle of the saddle. They secured the packs with ropes about six feet long that were "drawn as tight at every turn as the two men on the sides can pull it . . . diagonally across the packs as often as its length admits," made fast to one of the rings on the saddle, "and securely tied in a slip-knot." Marcy believed 125 pounds was an appropriate load for a mule on a long journey and advised that kettles, tin vessels, and anything that might rattle and spook the animals should be firmly lashed to the packs. A good packsaddle was essential, but Marcy found many so poorly designed that they were "mere instruments of torture upon the backs of the poor brutes, lacerating them cruelly, and causing continued pain." He recommended the packsaddles T. Grimsley made at Saint Louis. They were, he testified, the best he had ever seen.[198]

Until after the gold rush, improvised contraptions built from whatever wagon boards and spokes were available far outnumbered professional saddles like those Grimsley offered. "If a house or barn, or a bridge, was to be built, we had men who could have gone to work intelligently, but a pack-saddle—'that was a horse of another color,'" David Shaw wryly observed. Most of his companions had never seen a packsaddle, but they had watched Kit Carson mend his at Laramie in 1850 and every one was ready to do his part. "Two crosses, two feet in length and about fifteen inches apart, with a board beneath the lower extremities to rest upon either side of the animals' backs, and the upper projections upon which to hang our blankets, frying pans, coffee pots, etc., was what we evolved from our limited knowledge and common sense to constitute a pack-saddle," Shaw recalled.[199]

Many a greenhorn who took up packing left a comical account of learning to do it properly, and watching them do it "was better than a theatre," Mark Manlove recalled.[200] "It was but a few minutes before the packs began to turn; horses became scared, mules kicked, oxen jumped and bellowed, and articles were scattered in all directions," John Bidwell recalled.[201] "Not one of us had ever seen a mule packed before this morning," Edwin Bryant wrote after leaving Fort Laramie. New Mexican traders gave Bryant and his companions their first very valuable lesson, which was followed by extensive trial and error: he had not gone two miles before several of his bulky, unbalanced packs "were swinging under the bellies of the animals." Rearranging them "to the best of our poor skill, (and very poor skill it was)" did not help. To Bryant's credit, he was able to laugh at his ignorance and turn to a proper source for enlightenment. "The mules, stupid as

---

[198] Marcy, *The Prairie Traveler,* 98–100, 109, 118–19.

[199] Shaw, *Eldorado,* 44–45.

[200] Manlove, An Overland Trip to the California Gold Fields, California State Library.

[201] Bidwell, "The First Emigrant Train," in Nunis, *The Bidwell-Bartleson Party,* 113.

we regarded them, knew more about this business than we did; and several times I thought I could detect them in giving a wise wink and sly leer, as much as to say, that we were perfect novices, and if they could speak, they would give us the benefit of their advice and instruction. A Mexican pack-mule is one of the most sagacious and intelligent quadrupeds that I have ever met with," he wrote.[202]

A pack train's faster pace came at no small cost. "The pack mule companies are a pitiful set of slaves," Dr. Joseph Middleton observed. "They have to sit on their mules roasting in the sun all day. If they get down to walk or rest themselves they must be bothered leading the animals. When they stop at night they must unpack everything. In the morning they have to repack; when they noon they have to unpack, picket and repack. There is no shelter for them here."[203] Loading and unloading usually took longer than hitching a team to a wagon and demanded skills few pioneers possessed. Plus packing entailed substantial risk: you could not carry enough food for the entire trip or ride a mule after breaking a leg. Every early pack train ran out of food, sometimes long before reaching their goal: Lansford Hastings's 1845 party was in a starving condition when it reached both Fort Hall and Sutters Fort. "The truly impoverished condition of our larder," Edmund Bryant wrote while camped in the Sierra Nevada, "produced a slight sensation of uneasiness and regret."[204] Yet parties learned to deal with problems such as a disabling injury. Randolph Marcy described how to build a rectangular litter by lashing two twenty-foot poles with two three-foot crosspieces placed six feet apart. This supported a stout piece of canvas, blanket, or hide for a bed that could be carried between two horses or mules.[205]

In the early days of overland emigration, few parties left the frontier as pack trains, but all the first pioneering trains eventually had to abandon their wagons and resort to improvised packsaddles. Lansford Hastings complained that it took much labor and inconvenience to convert from wagons to packsaddles on his trip west in 1842.[206] The technique grew increasingly popular over time, especially for parties crossing west-to-east: during the gold rush it was the preferred way for single men to get to the gold fields. By the end of the 1850s, a properly organized and equipped pack train could travel with comfort and celerity, taking shortcuts and crossing the country in almost any direction without depending on roads, Captain Marcy wrote. And packers avoided "many of the troubles and detentions attendant upon the transit of cumbersome wagon trains."[207]

---

[202] Bryant, *What I Saw in California,* 28 June 1846, 114–15.

[203] Middleton, Diary and Letters, 30 July 1849, Beinecke Library, 52.

[204] Bryant, *What I Saw in California,* 27 August 1846, 235.

[205] Marcy, *The Prairie Traveler,* 150.

[206] Hastings, *The Emigrants' Guide,* 19.

[207] Marcy, *The Prairie Traveler,* 98.

Habited Like Myself, in Rags: Clothing

When Americans set out for Oregon or California, they usually dressed in the clothing they had worn at home. Farmers and their wives wore the clothes they used in the field or the kitchen, while doctors, attorneys, preachers, and gentlewomen donned more elaborate styles that reflected their social status—at least until such outfits fell apart. Women's fashions posed a number of challenges to prairie travel, as historian Margaret F. Walker observed, since they were purposefully designed to exaggerate and distort a woman's body "so that she had no choice but to be delicate, pure, and useful." A well-dressed mid-nineteenth-century woman was ensconced in a whalebone corset, as much as forty pounds of dresses and petticoats, and sleeves and sloped shoulders that made it impossible to bend over or raise her arms.[208] Rural women and men generally wore more practical clothing, but everyone dressed with a formality that would surprise a modern observer.

Based on standards of modesty in force throughout the trails era, both sexes wore clothing that covered them from ankle to wrist. Men and women concealed every bit of skin but their hands and faces, and women did their best to avoid exposing those to the sun, since suntans were not in style for anyone. Swiss emigrant Heinrich Lienhard's description of a "repulsive creature" he met on the trail reflects how those who defied these conventions appeared to their more prim contemporaries. "He was driving a yoke of oxen and a cart, was barefoot, his trousers had large holes in the knees that displayed his naked legs whenever he walked, and his shirt was even more ragged and barely afforded a covering for his arms."[209] Modesty had even sterner standards for women. "Rarely did we see any bright colors, even on rosy-cheeked girls," recalled Oregon emigrant Lucia Loraine Williams. "Flaming colors would not have been considered modest then."[210]

Convention played a much greater role in what emigrants wore on the trail than did convenience, but so did style. The traveling dresses of many of the very pretty young ladies he met on the trail in 1845, Lieutenant James Carleton reported, made "some pretensions to taste and fashion as well as comfort."[211] Captain Philip St. George Cooke heard the expedition spotted one young lady was "invested with a 'tournure'"—a bustle, sometimes stiffened with steel or whalebone strips, to accentuate a woman's backside. "Who would believe the tyrant Fashion held so wide a sway!" he marveled.[212]

---

[208] Walker, "All the Fantastic Costumes," 12–13. This article and Christina May's *Pioneer Clothing on the Oregon Trail* are the best studies of trail clothing.

[209] Lienhard, *A Pioneer at Sutter's Fort,* 160–61.

[210] Williams, "A Letter to My Mother," 16 September 1851, in Holmes, *Covered Wagon Women,* 3:153–54.

[211] Carleton, *The Prairie Logbooks,* 186.

[212] Cooke, *Scenes and Adventures,* 4 June 1845, 300.

As such comments indicate, women did not abandon their petticoats or corsets; practically everyone rigorously observed the era's strict standards of modesty, and chroniclers noted violations of the code. "The costume of these men," Edwin Bryant commented on meeting his first party of mountaineers, "was *outré* surpassing description."[213] As they approached Fort Laramie, Francis Parkman mourned that he and his companions "had grown rather shabby; our clothes had burst into rags and tatters; and what was worse, we had very little means of renovation." The men were "totally averse to appearing in such plight among any society that could boast an approximation to the civilized," and they stopped on the muddy North Platte "to make our toilet in the best way we could." The operation may not have improved their appearance much, but it gave them "a feeling of greatly increased respectability." Eventually Parkman gave up and adopted the red flannel shirt, moccasins, and buckskins of the trappers.[214]

Contemporaneous artwork shows that emigrants hewed to "civilized" standards of modesty. Trail wear had features that defy modern notions about what people wore on the frontier, as William Tylee Rainey revealed in his 1853 group portrait, "Advice on the Prairie," which pictured an emigrant family entranced by the stories of a veteran frontiersman dressed in moccasins and deerskin pants—but wearing a worn but formal frock coat. A male emigrant wears a vest and open collar, but the other two men wear frock coats, and even the boy listening in awe is sporting a tie. A young mother looks on, her head covered in a shawl and her full dress sheltering an unknown number of petticoats and undergarments.

Men's clothing was plainer than women's. The men he met marching up the Platte in 1845 generally "were clad in coarse homespun cloth, with broad brimmed glazed hats. Some had buckskin hunting frocks, but most of them wore loose blouses made of Kentucky jane," James Carleton wrote. "These were secured around their waists by the broad leathern belts—and outside all hung their powder horns and ball pouches."[215] Francis Parkman met the main body of California emigrants at Fort Laramie in 1846 as they were disposing of their "copious stock of Missouri whisky, by drinking it on the spot." These American backwoodsmen were clad in brown homespun, but their former leader, the tall, lank William Russell, harangued them while dressed in a dingy broadcloth coat and "drunk as a pigeon."[216]

"Hickory shirts," cheap shirts made of cotton with checked or pinstriped patterns, were particularly popular on the trail. "Let each man and lad be provided

---

[213] Bryant, *What I Saw in California,* 23 May 1846.

[214] Parkman, *The California and Oregon Trail,* chapter 8.

[215] Carleton, *The Prairie Logbooks,* 181–82. "Jane" was a fabric similar to today's denim.

[216] Parkman, *The California and Oregon Trail,* 72, 8, 121, 146, 156; and Parkman, *The Journals of Francis Parkman,* 28 June 1846, 447.

with five or six hickory shirts, one or two pair of buckskin pantaloons, a buckskin coat or hunting shirt, two very wide-brimmed hats, wide enough to keep the mouth from the sun," John Shively advised. He thought women needed nothing more than their ordinary clothing at home, but most women disagreed.[217] "Our clothing was made suitable for travling, dresses of plaid linsy, aprons of Scotch gingam, high in the neck, with long sleeves, belt waists and little collars. No more use for low necked, short sleeved, pretty little white dresses, with blue and pink sashes, and cute little slippers," recalled Virginia Reed Murphy, thirty-three years after she went west in 1846. "All those things were givin away. I remember when I first dressed up in my uniform for the planes, as we called it. How strangely I felt. The very clothing seemed to indicate that we were expected to endure something."[218]

Early recommendations about what clothing emigrants should take on the trail could be frustratingly vague. "Every person should be well supplied with boots and shoes, and in fact with every kind of clothing," Joel Palmer wrote in his 1847 journal of travels.[219] Experience improved the advice. "The coat should be short and stout, the shirt of red or blue flannel, such as can be found in almost all the shops on the frontier: this, in warm weather, answers for an outside garment," Randolph Marcy suggested. He recommended thick, soft woolen pants reinforced with soft buckskin where they came in contact with the saddle, which would make them more durable and comfortable. For a three-month expedition, a man should take four silk handkerchiefs; four pairs of woolen socks and two pairs of cotton; three pounds bar soap for washing clothes and one pound castile soap; three towels; two pairs of cotton drawers, "stout shoes," two flannel shirts and woolen undershirts; two toothbrushes; a broad-brimmed soft felt hat; a comb and brush; and a belt-knife and small whetstone. Marcy recommended using India rubber, a natural form of rubber introduced in 1843 and also known as gutta-percha, for ground-covers, knapsacks, tents, and ponchos. In addition, Marcy suggested carrying stout linen thread, large needles, beeswax, a few buttons, pins, and a thimble in a small buckskin or stout cloth bag. An awl and buckskin strings were essential for repairing clothing and footwear, and he recommended using green or blue-tinted wire-rimmed glasses, particularly to avoid snow blindness. These articles, with a coat and overcoat, he wrote, "complete the wardrobe."[220]

Not quite. J. Quinn Thornton considered one item essential to deal with the "intolerable" dust, which his party suffered from for weeks if not months. He

[217] Shively, "The Shively Guide," in Morgan, *Overland in 1846*, 736.
[218] Murphy to McGlashan, 8 June 1879, in Johnson, "1879," 3.
[219] Palmer, *Journal of Travels*, 259.
[220] Marcy, *The Prairie Traveler*, 39, 48, 136–37.

recommended buying several pairs of goggles for each member of a family to create "a reserve for any emergency." Thornton claimed dust had rendered one Mr. McKissick blind near Fort Laramie, and he noted that such eyewear could be purchased in the states for less than fifty cents, but at times he "would have given fifty dollars for a pair of goggles."[221]

Keturah Belknap described in detail how she prepared for a six-month trip in fall 1847, and her report conveys a sense of the endless work a woman tackled on the frontier. "There was nothing done or talked of but what had Oregon in it and the loom was banging and the wheel buzzing and trades being made from daylight till bed time," she wrote. The death of her infant daughter left her exhausted, but she was resolved to try to make enough clothes to last the rest of her family a year. She cut out four muslin shirts for her husband and two suits for her young son. "With what he has that will last him (if he lives)" until he had outgrown them, she wrote with a realistic fatalism. She worked through the winter spinning the wool for the men's outer garments. "The first thing is to lay plans and then work up to the program," Belknap reasoned, and her program included making a linen wagon cover and a number of large sacks.

She spun wool thread during the evening as her husband read to her, and her mother and a neighbor wove the thread into cloth. "I must work almost day and night to get the filling ready to keep the loom busy." After New Year she decided to make a muslin liner for the heavy linen wagon cover "so we can keep warm and dry," she wrote. "They both have to be sewed real good and strong and I have to spin the thread and sew all these long seams with my fingers, then I have to make a new feather tick for my bed. I will put the feathers of two beds into one tick and sleep on it." She dipped enough candles to last a winter, made two pairs of jeans, a vest, and a coat for her husband and traded dishes for her neighbors' sewing services. She washed and packed everything and decided to start out wearing old clothes "and when we can't wear them any longer [we] will leave them on the road." Finally, she cooked enough food to tide her family over until they got used to camp fare. She baked bread and crackers, fried donuts, cooked a chicken and boiled a ham, and stewed some dried fruits. "I think we are fixed very comfortable for the trip," wrote this remarkable woman, who gave birth to a son that summer in eastern Oregon.[222]

In contrast to Belknap's endless work, the prosperous Margaret Frink hired a seamstress to make her a full stock of clothing, and in addition to her clothes and her husband's, she "packed a trunk full of dress goods not yet made up." Frink

---

[221] Thornton, *Oregon and California in 1848*, 1:121–22.
[222] Belknap, "The Commentaries," in Holmes, *Covered Wagon Women*, 1:191, 213–15.

persisted in carrying a flatiron "across the plains with remonstrance" and felt vindicated when she came to the first mining camp in the Sierra Nevada, where a trader asked her if she had any flatirons to sell. She was delighted, since she now had a chance to at least make freight money, and she asked a "California price" for it, five dollars. The trader laughed and told her flatirons "were plentier than cobble-stones in San Francisco, having been shipped from the eastern cities in great quantities."[223]

"A suitable dress for prairie traveling is of great import to health and comfort," Captain Marcy advised. To a modern eye, covered-wagon women—in their heavy woolen clothing, long sleeves, and billowing dresses—appear as overdressed as Bedouins, but the woolens, sunbonnets, and long dresses that dominated styles from the 1840s to the 1870s proved practical for the rigors of overland travel. Like a Bedouin's robes, loose-fitting wool garments trapped perspiration but circulated air efficiently and helped prevent both sunstroke and dehydration. "Cotton or linen fabrics do not sufficiently protect the body against the direct rays of the sun at midday, nor against rains or sudden changes of temperature," Marcy wrote. "Wool, being a non-conductor, is the best material for this mode of locomotion, and should always be adopted for the plains."[224] Long dresses could be dangerous, since they caused any number of accidents by getting caught in a wagon's running gear, but they also protected a woman's legs from sagebrush and cactus. These fashions provided a measure of modesty, and when combined with split underwear, a long dress allowed a woman to relieve herself without undue exposure.

"Our 'slatted sunbonnets' were comfort and a protection as well," wrote Lucia Loraine Williams. "The sunbonnet kept the head from direct exposure to the heat and dust, protected the face and neck from tan, sunburn and freckles. They were a boon to women with delicate skin like my own. These head coverings were by no means beautiful in those days." Usually made of gingham or seer-sucker, most bonnets were brown, black, or gray. "Slat" bonnets inserted thin pieces of wood, whalebone, or another rigid material in the brim to extend it and provide more shade. Long "curtains" reached to the shoulders and neck, which sheltered a woman from the sun and offered some relief from the pervasive dust and alkali. "These old-fashioned sunbonnets may not have been beautiful," Williams observed, "but they were a godsend to women on that long journey."[225]

Stranded in Great Salt Lake City for the winter, Lucy Rutledge Cooke mourned that she was poorly off for clothing. She had worn her single pink bonnet "until it

---

[223] Frink, "Adventures of a Party of Gold Seekers," 5 September 1850, Ibid., 2:59, 157.

[224] Marcy, The Prairie Traveler, 37.

[225] Williams, "A Letter to My Mother," 16 September 1851, in Holmes, Covered Wagon Women, 3:15–54.

was really so mean looking I cant use it no longer." Once she arrived in El Dorado she would stop dressing as a poor woman, but among the Mormons she cared "little for appearances for there's no one here I care a snap for." Using her bonnet and a worn-out cloak, Cooke made her toddler, who was "a great hand to kiss," a black watered-silk hood and a petticoat. Cooke had saved a piece of red flannel to make the child a best dress. Clothing was extremely scarce in Utah, and she and her husband tried to sell "every thread" they could. Her husband traded his best coat for four hundred pounds of flour, and she hoped to trade a satin dress for a cow. She "swapt" a calico frock for a black alpaca dress. "I shall be glad of a black dress on the road," she wrote. "I am quite out of under clothes & cannot get anything in the city: theres not a yard to be bought." She did, however, make a chemise out of a large nightdress.[226]

The clothing of mid-nineteenth-century America may have adapted well to wagon travel, but the standard footwear was not up to the challenge. For horsemen, Randolph Marcy recommended "woolen socks and stout boots, coming up well at the knees, and made large, so as to admit the pants," which guarded against rattlesnake bites. He thought shoes were much better for walking than boots, since they were lighter and did not cramp the ankles, but both boots and shoes disintegrated when faced with a two-thousand-mile walk and challenging trail conditions.[227] One by one, Rachel Bond threw her seven pairs of shoes away because they hurt her feet so much, and she walked barefoot from South Pass to California.[228] "Everybody's shoes gave out and we bartered with Indians for moccasins," Harriet Scott Palmer recalled, "but that didn't help much about the prickly pears."[229] Whatever limitations moccasins might have, many emigrants arrived at their destination either barefoot or wearing the comfortable and tough moccasins they had purchased from Indians. Historian H. H. Bancroft noted that moccasins took the place of boots and shoes in Oregon in 1844 and were the almost-universal footwear.[230]

Waterproof rubber was available to help emigrants in their efforts to stay dry, and John C. Frémont took inflatable (and leaky) rubber boats on his second and third expeditions. Six days west of Fort Laramie, Narcissa Whitman wrote, "Our saddle blankets, with our India rubber cloaks, were our beds." On the Columbia River, she rolled her featherbed "and blankets in my India-rubber cloak, which preserved them quite well from the rain, so that nights I slept warm and comfortable

---

[226] Cooke to "Dearest Polly," October 1852, in Holmes, *Covered Wagon Women,* 4:270–71, 279–80.
[227] Marcy, *The Prairie Traveler,* 37, 39.
[228] Walker, "All the Fantastic Costumes," 13.
[229] Palmer, *Crossing over the Great Plains by Ox-Wagon,* 4.
[230] Bancroft, *History of Oregon,* 1:456.

as ever." (She also had a life preserver, "so that if we fall into the water we shall not drown. They are made of India-rubber cloth, air-tight, and when filled with air and placed under the arm will prevent one from sinking.")[231] While wintering in Salt Lake, Lucy Cooke's husband unwisely had traded away his overcoat and now wore a waterproof blanket "with a hole cut in the centre for his head to go through," which she said was the "Spanish fashion" in California.[232] Some overlanders even had air mattresses, for one group of Forty-niners tried to cross a river on their airtight India rubber beds.[233] Francis Parkman found that his India rubber ground cloth "excluded the water to admiration; but when at length it accumulated and began to run over the edges, they served equally well to retain it, so that toward the end of the night we were unconsciously reposing in small pools of rain."[234]

However carefully emigrants dressed for the journey, the trek left them ragged and dirty by the end of the trail. At Oregon City in fall 1843, a party of packers that had crossed the Cascade Range were compelled to buy back their livestock from Indians who had found or appropriated the animals. "Some of them had to give the Indians their shirts to have the animals brought back," Nineveh Ford recalled, "so that when they got in they had not any shirts themselves—only their coats on."[235] Upon reaching California in 1849, for Luzena Stanley Wilson the sight of a white shirt revived her "languishing spark of womanly vanity." In her embarrassment, she "drew down my ragged sun-bonnet over my sunburned face, and shrank from observation. My skirts were worn off in rags above my ankles; my sleeves hung in tatters above my elbows; my hands brown and hard, were gloveless; around my neck was tied a cotton square, torn from a discarded dress; the soles of my leather shoes had long ago parted company with the uppers; and my husband and children and all the camp, were habited like myself, in rags."[236]

After his 1853 trip, James Longmire recalled arriving in Oregon with "torn and ragged pants and coat, my cap tattered and torn, and with one boot on, the other foot covered with an improvised moccasin made of a piece of cowhide from one of the animals we had killed." Several gentlemen turned out to welcome his company. "My dress was a fair sample of that of the rest of our party, and when together, we felt pretty well, all being in the same fashion; but when brought face to face with well dressed men I must confess I felt somewhat embarrassed."[237]

---

[231] Whitman to "Dear Sister," 3 June 1836, in Eells, *Marcus Whitman*, 59.

[232] Cooke to "Dearest Polly," October 1852, "Letters on the Way to California," in Holmes, *Covered Wagon Women*, 4:271.

[233] Anonymous, Diary, 2 July 1849, in Mason Diaries, Beinecke Library.

[234] Parkman, *The California and Oregon Trail*, 59.

[235] Ford, The Pioneer Road Makers, Bancroft Library, 22–23.

[236] Wilson, *Luzena Stanley Wilson, '49er*, 9.

[237] Longmire, "James Longmire, Pioneer," *Tacoma Sunday Ledger*, 21 August 1892, 9–10.

James Nesmith came up with his own solution for his worn-out rags. After reaching Fort Vancouver in October 1843, his party spent most of their money on provisions and hickory shirts, "consigning those that had done such long and continuous service, with their inhabitants, to the Columbia."[238]

Do Not Depend on Game: Provisions and Supplies

During the first years of overland emigration, no one knew exactly how to prepare for the trip, or even how much food it would take to cross the plains, and few parties made it to Oregon with any food left. "I cannot urge you too strongly to be sure of plenty of provisions," warned Jesse Looney from Waiilatpu in 1843. "Do not depend on game, you may have some and you may not—it is uncertain." Looney had brought plenty of flour, "but most of the company were out long before they got here, and there is little or nothing in the way of provision to be had at the forts on the way." He advised overlanders to lay in food to last at least five months.[239] Trail veteran Peter Lassen provided a common sense way for travelers to calculate how much food they would need: "It is supposed that most men of family know what his family will use in a month;" Lassen wrote, "then he can calculate from 4 to 5 months on the road."[240]

Hard experience produced fairly useful advice. Emigrants took at least two hundred pounds of flour or meal, one hundred and fifty pounds of bacon, ten pounds of coffee, twenty pounds of sugar and salt, and "such other provisions as he may prefer," Lansford Hastings recommended in his 1845 guide. (Having provided such sound advice, the author ignored it and soon set out from Independence with a pack train that almost starved to death—repeatedly.) Hastings's list, and virtually every other catalog of recommended provisions, shows how much trail travelers relied on flour and pork, particularly cured pork.[241] "Bacon" in the 1840s included what emigrants called "fat bacon" (the product sold today), cured pork sides, and shoulders—virtually every part of a hog, except its head and hams. The spare ribs were left in while the bacon cured to prevent it from "rusting." Since it was pickled and smoked, it could endure almost anything almost forever.[242]

To make the trip, Joel Palmer estimated, each adult required two hundred pounds of flour, thirty pounds of "pilot bread" (hardtack), seventy-five pounds

[238] Nesmith, in Geer, *Fifty Years in Oregon*, 157.

[239] Looney to Bond, 27 October 1843, Oregon Historical Society.

[240] Lassen, "From the Emigrants," 16 July 1848, *The Brunswicker*, 9 September 1848, 1/2.

[241] Hastings, *The Emigrants' Guide*, 143–146.

[242] Williams, *Wagon Wheel Kitchens*, 24–25.

of bacon, ten pounds of rice, five pounds of coffee, two pounds of tea, twenty pounds of sugar, a half bushel of dried beans, a bushel of dried fruit, ten pounds of salt, about a half bushel of parched corn and corn meal, a small keg of vinegar, and two pounds of saleratus. (The saleratus—baking soda—only had to last until the mineral beds near Independence Rock, where emigrants could shovel it up. "If I were to tell you that we crossed a lake of saleratus, you would scarcely believe me," wrote Daniel Toole, "but it is true, we traveled over them with our teams; and used it in our bread, and it is as good, if not better than any you buy in the store."[243]) Palmer's diet provided at least a little variety, and he added an encouraging suggestion that travelers should take as many "good things" as they could carry, "for whatever is good at home, is none the less so on the road."[244]

Given the total absence of fruit, vegetables, and dairy products from most supply lists, it is a wonder more overlanders did not die of scurvy, let alone boredom. Knowledge of what to take improved over time, even if eating did not. "In the way of supplies there was flour, sugar, bacon and ham, tea, coffee, crackers, dried herring, a small quantity of corn starch, dried apples that we brought from Indiana, one bottle of pickles, cream of tartar and soda and that about made up the outfit," recalled Helen Carpenter. "One does like change," she noted after enduring the virtually changeless diet of a cross-country wagon trip, "and about the only change we have from bread and bacon is bacon and bread." (Carpenter protested that the boys had cooked so much bacon with Mrs. Dobbins's cold beans "that each bean had a rim of grease around it.")[245] One trail delicacy— bread dipped into hot bacon grease—was known as hot flour bread.[246]

Besides food, overland travel required a large pile of gear. Hastings recommended that emigrants take tents, tent poles, axes, spades, hoes, and sixty feet of strong rope for each horse or mule, with a supply of stakes, while physicians and surgeons should have a small assortment of medicine and a few surgical instruments. Tradesmen should take a few of their tools, which would always be needed along the way.[247] With a surprising nod to cleanliness, Lilburn Boggs recommended taking "dried fruit, beans, a good supply of hogs lard, and plenty of soap; the last article is important."[248] William Ide advised emigrants in 1845 to take fifteen pounds of tar and two pounds of rosin for each wagon, sixty-five feet of ¾-inch rope, one set of horseshoes and a hundred shoe nails for each horse,

[243] Toole to "Dear Brother," 2 August 1846, *Liberty Tribune*, 19 December 1846.

[244] Palmer, *Journal of Travels*, 260.

[245] Carpenter, "A Trip across the Plains," 93, 146.

[246] Williams, *Wagon Wheel Kitchens*, 23.

[247] Hastings, *The Emigrants' Guide*, 146.

[248] Boggs, "Route to the Pacific," *St. Louis Weekly Reveille*, 22 May 1848.

four ox shoes for each ox or cow, "and nails; one years clothing: tarpaulin, hat: one water proof cloak: one rifle 32 balls to the pound: 4 pounds of powder: ten pounds of lead: one thousand percussion caps: one belt, butcher knife, scabbard, shot pouch and powder horn: one canteen or tin cup, and two whips to each man: five pounds of salt to each head of cattle."[249] "Bring plenty of good strong rope, five or six hundred feet will not be too much," William Porter wrote in 1848.[250]

Elijah Bristow offered the folks back in Illinois advice on how to cross the plains in 1847: "Get good strong wagons, with five or six yoke of oxen to each, and make light yokes. Bale all your feathers, extra bedding, &c., by making a box to fit a mould." The bales should be as small as possible for easy handling. "Bring all your books in trunks or light boxes, your meat and flour (not superfine) in sacks," he recommended. "Rise early and keep moving. Do not push or fret your cattle by whipping them, for they will give out on the latter part of the road, where they are most needed—never get irritated. The road is the place to try men's souls; those who are clever there will be clever anywhere."[251]

Indian trade goods came in especially handy. John Wyeth described the cargo his cousin Nathaniel Wyeth hauled west in 1832 as "a gross of axes, a variety of articles, or '*goods*' so called, calculated for the Indian market, among which vermilion and other paints were not forgotten, glass beads, small looking-glasses, and a number of tawdry trinkets, cheap knives, buttons, nails, hammers, and a deal of those articles, on which young Indians of both sexes set a high value, and white men little or none."[252] Lansford Hastings recommended taking along beads, tobacco, handkerchiefs, blankets, butcher knives, fishhooks, and powder and lead. He suggested bringing "ready-made clothing," which was very much in demand by the tribes who were always eager to trade for "cheap, summer coats, pantaloons, vests and course, cheap shirts."[253] Samuel Hancock camped near a Platte River Indian village in 1845—it was probably a Lakota hunting camp— and his hosts showed him deer skins, buffalo robes, and many other "curious things" they wanted to trade. "They made us understand that they wanted any and every kind of clothing," he noted, "for which they would give us anything, in return."[254] Medorem Crawford advised his brothers to take a stock of common tobacco, plenty of ammunition, and as many small beads, strips of red cloth, flints, fishhooks, thread, coarse needles, and awls as possible, plus checked shirts and butcher knives "which you will need to buy ropes, moccasins, buffalo robes,

[249] Ide, "From Our Oregon Correspondent," 25 June 1845, *Sangamo Journal,* 4 September 1845.

[250] Porter to "Dear Father, Mother, Brothers and Sisters," 24 June 1848.

[251] Bristow, "For Oregon!" 4 April 1847, *Springfield Illinois Journal,* 11 November 1847.

[252] Wyeth, *Oregon,* 12.

[253] Hastings, *The Emigrants' Guide,* 146.

[254] Hancock, *The Narrative of Samuel Hancock,* 7.

salmon &c" from the Indians.[255] "You should bring some old flintlock guns to trade with the Snake Indians, they have the best horses on the route," Campbell Clarborne advised his family in 1845, "and some rings, trinkets and speckled calico shirts, cheap quality."[256]

The emigrants who went to Oregon with Andrew Jackson Chambers in 1845 "had spent, mostly, all their money for outfits and a great many even then, were very poorly provided with provisions for the trip."[257] In the early years of overland travel, however, cash was not very useful. "Money is of no value among the Indians," Edwin Bryant reported, although he thought traders would extort money from the emigrants whenever they could.[258] Lansford Hastings assured prospective travelers that if they equipped and supplied themselves according to his recommendations, they might embark "upon this wild, yet interesting excursion, with high prospects of enjoying many extraordinary and pleasing scenes;" and they could arrive at their destination "without suffering any of that extraordinary toil, unheard of hardship, or eminent danger." Best of all, an overland trip would cost the lucky emigrant "nothing but his time; for he can expend no money, as he travels entirely among tribes of barbarous Indians, who know nothing of money or its value."[259] The youthful Hastings (he was not yet twenty-five when he published his overland guide) was not the most unbiased or realistic of promoters, nor—as it turned out—the most trustworthy. Cash always made the trip substantially easier, and as trade and services such as ferries and bridges developed, it became a necessity.

"You may think the journey will be attended with many difficulties, but if you will fix as I advise it will be no killing job," wrote 1845 pioneer Elijah Bristow, with the optimism that permeated the first settlers of the Far West. "You will find the journey a summer excursion or a pleasure trip, if you are not too anxious. I have never repented for a single moment my undertaking; for it is the best effort of my life."[260]

JUMPING-OFF POINTS

Most travelers bound for Oregon or California in the 1840s set out from the complex of river towns that stretched north for more than two hundred miles along both banks of the Missouri River from Independence to Council Bluffs, including Westport, Fort Leavenworth, Weston, and—after 1843—Saint Joseph. Eventually, Fort

---

[255] Crawford to "Dear Brothers," 28 June 1845, in Stern, *Chiefs and Change in the Oregon Country,* 96.

[256] Walker to "Dear Brother, Sister and Friends," December 1845.

[257] Chambers, *Recollections,* 19.

[258] Bryant, *What I Saw in California,* 25 June 1846.

[259] Hastings, *The Emigrants' Guide,* 142, 146–47.

[260] Bristow, "For Oregon!" 4 April 1847, *Springfield Illinois Journal,* 11 November 1847.

Smith, Arkansas, competed with these northern "jumping-off points" as an outfitting center for expeditions to the West, but the first overland wagon parties set out from Independence. The farther north the departure point, the shorter the road to the Platte River, so the most popular jumping-off point gradually shifted north, first to Saint Joseph and by 1849 to Council Bluffs.

Sojourners bound for the Pacific could take their wagons across Missouri or Iowa to the frontier or book passage on a steamboat. A steamboat had first reached Council Bluffs in 1819, but twenty years later service was still sporadic. A few bold captains such as Joseph Sire went as far upriver as Fort Benton in present-day Montana, but many pilots considered Saint Joseph to be the head of navigation on the difficult and dangerous Missouri. During the opening years of overland emigration, most travelers drove their wagons to the frontier: only about a third of them arrived by steamboat.[261]

Since its founding in 1827, Independence had been the outfitting point for the caravans that served the Santa Fe and Rocky Mountain trade, so it was the logical place for wagon trains to start their journeys to Oregon and California. Its stores, stables, and blacksmith shops had long experience supplying western explorers and traders, and the town's merchants quickly adapted to equipping overland wagon trains. "Parties of emigrants, with their tents and wagons, would be encamped on open spots near the bank, on their way to the common rendezvous at Independence," Francis Parkman wrote as he traveled up the Missouri River. Every store was adapted to furnish outfits, and "the public houses were full of Santa Fe men and emigrants. Mules, horses, and waggons at every corner." Hardy, good-looking emigrants; "piratical-looking Mexicans" in broad, peaked hats; black slaves; and Delaware, Wyandotte, Osage, Sac and Fox, Shawnee, and Kanza tribesmen crowded the busy streets.[262]

J. Quinn Thornton called Independence "a great Babel upon the border of the wilderness."[263] Its population of about one thousand in 1846 lived around the courthouse on the public square, but solid frame and brick homes were replacing log cabins. An undulating and picturesque countryside blessed by "fat and exuberantly productive soil" surrounded the town and, as Edwin Bryant observed, in the spring every man in the vicinity of Independence seemed "to be actively and profitably employed."[264] The town site was more than three miles from the Missouri River,

---

[261] Faragher, *Women and Men on the Overland Trail*, 24–25.

[262] Parkman, *The California and Oregon Trail*, 11; and *The Journals of Francis Parkman*, 417, 419. Virtually every American account that mentioned Mexicans at Independence painted them as dark, dirty, and threatening. Conversely, Mexican descriptions of recent arrivals in California drew similar portraits of dark, dirty, and threatening Americans.

[263] Thornton, *Oregon and California in 1848*, 1:14.

[264] Bryant, *What I Saw in California*, 1.

which proved to be a disadvantage, and many overlanders preferred to land a dozen miles upriver at Westport, a village that Parkman thought bore all the characteristics of the extreme frontier.[265] The thirty or forty houses that made up this "border village" stood only a mile from the Missouri state line, and Westport was called "the usual rendezvous" for travelers bound for the Rocky Mountains as early as 1839.[266]

Thirty miles upriver from Westport stood the army's great citadel of the West—Fort Leavenworth, established in 1827. Four miles above the fort and across the river, former dragoon Joseph Moore founded Weston, Missouri, in 1837, and both sites became starting points for overland emigration after a wagon train first set out from the fort in 1844. Weston was a much better place to start the journey, wrote James Carleton, who accompanied the military expedition that improved the wagon road from Fort Leavenworth to the Oregon Trail in 1845. As he pointed out, the road began at the extreme western bend of the Missouri and avoided the Kansas River and several other bad crossings and "those notoriously adroit and impudent thieves, the Kanzas Indians" on the Independence Road. When the dragoons came in sight of a long train of wagons on the trace from Independence about 120 miles from the fort, Carleton learned it had been on the road for three weeks, while the soldiers had basically blazed their wagon road in six and a half days, traveling at a moderate pace to allow their horses to get accustomed to their change of diet from grain to nothing but grass.[267]

In 1843, Joseph Robidoux, then an old man but still "a very energetic, enterprising, shrewd business manager," founded Saint Joseph near his sixteen-year-old trading post in the Blacksnake Hills. Within a year of its birth, the boomtown began displacing Independence as the most popular outfitting depot.[268] When John Minto passed through on his way to join the 1844 emigration, he found a mere village of two or three stores and a single hotel, but by early 1846 the town's boosters were promoting it as the most "favorable point at which to rendezvous, and where all their necessary outfits can be procured, at the least possible expense." By then the town had about a thousand inhabitants and thirteen large stores that could furnish "every article in the Grocery and Dry Good line that may be required for an outfit, at prices as cheap, as the emigrant can bring them from St. Louis." Plenty of steamboats offered a passage to Saint Joseph for the same price as a ticket to Independence. There was a large flourmill within the city limits and a meatpacking plant that had slaughtered some five thousand

---

[265] Parkman, *The Journals of Francis Parkman,* 7 May 1846, 419.
[266] Wislizenus, *Journey to the Rocky Mountains,* 27.
[267] Carleton, *The Prairie Logbooks,* 170–71, 178–79.
[268] Lewin, Taylor, and Watkins, "St. Joseph, Missouri," 3.

hogs the previous winter. There were skilled blacksmiths, wagonwrights, saddle-makers, and mechanics who could "make or repair any article in their line, in a manner that will bear a successful comparison with similar establishments in the West, and at prices that will give satisfaction," advised "Friend of a Cause."

"Friend" claimed the "St. Joe Road" was one hundred miles shorter than any other approach to the Oregon Trail, which was not true, but he reported that about six hundred emigrants in 1844 and eighteen hundred in 1845 had outfit-ted at Saint Joseph, and they were happily writing back home and praising it as "being much the nearer and best route."[269] This enthusiastic booster was given to exaggeration, but whatever its actual merits as a place to start west, from the day it was founded Saint Joseph boomed. The town doubled its population between 1846 and the beginning of the gold rush, and then doubled it again before the frenzy was over.

The Independence Road and the St. Joe Road were the first major transporta-tion corridors to the Platte River, but soon a complex network of traces bound for the Oregon Trail crossed the northeastern corner of today's Kansas and south-eastern Nebraska. In terms of simple geography, Council Bluffs's location at the northern end of the jumping-off corridor had several advantages, especially for emigrants from Illinois and other northern states who could cross Iowa and reach the Platte River without having to detour south to Missouri. The region's mili-tary and trade history was even older than that of Independence. For decades the entire region was known as Council Bluffs after Lewis and Clark met with the Missouri and Otoe tribes in August 1804, although the treaty grounds were many miles north of today's city. American enterprise began in the region in either 1812 or 1814, when Manuel Lisa established a trading post about eleven miles north of present-day Omaha that became the headquarters of the Missouri Fur Company.

The War of 1812 made it clear to the federal government that the American West, especially its lucrative fur trade, needed protection from British interests. In 1818 President James Monroe proposed establishing two forts on the Missouri, one at the bluffs and the other at the mouth of the Yellowstone River. A talented army engineer, Stephen Long, suggested it could be done using the latest techni-cal innovation in transportation, the steamboat. The next year the army mounted a massive (for its time) expedition, sending Colonel Henry M. Atkinson, more than 1,120 men of the Sixth Infantry and the Rifle Regiment, and five steam-boats on the Yellowstone Expedition to carry out the president's plan. Two of the

---

[269] Minto, "Reminiscences of Experiences on the Oregon Trail in 1844," 124; and "HO! for Oregon or Califor-nia," *St. Joseph Gazette*, 6 March 1846, 3/1–2.

steamers never got past Saint Louis, while the *Jefferson* foundered near the mouth of the Osage River, becoming the first steamboat to sink in the Missouri. The *Johnson* broke down below the Kansas River, and the *Expedition* gave up about ten miles above the future site of Fort Leavenworth. Atkinson transported his men to the Council Bluffs in keelboats, where they established Cantonment Missouri and dug in for the winter.[270]

The army fared better with the 75 × 13–foot *Western Engineer,* a shallow-draft sternwheeler Major Long designed and built to navigate the Missouri's treacherous shoals. With its single tall mast and row of gunports, it looked nothing like the classic steamboat, but the vessel's distinctive dragon figurehead belched smoke, which mightily impressed the Natives and won it the name "Long's dragon." It became the first steamboat to reach the mouth of the Platte River. Long's men built Engineer Cantonment near Cantonment Missouri, and Long returned to Washington to get new orders. The following spring, he set out up the north bank of the Platte with fourteen men, an escort of seven soldiers, and two French guides to explore the Platte, Arkansas, and Red rivers. The expedition forded the Platte not far above its forks and followed the South Fork to the site of what is now Denver before heading south and getting lost on the Canadian River.[271]

Some 160 soldiers died during the army's first winter at Council Bluffs; the next summer the post was renamed Fort Atkinson. The government maintained this costly station until 1827, when it transferred the operation south to Fort Leavenworth. During that time, Council Bluffs became a key trading center and even the destination of envoys from New Mexico and the jumping-off point for American trading ventures that set off up the Platte for Santa Fe. Posts such as Cabanné's, Lucien Fontenelle's, and Bellevue on the west bank and François Guittau's 1824 settlement at Traders Point on the eastern shore soon became major fur-trade depots. Baptist and Presbyterian missions to the Otoe and Pawnees appeared during the mid-1830s, at first near the trading posts, but missionary Moses Merrill soon learned such an operation was "not a house of God, nor the gate of heaven. It is rather the house of Satan and the gate of hell."[272] Evangelists Samuel Parker and Marcus Whitman set out from Council Bluffs in 1835. Three years later, Pierre-Jean De Smet established the first Catholic mission in Nebraska among the recently displaced Pottawatomies. When overland emigration began, the area lacked the commercial development of Independence,

---

[270] Martin and Devereux, "The Omaha–Council Bluffs Area and the Westward Trails," 2–3.

[271] Ibid.; and James, *Account of an Expedition from Pittsburgh to the Rocky Mountains,* 112–14. Archaeologists believe they located the site of Engineer Cantonment in spring 2003. See Neurohr, "184 Years of Lost American History is Emerging from Local Missouri River Soil," *Omaha River Front,* 3 June 2003.

[272] Sheldon, *Nebraska, Old and New,* 140.

but the first party to cross Truckee Pass left Council Bluffs in 1844, and tens of thousands would follow in their wake.

The most popular jumping-off point shifted almost annually, but for three decades overland emigration was big business in the frontier towns along the Missouri. Trails historian Merrill Mattes identified eight major locations where emigrants crossed the river to begin their western journeys. The southernmost became Kansas City, and during the trail era it included Independence, Westport, Westport Landing, Kansas Landing, Kansasmouth, Liberty, and Parkville. Moving north, the next outfitting towns were around Weston and Fort Leavenworth, the settlement that became Atchison, Kansas, and then Saint Joseph. A string of "obscure places" upriver included Duncans Ferry, Oregon City, Iowa Point, and Rulo. At the next major crossing, the government in 1846 established what became known as Old Fort Kearny. To better manage relations between emigrants and Indians, the army wisely moved the post in 1848 to the head of Grand Island on the Platte, where the main overland trails converged. The old site on the Missouri evolved into the booming transportation center of Nebraska City: just to the north, the Mormons eventually built their own outfitting point at the town of Wyoming. A cluster of towns and trading stations surrounded the confluence of the Platte and Missouri rivers, including Plattsmouth on the Nebraska shore and Bethlehem on the Iowa. Another concentration of ferries began at Bellevue and anchored the northernmost of the jumping-off points around what became Omaha, Nebraska, and Council Bluffs, Iowa.[273]

THEIR LAST GOOD-BYE: LEAVE TAKINGS

The men and women who went west during the 1840s realized they might as well have stepped off the edge of the earth, for it was unlikely they would ever see again those they left behind. As A. H. Garrison watched his uncles bid good-bye to their kinfolk in the early 1840s, he saw "they realized it was their last parting, that this was their last good-by." After the men disappeared from sight, their mother went out to the road to look at their tracks, and then knelt down and prayed that God would guard them on their perilous journey.[274] Joseph Henry Brown described his family's parting on the morning of the ides of March as his party of thirteen wagons hitched up their teams and set out from Illinois in 1845. "Although I was quite young the scene was indelably fixed upon my mind," he wrote. "Tears were shed by mother and daughters as they embraced each other

---

[273] Mattes, *Platte River Road Narratives*, 617.
[274] Garrison, "Reminiscences of Abraham Henry Garrison," 11.

for the last time on earth, and the parting kiss was given as the last token of love from the hearts that knew the parting was forever. It was as solemn as a funeral, only the actors were in health, [but] the withdrawal from sight was as irretrivable as the clods upon the coffin."[275]

The homes they were forsaking haunted many women. "I have been often asked if I did not find many things to enjoy in our journey across the Plains," wrote Margaret M. Hecox, "and I have been obliged to answer, no." The scenery might have been beautiful, but Hecox was too tired or worried to care. Even the flowers reminded her of the home she would never see again, "and the antelopes told me we were far from civilization." Hecox recalled the dear home she was obliged to leave forever. "I can't tell you how I felt when I got into the wagon to leave there. I shed tears enough then and afterwards to make a river to carry me back to my mother."[276]

Catherine Sager recalled "a long farewell" as her family started west in 1844. "Some wept for departing friends, and others at the thoughts of leaving all they held dear for a long and uncertain journey, and the children wept for fear of the mighty waters that came rushing down and seemed as though it would swallow them up," she wrote. "Taken altogether, it was a sad company that crossed over the Missouri River that bright spring morning."[277]

"Some were laughing and some were crying," wrote Alice Rockefellow, recalling her family's departure for Oregon in 1853. "It was harder for the women than the men to leave their loved ones."[278] The fear that the trek west would break old family ties forever endured for decades. "Today we are to leave this place and home and friends and start upon a long journey, even to the land of gold," Delia Thompson Brown noted as she prepared to leave home in 1860. "Well, 'tis done—I have taken the parting hand with my mother who will be lonely, and kissed her a last good-bye—my heart was too full to speak," she wrote not long after the separation. "I have parted with my brothers and sisters dear, perhaps never more to meet, for this earth has many ways."[279]

Men, however, tended to depart with more bravado. Jesse A. Applegate recalled that when John East learned his party had crossed the Missouri state line, he turned to face the sunrise, pulled off his slouched hat, and waved it above his head, shouting, "Farewell to America!"[280]

---

[275] Brown, Recollection of 1847, Bancroft Library, 2–3.
[276] Hecox, "The Story of Margaret M. Hecox," 539, 542.
[277] Pringle, Across the Plains in 1844, Oregon Historical Society.
[278] Rockefellow, The Story of My Life, Southern Oregon Historical Society.
[279] Brown, Diary Kept of Delia Thompson Brown, 7 May 1860, Nevada Historical Society.
[280] Applegate, "Recollections of My Boyhood," 25.

CHAPTER 5

You Damn Yankees
Will Do Anything You Like

Opening Roads to the Pacific, 1842 and 1843

T he Territory of the United States commonly called the Oregon Territory," President John Tyler noted in his annual message to Congress in
1842, "begins to attract the attention of our fellow-citizens." The tide of
population that had subdued the Mississippi and Ohio valleys, the president said,
was ready "to flow over those vast districts which stretch from the Rocky Mountains to the Pacific Ocean."[1] During the next two years that tide would swell
from the handful of adventurers who set out for California in 1841 to a hundred
and then to almost a thousand Americans determined to take their wagons to the
Pacific "over a route so rugged and mountainous." The long and perilous journey
forever changed the people who made it, and the trails they forged transformed
the American West.

The man who drew the most attention to Oregon that spring was Dr. Elijah
White, who was actively encouraging good Christian people not under the influence of Methodism to join him in Oregon. After his banishment from the Methodist mission in 1840, White had allied himself with the Pacific mercantile firm
A. G. Benson and Bro. The Bensons helped him secure an appointment as United
States Indian subagent for Oregon.[2] (The doctor had lobbied to be named governor, but assigning an Indian subagent to a region it did not govern was as far as
the Tyler administration wanted to test the limits of the joint-occupancy agreement with Britain.) White could now return west as the first—and only—federal
official in Oregon and settle scores with his former evangelical comrades. Representative Caleb Cushing and Senator Lewis Linn gave added appeal to the remote
and romantic Eden by proposing legislation that promised 640 acres—a square

---

[1] Richardson, *A Compilation of the Messages and Papers of the Presidents*, 4:196.
[2] Clark, *Eden Seekers*, 153.

mile—of free land to Oregon emigrants. The act did not pass until 1850, but it helped lure thousands of Americans to the territory before it expired in 1855.

As 1842 came to a close, Secretary of State Daniel Webster suggested approaching the Mexican government with a proposal to cede Alta California to the United States.[3] In a revealing incident that autumn, the commander of the U.S. Navy's Pacific squadron, Commodore Thomas ap Catesby Jones, read in a Mexican newspaper that the two republics were at war. Acting on standing orders, Jones sailed to Monterey in October 1842, landed 150 marines and sailors, lowered the Mexican flag, and seized the capital of California. Jones soon learned that the report of war was false. He immediately restored Mexican authority and made diplomatic amends as best he could. The government relieved Jones of his command and disavowed his actions, but the incident made American intentions in California painfully obvious.

However transparent the United States government's ambitions for the Pacific Coast might have been, as long as Americans made up only a small fraction of the population of Oregon and California such dreams were empty fantasies. Oregon's missionaries and businessmen such as the Benson brothers had shown that a seaborne migration to the Far West was possible, but it was a risky and unappealing proposition for the farmers or craftsmen essential to such an undertaking. The only practical way to get large numbers of Americans to the Pacific Coast appeared to be overland by wagon, and as late as 1843 no one was sure such a feat was even possible.

OUR CHEERLESS JOURNEY: THE OREGON EMIGRANTS OF 1842

As he traveled to Independence in spring 1842, Elijah White lectured on the glories of Oregon and enlisted recruits, but most of the 112 or so people he found at Elm Grove had decided to go west on their own.[4] His sermons did, however, spread the growing contagion of Oregon fever that would achieve epidemic proportions the following year, and White organized the first overland company whose sole purpose was to take settlers to Oregon. The train's nineteen wagons lumbered west in mid-May. Women and children comprised almost half of the emigration of 1842, and attorneys and doctors made up a sizeable portion of the rest. One of White's recruits was a twenty-two-year-old Ohio lawyer, Lansford W. Hastings, who "had an anxious desire to visit those wild regions upon the great Pacific, which had now become the topic of conversation in every circle."[5]

---

[3] Webster to Waddy Thompson, 30 December 1842, *Correspondence*, 5:500–501.

[4] Bancroft, *History of Oregon*, 256n5, concluded the party picked up members on the trail, probably reaching McLoughlin's reported 137 on their arrival in Oregon.

[5] Hastings, *The Emigrants' Guide*, 5.

At the train's organizing meeting in mid-May, Hastings almost edged out White in the election of the train's captain, which the emigrant democracy decided would be held monthly. The next day the company set out, White recalled, "merrily singing or whistling to beguile their way."[6]

As the party approached the Kansas River, this happy unity disappeared when Captain White recommended destroying all the dogs in camp to prevent their contracting rabies. Bancroft noted that King Herod's infanticide order could scarcely have inspired a louder wail of lamentation than did White's directive. Since the train's "little government was purely democratic," the matter came to a vote, and surprisingly the majority supported White's decision. Twenty-two dogs died (although a few canines apparently escaped), resulting in a second referendum in which "the 'dog decree,' as it was called, was almost unanimously abrogated." Leadership of the party fell to Lansford Hastings at the next election. "He was rather an aspiring sort of man," Asa Lovejoy recalled, "and he worked it so that he got the command." But "Captain" Hastings and "Lieutenant" Lovejoy, another attorney, managed to get re-elected in July.[7]

In addition to White and Hastings, the 1842 emigration eventually comprised a number of men who would play prominent roles in Oregon and subsequent trail history, including Thomas Fitzpatrick, James M. Hudspeth, Stephen Meek, Sidney Moss, Hugh Burns, François Matthieu, Walter Pomeroy, James Robb, William O. Fallon, and Elbridge Trask. None, however, would make as continuing or enduring a contribution to Oregon as twenty-three-year-old Medorem Crawford, a former neighbor of Elijah White in Havana, New York. Crawford's daily journal provides far and away the best account of the trek.

Many of the party's experiences later became commonplace among overland companies, such as arguments over whether to wait for the sick to recover. The Lancaster family's only child died and her mother fell ill. The party debated whether to wait for her to get well: Columbia Lancaster resolved the situation when he decided to take his wife back to Missouri. (Lancaster journeyed west in 1847 with his wife and four-year-old daughter to become one of Oregon's first supreme court justices.) The train's encounter with vast herds of bison overjoyed the men: Crawford considered buffalo cow "decidedly the best meat I ever eat."

Personal conflicts raged continuously. A jury convicted Sidney Moss for refusing to stand guard and retried him when he declined to accept the verdict. After Hastings was elected captain, White and a few others formed their own company. The division lasted until the Laramie River, where Joseph Bissonette of

---

[6] Lavender, *Westward Vision*, 353.

[7] Bancroft, *History of Oregon*, 1:258; Hastings, *The Emigrants' Guide*, 7, 20; Lovejoy, "Lovejoy's Pioneer Narrative," 241; and Crawford, "Journal of Medorem Crawford," 8, 12.

Fort Platte advised them to reunite for safety. Here the party converted some of their wagons to carts "to expedite the journey," and F. X. Matthieu and a small band of trappers and veterans of the 1837 Canadian revolt joined the train. Just west of the fort, the emigrants fell in with Jim Bridger and Thomas Fitzpatrick. Acting as Indian agent, White engaged Fitzpatrick to guide the party to Fort Hall at government expense.[8]

"The accidental discharge of a gun," Lansford Hastings later advised, "is likely to be attended with serious and fatal consequences." At the Sweetwater on 13 July, a man named Bailey accidentally shot and killed Adam Horn. Four days later, someone shot one of Vardemon Bennett's small daughters in the foot. "Guns should never be carried capped or primed," Hastings cautioned, but he still recommended they should always be carried loaded and ready for action "upon a moment's warning."[9]

Even in July, the "nights are astonishingly cold & the days verry warm," Crawford noted. "Water in a pail froze ice like thick window glass" as the party approached the Continental Divide. Hundreds and finally thousands of Lakota and Cheyenne appeared along the Sweetwater River. John C. Frémont claimed their chiefs spent the night debating whether to attack the emigrants, and he thought the sojourners owed their lives to Fitzpatrick. Certainly Hastings and Lovejoy did, for after they lingered behind to carve their names on Independence Rock, the Sioux caught and detained them, but Fitzpatrick persuaded the tribe to let the men go. So the Lakota missed the chance to change history—Lovejoy went on to help found Portland, but in Hastings's case, the change might have saved lives.[10]

SCAMPISHLY INCLINED: RICHARD GRANT AND FORT HALL

After crossing South Pass on 28 July 1842, the main division of the fractured company began abandoning their wagons and carts. At Green River, White took Fitzpatrick and about two dozen men, leaving Hastings with eight wagons and Stephen Meek to guide his party to Fort Hall. Hastings and seven wagons caught up with White on the Snake River.

The post's new commander, Richard Grant, told the Americans "it would be impossible for us to take our wagons down to the Pacific," Hastings wrote. The most experienced hands at the post agreed, but some of them believed the emigrants might get their vehicles halfway. Once again, the traveling democracy held a meeting. Some thought the convenience of wagons warranted taking them as

---

[8] Crawford, "Journal of Medorem Crawford," 8, 9, 11; Hastings, *The Emigrants' Guide,* 7; Bancroft, *History of Oregon,* 1:259–60; Lovejoy, "Lovejoy's Pioneer Narrative," 243n15.

[9] Hastings, *The Emigrants' Guide,* 149.

[10] Spence and Jackson, *The Expeditions of John Charles Frémont,* 1:223; and Crawford, "Journal of Medorem Crawford," 12–13.

far as possible, but others pointed out that they could get something for them at the fort and nothing if they abandoned them on the trail. The party voted to leave the wagons. Grant purchased a few "for a mere trifle," but even Hastings conceded Grant bought them merely to accommodate the travelers. Many American overlanders deeply resented the Hudson's Bay Company. Despite such hostility, the Company's beneficence was essential to their survival. Grant welcomed Hastings's party at Fort Hall in the kindest manner, and they "received every aid and attention from the gentlemen of that fort."[11]

At age forty-eight, Chief Trader Richard Grant was already a veteran of twenty-seven years in the fur trade. George Simpson considered Grant poorly educated but well qualified to manage the affairs of a small trading post, finding him "active and bustling, but not Steady, would Drink if not under constraint, speaks at random and is scampishly inclined."[12] Despite Simpson's misgivings, the Company could not have found a better man to protect its interests in a remote and isolated country. Born in Montreal in 1794 to a French and Scottish family long engaged in the fur trade, Grant had served as a lieutenant in His Majesty's Second Battalion of Embodied Militia during the War of 1812.[13] He joined the North West Company at the war's end, transferred to the Hudson's Bay Company in 1821, and married Mary Ann de Breland. He worked his way up to command posts throughout Ruperts Land, such as Oxford House and Fort Assiniboine, and developed what historian Merle Wells called a gift for getting into unlikely situations. Following the death of his wife in 1832, Grant spent a year arranging for the care for his three young sons and a daughter in Montreal and then went north to manage a post on Lesser Slave Lake. He was at last commissioned a chief trader in March 1836. Although his official letters reflect a sharp eye and lively intelligence, Grant hated the paperwork that went with the promotion. "The Office to me is a dungeon," he told a friend in 1839, but he excelled "amidst Furs" managing the trade—"I am then in my element," he said, "but do the writing yourself."

The Columbia District was the reputed dumping ground for the Company's troublemakers. What earned Richard Grant a transfer to Oregon is unclear, but it happened shortly after he completed a difficult winter journey with even more difficult passengers from Oxford House to York Factory and back. "By the Bee that stung Adam," he swore, "I shall never again be persuaded to take in tow half-naked Ladies at such a cold season of the year as when I came up." Perhaps the assignment to a warmer climate was related to the rheumatism that tormented him from at least 1846. However he got there, Grant thrived in the Pacific Northwest. He

[11] Hastings, *The Emigrants' Guide,* 20.
[12] Simpson, "Servants Characters and Histories of Service, 1832," A 34/2, HBC Archives, 30–31.
[13] Grant, Oath on Military Service, 25 March 1847, D.5/19, HBC Archives, 437.

married the widow Eleanor MacDonald Kittson at Fort Vancouver in March 1845. The daughter of a Scottish trader and an Indian mother apparently of Iroquois and French heritage, she had been educated in an Ontario convent and was known as Helene Kittson. After Grant's transfer to the Columbia District in 1841, John McLoughlin sent him to replace Francis Ermatinger at Fort Hall and take command of the Snake Country.[14]

While directing Company operations at Fort Hall for a decade, Grant gathered his intriguing family around him. He managed to bring two of the four children from his first marriage, Stanislaus Richard and sixteen-year-old John Francis, overland in 1847 with Augustin Blanchet, the first Catholic bishop of Walla Walla–Nesqually. They worked with their father until a falling out in 1849, when the brothers struck out on their own as traders. By then "Johnny" was fluent in Shoshone, and Grant correctly concluded, "he has not want of life & I believe will hold his own, with either Indians or whites." Johnny Grant later reconciled with his father and they allied as trail entrepreneurs. The Grants were among the first pioneers of Montana, and Johnny's mansion still stands at Deer Lodge.[15]

Grant had a son by an Indian woman at Oxford House, which contributed to his exile to the Columbia District: this had been a common practice—even George Simpson had taken James Sinclair's sister as his mistress—but as a clerk wrote, Grant's "ideas about love and sex were too primitive to suit the atmosphere of the world as it is *now* about Oxford and Norway House."[16] Grant told Simpson he had a little son, James Cuthbert Grant, living among the Indians and asked him to authorize bringing the boy over the mountains—"the little fellow is between six and seven and will take up but little room," Grant begged. "I would consider it a great favor added to the obligations I am to you already much under." Simpson denied his request, but in 1846 John R. McBride saw a boy who "was evidently the pride of the Captain. He was about ten years old, spoke good English, and took me all over the quarters and was full of fire and energy as live boys are." Helene Kittson's two children—Eloisa Jemima, born in 1836, and Edwin, born late in 1839—joined their stepfather at Fort Hall, and she and Grant had three daughters, born at two-year intervals beginning in 1846: Helene Wilhelmina, Julia Priscilla, and Adeline.[17] Years later Helene fondly recalled the pet beaver she kept as a playmate. McBride apparently met Eloisa and guessed she was about fifteen: "She wore the Indian frock of dressed deer skin, but it was scrupulously

---

[14] Grant's story is taken from Merle Wells's sketch in Hafen, *The Mountain Men,* 9:165–186.

[15] Blanchet to Kendrick, 30 March 1848, Jesuit Oregon Province Archives, Gonzaga University; and Grant, *Very Close to Trouble,* 3, 10–12, 26n3.

[16] Van Kirk, *Many Tender Ties,* 160.

[17] Grant, *Very Close to Trouble,* 5n5, 11n4, 12n5, 26n3, 33n4.

clean and neat, and she was strikingly beautiful, with her long dark hair falling around her bare neck and shoulders."[18]

With the end of the rendezvous system, George Simpson hoped the Hudson's Bay Company could use Fort Hall to supply what was left of the Rocky Mountain fur trade, and he wanted to employ Jim Bridger as an agent. Bridger, however, proved to be an unwilling ally. Grant proposed trading arrangements to Bridger, but when "he returned no answer I concluded he did not wish to accept them." Joseph Williams, returning from Oregon in June 1842 after his adventures with the Bidwell-Bartleson party, "heard some dreadful oaths from Mr. Grant, about some threats which he had heard from Mr. Bridger, one of the American Fur Company, against Fort Hall." Grant charged that Bridger had stolen HBC goods, and he quickly devised a strategy to drive his competitor out of business.[19]

Grant could not have found a better rival for Jim Bridger than the character "generally known by the appellation of Peg Leg Smith from his having a wooden leg."[20] After his birth on a stormy night in Kentucky in 1801, Thomas L. Smith's first yelp was an Indian war whoop—at least according to legend, and most of Smith's life story reads like a legend. He left home at age sixteen, worked on Mississippi River flatboats, and the "wild, whooping, black-eyed, red-headed bull-shouldered youth" went west with Antoine Robidoux perhaps as early as 1820. He spent the next quarter century trapping beaver, fighting Indians, stealing California horses, and discovering mysterious gold mines. After an Indian skirmish at Browns Hole in about 1827, Milton Sublette amputated his mangled foot, although Smith later claimed to have done the job himself.[21]

Jim Bridger had equipped a fur brigade in 1842 that Smith led on a successful hunt deep into Mexican territory—the mysterious "Queaterra Country," perhaps in central or southern Utah. "From some misunderstanding or other on account of wages with Bridger," Grant wrote, "Old Gabe" and Pegleg had a falling out. Feeling Bridger refused to pay him a fair price, Smith sold his furs at Fort Hall. Grant quickly began a long-lasting commercial alliance with Smith, sending him to places such as Mexico or the Yellowstone where, Grant believed, "we are forbidden to go to." Smith delivered 460 beaver pelts to Fort Hall over the next year, and Grant soon had him "employed on our side [as] a severe thorn in the side of Bridger and the other traders, our opponents." Grant skillfully placed Smith in competition with Bridger and his partner, Louis Vasquez, who often was in charge of the establishment on Blacks Fork.[22]

---

[18] McBride, Recollections, in Morgan, *Overland in 1846,* 98.
[19] Hafen, *The Mountain Men,* 9:171–72; and Williams, *Narrative of a Tour,* 1 June 1842, 49.
[20] Grant to Simpson, 15 March 1844, D.5/10, HBC Archives, 426.
[21] Thrapp, *Encyclopedia of Frontier Biography,* 1336.
[22] Grant to Simpson, 15 March 1844, D.5/10, HBC Archives, 426.

Like other fur trade veterans in the early 1840s, Pegleg was casting about for a new source of income and quickly recognized the prospects of the emigrant business—his relationship with Grant and the Hudson's Bay Company gave him a reliable source of goods, and Pegleg prospered during this partnership. John Minto found him at Fort Hall in 1844 "neatly dressed in navy blue, and would have been judged a steamboat captain in Saint Louis."[23] For six years Pegleg was the most ambitious and active trader in the mountains. Before and during the gold rush, thousands of overlanders visited Smith's posts—he had established several trading stations on Bear River by 1848, one some four miles above the mouth of Smiths Fork and a "principle trading post" between today's Dingle and Montpelier, Idaho. Pegleg became a virtual trail landmark until he decamped for Sacramento late in 1850.[24]

The decade Richard Grant spent at Fort Hall made him the most influential figure on the Oregon Trail, and a giant of the overland era. With the Snake Country's fur trade in decline, the old trader quickly grasped the economic potential of the emigrants who arrived at his doorstep in 1842. He dealt fairly with his American customers, but he was not overly fond of them—particularly their leaders. "With regard to Dr. White," Grant informed George Simpson, "I can safely say for my own self that I never recognized either his authority or greatness, nor will I, with any of them untill ordered so to do by yourself, or the Gentlemen of the House in London."[25] An excellent judge of men, Grant identified White's worst flaw: his enormous ego. Sir George may have felt Grant lacked steadiness and was "scampishly inclined," but for ten years the savvy frontiersman exhibited character and competence his boss somehow overlooked.

THROUGH THE TRACKLESS DESERTS: REACHING OREGON, 1842

After nine years in the fur trade, Osborne Russell contemplated the state of the West at the end of 1841, recalling the large bands of buffalo that had filled the valleys near Fort Hall in 1836. Now, "the only traces which could be seen of them were the scattered bones of those that had been killed." The mountaineers' world had changed forever. "The trappers often remarked to each other as they rode over these lonely plains that it was time for the White man to leave the mountains as Beaver and game had nearly disappeared," he wrote. When Elijah White passed

---

[23] Camp, *George C. Yount*, 225, 233–34, 273; and Minto, "Reminiscences of Experiences on the Oregon Trail in 1844," 217.

[24] Smith, "A Journal of Scenes and Incidents on a Journey from Missouri to California, 29–31 July 1848." California State Library; Thrapp, *Encyclopedia of Frontier Biography*, 1336.

[25] Grant to Simpson, 15 March 1844, D.5/10, HBC Archives, 427–28.

through the next summer, Russell joined the migration, "determined on going to the Mouth of the Columbia and settle myself in the Willamette or Multnoma Valley."[26]

The party traded its "poor and way-worn horses" for better animals at Fort Hall "and having convinced ourselves that we were invincible," Lansford Hastings recalled, "we, once more, resumed our dangerous journey, over the burning sands, and through the trackless deserts of Oregon."[27] White's mule train left the fort soon after Hastings's wagons arrived and quickly had trouble with its packs. The greenhorns decided to wait for the annual Hudson's Bay caravan, but they soon found their cattle could not keep up with the veteran frontiersmen, who "drove on a trot nearly all day." After a man drowned while trying to catch up, White abandoned eight men without a pilot, including Medorem Crawford, and pressed on. The trip down the Snake passed through "country growing more barren not even producing sage," but Indians along the way traded both fresh and dry fish. At the still-unfinished Fort Boise, Francois Payette, the only white man at the post, provided them with a few provisions.

Leaving the Snake behind on 6 September, the party climbed Burnt River Canyon and the highest hills they had yet encountered. Two days later, the mountaintops looming on the western horizon "struck us with terror [for] their lofty peaks seemed a resting place for the clouds," Crawford wrote. "Below us was a large plain and at some distance we could discover a tree which we at once recognized as 'the lone pine' of which we had before heard." That evening the company camped at the "large Pine standing in the midst of an immense plain intirely alone. It presented a truly singular apearance and I believe is respected by every traviler through this Treless Country," he concluded.

The next day the emigrants crossed the Powder River and climbed over a series of ridges into the most beautiful valley Crawford had ever seen—the Grande Ronde, where they met Indians driving hundreds of horses over the mountains. "To our great joy they had pleanty [of provisions] and instead of starving as we expected we were able to trade enough fish to last us to Dr. Whitmans." An Indian guided the party over the Blue Mountains, and on 14 September 1842, the company arrived at the Waiilatpu Mission. "I was never more pleased to see a house or white people in my life," Crawford wrote. "We were treated by Dr. and Mrs. Whitman with the utmost kindness."[28] Elijah White, however, carried a sealed letter from the American Board of Commissioners for Foreign Missions directing Whitman to send home about half the mission's personnel and consolidate

---

[26] Russell, *Journal of a Trapper,* 125.

[27] Hastings, *The Emigrants' Guide,* 20.

[28] Crawford, "Journal of Medorem Crawford," 8–14 September 1842, 15–20.

its outposts into one station at Tshimakain, about twenty-five miles northwest of present-day Spokane.[29]

The grandiloquent Hastings skipped the details of "the residue of our cheerless journey" down the south side of the Snake River. Perhaps to avoid discouraging prospective migrants, he claimed it was less difficult than anticipated.[30] The emigrants reached the Willamette Valley as best they could. Some, like White, who was eager to claim his government office before Hastings's partisans could arrive, took boats down the river. Many made the difficult trek to The Dalles over roads "as bad and some worse" than anything they had yet encountered, with their "animals verry hollow and weak." Here some followed the Lolo Pass Trail around the north slope of Mount Hood, but the majority rafted down the great river. Most of the emigrants had reached the falls of the Willamette without accident by early October.[31] It had not been an easy trip, but more than one hundred Americans had successfully moved from the Missouri frontier to Oregon in a single season.

THE PATHFINDER:
EXPLORERS, EMIGRANTS, AND FRÉMONT'S FIRST EXPEDITION

To his admirers, John C. Frémont was "The Pathfinder"—a title he never claimed for himself—but his first expedition to the West found him doing what he always did best: following the tracks of an existing wagon road as he traveled behind the Oregon-bound trains of 1842. On his steamboat voyage up the Missouri, Frémont ran into a man who had spent half his life in the Far West, Christopher "Kit" Carson. "I had been some time in the mountains," Carson told him, "and thought I could guide him to any point he wished to go." Frémont made enquiries and then hired Carson for $100 a month. At Westport, Frémont assembled a party of twenty-one men, nearly all of French origin, who were the secret of the Pathfinder's success. He spoke excellent French, which helped him win over the French mountaineers who formed the largest non-Native population in the Far West. Through them he could communicate with almost everyone else, for his men spoke Spanish and a host of Indian languages. Frémont left the Missouri frontier on 10 June 1842 in command of the army's first topographical survey of the Oregon Trail, about three weeks behind the emigrants. His objective, Carson recalled, "was to survey the South pass and take the height of the highest peaks of the Rocky Mts."[32]

---

[29] Lavender, *Westward Vision,* 344.

[30] Hastings, *The Emigrants' Guide,* 20.

[31] Bancroft, *History of Oregon,* 1:261–62; and Crawford, "Journal of Medorem Crawford," 22–23.

[32] Carson, *Kit Carson's Own Story,* 50–51; and Spence and Jackson, *The Expeditions of John Charles Frémont,* 1:126, 169–70, 174–75, 189.

Frémont's leadership of three federal surveys of the West won him undying fame, due largely to the brilliant narrative of the first two—his *Report of the Exploring Expedition to the Rocky Mountains in the Year 1842, and to Oregon and North California in the Years 1843–'44* became the single most influential work ever published to encourage the settlement of the West. His impact on overland emigration extended even to the names applied to trail landmarks. Travelers did not settle on a name for Court House Rock, the first massive formation on the Platte River, Dale Morgan determined, until Frémont used it in his first report. Charles Preuss attributed the name to the Pathfinder's voyageurs, but not as explicitly as Captain Howard Stansbury, who said most of them came from Saint Louis and named it for its "fancied resemblance to a well-known structure in their own city."[33]

But Frémont's aloof manner, restless aspirations, and reckless actions launched endless controversy. His powerful family's partisan memories of dark conspiracies seeking to frustrate the young explorer's noble goals helped obscure the initial objectives of his topographical expeditions. His, and Thomas Hart Benton's, ambitions transformed Frémont's journeys from scientific undertakings seeking to extend America's limited knowledge of the West to geopolitical conquests. The ethics of these conquests were questionable, but his surveys would be of immense importance to western trails and the emigrants who followed them.[34] Historians tend to love or hate him, but whatever opinion one has of John C. Frémont, no other person had such a profound and enduring impact on the settlement of America's Far West.

The 1842 expedition produced much useful knowledge and the first scientific maps of the interior west, especially the maps Charles Preuss drew of the wagon road to South Pass. The summit of the pass proved so hard to detect that Frémont incorrectly placed the culminating point "between two low hills, rising on either hand fifty or sixty feet," soon to be known as the Twin Mounds, which was two-and-a-half miles east of the actual summit. Climbing the pass compared "to the ascent of the Capitol hill from the avenue, at Washington," the Pathfinder wrote, "and the traveller, without being reminded of any change by toilsome ascents, suddenly finds himself on the waters which flow to the Pacific ocean." The expedition pushed as far west as the Big Sandy.[35]

Although he exceeded his formal orders, Frémont finally established that South Pass was in the United States and not in Mexico, as many had believed. He

---

[33] Spence and Jackson, *The Expeditions of John Charles Frémont*, 9 July 1842, 1:215n37; and Stansbury, *Exploration and Survey*, 7 July 1849, 48.

[34] This analysis owes much to Volpe, "The Origins of the Fremont Expeditions," which makes the first use of the recently discovered 1842 Abert-Benton correspondence at the Southwest Museum.

[35] Spence and Jackson, *The Expeditions of John Charles Frémont*, 1:253–54.

explored the Wind River Range and conquered what he thought was the tallest mountain in the Rockies. Historians long suspected Frémont climbed Woodrow Wilson Peak, not the mountain now named for him, but the new consensus is that Frémont did climb Fremont Peak in what historian David Roberts called "the finest mountaineering feat performed to that time by Anglos in North America."[36] On its summit he unfurled an American flag emblazoned with a bald eagle clutching arrows and a peace pipe in its talons, a symbolic moment his report captured in all its drama. "As in so many places along Frémont's trail," his biographer notes, "the historical record by now lies hopelessly entangled in myth and lore."[37] Frémont's subsequent career suggests he would not rest until he had delivered the West into the eagle's grasp.

TRAILS EAST

No wagons headed to California from the Missouri frontier in 1842, but eastbound travelers returning to the United States made much significant overland trail history that summer.

After Elijah White delivered the American Board's sealed orders to close the missions at Waiilatpu and Lapwai, Marcus Whitman acted quickly. The missionaries, who had conflicts of their own, gathered at Waiilatpu in late September to resolve their differences and hear Whitman's plan for dealing with the crisis. He proposed returning east that winter to argue the case for keeping the stations open before the mission board. Promising to carry their letters home after finding someone to take over his duties at the mission, Whitman overcame his colleagues' reluctance to support his daunting proposal. Asa Lovejoy—who had spent only two weeks recovering at the mission from his trip west—volunteered to accompany the doctor. Whitman departed on 3 October before his replacement or his colleagues' letters could arrive.[38]

As Whitman and Lovejoy made their arduous winter journey via Fort Hall, Bear River, the Uinta Valley, and over the central Rockies to the Arkansas River and the Santa Fe Trail, they may have followed much the same route from Fort Hall as a band of returning Bidwell-Bartleson party veterans did in 1842. At least that was the course James Springer outlined in an 1856 letter describing a trip via Tejon Pass, Fort Hall, Green River, and Santa Fe—a very roundabout way to get back to Missouri. Perhaps mountain man George C. Yount had told Chiles about the Spanish Trail, as Doyce Nunis proposed, and the party used this route

---

[36] Roberts, *A Newer World*, 46–49, and caption 6 following 192.

[37] Chaffin, "How the West Was Lost," 138; and Chaffin, *Pathfinder*, 127.

[38] Lavender, *Westward Vision*, 358–61; and Drury, *Marcus and Narcissa Whitman*, 1:463–76.

far to the south of the Oregon Trail. Thirteen men left California in April 1842, including John Bartleson, Charles Hopper, Joseph Chiles, and Springer. Whatever route they took, they arrived in Independence on 9 September.[39]

Joseph Chiles visited the provincial capital at Monterey in 1841 and wrangled a promise for a land grant and mill site in the Sonoma Valley. Chiles, a six-foot-four-inch Kentuckian whose neighbors remembered him as a delightful fiddle player, was in his early thirties when he went west after the death of his wife. He had been a neighbor of George Yount's family in Missouri, and Chiles recalled how happy the old mountaineer was to hear from his children. Yount asked Chiles to bring his daughters from Missouri to California when he returned. He even gave Chiles and Hopper mules and supplies that Yount hoped his family could use to join their father in California.[40]

In keeping this promise in 1843, Joseph Ballinger Chiles set in motion the opening of the California Trail.[41]

A PROVISIONAL GOVERNMENT FOR OREGON

The Hudson's Bay Company charter granted it the right to govern Oregon—or at least the British citizens and other company retainers who were obliged to recognize its authority—but Americans in the Northwest were answerable to no legal power. When Ewing Young died in 1841 without a known heir, questions about how to divide his estate—particularly his large cattle herds—pointed up the lack of any system to handle such fundamental problems. After his funeral, settlers began debating whether to establish a government, and being Americans, they organized a committee to create a constitution. The committee never met, much to the disappointment of men like Jason Lee who wanted to establish an American-style government immediately. The settlers simply organized a court and appointed a probate judge.[42]

The arrival of the 1842 emigration increased agitation to create a more effective government, especially one that could issue land grants. That winter the Pioneer Lyceum and Literary Club debated and passed the resolution, "It is expedient for the settlers on this coast to establish an independent government."[43] Lansford

[39] Stewart, *The California Trail*, 33–35; and Nunis, *The Bidwell-Bartleson Party*, 200–202. History, George Stewart observed in recounting this episode, "is not really the story of what happened; it is necessarily the story of what is preserved in the record."

[40] Camp, *George C. Yount*, 165.

[41] Nunis, *The Bidwell-Bartleson Party*, 141.

[42] James M. Tompkins drafted this section based on his thesis, "Political Development in Oregon"; and his article, "The Law of the Land," 82–88.

[43] Carey, *The Emigrants' Guide*, xii–xiii.

Hastings, of course, argued for independence and warned John McLoughlin that the "Missionary Clan had petitioned the U.S. Senate to extend American jurisdiction over Oregon."[44] The Lyceum passed two other resolutions that winter, one directing that Oregon should set up a provisional government until the United States asserted its authority and one specifying that if the federal government did not act in four years, Oregon should become independent. A resolution urging immediate independence (and the election of Elijah White as president) failed miserably.

Jason Lee and his allies used several meetings held in early 1843 about a seemingly unrelated issue—wolves—to produce a government for Americans in Oregon. After the first "wolf meeting" at Lee's mission in February, the gathering got around to a problem they considered "worse than wild animals"—the British. The wolf meetings led to a general assembly at Champoeg to discuss forming a government in May 1843. Leery of American trickery, a number of Canadians came armed with instructions from McLoughlin to vote against a government. A vote to test the Canadians' strength went 52 to 50 against the Americans: considerable confusion and debating broke out until Joe Meek stood up (he later claimed) and boomed, "Its time for a divide. Those for a government over here with me." All three official records of the meeting agree that people moved to one side or another. Upon seeing their side was losing, those who opposed organizing a government went home. There was no count, but Joe Meek's biographer propagated the myth that two French-Canadians jumped sides to support the American position.[45]

The May assembly created a committee of nine men to draft a constitution. On 5 July 1843, four months before the arrival of the Great Migration, the settlers discussed and voted on the proposed organic laws, which largely dealt with filing land claims. By the time the 1843 trains arrived, it found a provisional bureaucracy in place. Peter Burnett had thought it was too early to attempt to organize a larger government, but he quickly concluded, "a government of some kind was inevitable. It grew out of stern, invincible necessity."[46]

MARCUS WHITMAN AND THE GREAT MIGRATION OF 1843

Marcus Whitman arrived at Independence in February 1843 with a caravan of Santa Fe traders and immediately departed for Washington and New York. With help from Samuel Parker, Whitman lobbied the government to promote overland emigration and pleaded with his mission board to renew its support. Whitman's

---

[44] McLoughlin, *The Letters of John McLoughlin from Fort Vancouver, 1839–44*, 251–52.

[45] Tompkins, "The Law of the Land," 86–88.

[46] "Oregon—Letter from Peter H. Burnett, Esq.," *St. Joseph Gazette*, 15 August 1845, 1/1.

superiors allowed the missions to stay open but withdrew all financial aid—the board would not even pay his travel expenses. Whitman's twelve-year-old nephew decided to return with him, and as they traveled west they saw the growing excitement about Oregon that was sweeping the frontier.[47] "It is now decided in my mind that Oregon will be occupied by American Citizens. Those who go only open the way for more another year," Whitman wrote from the Shawnee Mission in late May. "Waggons will go all the way I have no doubt this year."[48]

The romantic notion that the sudden surge of overland emigration in 1843 saved the Pacific Northwest for the American republic is overblown, but there can be no denying "the far-reaching significance of this first large and successful transcontinental emigration," the Great Migration of 1843. Something in the American westering spirit reached critical mass that spring, but the dismal state of frontier economics, rather than any sense of national destiny, probably inspired more people to move to a remote country about which they knew practically nothing. The nation had not yet recovered from the Panic of 1837 and the devastating depression that followed, while the boundless fertility of Missouri's farms and the lack of a commercial outlet had glutted the market for agricultural produce. Jesse Applegate reportedly sold a steamboat load of bacon and lard for $100, $25 less than it had cost him to raise it, only to see it burned as fuel. Many emigrants were hopelessly in debt and simply walked away from their farms and mortgages: Applegate did not even attempt to sell his farm. For many broke and desperate farmers, Oregon offered land for the taking and the chance to start a new life.[49]

About a thousand Oregon-bound travelers had gathered around Independence by May, along with William Drummond Stewart's band of some sixty wealthy British hunters and adventurers. Several lay brothers and Catholic missionary Fathers Peter Devos and Adrian Hoeken joined Stewart with their own Flathead pilot. "So we had doctors, Lawyers, botanists, Bugg Ketchers, Hunters, and men of nearly all professions," wrote William Sublette, Stewart's guide, who also brought two "Black boys of My Own, John, 14 years, and Lige, 11 years Old."[50] To complete the westbound throng, Joseph Chiles led a small California-bound contingent loaded down with trade goods and tools.

The most impatient adventurers, such as Overton Johnson and William H. Winter, set out in advance of the main emigration, but the large majority joined

---

[47] Bancroft, *History of Oregon*, 1:343–44.

[48] Whitman to "Brother Galusha," 28 May 1843, Shawnee Mission, in Hulbert and Hulbert, *Marcus Whitman, Crusader*, 2:217.

[49] Unruh, *The Plains Across*, 5; and Bancroft, *History of Oregon*, 1:391–92.

[50] Sublette, "A Fragmentary Journal of William Sublette," 102, 108.

the loosely organized Oregon Emigrating Company. The party included several men whose names would loom large in western history, including Peter H. Burnett, Isaac Williams, James Nesmith, John Myers, Samuel J. Hensley, and more than two dozen members of the Applegate clan, led by brothers Charles, Lindsay, and Jesse. According to John McLoughlin, when it reached Oregon the Emigrating Company consisted of about 875 souls. The train had some 113 wagons and perhaps five thousand cattle.[51] "It was all a private movement and we came on our own responsibility," Nineveh Ford recalled.[52] The party hired John Gantt, a former army captain turned fur trader, to guide the train to Fort Hall for a dollar per person.

The members of the Great Migration set out knowing they would have to answer a key question: could wagons and families reach Oregon from Missouri in a single season? The previous fall, Philip L. Edwards, a former companion of Jason Lee, had published a pamphlet praising Oregon but asserting that wagons could not travel more than two-thirds of the way there. Any party starting out with wagons should understand that they would have to be abandoned. Wagons

---

[51] Bancroft, *History of Oregon,* 1:395–96, 399.
[52] Ford, The Pioneer Road Makers, Bancroft Library, 9–10.

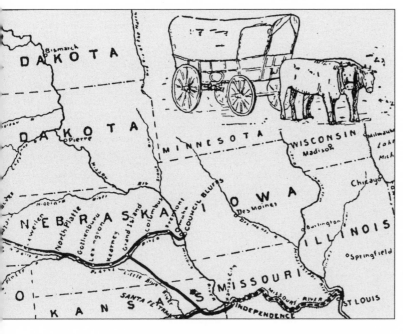

Map by Ezra Meeker.
From *Ventures and Adventures*
of Ezra Meeker or Sixty Years
of Frontier Life, Seattle, 1909.

or no, with women and children along the entire journey would take five or six months. At a gathering of prospective emigrants, Edwards spoke so eloquently against the undertaking that he discouraged all but six of the three hundred people recruited at Saint Louis from going to Oregon, John M. Shively recalled.[53] At a meeting on 18 May 1843, emigrants asked Marcus Whitman for his advice. The doctor assured them that wagons could make the trip.[54]

After a late start, on the first of June the main company stopped at the Kansas River to organize and elect officers. The aggravation that came with the title captain led Peter H. Burnett to quit after only a week, and the company elected "Colonel" William Martin and four captains in his place. On the Big Blue River it became clear that the train was much too large: the emigrants divided into a "light column" and a "cow column" that freed most travelers from the slow-moving cattle herd. West of Independence Rock, the columns regrouped into still smaller units.[55]

---

[53] Edwards, "Sketch of the Oregon Country," in White, *News of the Plains and the Rockies*, 2:292, 294–95.

[54] Lavender, *Westward Vision*, 367.

[55] Bancroft, *History of Oregon*, 1:395–97. P. B. Reading noted the division of "our company into four Marching divisions" on 2 June, five days before Burnett's resignation. As historian James M. Tompkins notes, immediately upon taking control of the families with herds, Applegate divided them into fifteen groups, each consisting of about four families. His organization allowed the "slower" column to keep pace and actually pass the "faster" column on occasion.

Frederick Piercy sketched a Mormon wagon train passing by the foot of Independence Rock in 1853. Ten years earlier, a future senator from Oregon recorded having "the satisfaction of putting the names of Miss Mary Zachary and Miss Jane Mills on the southeast point of the rock, near the road, on a high point. Facing the road, in all splendor of gun powder, tar and buffalo greese, may be seen the name of J. W. Nesmith, from Maine, with an anchor." From *Route from Liverpool to Great Salt Lake Valley,* author's collection.

Again trailing the emigrants was that dynamo of ambition John C. Frémont. The orders for his second expedition directed him to extend his 1842 reconnaissance to join Captain Charles Wilkes's naval survey, which had explored the Columbia River to Fort Walla Walla, "so as to give a connected survey of the interior of our continent." Frémont hoped to link "the frontiers of the Missouri with the mouth of the Columbia," filling in the gap in what he poetically called the Great West. The young lieutenant managed to exceed both his orders and his budget even before he left Saint Louis by requisitioning a brass mountain howitzer to "conduce" the safety of his party. The act brought a swift reprimand from his commanding officer, Colonel Abert, who pointed out that the purpose of Frémont's peaceful expedition was to collect scientific knowledge. Such war-like equipment, Abert feared, would defeat that purpose: to gather geographical information, not political intelligence. But by the time Abert's orders arrived in Missouri, Frémont and his thirty-nine men had left the frontier with their cannon. Once again his party consisted principally of "Creole and Canadian French," along with two Delaware hunters, a German artillery expert, and Jacob Dodson, a "free young colored man of Washington city" who volunteered to be Frémont's servant.[56] The indispensable Kit Carson, joined by Thomas Fitzpatrick, served as the expedition's guides.

Meanwhile, the columns of the Oregon Emigrating Company encountered storms, a battered Kanza war party, and the mutilated body of a Pawnee. One night on the Platte River a terrific storm blew over wagons and knocked down tents, "leaving the rudely awakened occupants exposed to the mercy of the elements."[57] Although the expedition found buffalo east of the Blue River, they were out of fresh meat by the time they reached Scotts Bluff, and farther west they found less game than expected, perhaps because of Captain Stewart's hunting safari. They spent four days preparing to cross the South Platte, using a rope to ferry the wagons and bullboats to haul the contents.

After visiting the frontier missions in Kansas, Marcus Whitman caught up with the light column at the crossing and almost immediately helped deliver a new member of the train. That "noble and devoted man," Jesse Applegate recalled, warned the emigrants to "travel, *travel,* travel,—nothing else will take you to the end of your journey; nothing is wise that does not help you along, nothing is good for you that causes a moment's delay." Whitman's medical services won the affection of many, although Pierson B. Reading complained that in bleeding him, the doctor "cut an orifice in my arm large enough for a beaver to make his ingress." Whitman

---

[56] Spence and Jackson, *The Expeditions of John Charles Frémont,* 1:343, 345, 426–29.
[57] Bogart, Reminiscences, Huntington Library, 1. Bogart's recollection is not without problems.

now helped John Gantt plot the best route; according to legend, he plunged into the river at Laramie to carry across a towrope. "I well remember when crossing the Platte river, which was both turbulent and high, Dr. Whitman doffed his outer garments (placing them in a wagon so as to have them dry to put on when he got over) and waded the river leading the first team by a rope attached to the oxen's horns, while the others closely followed," Nancy Hembree Bogart recalled sixty-seven years later. She claimed that if the missionary had not led them safely across a narrow stone ledge, the wagons "would have been submerged beyond their depth, causing the wagon beds to float off which would have meant great loss of life." Most emigrants fondly recalled the doctor as "that good angel." But Whitman and his nephew were traveling without supplies and relied on the kindness of strangers for their food: some would grumble for decades about the imposition.[58]

After sinking a wagon while fording the Laramie River at night, the next day the emigrants enjoyed hospitable treatment and a ball at Fort Platte, John Boardman recorded, and "some of the company got gay."[59] They crossed the sandy Black Hills, finding "the road bad; most rough and broken we have had since we started." On 18 July, six-year-old Joel Hembree fell off a wagon tongue and under its wheels, becoming perhaps the first of the many children who died on the Oregon-California Trail.[60] William T. Newby carved the headstone, which was a trail landmark for decades.

"We were not molested by the Indians beyond horse stealing and driving off cattle and having to pay to get them returned," Nineveh Ford recalled. "They were friendly generally. We saw but few. They appeared to be wild and shy and afraid of the wagons. Ours were the first wagons they ever saw."[61] At Waiilatpu that fall, Jesse Looney confirmed Ford's recollection. "We had no interuption of Indians, unless, indeed, they might have stolen a horse now and then to get a little something for bringing him in. Our greatest difficulty was in crossing rivers."[62] Matthew C. Field, a *New Orleans Picayune* correspondent traveling with the Stewart party, told a story about the Indian response to the migration. As the Sioux watched "the great number of wagons, and particularly white women and children," they began to think of occupying the homes the emigrants had abandoned in the states, "having seen, they supposed, *the whole white village* move up beyond the mountains."[63]

---

[58] Applegate, "A Day with the Cow Column in 1843," 130–31; Bogart, Reminiscences, 1; Reading, Diary, 1843, California State Library, 17; and Lavender, *Westward Vision*, 373–74.

[59] Boardman, "The Journal," 103, 104.

[60] Joel Hembree's grave was excavated in 1962 after Carl Porter discovered the headstone while digging a stock pond. See Duffin, "The Grave of Joel Hembree," 6–16.

[61] Ford, The Pioneer Road Makers, Bancroft Library, 3–4.

[62] Looney to Bond, 27 October 1843, Oregon Historical Society.

[63] Field, *Prairie and Mountain Sketches*, 29–30.

From the summit of Independence Rock, John Boardman admired the "wildest, rugged rocky mountains, thrown into all shapes and forms that the imagination can picture."[64] Typically, the ease with which they crossed South Pass astonished the travelers, and now Whitman's experience worked to their benefit. In 1836 he had crossed the north side of the pass, but Whitman knew the long, waterless crossing would play havoc with the train's livestock. The Flathead Indian guiding the Catholic missionaries had taken them southwest on a safer course along the tributaries of the Green and then into the shadows of the Uinta Mountains. Whitman learned of their route and sent word to the emigrants that the Native pilot had found a shortcut to the mountains. The trail to Blacks Fork and the Bear River was in fact some seventy miles longer than what became the Sublette Cutoff, but it spared the emigrants and their animals fifty barren miles without water.[65]

By chance, that summer a new attraction had opened for business on Blacks Fork, even though it was still "a shabby concern" built of poles and daubed with mud when emigrant Joel Palmer described the post two years later.[66] Jim Bridger and Henry Fraeb had started a trading station on the west bank of Green River in August 1841, not long after Fraeb's encounter with the Bidwell-Bartleson party. When Indians killed Fraeb while he was in the mountains "making meat" for winter, Bridger abandoned the site, moved to Blacks Fork, and started a trading post in partnership with Louis Vasquez.

In 1843 a contingent of Frémont's second expedition under Thomas Fitzpatrick "came nearly west along Black's Fork passing under the bluff on which Vasquez & Bridger's houses are built." It was, as Bridger noted that December, "in the road of the emigrants" at a beautiful location with fine, fresh water from the Uintas, its streams alive with mountain trout. It was also vulnerable to attack, as Arapaho and Cheyenne raiders demonstrated in August 1843 when they had "run off all the buffalo, killed 3 Snake Indians, and stolen 60 horses." Bridger had only a few Indian trade goods on hand when the wagon trains arrived that year, so he did not do much trading with them, but he noted they had plenty of "ready cash from the states" and needed horses, blacksmithing, and all kinds of supplies. He told a prospective partner he hoped to "have considerable business in that way with them" in the future. He also moved his fort to an island in Blacks Fork near the site of today's Fort Bridger, Wyoming.[67]

---

[64] Mattes, *Platte River Road Narratives,* 53; and of Boardman, "The Journal," 103, 104.

[65] Mattes, *Platte River Road Narratives,* 53.

[66] Palmer, *Journal of Travels,* 25 July 1843, 74.

[67] Gowans and Campbell, *Fort Bridger,* 11; Anderson, *The Rocky Mountain Journals,* 267; and Spence and Jackson, *The Expeditions of John Charles Frémont,* 1:462n40, 467n43.

Laying down the classic route of the Oregon Trail as they went, the emigrants left Blacks Fork, ascended the Little Muddy, and climbed over the Bear River Divide, the highest point they crossed on their journey. In late August, Frémont found the valley of the Bear "dotted with the white covers of the emigrant wagons," the women "occupied in preparing the evening meal, and the children playing in the grass." From here the travelers followed the Bear to Soda Springs, where John Boardman found a hot spring that "rumbles, roars, and gushes up water, much like in appearance, the puff of a high pressure steamboat." (Some of the boys made a futile attempt to plug Steamboat Spring.) They then turned northwest to strike the Portneuf River and follow it into the Snake River Valley.[68]

After the Oregon Company visited his post in late August, Richard Grant estimated that "No less than 130 & odd Waggons with nearly one thousand souls, besides several hundred head of horned Cattle, Horses, Mules &c. passed Fort Hall last Summer, on their way to Columbia, Calefornia & Flat Head Mission." He informed the Company that very few beavers remained in the Snake Country, but "something handsome I think might be made" by keeping "a good stock of flour, rice, coffee and sugar" to be sold to emigrants on their way to California and the Columbia. With only a few goods at hand, Grant reported sales of $1,350 to the emigrants "and other passants," plus acquiring a few furs and "several kind of horn Cattle & horses exchanged for others not in quite such good condition at the rate of two for one."[69]

The next summer Grant picked up a few hundred dollars from passing trains. But for years he was "left with hardly any goods and no horses to carry on trade" with anyone but Indians, and despite his best efforts, he could not persuade the Company to supply him with the "necessary articles of goods, groceries & provisions to meet the demands of the Emigrants."[70] James Nesmith complained about the fort's exorbitant prices, but P. B. Reading found Grant's hospitality almost extreme, "and it appears to give him much pleasure to have it in his power to serve them."[71]

The sojourners asked Grant's advice about the momentous decision they confronted at Fort Hall. "The migration of a large body of men, women, and children across the Continent to Oregon was, in the year 1843, strictly an experiment,"

---

[68] Ibid., 1:473–74; Boardman, "The Journal," 7 September 1843, 110; and Applegate, "Recollections of My Boyhood," 50.

[69] Grant to Simpson, 15 March 1844, D.5/10, HBC Archives, 427.

[70] Grant to Simpson, 31 January 1851, D.5/30, HBC Archives, 184–85. Today a replica of the fort stands in Ross Park, near downtown Pocatello. Nothing remains at the original site eleven miles west of the modern town of Fort Hall on the Shoshone-Bannock Reservation that became a National Historic Landmark in 1961. The tribes will arrange visits, but beware: it is still a paradise for mosquitoes.

[71] Nesmith, "Diary of the Emigration of 1843," 350; and Reading, Diary, 1843, California State Library, 20.

Jesse Applegate recalled. "It was the honest opinion of most of those who had traveled the route down Snake river that no large number of cattle could be subsisted on its scanty pasturage, or wagons taken over a route so rugged and mountainous."[72] Peter Burnett asked Grant if they could get their wagons to Oregon. Grant would not say it was impossible for Americans to make the trip, but he could not see how it could be done. He only knew the pack-trail, and he was sure no wagons could go that way, "but there might be a practical road found by leaving the trail at certain points."[73]

As Tallmadge B. Wood noted, Fort Hall was two-thirds of the way to the Willamette Valley, but the hard part of the journey had only commenced.[74] Grant "endeavored to dissuade us from proceeding further with our wagons, and showed us the wagons that the emigrants of the preceding year had abandoned, as an evidence of the impracticability of our determination," James Nesmith recalled in 1875. But Whitman persistently asserted wagons could go as far as The Dalles and be ferried down the river to the Willamette Valley, while livestock could be driven over the Cascades on an Indian trail.[75] The emigrants collected $400 to pay Whitman to guide them to the Columbia, a token of their admiration for the missionary doctor. Scouting ahead for the easiest routes and best campsites and sending dispatches up and down the line, Whitman repaid their confidence, offering information to all and encouragement to exhausted stragglers. He had concluded correctly that the emigrants had enough manpower to blaze a wagon road: subsequent events suggest that with enough strong backs, Americans could have built a wagon road to the North Pole.

It was not easy. Many emigrants reported that the trail to Fort Hall was much better than expected, but now they were truly pioneering a road, often through dense sagebrush. "We found no tracks. In some places we found an Indian trail and in other places not," Nineveh Ford told an interviewer in 1878, noting that an Indian trail often went straight up and down, "where wagons could not go," and the pioneer road builders preferred to seek out ridges and divides. "We seldom followed the trail. It was better traveling out of it than in it, it confused our teams." Worst of all was the "great deal of sage brush which was very hard to get over. We could not stop to chop it out. The wagons would bend it down but the ground was sandy and the wagons would sink deep into the sand and then rise high on the sage brush. The foremost wagons would mash it down. It tired the foremost teams very much."

[72] Applegate, "A Day with the Cow Column in 1843," 127.
[73] Burnett, *Recollections and Opinions of an Old Pioneer,* 117.
[74] Wood, "Tallmadge B. Wood Letter," 396.
[75] Nesmith, "Occasional Address," 47.

The trailblazers had to replace the lead team every day "and use the strongest teams and the strongest wagons to mash the sage brush down. We could do it however so that the next wagon could follow more easily. Frequently there would be a horseman ahead who rode where the wagons ought to go. If they found any obstacle in the way they would turn back and notify the train and turn them in [the] right direction."[76] That fall Jesse Looney advised his brother-in-law to wear good strong clothing or "the wild sage will trip you up." The sagebrush was hard on teams, especially those that had to break the trail, "but it will not be so bad on those that come next year," Looney wrote, "for we have left a plain well beaten road all the way."[77]

Not long after "some inconsiderate emigrant axe" felled the magnificent Lone Pine on Powder River that summer, bad news arrived from the missions that compelled Whitman to leave the emigrants to find their way to Waiilatpu, guided by Stickus, a Cayuse leader who had won his trust.[78] "Wherever he directed us to go there we went, without searching for any other route," Ford recalled, noting that although the road had since changed in many places, Stickus "found us a pretty fair route for getting through. The Indian did not look about much, he was familiar with the ground."[79]

After a hard crossing of the Blue Mountains, the emigration arrived in the Walla Walla Valley in the middle of October. Many arranged to trade their cattle to the Hudson's Bay Company and took canoes or rafted their wagons down the Columbia River to Fort Vancouver. Some pressed on with their wagons, but all their trials had "sorely taxed their powers of endurance," remembered Nancy Hembree Bogart, "so it was a sorry looking procession that wended its way into the place now called the Dalles," where they confronted the river and the volcano that separated them from the Willamette Valley.[80]

Whitman was absent from Waiilatpu when the emigration arrived, having been called east to Lapwai to treat the Spaldings for scarlet fever and deliver a baby for Myra Eells. Many of the emigrants bitterly resented the prices the mission charged for the few available provisions, and some of the packers robbed the Whitman home.[81] Ignoring such ingratitude, Whitman was proud of his accomplishment. His pioneers, he asserted, had "practically demonstrated that waggons drawn by horses or oxen can cross the Rocky Mountains to the Columbia River contrary to all the sinister assertions of all those who pretended it to be impossible."[82] The crowd that greeted Nineveh Ford and his companions made many

[76] Ford, The Pioneer Road Makers, Bancroft Library, 9–10.
[77] Looney to Bond, 27 October 1843, Oregon Historical Society.
[78] Lavender, Westward Vision, 379–80; and Spence and Jackson, The Expeditions of John Charles Frémont, 1:543.
[79] Ford, The Pioneer Road Makers, Bancroft Library, 12.
[80] Bogart, Reminiscences, Huntington Library.
[81] Boardman, "The Journal," 116.
[82] Whitman to Secretary of War, late 1843, in Drury, Marcus and Narcissa Whitman, 2:396.

comical remarks about the raft they floated down to Fort Vancouver, but John McLoughlin complimented their determination. "They beat any people for perseverance and enterprise that he ever saw or heard of," he said.[83]

"The road is good, much better than we expected, but it is long," Jesse Looney wrote from Waiilatpu that fall. He advised prospective travelers to take plenty of provisions, passing on one of the hard lessons members of Oregon's first large wagon train had learned. Looney concluded that the trip, however long and lonesome it might be, had been worthwhile. "This is a fine valley of land—excellent water, Good climate—and the finest kind of pine timber on the surrounding mountains and above all, a first rate range for stock, both winter and summer."[84] That wagons had reached the Columbia River now made the remote Eden all the more compelling.

Wagons would not climb over the mountains to Willamette Valley until 1846, but the Great Migration of 1843 answered the question of whether Americans could build a wagon road to Oregon. Fewer than three hundred of the emigrants were males over the age of sixteen, but there were still "men enough to make a wagon road where none existed."[85] They also laid the foundation for the myth that Whitman's actions and the arrival of large numbers of settlers "saved" Oregon for the United States.[86] Whitman came to believe the story himself, imagining that without his assistance the trek would have collapsed: by his "effort alone, the immigration was secured & saved from disaster," he argued in the last known letter he ever wrote.[87]

The tide of migration was now in flood. A year later, a Baptist minister at Fort Hall asked whether the emigrants could get to the Columbia River with wagons. "Mr. Cave, it's no use my answering your question. It's just a year since a lot of people came here just as you have done and asked me the same question. I told them 'No; that we found it very difficult to pass the narrow trails with our pack ponies,'" Grant replied. "They went on, just as you will do: just as if I had not spoken a word, and the next I heard of them they were at Fort Walla Walla. You ——— Yankees will do anything you like."[88] William Barlow recalled that when his father said he was going to drive his teams into the Willamette Valley, Grant remarked, "Well . . . if you say you will take your wagons over the mountains, you will do. The darned Yankees will go anywhere they say they will."[89] Eventually

---

[83] Ford, *The Pioneer Road Makers*, Bancroft Library, 18–19.

[84] Looney to Bond, 27 October 1843, Oregon Historical Society.

[85] Bancroft, *History of Oregon*, 1:395–96, 399.

[86] The classic statement of this theory is in Nixon, *How Marcus Whitman Saved Oregon*.

[87] Whitman to Greene, 18 October 1847, in Hulbert and Hulbert, *Marcus Whitman, Crusader*, 3:245.

[88] Minto, "Reminiscences of Experiences on the Oregon Trail in 1844," 217–18.

[89] Barlow, "Reminiscences of Seventy Years," 259. Rest assured that Richard Grant did not say "darned."

Grant concluded, "There is no place where you Yankees cannot carry a wagon, that I ever saw!"[90] Decades later, one overlander recalled the astonishment that greeted the first American wagons to reach Fort Vancouver: "Tut! tut! tut!" John McLoughlin allegedly said. "The damned Yankees would get to China with their ox wagons yet!"[91]

A Yankee ox wagon, however, had yet to reach California.

An Impracticable Barrier: Seeking a Way to California

John C. Frémont and his second expedition camped at Elm Grove on the last day of May 1843 with an emigrant party on its way to Alta California. Joseph Chiles was leading some thirty men and a number of women and children (including several accomplished, intelligent, "and very hand some young ladies") in his second attempt to reach California with wagons. The train was well equipped with trading goods, furniture, hardware, and—among other surprises—a complete sawmill. Chiles's overburdened party was poorly supplied with provisions, which they assumed could be hunted or purchased at trading posts. Chiles's venture seems to have been the first attempt to haul freight across the plains to take advantage of the phenomenal prices manufactured goods commanded in California, but it was a dangerously ambitious bit of trail enterprise. He started out behind the Oregon companies and, after picking up Marcus Whitman, caught up with them at the crossing of the South Platte, where eighteen Oregon-bound wagons joined his train. This consolidated company left the main emigration behind at the ford of the North Platte.[92]

In the Black Hills, the emigration met two traders, Joseph R. Walker and Louis Vasquez, on their way to Fort Laramie. Walker, "celebrated as one of the best and bravest" of the mountaineers, returned to Fort Bridger and joined the migration. By 15 August he had agreed to pilot Chiles to the "Point of the Mountains"—Walker Pass—but Fort Bridger had no supplies to sell the emigrants and Fort Hall had "neither meat, flour nor rice." Richard Grant was reluctant to part with any of his few cattle, and Walker refused to "start with the wagons till he has meat," John Boardman recorded. (Frémont also overestimated the availability of game and his men were already living on horsemeat.) Some of Walker's party talked of seizing the cattle by force rather than resort to eating horsemeat. Julius Martin and David McClellan were "unable to resist the clamors of their children

[90] Bruff, *Gold Rush,* 1:107.

[91] Stoughton, "Passing of an Immigrant of 1843," 209.

[92] Spence and Jackson, *The Expeditions of John Charles Frémont,* 1:343, 345, 429; and Reading, Diary, 1843, California State Library, 11, 12.

for food," Lieutenant Theodore Talbot of Frémont's expedition noted, and he promised to help the men if Grant refused to sell them provisions. They returned to the fort where "they boldly bearded the lion in his den and succeeded in frightening him into terms." Grant relented and sold Chiles four beeves at a high price. The next day, Chiles and Walker set out for California.[93]

The lack of provisions led the California-bound travelers to make an astonishing gamble. "Chiles talks of leaving his wagons, and packing through to California," John Boardman noted. "All are in a quandary to know how they are going to California." Chiles wanted Boardman and his companions to accompany him, but since no one knew the route, most of the travelers headed to Oregon.[94] As John C. Frémont pointed out, the great mass of mountains comprising the Sierra Nevada was considered "an impracticable barrier to wheeled carriages." Chiles decided to divide the California company, sending the women, children, and sawmill irons across the Great Basin with his partner, William Baldridge, and Joseph R. Walker, to blaze a wagon road, while Chiles himself sought "a more direct course" to the Sacramento.

Several factors led the emigrants to break up into two parties, Frémont wrote after talking to Walker the next spring. Thirteen men set out with Chiles's pack train bound for Fort Boise, where they planned to purchase supplies, head west, outflank the northern Sierra Nevada, and follow the rivers south to Sutters Fort. In California, they would secure a "reinforcement of animals, and a supply of provisions" and take them to meet the wagons at a predetermined rendezvous east of the mountains.[95]

The pack train made good time following the Oregon Trail to Fort Boise. "All felt elated when they came in sight of the Fort, supposing they would get plenty of provisions," John Boardman wrote, "but how soon were all hopes dampened when we learned the Oregon company had bought all that could be spared, and many of the company almost starved or suffering for want of provisions. No flour, meat, rice or sugar; but one beef to sell, and that for a horse." Instead, Chiles's party bought beef at seven cents a pound.[96] Turning west, the packers relied on Indian guides and advice from François Payette at Fort Boise to find their way through the deserts of southeastern Oregon to the head of the Sacramento Valley.

Now weak from starvation, the Chiles party butchered its dead animals and subsisted entirely on horse and mule flesh. As they struggled through the deserts

---

[93] Boardman, "The Journal," 111; Spence and Jackson, *The Expeditions of John Charles Frémont,* 1:508; and Talbot, *The Journals of Theodore Talbot,* 48–49. Editor Charles H. Carey identified McClellan as "F. McClelland." See Ibid., 127.

[94] Boardman, "The Journal," 13, 30 September, 1 October 1843, 111, 113–14.

[95] Spence and Jackson, *The Expeditions of John Charles Frémont,* 1:525.

[96] Boardman, "The Journal," 113. Hunger was often forgotten in the annals of the Great Migration, but many 1843 emigrants were "almost starved or suffering for want of provisions," Boardman noted.

and mountains of northern California, Indians filled some of their best animals with arrows. The angry Americans "swore vengeance against the Diggers," wrote Pierson B. Reading, and they resolved to kill every Indian they saw. At last, on 8 November they found cattle at "Capt Souters ranch," Hock Farm on Feather River. Two days later they reached their destination, John A. Sutter's "extensive Fort." Sutter's "truly beautiful estate," especially the fort, which was "large and imposing on its approach with its high walls, its bastions frowning with heavy cannon biding defiance to the enemy," astonished Reading.[97] Sutter was willing to share his bounty to provide relief to the families seeking to cross the Sierra with Joe Walker, but it was too late to hope that such an effort could succeed, for snow had already blocked the Sierra passes. Chiles and his companions could only hope Walker would bring their families and friends through the mountains alive.

PERSEVERANCE AND INDUSTRY AND ENTERPRISE: JOHN A. SUTTER

While men such as Lansford W. Hastings and Thomas J. Farnham dreamed of building empires in the West, a Swiss imposter with little more to rely on than charm, ambition, bluster, and Indian labor had conjured up his own fiefdom in the Sacramento Valley. In his early thirties John A. Sutter fled his creditors and abandoned his wife and children in Switzerland. After arriving in the United States in 1834, he established himself as a merchant, innkeeper, and Santa Fe trader on the Missouri frontier. For a time he prospered, but by 1837 he was deeply in debt. "It took him about eighteen months to gallop through his visible assets," recalled John C. McCoy. "Civil suits, attachments, and other legal contrivances made short work of his air castles." Sutter considered suicide, but in 1838 he again fled his creditors, who "could scarcely believe that such a noble foreigner would swindle them."[98]

Sutter joined Andrew Drips's fur caravan, and from the rendezvous he made his way to Fort Vancouver, Hawaii, and Russian Alaska before landing in California on 1 July 1839. In August he chartered four boats at Yerba Buena and set out to find the Sacramento River and found the first white colony in California's great Central Valley. "I had the best chances to get some of the finest locations near the settlements; and even well stocked ranchos had been offered to me on the most reasonable conditions," he later recalled, "but I refused all these good offers, and preferred to explore the wilderness, and select a territory on the banks of the Sacramento."[99]

[97] Reading, Diary, 1843, California State Library, 24, 31, 34.
[98] Staab, "Sutter in Westport," 99–101.
[99] Paul, *The California Gold Discovery*, 126.

A born opportunist, Sutter ("pronounced by himself Sooter") had brought "5 white men and 8 Kanacas (two of them married)" with him from Hawaii. His little party pushed up the river until they encountered some two hundred Indians ten miles below the confluence of the American and Sacramento rivers, "all armed & painted & looked very hostile." His white men soon wanted to know "how much longer I intended to travell with them in such a wilderness," he recalled. "I saw plain it was a Mutiny." He answered his men the next morning when he pitched his tents on the left bank of the American River. Only three whites stuck with him, but sheltered behind three cannons and a vicious bulldog, Sutter began building his dominion and an impressive adobe fort using Hawaiian workers and Indian labor acquired through alliances with local leaders or by simple violence.[100]

When Sutter arrived, perhaps as many as fifty thousand Natives lived in the Sacramento Valley. As historian Albert Hurtado observed, during the early 1840s Sutter was primarily engaged in "the Indian business." He ruthlessly exploited the valley's Natives and instructed his overseer to keep his Miwok and Nisean labor force "strictly under fear."[101] When he first saw the fort in 1846, Heinrich Lienhard recalled, "a gruesome sight met my eyes: the long, black hair and skull of an Indian dangling from one of the gateposts." Sutter eventually kept between six and eight hundred Indians "in a complete state of Slavery," James Clyman wrote in disgust, and fed them from wooden "troughs like so many pigs."[102]

By 1841 Sutter was a Mexican citizen and had wrangled a land grant of 48,827 acres from Governor Juan Bautista Alvarado, specifically "to prevent the robberies committed by adventurers from the United States, to stop the invasion of savage Indians, and the hunting and trading by companies from the Columbia."[103] He named his private empire New Helvetia after his homeland and raised an adobe fortress "in form of a parallelogram, 500 feet in length by 150 in breadth" near the mouth of the American River as his headquarters.[104] When Pearson B. Reading saw it in fall 1843, the fort had a gristmill, distillery, tannery, blacksmith shop, and a large mansion—a credit, Reading wrote, to Sutter's perseverance, industry, and enterprise.[105]

A number of ambitious foreigners converted to Catholicism and acquired substantial land grants in California's backcountry, notably Peter Lassen, John

---

[100] Owens, *John Sutter and a Wider West*, 4–5.

[101] Ibid., 51, 56, 63. Hurtado's magnificent *John Sutter: A Life on the North American Frontier* is the best study of Sutter's career.

[102] Lienhard, *A Pioneer at Sutter's Fort*, 3; and Clyman, *James Clyman, Frontiersman*, 21 July 1845, 174.

[103] Zollinger, *Sutter*, 80.

[104] "Capt. Sutter," *New-York Daily Tribune*, 7 April 1849.

[105] Reading, Diary, 1843, California State Library, 34. Kenneth N. Owens, *John Sutter and a Wider West*, reinterpreted Sutter's career.

Bidwell, and John Sinclair. Pablo Gutierrez secured a large grant on Bear River in 1844, and following his murder the next year, William Johnson, a New England mariner who came to California in about 1840, bought the ranch at auction. The ranch he built near what is now Wheatland became the first outpost early west-bound travelers came to after leaving the Sierra. Johnson and his partners sold the ranch late in 1849, but it was used as a store and remained an important trail site until about 1853.[106]

Sutter played to Mexican and American interests as they suited his needs, but his famous fort became the destination of Americans bound for California. Like John McLoughlin at Fort Vancouver, he offered food and work to the emigrants who often reached his outpost in desperate straits. But as Edward Kern noted after taking command of Sutters Fort during the War with Mexico, Sutter had "already lost much by his unbounded hospitality"—and he would ultimately lose much more.[107]

The Way to California

The trail to Oregon was challenging, but by 1840 fur traders had used it for more than a decade. Only one American party had ever traveled between the upper Snake River and the Mexican province of Alta California, when Joseph Walker returned from his expedition down the Humboldt and over the Sierra. The lack of geographical knowledge led some to conclude such a route would be extremely arduous and maybe impossible. "Westwardly from the Snake River there are sev-eral steep mountain chains with many glaciers, dividing this country from Cali-fornia and the Pacific Ocean," Frederick Wislizenus wrote in 1839. "The direct road to California is very difficult on account of these mountains. Even unloaded mules can cross them only with great effort." The doctor advised those going to Alta California to go to the Columbia River and then head south.[108]

From its parting with the Oregon Trail, the best natural wagon road to Cali-fornia headed southwest up the Raft River Valley to "Silent" City of Rocks, a startling collection of ancient granite monoliths eroded into fantastic shapes that evoked pyramids, steeples, fortresses, and temples. Below two towering rocks that overlooked the route like twin sisters was a natural junction for trails to the Great Salt Lake and the headwaters of the Humboldt River. Located near the intersection of today's Idaho, Nevada, and Utah borders, City of Rocks lies just north of the 42nd parallel, the international boundary in 1840: from the summit

---

[106] Steed, *The Donner Party Rescue Site*, 3–4, 39–40, 124–26.
[107] Kern to Hull, ca. 29 January 1847, Huntington Library.
[108] Wislizenus, *Journey to the Rocky Mountains*, 108.

Historian David E. Miller's photograph shows the Salt Lake Cutoff as it approached its junction with the California Trail near the City of Rocks formation known as the Twin Sisters. Courtesy Utah State Historical Society.

of Granite Pass a view of northern Mexico and its apparently endless ranges of mountains spread out to the horizon, shrouded in a blue haze.

After a precipitous descent from the pass, Goose Creek and its upper fork provided a path through this alpine maze, leading back over the rim of the Great Basin to Thousand Springs Valley. A spectacular set of hot and cold springs bubbled up from a meadow at the valley's southern end. Brush Creek Draw led to the ridge dividing the Great Salt Lake Basin from the headwaters of Peter Skene Ogden's Unknown River.[109] Joseph Walker's party had called it the Barren River, but most trappers and traders knew it as Ogdens River, for obvious reasons, or Marys River, a name that was said to honor Ogden's Indian wife. John C. Frémont renamed the river for his hero, Alexander Humboldt, the German naturalist: it was at best a dubious honor, given the contempt sojourners had for the watercourse they denounced as "the Humbug."

Other than Ogden's Hudson's Bay Company brigades, only a handful of white fur hunters had ever laid eyes on the desert river that was the key to opening a wagon road to California. As the view from Granite Pass revealed, the Great Basin's mountain ranges ran north and south, creating a basin-and-range pattern as regular as a washboard. The valley of Marys River cut through the washboard's ridges, providing the only reasonable east-to-west path across the central Great Basin. From the Hot and Cold Springs in Thousand Springs Valley, there were two approaches to the river: a direct route down the scenic but narrow Bishop Creek Canyon, and a more roundabout way to the river's other headwaters at a group of pools soon known as the Wells.

At first, the mountain-born river passed through broad, grassy valleys under the shadow of majestic snowcapped peaks. At the foot of Elko Mountain, a hot spring spewed "forth volumes of steam like a cauldron of boiling water" that could be seen for miles; it proved a fine place to do laundry.[110] A few miles farther on, the South Fork and its winding canyon joined the river, which then cut through five miles of the Adobe Range to form Carlin Canyon. To avoid Palisade Canyon's four river crossings, travelers crossed Emigrant Pass and returned to the river at Gravelly Ford. From the ford, both sides of the river provided a tolerable to very good road, but places such as Stony Point and Iron Point soon earned a reputation for violence.

After a big bend north to the confluence of the Little Humboldt—so little it was usually reduced to a trickle during the summer—the river turned southwest. Another fifty miles brought travelers to a meadow on the edge of the Black

---

[109] Ogden said it was also "known as *Swampy River* or *Paul's River*." See Ogden, *Peter Skene Ogden's Snake Country Journals,* 2 June 1829.

[110] Batchelder, Journal, 5 September 1849, Bancroft Library.

Rock Desert, known after 1848 as Lassens Meadow, which offered the last good grazing until the river's end. The playa to the west promised a chance to escape the river and outflank the Sierra Nevada and the Cascades, or at least a place to make a relatively easy crossing of the mountain wall that barred a passage to the coast as effectively as it bottled up the waters of the Great Basin. No other spot offered such a seductive opportunity for a shortcut to the valleys of Oregon and California. On leaving the meadow, the desolate river turned directly south, diminishing in size and quality as it passed through blasted peaks languishing like so much broken crockery in the rain shadow of the Sierra Nevada. The landscape grew increasingly harsh: "naked, barren mountains, and mountains beyond and on the top of the mountains, and all void of vegetation of any kind."[111]

At last the dying river spread out to form a grassland marsh called the Big Meadows. The river valley offered better grazing in 1840 than it does today, especially in its many vanished sloughs and wetlands, now lost to irrigation. Getting there required a dry, rocky, and dusty forty-mile trek with the only water being the miserable dregs of the river, now "bad enough to kill the devil," one traveler complained.[112] Below the marsh the river's mineral-laden waters came to rest in the Humboldt Lake, a shallow lagoon created by a huge natural dike. By summer the lower lake was usually a brilliant white playa, an alkaline flat known as the Sink. The dike marked the terminus of the river and the beginning of the Forty-mile Desert. From here two long, hard drives led to grass and flowing water: a southwestern route to the Truckee River and a more southerly crossing to the Carson River. Sandhills and sagebrush made either trek miserable. About midway on the trail to the Truckee, boiling alkaline pools bubbled up from fragile crevices that were prone to swallow dogs and mules. Otherwise both trails were waterless and a bit longer than forty miles.

Ascending the Truckee River's winding canyon led to another Big Meadows in the valley below the Sierra foothills, where Reno now stands. The trail up the Carson River made a longer, drier passage to a well-watered and forested valley that led to the narrow canyon from which the Carson's west fork escaped the mountains. Both rivers opened narrow gateways into the single greatest challenge on the entire trail: the granite wall of the Sierra Nevada.

This imposing mountain barricade appeared impenetrable to anything on wheels. No known European had crossed it by any means before Jedediah Smith did so on horseback in 1827, and only a handful of hardy souls had ever surmounted the barrier until well into the 1840s. Several life-giving rivers flowed

111 Hale, "Diary of a Trip to California," 10 August 1849, 105.
112 Hanna, Diary, 25, 29 July 1850, Bancroft Library.

into the Great Basin, and the Truckee and the Carson canyons offered the most
promising portals into California, but the Truckee route required crossing a
7,239-foot pass and the Carson route's West Pass topped out at 9,600 feet elevation. The southernmost of these watercourses, the Walker River, lured some of
the first overlanders up its canyon and eventually found limited use as a wagon
road, but its passes proved to be even higher and harder than those on the Carson
route. The "bald and inaccessible summits of the Sierra," Edwin Bryant observed,
formed a "formidable and apparently impassable barrier erected by Nature."[113]

A LONG AND A HAZARDOUS JOURNEY: JOSEPH R. WALKER

As John C. Frémont observed, when the small wagon train set out for California
with Joseph R. Walker in 1843, they began "a long and a hazardous journey for a
party in which there were women and children."[114] The emigrants were extraordinarily lucky that a man with Walker's unique qualifications agreed to guide
them, since he was one of the few men alive who had crossed the Great Basin and
the Sierra. Given the arduous nature of that venture, it must have been the lure of
California that persuaded him to undertake such a difficult journey again.

Walker left the Portneuf on 17 September with his nephew, David McClellan; three mule-drawn wagons; fifteen other men; four women; and five children. Elizabeth McPherson, wife of Julius Martin, was the mother of three small
daughters, Mary, Arzelia, and Martha. Frances Vines, the wife of Bartlett Vines
and mother of two children, and her unmarried sister, Elizabeth Ann, were the
daughters of George Yount whom Joseph Chiles had promised to bring to California. The somewhat mysterious Miss Ayers (or Ayres), surely one of the "very hand
some young ladies" who had caught Pierson B. Reading's eye at the South Platte
ford, was probably the daughter of Miles Ayres, who had left her father at the end
of August for beating her and went on to California with Julius Martin.[115]

Not far behind Walker, John C. Frémont reached Raft River after visiting Fort
Hall. The Pathfinder followed "a plain wagonroad leading up this stream" until
he realized the trace was heading directly south. "We were on a trail formed by
a party of wagons," he wrote, "with whom we had encamped at Elm grove, near
the frontier of Missouri, and which you will remember were proceeding to Upper
California under the direction of Mr. Jos. Chiles." They still had to cross the
Sierra Nevada—*"the Great California mountain"*—which was said to be impassible

---

[113] Bryant, *What I Saw in California*, 26 August 1846, 230.

[114] Spence and Jackson, *The Expeditions of John Charles Frémont*, 1:525.

[115] Stewart, *The California Trail*, 47; Camp, *George C. Yount*, 165; Reading, Diary, 1843, California State Library,
11; and Bancroft, *History of California*, 4:393, 399–400, 732; 5:764.

for anything on wheels. Chiles's party later divided, and "a greater portion of the camp, including the wagons, with the mail and other stores, were now proceeding under the guidance of Mr. Joseph Walker, who had engaged to conduct them, by a long sweep to the southward, around what is called the *point of the mountain;* and, crossing through a pass known only to himself, gain the banks of the Sacramento by the valley of the San Joaquin." As Frémont noted, the route lay through country with very poor game and "inhabited by wild and badly disposed Indians." Walker, however, possessed "great and intimate knowledge of the Indians, with an extraordinary firmness and decision of character."[116]

Retracing the trail he had explored ten years earlier, Walker guided his charges up the Raft River Valley, over the rim of the Great Basin to Goose Creek, across the rim again to Thousand Springs Valley, and down Bishop Creek Canyon to the Humboldt River. Walker's 1834 trail proved to be the best way to get wagons from the Snake River to the Humboldt, and the Humboldt was the key to crossing the Great Basin with wheeled vehicles.

From the Humboldt Sink, Walker turned southwest along the trail he had used to leave California in 1834. The wagons entered the pass that now bears his name, far to the south of what soon became the major portals of the Sierra. Suffering "infinite hardships," the emigrants abandoned their wagons and cached Chiles's sawmill a day's drive from Owens Lake. On horseback they crossed the southern Sierra Nevada and entered the arid plain of the great Central Valley of California. From here the migrants wandered into the Coastal Range to reach the Salinas Valley in January.[117]

Walker Pass proved to be an impractical road (and an elusive goal to many later would-be pathfinders), but in blazing a wagon trace from Raft River to the Forty-mile Desert, Walker established the basic route that tens of thousands of emigrants would later take to El Dorado. Still, sheer distance meant that any attempt to open a wagon road that outflanked the heights of the central Sierra was doomed to failure. But Captain Walker had demonstrated that wagons could reach the "impracticable barrier" of the California mountains, and he had done it without losing a single member of the party.

But so far, all the wagons that had entered the Sierra Nevada had not come out, and no one had yet taken an American wagon into the valleys of California.

---

[116] Spence and Jackson, *The Expeditions of John Charles Frémont,* 26 September 1843, 153–55.
[117] Bancroft, *History of California,* 4:394–95.

CHAPTER 6

THE RESTLESS ONES

The Swelling Tides of 1844 and 1845

With the success of the Great Migration to Oregon and the blazing of a practical wagon road across the Great Basin to California in 1843, the next two years saw the floodtide of overland migration run strong: it almost doubled in size in 1844, and added another thousand souls in 1845. As Americans grew increasingly concerned about the fate of the Pacific Coast, and for the first time expansionism became a major issue in a presidential election, these treks took place against a dramatic political backdrop. The results of John C. Frémont's first expedition to South Pass, including the spectacularly popular report it produced, encouraged both the government and the energetic young explorer, who completed his second western journey in 1844, published his second report, and launched his third expedition in 1845. That year Colonel Stephen W. Kearny led the first military expedition up the North Platte—the undertaking impressed the Indians, but other travelers sharing the road did not entirely appreciate the army's presence. Schemer Lansford Hastings returned in 1844 from Oregon and California fired with ambition and within a year had published a guidebook that proved to be as reckless as it was influential. Another charming but untrustworthy young promoter-frontiersman, Stephen Meek, persuaded the first large wagon train to gamble on an unexplored shortcut, establishing a pattern of disastrous experiments that would affect hundreds of sojourners for the rest of the 1840s. In two short years, America's knowledge of the West increased dramatically, and a new catchphrase captured a rapidly changing society's restless impulses: Manifest Destiny.

THE TEXAS GAME AND THE POLITICS OF NATIONAL EXPANSION

The election of 1844 brought the American West to the forefront of presidential politics, and that year's migration reflected the nation's growing interest in Oregon and California. More people went west in 1844 than in the previous three years combined. Some fifteen hundred men, women, and children, half again as many settlers as had departed in 1843, set out for Oregon that spring. The number of California-bound travelers remained a small fraction of the total exodus, but when these fifty-odd adventurers worked out a wagon road over the Sierra Nevada, they accomplished what had long seemed impossible.

A number of critical developments transformed the jumping-off towns at the start of the overland trail. Joseph Robidoux had been trading in the Black Snake Hills, sixty-five miles north of Independence, since at least 1826, and he formally founded Saint Joseph in 1843. The next spring wagons departed for the first time from the new town, which was close to the Platte Purchase, the former home of many early emigrants.[1] Equally important, parties originating in Iowa Territory set out from Council Bluffs, taking the first emigrant trains along the north bank of the Platte.[2] Like tens of thousands who later followed them, many of those who left Council Bluffs were bound for California.

President Tyler's covert operation using a private business and the American Navy revealed his secret support for emigration to the Pacific Coast, but American settlers in Oregon were getting impatient at the inaction of Congress and the diplomatic failure to sort out who owned what in the Pacific Northwest. There was growing agitation in the West to create an independent Republic of Oregon. "The population of this country are no doubt desirous to live under the government of the United States," Peter Burnett wrote from Oregon on the eve of the presidential election, "but if she will never do anything for us, we must, and will do it for ourselves."[3]

The Mississippi Valley's growing political and commercial power helped make western expansion a national issue in 1844. The Republic of Texas had applied for admission to the Union, and its request and the unsettled status of Oregon turned the race into a referendum on the future of the country. Martin Van Buren's opposition to the annexation of Texas cost him the Democratic nomination, but the Whigs believed that a continental nation would be too large to govern and stoutly resisted the swelling support for enlarging the nation's borders. Their nominee, Henry Clay, lost votes with his awkward attempt to straddle the Texas issue. The nation's first dark-horse candidate, James Knox Polk, pledged to assert America's claim to "the whole of the Oregon Country" from the 42nd

---

[1] Lewin, Taylor, and Watkins, "St. Joseph, Missouri," 2–3. Lewin and Taylor, *The St. Joe Road,* describes the wagon trail in detail.

[2] The Spalding and Whitman missionary families had already taken two wagons up the north bank of the Platte in 1836 with Thomas Fitzpatrick's American Fur Company caravan. See Drury, *Marcus and Narcissa Whitman,* 1:177–83.

[3] "Oregon—Letter from Peter H. Burnett, Esq." 4 November 1844, *St. Joseph Gazette,* 15 August 1845, 1:1–2.

parallel to the southern border of Russian Alaska at 54°40' north latitude. After a vicious campaign Polk won the election by a razor-thin margin.[4] Western politicians such as Senators Thomas Hart Benton and Lewis Linn of Missouri and their commercial allies in the east, notably Caleb Cushing, had yet to pass a single piece of legislation benefiting Oregon, but their vision of an empire in the West was winning the hearts of the American people.[5]

In his inaugural address, written by political fixer Amos Kendall, Polk said it was his "duty to assert and maintain by all constitutional means the right of the United States to that portion of our territory which lies beyond the Rocky Mountains." The American title to Oregon was clear and unquestionable: already, the new president noted, "are our people preparing to perfect that title by occupying it with their wives and children." Polk was prepared to compromise on the boundary question, but his public rhetoric grew increasingly aggressive. Believing England would not go to war over a prize as remote as Oregon, his brinksmanship was intended to convince the British to abandon their hopes for a border on the Columbia River and accept the 49th parallel as a boundary.

Privately, Polk planned to press and press hard for the American acquisition of California. Securing California and resolving the Oregon question were two of the four goals he had set for his administration, Polk confided to Secretary of the Navy George Bancroft. He hoped to purchase the province from Mexico or encourage the Californians to establish a republic that would eventually be annexed to the United States—a strategy the press already called "the Texas game."[6]

Early in 1845, the *Baltimore American* explicitly described how the process worked: "A more convenient route of conquest was never devised than the one which has given us Texas, and which promises to secure California. Our settlers go into a Mexican province and take up their abode; others follow them; they take occasion to rise against the local authorities, sure of assistance from their countrymen in the United States; the struggle is for liberty," the paper said righteously, even though the objective resembled a land grab more than a war of liberation. "They prevail, and then they and the country are in a condition to be annexed. This is more convenient than a warlike invasion."[7]

---

[4] "Fifty-four Forty or Fight!" was not used as a campaign slogan and only became popular the year after the 1844 election. See Miles, "Fifty-four Forty or Fight," 291.

[5] For the classic economic interpretation of Manifest Destiny, see Graebner, *Empire on the Pacific*.

[6] The *New Orleans Tropic* proclaimed, "Once let the tide of emigration flow towards California, and the American population will soon be sufficiently numerous to play the Texas game!" "California," *Niles' National Register,* 17 May 1845.

[7] *Gettysburg Adams Sentinel,* 28 April 1845, 1/6, citing the *Baltimore American.*

A SHOWER OF JAVELINS:
THE DISCONSOLATE 1844 OREGON EMIGRATION

Four wagon trains headed west in spring 1844.[8] Cornelius "Neal" Gilliam, "an intrepid and well known soldier of the South" was a preacher, sheriff, and legislator; and he had served as a militia commander in Missouri's "Mormon War" of 1838. Gilliam, said to be a personal friend and political ally of James Monroe and James K. Polk, assembled some three hundred people north of Fort Leavenworth and pioneered an early version of what became known as the St. Joe Road. "He was used to having people do what he said," Gilliam's daughter recalled. Bancroft described him as a "brave, obstinate, impetuous, and generous" frontiersman who was poorly educated but was "just the robust, impulsive, sympathetic, wilful, and courageous leader the men of the border would choose."[9] His "Independent Colony" adopted an elaborate organization, with Gilliam elected "general," and Robert Wilson Morrison, William Shaw, Allen Saunders, and Richard Woodcock elected captains of four companies. Meanwhile, "Colonel" Nathaniel Ford led five hundred sojourners northwest from Independence. Companies under John Thorp and Elisha Stephens set out from Council Bluffs, and finally, Andrew Sublette left Westport with twenty-two men, half of whom were traveling west to regain their health—or, at least, sobriety.[10] These divisions, historian Bancroft noted wryly, "appear not to have found it necessary to burden themselves with too many regulations, and progressed well without them."[11]

Emigrants could already appreciate the value of an early start, but six weeks of hard rain produced flooding that became legendary on the Missouri frontier. Several parties set out in mid-May and reached Wolf Creek, where most of the wagons crossed, but some had to camp on the east bank and endured a deluge such "as no Webfooter ever saw in this country," T. C. Shaw recalled. The advance party waited for the rest of the wagons to cross the stream, but by the time they caught up, it had rained day and night for almost a week: "the mud was consequently past any reasonable calculation."[12] The flood caught Gilliam's train at the Vermillion River, where their worst troubles began. They had camped a mile and a half from the stream, but the next morning the rain began falling in torrents. "This little stream that at low water could be stepped over," Gilliam's son remembered, "detained us seventeen

---

[8] The most comprehensive study of the 1844 emigration is Thomas A. Rumer's *The Wagon Trains of '44: A Comparative View of the Individual Caravans in the Emigration of 1844.*

[9] Bancroft, *History of Oregon,* 1:449.

[10] Clyman, *James Clyman, Frontiersman,* 57–58, 267, 317n84; and Minto, "Reminiscences of Experiences on the Oregon Trail in 1844," 135.

[11] Bancroft, *History of Oregon,* 1:450.

[12] Shaw, "Reminiscence of 1844," *Oregon Statesman,* 22 May and 12 June 1885.

days in one camp."[13] The swollen creeks washed out bridges and kept some of the emigrants from reaching the Platte River until late June.

Again, mountaineers led the way. James Clyman, one of the men who rediscovered South Pass in 1824, traveled west with Ford's party, along with fellow Black Hawk War veteran Levi Scott. Moses "Black" Harris served as guide, but Clyman felt his advice was perfectly useless. Harris left at Fort Laramie, but Joseph R. Walker led a number of emigrants on to Fort Bridger.

Perhaps the most intriguing sojourner of 1844 was Missourian George Bush, a freeman of black and Irish ancestry who "had means, and also a white woman for a wife, and a family of five children. Not many men of color," John Minto recalled, "left a slave state so well to do, and so generally respected." Bush told Minto that if he were not given a freeman's rights in Oregon he would seek them in Mexico. "It was not in the nature of things," Minto wrote, "that he should be permitted to forget his color."[14]

Except for the horrendous weather and the rains that hammered down "like a shower of javelins" on the road to the Platte, the emigration fell into what were already becoming familiar patterns: births and deaths, peaceful trading encounters with Indians and aggravating raids on livestock, and amazement at the landscape.[15] The large wagon trains organized in Kansas quickly broke up into smaller units that were less contentious and easier to manage. On the Platte River plain, which Samuel Crockett called "the best natural road that I ever traveled," both men and women shot large numbers of bison with unrelenting enthusiasm. "Hunting Buffalow is the greatest sport that can be conceived," Crockett wrote from Oregon the next spring.[16]

The rains delayed the entire migration, which was at least a month behind the pace of the previous year's trains.[17] The wasted days left many emigrants desperate for supplies long before they reached their destination. Some ran out of staples before reaching Fort Laramie, where they found the post charging thirty and forty dollars a barrel for flour. Beyond South Pass, the host that had set out with such high hopes began to flag. Two days west of Fort Bridger, men without families began abandoning their wagons, and others left them behind at Fort Hall

---

[13] Gilliam, "Reminiscences," 203.

[14] Minto, "Reminiscences of Experiences on the Oregon Trail in 1844," 212. Bush's middle name is sometimes given as Washington, an assumption made by later historians. When Bush arrived in Oregon, the commonwealth was considering exclusionary laws against blacks, identical to those in Indiana and Illinois. This prompted Bush, a former HBC employee, to settle north of the Columbia, where he became the first American pioneer. He established what is now Bush Prairie, near Olympia, and founded the town of Centralia. Bush's son served in the legislature that created Washington State University.

[15] Nichols, "Across the Plains in 1844," chapter 3.

[16] Crockett to "Dear Friends," 16 February 1845, Oregon Historical Society.

[17] Clyman, James Clyman, Frontiersman, 118.

in mid-September and took to packing. There Gilliam's party found a letter from Peter Burnett advising the emigrants to send word to the settlements if they needed assistance. An advance party of young men including John Minto, Samuel B. Crockett, Daniel Clark, and three men from Nathaniel Ford's company crossed the burning plain of Snake River "where nought but sand and wormwood appeared to the eye." They reached Oregon City in mid-October, but the trains they left behind were already in dire straits.[18]

Snow caught the wagons as they struggled over the Blue Mountains. Joseph Watts, a bachelor who struck out on his own after the family he was working for ran out of supplies, recalled "there were snow-flakes as large as my hat, and it was damp snow." The Cayuses provided the cold and starving travelers with wheat, corn, and potatoes in exchange for clothing and other trade goods, but when the emigrants refused to accept the drafts federal agent H. A. G. Lee had distributed to the Indians to use as payment for cattle, the Cayuses simply stole them.[19] But again, the Cayuse leader Stickus arrived in the Blues to lead "these first teams of 1844 to cross these mountains." John Minto ranked Stickus with Marcus Whitman as a man entitled "to the remembrance of Oregonians."[20]

"The misery entailed upon the belated travellers by the change to winter weather was indescribable," H. H. Bancroft wrote. "The road from Burnt River to the Dalles was a panorama of suffering and destitution." Those who reached the Cascades were too exhausted to cross the mountains and resorted to eating their dogs. "There was scarcely a dry day," John Minto recalled after he brought supplies to the stranded travelers, "and the snowline was nearly down to the river." The last of the wagons camped at the Whitmans' over the winter. The Hudson's Bay Company provided boats to ferry some of the stranded Americans from The Dalles. Few of the emigrants had died during the arduous trek, but many arrived in Oregon sick and exhausted, and the great loss of property, cattle, clothing, and household goods was ruinous. Fortunately, there was enough food to go around, and John McLoughlin made sure that no one starved.[21] A few parties that had detoured far from the trail to Browns Hole on Green River and to the missionary station at Lapwai did not reach the Willamette Valley until the next spring. J. S. Smith recalled arriving Oregon City on 22 May 1845, "just a year to the day from the time I left Missouri."[22]

---

[18] Crockett to "Dear Friends," 16 February 1845, Oregon Historical Society; and Bancroft, *History of Oregon,* 1:451–52.

[19] Ibid., 1:452–55.

[20] Minto, "Reminiscences of Experiences on the Oregon Trail in 1844," 224–25.

[21] Bancroft, *History of Oregon,* 1:452–56.

[22] Rumer, *The Wagon Trains of '44,* 193–95.

We Traveled a Rough Road: The Sager Children

"My father was one of the restless ones," Catherine Sager Pringle recalled after going west in 1844, "who are not content to remain in one place long at a time." Inspired by Marcus Whitman's gospel of Oregon, German immigrant Henry Sager sold his property in the Platte Purchase, moved near St. Joseph, and in April started across the plains with William Shaw's train. His family included his pregnant wife, Naomi, and six children: daughters Catherine, Elizabeth, Matilda Jane, and Hannah Louise; and two boys, John and Frank, who were "hardly old enough to be any help."[23]

On the North Platte, a wagon wheel crushed Catherine Sager's leg. West of Laramie, all the Sager males fell ill, and by the time the party crossed Green River, Henry Sager realized he was dying. He "could not be reconciled to the thought of leaving his large and helpless family in such precarious circumstances," his daughter recalled. Sager begged Captain Shaw to take charge of his family "and see them through." He died on 28 August and was buried on the banks of Green River.[24] His widow, just recovering from childbirth, did not long survive him. With the help of a German surgeon, Theophilos Dagon, the family pushed on, but west of Fort Bridger, Mrs. Sager fell into a delirium, sick from exposure, camp fever, and a sore mouth, perhaps due to scurvy. "We travelled a rough road the day she died," Catherine remembered, "and she moaned fearfully all the time." West of Salmon Falls, her journey came to an end on 25 September 1844. "Oh, Henry!" she said as she died, "If you only knew how we have suffered." The emigrants buried her the next morning. Her daughter Henrietta was only four months old.[25]

"So in twenty-six days we became orphans," Catherine wrote. "Seven children of us, the oldest fourteen and the youngest a babe." Their mother had asked Dr. Dagon and Captain Shaw to care for the orphans, "and all were literally adopted by the company. No one there but was ready to do us any possible favor." Shaw and his wife treated the orphans as their own, dividing their last loaf of bread with the children, who returned the love of Uncle Billy and Aunt Sally.

Misfortune dogged the children to the Grande Ronde, where Elizabeth's skirt caught fire. The doctor saved her, but Dagon's hands were so badly burned he was unable to drive a team. Shaw rescued Louise after she wandered away into the freezing night, searching for her mother. Frank Sager survived the explosion

---

[23] Pringle, Across the Plains in 1844, Oregon Historical Society. For the best telling of the Sager saga, see Thompson, *Shallow Grave at Waiilatpu*.

[24] Ibid.; and Minto, "Reminiscences of Experiences on the Oregon Trail in 1844," 163.

[25] Rumer, *The Wagon Trains of '44*, 113–14.

As the daughter of a man who was "one of the restless ones," Catherine Sager Pringle survived a series of devastating disasters: she lost both parents on the trail to Oregon in 1844 and she witnessed the murder of her legal guardians, Marcus and Narcissa Whitman, in 1847. Courtesy Stafford Hazelett.

of his powder horn. "Such were the incidents and dangerous and humorous features of the journey," Catherine remembered. At the Umatilla River, Sally Shaw
watched the orphans depart for the Whitman mission, thinking she had never
seen "a more pitiful sight than that cartful of orphans going to find a home among
strangers."

Narcissa Whitman greeted the children at Waiilatpu: they thought she was
the prettiest woman they had ever seen. Despite the doctor's reluctance, Captain
Shaw persuaded Marcus Whitman to take charge of the orphans. The children
were extremely shy and wary of their new mother, but Mrs. Whitman's gentle
demeanor won them over. She showed them the grave of Alice Clarissa, her two-
year-old daughter who had drowned in the Walla Walla River, and introduced
them to their foster sisters, Helen Mar Meek and Mary Ann Bridger, the daughters
of Joe Meek and Jim Bridger. "We were a sight calculated to excite surprise, dirty
and sunburned until we looked more like Indians than white children," Catherine
Sager recalled. The children soon adapted to the discipline of the mission and
formed a warm attachment to the Whitmans. Like the other children, they began
to call Narcissa and the doctor mother and father. "From morning until night,"
Catherine recalled, "our adopted parents labored to promote our happiness." The
next spring, Marcus Whitman became the children's legal guardian. Still, the
addition of such emotional burdens and the carping demands of desperate travelers made Narcissa Whitman dread the arrival of the annual emigration.[26]

Mr. Hitchcock, Elisha Stephens, Old Greenwood, and Chief Truckee

"There were above 150 waggons started from Missourie last spring," Samuel B.
Crockett informed his friends early in 1845, "eleven of which went to California."[27] The men and women who pioneered the trail over the Sierra via the Truckee, Yuba, and Bear rivers made up one of the most interesting parties ever to
cross the plains. Only a few newspaper stories and a handful of recollections,
notably those of Moses Schallenberger, a teenager at the time, tell the story of
this epic trek, so it retains elements of mystery and legend.[28]

The company of twenty-seven wagons was the first emigrant train ever to set out
from Council Bluffs. It followed the north side of the Platte, tracing the line the

[26] Drury, *Marcus and Narcissa Whitman,* 2:116–21.

[27] Crockett to "Dear Friends," 16 February 1845, Oregon Historical Society. The sentence ends, "the balance
came to Oregon except a few that were left [at Fort Hall]."

[28] Dale Morgan collected most of the "fugitive and difficult" sources for the 1844 emigration in Kelly and Morgan, *Old Greenwood.* George R. Stewart, Jr., annotated Shallenberger's narrative in *The Opening of the California Trail.*

Long Expedition had explored in 1820 and the Whitmans had taken west in 1836. Although the extended family of fifty-eight-year-old Irish emigrant Michael Murphy comprised more than half the party, the sojourners elected a taciturn blacksmith as their captain: Elisha Stephens's long service at Indian agencies around Council Bluffs probably influenced the decision. Still a bachelor at age forty, Stephens was "an Experienced Mountaineer," said to have been a trapper for twenty-eight years, although he only knew the way to Fort Laramie.[29] The choice is still something of a puzzle, since two ancient veterans of the fur trade also joined the train.

Caleb Greenwood was over eighty years of age and had first gone west with the Astorians. He was already legendary as "Old Greenwood." John and Britton, sons by his Crow wife, accompanied him. Greenwood guided the party from Council Bluffs to the Rockies, Moses Shallenberger recalled, but his services were sporadic.[30] At sixty-four, Isaac Hitchcock was far less renowned, but his knowledge of the West proved crucial to the expedition's success. He had accompanied one of the Sublette family's western ventures, was familiar with the Great Basin, and a family tradition recorded in 1941 claimed he had visited California in 1833 with Joseph R. Walker.[31] Hitchcock's widowed daughter, Isabella Patterson, joined the party with her four children—Isaac, Lydia, Margaret, and Helen.[32] One recollection credited Hitchcock with leading the party over a shortcut to Green River, the route William Sublette had used the previous year. This arduous desert crossing became known as the Greenwood Cutoff and later as the Sublette Cutoff, but perhaps Old Greenwood had less to do with bringing the first emigrant party over it than the name indicated.[33]

The Martin, Miller, Montgomery, Sullivan, and Townsend families, plus a few single men, made up the balance of the company that turned south at the mouth of Raft River. Some forty-six emigrants followed the path Joseph Walker's wagons had laid down the previous year. Frontier doctor John Townsend had brought along a small library and a load of silks and satins as trade goods, perhaps to provide unemployment insurance if the tales of the incredibly healthy conditions prevailing in California should prove true. The company became known as the Stephens-Murphy-Townsend party.[34]

---

[29] Kelly and Morgan, *Old Greenwood*, 94–97; Edward Bray in 1872 and perhaps Sarah Montgomery in 1864, in ibid., 323, 326.

[30] Stewart, *The California Trail*, 57; and Bray in Kelly and Morgan, *Old Greenwood*, 102, 326.

[31] Gail Darling to Will Bagley, Overland Trails e-mail list, 9 Feb 2002.

[32] Clyman, *James Clyman, Frontiersman*, 323n132.

[33] Dale Morgan traced the origin of the term Sublette Cutoff to Joseph E. Ware's use of Solomon Sublette's name in his influential *Emigrants' Guide to California* of 1849. See Kelly and Morgan, *Old Greenwood*, 108–10.

[34] Stewart, *The California Trail*, 62–63. Several authors (and the name of Stevens Creek Boulevard in Silicon Valley) use the spelling Stevens, but contemporary documents are signed Stephens.

The party's eleven wagons took Walker's wagon trace to the headwaters of the Humboldt River.[35] They followed the diminishing river down to the Sink, where the emigrants met a Northern Paiute leader they called Truckee, for the phrase he used to answer all their questions: it apparently meant "all right." With Caleb Greenwood interpreting as best he could, they learned that fifty or sixty miles to the west a river flowed out from the Sierra that was lined with large trees and good grass. While the company rested, Stephens, Townsend, and Joseph Foster explored the desert to the south. Days later, they "found the river just as the Indian had described it," Schallenberger recalled. In appreciation, Townsend reportedly named the river after Truckee.[36]

After making the first known crossing of the Forty-mile Desert directly to the Truckee, the party ascended its canyon to the site of what is now Reno, Nevada, and then climbed the stream into the foothills of the Sierra Nevada. Soon the country was "so rough and broken that they frequently had to travel in the bed of the stream," wreaking havoc on the feet of their oxen. The arduous ascent exhausted emigrants and animals. Snow began to fall, limiting the food supply for stock to reeds, and it took most of a month to reach the site of present-day Truckee, California, on 14 November.[37] Here the company divided, perhaps by accident. Riding ahead of the wagons Daniel, John, and Ellen Murphy; Mrs. Townsend; her black servant Francis Deland; and Oliver Magnant followed the main branch of the Truckee to become the first non-Indians to see the "Mountain Lake," Tahoe. They probably followed the Rubicon and the Middle and North forks of the American River to reach the Sacramento Valley, arriving at Sutters Fort by 10 December 1844.[38]

The rest of the company climbed to Truckee Lake and searched for a way to take their wagons over the granite wall of the Sierra. After several days, the weary emigrants found what would later be called Donner Pass. Leaving six wagons at Truckee Lake, they doubled their teams and, one by one, hauled their empty wagons over a ten-foot escarpment, crossing the summit on 25 November. Amid the accumulating snows, they finally reached the South Yuba River, where the men were compelled to build a cabin and leave the women and children behind while they went for help in the valley. At Sutters Fort, the men became entangled in civil warfare between Mexican officials. Only in February were they able to rescue their wives and Moses Schallenberger, who had been left alone to guard

[35] Most accounts refer to eleven wagons, but when he passed Raft River on 13 September, Clyman reported Hitchcock went south with thirteen wagons. See Clyman, *James Clyman, Frontiersman,* 103.

[36] Kelly and Morgan, *Old Greenwood,* 120; Morgan, *Overland in 1846,* 19–20; and Schallenberger, in Graydon, *Trail of the First Wagons over the Sierra,* 7. The 1882 *Illustrated History of Plumas, Lassen and Sierra Counties* credited the name to Baptiste Truckee, who allegedly discovered the river while on Joseph R. Walker's expedition. The story is apocryphal.

[37] Schallenberger, in Graydon, *Trail of the First Wagons over the Sierra,* 7–9.

[38] Kelly and Morgan, *Old Greenwood,* 124–26.

the wagons abandoned at Truckee Lake. In June 1845 they retrieved their possessions and brought the first American wagons into California. Amazingly, not only
had they done it without a casualty, but two children, Elizabeth Independence
Miller and Elizabeth Yuba Murphy, were born on the way.[39]

The Stephens-Murphy-Townsend party brought the first wheeled vehicles over
the crest of the Sierra, blazing a rough but practical wagon road from the Missouri to the Sacramento. The Truckee Pass route would be the only wagon road
across the mountains until 1848, and the Transcontinental Railroad and Interstate
80 both followed its path. While spending his last years in hermitlike solitude on
the Kern River, Elisha Stephens justly complained that Donner Pass should have
borne his name. In recognition of his role in pioneering the California Trail,
on 24 September 1994 the Nevada County Historical Landmarks Commission
named a peak below Donner Summit and immediately west of Rainbow Bridge
on Old Highway 40 Mount Elisha Stephens, and nearby the Oregon-California
Trails Association dedicated a marker in his honor.

FRÉMONT'S SECOND EXPEDITION AND REPORT, 1843–1844

After following the Great Migration of 1843 to Soda Springs, John C. Frémont
quickly surveyed of the Great Salt Lake and then rode north to reunite with
the main party of his second expedition. At Fort Vancouver, John McLoughlin
reported that "a Lieut Fremont of the Typographical [sic] Corps of Engineers"
arrived with the emigration, got some supplies, "and left this on the 15th Nov—
he expects to be at Washington in March and return here this season to finish his
survey and it is said a large immigration will accompany him to this country."[40] As
Colonel Abert had feared, Frémont's mountain howitzer raised questions among
the Hudson's Bay officials about the scientific nature of his expedition.

Returning to the eastern slope of the Cascades, Frémont followed the tracks of
Peter Skene Ogden south to the Great Basin, turning west at the Carson River to
cross the Sierra in mid-December. After five weeks of intense cold and hunger and
the loss of his controversial howitzer, all his men reached Sutters Fort, where the
expedition headed south through the Central Valley to cross the southern Sierra
at Oak Creek Pass. They struck the Spanish Trail and followed it until the expedition turned north to Utah Lake. After crossing the Wasatch Range, the Uinta
Mountains, and the Three Parks of the Rockies, Frémont reached Bents Fort and
the Santa Fe Trail. He arrived at the Missouri on 31 July 1844 and headed for
Washington.

[39] Schallenberger, in Graydon, *Trail of the First Wagons over the Sierra*, 9–10; and Stewart, *The California Trail*, 73.
[40] McLoughlin to Simpson, 20 March 1844, D.5/10, HBC Archives, 483.

Nowhere is his amazing energy more evident than in Frémont's achievement during the next few months. With occasional help from his wife, Jessie Benton, Frémont drafted and published the report of his circuit of the Far West in 1843 and 1844. The published account was a sensation, winning him widespread fame as an explorer and inspiring thousands to follow in his footsteps. The adventure made splendid reading, providing a romantic description of the trail and a stirring account of the young lieutenant's exploits.

In Washington Frémont worked feverishly to launch another expedition. His newfound fame preceded him to Missouri and he had to employ guards to fend off his admirers. Once again many of his old comrades joined him, and he purchased a dozen rifles, "the best that could be found," to offer as prizes to the best marksmen among them. The third expedition assembled at Westport and made a late start on 26 June 1845. Two days earlier, Secretary of the Navy George Bancroft had sent orders to Commodore John Sloat on the Pacific Coast, directing that should he "ascertain beyond a doubt" that Mexico and the United States were at war, his squadron was to seize San Francisco immediately.[41]

Brevet Captain Frémont set out with sixty-two experienced frontiersmen and two Delaware scouts, and he recruited veteran mountaineers such as Kit Carson, Joseph R. Walker, Dick Owens, and Bill Williams as he marched up the Arkansas River to the Rockies.[42] His official orders merely directed him to locate the headwaters of the Arkansas River and explore "within a reasonable distance of Bent's Fort . . . the streams which run east from the Rocky Mountains," but he later insisted he was authorized to extend his survey to California. His actual orders said nothing about entering Mexican territory and would have kept the expedition within the United States. Frémont may have had verbal permission to extend this very limited charter 1,200 miles west to the Pacific Coast, but the young officer had demonstrated his ability to ignore orders when they conflicted with his ambitions. It is possible Frémont informed only Senator Benton and his personal confidants of his plans. In any case, by July the Missouri newspapers reported he intended to winter at the American settlements in Alta California. As the editors of his contradictory records note, "knotty questions about secret instructions or lack of instructions" cloud the exact nature of Frémont's orders.[43]

---

[41] Rolle, *John Charles Frémont,* 68; Harlow, *California Conquered,* 116–17; and Spence and Jackson, *The Expeditions of John Charles Frémont,* xxii, 9.

[42] Spence and Jackson, *The Expeditions of John Charles Frémont,* 2:5; Rolle, *John Charles Frémont,* 68–69. Tracking Frémont's rank can be confusing. Commissioned a second lieutenant in July 1838, he received his brevet promotion to captain 31 July 1844 for gallantry and meritorious service during his first two expeditions. (A brevet commission gave an officer a higher nominal rank without the accompanying pay raise.) Congress appointed Frémont lieutenant colonel of the newly created regiment of Mounted Riflemen in May 1846. See Heitman, *Historical Register,* 1:436.

[43] Spence and Jackson, *The Expeditions of John Charles Frémont,* 2:xix, xiii, xxiii, 9.

Now You Must Die:
Yellow Serpent and the Murder of Elijah Hedding

Well into the mid-1840s, American emigrants experienced "no serious difficulty" with Oregon's tribes, but "that their passage is becoming more and more a subject of interest to the Indians is abundantly manifest," H. A. G. Lee observed in spring 1845. "They collect about the road from every part of the country, and have looked on with amazement; but the novelty of the scene is fast losing its power to hold in check their baser passions." Lee made a dark prediction to Indian agent Elijah White about the future as the tide of newcomers increased: both sides had been "provoked and exasperated" and such conflicts multiplied every year. "Much prudence is required on the part of the whites, and unfortunately they have very little by the time they reach the Columbia Valley," Lee observed.[44] And among the tribes of the Columbia Plateau, patience with the white intruders was wearing very thin. A murder at Sutters Fort inflamed Oregon's Indians and set off a string of events with dire consequences for Natives and newcomers alike.

"In the autumn of 1844 a number of Cayuse, Nez Percé, and Wallawalla chiefs decided to visit the California settlements in order to trade for cattle," Joel Palmer reported. The Indians said John Sutter invited them.[45] Some forty men and their families from the Cayuse, Nez Perce, Umatilla, Walla Walla, and Spokane nations set out for California. They included such notable Christians as Spokan Garry of the Spokanes, Ellis of the Nez Perces (another man the Hudson's Bay Company sent to Red River to acquire an education), Young Chief of the Cayuses, the Walla Walla leader Peupeumoxmox, better known as Yellow Serpent, and his son, Elijah Hedding, who had been educated at the Chemeketa mission. The leaders, Elijah White reported, set out on "the hazardous, but grand and important enterprise, of going directly through the Indian country to California, with a view of exchanging their Beaver, Deer, and Elk skins, together with their surplus horses," for cattle—and any slaves they could acquire by force or barter along the way. "They were well mounted and equipped, the chiefs clad in English costume," the agent wrote.[46]

Indians from Oregon had been trading in California for more than half a century, but as H. H. Bancroft observed, their journey was still fraught with danger. When they arrived at Sutters Fort in the fall, Sutter welcomed them, for he had met many of the delegation's leaders on his way to Fort Vancouver in 1838. "I received these people well and with great hospitality," Sutter later wrote, and he gave them passports and permission to hunt. Their mountain hunt proved successful, and they

---

[44] Lee to White, 4 March 1845, in Gray, *History of Oregon,* 415–16.
[45] Palmer, *Journal of Travels,* 26 March 1846, 229–30.
[46] White to Secretary of War, 4 April 1845, in "The Wallawalla Indians," *Californian,* 19 September 1846, 1/1.

captured twenty-two stolen horses and mules from a band of "freebooters." When Sutter returned from a visit to Monterey in October 1844, he found the Natives again camped at his fort but now embroiled in conflict with American settlers who wanted to reclaim their stolen livestock: by their customs, the Indians believed they owned the horses. Sutter tried to negotiate a compromise, but hotter heads prevailed. Grove Cook, a veteran of the Bidwell-Bartleson party, claimed one of the mules. Elijah Hedding calmly loaded his rifle and said to Cook, "Go, now, and take your mule." Outraged, Cook left, but negotiations began to trade the recaptured horses for ten or fifteen cows.[47]

The Sunday after Cook and Hedding had their confrontation, the Indians attended church at the fort. After the service Sutter invited them into his office to settle matters, "and while there in an unarmed and defenceless condition," some fifteen "foreigners" began threatening Hedding. Sutter was called out to meet with the Russian Fur Company agent, and the Americans began calling the Indians thieves and dogs. Cook drew a pistol and said, "Yesterday, you were going to kill me, now you must die." Hedding asked, "Let me pray a little first," and knelt down. As the Indian prayed, Grove Cook shot him "dead upon the spot." Fearing for their lives, the rest of the band fled, leaving behind the leather goods, buffalo robes, and curiosities they had hoped to trade for cattle.[48]

Sutter claimed Elijah Hedding was a menace who "behaved very saucy and haughty & more independent than the chiefs, in the first place he killed a young man of his own people" while camped near the fort. (The "body was ate up by the hogs" before anyone discovered it.) "This boy was the terror of the old chiefs, and he had the whole rule over them, and no doubt would have become a great tyrant among his people," Sutter complained. The Californians thought the young man got his just deserts: "We believe here all," Sutter wrote, "that Elijah was a great rascal."[49] Elijah White, in contrast, felt the young man was a saint, and, thanks to Grove Cook, a martyr.

On reaching Oregon, the Indians delegated Ellis to take their complaints to Sub-Indian Agent White, and the Nez Perce leader accompanied Richard Grant to Vancouver. Meanwhile, Marcus Whitman sent White a "hasty communication, written in excitement," expressing his fear that the Indians, "all excited by reason of the violent and treacherous death of this educated and accomplished young chief," would take revenge on the whites. Ellis met with White about the first of March 1845: before White returned to the states, he sent messages to California with James Clyman and alerted the secretary of war to the problem. Instead of

[47] Bancroft, *History of Oregon*, 1:285–89; and Sutter to Larkin, 21 July 1845, in Larkin, *The Larkin Papers*, 3:279–80.
[48] Larkin, *The Larkin Papers*, 3:279–80; and "The Wallawalla Indians," *Californian*, 19 September 1846, 1/2.
[49] Sutter to Larkin, 21 July 1845; *Californian*, 19 September 1846, 4/1–2.

defusing the crisis, the incompetent agent merely inflamed matters.[50] The murder, Richard Grant reported early in 1845, "created much agitation among the Indians" on the Upper Columbia. "I firmly believe they are not the most friendly towards Americans, what the result will be time will tell."[51] Time would tell a very hard story.

OREGON FEVER, 1845

The dramatic surge in emigration in 1845 fundamentally changed the nature of overland travel. The rising tide transformed the experience from the struggles of individual wagon parties to overcome nature and the elements into a national movement. The news that wagons had successfully reached the Columbia, a fact unknown to the emigrants of 1844, helped persuade some 2,750 Americans to head west the next spring. Fueled in part by Frémont's first report, the increasing intensity of "Oregon fever" reflected a growing public passion. The *St. Joseph Gazette* reported that the migration setting out from Saint Joseph alone consisted of 223 wagons, 954 people, 545 firearms, 9,425 cattle, and 168 horses and mules. It estimated that "the whole wealth of the company" was near $130,000.[52] On their march to South Pass, the First Dragoons passed 460 wagons, 850 men, 1,475 women and children, 400 horses and mules, and 7,000 head of cattle.[53] In addition, the migration included more than 1,000 goats.[54] Families again made up most of those going west, and Samuel Hancock found the women in his party "comprised decidedly the most interesting portion of our company."[55]

Guided by Thomas Fitzpatrick, Colonel Stephen Watts Kearny led five crack companies west that summer to display the army's power to the tribes. Except for topographical surveys, the expedition represented the army's second military venture on the overland trail: Kearny himself had accompanied Colonel Henry Dodge's march up the South Platte in 1835. As H. H. Bancroft observed caustically, the army's purpose in 1845 was "theoretically perhaps to protect the emigrants, and practically to eat up the grass and consume the water at all the best camping spots in advance of them."[56] With their cannons and rockets the dragoons made a powerful impression on the Indians, and Kearny succeeded in

---

[50] Ibid., 1/2–4/1.

[51] Grant to Simpson, 11 March 1845, D.5/13, HBC Archives, 292.

[52] "The Oregon Emigrants," *St. Joseph Gazette,* 2 May 1845, 2/3.

[53] Kearny, "Report of a Summer Campaign," Serial 480, 212.

[54] On the Meek Cutoff, in addition to the three thousand cattle and oxen, "1,051 Gotes also consume A heap of water," Samuel Parker complained. Parker, Diary, 16 September 1845, Oregon Historical Society, 11.

[55] Hancock, *The Narrative of Samuel Hancock,* 9.

[56] Bancroft, *History of California,* 4:574.

overawing the tribes that gathered at Fort Laramie to council with him. "I am opening a road for the white people, and your great father directs that his red children shall not attempt to close it up," Kearny warned. But he also promised that the Americans were only passing through Indian lands: "There are many whites now coming on this road, and moving to the other side of the mountains; they take with them their women, children, and cattle. They go to bury their bones there, and never return. You must not disturb them."[57]

The emigration was large but respectable and increasing rapidly, reported the *St. Joseph Gazette*. "They are sufficiently strong to travel thro' the Indian country. It gives me pleasure to be able to state that the emigrants this spring are well prepared in every way for the expedition. They seem to be quite cheerful and agreeable," wrote W. P. Richardson after watching them pass the Nemaha Agency. "The character of the emigration is very much improved from last year."[58] The first trains to arrive at the junction of the Independence and Saint Joseph roads in early May could tell they were a month ahead of the parties of 1844 from the dates cut on trees. "Burnetts Trace," the name emigrants often used for the Independence Road, was deeply rutted, a legacy of the previous year's torrential floods.[59]

William B. Ide thought the sojourners numbered between six and seven thousand, an astonishing overestimate, but they were "all in good health and spirits."[60] One of them, William Barlow, left Illinois with a three-hundred-pound box filled with fruit-tree grafts. Men familiar with the trail ultimately convinced him to dump them at Independence Rock, but he saved a bag of seeds and quickly sold 15,000 seedlings in Oregon the next spring.[61]

The migration soon fell into what were by now established patterns, partly enforced by the monotony of the routine that characterized plains travel. The early arrival of the wagons surprised traders and mountaineers along the way, but otherwise the passage of the dragoons and the extraordinary number of children injured under wagon wheels were what primarily distinguished the 1845 migration up the Platte. "The Indians did not disturb us at all," wrote Mariah King, except for stealing horses, but whooping cough and measles swept through her camp.[62] James Field thought the Lakota bands he met at Fort Laramie were "as intelligent, cleanly-looking Indians as ever I saw anywhere." Field noted a number of mixed-race children among them and reported their preference in firearms:

[57] Kearny, "Report of a Summer Campaign," 215.

[58] "Oregon Emigration," *St. Joseph Gazette,* 6 June 1845, 2/1.

[59] Field, Crossing the Plains, 13 May 1845, Oregon Historical Society.

[60] "The Emigrants to Oregon," *New-York Daily Tribune,* 16 June 1845, 2/2.

[61] Tadlock, "The Migrating Orchard," 22.

[62] King to "Dear Mother, Brother, and Sisters," 1 April 1846, Oregon Historical Society.

"The only guns among them, or that they will have, are short, large-bored shot-guns, and they don't want a rifle at any rate."[63]

West of the fort, William Tustin camped for a day to recruit "the spirits of our cattle, as they had not been in good feed for a long time": Kearny and his dragoons were now behind him. Tustin found "tedious travelling" in the Black Hills, "ups and downs, crossing deep gullies, and the dust was dreadful, almost impossible to keep from smothering to death. Water was very scarce."[64] As they pressed on, the Oregon travelers divided into smaller and more manageable units under captains such as Samuel Parker, Alexander Ligget, Levin English, Alexander McNary, John Stewart, Solomon Tetherow, James B. Riggs, and Abner Hackleman, whose refusal to travel on Sundays worked to his followers' great good fortune. The trains sometimes jockeyed to take the lead, "racing and crowding" each other. "Not less than 456 waggons besides several packing parties passed here on their way to Columbia & Calefornia with thousands of cattle," Richard Grant reported from Fort Hall, surprised the emigration had arrived so early.[65] On the sage-brush-choked road up the Snake River, James Field saw English's company rush through sagebrush to take the lead, but soon "their teams [were] cut up so that they can hardly travel."[66]

At Burnt River on 1 September, the Barlow, Knighton, and McDonald parties and their eighty-seven wagons met Agent Elijah White, Moses Harris, and their small pack train bound for the states with a petition for Congress. White found them "all in good health and fine spirits, representing the difficulties of the route as nothing in comparison with what they had expected."[67] Those who stayed on the main trail had little trouble reaching the Columbia, but at The Dalles they faced an immense barrier: Mount Hood. There was still no wagon road to the Willamette Valley, and goods and most people went down the river on rafts or HBC bateaux. New arrivals could guide their animals down a narrow trail along the south bank, but at least twice the ledge disappeared and they were forced to swim the river. Stock could be driven overland from Dog River, up the west fork of today's Hood River, and over Lolo Pass and a rough trail Lansford Hastings surveyed for the Hudson's Bay Company around the north flank of Mount Hood to the Sandy River, where traces led to the settlements—but none of these trails was easy.

---

[63] Field, Crossing the Plains, 20 June 1845, Oregon Historical Society.

[64] Tustin, "California & Oregon." 1 May 1846, *Illinois Gazette,* 26 February 1848.

[65] Grant to Simpson, 2 January 1846, D.5/16, HBC Archives, 425.

[66] Field, Crossing the Plains, 12 August 1845, Oregon Historical Society.

[67] White, "Overland Mail from Oregon," *Independence Express,* 17 November 1845, reprinted in *Times and Seasons,* 1 December 1845, 1045.

A Burning World: Meeks Cutoff

The lure of finding a more direct route to Oregon than the arduous road up the Snake and down the Columbia was so seductive that even Colonel Stephen W. Kearny could not resist speculating on a course that might spare emigrants the trip. "There is little or no doubt that a distance of about 400 miles can be saved for them," Kearny wrote, "and a much better route for them to pass over, by leaving the trail on Bear river—pass north of Lake Booneville to Ogden's or Lost river—cross Wyhee river and Blue mountains north of Clamet lake, and then fall on the headwaters of the Wilhamet." Kearny recommended Thomas Fitzpatrick for the job of exploring such a road, but even the legendary "Broken Hand" could not have taken wagons over the path Kearny described.[68]

As Kearny filed the report of his march, others actively sought a shortcut to the Oregon settlements. At Fort Boise, fur-trade veteran Stephen H. L. Meek persuaded some two hundred families to follow him west on a shortcut to either The Dalles or the Willamette Valley—exactly where Meek intended to go is not clear. The most dramatic episode in the story of the 1845 Oregon migration would establish a template for similar disasters in later years. Instead of finding an easier and shorter road, Meek led his followers into a nightmare that contributed to scores of deaths and came close to cutting Meek's own life short at the end of a rope. The story of a charismatic frontiersman whose bright promise of a cutoff led to suffering and sometimes death would be repeated on the South Road to Oregon and the Hastings Cutoff in 1846, by the lost wagon train of 1848, and again the next year by the Forty-niners who gave Death Valley its name.

By his own account, Stephen Meek had "commenced that wild life of adventure" he led for many years in about 1830. With his younger brother Joe, Meek went to California with Joseph Walker in 1833 and the next year trapped in eastern Oregon with Captain Bonneville. He led trains down the Santa Fe Trail and joined scalp hunter James Kirker for a time. In March 1845 Meek collected letters of recommendation from Thomas Fitzpatrick, William Sublette, and Robert Campbell that got him hired as "guide to the immense emigrant train of 480 wagons then preparing to go to Oregon." The party set out on 11 May 1845, "on which day I first saw Elizabeth Schoonover, whom I married a week later."[69]

Meek's piloting services ended at Fort Hall. He rode up the Snake with his bride and began recruiting emigrants "who wanted to avoid all trouble and danger by taking a route over which he could guide us from Fort Boise to the Dalles,"

---

[68] Kearny, "Report of a Summer Campaign," 213.

[69] Meek, "A Sketch of the Life of the First Pioneer"; Thrapp, *Encyclopedia of Frontier Biography*, 968; and Henry E. Tobie's life sketch in Hafen, *The Mountain Men*, 2:225–50.

William Goulder recalled. The proposed cutoff would have saved many difficult miles, but Meek had never crossed it, although he apparently had some experience in the country and seems to have worked out a plausible route.[70] He "engaged to pilot the leading company . . . through to the Dalles of the Columbia river by a new and near route," James Field recorded, "cutting off between 100 and 200 miles' travel."[71] Meek "said he could take us [by] a new route across the Cascade mountains to the Willamette River in 20 days," Mariah King reported the next spring. A large company "of a hundred fifty to two hundred wagons left the old road to follow the new road and traveled for 2 months over sand, rocks, hills and anything else but good roads."[72]

Meek "represented that this route was much shorter than the other, and that there was no danger from the Indians, as this way did not lead through the Snake River Indians' territory," Lucy Jane Burnett wrote fifty years later. She remembered the company voted to follow Meek and signed a contract to pay him. "He agreed to pilot the company safely through in thirty days, or, as was written in his own words, give his head for a football."[73]

Meek's promises indicate he was betting he could find an easy way to cross the Cascades. The prospect of eliminating all those miles and avoiding the dangerous passage down the Columbia proved compelling to the exhausted emigrants. One party agreed to pay him fifty dollars to guide them to The Dalles on a trail they believed was 150 miles "nearer than the old route."[74] Rumor said the Walla Walla Indians, outraged by Elijah Hedding's "violent and treacherous" murder by a worthless white man at Sutters Fort, intended to close the trail through their land, which made Meek's proposal even more seductive.[75] Starting on 25 August, between a thousand and fifteen hundred people followed Meek west from present-day Vale, Oregon, and disappeared into the desert.[76]

It was a hard road from the beginning, with "an abundance of small, sharp stones in it, black and hard as iron," and it grew progressively worse. When Meek turned southwest, James Field suspected he intended "to take us over onto the head of the Willamette if he can find a place along the Cascades which will admit of the passage of wagons through." The scattered parties struggled over the Stinking Water Mountains into Harney Valley, drank the "miserable, stagnant water"

[70] This quotation is from the Clark and Tiller classic, *Terrible Trail, 1845,* 15.
[71] Field, Crossing the Plains, 24 August 1845, Oregon Historical Society.
[72] King to "Dear Mother, Brother, and Sisters," 1 April 1846, Oregon Historical Society.
[73] Burnett, "Reminiscences of a Trip across the Plains in '45," 27.
[74] Herren Diary, 23 August 1845, in Clark and Tiller, *Terrible Trail, 1845,* 261.
[75] White, "Overland Mail from Oregon," *Independence Express,* 17 November 1845, in *Times and Seasons,* 1 December 1845, 1045.
[76] Clark and Tiller, *Terrible Trail, 1845,* 16, 20–21.

at Harney Lake, marched up to Silver Lake, and then endured a twenty-five-mile waterless passage to Wagontire Mountain.[77] "It had become more and more evident to us that Meek had no more knowledge of the country through which we were passing than we did ourselves," William Goulder recalled.[78] "Some talk of stoning and others say hang him," John Herren wrote on 3 September. "I can not tell how the affair will terminate yet."[79]

"One day, after three weeks' travel on our new route, our guide suddenly and excitedly exclaimed, 'My God, we are lost,'" Lucy Jane Burnett recalled.[80] He was right: the mountains and deserts had completely bewildered him, but Stephen Meek put up a brave front. "I have brought you here," he told Samuel Hancock, "and will take you off, if you will go." By now none of the emigrants had the slightest confidence in their guide, Hancock wrote. Meek finally had to leave Wagontire hidden in Hancock's wagon. Some of the emigrants were running out of food. Several children had already died, but "a good many of our company were sick, not only of heart, but body also." Finally, after days of searching, scouts found water some twenty-five miles to the north and that night the beleaguered parties made another dry crossing.[81]

Many of the emigrants took refuge in what became known as the Lost Hollow. Their scouts "traveled forty of fifty miles in search of water, but found none. Go back we could not, and we knew not what was before us," wrote Betsey Bayley. "Our provisions were failing us. There was sorrow and dismay dipicted on every countenance. We were like mariners lost at sea, and in this mountainous wilderness we had to remain for five days."[82] Lucy Jane Burnett remembered sending the scouts on a desperate quest for water. "If any was found a signal of three shots was to be fired in quick succession; if not three shots at intervals." The train heard nothing at dawn and set out "through sage brush and across dry creek beds which mocked our thirst." At noon, the party heard three shots at intervals; "like a death knell they sounded. The men stood in groups talking over the situation, the mothers, pale and haggard, sat in the wagons with their little ones around them." At last, at nightfall the train heard three shots in quick succession, "which proclaimed that water had been found. All pushed forward with renewed energy." Sensing relief, "the thirsty oxen broke into a run and rushed into the water and drank until they had to be driven out." Burnett recalled that Stephen Meek cried, "We are saved, we are saved! Thank God! for now I know the way."[83]

---

[77] Field, Crossing the Plains, 27 August, and 3 and 6 September, Oregon Historical Society.

[78] Clark and Tiller, *Terrible Trail, 1845*, 43–44.

[79] Herren Diary, in Clark and Tiller, *Terrible Trail, 1845*, 266.

[80] Burnett, "Reminiscences of a Trip across the Plains in '45."

[81] Clark and Tiller, *Terrible Trail, 1845*, 49.

[82] Bayley to Griffith, 20 September 1849, in Holmes, *Covered Wagon Women*, 1:36–37.

[83] Burnett, "Reminiscences of a Trip across the Plains in '45," 27.

The weary travelers found water at Buck and Camp creeks, and an Indian led the wagons with Meek to the Crooked River. The lost emigrants staggered northward, burying their dead as they wandered from spring to spring. "The mountains looked like volcanoes and [gave] the appearance that one day there had been an awful thundering of volcanoes and a burning world," wrote Betsey Bayley.[84] They divided into two smaller companies and each set about finding its own way. The jagged ridges of the Cascades appeared on the western horizon, and at last they struck the barrier of Deschutes Canyon. Incredibly, the exhausted wayfarers managed to cross the gaping canyon and its torrential river, "stretching a large rope from bank to bank and suspending a wagon bed beneath to work on rollers," Samuel Hancock recalled. With this aerial rope ferry the emigrants "were enabled to cross without being exposed to the water."[85]

Many believed he had abandoned them early on, but Meek stayed with the emigrants until they reached the Deschutes crossing. According to one account, before the ferry went into operation, a messenger "rode up in great haste and informed our guide that he would have to leave immediately." A man attributed the deaths of his two sons to Meek's incompetence, "and their father had taken an oath that the guide should die before sundown." Meek understood and asked some Indians to help him and his wife cross the river "at all hazards." An Indian crossed the river with a rope in his mouth and towed Meek across with his wife, who had shown great courage throughout the ordeal. The Meeks escaped without changing their clothes. They "had not been gone more than fifteen minutes when two men rode up with rifles and inquired the whereabouts of the guide. Being told that he had gone in the direction of our destination, the old man replied that it was perhaps well, as his sons were now buried."[86]

After crossing the Deschutes, it still took the emigrants at least five days to traverse the last thirty miles to The Dalles. "Mr. Meek would certainly have given his head for a football, had not he and his wife made their timely escape," Lucy Jane Burnett recalled. "We did not hear of the Meeks for more than a year after this," she said. "We were lost in the mountains six weeks. The way was rough beyond description. The women and children walked most of the way."[87]

Death stalked the travelers, who came to be known as "the Lost Meeks." Contemporaneous accounts report twenty-four deaths on the trail between 8 September and 5 October. "After we took the new route a slow, lingering fever prevailed," Mariah King wrote. "Sickness and death attended us the rest of the way. . . .

[84] Bayley to Griffith, 20 September 1849, in Holmes, *Covered Wagon Women*, 1:36–37.

[85] Hancock, *The Narrative of Samuel Hancock*, 34.

[86] Clark and Tiller, *Terrible Trail*, 105–106. The grief-stricken father was perhaps Henry Noble.

[87] Burnett, "Reminiscences of a Trip across the Plains in '45."

Upwards of fifty died on the new route."[88] Hiram Smith sent a bitter letter to Missouri saying the 214 wagons of the Saint Joseph Company "had been led astray by a pilot by the name of Stephen Meek." He described their "intense suffering, and the loss of near 50 souls, young and old. The greatest number that died were children." A startling percentage of the shattered survivors died after reaching the Columbia. They were, J. M. Bacon recalled, "the most desolate looking people I ever saw in my life." All told the total number of victims of Meek's experiment almost certainly exceeded the forty-two deaths in the Donner party. "Those that traveled the old road," wrote Hiram Smith, "got in well and in good time."[89]

Forty years later, an old frontiersman, who still made his living trapping and guiding hunting parties, recounted his glory days. One third of the train had set out to California from Fort Hall, "guided by the old trapper, Greenwood," Stephen Meek recalled. "The remainder, I conducted safely to Oregon, the first large train of wagons ever taken there."[90] Others remembered the story very differently. "He said he knew every trail and camping ground from Fort Laramie to Vancouver, west of the Cascade mountains," William Barlow wrote of Meek. "But he proved himself to be a reckless humbug from start to finish."[91]

Somewhere in the wanderings of the lost wagons, legend has it that a little girl fetching water loaded up her blue bucket with shiny rocks. A blacksmith pounded some of them into fishing weights and tossed them into his toolbox. The child had to leave the rest of her pretty rocks behind, but after the California gold discovery someone identified the blacksmith's weights as gold. Nonsense or not, the legend of the Blue Bucket Mine entered western folklore and sparked innumerable prospecting trips through the deserts of eastern Oregon. In 1868, Stephen Meek led a party up from his home in California to hunt for the lost riches. The expedition was, of course, a failure.[92]

We Could Go Almost Anywhere: Blazing the Barlow Road

"There were a few row boats at The Dalles to take the emigrants down the Columbia and up the Willamette, as that was the only way to reach the Willamette Valley with wagons at that time," Miriam Tuller recalled. By 1845 there were so many emigrants "it would take too long for all to go in those small boats, so some concluded to go through the Cascade Mountains. S. K. Barlow was the

[88] Mariah King to "Dear Mother, Brother, and Sisters," 1 April 1846. Oregon Historical Society.
[89] Clark and Tiller, *Terrible Trail,* 114–18. Clark and Tiller regard the contemporary death toll of fifty with some skepticism, but the documented deaths suggest the number may be accurate.
[90] Stephen Meek, "A Sketch of the Life of the First Pioneer," 1885.
[91] Barlow, "Reminiscences of Seventy Years," 254.
[92] Clark and Tiller, *Terrible Trail,* 91.

moving spirit in this undertaking," she said.[93] In late September Samuel K. Barlow began resolutely searching out a wagon road over the south side of the volcano. "God never made a mountain that He had not made a place for a man to
go over it or under it, if he could find the place," Barlow reportedly said. "I am
going to hunt for that place."[94] The energetic Joel Palmer found the boats offering
transportation down the Columbia exorbitantly expensive and all booked for at
least ten days. "We then determined to make a trip over the mountains," he wrote
in his journal. He ascertained that Barlow's men had "penetrated some twenty or
twenty-five miles into the interior, and found it impracticable." They had been
in the mountains for six days with seven wagons, "intending to go as far as they
could, and if found to be impracticable, to return and go down the river." Palmer
persuaded fifteen families to join "in our trip over the mountains." On 1 October,
he set out with about thirty wagons.[95]

Palmer soon found the advance wagons and learned Barlow and a small party
had pushed ahead to search for a crossing. Barlow discovered a route he thought
would be practical for wagons, and Palmer said Indians told of "a trail to the
north, which ran over Mount Hood, and thence to Oregon city." The road blaz-
ers sent their loose cattle ahead with a few men who were "to procure provisions
and assistance, and meet us on the way." By 10 October, Barlow and Palmer had
cut a road to the top of the ridge, but the descent "was covered with a species of
laurel bush, and so thick, that it was almost impossible to pass through it, and as
it was very dry we set it on fire." By dawn, the fire had cleared the road down
the precipitous pitch later known as Little Laurel Hill—but Laurel Hill, the even
more infamous descent down the side of Mount Hood, still lay ahead.[96]

"We had overcome so many difficulties that we felt quite sure we could go almost
anywhere," Miriam Tuller recalled.[97] Palmer and Barlow climbed the south shoulder of Mount Hood nearly to the top of Oregon's tallest volcano, reaching an area
now called Palmer Glacier. "From this peak, we overlooked the whole of the mountains," Palmer reported. Leaving his companions behind, he climbed above the tim-
berline and saw what seemed to be a route wagons could use to get to the Sandy
River Valley. But now time was working against them: on 13 October the weather,
which had been clear for months, began to cloud up, and the men realized that if the
winter rains began, their families would be trapped in the mountains.[98]

---

[93] Tuller, "Crossing the Plains in 1845," 88.

[94] Barlow, "Reminiscences of Seventy Years," 260.

[95] Palmer, *Journal of Travels,* 30 September 1845, 120–21. Palmer provides the best account of blazing what
became the Barlow Road.

[96] Ibid., 1–10 October 1845, 127–30.

[97] Tuller, "Crossing the Plains in 1845," 89.

[98] Palmer, *Journal of Travels,* 10–30 October 1845, 130–55.

"The men worked on the road for about two weeks, but gave up hope of getting the wagons through that fall, as it was now October, and concluded it was best to send the women and children out of the mountains," Miriam Tuller remembered. Assigning guards to watch their property, most of the emigrants began packing to the settlements. Tuller mounted a Cayuse pony and set out with Palmer's party, leaving "husband and camp—everything—but a few clothes and a little provisions, to try to reach some place before the rain set in. The first night after we left camp rain commenced and it rained all the time until we got through the mountains." Relief parties reached the soaked and hungry sojourners with provisions provided by their future neighbors in the Willamette Valley.[99] Barlow left on another scouting trip on 16 October, eventually reached the settlements, and met Palmer on his return. The two men led the remaining families out of the mountains, reaching the settlements in November, leaving men behind to guard goods cached in a rude cabin at "Fort Deposit."

Soon after reaching the settlements, Barlow persuaded Oregon's provisional legislature to grant him a charter to construct the Mount Hood Toll Road and the right to charge $5 for wagons using it. As soon as it opened in 1846 the rough trace became known as the Barlow Road.[100] Clarborne Walker described the prospects for the route not long after he and his brother reached the Willamette Valley. Barlow and his partners said "they will get a road through that will be practicable for wagons. The hills are not as bad as anticipated. Dense forest of timber to cut through, the greatest obstacle in the way," Walker reported. Others laid plans "to cut a road through the Cascades about 50 miles south of this road but whether it will be done is uncertain," although already some were talking about trying to blaze a direct trail to Fort Boise the next spring. "Mountaineers say there can be a good road got through this way," Walker observed, "but in general they are such liars there is no certainty in what they say."[101]

The Declivity of the Back Bone: The California Trail in 1845

The California emigration of 1845 began when Caleb Greenwood and his sons set out from Sutters Fort with a party of twelve men on 12 May, bound for Fort Hall, where he offered his services as a guide to westbound trains. For the Greenwoods, it may have been a simple moneymaking expedition. Some believe John Sutter employed Greenwood to divert Oregon-bound emigrants to California, but Sutter mentioned nothing about such an arrangement in his letters that spring.

---

[99] Tuller, "Crossing the Plains in 1845," 89.
[100] James M. Tompkins's *Discovering Laurel Hill and the Barlow Road* is an excellent tour guide.
[101] Walker to "Dear Brother, Sister and Friends," 1845, Purvine Family Records.

Greenwood appears to have acted on his own initiative and may have journeyed to Fort Hall to meet his youngest children.[102]

William H. Winter chronicled his journey east with Greenwood in the guide-book he published with Overton Johnson in 1846. John Greenwood apparently improved the trail opened the previous year by discovering a practical wagon route that bypassed the treacherous climb up Truckee Canyon and approached the mountains through Dog Valley. The party reached Fort Hall forty days after leaving Sutters Fort. Neither the Great Basin nor its inhabitants impressed Win-ter: he saw no game between the Sierra and the Snake except a few antelope, and beyond the headwaters of the Sacramento the country was either broken by mountains or "covered with extensive wastes of sand and volcanic desolation." Winter thought it could never be inhabited by any "people much superior to the insect and reptile eating savages."[103]

By the end of July, the Greenwoods were at Soda Springs. According to some accounts, a third son had joined them. The old man and his sons were "well posted on the route," leading Solomon Tetherow's company over a shortcut to Fort Hall, "an easy, level way" with excellent campgrounds that James Field thought "must cut off at least nine or ten miles." The traders at Fort Hall said the first trains "took them by surprise, being a month earlier than companies had ever reached the fort before."[104]

A tale told about Fort Hall that summer would be echoed in folktales and pioneer recollections for decades. Aware of the Native custom of presenting a bride's family with horses as a dowry, David Dodge "All-in-a-Joke" Bayley asked an Indian how many horses he would give for his daughter. The Indian offered three, and Bayley said for six horses he could have her. "The next day he came after her, and had the six horses, and seemed determined to have her," her mother wrote. "He followed our wagons for several days, and we were glad to get rid of him without any trouble. The Indians never joke, and Mr. Bayley took good care ever after not to joke with them."[105]

With Richard Grant's support, Caleb Greenwood began aggressively recruit-ing emigrants to follow him to California. Joel Palmer believed the old moun-taineer was "well stocked with falsehoods" about the trail to Oregon, so that the "perils of the way were so magnified as to make us suppose the journey to Oregon

---

[102] Kelly and Morgan, *Old Greenwood*, 132–34, 149–50.

[103] Johnson and Winter, *Route across the Rocky Mountains*, 105–106.

[104] Field, Crossing the Plains, 29 and 31 July 1845, Oregon Historical Society.

[105] Bayley to Griffith, 20 September 1849, in Holmes, *Covered Wagon Women*, 1:36–37. Holmes pointed out, "This contemporary document is a corrective for the tall tales of later years." In Oregon folktales the number of horses grew to sixty and the girl had to be rescued from an Indian camp.

almost impossible." Palmer thought Greenwood "had been dispatched from California to pilot the emigration through."[106]

"There appears to be a great anxiety on the part of the Hudson's Bay Company, to turn as many of the Oregon people to California as possible," A. H. Thompson wrote near Fort Boise. Officers like Grant "employed some of the worst rascals in the mountains, to intercept the emigrants at Fort Hall and turn as many to California as they can," he charged. These agents claimed the Oregon road was "utterly impassable on account of rocks and mountains, and that Snake river never has or can be forded with wagons; all of which we all know is false." In contrast, the promoters praised the road to California as "one eternal pasture." Thompson claimed these guides persuaded "52 wagons belonging to the more timid and fickle-minded of the people" to abandon their plans to go to Oregon. In return, the guides were "paid a premium for all that go, by the company, and demand also $1.25 per head of the emigrants themselves, for pilot money."[107]

Grant did, in fact, have "the worst rascals in the mountains"—or at least the cagiest traders—in his employ. He had ample reasons to try to deflect American emigrants away from Oregon, but he does not seem to have been acting on an official directive. His alliance with Pegleg Smith had proved highly profitable and effective in reducing competition. Louis Vasquez had few trade goods at Fort Bridger, Smith reported in January 1844, and Grant mentioned Miles Goodyear, another "petty trader" who had done business with the Company but now was supplying himself from Taos, "wherefrom he smuggles as much Liquor as he pleases." Grant believed American traders such as Goodyear and William O. Fallon offered trifling competition, but "trappers of the mountains will do any thing and go any where for Liquor," which HBC policy forbade selling. Grant was sure his smalltime competitors did "a great deal of harm and are the cause of a good many beaver skins not coming our way."[108]

The Snake Country produced £3000 worth of furs for the Hudson's Bay Company during 1845, "besides a few hundred dollars picked up among the Emigrants passing here on their way to Oregon and Caleforina." Chief Trader Grant had "kept good friends or rather on good terms with them all but I assure you they are

---

[106] Palmer, *Journal of Travels,* 8 August 1845, 87–88.

[107] "From the Oregon Emigrants," *Boston Cultivator,* 20 December 1845, courtesy of James M. Tompkins.

[108] Grant to Simpson, 15 March 1844, D.5/10, HBC Archives, 426. Redheaded Miles Morris Goodyear (1817–49) of Connecticut went west in 1836 with Marcus Whitman and accompanied William Drummond Stewart to Green River in 1843. Grant's comment is the first evidence he was engaged in the New Mexico trade, importing the infamous "Taos Lightning" so popular in the Rocky Mountains. In fall 1846, Goodyear and British Army veteran "Captain Wells" founded Fort Buenaventura on the site of present-day Ogden, Utah. Their trading post and garden on the Weber River showed that permanent agricultural settlements could survive in the Great Basin. Goodyear sold his establishment to the Mormons late in 1847 for $1,950 and died on the Yuba River in California two years later.

a rough and uncouth set, it requires all my Yankeeship and Knowing them and their ways of days past." Grant felt "that there is all the appearance of war between Great Britain and the United States," and there was no shortage of people who were eager for war "to have an excuse to come here & help themselves."[109]

Old Greenwood's siren song was not very effective: in 1845 only about one in ten overland wagons turned south for California. A mysterious party may have left Fort Hall with five wagons at the end of July, but Jacob Snyder chronicled the journey of the dozen young men in a pack train that otherwise led the way. Writing to his father the next spring, William L. Todd (Mary Todd Lincoln's cousin) said he left Fort Hall on 9 August with ten wagons and fell in with fifteen more on the Humboldt. This was the third company of some one hundred souls that met Snyder's packers a day's journey from Fort Hall. Old Greenwood and his sons guided this party—sometimes known as the Grigsby-Ide company for its two most prominent members, John Grigsby and the "well provided" William Ide. "There was in our train about thirty wagons," Eliza Gregson remembered. They needed a guide "for the road was new & was but little known to any but the trappers." Greenwood "got $2.50 a piece to pilot us in to California," John Gregson recalled.[110]

The travelers left the Oregon Trail and headed up the Raft River on what was now the main route to California. Although Joseph R. Walker and Greenwood had taken wagons over the trace, Jacob Snyder recalled, "There was no trail or the sign of any where we passed" between the Raft River to the head of the Humboldt.[111] Greenwood led the wagons to the singularly shaped formations at City of Rocks (Snyder thought one of them looked like the Ace of Spades). As they approached the Humboldt, Greenwood took a new route down Town Creek said to be two days shorter than the original road down Bishop Creek Canyon. This trail met the headwaters of the river at what is now Wells, Nevada, and was longer but much easier for wagons. As they approached today's Elko, "friendly Indians" (probably Western Shoshones) warned that over the mountains they would find Indians who would steal and shoot their horses. "The Snakes have been driving the Diggers out of the country for some offense," Snyder noted, and the emigrants passed deserted villages that appeared to be hastily abandoned. Such intertribal warfare did not prevent the Paiutes from attending to their immediate needs, and the party began to lose horses and find their oxen filled with arrows.[112]

---

[109] Grant to Simpson, 2 January 1846, D.5/16, HBC Archives, 424.

[110] Kelly and Morgan, *Old Greenwood*, 143, 151–53. Mrs. Gregson recalled there were forty wagons; Pat McChristian told Bancroft there were forty-one.

[111] Simpson, *Report of Explorations across the Great Basin*, 22, citing "a letter dated San Francisco, November 3, 1860, from Maj. J. R. Snyder."

[112] Kelly and Morgan, *Old Greenwood*, 155–63.

On the edge of the Black Rock Desert, John Greenwood murdered an Indian. According to Benjamin F. Bonney, Greenwood shot the man in the back after he had surrendered and turned to run. The callousness of "this most wanton and dastardly" murder shocked the emigrants, who tried to make the wounded man's last moments comfortable. When Old Greenwood came up, he told Britton, his other son, to "shoot the Indian through the head to put him out of his misery." When he reached the emigrant camp, the old trapper said, "The man who killed that Indian must die." When he learned that his own son had viciously killed the man, Greenwood ordered "whoever saw John to shoot him on sight as they would a wild animal."[113]

By the middle of September the emigrants had reached the Truckee River. Jacob Snyder and the packers left the wagons behind to cross the "declivity of the Back Bone of the California Mountains." John Greenwood and a small party arrived at Sutters Fort on 27 September, and the next day emigrants "kept coming in all day." Solomon Sublette appeared with another mounted party on 7 October. He told Sutter there were sixty more American wagons in the Sierra bound for his fort.[114]

"When we struck the main ridge of the mountains, every heart was filled with terror at the awful site," William Isaac Tustin wrote home. The path to the summit was about two and a half miles: "It was solid rock from bottom to top; some places were almost perpendicular to descend; others so smooth an ox could hardly stand; other places where sharp rocks cut the cattle's feet and legs, till they bled in streams." It took four days of hard labor for most of the Grigsby-Ide party to reach the summit. "The mountain was smeared with blood and hair from bottom to top.—it was the most awful sight I ever saw," Tustin said.[115]

"Tribulation in the extreme" attended crossing the Sierra with wagons, William Todd wrote next spring: it required "jumping from one rocky cliff to another." In places the travelers had to lift their wagons over a ledge of rocks by main force. William Ide reportedly devised new techniques, probably involving a block and tackle, that reduced the difficulty of crossing the passes. "You never saw a set of fellows more happy," Todd said, "than when we reached the summit." One party experienced considerable excitement when a keg of gunpowder exploded and blew a wagon apart, but at midnight on 16 October, the first wagons to cross from the Missouri to the Sacramento in a single season arrived at Sutters Fort.[116]

---

[113] Ibid., 163, 166, 168. Dale Morgan noted, "It is difficult to know how much faith should be placed in this dramatic tale." Some of Bonney's details are clearly incorrect.

[114] Ibid., 172, 174–75.

[115] Tustin, "California & Oregon," 1 May 1846, *Illinois Gazette,* 26 February 1848. Courtesy of Kristin Johnson.

[116] Bancroft, *History of California,* 4:579–80; and Todd, "Interesting from California," 17 April 1846, *Sangamo Journal,* 13 August 1846.

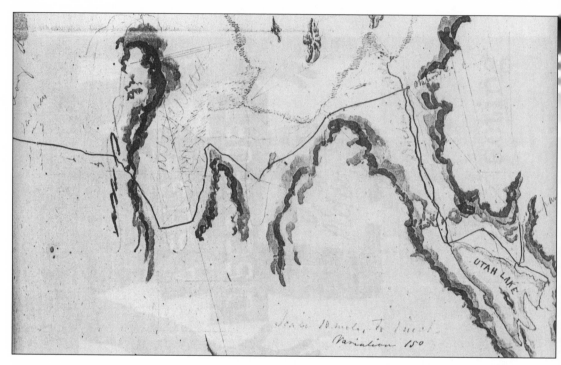

Edward Kern accompanied John C. Frémont's third expedition. This map of the Great Salt Lake in his 1845 journal shows the route Lansford W. Hastings followed the next year for his disastrous cutoff. Courtesy Beinecke Library.

Grim news greeted the California emigrants. "The Mexicans talk every spring and fall here of driving the foreigners out of the country," Todd wrote. "They must do it this year, or they never can do it." If any official dared ask for his passport, Todd said he would "shew my rifle."[117] But on 21 October, the day after Todd arrived at his fort, John Sutter received orders from the Mexican government to stop emigration from the United States. The two countries, his dispatches said, were at war.

For Wagons, the Road Is Decidedly Better: Frémont's Third Expedition

Despite intense agitation in both countries, Mexico and the United States were at peace in 1845. On 10 July the Mexican government ordered Americans from Oregon and Missouri not to enter Alta California, but local officials did nothing to enforce the decree after publishing it in the province on 12 September. Two months later, Prefect Manuel Castro, "with the spirit of hospitality which distinguishes the Mexicans," suspended the order.[118] While tension mounted in California, the armies of both nations took up positions in Texas along the contested border. The arrival of Brevet Captain John C. Frémont at Sutters Fort on 10 December 1845 did nothing to defuse the explosive situation.

Frémont's third expedition left Bents Fort on the Arkansas River on 16 August 1845 on what his powerful father-in-law said "the adventurous explorer" intended "to be the crowning work of his labors."[119] The men pushed hard, traveling at what Henry King called "a pretty swift rate." The pace winded their animals—King said he "rode down" three horses between Westport and the "lower point of the Cordilleras," apparently referring to the Sierra Nevada.[120] The expedition crossed central Colorado and the Uinta Basin and entered the Great Basin near the headwaters of the Provo River, which Frémont followed to Utah Lake. Moving north, he camped on the future site of Salt Lake City on 14 October. Six days later, Frémont began his only pathfinding that actually blazed a wagon road.

"The most direct route, for the California emigrants," guidebook author Lansford W. Hastings had speculated early in 1845, "would be to leave the Oregon route, about two hundred miles east from Fort Hall; thence bearing west southwest, to the Salt lake; and thence continuing down to the bay of St. Francisco."[121]

---

[117] Ibid.

[118] Bancroft, *History of California*, 4:605–606.

[119] Benton, "Speech of Hon. T. Benton," 2 February 1847, *Congressional Globe* (29:2), vol. 16, appendix, 135.

[120] King to "Dear Parents," 30 March 1846, "Copy of Henry King's Letter from California," *Congressional Globe* (29:2), vol. 16, appendix, 137. Frémont forbade members of his Third Expedition from keeping diaries, and his own journals went up in smoke, so the record of the trek is, as Dale Morgan observed, remarkably barren, increasing the value of King's overlooked letter.

[121] Hastings, *The Emigrants' Guide*, 137–38.

Hastings was pointing out the obvious: going straight west from Fort Bridger to the Humboldt River would be the shortest distance between the two points and would eliminate the long detour north to Fort Hall. On a map, it looked like a simple way to save several hundred miles' travel. Frémont's mountaineers, however, knew that the Great Salt Lake Desert was some of the most forbidding country in the West. "It had never before been crossed by white man," Kit Carson recalled. "Old trappers would speak of the impossibility of crossing, that water could not be found, grass for the animals, there was none."[122]

Frémont's frontiersmen crossed the eighty-three waterless miles between Skull Valley and Pilot Peak (which he named) at the cost of at least ten mules and several horses.[123] Here they struck the tracks of the Bidwell-Bartleson party, whose trail marked the end of Frémont's contribution to original trail exploration in the Great Basin. He had shown that disciplined horsemen could cross the Great Salt Desert playa, but his loss of animals made clear that this was not a practical wagon road.

The expedition divided at Mound Springs, south of present-day Wells, Nevada. Frémont and Kit Carson led a contingent of ten men south from Ruby Valley to Walker Lake, while Lieutenant Theodore H. Talbot followed Joe Walker across Secret Pass to the Humboldt River and then down the California Trail. From the rendezvous at Walker Lake, Talbot's detachment entered the Sierra via the Walker River, while Frémont turned north to examine the new emigrant road over Truckee Pass. Following wagon tracks to the settlements, he reached Sutters Fort on 10 December 1845. Three days later, he left to meet Walker and his thirty men, who had eaten all their cattle and most of their mounts. As ordered, Walker's party waited for twenty days and then crossed the Sierra via Owens Lake. This took the party too far south, and Walker mistook the Kern River for Kings River, where the men planned to rendezvous with Frémont. It was another hard journey that left Henry King with "some very tough yarns to tell." Before the expedition reunited, he spent nine days without anything to eat. "My hip bones became so sharp that I could not sleep for several nights," he complained. Frémont, meanwhile, had "attempted to take a short cut across to head us off on the other side, but got into the snow and lost everything, animals and all, and had to go back again on foot," King reported.[124]

The young explorer's presence again raised questions about American plans for the Pacific Coast. "The arrival of Captain Fremont has revived the excitement

---

[122] Korns and Morgan, *West from Fort Bridger,* 10.

[123] Madsen, *Exploring the Great Salt Lake,* 182.

[124] King to "Dear Parents," 30 March 1846, 138. Frémont did lose all his cattle trying to ascend King's Canyon, but he apparently saved at least some of his horses. See Spence and Jackson, *The Expeditions of John Charles Frémont,* 2:40–42. Henry King was one of the men who lost his life on Frémont's disastrous fourth expedition in 1848.

After the "Long Hard Drive" of more than eighty waterless miles, travelers on the Hastings Cutoff at last found relief at Pilot Springs, at the foot of Pilot Peak on the present-day Utah-Nevada border. Now known as Donner Spring, the site is shown as it was in 1994, shortly after members of the Oregon-California Trails Association fenced and restored the historic waterhole. Courtesy W. L. Rusho.

in California respecting the Emigration," American Consul Thomas Larkin later reported to Secretary of State Buchanan, "and the fear of the Californians losing their country."[125] Frémont soon proved their fears were well justified.

A Road through the Stony Mountains:
The Return of Lansford W. Hastings

On Christmas Day, 1845, the last of the year's overland travelers reached Sutters Fort. After months of bombarding his allies in California with letters boasting that he would lead at least two thousand Americans "mostly of good character & some property" to California that season, Lansford W. Hastings arrived at the head of a party of only ten men. Undeterred, within three weeks Hastings was claiming he had "found a road through the Stony Mountains 400 miles shorter than has ever been traveled. A Larg Emigration will be through this summer."[126] Hastings had in fact found nothing: he had actually stayed on the established trail through Fort Hall and was apparently referring to Frémont's recent discoveries. By year's end, Hastings had secured a land grant of half a square mile from Sutter, and he and John Bidwell surveyed a site on the Sacramento River for "Sutterville" three or four miles below the mouth of the American River in January 1846, which was "intended for a Mormon town."[127]

After leaving California, Hastings had visited Mexico City and Vera Cruz and then sailed for New Orleans. He reached New Madrid, Missouri, by 19 March 1844, and there he wrote John Calhoun an audacious letter: "There are some revolutionary arrangements, now being made, in California, of which I stand fully advised." Hastings reported great dissatisfaction at the United States government's "seeming neglect" of American settlers on the Pacific. Remarkably, this twenty-five-year-old adventurer then warned the secretary of state, "If the U.S. does not give the people of Oregon, a government of some kind soon, an attempt will be made at an organization of an independant government." To the press, Hastings announced "he proposed to publish a small work in pamphlet form, to be entitled 'The Emigrants' Guide to Oregon and California.'"[128]

---

[125] Larkin to Buchanan, 2 April 1846, in Larkin, *The Larkin Papers,* 4:276. President Polk appointed Larkin a "Confidential Agent for California" in October 1845, but news of the assignment did not reach Larkin until June 1846. The same letter said Polk would "make no effort and use no influence to induce California to become one of the free and independent States of this Union," but "if the People should desire to unite their destiny with ours, they would be received as brethren." See Buchanan to Larkin, 17 October 1845, in ibid., 4:45–46.

[126] Leese to Larkin, 12 January 1846, in Larkin, *The Larkin Papers,* 4:161.

[127] Bidwell, "Life in California before the Gold Discovery," 180–81; and Bancroft, *History of California,* 3:778.

[128] Hastings to Calhoun, 20 May 1844, in *Annual Report of the American Historical Association* (1929): 234–35. Calhoun became secretary of state on 1 April 1845. Hastings's subsequent letters indicate Calhoun sent him an encouraging reply, but no such letter appears in Calhoun's published correspondence.

Hastings released his famous guidebook in Cincinnati in April 1845.[129] The volume was not admired in the West. "No general English reader will read one quarter of the Book," Thomas Larkin scoffed.[130] The *California Star* sneered at Hastings's history of California as taken from hastily jotted notes and written "in his own big easy chair in the city of Cincinnati."[131] However preposterous Hastings's boasts might appear on the West Coast or to his future critics, in 1845 they had considerable appeal in America's borderlands, and Hastings hoped his guide would ignite a massive emigration to California. The book did persuade some Americans to go west, but not nearly as many as Hastings and his friends had dreamed.

A Pittsburgh newspaper editor met Hastings on the Ohio River in May 1845, shortly after the guide's publication. Seven thousand souls had already left Missouri for Oregon and California, Hastings claimed, and he had supplied them with two thousand copies of his book, which would have been almost enough to provide every man, woman, and child actually headed west with their own copy. The American residents of California "had fully resolved to throw off the Mexican yoke, and that the independent government would be formed next fall in September or October" by a "bloodless revolution." The young promoter was on his way to Saint Louis, "consummating his plans" to return to California "with a company of emigrants, mostly enterprising young men, who are going by sea." On the same trip, Hastings apparently met New York publisher Samuel Brannan, who was traveling to the Mormon capital at Nauvoo, Illinois, and who may have already conceived a plan to lead a shipload of Mormon emigrants to California.

The editor suspected the ship would carry "the means of overturning the Mexican government in California, and that she will be freighted with ambitious youths, who design to be Presidents, Governors, Judges, Legislators, and home and foreign ministers in the new Republic. Indeed," he concluded, "I strongly suspect that Captain Hastings aims at the highest executive office himself."[132]

THE IRRESISTIBLE ARMY OF ANGLO-SAXON EMIGRATION:
THE SCHEMES OF 1845

The schemes of a small group of adventurers, politicians, and businessmen in the city of New York during the sweltering summer of 1845 might seem peripheral to the history of overland emigrant trails, but the ambitious young men who

---

[129] Cumming, "Lansford Hastings' Michigan Connection," 20.

[130] Larkin to Buchanan, 2 April 1846, in Larkin, *The Larkin Papers*, 4:276.

[131] Hastings, *The Emigrants' Guide*, 20, 137, 143–52; and "Yerba Buena and San Francisco Bay," *California Star*, 30 January 1847. For a defense of the book, see Andrews, "The Controversial Hastings Overland Guide," 21–34.

[132] "Oregon and California," Correspondence of the *Pittsburgh Gazette*, from the senior editor, dated Louisville, May 16, reprinted in *Camden Ohio Repository*, 29 May 1845. Courtesy of Kristin Johnson. For Brannan's plans, see Brannan, *Scoundrel's Tale*, chapter 3.

Charles Kelly got the only known image of adventurer
Lansford W. Hastings from his descendants in the 1920s.
Author's collection.

sought to determine the fate of California had a surprising influence on subsequent events. As historian Dale L. Morgan observed about their tangled plots, "There is a great deal more here than meets the eye."[133]

After reaching New York from Saint Louis via the Great Lakes in June, Lansford Hastings touted his *Emigrants' Guide* in three lectures at Croton Hall "to put forth *in their true light* the advantages and inducements" Oregon and California held out to the "immigrating community." Based on his "thorough knowledge of both the route and the method of traveling," Captain Hastings confidently assured all comers he would lead them to either Oregon or California in only three months "with entire safety," to prove that emigrants could leave the frontier as late as August first with every assurance of reaching the coast successfully.[134] Hastings's braggadocio hid the fact that he had left California before anyone knew whether it was possible for a wagon to cross the Sierra in *any* length of time.

The summer of 1845 was a heady moment in the history of the young American Republic. Texas accepted admission to the Union on the Fourth of July, and Mexico recalled her minister to Washington to protest the annexation. On a second front, President Polk was pressing Britain so aggressively to settle the "Oregon Question" that his tactics resembled what became known as brinksmanship. That July in New York, John L. O'Sullivan's *United States Magazine and Democratic Review* proclaimed it was America's "manifest destiny to overspread the continent allotted by Providence," coining a phrase that captured the spirit of the times. Historians have long assumed O'Sullivan wrote the editorial, but new evidence indicates it was actually the work of his political editor, Jane McManus Storm Cazneau. Whoever coined it, the redundant phrase evoked the powerful public sentiment about America's divine mission to bring the blessings of republican democracy to her benighted neighbors in Mexico and Canada. "The advance guard of the irresistible army of Anglo-Saxon emigration," the editorial argued, had established the right "to the possession of the homes conquered from the wilderness by their own labors and dangers, sufferings and sacrifices—a better and a truer right than the artificial title of sovereignty in Mexico."[135]

Hastings's New York allies included fellow author-attorney-promoter Thomas Jefferson Farnham, Mormon official Samuel Brannan, Oregon entrepreneurs and emigration agents Arthur W. and Alfred G. Benson, and, most remarkably, politician Amos Kendall. As Andrew Jackson's postmaster general, Kendall had revolutionized mail delivery and, having drafted Polk's inaugural address the previous

---

[133] Morgan to Virginia Sorenson, 29 December 1943, Morgan Papers, Bancroft Library.

[134] "Oregon and California," *New-York Daily Tribune*, 24 June 1845, 2/2.

[135] O'Sullivan, "Annexation." Linda Hudson's *The Mistress of Manifest Destiny*, 60–62, 209, presents compelling evidence Cazneau wrote the editorial. During the Mexican-American War the remarkable Jane Cazneau conducted a peace mission for Polk.

March, was now embarked on a career as one of America's earliest, if not its first, lobbyist. It seems Kendall acted as a "ringmaster behind the scenes," looking out for the president's complicated California policies. Polk was already working on a variety of plans to acquire the province by purchase, diplomacy, or war, and Kendall provided the president with the latest reports from the Pacific.[136]

Like Hastings, Farnham was an attorney and the author of racist books based on brief visits to Oregon and California. He had recently published *Travels in the Californias* about his 1839 adventures with the Peoria Party, and he too was interested in promoting an American takeover of the Pacific coast. Farnham was no doubt intrigued by Hastings's claim that "the independence of California, as respects Mexico, has been settled in the minds of her people," who had resolved to have a government of their own or unite with Oregon as "one Free Republic."[137]

In May Hastings had announced his plans to return to California by sea, but in New York he decided to offer the large number of emigrants who had gathered at Independence that summer "the earliest opportunity of setting out for Oregon or California" with him as their guide.[138] That fall, Mormon preacher and newspaper publisher Brannan successfully recruited the first shipload of American emigrants to go to California via Cape Horn: in February 1846 some 230 Mormons set sail for San Francisco. "As a blind" their ship, the *Brooklyn,* flew a flag proclaiming it was bound for Oregon.[139]

Sam Brannan claimed his followers' bloc votes had delivered New York and the presidency to James K. Polk: he boasted he had met with the new president shortly after his inauguration.[140] It appears Brannan introduced Hastings to the Benson brothers, who had helped Hastings's old rival Elijah White win his appointment in 1842 as Oregon's first federal official. For four years the Bensons had vigorously fulfilled their confidential arrangement with John Tyler to ship supplies to the Pacific Squadron and fifty American emigrants to Oregon. Tyler himself believed the Bensons had faithfully executed their contract. To expand their operations in the West, at government expense the brothers sent F. W. Pettygrove with $15,000 in trade goods to stock a store on the Willamette.[141]

Through the alliance they formed with Kendall, Brannan, and Hastings, the Bensons sought to extend their commercial enterprises to California, but their scheme encountered a more pressing problem. The interests of Benson and Co. collided with the Polk administration when the new secretary of the Navy, George

[136] DeVoto, *The Year of Decision,* 240.

[137] "Oregon and California," *New-York Daily Tribune,* 11 June 1844.

[138] "Oregon and California," *New-York Daily Tribune,* 24 June 1845.

[139] Brannan, Fragmentary remarks, Brannan Collection, Huntington Library.

[140] Brannan, *Scoundrel's Tale,* 58, 143.

[141] "Letter from the Secretary of the Navy," 3 March 1845, House Doc. 161 (28-2): 21–22; and Bancroft, *History of Oregon,* 422.

Bancroft, reviewed the Bensons' lucrative contract in March 1845, concluded it was "unauthorized by law," and canceled it. The Bensons turned to Amos Kendall to win it back. Kendall sprang into action and began lining up political support to revive the Bensons' sweetheart deal.[142]

"In the present position of the Oregon question," Kendall argued in a letter to the president, "it was exceedingly unpolitic to disturb that arrangement," especially since it had been in operation for years. He warned that Senator Sidney Breese of Illinois was infuriated and had written, "When I return to Washington next winter I intend the administration shall know there is a *west* & possessed of important interests." Kendall told Polk "our leading friends in the West" had long known about the contract and assured emigrants they could buy axes, plows, hoes, and other farming utensils at the Benson brothers' store in Oregon. He quickly forwarded Breese's angry letter to the president. "Rely upon it," Kendall assured Polk, "the utmost response is required to prevent a general outbreak of similar feeling among the western friends of Oregon."[143]

Hastings and Farnham claimed they could inspire as many as twenty thousand Americans to head for California in 1846.[144] With this support, they would declare independence from Mexico and establish a Republic of California. When Hastings left New York on 6 July 1845, he carried a letter from Farnham to Dr. John Marsh at Mount Diablo. Farnham assured Marsh that "the strongest desire of my heart" was "that the 'Republic of California' should arise." He described the plan: "From 10 to 20 thousand emigrants will enter California next summer. There will then be population enough to authorise the step; & we shall have force for any contingency." Farnham even outlined a schedule: "Neither Europe or the States are yet prepared for that event. The excitement consequent on the admission of Texas into the Union must have time to abate. The winter of 46 will do."[145]

On his way west Hastings hoped to visit Nauvoo, Illinois, to consult with senior Mormon leaders who were then planning to move their followers to Alta California the next spring, but he cancelled the trip.[146] Hastings intended to lecture in

---

[142] Webster to "Dear Caroline," 24 June 1849, *Correspondence*, 6:343. The Bensons were finally awarded $10,792 in March 1851 for breach of their transportation contracts. See ibid., 6:344n1; and Senate Reports, 31st Cong., 2d sess., Serial 593, Doc. 319, 31 March 1851.

[143] George Bancroft to Sidney Breese; Breese to E. D. Taylor, 18 May 1845; and Kendall to Polk, 8 June 1845, James K. Polk Papers, Library of Congress.

[144] H. H. Bancroft estimated California's European population was 14,000 souls between 1845 and 1848, but more recent calculations put the total non-Indian population in 1848 at 7,600, including 700 foreigners, mostly Americans. See Bancroft, *History of California*, 5:643; and Holliday, *Rush for Riches*, 26.

[145] Hastings to Marsh, 26 March 1846; Farnham to Marsh, 6 July 1845, in Hawgood, *First and Last Consul*, 23–24, 52.

[146] Brannan to Young, 22 July 1845, Brigham Young Collection, Family and Church History Department Archives, The Church of Jesus Christ of Latter-day Saints, Salt Lake City, Utah. When Brannan's *New York Messenger* serialized Hastings's book, the *Nauvoo Neighbor* reprinted the introduction, "Mr. Hastings has recently been lecturing in this city," without citation, leading some to believe Hastings visited Nauvoo. An 1861 Hastings letter to Brigham Young shows otherwise.

the "principal cities" on his route, and he at least promised to speak in Saint Louis on 25 July. The *Western Expositor* reported he left Independence for California on 15 August 1845 with twenty-three men, but thirteen left him before he reached Fort Laramie.[147] After three months on the trail, his starving pack train straggled into Fort Hall in November. Hastings claimed "several thousands of Mormons were making great preparations in the States to steer their course [this] ensuing summer to the Promised Land which they say is Calefornia," Richard Grant reported. At John McLoughlin's request, Grant provided supplies to the packers at the cost of "a pretty heavy debt to a Lawyer of the name of Hastings."[148]

After 132 days on the trail, Hastings's party reached Sutters Fort just as snow began to fall in the Sierra Nevada, ending, as Dale Morgan concluded, a foolhardy undertaking that summed up Hastings's extensive ignorance. His rash gamble had paid off this time, but his arrogant disregard of the weather in the Sierra would soon have grim—and fatal—consequences.

CALIFORNIA MUST BELONG TO THE AMERICANS

By the end of 1845, American emigrants had proven that wagons could reach both Oregon and California in a single season. They had done so with practically no help from their government, but now an American president would take a much more active interest in realizing his vision of a continental nation. James K. Polk first informed his cabinet of his desire to acquire California for the United States on 16 September 1845. A letter from American consul Thomas Larkin arrived at the state department in October: it galvanized the administration into action, for Larkin reported that the Hudson's Bay Company and British government were interfering in California's affairs.[149]

The U.S.S. *Congress* sailed from Hampton Roads, Virginia, for California on 25 October 1845 "with *sealed orders*" for the new commander of American naval forces in the Pacific.[150] Commodore Robert F. Stockton, a wealthy capitalist and ardent expansionist known to his sailors as Fighting Bob, had spent the previous spring in the Gulf of Mexico commanding U.S.S. *Princeton,* the most sophisticated warship in the American fleet. Anson Jones, president of the Republic of Texas, told his colleagues that the commodore, acting for the United States government, wanted him "*to manufacture a war* for them."[151] Stockton suggested

---

[147] "Oregon and California," *New-York Tribune,* 24 June 1845, 2; and Morgan, *Overland in 1846,* 28, 30.

[148] Grant to George Simpson, 2 January 1846, D.5/16, HBC Archives, 425; and 4 January 1849, D.5/24, HBC Archives, 227. It is not clear if Hastings ever paid his debt to the Hudson's Bay Company.

[149] Hussey, "The Origin of the Gillespie Mission," 44, 46.

[150] Bayard, *A Sketch of the Life of Com. Robert F. Stockton,* 95–97.

[151] Price, *Origins of the War with Mexico,* 112.

Texas troops occupy the disputed territory between the Nueces and Rio Grande rivers and informed George Bancroft that the Texas militia would "call out three thousand men & 'R. F. Stockton Esq' will supply them in a private way with provisions & ammunition." Texans declined Stockton's offer to finance a war for them, and he had to be content to return to the states with "the glad tidings of annexation."[152] As Stockton weighed anchor, Secretary of the Navy George Bancroft ordered Lieutenant Archibald H. Gillespie, USMC, to cross Mexico incognito bearing official correspondence for Thomas Larkin and John C. Frémont in California. Gillespie also carried private letters to the explorer from Mrs. Frémont and Senator Thomas H. Benton.[153]

That autumn, Amos Kendall introduced Samuel J. Hastings, a Boston seafarer and veteran of the California trade, to President Polk, who "talked with him for two hours and questioned him closely about the country." A new flag would fly over California, the sea captain informed Thomas Larkin in November 1845, and it would be "an American one or a new one and American Agents and American capital will be at the bottom of it." Samuel Hastings noted, "California must belong to the Americans. So say the knowing ones at Washington & even Mr Polk thinks it must come to pass. Whether in his time or not he did not say."[154]

---

[152] Stockton to Bancroft, 27 May 1845, in ibid., 122. Sellers, *James K. Polk,* 224–25, disputed the Stockton intrigue argument.

[153] Harlow, *California Conquered,* 78, 84; and Bancroft to Gillespie, 28 October 1845, Gillespie Papers, UCLA.

[154] Larkin, *The Larkin Papers,* 5:290, 4:92, and 4:177.

CHAPTER 7

All Very Much the Same

Life on the Early Trails

Ｉt is four o'clock A.M.; the sentinels on duty have discharged their rifles—the
signal that the hours of sleep are over," Jesse Applegate wrote in a romantic
recollection of the start of a typical day's travel during the Great Migration
of 1843. "Every wagon and tent is pouring forth its night tenants, and slow-kin-
dling smokes begin largely to rise and float away on the morning air."[1] The common experiences of daily life are often lost to historians, but overland travelers
like Applegate left behind thousands of narratives that provide surprising details
about what life was like on "the long and hazardous journey across the plains."[2]

In ways, day-to-day life on the trail resembled an extended camping trip.
When most of the dear old emigrants recalled their trek west, William Barlow
knew, they emphasized "the privations and starvations," but Barlow felt differently. "I will now say again, for myself and our company, that I never passed a
more pleasant, cheerful and happy summer in my whole long life."[3] The trek
could be an ordeal or a pleasure, and for many overlanders it was both, especially
for children. "A person that has never made such a journey cannot imagine the
trials and hardships that they have to endure," wrote Mary Marsh Cason, who
lost her mother on the trek in 1847. "I, myself, cannot realize them for I was too
young. It was more of a pleasure trip for me."[4]

Emigrants often expected to enjoy the trek and some were surprised it was
not as difficult as they had anticipated. "I never could have believed we could have
travelled so far with so little difficulty," Tamsen Donner wrote from the forks of
the Platte. "Indeed, if I do not experience something far worse than I have yet

---

[1] Applegate, "A Day with the Cow Column in 1843," 127. Applegate's 1868 memoir was probably the single most
widely quoted overland account. See Unruh, *The Plains Across,* 5. How much Applegate or his editor, Bret Harte,
idealized life on the trail is open to question.

[2] Ignatius Smith to Mr. Gillis, 7 March 1911, California State Library.

[3] Barlow, "Reminiscences of Seventy Years," 258.

[4] Cason, "The Whitman Massacre as Recalled by Mary Marsh Cason," Oregon State Archives.

done, I shall say the trouble is all in getting started."[5] Others managed to take pleasure from the trip despite its trials, but early overland journeys were a test of character. A trip to Oregon in 1843 was not beset with very great perils, Peter Burnett noted, but it "was exceedingly severe upon the temper and endurance of people. It was one of the most conclusive tests of character, and the very best school in which to study human nature. Before the trip terminated, people acted upon their genuine principles, and threw off all disguises."[6]

Missionary Henry Spalding described his fur-trade caravan's daily routine in 1836, and it hardly changed over the entire trails era. Travelers rose long before dawn, turned their mules out to graze, cooked and ate breakfast, harnessed their teams, and began moving at 6:00 A.M. They rested or nooned at midday for two hours, camped at six o'clock, picketed the animals at 8:00 P.M., and mounted "a constant guard night and day. The intervals were completely taken up in taking care of animals, getting meals and seeing to our effects, so that we had no time for rest from the time we left one post till we reached another." The missionaries and their livestock were nearly exhausted by day's end, he wrote, and Eliza Spalding and Narcissa Whitman "endured the fatigues of the march remarkably well."[7] Experienced camp attendants and cooks served the caravan, but when overland wagon travel began in 1840, all the cooking, washing, cleaning, and child tending fell to the women.

Life on the trail revolved around the needs of the draft animals. On his "tedious and tiresome journey" to Oregon, John Boardman observed that an emigrant had to devote his full attention to "his animals (as all depends on them), whether they may not be stolen or get away, perhaps turn their packs and lose part of the things, or break something; and when near camping time, he is all anxiety to get good grass, wood and water." In the evening, a prairie traveler needed to collect firewood, build a fire, cook and eat, and "then mend pants, moccasins, pack-saddles, cruppers, lash-rope, girths, &c, or alter his packs, as one too heavy hurts the mule's back. Then comes making bed, and by that time, one only thinks of enjoying repose, and so sweet and undisturbed that he cannot even dream of his native land or those he loves." As one sojourner complained, the trek overland could be "long, tedious and tasteless," but for some the relentless monotony of the endless cycle provided comfort.[8] "The days settled down into a tiresome routine," Margaret Hecox wrote. "I was thankful for this; I knew any change would be for

[5] Donner to "My Old Friend," 16 June 1846, in Morgan, *Overland in 1846*, 562.
[6] Burnett, *Recollections and Opinions of an Old Pioneer*, 99.
[7] Spalding, "A Letter by Henry H. Spalding from the Rocky Mountains," 11 July 1836.
[8] Boardman, "The Journal," 24 September 1843, 112–13; and N. Simons, Letter, ca. 28 June 1854, BYU Library.

the worse." But she found "the terrible trip across the Plains" was a long, hard tramp.[9] "It took us seven months and twenty-one days to reach Oregon from Missouri," Betsey Bayley reported. "This was along time to live in a wagon."[10]

ARISE! ARISE! BREAKING CAMP

"In the morning as soon as the day breaks the first that we hear is the words, 'Arise! Arise!'—then the mules set up such a noise as you never heard, which puts the whole camp in motion," wrote Narcissa Whitman.[11] A day on the trail often began with a bugle call or a gunshot sometime before first light, or as emigrants calculated time, about 4:00 A.M. Breakfast was usually very simple, consisting of biscuits and bacon: "Let your minds take in the idea of the number of mornings and nights that plain middling meat, crackers and heavy biscuit comprise our fare," mourned George Curry in 1846, but he also had "ripe strawberries upon the prairies—we eat them with cream, too, think of it."[12] Sometimes the meal was surprisingly creative. "Stewed apples and peaches and made light bread," wrote Virginia Fackler Creel. "Dressed birds and rabbit for breakfast; won't we feast?"[13] Men tended to make less elaborate preparations: as Edwin Bryant wrote, the meal often "consisted of badly-baked corn-bread, bacon, and coffee."[14]

Many early trains kept their livestock inside the wagon corral but turned them loose not long before dawn. While women rekindled the campfires to prepare breakfast, herders collected the animals that might have grazed as far as a mile or two away and drove them to camp, where teamsters would select their teams for the day. "Breakfast was over by daylight," A. H. Garrison recalled, "and soon our team were hitched to the waggons, the stock was driven from the pasture and all was ready for the start."[15] Locating lost animals or recovering from a stampede could be a difficult and time-consuming process and was the leading cause of delay in getting a large train underway. "Some of our cattle are still lost and we are detained hunting for them," Samuel Crockett complained one morning.[16]

Marcus Whitman's advice—"travel, *travel,* travel"—was as highly regarded as it was true.[17] Trains liked to be underway by at least 7:00 A.M. After breakfast the camp became "a scene of confusion, men and boys running hither and yon, looking

[9] Hecox, "The Story of Margaret M. Hecox," 535, 541.

[10] Bayley to Griffith, 20 September 1849, in Holmes, *Covered Wagon Women,* 1:38.

[11] Whitman to Sister Harriet, 4 June 1836, in Eells, *Marcus Whitman,* 61.

[12] Curry to the St. Louis *Reveille,* 15 May and 12 June 1846, in Morgan, *Overland in 1846,* 540, 553.

[13] Creel, Diary, 4 June 1864, Western Historical Manuscript Collection.

[14] Bryant, *What I Saw in California,* 6 May 1846, 21.

[15] Garrison, "Reminiscences of Abraham Henry Garrison," 11.

[16] Crockett, "Diary," 13 May 1844.

[17] Applegate, "A Day with the Cow Column in 1843," 132.

for their oxen, a great many of them not yet broken sufficiently to be readily yoked." This "added greatly to the uproar; the women hastily packing away cooking utensils, or frantically calling out to some child that was disposed to get within dangerous proximity to animals heels; all was hurry and bustle," Joseph Henry Brown wrote. "The teams would be yoked and hitched to their respective wagons and the word would be given for some family team to take the lead for the day, which would of course take its place in the rear the next. The train would soon be on the move stringing along the road with the loose cattle in the rear."[18]

I Walked Half of the Way to Oregon: The March

Americans who still make their living doing arduous physical labor can appreciate the toil involved in walking from Missouri to Oregon. Many more of us can connect with the basic trail experience because, as historian Elliot West observed, the people who went west in wagons accomplished "something close to epic, and they did it through a perfect metaphor for how each of us makes it through every day: by putting one foot in front of another."[19] Although the pioneer families of Hollywood wagon trains are often shown happily riding west in a wagon, overland emigrants who did not ride a horse or mule usually walked virtually the entire "plains across." Until the 1850s, most wagons had no springs, and the ride of a wagon with no suspension system must be experienced to be appreciated. Walking all day might have been exhausting, but it was preferable to the bone-rattling pounding a wagon inflicted on its passengers.

"Mother and I walked most of the way to California," James Newton Angel remembered. "It is not necessary to detail the hardships and monotony of a trip across the plains, where one day was just like another, week after week."[20] What Eliza Burnett said was true of the trail in general: "The women and children walked most of the way."[21] The children in her company walked many, many miles, Mary Munkers Estes recalled. "Sometimes I think I walked half of the way to Oregon!" She probably walked farther than that.[22]

Organized companies usually rotated their order of march so that no wagon would be permanently consigned to the rear amid the clouds of dust that bedeviled overland trains. One captain of an 1846 train ordered every team to be ready to start at 6:00 A.M., and those not ready were left behind and not allowed to

---

[18] Brown, Recollection of 1847, Bancroft Library, 7.
[19] West, "American Pathways," 23.
[20] Angel, Memoir of 1847, NFTC Manuscripts, Mattes Library, 1.
[21] Burnett, "Reminiscences of a Trip across the Plains in '45."
[22] Estes, Crossing the Plains in 1846.

rejoin the company. "The order was to march in four platoons. Four wagons should start together, keeping twenty feet apart. Then four more should move in the same manner, and so on till all were under way," Jacob Harlan recalled.[23] James Field found the dust along Oregon's Malheur River was "frequently more than shoe deep, and if the wind happens to blow length-wise with the road, it raises such a fog you cannot see the wagon next in front."[24] The clouds of dust were often so dense, B. F. Nichols remembered, that a teamster could not see the oxen he was driving.[25]

"Our people had halted for lunch at noon, and to rest the teams and allow the oxen to graze," Peter Burnett wrote about "nooning," as Tamsen Donner and her daughter called the midday break. "At nooning our teams stood in line on the road chewing the cud and taking their breathing spell," is how Eliza Donner Houghton recalled this "necessary nooning."[26] It provided a break for both travelers and their animals and gave people time to eat their midday meal. More importantly, it allowed the draft animals to rest and graze during the hottest part of the day. "Between 12 o'clock and one o'clock the train is halted in the road for the oxen to breathe," Edwin Bryant reported. "There is a delay of an hour, during which each person partakes of such refreshment as has been provided for him before leaving camp in the morning."[27] Daniel H. Budd called one such respite "our noon spell," which lasted about half an hour.[28] Sometimes, especially on hot days, the break could last up to eight hours.

The rest offered an opportunity for fun or mischief. A few days west of Chimney Rock in 1846, A. H. Garrison recalled nooning at a large spring filled with "a big lot of suckers." He and his young friends "tied lines with hooks on our whipstocks and was catching the suckers by hooking them." Another boy stole his fishing rod, and not wanting to lose his whipstock, which he had carried all the way from Missouri, Garrison hit him. "Well we knocked each other about for a while, when we discovered there was another fight on our hands," for one of the Garrison's teamsters had stopped the boy's brother from clubbing him, and the boy's father joined the fray. The teamster "done him up well," and the party moved out of the fighting camp.[29]

At day's end large trains often corralled their wagons in a circle or U-shaped formation. Fur-trade caravans developed the basic wagon corral, but they preferred a

---

[23] Harlan, *California '46 to '88*, 34.

[24] Field, Crossing the Plains, 25 August 1845, Oregon Historical Society.

[25] Nichols, "Across the Plains in 1844," chapter 8.

[26] Houghton, *The Expedition of the Donner Party*, 38/14, 76/46.

[27] Bryant, *What I Saw in California*, 6 June 1846, 75.

[28] Budd, Journal, 22 June 1852, Mattes Library.

[29] Garrison, "Reminiscences of Abraham Henry Garrison," 16.

hollow square formation.[30] Joseph Henry Brown recalled how Captain Bradshaw, a fur-trade veteran, showed his company how to do it in 1847. After selecting a camp, the two leading wagons stopped, "with the forward wheels of the first wagon nearly even with the hind wheels of the next wagon, and the third wagon assuming the same position to the second and so on through the train; forming a circle when the train had all assumed their positions," with the teams inside the corral. After they had been unyoked and driven out of the circle, "the tongues were chained to the preceding wagons, thus making a barricade of great strength in which to keep the stock during the night and to resist an attack by Indians."[31]

"The Capt. Leads to the water at a distance ahead [and] when he reaches the intended encampment he turns his horse or mule broad side (as a Signal)," the colorful Richard Martin May wrote. "Then gee, haw; go along as the case may be. The whip is Cracked as a token of gladness." Upon reaching the camp, "the Foremost drives around the ring and Stops So as to be hindmost, each man driving his wagon So as to Stretch a chain from one wheel to another Thereby making a good fence for Coreling." More formally, Jesse Applegate recalled, "The corral is a circle one hundred yards deep, formed with wagons connected strongly with each other; the wagon in the rear being connected with the wagon in front by its tongue and ox chains," creating "a strong barrier that the most vicious ox cannot break, and in case of an attack of the Sioux would be no contemptible entrenchment." Especially in Indian Country, emigrants corralled their animals inside the wagon circle and camped outside the circle, often in tents. Other companies grazed their livestock outside the corral and camped inside. The next morning, the cry was "yoke up boys and drive out and take your respective places in the road."[32]

A Splendid Affair for the Plains:
Camp Life, Music, and Dance

As noted, a good campsite had three essential attributes: good grass, good water, and plenty of wood, or at least an acceptable substitute. An ideal campsite might offer shade and shelter and enough water to bathe or wash clothes, but water for

---

[30] Parker, *Journal of an Exploring Tour*, 1 July 1835, 49. Parker's caravan formed "a large hollow square, encompassing an area of about an acre, having the river on one side." William Sublette formed his camp "in a manner to leave a large hollow square, the stream forming one side," John Ball reported. Parker's caravan formed "a large hollow square, encompassing an area of about an acre, having the river on one side." See Ball, "Mode of Encampment," in *Autobiography of John Ball*, 67.

[31] Brown, Recollection of 1847, Bancroft Library.

[32] May, *The Schreek of Wagons*, 22 June 1848, 40; and Applegate, "A Day with the Cow Column in 1843," 128. These emigrants' fears and Hollywood to the contrary, no Lakota war party ever attacked circled wagons during the 1840s or 1850s.

people and animals and grass to feed the livestock were close to indispensable: no one wanted to make a dry camp. William Porter's journal describing his trip down the Snake River can best be described as terse: its longest entry described the losses he and his brother suffered when they "made a dry camp at which two of my oxen gave out and Stephen lost one, to-wit, Old Tom."[33]

The bivouac of a large train was "a very picturesque sight, the white covers of the wagons and new tents resembled a small village, while the camp-fires shed their ruddy light on the surrounding darkness with its ever changing hues and making the increasing darkness still more impenetrable," Joseph Henry Brown recalled. After clearing away the evening meal, women would often prepare the next morning's breakfast. Men not standing guard gathered around the fires, "smoking and recounting the incidents of the days travel, singing songs, telling jokes at each others expense; while in another part of the camp, the violin would enliven the air with its notes, to which young and agile feet were keeping time in the merry dance on the soil of the plains."[34]

Peter Burnett painted an equally romantic portrait of his train's first stop at Elm Grove. "The place where we encamped was very beautiful; and no scene appeared to our enthusiastic visions more exquisite than the sight of so many wagons, tents, fires, cattle, and people, as were here collected. At night the sound of joyous music was heard in the tents." Burnett, however, tempered the portrait with this reflection: "Our long journey thus began in sunshine and song, in anecdote and laughter; but these all vanished before we reached its termination."[35]

"The company that I was in made it a rule that if they could find a suitable place to camp they would always lay over one day in every week in order to rest up and do their washing," wrote David Campbell, recalling his trip in 1846. "We aimed to travel twelve miles each day stopping when a good camping place was found."[36] If making camp signaled an end to a day of walking, it began another round of chores—unyoking animals and turning them loose to graze, setting up tents or making beds in or under wagons, gathering firewood and preparing supper, and cleaning up.

"There were several musical instruments among the emigrants," Catherine Sager remembered, "and these sounded clearly on the evening air when camp was made and merry talk and laughter resounded from almost every camp-fire."[37] At a time when families provided their own entertainment, music and dance were

[33] Porter, Oregon Trail Diary, 7 August 1848.

[34] Brown, Recollection of 1847, University of Oregon, 5.

[35] Burnett, *Recollections and Opinions of an Old Pioneer,* 22 May 1843, 102.

[36] Campbell, "Pioneer of 1846," *Porterville Recorder,* 11, 12, and 13 August 1910.

[37] Pringle, Across the Plains in 1844, Oregon Historical Society.

an invaluable form of relaxation and recreation, and from the beginning, music was an integral part of an overland trek. At Independence Rock on the Fourth of July, 1841, "the sound of the violin" entertained the Bidwell-Bartleson party.[38] "Every night when we encamp we make quite a village, but take it up the next day," Elizabeth Geer Smith wrote on 19 June 1847. "We have plenty of music with a flute and violin and some dancing."[39]

Given the physical challenges emigrants faced every day, the variety of their social life is surprising. Many travelers could walk all day and dance far into the night—at least at the start of their journeys. "Every night we young folks had a dance on the green prairie. Our musician was usually a young fellow named Frank Kellogg, who played the fiddle pretty well, but from time to time, as our musician, we would get Ann Eliza Fowler," recalled Jacob Harlan, revealing that women joined in the fun. "In playing the fiddle she could just knock the hindsights off Frank or any one in the train," Harlan wrote. He later married her.[40]

"Our evenings were spent quite pleasantly around the campfires in telling stories, singing and often dancing on the green prairie," recalled Mary Ann Harlan Smith. "Our musicians were a couple of young men who played 'The Arkansas Traveler,' 'Money Musk,' and the 'Virginia Reel.'"[41] Not everyone appreciated the treat or approved of such profane songs. Joseph Williams found that the "coarse violin" he heard a missionary play at Waiilatpu "was poor music on Sunday."[42] John Hudgins's party had a drum, fife, coronet, and fiddles, "and some nights they would give a concert that would annoy our guard and divert the wolves."[43] It seemed to Samuel Hancock as if all the wolves for a thousand miles around had congregated around his camp on the Little Blue and "made the night hideous with their yelling," which was "anything but musical." As the packs scattered in the morning, he commented, "we were by no means loth [sic] to part with these 'traveling musicians.'"[44]

The Fourth of July was celebrated with gunpowder, alcohol, and "more spirit and zest, than it usually is in the crowded cities of the States," but as Edwin Bryant pointed out, "The pageantry, of course, was not so imposing." J. Quinn Thornton fired his rifle and revolver "at the dawn of day, in honor of the anniversary of the Declaration of American Independence." Several 1846 companies gathered in a grove near their camp on Deer Creek and fired a small arms salute at 9:00 A.M.

[38] Williams, *Narrative of a Tour*, 29.

[39] Smith to Foster and LaPorte, 25 May 1848, in Geer, *Fifty Years in Oregon*, 135.

[40] Harlan, *California '46 to '88*, 36.

[41] Smith, "Recollection of a Pioneer Mother," 29.

[42] Williams, *Narrative of a Tour*, 47.

[43] Hudgins, "California in 1849," Western Historical Manuscript Collection, 3.

[44] Hancock, *The Narrative of Samuel Hancock*, 5.

"Our Tent & Camp in '46." Pherne Brown Pringle made this sketch of the domestic comforts some overlanders brought with them on the road across the plains. Cooking over an open fire made of whatever fuel was available posed special challenges. Bush House Museum, Salem Art Association, Salem, Oregon. Courtesy Stafford Hazelett.

They formed a procession and marched around their corralled wagons and then went back to the grove to hear the Declaration of Independence read and a speech by Colonel Russell. James Frazier Reed "had preserved some wines and liquors especially for this occasion." After the ladies of the encampment served refreshments, the men made patriotic toasts that "were given and drunk with much enthusiasm, a discharge of musketry accompanying each sentiment." Mr. Bryant and several gentlemen sang a few patriotic and sentimental songs. The travelers then listened to music performed on a "fiddle, flute, a dog drum—the dog from which the skin was taken was killed, and the drum made the night previous." The celebration ended with the discharge of all the guns of the camp and created, Charles Stanton wrote the next day, "one of the most pleasurable excitements we have had on the road."[45]

Heinrich Lienhard described the music he heard while working at Sutters Fort. "At all local dances music was provided by a harp, a violin, and a guitar. I enjoyed the trios immensely, for the musicians played very well indeed. With the addition of the flute, these were the only musical instruments used in those days in California, and tunes played on them were always popular, for early settlers seemed to be universal lovers of music."[46] Others found melodic consolation elsewhere. "To me every thing in nature, in the wilderness, was musical, if it had a voice at all," wrote J. Quinn Thornton, recalling the chirp of the cricket and the call of the whippoorwill, which "produced sensations of pleasure that were inexpressible. The sound fell upon my ear as I reposed upon my rude bed at night, and it ran along every nerve of my body, reaching even to my fingers' ends, like the vibrations of a harp string."[47]

TO KEEP OFF THE WOLVES: GUARD DUTY

For many overlanders, there was no rest at the end of a day's journey. Women had to cook and make camp, while men had to care for and guard the livestock, often in trying circumstances. Besides exhaustion and "skulking Indians," guards had to contend with challenges such as cold and soaking rain, hungry and howling wolves, and hordes of relentless mosquitoes.[48]

From the beginning of overland travel, men often had to guard their livestock through the night in addition to their other tasks. Joseph Williams recalled standing

---

[45] Thornton, *Oregon and California in 1848*, 4 July 1846, 119; and Charles to Sidney Stanton, 5 July 1846, in Morgan, *Overland in 1846*, 586.

[46] Lienhard, *A Pioneer at Sutter's Fort*, 28.

[47] Thornton, *Oregon and California in 1848*, 17 May 1846, 32.

[48] Hewitt, *Across the Plains*, 138.

guard every fourth night with the Bidwell-Bartleson party.[49] Generally the guard was intended to protect livestock from Indian raiders, but Samuel Hancock recalled that his 1845 party "detailed a guard to keep off the wolves while our cattle were feeding, eventually corralling for the night."[50] Due in large part to the threat from Pawnee raiders—Benjamin Lippincott described them "as grand a set of double refined horse thieves as the Prairies can produce"—wagon parties tended to start out with rigorously scheduled guard duty for all able-bodied men.[51] "We have divided our men into seven guards or watches, three of which come on each night to guard the cattle and wagons," William Porter wrote in 1848. "This division operates equally upon all."[52]

Such vigilance, along with general camp organization and discipline, usually declined upon reaching the Platte River and sometimes sooner. "Every man was well armed and watchful for two weeks," John Berry Hill recalled. "Then some of the men refused to stand watch. As we were not sworn to obey orders, we did as we pleased and volunteers had to go on duty. After three weeks we quit guarding our stock and let them shift for themselves."[53] T. J. Van Dorn's party heard of a few Indian depredations. "Still, it has been our good fortune to meet none, nor do we keep any guard," he wrote. "The cattle once out of the yoke are turned into feed and no more attention is paid to them until morning."[54]

Even old trail hands felt that wagon trains could relax their vigilance once they left the frontier. "I should advise all companies coming over the mountains to take good care of their stock on the way, guard them every night strictly, until they reach the Platte river. It will prevent them from getting off, perhaps returning home, or straggling off and giving a great deal of trouble in their collection," wrote Peter Lassen. "After reaching the Platte it will be sufficient to guard the camp."[55] The traders at Fort Laramie assured Jacob Wright Harlan's party that they did not need to fear the Indians would steal their animals. "We made some presents to the old chief, which pleased him much, and he told us through an interpreter that our stock was safe, and that we need not guard it," Harlan recalled. "We found this to be true, and lost no animals by those Indians."

This lax policy usually changed once California-bound parties reached the Humboldt River, where the tribes seized livestock whenever they had a chance.[56] Trav-

---

[49] Williams, *Narrative of a Tour,* 28.

[50] Hancock, *The Narrative of Samuel Hancock,* 10.

[51] Lippincott to John L. Stephens, 6 February 1847, Bancroft Library.

[52] Porter to "Dear Father, Mother, Brothers and Sisters," 24 June 1848.

[53] Hill, *A Gold Hunter,* 21.

[54] Van Dorn, Diary, 15 August 1849, Beinecke Library, 35.

[55] "From the Emigrants," 16 July 1848, *The Brunswicker,* 9 September 1848, 1/2.

[56] Harlan, *California '46 to '88,* 39–40, 45–46.

elers on the Oregon Trail often resumed the practice upon reaching the Columbia. After camping on the John Day River, Elizabeth Dixon Smith's party once again "put out a guard for fear of Indians, which we have not done for 3 months before."[57] Near the end of the trail, even in dangerous country some sojourners no longer had the will or the wisdom to post a proper guard: others considered it pointless. "My father did not have his men stand guard over the stock at night," James Madison Goode recalled. "He argued that if the Indians wanted to stampede the stock they could and would do so and would probably kill all the guards and he said he valued his men more than the stock. We were not molested by Indians, and were menaced only once."[58] Others literally poked fun at the guards and their tendency to fall asleep. Ezra M. Hamilton remembered poking an emigrant guard with a stick, "and to this day he believes he was shot by an Indian."[59]

DEMOCRACY ON WAGON WHEELS

From the very beginning of western migration, Americans carried the spirit of Jacksonian democracy across the Missouri River. The first overland wagon party elected a captain at Sapling Grove, a vote John Bartleson won with some heavy-handed politicking. John Bidwell, who was elected secretary of the party, recalled that Benjamin Kelsey's skill at "finding the way" eventually made him the train's de facto leader.[60] The self-obsessed chiefs of the 1842 trek to Oregon, Elijah White and Lansford Hastings, spent more time electioneering than they did scouting the trail. "We had proceeded only a few days travel, from our native land of order and security, when the 'American character' was fully exhibited," recalled Hastings, who talked his way into the "first office" of this "infant republic." After his election, "the disaffected and disappointed office-holders and office-seekers"—a jab at Elijah White and his allies—separated from the main body. "All appeared to be determined to govern, but not to be governed," Hastings complained.[61]

James W. Nesmith recalled how a motley crowd "from all the States and Territories, embracing all nationalities" organized in May 1843. Most of them came from Missouri, Iowa, Illinois, and Arkansas, "all strangers to one another, but deeply impressed with the imperative necessity for mutual protection against the hostile Indians inhabiting the great unknown wilderness, stretching away to the shores of the Pacific." (This abiding fear was a widely held illusion.) Candidate

---

[57] Smith, "Diary of Elizabeth Dixon Smith," 21 October 1847, in Holmes, *Covered Wagon Women*, 1:138.

[58] Goode, Recollection of 1849 and 1853, California State Library.

[59] Hamilton, Reminiscences [1853], Ezra Hamilton Collection, California State Library.

[60] Nunis, *The Bidwell-Bartleson Party*, 118.

[61] Hastings, *The Emigrants' Guide*, 9.

"Pete" Burnett, an affable Missouri lawyer, mounted a log and "the glib-tongued orator delivered a florid, glowing address." The lands they were leaving lacked "sufficient elbow room for the expansion of their genius and enterprise, and that it was a duty they owed to themselves and their posterity to strike out in search of a wider field and a more genial climate," he flattered his fellow travelers. In his projected Eden, the soil would yield the richest return for the smallest effort and trees would be loaded with perennial fruit and "a good substitute for bread, called *La Camash,* grew in the ground, salmon and other fish crowded the streams, and where the principal labor of the settler would be keeping his gardens free from the inroads of elk, buffalo, deer and wild turkeys."

Burnett appealed to his comrades' patriotism and evoked the glorious empire they, with their trusty rifles, would establish on the Pacific Coast. They would drive out the "British usurpers," defend Oregon from the avarice and pretensions of the English lion, and posterity "would honor us for placing the fairest portion of our land under the dominion of the stars and stripes." He finally said he did not expect to meet any tribe of noble "red men" that the valiant and well-armed crowd could not vanquish in a single encounter. Naturally, after the votes were counted, "the meeting, as primitive and motley a one as ever assembled, adjourned with 'three cheers' for Captain Burnett and Oregon." The Great Migration of 1843 then elected nine councilmen and Nesmith as orderly sergeant.[62] Burnett adopted rules and tried to enforce them in the face of stiff opposition: he resigned after only a week in office. As predicted, the party divided into smaller and more manageable units. Many wagon train captains found the honor hardly worth the aggravation and followed Burnett's example.[63]

"Once people find out how much easier it is traveling in small companies," James Field observed in 1845, "it is not easy work to keep them in a large one."[64] In the early 1840s, the annual migrations usually started out as one or more massive confederations, but such unwieldy organizations quickly disintegrated. "Avoid large parties," advised 1844 overlander Nathaniel Ford. "As soon as some 10 or 15 wagons, and some 20 or 25 armed men, can unite, they should travel on."[65] After the 1845 emigration had passed the Rocky Mountains, its leaders abandoned any attempt to keep large companies together.[66]

J. M. Shively told emigrants they did not need military array, officers, and non-commissioned officers: "all this is folly."[67] Until after the gold rush, few heeded

---

[62] Nesmith, *Two Addresses,* 9–10.

[63] Burnett, *Recollections and Opinions of an Old Pioneer,* 102.

[64] Field, *Crossing the Plains,* 16 August 1845, Oregon Historical Society.

[65] Ford, "Letter from Oregon," 6 April 1845, in Clyman, *James Clyman, Frontiersman,* 271.

[66] Bancroft, *History of Oregon,* 1:450.

[67] Shively, "The Shively Guide," in Morgan, *Overland in 1846,* 734.

his advice. "We organized by selecting John Purvine Captain and William Porter Lieutenant," Porter wrote from the North Platte Ferry in 1848. "We divided our company into six messes or divisions, each one takes his turn to lead."[68] Drudgery and exhaustion made it difficult to find enough men to perform guard duty, especially when the expected threat from "lurking savages" failed to materialize. Abuses of authority, such as ordering everyone's dogs shot or sentencing a man "to be tied and staked out in the hot sun from 11 A.M. until the going down thereof" for violating an 1844 train's martial law, contributed to the general failure of such military organizations.[69]

Over time, small, fluid associations replaced oversized and unwieldy trains, and the number of families who joined no formal group increased as the trail became safer. "No company of forty waggons have ever traveled to Oregon without dividing," William Ide wrote in 1845.[70] The fascination with elections, regulations, and proto-military organizations declined as knowledge spread of the practical realities of wagon travel over the plains.

Several emigrants recalled holding votes on practical matters, such as which course to take when they reached a fork in the road. "When we arrived at the turning-off point a vote was taken," James Field wrote west of South Pass, and his party chose to follow the new route—the Greenwood Cutoff—west from the Parting of the Ways. Other travelers recalled voting to take any number of ill-advised cutoffs and living to regret it. New routes and their promised shortcuts appear to have carried most of these votes, but despite obvious problems with such electoral decision making, Americans refused to leave their democratic sympathies behind.[71]

HIS UNERRING AIM: HUNTING ON THE EARLY TRAIL

The importance of hunting as a food source for overland travelers has been exaggerated—the average party spent considerably more time hunting grass or stray oxen than game—but there is no question that it played an important and colorful role in emigrant social life. Martha Williams Reed recalled that the Bidwell-Bartleson party "saw thousands upon thousands of Buffalo and we had fresh meat all the way across the plains," but until the travelers reached the Platte River, Joseph Williams observed that game was very scarce. Beyond the Sweetwater

---

[68] Porter to "Dear Father, Mother, Brothers and Sisters," 24 June 1848.
[69] Willard Rees, Recollections, in Mattes, *Platte River Road Narratives,* entry 114, 60; and Rumer, *The Wagon Trains of '44,* 217. Accounts vary, but Clark Eads had either threatened or actually shot at another member of the party. His "sentence was duly executed."
[70] Ide, "From Our Oregon Correspondent," 25 June 1845, *Sangamo Journal,* 4 September 1845.
[71] Field, Crossing the Plains, 14 and 24 July 1845.

River, Williams did not expect to find much more wild food, and the company's California contingent only survived their crossing of the Sierra Nevada by eating their oxen.[72] Even during the 1840s travelers who intended to rely on hunting for their food supply soon learned it was a dangerous gamble. Still, wild game was a valuable source of protein on the trail. "Our father would get some one to drive his team and start on the hunt, for he was enthusiastic in his love of such sport," recalled Catherine Sager. "He not only killed the great bison, but often brought home on his shoulder the timid antelope that had fallen at his unerring aim, and that are not often shot by ordinary marksmen."[73]

As early as 1842 Joseph Williams heard the Indians of Oregon complain that "the white people are killing all their game."[74] The trail quickly had an impact on wildlife and the peoples who depended upon it for their livelihoods. A variety of conditions—location, timing, weather, hunting pressure—affected the availability of game, but western travelers reported a pronounced decline in the number of antelope, deer, and bison between 1840 and 1870. Many of the earliest descriptions evoke the image of a wild Eden on the plains. But from the earliest days of overland travel, veterans warned that hunting distracted overlanders from their main task: reaching the Pacific. Make "no calculation on getting buffalo or any wild meat, for you are only wasting time," Samuel Gilmore warned.[75] The Plains Indians soon recognized the threat that wagon trains posed to their main food supply and quickly devised strategies to minimize their losses. Jesse Applegate noted that "the unfriendly Sioux have driven the buffalo out of the Platte, and the hunters must ride fifteen or twenty miles to reach them."[76]

The Comforts of Religion: Faith on the Road West

On the last Sunday before they set out on their arduous journey, J. Quinn Thornton and his ailing wife attended a Methodist service. "We believed that it was probably the last time that we should hear preaching until after our arrival in Oregon. It is not wonderful, therefore, that we felt not only solemn but sad," he wrote after listening to the "potent and sublime truths." Subsequent experiences convinced him "that Christianity is adapted to the peculiar condition and wants of the emigrant in the wilderness." It was not the last homily the Thorntons would hear on the road to Oregon—they listened to Rev. J. A. Cornwall preach

---

[72] Reed, "Old California Pioneer Passes Away"; and Williams, *Narrative of a Tour,* 27, 30.

[73] Pringle, Across the Plains in 1844, Oregon Historical Society.

[74] Williams, *Narrative of a Tour,* 25 January 1842, 41.

[75] Gilmore, "Letter from Oregon," 11 November 1843, 282.

[76] Applegate, "A Day with the Cow Column in 1843," 128.

"an impressive and eloquent sermon" beside the grave of Sarah Keyes at Alcove Springs—but like many other deeply religious prairie travelers, they struggled to live their religion as they headed west. It was not easy to do so in the rough-and-tumble society of a wagon train, Thornton learned: he did not believe in traveling on the Sabbath, "and desired to remain in camp; but the company having no scruples of the kind, determined otherwise."[77]

"It has long been one of Uncle Sam's legends," trail veteran Gilbert L. Cole recalled in 1905, that "he who starts across the continent is most sure to leave his religion on the east side of the Missouri river."[78] A number of early westerners were irreligious—Methodist minister Joseph Williams complained that the Bidwell-Bartleson party was "mostly composed of Universalists and deists"—but when he proposed having prayers on the Fourth of July in 1841, a Sunday, "several of the wicked class came up."[79] Many emigrants felt that they were entering a godless wilderness when they left the frontier, and the deeply religious Peter Burnett despaired that in California, "in the absence of female influence and religion, the men were rapidly going back to barbarism."[80]

Men and women who had little or no use for organized religion sometimes poked fun at those who did. Two Roman Catholic clerics who accompanied an 1847 train found half their oxen mired fast in the mud, one emigrant noted. They stalked "around among the men with their long robes on and their bibles under their arms praying to God to help them out. He didn't."[81] Many left both God and morality behind them; and despite the deep faith often expressed by literate emigrants, their journals despaired over the general disregard for religion. "Along all this road I have seen none that loved God, but that woman who was sick on Platt River," Julia Wood mourned, recalling a woman who told her she was ready to die if it was the Lord's will. "How my heart aches for them. There are 36 of us and of all that number, none love the Lord. All but our company profane His Holy name." Yet Wood could say of her trail experience, "I never felt the value of religion as I do now."[82]

Faith sustained many overlanders through trials that would destroy most people. "I suppose you heard of my trouble and deaths on the plains in loosing my wife and children," wrote Fielding Lewis. "I have no words to express my trubble my loss was great in property but nothing to that of a loving wife and children but

---

[77] Thornton, *Oregon and California in 1848,* 13–14; and 16 May 1846, 28, 55.

[78] Cole, *In the Early Days along the Overland Trail,* 77.

[79] Williams, *Narrative of a Tour,* 29.

[80] Burnett, *Recollections and Opinions of an Old Pioneer,* 283–85, 299.

[81] Coon and Coon, Diary, 7 June 1847. One of the clerics may have been A. M. Blanchet, Bishop of Walla Walla.

[82] Wood, Diary of Mrs. Julia Newton Wood, 19, 27, 30 May and 14 August 1853, Mattes Library.

it is the lord that gave [and] the lord that taketh."[83] And as Patrick Breen recorded during its darkest days in 1846, the Donner party "offered our prayers to God this Christmas morning; the prospect is appalling, but we trust in Him."[84]

Drenching Them with Lard and Gunpowder: Animal Doctoring

Given the primitive state of human medicine, it is no surprise that animal doctoring on the trail was a hit-or-miss proposition. The leading causes of illness among livestock were bad water, starvation, infection, exhaustion, and changes in water and feed that produced colic. "You should have Plenty of cotuck assid [caustic acid] in case of any of your Cattle getting alcolicd [colic] you ma[y] be able to give them relief immediately for cosid [caustic] is a good remidy," advised one spelling-challenged trail veteran.[85] Even modern trail expeditions lose animals: On the California National Historic Trail wagon train in 1999 a probable bowel obstruction killed a mule that was healthy one morning and dead the next.[86]

Trail journals are filled with folk remedies for animals. After a horse in Thomas Christy's party drank alkaline water, Christy gave him vinegar and acid, which probably countered each other's effects. But that night they feared that their cattle had been poisoned and "went to work drenching them with lard and gunpowder," which surely did them little good.[87]

In a letter home, California pioneer B. T. McClenny described two dreadful folk diseases, "hollow horn" and "foot evil," which he said were common complaints amongst cattle on the plains. "They are subject [to] get the hollow horn and many cattle die of it and nobody knows what is the matter with them. I had like to have lost one of my Best oxen by it Before I knew what was the matter with him. You would do well to look well to it if any of your Cattle Begins to fail to see if they have not got it." Apparently unaware that even a healthy cow's horns are hollow, William Stillwell blamed the condition on "the sudden change from wet and mud to the dry, hot sand and alkali plains." The imaginary affliction became so widespread in his 1844 company "that it threatened to become a serious matter, and retarded their progress very much." McClenny advised having plenty of turpentine and calomel, as they were the best remedies for foot evil.[88]

---

[83] Lewis to "Dear Cosin," 8 May 1852, NFTC Manuscripts, Mattes Library.

[84] Breen, Diary, in Bryant, *What I Saw in California,* 258. Breen actually wrote, "offerd. our prayers to God this Cherimass morning the prospect is apalling but hope in God Amen."

[85] McClenny to "Dear Sister and Brother," 12 February 1859, Missouri Historical Society.

[86] Threlkeld, Trail Journal, 6 and 7 August 1999.

[87] Christy, *Thomas Christy's Road across the Plains,* 9 June 1850, 37, 38.

[88] McClenny to "Dear Sister and Brother," 12 February 1859, Missouri Historical Society; and William D. Stillwell biography, in Elwood et al., *History of the Pacific Northwest.*

Both hollow horn and what R. F. Neslen called "the fouls of foot evil" had a variety of other folk remedies.[89] Clarborne Walker's cattle had "the foot evil considerable on this trip [and] a great many are left on this account." He felt the best cure was a powder mixed with old bacon fat and put on moderately warm.[90] Mormon pioneer Joseph Orton "gave the old cow grist salt, 3 spoonsful each of 3 eggs and one spoonful of copra mixed with flour. I put red pepper and vinegar and butter simmered together in her ears for the disease of hollow horn."[91] Thomas Cramer burned his "young cattle's feet with hot grease and tar to cure the disease 'Foot Evil,' which is caused, I think chiefly by traveling in the mud too much"—could the cure have been worse than the affliction?[92]

Country doctor W. J. McKnight cast a jaundiced eye on maladies such as hollow horn and "wolf in the tail," which he believed were the result of starvation. "If they had called it hollow belly and wolf in the stomach they would have been nearer the truth," he wrote. The remedy for hollow horn was to bore a gimlet hole in the horn near the head and wrap a turpentine-soaked cloth around the horn. McKnight correctly diagnosed why such "cures" were popular: if the critter recovered, it was the right remedy; if it died, the remedy had been used too late. "Of course," wrote the doctor, "these conditions were all imaginary. They were only diseases resulting from exposure and want of nourishing food."[93]

A VAST DISTANCE BETWEEN US: COMMUNICATIONS

In the first years of overland emigration, communications between the United States and the West Coast posed an enormous problem. "There is a vast distance between us," 1845 Oregon emigrant Betsy Bayley wrote to her sister. "I don't know whether I am writing to the dead or the living."[94] Before the development of routes over the isthmuses of Central America, messages from Oregon or California had to be carried overland or around Cape Horn, and a quick passage required almost six months. A few adventurers, such as Lansford Hastings, were able to reduce this time by crossing Mexico, but using a similar route, Lieutenant Archibald Gillespie took six months to deliver an urgent presidential message to northern California. Two years and nine months passed, A. H. Garrison recalled, before his family in Missouri learned their relatives had reached Oregon.[95]

[89] Neslen to Brigham Young, 7 August 1859, Brigham Young Collection, LDS Archives.

[90] Walker to "Dear Brother, Sister and Friends," 1845, Purvine Family Records.

[91] Orton, History of Joseph Orton, 13 April 1859, BYU Library.

[92] Cramer, Overland Journey from Kansas to California, 9 June 1859, Beinecke Library.

[93] McKnight, *Pioneer Outline History of Northwestern Pennsylvania*.

[94] Bayley to Griffith, 20 September 1849, in Holmes, *Covered Wagon Women*, 1:35, 38.

[95] Garrison, "Reminiscences of Abraham Henry Garrison," 11.

Travelers setting out from the Missouri in 1845 had no information about the fate of the previous year's emigration, and all overland communications were uncertain at best. "I am fearful that you will not receive my letter in consequence of our having no other means of conveyance than private travelers, which cannot be relied upon with any degree of confidence & Safety as where we have the prevelige of Public posts," Willard Rees wrote early in 1846. He had sent several letters east with Elijah White the previous fall, but rumor said White's party had been "captured and put to death by the Soux Indians consequently the papers & letters intrusted to their care ware all lost." Some of them, Rees felt, were "of Vital importance to Oregon."[96] In truth, the Pawnees captured White's pack train "and pillaged of everything of value; not even letters to people in the States were omitted." White "lost many of his most valuable papers, and some twenty letters," but he mailed more than five hundred letters when he reached Independence.[97]

"There were no mail facilities whatever," Joseph Henry Brown complained after he reached Oregon in 1847. "We only received newspapers by the Missionary ships once a year, and letters from friends by emigrants across the plains, and the war with Mexico had been closed some six months before we heard of it." It required at least two years to send a letter home and receive an answer back from the United States. When mail service opened across Panama, Brown wrote, "we hailed it as one of the remarkable achievements of the day; we were then able to hear from our friends once every three months."[98]

President Polk called on Congress to provide mail service "to our citizens west of the Rocky Mountains" in August 1846, and next March the Post Route Bill directed the U.S. Post Office to initiate service from South Carolina "across the isthmus to Panama, and from thence to Astoria, or the mouth of the Columbia river, touching at Monterey, St. Francisco, and such other places on the coast as the Postmaster General may direct" by steamships going each way once every two months.[99] The *California,* the Pacific Mail Steamship Company's first vessel, left the East Coast for San Francisco on 6 October 1848. The previous April American military authorities sent Kit Carson east with the first official U.S. mail, but it would be ten years before a regular overland mail route opened across the Southwest.

Mormon settlers in the Salt Lake Valley sent the first private mail party east early in 1848, and public mail began even before the creation of Utah Territory when Samuel H. Woodson started service on 1 July 1850 for $19,500 per annum.

[96] Rees to "Mother," 20 March 1846, NFTC Manuscripts, Mattes Library.
[97] White, "Overland Mail from Oregon," 1048.
[98] Brown, Recollection of 1847, Bancroft Library.
[99] "An Act to Establish Certain Post Routes," U.S. Congress, 3 March 1847.

Distance and weather made the route unprofitable for private contractors, and Woodson abandoned the business early in 1854.[100] Virtually all overland mail, however, was transported by individuals or private express companies rather than by the federal government. Emigrants reported sending letters back home with discouraged companions who had given up the trip, fur traders, parties returning from Oregon and California, and Indians. All these delivery systems had their problems, but most of these epistles reached their destinations.

"Just as we camped, three gentlemen from Fort Larimie, returning to the States, came to camp, and spent the night with us," James Field recalled. "They told us they would take on all letters written, and next morning received a good-sized packet of them."[101] Edwin Bryant met two eastbound Shawnees carrying "a large budget of letters" from emigrants. This traffic between emigrants and Indians worked both ways: John Wolf, a Shawnee, had already asked Bryant to write a short letter reporting the deaths of several Shawnee leaders and a relative and "carry it westward to some great Indian captain of his tribe." Bryant, however, could never find Black Poddee, the recipient, "and consequently the brief epistle was never delivered." The previous winter travelers had converted a trapper's cabin at Ash Hollow into "a sort of general post-office," Bryant reported. There he found "a large number of letters deposited, addressed to persons in almost every quarter of the globe, with requests, that those who passed would convey them to the nearest post-office in the states."[102]

Surviving letters reveal how much settlers treasured mail or news of any sort from home. "I would give One Dollar for a newspaper, Five for a letter and Fifty to see our friends," Amasa Morgan wrote after experiencing the hardest time of his life on the Humboldt River.[103] Daniel Budd received a letter "from my dear old chick" after reaching California. "Never devoured a letter so eagerly as this one before in my life."[104] Some travelers wrote home whenever the opportunity presented itself. "This I write using my saddle for a desk," Andrew Cooper scrawled from western Nebraska. "When you get this I want you to wright me a lengthy letter give me all the news. Anything will be news to me. . . . I am counting letters now."[105]

Wagon trains devised a variety of ways to communicate with each other. "Doctor Whitman used to put up notices directing us from one notice to another," Nineveh Ford recalled.[106] "A sort of post-office communication is frequently

---

[100] Mortensen, "A Pioneer Paper," 78; and Hafen, *Overland Mail*, 37–38, 41, 54–55.
[101] Field, Crossing the Plains, 15 June 1845, Oregon Historical Society.
[102] Bryant, *What I Saw in California*, 16 May, 3 and 19 June 1846.
[103] Morgan, Diary, 10 July 1849, Bancroft Library.
[104] Budd, Journal, 15 September 1852, Mattes Library.
[105] Cooper to Mr. & Mrs. Hieronymous & Molly, 12 June 1864, Mattes Library.
[106] Ford, The Pioneer Road Makers, Bancroft Library, 8–9.

established by the emigrant companies," wrote Edwin Bryant in 1846. "The information which they desire to communicate is sometimes written upon the skulls of buffaloes,—sometimes upon small strips of smooth planks,—and at others a stake or stick being driven into the ground, and split at the top, a manuscript note is inserted in it. These are conspicuously placed at the side of the trail, and are seen and read by succeeding companies." Bryant met Wales Bonney on the Sweetwater River carrying an open letter from Lansford Hastings inviting emigrants "to concentrate their numbers and strength" and try his new route "by which the distance would be materially shortened."[107]

On new routes, trailblazers used these techniques to pass on important information to those who followed, as the dramatic story of the Donner party illustrates. As the last train that took Hastings's unproven shortcut, the Donner wagons periodically received confusing directions posted on trail signposts. Hastings left a letter on a clump of sagebrush at the head of Echo Canyon promising the Donner party "that if we Came after him he would return and Pilot us through his new and direct rout to the South end of the Salt Lake," James Frazier Reed wrote.[108] Eliza Donner later told how her mother assembled a note crows had ripped to pieces from a "guide board" and deciphered Hastings's warning about the long hard drive across the Salt Desert.[109]

Animal skulls became renowned as the "post office of the plains." The road was strewn with plenty of white bones, mostly of buffaloes and oxen, and passing pilgrims could pencil a message on one, put it in a conspicuous place, and leave behind an open letter for all to read. "If anyone is lost from his train the company with whom he has been traveling will write on the forehead of these skull bones the name of the company, date of camping and other information pertinent to the question and set the head up on its horns in some prominent place by the roadside," John Hawkins Clark reported.[110]

"Sometimes the lack-luster skull would inform John [that] Mary was all right, or a shoulderblade would inform Polly that James was going to take the California road, assuring her that wood and water were better on that route. Information about the Indians was also conveyed," George B. Curry wrote. "The means of communication with the trains in front was the 'Bone Express.'"[111] Near the Upper Platte Crossing, "a letter written on a bone and placed on the side of the road on which the drivers walk, was picked up," Lydia Milner Waters recalled. It warned that a war party led by a "white Indian" named London "Black" Jack,

[107] Bryant, *What I Saw in California,* 9 June, 10 July 1846, 79–80, 127.

[108] Korns and Morgan, *West from Fort Bridger,* 211n9, 213.

[109] Mullen, *The Donner Party Chronicles,* 135.

[110] Clark, "Overland to the Gold Fields of California," 29 May 1852, 245.

[111] Curry, "Occasional Address," *Transactions of the Oregon Pioneer Association,* 1887.

had raided a train, wounded a teenage girl, and run off its livestock.[112] The buffalo skull registry recorded thousands of names and dates, James Henry Elgin recalled, some dating back several years, and weary travelers often found "the names of some friend in the van of the emigration and the dates telling the number of days he had been preceded by his relative or friend."[113]

WHERE HE COULD GO I COULD: WOMEN ON THE EARLY TRAIL

Women, of course, arrived in the American West with the first men. The earliest American and British males to settle in the region, including such notables as Jim Bridger, Richard Grant, and Kit Carson, married Indian and Mexican women who evoked considerable commentary from both male and female emigrants, much of it critical and often downright racist. Women of northern European descent left almost all of the surviving reports, but between 1840 and 1870 overland emigration included both slave and free black women, Mormon women from the Waldensian valleys of northern Italy, Métis women from Canada, and eventually even Shoshone and Lakota women joined wagon trains with their French husbands.

Once a man decided to seek better prospects in the West, a woman either sent him away or left their home and went to make a new life. "There was nothing to do but bear my lot, I determined to do my best," Margaret Hecox wrote. She hid how unhappy she was when separated from her husband: she "tried to seem cheerful, and I don't think he ever realized what a hard time I had."[114]

Not all women made the overland trek as unwilling chattel, and some simply refused to let mates afflicted with western fever abandon them. "Where my husband goes I can go," Nancy Kelsey resolved in 1841. "I can better endure the hardships of the journey than the anxieties for an absent husband."[115] Some women made it clear they would not accept such a fate. "I would not be left behind. I thought where he could go I could," recalled Luzena Stanley Wilson, "and where I went I could take my two little toddling babies."[116] Despite their reluctance or even resistance, women were often compelled to follow their husbands west, like Mary Annie Jones, who pleaded with her spouse not to go to California in 1846. "It made no difference. We sold our home and what we could not take with us and what we could not sell we gave away," she recalled.[117]

---

[112] Waters, "Account of a Trip," 58–79.

[113] Elgin, "To the Oregonian," 1902.

[114] Hecox, "The Story of Margaret M. Hecox," 535–36.

[115] Joseph Chiles, in Nunis, *The Bidwell-Bartleson Party*, 142.

[116] Wilson, *Luzena Stanley Wilson, '49er*, 1.

[117] Jones, Story of My Life, Papers Relating to California Pioneers, Bancroft Library.

For Eliza Gregson, poverty, bad health, and the awful climate of the Midwest helped persuade her to go west with her husband. There was so much malaria in Illinois afflicting the Mississippi bottomlands, she remembered, "we could not stand that. We could make a good living if we could only keep from shaking," she recalled, "so missfortuns seldom come alone." Her first child was born in September 1844, but the sweet little babe died three months later. Her extended family spent the winter in a ramshackle cabin with "holes in the sides that you could throw your hat through": no wonder, she concluded, that the family was sick or that her baby died. "There was no help for it," she recalled. "We were geting poorer every day." The next spring the Gregsons set out for Oregon, and six months later they found themselves in California.[118]

Women such as Elizabeth Markham could count the cost of crossing "mountains high and burning plains," but children usually remembered thoroughly enjoying the trip.[119] "I've often been asked if we did not suffer with fear in those days but I've said no, we were not old enough and did not have sense to recognize the danger," Nancy Hembree Bogart wrote. She recalled that her trip to Oregon started on her sixth birthday in 1843. "*We* just had the times of our lives; but since I've grown older and could realize the danger and feelings of the mothers, I often wonder *how* they really lived through it all and retained their reason."[120]

Like the Devil among Angels:
Skinny Widows and Single Women on the Early Trail

Most unmarried women who went west before 1849 did so within the safety of their extended families. Single women and widows such as Narcissa Burdette Land Ashcraft made the trek without anyone to protect them; they did not have an easy time. Heinrich Lienhard met Lucinda Jane Saunders, a "husky servant girl," on the trail in 1846. An unmarried, illiterate woman in her late twenties, Saunders was working for Jacob Hoppe's family, but this "strong, two-legged animal" volunteered to do laundry for Lienhard and the four "German Boys" who shared his wagon. "Lucinda's quick readiness to do my wash came as a bit of a surprise to me," he recalled. "She was a person who had a way of attracting attention to herself, though not always in a favorable way."

The German boys proceeded to make the "the notorious Lucinda" the butt of several cruel jokes. One evening the young men in his train "were anxious to arrange some kind of gay entertainment," Lienhard recalled, so they staged a fake

---

[118] Gregson and Gregson, "The Gregson Memoirs," 113–43.

[119] E. M., "Road to Oregon," *Oregon Spectator,* 9 January 1851, in Holmes, *Covered Wagon Women,* 1:155.

[120] Bogart, Reminiscences, Huntington Library, 2.

wedding between "the marriage mad" Lucinda and George Zins, one of the German Boys. Zins "just wanted to have a little fun," Lienhard said, and "the affair ended amidst general hilarity, and Lucinda returned to the wagon where she kept her few miserable belongings." The disappointed bride left the Hoppe wagon and joined the Harlan family, where she attempted to marry a young teamster—a union that dissolved within twenty-four hours. One train allegedly left Lucinda Jane with an Indian tribe. The next day, the weary and beleaguered band overtook the wagon train and gave her back.[121]

The unsympathetic Lienhard, who mercilessly ridiculed "the ever eager-for-marriage" woman, is the sole source for Lucinda's story. He recounted her later tribulations on the Hastings Cutoff in mid-August, and summarized her subsequent career. After rejoining the Hoppe family, she "cast an eye, if not two, on the large, good looking man, Mike, who drove the other wagon," but he escaped her "pressing attentions." Lucinda again found shelter with the Harlans and apparently accompanied them to California, where she soon "married a hefty young man; this fellow, however, soon turned sickly and died!" While Lienhard was superintendent of Sutters Fort in 1847, Lucinda took up with Edmund Bray, "a rather thin Irishman" who had come overland in 1844. He "shortly appeared to be doubtful whether upon taking her as his wife, he would be able to fulfill his duties as a husband. In view of such doubts it seemed that his first ardent desire to be married suddenly cooled and he decided that he preferred to continue a while longer in his proud bachelorship." Lucinda next moved to San Jose and "reportedly put an end to her widowhood by marrying a sailor," an experiment Lienhard claimed she repeated three times over six weeks. The documentary record apparently supports some of Lienhard's story. The Donner Marriage Book preserved at Sutters Fort recorded the marriage of William Thompson to Lucinda Jane Saunders at the fort on 14 April 1847, and the *New Helvetia Diary* contains three references to a Lucinda.[122]

Another target of Lienhard's ridicule was a "skinny widow with two children." She started the trek in a small wagon with a man assumed to be her husband, but he soon abandoned her. "He had confided in some of his friends that he could not stand it any longer with that woman," Lienhard alleged. "After he had driven the wagon all day and walked most of the time, he wanted to have some rest during the night. But it was seldom he could get it." She was left to drive the wagon herself. Lienhard's

---

[121] Lienhard, *From St. Louis to Sutter's Fort*, 14, 18, 21–22. Lienhard identified these women only as "Lucinda" and "the widow." Various E Clampus Vitus websites also tell Saunders's story.

[122] "The Journal of Heinrich Lienhard," in Korns and Morgan, *West from Fort Bridger*, 16 and 20 August 1846, 154, 164–66n55; and Lienhard, *From St. Louis to Sutter's Fort*, 121n74. Presumably all these Lucindas are the same woman.

story of the "notorious widow" ended at Fort Laramie, where she "declared she had decided to stay at the Fort if no man would take care of her." A Mr. Wright tried to persuade the German Boys and others to help her, and finally declared that he would look out for her. His wife, however, would have none of it: "If you take this person along, I'll stay here," she announced. Wright looked at his wife in astonishment and finally said, "I did it in good faith. But I can see I cannot be of help to the woman."[123]

That night, the emigrants had a ball at the fort. "Such belles!" declared Francis Parkman. "One woman, of more than suspected chastity, is left at the Fort; and Bordeaux is fool enough to receive her."[124] Two days later, J. Quinn Thornton reported "a worthless white woman, who had been in one of the forward companies, had stopped at this place."[125]

The anecdotal experiences of these two unfortunate women may not be typical, but they do reflect the deep-seated hostility, if not outright fear, such independent females inspired among male observers. Both are portrayed as immoral, oversexed, and man crazy. Lienhard disguised how uncomfortable these women made him with mockery and rough humor, but his tales betray an unfortunate antagonism to women. In a letter to his father, Parkman offered a more sympathetic view of the widow's plight. She had become a scandal to her party, he wrote, and "what had probably much greater weight, caused them trouble to feed and take care of her." She had taken lodging at the fort in what Parkman called "a pitiful situation," for it was quite impossible she could return to the settlements for many months, and "meanwhile, she is left alone among the Indian women, and the half-savage retainers of the Company—for there are no white women, and very few civilized white men in the country." Dale L. Morgan, suggested that the outcast did much better than the young aristocrat anticipated, for "in all probability the widow was espoused by a prominent mountain man." Lacking definitive evidence, Morgan declined to name her husband, but he was no less a figure than fur-trade veteran Pierre Louis Vasquez, who was outfitting several supply wagons at Laramie that June and was "about to set out for a remote post in the mountains" that he ran on Blacks Fork with Jim Bridger.[126]

Narcissa Burdette Land accompanied Vasquez to Fort Bridger that fall. Born in Kentucky on 4 October 1819, she married John Coldwell in 1837 in Jackson

---

[123] Ibid., 54–56, 68.

[124] Parkman, *The Journals of Francis Parkman,* 26 June 1846, 447. The American Fur Company appointed P. D. Papin factor at Fort John in 1845, but James Bordeaux remained in practical command of the post until it was sold to the U.S. Army in 1849. Known to his Lakota in-laws as "Bear," his good relations with the tribe were a key to the fort's success.

[125] Thornton, *Oregon and California in 1848,* 28 June 1846, 1:115.

[126] Morgan, *Overland in 1846,* 109n48; and Parkman, *The California and Oregon Trail,* 126.

County, Missouri, and Joseph Ashcraft about 1840. Hiram Washington, her son by Ashcraft, was born in 1843, and his father may have been the man who abandoned Narcissa in 1846. Vasquez adopted his wife's two small children, and Louis Vasquez, Jr., was born at Fort Bridger on 7 July 1847. Jacob Gates described her in September as a "white woman who was left by the Oregon com[pany] about a year ago. She married a frenchman & has one child." The couple had six more children during their long marriage.[127]

Alonzo Delano met the family in their "grand lodge" at South Pass: he was surprised to find "a fine carpet spread on the ground, a comfortable camp bed, several chairs, among which was a nice cushioned rocking chair, several volumes of standard books, and last though not least, a rather pretty and well dressed American woman, with an easy, pleasant address—the companion of the gentlemanly proprietor of the post." Delano thought it strange "that a woman of her apparent character, could be content to pass her life in such a wild country, and among such an uncouth set of companions."[128] Perhaps Mrs. Vasquez found her new friends more personable than the American women who had abandoned her in 1846.

Father De Smet baptized Narcissa and solemnized her marriage to Vasquez on 25 September 1851 at the Horse Creek Treaty negotiations: he also baptized Louis, Jr., and Mary Ann Vasquez. Louis Vasquez was wealthy enough to retire in 1855, and he died at Westport, Missouri, in 1868. The next August, the widow married Julius Grenflo in Jackson County, but in 1871 she moved to Huerfano County in Colorado Territory with her son Hiram Vasquez. There she married her fifth and last husband, James H. Buchanan, but she usually lived with her sons and daughters. "Described as a petite woman with a lovely smile," Narcissa Vasquez was said to have been gracious and possessed of an effervescent personality. She smoked a clay pipe, crossed the country many times by horse, mule or wagon and walking, and said she had "lived in dugout houses, forts, stately homes and ranches." She died on 23 October 1899 of "old age and exhaustion," one of many old pioneers who ended their days at the Pueblo Insane Asylum.[129] She had earned her rest.

Unlike the redoubtable Mrs. Vasquez, Lucinda Jane Saunders disappeared into the chaos of the California gold rush: she may have ended her days as wife and society matron, or as a prostitute. Despite Heinrich Lienhard's ridicule, however, her place in history is not entirely without honor, for her name adorns the Elko, Nevada, chapter of that famous gold-rush fraternal organization, E Clampus Vitus.

---

[127] Gates, Journal, 22 September 1847, LDS Archives. LDS records date Land's birth to April 1819. According to LeRoy Hafen, the Vasquez family Bible reported that the forty-eight-year-old Louis married Narcissa Land Ashcraft in Saint Louis in 1846. See Hafen, *The Mountain Men*, 2:333. No record of such a ceremony survives.

[128] Delano, *Life on the Plains*, 28 June 1849, 109–10.

[129] Albright, *One Man's Family*, 158.

Francis Parkman was convinced Narcissa Burdette Land Ashcraft was doomed when her overland company ostracized her at Fort Laramie in 1846, but she made a very good match with the legendary frontier entrepreneur Louis Vasquez, who adopted her children and took them to his trading post at Fort Bridger. Father De Smet married the couple in 1851. Courtesy Utah State Historical Society.

WRITING THIS NONSENSE: DIARIES AND JOURNALS

"Mounted on the baggage wagons, and seated on a half barrel of bacon which forms part of our stores, I am endeavoring to commit my ideas to paper, on the cover of the cigar box resting on my knees," wrote naval officer Selim Woodworth in 1846. Later he drew a somewhat comical sketch of the challenge of writing on the trails. "I did promise to write you long letters, but I was not then aware of the difficulties attending such labours on the prairie," noted the beleaguered midshipman. "We have no tables—no *escritoires*—no editorial chairs—and it sometimes rains and blows in these regions. I am at present quite luxuriously accommodated, as I have, by great good luck, secured a tub of 'salt-horse' to sit upon, and an inverted water-bucket for a writing desk!—an 'iron-bound-bucket' at that."[130]

We owe our knowledge of the trails to Oregon and California to a hardy band of letter writers, journal keepers, and memoirists who chronicled their experiences crossing the continent. "Perhaps no mass movement in history has been better recorded than the migration of Americans across the continent during the 1840s, 1850s, and 1860s," historian Sandra Myres observed.[131] Since diarists were literate and many hoped to publish their reports, these records reflect their superior social status and offer a skewed perspective of the venture. But they produced a surprising number of first-rate narratives, often written under extraordinary circumstances that capture the risky nature of the entire enterprise. After camping near the graves of two emigrants, Edward Jackson began to "see my journey in its true light" and concluded that if he survived the journey, "the pages of my journal will tell a fearful tale."[132] As Mary Burrell made clear, these records were often created at no little cost: "Ike Standing at the wagon foolin. Stucky laying in the tent singing. Put & Frank gone for good water. Ed gone to buy oxen. Louisa doing I dont know what. Myself sitting on the edge of the wagon box until it hurts me and what am I doing? Writing this nonsense—"[133]

"I could have writen a great deal more if I had the opertunity. Some times I would not get the chance to write for two or three days and then would have to rise in the night when my babe and all hands was a sleep [and] light a candle and write," recalled Elizabeth Dixon Smith, who shepherded eight children over the trail after the death of husband in 1847. "Oh that I had the time and talent to describe this curious country," she wrote after crossing South Pass.[134] From Saint

---

[130] Woodworth, "Letter from an Officer of the Navy," 14 May 1846; and "Letter from Oregon," 15 June 1846.
[131] Myres, *Westering Women and the Frontier Experience,* 98.
[132] Jackson, Journal, 20 May 1849, BYU Library.
[133] Burrell, "Council Bluffs to California," 3 July 1854, 243.
[134] Smith, "Diary of Elizabeth Dixon Smith," 29, 31 July 1847, in Holmes, *Covered Wagon Women,* 1:126–27.

Joseph in 1849, Epaphroditus Wells sent his wife a letter written in his wagon with the paper lying on a bag of beans.[135] "I must now give up writing," George Bonniwell scribbled while camped on the Carson, "as it is time to go and get our horses from over the river."[136]

The great trails historian Merrill Mattes estimated that of the almost 500,000 sojourners who traveled on the Great Platte River Road between 1812 and 1866, about 1 in every 250 left some sort of meaningful record of their adventure.[137] The writers themselves felt it was a hit-or-miss proposition: "I was obliged to give up keeping a journal, there was not sufficient idle time for me to write every day, so that I would get behind, then could not fill up the space, so concluded to let it go altogether," Eugenia Zieber explained after reaching Oregon.[138] Thomas Galbraith kept a faithful diary of his trek until he came to the Truckee River in August 1849: "After this the roads were so rough and difficult and our team so worn down," he wrote, "that any man ought to be called crazy who would attempt to keep a journal."[139]

Some diarists pleaded for forgiveness for the limitations of their literary efforts: "You must excuse all errors, as I write seated upon a bucket, with a board on my knees, a candle in a lantern, with the wind blowing, and extremely cold," James Abbey wrote in 1850.[140] "I must claim the indulgence of my readers for these badly written sketches. No one, but a person who has crossed the Plains, can imagine the difficulty with which I have written," Edwin Patterson noted in 1850. "Sleep is all we ever desired, after supper, or when we were resting during the day, and I have had to snatch from my covetous eyelids, what little time I devoted to this journal.—I thought I could have made an interesting book. My material was ample, and had I been seated in My sanctum, I might have made my 'impressions' readable—as it is, I have done my best."[141]

The contrast between the documents written on the trail and the recollections recorded long after the journey's end reveal how time transformed the pioneers' view of their experience. The diaries and letters describe a hard, dirty, and often harrowing venture, while the reminiscences usually soften the hard edges of the

---

[135] Wells, Letters to Wife, Missouri Historical Society.

[136] Bonniwell, The Gold Rush Diary, 4 August 1850.

[137] Mattes, *Platte River Road Narratives*, xiv. Mattes cataloged 2082 narratives in his essential annotated bibliography, including a few that were fictional. Casting a broader net for overland sources, John Townley listed more than five thousand works in *The Trail West*. More than five hundred previously uncataloged non-Mormon Platte River Road narratives have appeared since publication of these bibliographies in 1988. In addition, the LDS church has posted more than three thousand overland sources on its Mormon Pioneer Overland Travel, 1847–1868, website.

[138] Zieber, "Journal of Our Journey to Oregon," 21 October 1851, 200–201.

[139] Galbraith, Journal of Mess Number Twenty-seven, entry following 26 August 1849, Mattes Library.

[140] Abbey, *California. A Trip across the Plains,* 31 May 1850.

[141] Patterson, Diary and Letters, 16 July 1850, Mattes Library.

story and often celebrate a march to glory. Memory distorts events, and a lack of education, social conventions, and fading recollections embarrassed many chroniclers. "I have written an account of my trip across the Plains, I know it is badly written ungrammatical and badly Punctuated," Ignatius M. Smith apologized in 1911. "You must excuse a Man who is Seventy two years old and writing about something that happened nearly fifty-two years ago."[142]

"I now must close this book, and I hope that all that reads it will excuse all bad writing, spelling, and as I find by looking at it, there is plenty I should have corrected it before I set it down, but had not time," George Bonniwell wrote at the end of his journal. "I hope every allowance will be made."[143] Such pleas for mercy are unnecessary: the literary legacy of the overland trails forms an important part of America's collective memory, and these documents constitute a national treasure. Beginning with the accounts of Joel Walker, John Bidwell, Joseph Williams, and Martha Williams Reed, the letters and journals describing the emigrant experience of the 1840s are dramatic and revealing human documents. The narratives of Joel Palmer, Edwin Bryant, Heinrich Lienhard, Sarah Royce, J. Goldsborough Bruff, William Kelly, and Alonzo Delano are all great human documents; and the journals and memoirs of Edward Smith, Aretas J. Blackman, Delia Thompson Brown, Daniel H. Budd, William Lorton, Joseph Middleton, Alexander B. Nixon, Pardon Dexter Tiffany, Washington Peck, Jacob Pindell Prickett, and Mary Stone Smith are uncut jewels awaiting publication.

"For all its multiple uses, the overland journal merits appreciation in and of itself," historian Dale L. Morgan wrote in 1961. "And each overland journal is a reflection of a folk experience and a time spirit. In their journals Americans set down a collective self-portrait, a mosaic in words. This mosaic can never be altogether filled in, never amount to a final creation. Each journal that is found alters some detail, and gives fresh play to our imagination as well as our understanding. It is rather wonderful to think that this can go on forever."[144]

---

[142] Smith to Mr. Gillis, 7 March 1911, Bio Letter File, California State Library.

[143] Bonniwell, The Gold Rush Diary, 24 September 1850.

[144] Morgan, "The Significance and Value of the Overland Journal," 33–34.

CHAPTER 8

GRASPING AND UNSCRUPULOUS

Peace in Oregon, War in California, 1846

Between 1846 and 1848, American adventurers, pioneers, and soldiers transformed not only the trails to the West but the United States itself. As James K. Polk realized his dream of forging a continental nation reaching from the Atlantic to the Pacific, a series of tumultuous events answered the questions of war and peace that would determine the future of the young republic. The resolution of these conflicts did not come easily: in 1846 a collection of scoundrels and schemers hitched their personal ambitions to the dreams of aspiring politicians and capitalized on the sacrifices of the hardworking farm families who went west to find a better life. As American and British diplomats resolved their longstanding differences over Oregon and the U.S. Army marched on Mexico City, a restless nation converted covered wagon trails from pathways of colonization to roads of conflict and conquest.

By 1845, California chronicler H. H. Bancroft observed, the road to Fort Hall was a great national highway, "without hardships or dangers so excessive as to prevent the travellers from being born and married and buried on the way."[1] Over the next three years the United States established its sovereignty over Oregon and the Southwest, the Latter-day Saints established the first major settlement along the trail, and the tenacity, suffering, and endurance of ordinary American families captured half a continent, finished forging the road across the plains, and opened all the primary routes of the Oregon-California Trail.

BY ANY AND ALL MEANS NECESSARY:
THE ANSWER TO THE OREGON QUESTION

On Washington's Birthday in 1846, the crack in the Liberty Bell became so pronounced that it never rang again. During this pivotal year, many citizens feared

---

[1] Bancroft, *History of California*, 4:575.

that the sitting president's militant pursuit of Manifest Destiny and western lands would fracture the republic in a similar fashion. "Will the People of the United States support an expensive & bloody war, merely for conquest and aggrandizement?" asked Daniel Webster. If, as he feared, the United States waged war "for the real purpose of conquest, or of unjustly wrestling territory from neighboring States, then grave & important questions will arise."[2] The most significant of those questions would be the future of slavery in the new lands.

Webster believed the election of a Locofoco president—that is, the radical Democrat James K. Polk—would prove disastrous for the country. Polk's inaugural address and its aggressive stance on Oregon evoked a heated reaction: Foreign Secretary Lord Aberdeen told parliament Britain had "clear and unquestionable" rights in the contested country. "Oregon will never be wrested from the British Crown, to which it belongs, but by war," the *London Times* threatened. Webster feared "that England & the European nations regard our annexation of Texas, our migrations to Calafornia, our inordinate appetite for the whole of Oregon, as decisive evidence of our grasping & unscrupulous disposition to enlarge our territories by any & all means necessary." Behind the rhetoric, both countries searched for a compromise, and the obvious solution was to extend the existing 49° boundary. This, however, required Britain to abandon its longstanding claim to the Columbia River and would force the United States to renounce its assertion that southern Russian Alaska was the proper northern border, the foundation of the slogan "Fifty-four Forty or Fight!" Despite his public support for the acquisition of "all Oregon," Polk was actually maneuvering to persuade England to accept the 49th parallel as the border. Diplomats had fashioned such a compromise, but miscommunication led the British to reject the proposal in late July 1845, creating a crisis.[3]

Polk played a dangerous game, taking aggressive actions that seemed calculated to provoke war with both Mexico and Britain. On 30 July 1845 Secretary of State James Buchanan delivered an "all of Oregon" proposal to the British ambassador that Buchanan himself feared would derail negotiations and lead to war. The same day the president sent orders to General Zachary Taylor to engage any Mexican force that crossed the contested border at the Rio Grande.[4]

The president's calculated risk paid off. As Oregon became increasingly important to the American public, interest in England declined. "At present the shores of the Pacific are not worth fighting for," the *Times* of London wrote. "Their dis-

---

[2] Webster to Ambrose Spencer, 16 May and 28 May 1846; and Webster to Anthony Colby, 20 May 1846, *Correspondence*, 6:165, 157, 160.

[3] Ibid., 6:157; and Sellers, *James K. Polk, Continentalist*, 235–36, 244.

[4] Ibid., 253.

tance, their vastness, and their comparative solitude render them almost incapable of military conquest or occupation." The American press echoed Polk's hope "that, in this enlightened age, these differences may be amicably adjusted."[5]

Many but not all of the Americans on the West Coast shared this view. California's first newspaper concluded there was but little doubt that the two nations would come to an amicable adjustment of the Oregon question. "Neither country in this matter has much to gain by obstinacy, and both have much to lose by war."[6] But well into 1845, Hudson's Bay Company officers at Fort Vancouver hoped to hold on to at least part of their Oregon empire. They received assurances that summer from the Royal Navy's Pacific command that Britain "will maintain her rights to oregon happen what may." They also recognized it would be futile to resist a military occupation by the United States. If American troops arrived at Fort Hall, the Company directed Richard Grant to verify that it was a government force and make "a correct account of everything in the fort in case of surprise so as to be able to swear to what was taken if they did so." He should then "have the Gates open and hoist no flag and let them come in. You are a civilian and have nothing to do with war."[7] Characteristically, Grant was not pleased with his orders: he feared critics would "throw up to my face that I have given up my post like an old woman."[8]

In his first annual message, President Polk took a hard line on Oregon, calling on Congress to give the year's notice required to terminate joint occupancy. To protect emigrants, he proposed establishing a regiment of mounted riflemen to garrison forts along the Oregon Trail. Polk hoped to compel the British to compromise, but he was prepared to back up his Oregon claim by force. On 5 December 1865, Secretary of the Navy George Bancroft ordered Commodore John Sloat, naval commander in the Pacific, to provide "any rifles or other small arms on board your ships" to American settlers in Oregon. "These orders you will keep secret," Bancroft directed. Lieutenant N. M. Howison of the schooner *Shark* sailed up the Columbia River to carry out this mission. Whether he distributed the arms before the *Shark* wrecked on the Columbia bar remains a mystery, but he assured his countrymen "that the United States would never accept of any boundary short of 49°." This inspired "the whole host of Yankee speculators" to head north of the Columbia "to take possession of every acre of land" in defiance of the Hudson's Bay Company's rights, its officers complained.[9]

[5] "The Oregon Matter," *Boston Cultivator,* 20 December 1845, quoting the *National Intelligencer.*

[6] "Oregon," *Monterey Californian,* 12 September 1846, 3/1.

[7] McLoughlin and Ogden to Grant, 25 August 1845, D.5/16, HBC Archives, 27.

[8] Grant to Simpson, 2 January 1846, D.5/16, HBC Archives, 424.

[9] Sellers, *James K. Polk, Continentalist,* 341; Merk, *Manifest Destiny and Mission in American History,* 65–68; and Merk, *The Oregon Question,* 242.

Polk's aggressive policy panicked Wall Street but led Britain to compromise. It was, as Lord Aberdeen said, absurd to go to war "for a cause so preposterous as a few miles of pine swamp," and a famine in Ireland confronted England with a crisis much closer to home. In late April 1846 Congress authorized Polk to give notice of termination of the Oregon agreements. The action forced British ambassador Richard Pakenham to offer another proposal that put the border at the 49th parallel and granted navigation rights on the Columbia to the Hudson's Bay Company, not to Britain. The Senate ratified the treaty on 15 June 1846 and settled the Oregon question on essentially the terms proposed in 1818.[10]

It was politics and not population that drove the compromise. Early Oregon settlers (most notably Marcus Whitman) assumed that their numbers would resolve the question of sovereignty, and historians long presumed that America's success was largely due to Oregon's pioneers. As historian Frederick Merk demonstrated long ago, this was an illusion. England and France had set the 49th parallel as a boundary line in 1713 in the Treaty of Utrecht, and Britain offered to concede territory north of the Columbia to the United States as early as 1826. The fact that only a handful of Americans lived north of the Columbia in 1846—Merk counted a total of eight—confounds the illusion that five thousand American settlers "wielded the pen" that wrote the Oregon Treaty. Although it had failed to attract large numbers of British subjects to the territory, the Hudson's Bay Company and the attractions of the Willamette Valley proved remarkably successful in containing Americans to the south of the river.[11]

Ten days after the steamer carrying the British compromise offer left Liverpool, word arrived that Mexico was at war with the United States. A delay of only a few days in the ship's departure might have substantially affected the favorable terms England offered to settle the Oregon question.

A VERY GOOD ROAD: OVERLAND IN 1846

Eighteen forty-six settled the dispute over Oregon but raised the "grave & important questions" Daniel Webster feared would set the course of American history. As Dale Morgan noted in his classic documentary history of the 1846 trek, the year was "one of the most remarkable and varied in the annals of overland emigration." Bernard DeVoto called 1846 the year of decision, since he believed the continental nation born during those twelve months intensified the conflict over slavery that inevitably led to the Civil War. However that may be, "comedy,

---

[10] Sellers, *James K. Polk, Continentalist*, 357, 373, 397; and Merk, *The Oregon Question*, 413, 417.
[11] Ibid., 234–36, 395.

tragedy, high adventure, achievement, and frustration" characterized this year's dramatic migration.[12] It saw the opening of two problematic cutoffs that led to the best-known tragedy of the trails—the Donner party disaster—and a largely forgotten drama, the blazing of the southern road to Oregon.

The 1846 emigration produced a shelf of classic overland narratives, most notably Francis Parkman's *The Oregon Trail,* Edwin Bryant's *What I Saw in California,* and J. Quinn Thornton's *Oregon and California in 1848.* The year witnessed the publication of some of the first trail guidebooks, including J. M. Shively's *The Road to Oregon and California across the Rocky Mountains* and Overton Johnson and William H. Winter's *Route across the Rocky Mountains.* Several people going west that year carried Lansford Hastings's 1845 *The Emigrants' Guide, to Oregon and California.*

The resolution of the Oregon question assured peace with Britain, but relations with Mexico had festered after the annexation of Texas in February. The president had tried repeatedly to acquire California peacefully: his 1845 offer to pay $40 million for the territory exemplified his preference for peace over war. Polk knew that the illegal aliens—Americans—who were flooding across the Sierra would soon hold the balance of power in the province, but he feared that a third power would seize the country before the "Texas game" had played out. When Mexico rejected his overtures, Polk ordered the army to occupy southern Texas, even though he knew Mexico would regard the presence of American troops south of the Nueces River an act of war. After General Zachary Taylor marched into the disputed territory, Mexican cavalry attacked an American scouting party on 25 April 1846, and Congress declared war on 13 May 1846.[13] Mexico's national honor compelled her to succumb to the provocations and ignite a war that was a political disaster for the unstable republic.

Most emigrants left the frontier knowing that Congress had given notice to terminate the joint-occupancy agreement with Britain, which many believed would lead to war over Oregon. The first overlanders to arrive at Oregon City on 26 August, however, brought news "that there is war between Mexico and the United States." The vast hordes that promoters such as Hastings and Thomas Farnham had speculated would crowd the trails in 1846 failed to materialize. Instead, some twenty-seven hundred people assembled at three Missouri River jumping-off places—Independence/Westport, Saint Joseph, and for the first time at a site some thirty miles south of Council Bluffs that would eventually be named Nebraska City. The Missouri borderlands were alive with rumors that "large bodies of Mormons, well armed" were "swarming" across the river at Council Bluffs.

---

[12] DeVoto, *The Year of Decision, 1846;* and Morgan, *Overland in 1846,* 6.

[13] Ibid., 48–49. When news of the attack on American forces arrived, Polk had already prepared a request for a declaration of war based on the pretext that Mexico had refused to pay its debts.

These generated fear all along the frontier and diverted Pacific-bound emigrants away from Council Bluffs.[14]

The Latter-day Saints, as they preferred to be known, already had a contentious reputation, having been driven from their settlements in Missouri to Illinois following a bloody conflict in 1838. A mob murdered Joseph Smith, their young prophet, in 1844, and two years later his followers agreed to abandon their homes in Illinois to avoid a civil war. The Mormons' new leader, Brigham Young, was determined to shake the dust of the United States off his boots. Having closely studied reports from the West, he planned to establish an independent state in the unsettled interior of Alta California. In addition, a U.S. district court had indicted Young and four of his fellow apostles for counterfeiting, and they sought to avoid any interference with their plans. He began moving his people west in February 1846, hoping that the early start would allow them to establish supply stations along the northern shore of the Platte River.[15]

"No one could predict what would be the result, when large armed bodies of these fanatics should encounter the most impetuous and reckless of their old enemies on the broad prairie, far beyond the reach of law or military force," Francis Parkman observed: he heard the emigrants had requested an escort of dragoons from Fort Leavenworth to take them to the Platte. The army refused, and it turned out the Mormons felt "quite as much awe of the 'gentiles' as the latter did of them."[16] On her way to Saint Joseph, Margaret Hecox met a Mormon woman who told her that Brigham Young was a great and good man, and "even more than a man, because he had his instructions directly from God,—that he was going to found a Kingdom for the Saints where all would be good and happy." The men in her party were more afraid of the Mormons than she was, Hecox recalled. "They thought we might have to fight our way through, but we had no trouble whatever. In fact, when we arrived at the place where they were supposed to be camped in great numbers, we found they were all gone."[17]

Most of the Mormon refugees did not reach Council Bluffs until June, so exhausted and impoverished that they were unable to send scouts to the mountains that year. Only nineteen misguided wagons from Mississippi joined the trek at Independence, having failed to learn of Brigham Young's change of plans. These lost

---

[14] Ibid., 528, 537, 549, 773.

[15] DeVoto, *The Year of Decision*, 75–101; and Bennett, *We'll Find the Place*, 1–116. Two days after he crossed the Mississippi on 15 February 1846, Brigham Young received a contract from Samuel Brannan in New York, allegedly drafted by Amos Kendall and signed by A. G. Benson, promising to "prevent any authorized interference" by the government to stop the Mormon exodus in exchange for half the lands they settled. Brigham Young refused to sign "any such unjust and oppressive agreement." See Tullidge, *Life of Brigham Young*, 20; and Roberts, *History of the Church*, 7:588–91.

[16] Parkman, *The California and Oregon Trail*, 50.

[17] Hecox, "The Story of Margaret M. Hecox," 541.

sheep were enough to feed rumors that the Mormons were moving west in force. False reports later reached the river towns that they had murdered the most famous member of the emigration, former governor Lilburn Boggs, in retribution for his 1838 extermination order that had ejected the Mormons from Missouri.[18]

Poverty and mud stopped the Mormons at the Missouri, and for the first time in two years no one went west along the north shore of the Platte. Perhaps due to the rumors of war that had swept the country for almost a year, the number of emigrants fell far short of the previous year's total, but for the first time since 1841 most of the travelers went to California.[19] A party of "Arkansas Californians," apparently including freebooter T. J. Farnham, left Fort Smith in April. Only eleven of the one thousand men he had anticipated joined him. Farnham and friends disappeared after writing a letter from Santa Fe in June, but his departure represented the first of hundreds of outfits that would leave the southern frontier for California over the next decade.[20]

Despite the failure of various wild prophecies, the pace of westward expansion was accelerating. For the first time, news reached the frontier that wagons had actually made it all the way to California, when E. A. Farwell's letter appeared in the *Missouri Republican* on 5 May 1846, early enough for late-starting emigrants to see it. A small party led by Townsend and Stephens in 1844 had discovered and traveled "a very good road," Farwell wrote. On 22 April the *New Orleans Picayune* reported a conversation with a gentleman "direct from California" who described Frémont's purported discovery of "a new route, or pass, by which California can be reached by emigrants in sixty days less time than by the old route via Oregon." This perfectly practicable route, the traveler predicted, would "give a renewed impetus to emigration to California." But as their wagons prepared to cross the Kansas River in the middle of May, a man overtook them with a copy of the *Missouri Republican* "containing an account of the defeat and capture of Captain Thornton and his command by the Mexicans" on the Rio Grande.[21]

Polk had successfully provoked Mexico, and America was at war.

GOOD HEALTH AND FINE SPIRITS: THE OREGON EMIGRATION, 1846

A successful and uneventful episode is never as dramatic as a spectacular failure, and the lack of any diary by the first overlanders bound for Oregon in 1846 has left

---

[18] Morgan, *Overland in 1846,* 528, 537, 549.

[19] Stewart, *The California Trail,* 145; and Unruh, *The Plains Across,* 119.

[20] Morgan, *Overland in 1846,* 459, 477–79, 488.

[21] Thornton, "Occasional Address," 37; and *Oregon and California in 1848,* 1:26.

few details of their adventures. From the newspapers and reminiscent accounts like that of John R. McBride, it appears the advance elements left the Missouri frontier in mid-April and made excellent progress over the entire route. The most interesting incidents of the trip were encounters with mountaineers such as Pegleg Smith and Jim Bridger and meetings with returning Oregonians, notably Wales Bonney (who some reported had killed a man before fleeing Oregon) and Joel Palmer.

Palmer started from Oregon City on 5 March to bring his family from the states, and his eastbound journal provides one of the most vivid accounts of that year's westering. Palmer's party met the advance companies at Fort Laramie in the middle of June. Some of the Oregonian's faces were frostbitten from crossing the mountains, Jessy Quinn Thornton recalled, and one man gave an evil report of Oregon, saying "it rained so much and so continuously that a goose could not get to grass." For the next two hundred miles Palmer encountered companies of 6 to 40 wagons and people "generally in good health and fine spirits." Palmer counted 541 wagons, and the drivers of 212 of them said they were bound for California. As he later learned, many of them changed their minds and went to Oregon.[22]

Recollections provide anecdotes about the trek. Seventy years after reaching Oregon, Mary Munkers Estes described a storm on the Platte River: "The wind blew a hurricane! Thunder roared and lighting flashed! It was as dark as Egypt. The rain poured like it was being emptied from buckets." The gale blew down every tent, but no one was injured. "The men chained the wagons together to hold them from being blown into the river," she remembered. "Our camp belongings were blown helter skelter over the country around about and our stock was stampeded 'till it took all the next day to get them rounded up."[23]

At Soda Springs, "we sweetened some of the water with honey and it foamed up in great shape," recalled Elizabeth Foster Currier, a memory that Daniel Toole confirmed in a rare contemporary letter describing Steamboat Spring.[24] "The soda springs are a curiosity indeed; the water of these springs tastes a good deal like soda, and boils up like soda when the acid is mixed. Just below these soda springs is a boiling spring, which comes up through a hole in the rock; it makes a noise like it was boiling, and can be heard a quarter of a mile off," Toole wrote from Fort Hall. "The water foams like suds, and is a little above milk warm."[25] In contrast to these pleasant stories, California pioneer David Campbell recalled that after leaving Fort Hall, mountain fever began to ravage his party, and, lacking a doctor, a great many people died. At the parting of the trails to Oregon and

[22] Palmer, *Journal of Travels,* 250; and Thornton, "Occasional Address," 45.

[23] Estes, Crossing the Plains in 1846.

[24] Currier, "Crossing the Plains in 1846," Oregon Historical Society.

[25] Toole to "Dear Brother," 2 August 1846, *Liberty Tribune,* 19 December 1846.

California, "about fifty wagons concluded they would go to Oregon, as they had so many deaths in their families."[26]

Those who kept to the old road to the Columbia made excellent time: Pack trains reached Oregon City by 25 August, and Joseph Waldo arrived from Independence in four months and nine days. Both parties had come by the Barlow Road, the eighty-mile wagon trace over the southern shoulder of Mount Hood and the Cascades that Samuel K. Barlow and Joel Palmer had laid out the previous fall and which Barlow completed—after a fashion—during the summer. J. W. Ladd (or perhaps Reuben Gannt) brought the first wagon over the road to Oregon City by 13 September, "at least two months in advance of any previous emigration." The Barlow Road probably constituted the single most significant improvement ever made to the Oregon Trail, which at last was truly a wagon road—though still a very rough trace—to the Willamette Valley. By the end of October, the *Oregon Spectator* reported that 152 wagons had crossed the mountains over the new road.[27]

Among the first arrivals was Midshipman Selim Woodworth, ordered west with dispatches for American naval forces in the Pacific. Woodworth's pomposity and incompetence—he could not saddle his own horse—entertained and aggravated westerners from Missouri to Oregon. One of his men complained he acted like a lost puppy in tall rye, while John R. McBride described the results of his orders as "very much like a shipwreck on a rough coast." Woodworth reached Oregon City on 19 August, having left the frontier on 14 May, completing the trip in ninety-eight days, "being about thirty days less time than it has ever before been accomplished in, to my knowledge," he claimed.[28]

"All were anxious to trade with the emigration," a visitor at Fort Hall reported in fall 1846. After the trains appeared, "Mr. Grant had scarcely time to take his meals."[29] Richard Grant kept on friendly terms with the emigrants, the trader wrote from his post, but he had to "pass over and put up with things that in any civilized part of the World would hardly go down," but the "rough Citizens of the Mountains and Emigrants from the borders & wilds of the United States some times bark loud but very seldom bite."[30] About half the Oregon-bound migration had passed Fort Hall by 8 August 1846 when Jesse Applegate arrived from the Great Basin, where he claimed to have found a better road to the Willamette Valley—"the distance is considerably shortened, the grass and water plenty"—than the trail down the Snake River.[31]

---

[26] Campbell, "Pioneer of 1846," *Porterville Recorder,* 11, 12, and 13 August 1910.

[27] James M. Tompkins, comments to the author; and Morgan, *Overland in 1846,* 662–63, 687.

[28] Ibid., 98–99, 656; and Woodworth, "Letter from California," 6 February 1847, *The Home Journal,* 31 July 1847, 2.

[29] Joseph Burke to Sir William, 17 October 1846, Morgan Papers, 56:115.

[30] Grant to George Simpson, 1 April 1847, D.5/19, HBC Archives, 443.

[31] Morgan, *Overland in 1846,* 87, 637.

THE SOUTH ROAD EXPEDITION: BLAZING THE "APPLEGATE TRAIL"

The call to open a road to the Willamette Valley that circumvented the Cascades and the Columbia Gorge grew louder with each year's migration. "All are impressed with the conviction," editorialized the *Oregon Spectator* on 25 June 1846, "of the vast importance of obtaining an easy and safe road to the Willamette Valley, by a southern route, and thus avoiding the numerous and heartbreaking difficulties of the Columbia." As war with Britain loomed, Americans feared that the Hudson's Bay Company could sever their only road to the states, fueling the urgency of finding an alternate route to the Willamette. Before other distractions intervened, John C. Frémont intended to ascend the Sacramento River in 1846 and "go from the Tlamath Lake into the Wahlahmath valley." He would explore a trail "making the road into Oregon far shorter, and a *good* road in place of the present very bad one down the Columbia."[32] Peter Skene Ogden had explored the route in 1827 that Frémont proposed to find almost two decades later. Americans traveling between Oregon and California had used this rough trace over the Siskiyou Mountains since 1834—but no one had located a practical way to get over the Cascades and connect the trappers' trail with the Humboldt River.[33]

Elijah White and Moses "Black" Harris ascended the Santiam River in 1845 to "look out a road across the Cascade mountain," but gave up after a month-long search for a pass. A committee began collecting money in February 1846 "to explore and open a wagon road." In late March a band of prominent Oregon Trail veterans, including Nathaniel Ford, Cornelius Gilliam, Stephen Meek, and Harris, announced plans "to examine for a practicable wagon road" south from the Willamette.[34] A party of fifteen men left the settlements in mid-May, but dissension and the complex terrain of southern Oregon discouraged the explorers and they returned home.

Late in June 1846, another fifteen men, now including Jesse and Lindsay Applegate, set out from near present-day Dallas on what they called the South Road Expedition. The Applegates had both lost sons to the rapids of the Columbia: as Lindsay later wrote, "We resolved if we remained in the country, to find a better way for others who might wish to emigrate." The explorers included Levi Scott, his son John, David Goff, and the ubiquitous Moses Harris. Believing that a lack

---

[32] Frémont to Jessie Frémont, 24 January 1846, in Spence and Jackson, eds., *The Expeditions of John Charles Frémont*, 47–49, 570.

[33] Jeff LaLande's 1987 study, *First over the Siskiyous*, reinterpreted Peter Skeen Ogden's first expedition into the Oregon-California borderlands, accurately describing his route in 1826 and 1827 for the first time. As LaLande's work shows, the South Road survey's only trailblazing was between Klamath Lake and the Humboldt. For an excellent summary, see Ross A. Smith's "The Southern Route Revisited," 292–307. Much of this section is based on Stafford Hazelett's research, which he generously shared with the author.

[34] Morgan, *Overland in 1846*, 32n12, 70, 490, 493–94, 739.

of a clearly defined command had contributed to the dissolution of the previous survey, they chose Jesse Applegate to lead them.[35] Over the next six weeks, the men followed Ogden's trail over the Calapooya Mountains and south, repeatedly encountering small parties coming from Sutters Fort. At the forks of the South Umpqua River at what is now Canyonville, they followed the pack trail up the brush-and-boulder-choked Canyon Creek, leaving Ogden's trace near today's Ashland. Up to this point, the surveyors had relied on existing trails, but now they entered uncharted territory. Following a map Ogden had given Applegate and information about the area picked up from a party of southbound French mountaineers, the road finders headed up Emigrant Creek, across the eastern Siskiyou Mountains, and into the Cascades until the Klamath River's deep canyon blocked progress. Some of the men proposed giving up, but Levi Scott and three scouts climbed a butte and spied out a route they felt could penetrate the densely forested mountains to reach the open country that lay beyond.

The men explored "the valleys of the Umpqua, Rogue river, Clamet and Sacramento," Jesse Applegate wrote the next March, confusing the Sacramento with the Lost River, where an Indian showed them a natural stone bridge across the otherwise unfordable river. Their way-worn animals enjoyed a few days of good grazing before enduring several dry marches to get around the Lower Klamath, Tule, and Clear lakes: disgusted at the resulting complaints, Jesse Applegate resigned as leader, but after talking it over, Levi Scott and David Goff agreed to share the burdens of command. From Goose Lake, the road hunters headed southeast, crossing the Warner Mountains and Surprise Valley to High Rock Canyon, where they turned south to Mud Meadows and the increasingly parched desert until they reach the great spring at Black Rock, at the edge of a wide, dry playa.

Here the party's leaders debated how to cross the wastes that lay before them. Applegate thought he could see a pass bordering the desert and set off to the southeast with five men; Scott, Goff, and the rest took a more southerly course. They found water on their first two days on the Black Rock Desert, but the last half of the trip was another dry passage. Scott's party reached the Humboldt and the California Trail well south of present-day Rye Patch Reservoir: after slaking their thirst they began searching for Applegate's men, whom they found in desperate shape.[36]

Jesse Applegate and four companions headed for Fort Hall, while Levi Scott and nine men stayed behind to work out a reasonable route for wagons across the Black Rock Desert. Before splitting up, Scott recalled, the surveyors estimated it would take thirty properly equipped men to open the road, which had not

---

[35] Applegate, "Notes and Reminiscences," 14. Although attributed to Lindsay Applegate, this memoir was probably written by his son, O. C. Applegate.

[36] Morgan, *Overland in 1846*, 73, 86.

even been marked—and Applegate agreed that if he could not recruit enough volunteers to do the job, he would not encourage emigrants to risk the new trail. Given the repeated challenges of the terrain, notably the precipitous descents to Jenny, Keene, and Tyler creeks, not its mention the route's extreme aridity—it is a testament to pioneer optimism that anyone could believe even an army could open a reliable wagon road. Scott's men worked out a difficult but not impossible crossing from what became known as Lassens Meadow to Antelope, Rabbithole, and Black Rock springs, and his surveyors then headed east on the California Trail to meet Applegate and the parties he had presumably recruited.

Years later, Lindsay Applegate recalled that while hunting antelope on the California Trail, he and Levi Scott had discovered the wreckage of several burned wagons—perhaps those of the unknown party that left Fort Hall in advance of the other 1845 companies—whose owners appeared to have been murdered. The new road had a host of other problems: it avoided the challenges of the Snake and Columbia rivers and the deserts of eastern Oregon, but Jesse Applegate's promise that those who followed it could reach the Willamette in time to build a cabin and sow wheat before the rains came proved to be a cruel fantasy.[37]

After encouraging parties he met heading west on the California Trail to the try the new route, Jesse Applegate appeared at Fort Hall on 8 August. Like other promoters excited by the discovery of a shortcut, he seemed compelled to exaggerate its benefits and downplay its many challenges: "The advantage gained to the emigrant by this route is of the greatest importance—the distance is considerably shortened, the grass and water plenty, the sterile regions and dangerous crossings of the Snake and Columbia rivers avoided, as well as the Cascade Mountain—he may reach his place of destination with his wagon and property in time to build a cabin and sow wheat before the rainy season," he announced in an open letter. "This road has been explored, and will be opened at the expense of the citizens of Oregon, and nothing whatever demanded of the emigrants." Despite Applegate's claims, the southern route was much longer than the road down the Columbia: geographer Richard Rieck calculated that by the old trail it was 730 miles from Fort Hall to Oregon City, while by the South Road it was 985 miles. A year later, after an explosion of controversy, Applegate told his brother Lisbon he had been fully convinced of his new road's advantages, but claimed he "made no effort to induce emigrants to travel the road."[38]

But Applegate was persuasive, and many of those who took the new trace thought otherwise. "There were some men who met us near Fort Hall and through

[37] Ibid., 634, 637–78; and Bancroft, *History of Oregon*, 552, 557. Scott says nothing about this in his memoir.

[38] Smith, "The Southern Route Revisited," 305; and Morgan, *Overland in 1846*, 637–38, 768.

their persuasion we took the new route," John E. Lose wrote next spring, framing a telling indictment of the South Road: "The roads were very bad, pasture indifferent, having heavy beds of sand without wood, water or grass, for 45 or 50 miles, to travel through; the dust was intense, the sand appears to be mixed with lime and salt, and both man and beast had to cough and sneeze, the cattle would frequently bawl from suffering." The Black Rock Desert formed a waterless barrier that killed many oxen, and Applegate seemed unaware of the hostile Indians who lined virtually the entire route. The Natives "killed some of our men, and we in return killed them, for our feelings were not friendly towards each other," Lose reported.[39] "Three or four trains of emigrants were decoyed off by a rascally fellow that came out from the settlement in Oregon, assuring us that he had found a *near cut-off*," Tabitha Brown recalled in 1854. The scoundrel said "that if we would follow him we would be in the settlement long before those who had gone down the Columbia."[40]

Applegate had raised a few volunteers to help open the road, one of them recalled years later, but the emigrants could spare few able-bodied men. "About 100 wagons with 400 or 500 people turned from the old route to follow him," Truman Powers wrote. Applegate advised them "it would be necessary for a party to precede the wagons and open the way for them through the timber, and he called for volunteers from among the immigrants for this work." Powers signed on, and recalled that Applegate recruited "a company of twelve as a road party, and they were furnished with axes from the wagons. These were all the tools that could be furnished for road making."[41]

The surveyors—at least those who had not disappeared for points unknown—reunited in Thousand Springs Valley, where on 13 August, Captain Applegate forged ahead "to mark and open the new road." Levi Scott and David Goff stayed to guide the wagons, which followed in small detachments. Lacking enough supplies and manpower, and clearly in a hurry to get back home, Applegate and a few men covered an average of twenty-four miles a day over critical sections of the trail, and the handful of volunteers they left behind to work on the road had little actual impact on the rough terrain. "We found nothing to dishearten us, until we came to the canyon in the Umpqua mountain," Truman Powers recalled, referring to the canyons of Canyon Creek and the South Umpqua, the roughest section of the trail, which won the name "Terrible Canyon" that fall. Jesse Applegate arrived home in late September: his notice about the new road appeared in the *Spectator* on 1 October, before the first wagons had reached the Klamath

[39] Lose, "From Oregon," *Defiance Democrat*, 25 November 1847, 3/1–2, courtesy of Kristin Johnson.
[40] Brown, "A Brimfield Heroine, Tabitha Brown," *Covered Wagon Women*, 1:52.
[41] [Powers], "A Pioneer's Reminiscence," *Morning Oregonian*, 12 March 1879, 1/2.

Tabitha Moffatt Brown was born in Massachusetts during the American Revolution. She was almost sixty-
six, and had a bad hip, when she set out for Oregon in
1846 with her seventy-seven year old brother-in-law,
John Brown, a former sea captain, and their extended
family. She rode through the Umpqua Mountains "in
three days at the risk of my life, on horseback, having
lost my wagon and all that I had but the horse I was
on." Brown returned to school teaching and became
a founder of Pacific University. She died in 1858 and
is buried in Salem's Pioneer Cemetery. The state
legislature recognized her as the "Mother Symbol of
Oregon" in 1987. Courtesy Stafford Hazelett.

River, at which point they had already traveled as many miles as it would take to reach Oregon City on the old road—and they were still hundreds of hard miles from the nearest settlement, and much of that distance through forested land that provided no forage for draft animals. The last of the road builders secured a few bushels of supplies from an HBC trading post, but when they ran out, they set out for the settlements, almost immediately meeting the "strong and resolute" Solomon Tetherow and John Owens with provisions enough to let them return "to the work with renewed courage" for another twelve days.[42]

Working backward, the road crew found no wagons when they reached the Rogue River and headed for the settlements. Powers believed that had the wagons gotten that far, "they could have passed through the canyon without loss, as no rain had fallen at that time": but the road builder's work proved insufficient. Meanwhile, Scott struggled to build a road as all the trains backed up, creating a logjam.

Getting wagons over the rough trace demanded huge efforts, especially at the harrowing descent into Canyon Creek Canyon and what Jesse Applegate called "the dividing ground between the waters of the Rogue river and Umpqua," where he admitted his road builders "were unable to make this road properly" due to a lack of tools and provisions: they "attempted only to make it passable with as little labor as possible." Then, as October ended, "The difficulties of the road were much increased by the rains commencing about the time the first wagons were crossing the mountain," Applegate wrote next spring. When winter set in with most of the emigrants scattered along seventy miles of trail, most only a hundred miles from the safety of the settlements. As the weather worsened, the wagon companies disintegrated and the wretched survivors struggled into the Willamette Valley as best they could.

Learning of the emigrants' plight from the first of the desperate overlanders to reach the settlements in early October, Oregonians launched a concerted rescue effort. Applegate's role in the relief is ambiguous: help reached the last emigrants stranded in the Rogue River Valley in December, but some only made it to the Willamette the next spring. That fall, Jesse Applegate blamed those who had suffered on the South Road "for want of energy and diligence in travelling," and later chroniclers reported that the exhausted emigrants had "lingered too long in this beautiful country," but "lingering" hardly describes the experiences of these starving people and their dying animals.[43] The rising waters of Canyon Creek made travel either painfully slow or impossible, trapping many families for

---

[42] Ibid.; Smith, "The Southern Route Revisited," 298–300; and Bancroft, *History of Oregon*, 1:558.

[43] Morgan, *Overland in 1846*, 767; and Bancroft, *History of Oregon*, 1:562. The chronicler was Frances Fuller Victor.

weeks. "I rode through in three days at the risk of my life, having lost my wagon and all I had but the horse I was on," Tabitha Brown recalled. Her party led the way down the canyon and managed to get through the mud and rocks with less difficulty than those who followed, but Brown said only one wagon came through without breaking. "The Canyon was strewn with dead cattle, broken wagons, beds, clothing and everything but provisions of which latter we were nearly destitute." Despite the relief effort, hunger haunted the emigrants as they began to divide their last supplies. "The word was *Fly,* everyone who can, from starvation," Brown wrote.[44] Moses Harris and Thomas Holt led parties whose prodigious efforts undoubtedly reduced the loss of life, but the eyewitness accounts contain grim tallies of the casualties.

Literary warfare over who was to blame for the catastrophe erupted in the *Oregon Spectator* almost immediately. J. Quinn Thornton denounced the road builders as "outlaws and banditti," while Applegate and his allies mounted a stout defense. "That the road through the Umpqua mountain is at present a bad one, no one has denied or wishes to deny; and that the necessary labor will make it a good one is as generally conceded," asserted a letter signed by the illiterate David Goff but written by James Nesmith, Goff's son-in-law. The lost property and severe suffering was to be regretted, the letter admitted, "but that the road hunters are to blame for it, none but fools believe or liars assert."[45] Many disagreed. "The route through which we travelled is about 1200 miles from Fort Hall to Oregon, and through the old route it is but 750," observed John E. Lose, reporting that "about 100 of our company died on the road." Historian Ross A. Smith concluded that that only a dozen or more emigrants died, but Lose framed the case against "the new route, an off cut as it was called," persuasively: "Our miseries were almost inconceivable in consequence of going the lower route.—Those who went the old route fared well, and arrived September; but we did not arrive until January."[46] Even Jesse Applegate admitted he would hesitate to advise emigrants to take the new route, since there was nothing to restrain hostile Indians "from the exercise of their natural disposition to plunder."[47]

Levi Scott headed east again over the southern route early in 1847. He returned in the fall, and his wagons reached the settlements "in good season and in good condition." The provisional legislature appointed Scott road commissioner, but the southern route never replaced the Oregon Trail as a way to the Willamette: it was simply too long. Peter Lassen incorporated segments of it in his own

---

[44] Brown, "A Brimfield Heroine, Tabitha Brown," *Covered Wagon Women,* 1:52–53.

[45] Morgan, *Overland in 1846,* 682.

[46] Smith, "The Southern Route Revisited," 292; and Lose, "From Oregon," *Defiance Democrat,* 4 November 1847, 3/2.

[47] Bancroft, *History of Oregon,* 1:562; and Morgan, *Overland in 1846,* 77, 682.

extended shortcut to the Sacramento in 1848, while during the California gold rush Oregonians bound for the mines used some of the trail, but the road fell into disuse in the 1850s. "This chronicle records the first trip in 6 years (since 1853) over the Applegate cut-off, or 'Death route,'" Charles J. Cummings wrote in his 1859 journal.[48] Today major highways follow Peter Skene Ogden's trapper trail through southern Oregon, but to this day no paved road crosses the route the South Road Expedition blazed from Rogue River to the Klamath and across the Black Rock Desert to the Humboldt.

Controversy over opening the trail has endured into the twenty-first century: the memory of their ancestors' hard road still pains some Oregonians. Many of those who used the cutoff did not have a high opinion of the expedition's leader, but like other early overlanders, most accepted responsibility for their own decisions. Jesse Applegate's reputation fared less well with their descendants, especially the family of Ellen Skidmore Smith. Her daughter Angeline Smith Crews, who had been nine years old in 1846, claimed the promoters "Robbed the Emegrants and left them in the Wilderness to starve [and] never dun a lick of work to open the Road." Jesse Applegate collected a toll from each wagon, Crews recalled, which would have been standard operating procedure for cutoff discoverers, but she charged he "told them that he would see that the Road was Worked and Put in good shape." The promised good roads came to an end "hardley be fore they started and thay saw no more of there tole collector and the Man that was to see them through." To compound the outrage, starving emigrants were compelled to buy flour from "Jess Applegate the trator that had misslead them"—a charge that apparently is not true.[49]

Today the name "Applegate Trail" has been applied to "to virtually every old wagon road within the general corridor of travel from Ashland to Dallas," as Stafford Hazelett observed. Descendants of those who suffered in 1846 sometimes resent the route's official name, "Applegate Trail," even though no less an authority than John McLoughlin referred to it as "the Applegate Road" and called it "the Best Route from Fort Hall to this place" in 1847.[50] Early on, the name stuck: gold rushers such as Abram Minges called it "Applegates rout to oragon." The family was among the first to settle along the southern road, remaining pioneers till the end, and their literary talent and devoted progeny helped protect

[48] Cummings, Diary, 26 April 1859, Beinecke Library.

[49] Smith, A Brief Sketch and History of an Oregen [sic] Pioneer, Huntington Library, 6–7, 9. See also Angeline Smith Crews, Typescript Recollection, ca. 1916, William Smith Family Papers, Oregon Historical Society. Although attributed to both Smith and Crews, both documents are variants of the same narrative. The Huntington manuscript was allegedly "Copyed From Mrs Ellen Smith's Direy."

[50] Hazelett to Bagley, 21 October 2008; and McLoughlin, *John McLoughlin's Business Correspondence, 1847–48*, 66.

their ambiguous legacy.[51] A peak, pass, river, valley, Civilian Conservation Corps camp, dam, and even a metamorphic rock group in the Klamath Mountains eventually bore the name Applegate, so it seems pointless to begrudge applying the name to another cutoff to disaster.

The Promised Land: California Fever

The stories that played out on the California Trail in 1846 are even more compelling than the dramatic events on the new road to Oregon. During the winter and spring, California's boosters laid plans that would profoundly affect the fate of that year's emigration.

After failing to rendezvous with Joseph R. Walker's detachment of his third expedition, John C. Frémont returned to Sutters Fort on 15 January 1846. Nine days later he sent his wife a letter that "verged upon dangerous nonsense," as Dale Morgan observed. "Instead of a barren country, the mountains were covered with grasses of the best quality, wooded with several varieties of trees," the captain reported. By the route his men had explored the previous fall, Frémont claimed he could ride from the Front Range of the Rockies to Sutters Fort in thirty-five days. For wagons, he boasted, the road, was "decidedly better" than the established trail. Frémont contradicted himself in 1848 when his abbreviated scientific report characterized the eighty waterless miles across the Great Salt Desert as "destitute of any vegetation except sage-bushes, and absolutely bare and smooth." The ambitious young explorer apparently told this calculated lie to encourage emigration to California with an eye to its conquest.[52]

There is no written evidence that they actually met, but Lansford W. Hastings and Frémont spent four days together at Sutters Fort. It is hard to believe that two men with such strong mutual interests would not have exchanged information and ideas, since their descriptions of the Salt Desert route were so alike. Both used strikingly similar rhetoric when promoting the cut off, while Hastings repeatedly invoked Frémont's name to recruit emigrants to test his shortcut to the Humboldt. But the subsequent actions of Frémont and Hastings are so confusing that it appears neither man had thought carefully about what it would actually take to conquer California. Both initially stated they intended to go to Oregon. For unknown reasons,

[51] Minges, Journal, 13 August 1849, Bentley Historical Library; and Bancroft, *History of Oregon*, 1:568–72. Promoter Walter Meacham of The Old Oregon Trail Association essentially invented the name Applegate Trail in 1947 when he published a pamphlet with that title that was distributed to all the public schools in Oregon. State officials long resisted using term, but after a hasty local review, the Applegate Trail was named in the 1992 Congressional legislation that created the California National Historic Trail.

[52] Korns and Morgan, *West from Fort Bridger*, 12–13; and Morgan, *Overland in 1846*, 48–49.

Frémont led his men to the coast in an apparent attempt to provoke a military confrontation with the Mexican authorities. When they ordered him to leave, Frémont
fortified a mountaintop near Monterey to defend against an imaginary attack. After
four days, Frémont got hungry, retreated, and marched north. Apparently unable
to persuade anyone to accompany him to Oregon, Hastings left Sutters Fort on 11
April with James M. Hudspeth and an Indian vaquero to join a party of Americans
at Johnsons Ranch to return to the states. Hastings hoped to persuade emigrants to
try "a new route Discovered by Capt. fremont which is about 3 or 400 Miles shorter
as the old route over fort Hall," Sutter reported.[53]

Hastings told any number of interesting tales during his visit to California.
"The tide of emigration to both, this country and Oregon, is unparalleled in the
annals of history. The eyes of the American people are now turned westward,"
he told American Consul Thomas Larkin on 3 March 1846, predicting the influx
that year would "not consist of less than *twenty thousand* souls." The Benson brothers planned to establish a commercial house and "proposed to bring all emigrants
to this country, and to Oregon, free of charge," Hastings claimed. "This latter arrangement is a confidential, governmental arrangement. The expense thus
incured is not borne by that house, but by our government, for the promotion of
what object, you will readily perceive." Thus, said the young promoter, "a new
era in the affairs of California, is about to arise."[54]

Hastings was "laying off a Town at New Helvetia for the Mormons," Larkin
informed Secretary of State James Buchanan, while at the same time spreading
rumors that an oncoming horde of Latter-day Saints was bound for California.
The Mormons would "march towards California, which has been designated to
them as the promised land where they are to develop their belief and multi-
ply their posterity," the French consul reported in late March. "This invasion,
announced for the next summer, has thrown fear and anxiety into the minds
of the Californians."[55] John A. Sutter wrote, "The next fall will be a powerfull
Emigration here. It is started [*sic*] from 10 to 20,000 which hardly I can believe. I
think if 2 or 3000 would come it would be a great many."[56]

Hastings had aroused deep resentment in Oregon. Truman and James Bonney
claimed he "told us publicly that he and Captain Suter intended to revolutionize
the country, as soon as they could get sufficient emigrants into California to fight
the Spaniards; this plan was laid between Captain Suter and L. W. Hastings,

[53] Ibid., 42, 43, 47.

[54] Hastings to Larkin, 2 March 1846, in Larkin, *The Larkin Papers*, 4:220–21.

[55] Nasatir, "The French Consulate in California, 1843–56," 355.

[56] Sutter to Larkin, 2 March 1846, in Larkin, *The Larkin Papers*, 4:219. Sutter was correct: the 1846 overland
emigration to California totaled about 1,500 souls. See Morgan, *Overland in 1846*, 116.

before said Hastings published his book of lies."[57] The promoter had also made his
share of enemies in California. "I am afraid we shall see a great deal of trouble in
California this year," W. D. M. Howard wrote. "There are 7 or 8000 emigrants
from the U.S. expected and this Hastings who has written a book about California is determined, I think, to kick up a row."[58] John Sutter was relieved to see
Hastings depart and suggested hopefully to John Marsh that "perhaps nobody
will see him here again, as his life will be in danger about his book, making out
California a paridise." Emigrants had threatened him, and his "impudent writing"
made him an enemy to many people. "I like to be hospitable," wrote Sutter in his
broken English, "but I am very glad when Capt. Hastings is gone."[59]

The unpopular promoter left Johnsons Ranch on 23 April in company with
nineteen men and boys, three women, two children, and about 150 mules and
horses. Mountaineer James Clyman feared it was "too many for this rout at so early
a season."[60] The Greenwood clan traveled with them, bound for Fort Hall to ply
their trade as guides and perhaps again seeking to reunite with family members.
Upon reaching the Humboldt's north fork on 21 May 1846, Hastings headed east
to find Frémont's trail across the Salt Desert to the Salt Lake Valley. After "long
consultation and many arguments for and against," about half the party, including
a woman and child, took the alleged shortcut, despite James Clyman's conviction
it was "very little nearer and not so good a road as that by fort Hall."[61]

It took Clyman's little band more than two weeks to reach Fort Bridger. They
crossed the Salt Desert's "boundless salt plain" in two days, spending thirty hours
without water on the dry *jornada*. Clyman understood that "if we could follow
Mr Fremonts trail we would not have more than 20 miles without fresh water."
Since the actual distance between springs is eighty-three miles, this telling piece
of misinformation raises questions about what Frémont told Hastings. Clyman
guided the company through the Wasatch Mountains, crossing the tangled terrain via East and Echo canyons to find Bridgers Fort abandoned. "Nothing can be
mor desolute and discouraging," Clyman wrote, "than a deserted fort whare you
expect relief in a dangerous Indian country."[62]

The company split up. Hastings, Hudspeth, and their Indian companion crossed
the Rockies and "encamped at a place where the Sweet Water breaks through a
cañon, at the point where the emigrants leave that river to enter the South Pass,"

[57] The *California Star*, 27 February 1847, claimed this statement was "probably made without any personal knowledge of [Hastings's] intentions." See Morgan, *Overland in 1846*, 568, 750.

[58] Howard to Stearns, 21 April 1846, in Hawgood, *First and Last Consul*, 54.

[59] Sutter to Marsh, 3 April 1846, in Morgan, *Overland in 1846*, 42.

[60] Clyman, *James Clyman, Frontiersman*, 209, 211.

[61] Morgan, *Overland in 1846*, 42; and Korns and Morgan, *West from Fort Bridger*, 29–30.

[62] Ibid., 32–34, 42.

presumably below Rocky Ridge.[63] There he waited, recruiting overlanders bold enough to risk his untested trail. Hastings planned to meet "the emigration," but much evidence suggests he was waiting for Brigham Young and the Mormons, who were widely expected to trek to Alta California in 1846. The speculative estimates he made of how many Americans would come to California that year bore a suspicious resemblance to the number of Latter-day Saints projected to head west that season. When Clyman reached Saint Louis, he told a reporter, "Mr. Hastings had been looking for some force from the United States, with which he designed to revolutionize California, but in this he had been disappointed. He was then, it seemed, awaiting the action of the American Government, in taking possession of that country—of which he appeared to have some intimation."[64]

A Distrissing Bad Road: The 1846 California Emigration

"How are ye, boys?" was the way a half-dozen cursing, shouting, and "yellow-visaged" Missourians greeted Francis Parkman at the crossing of the Blue River. "Are ye for Oregon or California?"[65] The young Bostonian was headed no farther west than Fort Laramie, but as the first wagons left the frontier in April and May 1846, California had become the destination of the majority of those headed for the new lands, at least in the opinion of newspaper editors. By the middle of May, travelers learned of the War with Mexico, but the news caused little alarm. Instead, many westbound men appeared to be spoiling for a fight. One overlander wished that Congress would "authorize them to make the conquest of Mexico." As Oregon emigrant George L. Curry wrote, "Texas is ours—is it impossible that California can be?"[66]

As in previous years, the emigration began with enormous wagon trains that quickly broke into more manageable parties. The largest company elected Kentucky Colonel William H. Russell its leader by a large majority over former Governor Lilburn Boggs, perhaps because Russell got his supporters slightly inebriated. "My duties as commandant are troublesome beyond anything I could conceive of," Russell soon complained.[67]

The wagon trains fell into the familiar patterns of overland travel and its attendant births, marriages, and deaths. Near Fort Laramie emigrants began to meet parties returning to the states. Noted mountaineers such as James Clyman and Joseph R. Walker were on their way to Missouri, and they gave the California

---

[63] Thornton, *Oregon and California in 1848*, 2:95.

[64] Clyman, *James Clyman, Frontiersman*, 231.

[65] Parkman, *The California and Oregon Trail*, 72.

[66] Morgan, *Overland in 1846*, 528, 537, 546, 549.

[67] Ibid., 537–38, 541, 557.

companies mixed reports about the country but a very clear message: ignore any claim that Frémont's trail across the Salt Desert was a viable wagon road. Walker "spoke discouragingly of the new route via the south end of the Salt Lake," Edwin Bryant noted. This excellent advice failed to convince those sojourners (including Bryant) who were eager to find a shortcut. Many of the companies that stuck with the main trail met Caleb Greenwood, who had parted ways with Clyman and Hastings on the Humboldt. Greenwood went as far east as the Sweetwater, perhaps seeking his younger children, who apparently headed west that year. By late July, he was back at Fort Hall, again encouraging emigrants to follow him to California. But the breakup of large parties into small ones may have made it difficult to assemble a train big enough to pay a respectable fee for a guide.[68]

After following the Humboldt River until it disappeared into the sand, emigrants again persuaded "Old Truckee" to pilot them across the Forty-mile Desert. Joseph Aram's geographically confused recollection claimed Greenwood left his party at the Sink, but Truckee and his brother joined the train and proved "of much service to us." After Indians stole five oxen, Truckee said they were Shoshones and not his people, an unlikely tale.[69] In revenge, the emigrants burned the first Indian camp they came to.[70]

Continuing the trail's dynamic evolution, the emigrants pioneered two routes over the crest of the Sierra, "up the worst mountain that waggons ever crossed," as William E. Taylor wrote.[71] The new paths rounded the south side rather than the north shore of Truckee Lake and climbed Coldstream Valley to its head at Emigrant Canyon. Joseph Aram's company may have opened the first trail with the help of Chief Truckee. "We spent three days there exploring the mountains to find a pass where we might make a crossing. A party of us took our horses and went to the summit, traced it both ways and finally decided on the place to make the crossing," Aram recalled. "It was quite an undertaking to get our wagons up. We put about five yoke on a wagon, and had as many men with it as was necessary to keep it from sliding sideways. Then with five yoke on the summit letting down our long one hundred and fifty feet of rope, and hitched it with the leaders that were on the wagon, [and] by this process, we succeeded in getting all the wagons up safely."[72] At 7,812 feet above sea level, Coldsteam Pass lay between Mount Judah and Donner Peak, about a mile and a half south of what is now called Donner Pass.[73]

[68] Kelly and Morgan, *Old Greenwood*, 205.

[69] Aram, "Across the Continent in a Caravan," 16. As Dale Morgan noted, "the Aram account is full of misinformation, and no credence can be given to his particular statements." See Morgan, *Overland in 1846*, 385n36.

[70] Kelly and Morgan, *Old Greenwood*, 207, 209–210.

[71] Taylor, "Diary of William E. Taylor," 28 August 1846, in Morgan, *Overland in 1846*, 129.

[72] Aram, "Across the Continent in a Caravan," 16.

[73] Elevations are from Fey, King, and Lepisto, *Emigrant Shadows*, 98.

Several weeks later, another party opened a crossing that left Emigrant Canyon. Caleb Greenwood "advised us to follow the counsel of our fellow traveler, Mr. Judson Green, who had proposed to make a roller, and fasten chains to the wagons, and pull them over the mountain with the help of twelve yokes of oxen," Nicholas Carriger recalled. His wagons apparently crossed the 7,860-foot saddle between Mount Judah and Mount Lincoln about two miles south of Donner Pass. "I consider it needless to say that Mr. Green's plan worked admirably, and in a few days the whole of our party was safely placed on the top of the mountain," Carriger wrote in his memoir, but his diary called it "a distrissing bad road."[74] The new route became known as Roller Pass. Both summits were almost eight hundred feet higher than Donner Pass, but the approaches were so much easier that they became the preferred ways to surmount the imposing granite wall.

John Craig and Larkin Stanley brought the first two wagons of 1846 over the trail in record time—by Craig's calculation, they reached the California frontier on 13 September in four months and ten days.[75] But several hundred wagons were behind them, and many of them would never reach the valley of the Sacramento. Those that did faced a long, hard road: Daniel Rhoads told his in-laws he had "traveled hundreds of miles without seeing a stick of growing timber" over "exceeding good roads" until they reached the Truckee River: from that point the "last 300 miles is verry near all rocks. The nearer California the wors the road." It took his party three days to get over the summit: "The oxen could be trailed from bottom to the top by the blood." His family had to subsist on boiled corn and his oxen on "nothing but oak bushes" for the last three days of the trek.[76] For most, the toil paid off. "When we had our first view of the grand Sacramento Valley and saw the pastures covered with fat cattle and horses, we thought we had reached the promised land!!" recalled Mary Ann Harlan Smith.[77]

THE FEARFUL LONG DRIVE: HASTINGS CUTOFF

The January letter John C. Frémont wrote promoting his newly discovered shortcuts to Oregon and California appeared in *Niles' National Register* on 16 May. The young explorer made astonishing claims about his recent expedition to California and his plans for Oregon, which included his ambitious hope to open "a *good road*" into the south end of the Willamette Valley.[78] Jesse Applegate and Levi Scott were already proving the dubious nature of this particular speculation. In

---

[74] "Diary of Nicholas Carriger," 24 September 1846, in Morgan, *Overland in 1846*, 146, 158.

[75] Ibid., 135.

[76] Daniel Rhoads to "Dear Parents," 1847, Bancroft Library courtesy of Bernie L. Rhoades.

[77] Smith, History of George Harlan.

[78] Frémont to Jessie Frémont, 24 January 1846, in Morgan, *Overland in 1846*, 47–49.

St. Louis, when Thomas Fitzpatrick saw the *Washington Union*'s report about Frémont's "new and better route" to Oregon, the veteran frontiersman expressed his
skepticism: "This I think is a mistake."[79]

In late June or early July at the Last Crossing of the Sweetwater, the leading
trains met "a tall, fine-looking man, with light brown hair and beard, dressed in a
suit of elegant pattern made of buckskin, handsomely embroidered and trimmed
at the collar and openings, with plucked beaver fur." Lansford Hastings cut a
dashing figure, John R. McBride thought—"an ideal representative of the mountaineer."[80] Captain Frémont had discovered a cutoff much nearer and better than
the old road to Fort Hall, Hastings told travelers. He claimed "there was an abundant supply of wood, water, and grass upon the whole line of the road, except one
dry drive of thirty-five miles, or of forty at most: that they would have no difficult
cañons to pass, and that the road was generally smooth, level, and hard." Despite
the barren country he had seen with Clyman, Hastings seemed oblivious to the
risks of taking wagons over mountains, down canyons, and across deserts where
no wheel had ever rolled before.[81]

James Clyman had no illusions about the new route. In his old age, Clyman
recalled meeting his friend from the Black Hawk War, James Frazier Reed, who
asked about the shortcut. Clyman told him to "take the regular wagon track and
never leave it—it is barely possible to get through if you follow it—and it might
be impossible if you don't." Reed replied, "There is a nigher route, and it is of no
use to take so much of a roundabout course." Clyman admitted this was true,
"but told him about the great desert and the roughness of the Sierras, and that a
straight route might turn out to be impracticable."[82]

At South Pass Hastings persuaded the eastbound Wales Bonney to carry a letter to the rearguard of the emigration promoting the new cutoff and his plans.
No copy of the letter survives, but Charles Putnam read it and said if Hastings
intended "to aid in revolutionizing the country & get us to aid him in *immortalizing*
himself, he will find himself vastly mistaken."[83] Hastings's letter hinted that the
Mexican government would probably oppose the entry of American emigrants,
Edwin Bryant reported, "and invited those bound for California to concentrate
their numbers and strength" on his route.[84]

Hastings returned to Fort Bridger on 16 July, having persuaded some forty
wagons to try his cutoff. Another forty-odd wagons later followed his trail, but

---

[79] Fitzpatrick to Abert, 12 May 1846, Abert Family Papers, Missouri Historical Society.
[80] McBride, "Pioneer Days in the Mountains," 317.
[81] Thornton, *Oregon and California in 1848*, 2:96.
[82] Clyman, *James Clyman, Frontiersman*, 266.
[83] Charles to Joseph Putnam, 11 July 1846, in Morgan, *Overland in 1846*, 604.
[84] Bryant, *What I Saw in California*, 127.

not everyone believed the charming promoter's promises. "On arriving at Bridger's trading post on the Black fork of the Rio Colorado of the west—we found Lansford W. Hastings author of a work on California & Oregon, who had discovered a nearer route by some 300 miles, by way of the Salt Lake & great desert leaving the old route & Fort Hall to the North," Benjamin S. Lippincott wrote the next winter. "He succeeded in inducing ½ of the emigration to follow him, but his statements to me was so unsatisfactory, concerning the route that our company followed the old trail, knowing that was passable."[85] Tamsen Donner "was gloomy, sad, and dispirited in view of the fact that her husband and others could think of leaving the old road, and confide in the statement of a man of whom they knew nothing, but was probably some selfish adventurer."[86]

Four major groups gambled on Hastings's unproven shortcut. On 20 July Bryant's eight Kentuckians and three scouts left Fort Bridger on muleback, with James Hudspeth as their guide. A second company of about forty wagons and two hundred souls, often called the Harlan-Young party, left the fort with Hastings the same day. A third train of about twenty wagons, including Jacob D. Hoppe, diarist Heinrich Lienhard, and mapmaker T. H. Jefferson, followed six days later. "Although Mr. Hoppe was not always our captain," Lienhard wrote, "our party was known as Hoppe's Company."[87]

James Hudspeth returned in time to lead the first wagons into the Wasatch Mountains, while Hastings backtracked to try to shorten the road from Fort Bridger to Bear River, "riding up and down the line," as historian Charles Kelly commented. Hastings advised the first companies that on reaching the Weber River, they "should turn to the left which would bring them by a shorter route to the Salt Lake." He apparently failed to mention that this would involve blazing a wagon road over the mountains. As Hastings worked on improving the trail to Yellow Creek, Hudspeth led the Harlan-Young party directly down the Weber River. Its steep and constricted canyon, especially near its mouth at the narrows called Devils Gate, made it a hard route: at times the wagons had to travel in the riverbed, playing havoc with the hooves of the draft animals. But Heinrich Lienhard's company "made the passage of the dreaded places without any particular difficulty" in less than four days.[88]

Hastings, however, considered the route so difficult that he posted a note at the mouth of Echo Canyon directing the last wagons to go across the mountains and not down the river. As Charles Kelly observed, he "would have done better if he

[85] Lippincott to John L. Stephens, 6 February 1847, Bancroft Library.

[86] Thornton, *Oregon and California in 1848,* 19 July 1846, 142–43.

[87] "The Journal of Edwin Bryant," in Korns and Morgan, *West from Fort Bridger,* 77n49.

[88] Korns and Morgan, *West from Fort Bridger,* 140–43.

had stayed with the lead wagons and done some real guiding."[89] Hastings's failure to explore the trail adequately and make his intentions clear to Hudspeth left the task of building a thirty-five-mile road across the imposing Wasatch Mountains to the twenty-nine able-bodied men traveling with the last wagons following his alleged shortcut.[90]

The last train was so far behind the other companies that only a few of its members ever saw Lansford Hastings. When the Graves family caught up with them in the Wasatch Mountains in mid-August, the Donner-Reed party completed its roster of twenty-three wagons and eighty-seven people, including many women, children, and old men. They reached the mouth of Echo Canyon only a few days behind the companies that had gone down the river to find the note Hastings had left "on the road that if we Came after him he would return and Pilot us through his new and direct rout to the South end of the Salt Lake." Unable to fathom what the note meant, James Reed set out with two companions to find Hastings, finally catching up with him two days later at what is now Grantsville, Utah. They persuaded the reluctant trailblazer to return and show them his better route. Hastings went back as far as Big Mountain to lay out the line of the wagon road they would have to build across the Wasatch.[91] After more than two weeks hacking out a road through brush-choked canyons and up and down precipitous mountainsides, the exhausted company staggered into the Salt Lake Valley on 22 August, still faced with an even more horrendous ordeal: crossing the Salt Desert.

Despite his cutoff's problems and his failings as a guide, Hastings apparently led the first sixty or so wagons over it to the Humboldt without loss of life. It was a difficult trek, but the route's key problem was obvious. Heinrich Lienhard met a small company that had left Fort Bridger twelve or thirteen days after he did "and were now just as far advanced as we." The Hastings Cutoff, Lienhard caustically observed, "might be better called *Hastings Longtripp.*"[92] According to mapmaker T. H. Jefferson's calculations, the purported shortcut from Fort Bridger to the Humboldt River was 479¾ miles long, about ten miles longer than the much easier Fort Hall Road.[93]

Hastings Cutoff almost immediately earned a bad reputation. "Some few have passed by a new route to California called the Hastings cut-off by the south border of the Salt Lake," Brigham Young warned in August 1847. "It is not a safe

[89] Kelly to Morgan, 27 July 1951, Charles Kelly Collection, Utah State Historical Society.

[90] Korns and Morgan, *West from Fort Bridger,* 140, 200, 204.

[91] Ibid., 211–13. The name "Donner-Reed party" may be a more accurate name for the West's most famous wagon train, but this work uses the traditional name, Donner party.

[92] Ibid., 176.

[93] Ibid., 190. Based on tables in Shively's *The Road to Oregon and California* and Isham's *Guide to California and the Mines,* the distance from Fort Bridger to the mouth of South Fork Canyon on the California Trail via Fort Hall is about 470 miles.

Lovina Graves, about 1850. According to Lovina Graves
Cyrus's granddaughter, after her family joined the Donner
party, "all was trouble." Both parents and three of the family's nine children died, and those who survived were impoverished. Lovina married fellow Hastings Cutoff veteran John
Cyrus in 1855 and settled in Calistoga. The mother of six
children, Lovina died in 1906. Courtesy Kristin Johnson.

route on account of the long drive without water."[94] Travelers used the Salt Desert trail sporadically until 1850, but the route served none of them well.

Little is known about what happened to the advance elements of Hastings's followers. Hastings apparently intended to leave the emigrants as soon as he returned to the main trail, where he may have heard that events had overtaken his dream of leading a revolution in California. Perhaps he met the messenger Stephen Cooper encountered while traveling with a "demoralized lot, slowly creeping down the valley" of the Humboldt. Cooper suddenly spotted a lone rider "galloping up the valley, shouting, swearing, and praying, all in one breath," lashing his horse and cheering for Frémont, California, and America. When the rider reached him, Cooper got off his wagon and asked what was the matter. "He acted like a madman, shouting until I threatened to thrash him unless he spoke sense. Then he told me that Fremont had captured California."[95]

As the Donner party blazed a wagon road into Salt Lake Valley, Hastings left the leading wagons on the Humboldt and rushed on to California. He apparently gave little thought to the last train, still struggling on his shortcut.

ATROCIOUS AND INFAMOUS: THE CONQUEST OF CALIFORNIA

With his black servant, Benjamin Harrison, and Peter Lassen for a guide, Archibald Gillespie at last caught up with John C. Frémont on 9 May 1846 at a camp on Oregon's Upper Klamath Lake. The Marine lieutenant had left Washington in October 1845, bearing the Polk administration's official correspondence to American Consul Thomas Larkin at Monterey. He now delivered the same dispatches to Frémont, plus private letters from the explorer's wife, Jessie, and father-in-law, Senator Thomas H. Benton. The two men talked late into the night. Frémont failed to post a guard, and about midnight, Indians attacked the camp and killed three men.[96]

What Gillespie told Frémont that night remains a matter of debate, but it is not an impenetrable mystery. Larkin's orders directed him to act if foreign powers (meaning Britain or France) threatened to seize California, but they contained no specific orders for Frémont. Years later Benton claimed that the purpose of his "somewhat enigmatical" and now vanished letter to his son-in-law was "to save the administration from responsibility for what might happen." Polk denied in 1848 that he had given the young captain "the authority to make the revolution" that followed Gillespie's arrival, but Benton asserted the president had asked him to write the letter that inspired Frémont's subsequent actions in California. Frémont

---

[94] Bigler and Bagley, *Army of Israel,* 356.
[95] John Bidwell, memoir in Rogers, *Colusa County,* 359.
[96] Harlow, *California Conquered,* 78, 84.

and his supporters insisted Gillespie had delivered verbal orders from the president authorizing him to use violence against the Mexican government. The evidence, however, reveals that Frémont operated on his own initiative when he returned to California. Gillespie himself conceded Frémont told Commodore John Sloat he had "acted upon his own authority, and not from orders to the government."[97]

The several enterprises involved in James K. Polk's multifaceted plots to acquire California had an unfortunate tendency to collide with each other. As Benton observed about Polk and his ministers, "Never were men at the head of a government less imbued with military spirit, or more addicted to intrigue."[98] Despite his fondness for secrecy and scheming, Polk's diary and public statements reveal his belief that expanding the borders of the United States would extend the benefits of democracy and freedom, a conviction he shared with many overlanders. But as his secretary of state told Consul Larkin, the use of force "to extend our Federal system over more Territory" would be "repugnant both to the policy and the principles of this Government." Polk was determined, however, to defeat any attempt by a foreign power to seize California, and in appointing Larkin as a confidential agent, the administration directed that if California should assert its independence, "we shall render her all the kind offices in our power as a Sister Republic."[99]

California was awash with wild rumors, but in June Americans in northern California did not know that a state of war already existed. This detail did not prevent John C. Frémont from taking up arms against the Mexican government. To justify his actions, he claimed he was responding to official threats against American settlers, but, as John Bidwell pointed out, "this was simply a pretense to justify the premature beginning of the war."

On Frémont's return to California in late May, Americans flocked to his camp. "Some were settlers, some hunters; some were good men," Bidwell wrote, "and some about as rough specimens of humanity as it would be possible to find anywhere." A band of these "promiscuous people" left Frémont's camp to launch a ragtag revolt with the theft of a horse herd from Mexican officers near Sutters Fort. "Thus, without giving the least notice even to Sutter, the great friend of Americans, or to Americans in general, scattered and exposed as they were all over California," Bidwell observed, Frémont "precipitated the war."[100]

After the triumphant horse thieves drove their stolen mounts into his camp, Frémont sent his partisans to seize General Mariano Vallejo and his forces at Sonoma. The celebrated Bear Flag Revolt that transpired there early on the morning of 14

[97] Royce, *California,* 45; and Spence and Jackson, *The Expeditions of John Charles Frémont,* 2:xxix, xxxi, xxxii.

[98] Benton, *Thirty Years' View,* 2:680.

[99] Larkin, *The Larkin Papers,* 4:44–46.

[100] Bidwell, "Fremont in the Conquest of California," 519–22.

June 1846 would be, as historian Josiah Royce observed, "unspeakably ridiculous, as well as a little tragical, and for the country disastrous."[101] Some one hundred Americans, "well skilled in the use of the rifle," surprised Vallejo and accepted the surrender of the handful of troops at Sonoma. "Feeling confidence in their intrepidity and contempt for the Californians," wrote midshipman Alonzo Jackson, the men "hoisted a standard of their own, elected a president and declared themselves independent. Their flag was a Grizzly bear in a white field."[102]

The rebel president, William B. Ide, set about writing a windy proclamation. William Todd adorned "a piece of brown cotton, a yard and a half or so in length, with old red or brown paint that he happened to find, what he intended to be a representation of a grizzly bear." According to legend, Nancy Kelsey helped stitch the banner together. The crude image on the rebels' flag puzzled the local Californios, John Bidwell recalled. They wondered why the Americans had chosen a pig to decorate their banner.[103]

The Bear Flaggers sent Vallejo and their other prisoners to Frémont, who locked them up at Sutters Fort. Frémont's treatment of General Vallejo, who had always been a firm friend of the settlers, was more than insulting: it was tragic. The precipitous actions of the rebels upset the delicate negotiations of Thomas Larkin, who was quietly orchestrating a peaceful transfer of power in California. The American diplomat had persuaded the most influential men in the province, including Vallejo, to support a declaration of independence from Mexico. Governor Pío Pico had called for a meeting on 15 June in Santa Barbara that was "confidently expected to declare Alta California independent." Frémont's actions "came as a complete surprise to Larkin and upset all his plans, for Vallejo had been the most pro-American of the California leaders." Pico had already canceled the meeting, but the incident at Sonoma ended forever the chances the United States could acquire California through negotiations rather than through an act of war.[104] In a letter to Larkin at the end of June, Pico denounced the act as "the most atrocious and infamous that can be imagined, so much so, that the like is not seen even among barbarians." The "base management" that characterized the revolt "highly compromises the honour of the United States, and if it shall have such a stain upon itself, there is no doubt that it will be graven eternally in the remembrances of all nations, and will cause it to be despised."[105]

The American conquest proceeded apace. Commodore John D. Sloat received word at Mazatlán on 6 June 1846 that war had broken out on the Texas border

---

[101] Royce, *California*, 49.

[102] Jackson, "The Conquest of California," 55.

[103] Bidwell, "Fremont in the Conquest of California," 520.

[104] Hawgood, *First and Last Consul*, 51.

[105] Pico to Larkin, 29 June 1846, in Larkin, *The Larkin Papers*, 5:82.

and acted on his standing orders to occupy the ports of California. He anchored off Monterey on 2 July, and with Larkin's assistance planned the annexation and exchange of courtesies with the Mexican officials. On 7 July Sloat's men marched to the Custom House, raised the American flag, and declared California part of the United States. Two days later Commander John B. Montgomery of the U.S.S. *Portsmouth* seized San Francisco.[106]

As John Bidwell noted, except for two minor skirmishes, the conquest of California was achieved without a battle. "We simply marched all over California, from Sonoma to San Diego, and raised the American flag without opposition or protest," he recalled. "We tried to find an enemy, but could not." Commodore Robert F. Stockton arrived, replaced Sloat as the senior American military officer, and sent Kit Carson east with dispatches announcing the conquest. Stockton appointed Frémont governor, and the Americans left small garrisons at Los Angeles and Santa Barbara. The arrogance of the occupying forces insulted the local citizens, and in October 1846 they rose in revolt, driving Archibald Gillespie and his garrison from Los Angeles. Soon, John Bidwell recalled, "the whole country south of Monterey was in a state of revolt." Stockton's forces failed to recapture Los Angeles during the fall and "for the first time there was something like war."

General Stephen W. Kearny and a contingent of his Army of the West arrived in California in December, but at San Pasqual, Californio lancers badly mauled his small command. Meanwhile, in northern California, Frémont recruited the California Battalion "principally from the large Hastings immigration at Sacramento, and marched south" with "450 as hawkeyed riflemen as ever pulled triggers." The combined forces of Stockton and Kearny fought two skirmishes with Mexican forces near Los Angeles, and the defeated rebels signed the Treaty of Cahuenga on 13 January 1847, surrendering to the California Battalion. "The terms of surrender," Bidwell recalled, "were so lenient that the native Californians from that time forth became the fast friends of Frémont."[107]

I Demand Justice! The Return of Yellow Serpent

After the murder of his son, Elijah Hedding, at Sutters Fort early in 1845, Yellow Serpent "felt great rage and grief, and swore to extract vengeance." John McLoughlin refused to give him arms and ammunition and strongly advised him not to return to California. Elijah White apparently placated him for a time and diffused a potential campaign against Americans in Oregon, but Yellow Serpent

---

[106] Meyers, *Naval Sketches of the War in California,* introduction by Franklin D. Roosevelt.

[107] Bidwell, "Fremont in the Conquest of California," 524; and Lippincott to E. H. Williams, 22 March 1847, Bancroft Library.

was still bitter.[108] "The chief's feelings were excited against all Americans," Joel Palmer wrote. When Palmer camped on the Walla Walla River in late March 1846, he and his companions fortified their camp after hearing Yellow Serpent's people perform what sounded like a war dance, "giving most hideous yells." The old chief and a few of his principal men visited the next morning and appeared friendly, but he told Palmer he was determined to return to California.[109]

Amid the chaos of the American conquest, rumors swept northern California that thousands of Oregon's outraged Indians were preparing to invade. In September, California's first newspaper printed Indian Agent Elijah White's inflammatory April 1845 letter to the secretary of war reporting that the aggrieved Walla Wallas wanted to raise two thousand Cayuse, Spokan, Kalispel, Salish, Nez Perce, and Shoshone "warriors of these formidable tribes and march to California and then by plunder enrich themselves by the spoils."[110]

Early in September, Yellow Serpent and about forty warriors and their families appeared at the door of Mrs. William B. Ide's isolated adobe overlooking the Sacramento River near present-day Red Bluff: her husband, the former president of the Bear Flag Republic, was not at home. The Indians asked if she and her children belonged to Captain Sutter. "No," said Mrs. Ide's daughter Sarah, "we belong to our father." They asked about Sutter's fighting strength and looked closely at the firearms in the cabin. After consulting among themselves, they mounted their horses and rode off singing.[111]

Despite his later denials, Yellow Serpent probably intended to kill Grove Cook to avenge the murder of his son. His band's actions, however, were entirely peaceful. Whatever their plans, the Walla Wallas touched off panic when they arrived in California. By the middle of September, "All available forces have been moved up the Valley to support Fort Helvetia," *The Californian* reported, even though the Indians had committed no act of hostility. Commodore Stockton deployed men to deal with the threat, while General Mariano Vallejo immediately offered his services to respond to the rumors "that 2000 Wallawalla braves, had entered the country on a hostile visit." Within a few days, "Every man North of the Bay was ready for the march." By mid-October, however, the newspaper finally reported that the "bloody rumor about the Wallawalla Indians" had been very much exaggerated: the invading horde had "dwindled to forty, on a peaceful trading expedition!"[112]

---

[108] Heizer, "Walla Walla Indian Expeditions to the Sacramento Valley," 2.

[109] Palmer, *Journal of Travels,* 26 March 1846, 230–31.

[110] "The Wallawalla Indians," *Californian,* 19 September 1846, 1/2–4/1.

[111] Hussey and Ames, "California Preparations to Meet the Walla Walla Invasion," 9.

[112] "Wallawalla Invasion," 26 September 1846, 1/1; "Commodore Stockton's Reply," 24 October 1846, 4/2; "General Mariano G. Vallejo," 3 April 1847, 3/2, 143; and "The Disturbance," 10 October 1846, 2/1, all in *The Californian.*

Lieutenant Joseph Revere, usn—a grandson of Paul Revere—met with Yellow Serpent and his band and found their "disposition entirely pacific." The Walla Wallas wanted Grove Cook and compensation for the goods they had left with Sutter in 1845, but the presence of women and children made it apparent, as their leader pointed out, "we did not set out on a hostile expedition against your countrymen." Practically every Indian was sick with malaria, Revere reported. Yet Yellow Serpent made his case. "I have not traveled thus far only to mourn," he told Revere. "I demand justice! The blood of my slaughtered son calls for vengeance!" Not surprisingly, Yellow Serpent got neither justice nor revenge. Revere, however, authorized the enlistment of thirty of the band's warriors, and at least ten of them served with distinction in Frémont's California Battalion. They mustered out in 1847, and Frémont paid them in government horses.[113]

When they returned home, however, the Walla Wallas brought back more than California horses and cattle to Oregon: they brought measles.

This Tale of Horror: The Donner Party

Drought in California and a string of mild winters during the early 1840s gave Americans the impression that the Sierra's passes remained open until December, but when the rearguard of the California emigration reached Truckee Lake on 28 October 1846, it began to snow, as it usually did that time of year. (This was the same system that Jesse Applegate reported caught "the emigrants who travelled the Southern rout to Oregon" in "rains which were of unusual severity.")[114] Charles Stanton, William McCutchan, and James Reed had already carried word of the emigrants' plight to Sutters Fort. Sutter dispatched Stanton, two Indian vaqueros, and seven mules loaded with supplies. The relief reached the emigrants near present-day Reno, Nevada, where they were resting to prepare to cross the mountains.

Sutter concluded the stranded sojourners could survive the winter by butchering their livestock. Unfortunately, when storms struck the emigrants, some wanted to kill the oxen immediately, "but several men owning animals believed weather conditions might improve and did not favor this plan. They wanted to save pet animals they had brought from the States, and could not come to a mutual decision," Heinrich Lienhard wrote. "One night a heavy snow fell, and by morning the ground was a blanket of white; in the darkness the oxen, searching for food, broke away." The heavy snowfall covered their tracks and most of their carcasses disappeared until

---

[113] Hussey and Ames, "California Preparations to Meet the Walla Walla Invasion," 15–17; and Heizer, "Walla Walla Indian Expeditions to the Sacramento Valley," 3.

[114] Morgan, *Overland in 1846,* 767.

next spring.[115] "Instead of killing their cattle and saving their meat they remained and were soon left without food," Antonio B. Rabbeson remembered. "If they had had any body with them posted as to the country, or climate, or what they had to expect there, they would have killed their cattle at once."[116]

The party built cabins and killed their remaining cattle, "but there was not enough [food] in the company to last half of the winter, and no game," Sarah Fosdick recalled the next spring. "We were 150 miles from the settlements with snow thirty feet deep to cross."[117] By early November, blizzards had stranded sixty people in three cabins at Truckee Lake, and an additional twenty souls in three hastily constructed shelters at the Donner family camp about six miles east of the lake on Alder Creek.

"It is with feelings of deep sympathy I hasten to inform you of the Melan Choly fate of a portion of the late Emigration from the U. States, who, unable to reach the valley, had proposed wintering in the Mts," Lieutenant Edward Meyer Kern wrote from Sutters Fort in January 1847. Kern had learned that a few of these unlucky souls had straggled into Johnsons Ranch on Bear River "in a highly pitiable condition."[118]

Ten men, five women, and Sutter's Indian vaqueros "left what is called Reid's party of emigrants, who have been detained in the mountains by the snow, with intention of reaching this settlement." Two of the men turned back, John Sinclair wrote, but those who trudged on were "driven to this course by the certain death which awaited them in this mountains." Faced with starvation, they left Truckee Lake "with but a scanty supply of provisions & poorly clad."[119] Years later, Donner party chronicler C. F. McGlashan dubbed this desperate gamble the "Forlorn Hope." Four months after reaching safety, Sarah Fosdick recalled how they had made snowshoes and set out in the middle of December "with about eight pounds of dried meat, without knowing the road." They soon lost the heroic Charles Stanton, who had selflessly returned with Sutter's provisions.[120]

The exhausted refugees were obliged to throw away most of their blankets and soon ran entirely out of provisions. "On the eighth day of our travels we got lost but resolved to push on, for it was but death any way. The ninth day it commenced raining and we were obliged to lay by, for we could not keep our course," Fosdick recalled. "It rained that day and night and then snowed for three days and all of this time we were without fire or anything to eat. Father perished

---

[115] Lienhard, *A Pioneer at Sutter's Fort,* 168.

[116] Johnson, "An Overland Emigrant of 1846."

[117] Fosdick, "Going to California," *Davenport* [Iowa] *Gazette,* 10 February 1848, 1/5–6. Courtesy of Kristin Johnson.

[118] Kern to Hull, ca. 29 January 1847, Huntington Library.

[119] Sinclair to Bartlett, "Sufferings of the California Emigrants," 29 January 1847, reprinted in *Crossroads* 8, no. 4 (Fall 1997).

[120] Ibid.; and Fosdick, "Going to California," *Davenport Gazette,* 10 February 1848, 1/5–6.

in the beginning of this storm, of cold; four of our company died at that place." For three days and nights "they sat huddled together in the snow, their heads resting upon their knees, exposed to the pitiless storm! Great God! Who can imagine the sufferings of these helpless, houseless beings, at that time, without food and without fire?—no prospects before them but death, and that death the most horrible which can fall to the lot of man!" Sinclair wrote sympathetically. In desperation, Kern reported, the survivors "agreed to draw lots as to who should die to save the remainder—as several died from hunger and exhaustion this was unnecessary—And they lived on the dead bodies of their friends—drying the meat when one perished—and wandering a month in snow." Sinclair made the same evaluation: "Yes, stern necessity, and that love of life which even sufferings the most intense cannot vanquish, compelled them to devour their dead."[121]

Sarah Fosdick told this grim story quite simply: "As soon as the storm ceased we took the flesh of the bodies what we could make do us four days, and started. We travelled on six days without finding any relief. On the night of the 6th of January, my husband gave out and could not reach the camp;—I staid with him without fire; I had a blanket and wrapped him in it sat down beside him, and he died about midnight, as near as I could tell."[122]

That same day William Eddy killed an emaciated deer that fed his companions for four days. When the venison ran out, the survivors ate Sutter's vaqueros: the emigrants murdered the men while they slept.[123] "These lasted until we came to some wild Indians with whom we staid nine days, with nothing but acorns to eat," Fosdick recalled. "Seven out of fifteen got in to tell the sufferings of the camp."[124] Five of the seven were women. The survivors were barely able to walk by the time they reached Johnsons Ranch on 17 and 18 January 1847, Kern wrote. "Those who escaped arrived with hardly sufficient clothing to cover their nakedness, their clothes being nearly burnt from their backs by keeping as close to their fires, and most of them having their feet badly frozen," Sinclair added.

Kern's letter was distressing news for American commanders in northern California, since most of their forces were in Los Angeles suppressing the Mexican uprising. "There are yet 60 souls remaining behind the major part of which are women and children with sufficient provisions with economy to last until the middle of February," Kern reported. Any supplies would have to be packed in by men, since the snow was too deep for animals. With his usual generosity, John Sutter offered to do everything in his power to relieve their suffering. "He has

---

[121] Ibid.; Kern to Hull, ca. 29 January 1847, Huntington Library; and Sinclair to Bartlett, 29 January 1847. Since it is not generally known to trail scholars, Kern's letter is quoted in detail.

[122] Fosdick, "Going to California," *Davenport Gazette,* 10 February 1848, 1/5–6.

[123] Kern to Hull, ca. 29 January 1847, Huntington Library.

[124] Fosdick, "Going to California," *Davenport Gazette,* 10 February 1848, 1/5–6.

Nancy Graves was only eight years old when she crossed the plains with the Donner party in 1846. She married the Reverend Richard S. W. Williamson in 1855 and became the mother of nine children before her death in 1907. Courtesy Kristin Johnson.

already lost much by his unbounded hospitality—and in the present case will be minus several hundred dollars besides the loss of his servants whose melancholy fate he deeply regrets." Californians already knew that the last emigrants of 1846 were trapped in the mountains, but everyone assumed they had supplies. When the seven specters staggered out of the Sierra and brought word of the desperate situation at Truckee Lake, many felt that "had more caution been used by them they would have had plenty of provisions."[125]

The winter of 1846–47 assaulted the entire West Coast with pounding rain, the interior with intense cold, and the mountains with sustained blizzards. Peter Burnett considered it "the most extraordinary winters [sic] ever seen in Oregon, within the memory of man." Richard Grant feared the snow would stop him from crossing the Blue Mountains with the Snake Country returns. He finally left the furs with two men at Grande Ronde and crossed the mountains on snowshoes. Both Fort Hall and Fort Bridger "sustained an exceedingly heavy loss in stock and horses": Grant estimated the Shoshones lost at least six thousand head. Hard weather and slow business inclined Grant to think that "my opponents, Bridger & Vasquez, will have to give up this year."[126] Travelers stranded on the southern route to Oregon recalled "the shivering and frezing children."[127]

Americans at Sutters Fort immediately began organizing a rescue operation. John Sinclair hoped by early February "about fourteen men will be able to start, which will be nearly every able-bodied man in the vicinity."[128] In response to an appeal from James Reed, San Franciscans raised hundreds of dollars to finance relief efforts, but bad weather delayed any operations. McCutchan and Reed finally launched an expedition equipped by John Sutter. Through driving rain and increasingly deep snow, they battled their way to the ridge overlooking the Yuba River, only a dozen miles from the summit. Along the way they rescued a couple trapped in Bear Valley, where they had hoped to find their families. When the defeated rescuers returned to Sutters Fort, Captain Sutter assured them the company had enough resources to survive until rescue parties could cross the mountains.[129]

Reed "was determined, at all hazards, to return to his family, or perish in the attempt," wrote Selim Woodworth. With typical ineptness, the midshipman assumed command of the initial relief parties, which consisted "of hunters, trappers and mountaineers—all hardy, vigorous fellows, used to hardships of every description."[130] The Donner party rescue was an epic of horror and heroism,

---

[125] Kern to Hull, ca. 29 January 1847, Huntington Library; and Sinclair to Bartlett, 29 January 1847.

[126] Grant to Simpson, 1 April 1847, D.5/19, HBC Archives, 444–45.

[127] Crews, Recollection of 1846, Oregon Historical Society; and Morgan, *Overland in 1846*, 690.

[128] Sinclair to Bartlett, 29 January 1847.

[129] Stewart, *Ordeal by Hunger*, 76–82.

[130] Woodworth, "Letter from California," 6 February 1847, *The Home Journal*, 31 July 1847, 2–3.

but some of the emigrants were beyond saving and many of the rescuers almost
starved themselves. "Ten men started to their relief. A good many had starved
to death. Mother and the children were all alive, but there were too few men
to carry the little children, and mother and the little ones were all left," wrote
Sarah Fosdick. A second party under James Reed "started and found them all
alive; started with them and got about eight miles from the camps when there
came up a snow storm that lasted four days. All of this time they were out of
provisions, and being weak, could not go any farther; they were left, and before
relief reached them mother and Franklin died."[131] Almost half of the party had
died of starvation before a fourth expedition brought in the last of the survivors
in April 1847. The appalling details of their ordeal appeared in *The California Star*
and quickly spread to papers throughout the United States.

Who was to blame? Lansford Hastings had little to say about his part in the
Donner disaster, but he expressed his regrets at least once. Jacob Harlan recalled
meeting Hastings at San Jose. "I told him of our troubles, and of the Reed and
Donner calamities, which resulted from following his advice. Of course he could
say nothing but that he was very sorry, and that he had meant well," Harlan
remembered. Harlan faulted Reed for not going down Weber Canyon but wrote
that Hastings was not to blame for the debacle, since he had told Reed and Donner he did not know the route and had never been over it.[132] When the adventurer
found young George Donner selling papers in San Francisco, "Lawyer Hastings
(the Path Finder) gave him his clothes."[133]

Other veterans of the 1846 trek did not hesitate to place blame for the disasters
that haunted the trail that season. "It can be shown that there has been a greater
loss of life and property, in one year, resulting from abandoning the regular
route, than has ever been sustained at the hands of all the savage tribes between
the borders of the western states and the Pacific coast," wrote J. Quinn Thornton. He estimated that half of the 1846 Oregon emigration lost their property
after placing confidence in a man who beguiled them into leaving the old road to
try his short cut. The "miserable and unfortunate survivors" of the Donner party
lost much more due to their trust in a similar character, Thornton observed.
"These companies would have arrived, each at its place of destination, safely and
in season, had they pursued the regular route."[134]

Survivor Virginia Reed came to her own conclusions. "Never take no cutofs,"
she warned her cousin, "and hury along as fast as you can."[135]

[131] Fosdick, "Going to California," *Davenport Gazette*, 10 February 1848, 1/5–6.

[132] Harlan, *California '46 to '88*, in Johnson, *"Unfortunate Emigrants,"* 261.

[133] Brown, *Reminiscences and Incidents of Early Days of San Francisco*, 62–64.

[134] Thornton, *Oregon and California in 1848*, vol. 2.

[135] Korns and Morgan, *West from Fort Bridger*, 238.

A Vast Country Which Was Almost Entirely Unknown:
Frémont's Legacy

Having captured California, the conquerors set about fighting among themselves. Both John C. Frémont and Stephen W. Kearny claimed to be governor of the province, but Captain Frémont declined to obey General Kearny's orders. Under virtual arrest for his conduct, Frémont returned to the states in 1847 with Kearny. When they arrived at Fort Leavenworth, Kearny charged Frémont with mutiny and insubordination. His court-martial began in early November, lasted for three months, and ultimately convicted him of mutiny, disobeying a lawful command, and conduct prejudicial to good order. The sentence dismissed Frémont from the army, but acting upon the court's recommendation, President Polk pardoned the young celebrity.

Convinced he had suffered a great injustice, Frémont resigned his commission. He wrote the brief *Geographical Memoir,* describing the Great Basin and celebrating California's position "on the line of an American road to Asia."[136] He never submitted a formal scientific report documenting his third expedition. The Pathfinder led two private surveys in 1848 and 1853 seeking a central route for a transcontinental railroad: both ventures ended in disaster. He served briefly as one of California's first senators, and the gold deposits on his vast estate in the Sierra foothills made him rich, but his local reputation dogged him. "The Col. is not very popular in California," wrote Robert J. Boylan. "The miners dug out all the placers in the immediate vicinity of his ranch and only laughed at him and his agents [when they] wished to lease the privilege of mining."[137]

In 1856 Frémont was the Republican Party's first presidential candidate: H. H. Bancroft thought his campaign biographer ruined his reputation among California's pioneers, and Frémont's Civil War service was disastrous. His postwar speculations in mines, land, and railroads were no more successful than his military career, and after losing his fortune, he served as a controversial governor of Arizona Territory. Suffering from a debilitated memory, he wrote a memoir with the help of his wife, Jessie, seeking to establish his place in western history. But in 1890 Frémont died in New York, alone and in virtual poverty.

Frémont's legacy was as controversial as his legendary life, which became a symbol of Manifest Destiny. Peter Burnett called him "the cool, determined, yet prudent Fremont," but his political acts in Oregon and California are now widely regarded as disastrous. Many of Frémont's colleagues and fellow army officers believed his ambitions outstripped his talents, especially in science—his astronomical readings exhibit such wild variations that it appears he never mastered

---

[136] Spence and Jackson, *The Expeditions of John Charles Frémont,* 3:546.
[137] Boylan, *Gold Rush Letters,* 18 May 1852, California State Library.

the use of a sextant, and army maps faithfully repeated his misplacement of Lake Tahoe entirely in present-day Nevada for more than a decade. "That fellow knows nothing about mineralogy or botany," charged his cartographer, Charles Preuss, who devoted much ink in his irascible diaries to complaints about his boss's many failures.[138]

Others were more favorable in their assessment of the colorful young luminary, including Peter Burnett, who traveled with the explorer for about ten days in Oregon in 1843. "He was then about thirty years old, modest in appearance, and calm and gentle in manner," Burnett recalled. "His men all loved him intensely. He gave his orders with great mildness and simplicity, but they had to be obeyed. There was no shrinking from duty. He was like a father to those under his command." Frémont was small and slender, but he could endure hardships that killed hardened frontiersmen. "I never traveled with a more pleasant companion," Burnett concluded.[139] Frémont inspired intense devotion among his men, including such old veterans as Kit Carson, and he narrated his reports "with modesty and full credit to those who preceded and accompanied him." As Bancroft acknowledged, "As a pioneer of scientific exploration in the far west, he deserves only praise."[140]

Ironically, despite his reputation as a trailblazer, Frémont felt his status prevented him from mingling with the emigrants. Many of them were not impressed when they met him and carried their low opinion of the man to their graves. He hired Joseph Chiles to hunt for him in 1843, and when Frémont took the best parts of a deer Chiles had killed and left the emigrants only the forequarters, Chiles was disgusted with his arrogance and quit.[141] "Frémont has not been a popular man among the pioneers and mountaineers of California," wrote Bancroft, who denounced him "as a vain, incompetent, and pretentious charlatan." The historian's directness outraged many readers, who failed to appreciate his praise of the explorer's talent that made his reports "at once fascinating, terse, and strong." Frémont acknowledged "over and over again that the trappers and immigrants had everywhere preceded him." Most historians today share Bancroft's disdain for this "adventurer of marvelous good fortune"—and the bitter feelings Frémont provoked with his needlessly violent conquest of California had catastrophic and enduring consequences.[142]

However problematic his character or irresponsible his actions, Frémont's contributions to the American West endure. His maps made the secrets of the moun-

[138] Preuss, *Exploring with Frémont*, 5 August 1842, 35.
[139] Burnett, *Recollections and Opinions of an Old Pioneer*, 135.
[140] Bancroft, *History of California*, 3:747.
[141] Stewart, *The California Trail*, 41.
[142] Bancroft, *History of California*, 3:747, 749; and 4:440–43.

taineers into common knowledge. For five years he was a dynamo of energy: his tenacity won the respect and devotion of leading frontiersmen, and his colorful prose still animates a vanished time and place. No one did more to encourage overland emigration and the settlement of the West, and while he had little to do with the creation of the Oregon and California trails, John C. Frémont made them a success.

Frémont's legacy as a boyish national hero long outlived his tarnished exploits as an adult. "You have displayed a noble courage in distant expeditions," the most renowned scientist of his age said in 1850, as he presented California's young senator with a gold medal from the King of Prussia. Frémont had "braved all the dangers of cold and famine, enriched all the branches of the natural sciences," Alexander von Humboldt said, and he "illustrated a vast country which was almost entirely unknown."[143]

---

[143] Spence and Jackson, *The Expeditions of John Charles Frémont,* 3:206.

CHAPTER 9

A WILD LOOKING SET

Society on the Trails

W hen they crossed the Missouri and the threshold of Indian Country, most overland travelers believed they were about "to enter the wilderness, where nothing living could be found but wild animals and Indians."[1] In truth, they came into a region humans had occupied for more than ten thousand years. It was home to a large Native population and, since Spanish soldiers and French traders arrived in the seventeenth century, a host of strangers had come to visit and sometimes stay in the plains and Rockies. Their arrival and the diseases and technology they brought with them ignited generations of cultural turmoil and, long before the first wagons headed west, began a radical transformation of the lives of the first Americans.

Ancient North America was a cauldron filled with a stew of different cultures, peoples, and languages. The tribes of Kansas and Oregon were as different from one another as the citizens of France were from the subjects of Russia. The arrival of Europeans, Polynesians, and, by early 1848, "two or three of the 'Celestials'"—Chinese—further diversified a region that was already home to dozens of Native cultures.[2] The revolution European horses, weapons, and diseases launched in North America intensified during the 1840s as Indian peoples along the emigrant trails experienced an era of crisis and transmutation.

Every wagon train that headed west during the 1840s formed a miniature society. The citizens of these rolling villages reflected the convictions and passions of Americans of their time, with a fervent belief in democracy and individual responsibility. Ralph Geer thought the ninety-nine wagons and four hundred–odd souls ranging in age from six days to sixty years he joined to go west in 1847 was the finest camp of pioneers he ever saw, and it boasted members of nearly every profession, trade, and occupation. "We had preachers with their bibles and

[1] Stabæk, "An Account of a Journey to California," 104.
[2] "China," *The California Star,* 1 April 1848, 2/3.

psalm books, doctors with their medicine chests, lawyers with their law books, school teachers, anxious to teach the young." Geer's town-on-the-march included "merchants with their goods, nurserymen with their trees and seeds, stockmen with their fine horses and cattle, millers, millmen, millwrights, wheelwrights, carpenters, cabinet makers with their chest[s] of tools, blacksmiths with anvils, bellows, hammers and tongs ready and willing to do all kinds of repairing at any time and place, gunsmiths and silversmiths with their fine tools." His list concluded with "shoemakers with the lasts, awls, hammers and bristles, saddlers with their tools, dressmakers and milliners with their needles, thimbles and patterns, a lumberman with his heavy log wagon, and last, though not least, farmers with and without families."[3]

Most overland trains formed from some sort of association of kinship or community: the closer one examines any overland company, the more complicated the bonds of blood and marriage, and sometimes one finds friends and families who had migrated west together. The trials of crossing the plains in what Heinrich Lienhard called a wagon village could destroy old friendships, but often the experience created enduring bonds. "You don't know who your friends is unless you come acrost the plains once and then you will find out," Lydia B. Atkinson wrote.[4]

One aspect of this shared ordeal helped ensure the success of subsequent migrations: people who had made the journey empathized with those who followed. Early overland accounts are replete with descriptions of the substantial aid generously sent from the raw settlements in Oregon and California to exhausted and starving trains caught in the deserts or mountains at the end of the trail. When disaster struck, frontier communities would immediately rally to send wagon loads of supplies to emigrants who had been pushed beyond the limits of human endurance.

They Sung For Us: Mexicans and Spaniards

Hispanics were a pervasive presence on the frontier throughout the trails era: early overland narratives are filled with references to Spaniards and Mexican-Americans. Trade along the Santa Fe Trail ran both ways, and caravans from New Mexico brought a host of experienced Spanish-speaking frontiersmen to the jumping-off points in Missouri, while others drifted northward from the Mexican frontier along the Trappers Trail that connected Taos and Fort Laramie.[5] Latinos made an enormous contribution to the fur trade. For example, they provided

---

[3] Geer, "Occasional Address for the Year 1847," 33–34.
[4] Atkinson to Anna Knox, 15 October 1852, NFTC Manuscripts, Mattes Library.
[5] Whiteley, "The Trappers Trail," 2–5.

most, if not all, of the skilled labor that built the West's adobe trading posts, including Fort John and Fort Platte. The walls of Fort Laramie were "built of clay, after the fashion of the Mexicans, who are generally employed in building them," John C. Frémont reported in 1842.[6]

Having been an important presence in the West since Spanish colonists founded New Mexico in 1598, Hispanics possessed expertise that proved invaluable in the fur trade and later on the trail. Zenas Leonard celebrated the Fourth of July in 1834 with Joseph Walker's California expedition, "drinking toasts, singing songs, shooting at mark, running, jumping, and practising on our horses." His fellow trappers picked up primitive rodeo skills from two deserters from the Mexican Army, "who learned us many singular pranks, and were a valuable addition to our company, as they created a great deal of fun, and were always in a good humor."[7]

Hispanics were famous for their horsemanship. "The mules are herded in the plains by Mexicans each of whom have a fleet horse saddled & bridled," wrote Pardon D. Tiffany in a detailed account of these vaqueros and how they lassoed and broke mules. "It was great sport to see them catch & harness wild mules. They treat them cruelly, but it appears to be the only way such untamable & obstinate animals can be subdued. They coil up one end of the rope in the left hand then open the noose at the other end of the rope & swing the noose around their own heads to give it velocity. They mark their animal let go of the noose & it flies over the head of the mule. Then sometimes 5 or a dozen men seize the rope which draws tight around the animals neck & chokes him. They then put on the harness. Some will stand quietly."[8]

Mexican frontiersmen were especially in demand during the gold rush. A large company of traders from Santa Fe rode by William Johnston's camp at Independence in April 1849. Their wagons were drawn by as many as ten mules, and it is doubtful that any of the Americans who went west in the early 1840s had the benefit of such competent wagon masters.[9] Several Independence businessmen had guided small parties to California for several years, Samuel Mathews heard. "One of them is a Mexican, who lassos mules handsomely," he wrote.[10] Near South Pass in June, Peter Decker "met a Mexican family from St. Louis, formerly from San Antonio, with an old poor grey horse packed for California, all alone, very dark skinned," who had left the train with which they had been traveling.[11] William Watson called the fourteen hundred residents of Oregon City "a mixed multi-

---

[6] Spence and Jackson, *The Expeditions of John Charles Frémont,* 15 July 1842, 1:218.

[7] Leonard, *Narrative of the Adventures of Zenas Leonard,* 217.

[8] Tiffany, Diary and Letters, 10 May 1849, Mattes Library, 13–14.

[9] Johnston, *Experiences of a Forty-niner,* 45.

[10] Mathews to "Dear Huldah," 30 April 1849, in *The Mathews Family in America,* 295.

[11] Decker, *The Diaries,* 15 June 1849, 97.

tude; Sandwich Islanders, Indians of several tribes, Mexicans and Spaniards."[12] Watson's reference to Mexicans and Spaniards suggests he met Hispanics who included emigrants from Central and South America—but anyone who spoke Spanish tended to be identified as Spanish, and until the California gold rush brought a substantial number of prospectors from Peru and Chile, most people so identified were probably Mexican, with a large proportion of them being New Mexicans and Californios.

Many trail references to Hispanics were subtly or overtly racist. At the Upper Platte Bridge in 1853, "There was a great many Spainards there, and all of them had squaw wives," Agnes Stewart wrote.[13] When Thaddeus S. Kenderdine came upon a camp of Mexicans on the wagon road to Los Angeles in central Utah in 1858, he thought "they looked like a pack of land-pirates, with their knives, broad hats, and heads stuck through the centres of their blankets."[14] Expressing the prejudice common to the times, Forty-niner Charles Boyle described meeting "one or two Mexican greasers, yellow and ugly," at Independence. Yet when he overtook a lone Mexican in the Wind River Mountains (perhaps the man whose family Peter Decker also met), the man's courage seemed to impress him, since "he had started with the Telegraph train but had left them on account of bad usage."[15] Not all such encounters were hostile: on the Blue River in 1860 John Melvin Graham visited a Mexican train bound from New Mexico to Kansas City, and "they sung for us."[16]

Those Interesting Islanders: Kanakas

"Here are half breeds, and Indians, and French, and Wyhees, all together," Joseph Williams wrote as he passed American Falls in 1841.[17] These "Wyhees" were Hawaiians, some of the most surprising early residents of the American Far West. Occasionally referred to as Blue Men (allegedly because their skin took on a bluish hue during the winter), they were almost universally known as Kanakas, a term apparently derived from *kanaka maoli,* Hawaiian for "true human being." Hawaiians visited England with Captain Cook and had been involved in western exploration and commerce since 1788. John Jacob Astor's Pacific Fur Company employed more than thirty-two "Owhyhees" to work on Fort Astoria after the *Tonquin,* the company's supply ship, stopped in the islands in 1811, while at least twenty Hawaiians participated in the Astorians' expedition to the Spokane River

[12] Watson, *Journal of an Overland Journey to Oregon,* 13 September 1849, 48.
[13] Stewart, Diary, 1853, Oregon Historical Society, 8.
[14] Kenderdine, *A California Tramp,* 132.
[15] Boyle, Diary, 15 April and 15 June 1849.
[16] Graham, Diary, 1 May 1860, Mattes Library.
[17] Williams, *Narrative of a Tour,* 21 August 1841, 33.

in 1812.[18] Of the Hudson's Bay Company's four hundred employees in the Oregon County in 1846, 152 were "Sandwich Islanders."[19]

On his way to Fort Vancouver in 1832, John Ball met "two strange looking men, [and] saw at once they could be neither Caucasian, Indian or African. And so it proved, they were Kanakas." Often identified as Sandwich Islanders, the name given the islands by Cook, the Hudson's Bay Company brought them to the Columbia River as low-paid workers.[20] The Owyhee River in Oregon and Kanaka Rapids on the Snake River were named after three Hawaiians killed nearby while working for the Company. James Keith's Fort George memorandum book dates the event to 1820 and reports that one Owhyhee "in the Snake Country was destroyed by the Natives" in 1819.[21]

Twenty Hawaiians came to Oregon in 1834 with Nathaniel Wyeth's supply ship. Wyeth sent Joseph Thing, twelve Sandwich Islanders, and six whites to reinforce Fort Hall, while he followed with a party that included four more Hawaiians. The Polynesians deserted Thing, and in March Wyeth seized seven of them on the Columbia. Of the rest, two were killed by Indians, one drowned, one froze to death, and two were unaccounted for, Wyeth wrote.[22] Hawaiian men and women helped John Sutter found New Helvetia in 1839, and Heinrich Lienhard recalled that for some time "these Kanakas were his only companions."[23] Both Marcus Whitman and John McLoughlin employed them in large numbers. Of the twenty-five paid servants at Fort Hall in 1846, at least ten had Hawaiian surnames.[24] "Here we bought two ponies of some Sandwich Islanders, who could talk English tolerable plain: they were stout made, having long, black, curly hair," wrote William J. Watson at Fort Boise in 1849. "I sold them a pair of cotton pants and a vest for ten dollars."[25]

When the measles epidemic of 1847 struck Fort Vancouver, clerk Thomas Lowe recorded the deaths of five "Kanaccas" in December. "Old Cox, a Sandwich Islander who has been a long time in this Country in the Company's employ died here yesterday afternoon," Lowe wrote on 1 February 1850. "He was in England and Canada, and was about 12 years old when Captain Cook was killed at Owhyhee."[26] John Coxe had come to Oregon in 1811 with the Astorians, and

---

[18] Ross, *Adventures of the First Settlers on the Oregon or Columbia River,* 251; and Hafen, *The Mountain Men,* 7:76, 84, 284. For more on Hawaiians in the early West, see Koppel, *Kanaka;* and Duncan, *Minority without a Champion.*

[19] Swagerty, "'The Leviathan of the North."

[20] "Fort Vancouver, 1832," Ball, *Autobiography,* 90.

[21] See Lloyd Keith to H-Net Western History List, 21 April 2005. Alexander Ross corroborates the 1820 date in *The Fur Hunters of the Far West.*

[22] Hafen, *The Mountain Men,* 1:199, 200; Wyeth, *The Journals of Captain Nathaniel J. Wyeth's Expedition to the Oregon Country,* 83–84, 127.

[23] Lienhard, *A Pioneer at Sutter's Fort,* 76.

[24] Statement of Servants, Snake Country Outfit 1846, Columbia District, HBC Archives.

[25] Watson, *Journal of an Overland Journey to Oregon,* 9 August 1849, 36.

[26] Lowe, Private Journal, British Columbia Archives and Records Service, 62, 73.

he transferred to the North West Company when it bought out Fort Astoria in 1812. The company sent him overland to Canada and then to England, and he sailed for Oregon aboard H.M.S. *Raccoon* in 1813. He returned to Hawaii in 1814 but ultimately settled in the Northwest and spent his old age as a swineherd at Fort Vancouver.[27]

Herbert Beaver, the Anglican chaplain at Fort Vancouver from 1836 to 1838, denounced the Hudson's Bay Company's treatment of Indians in an 1842 letter to the Committee of the Aborigines' Protection Society. The company also had Sandwich Islanders "scattered all over the continent, from twelve to twenty being imported about every other year from their native country," he reported. Their condition, Beaver wrote, was "little better than that of slavery, being subject to all the imperious treatment which their employers may think fit to lay on them, whether by flogging, imprisonment, or otherwise, without a possibility of obtaining redress." The Hawaiians were paid more than other HBC employees, but they were charged much higher prices for clothing and supplies than their white colleagues and lived in perpetual debt to the company. They were prevented from being "cognizant of the deception and imposition thus shamelessly practised upon them." Few of "those interesting islanders" ever returned home.[28]

VIRULENT PREJUDICE AGAINST HIS RACE: BLACKS ON THE TRAIL

In the early days, Sarah Winnemucca recalled, wagon trains caused great excitement among the Paiutes, and one winter her people "talked of nothing but their white brothers." News arrived the next year that the emigrants were on their way "and had something among them that was all in a blaze." The scouts said it looked like a man—it had legs, hands, and a head, but the head had quit burning and was quite black. "There was the greatest excitement among my people everywhere about the men in a blazing fire," Winnemucca remembered, but these supernatural beings turned out to be "two negroes wearing red shirts."[29]

Although their contributions have long been ignored, African Americans participated in overland exploration and emigration from its earliest days. William Clark's slave York traveled to Oregon with the Corps of Discovery, becoming one of the first Americans to cross the North American continent. "A black man" named Hinds accompanied the Whitmans to Oregon from the 1836 rendezvous: he and "Owyhees" provided some of the labor to build their mission.[30] Blacks

---

[27] Clark, "Hawaiians in Early Oregon," 22–27.

[28] Pipes, "Indian Conditions in 1836–38," 339–41. Beaver, "Indian Conditions in 1836–38," 333–38, describes the chaplain's work at Fort Vancouver.

[29] Hopkins, *Life among the Piutes,* 3.

[30] Drury, *First White Women over the Rockies,* 1:110, 121.

served in Frémont's expeditions as servants and cooks. A negro accompanied
Joseph Chiles when he came to ask for permission to build a sawmill, Mariano G.
Vallejo recalled, and the same man returned with Chiles in 1843.[31] The Stephens-
Murphy-Townsend party included at least one black, Francis Deland.[32] In the
Cascades in 1843 a black servant of the Burnett family "went out into the canoe
to dip up some water, and the canoe sheered from under her and she fell in and
disappeared," Nineveh Ford remembered. "She was never seen again."[33]

Just outside Independence, Edwin Bryant's wagon stalled in mud, and he was
unable to budge it until "fortunately a negro man with a well-trained yoke of oxen
came down the road . . . and hitching his team to ours the wagon was immediately
drawn out of the mud."[34] Francis Parkman met a runaway slave who had gone to
work for a French trader. He had been reduced to "a wretched negro" after getting lost: he survived for thirty-three days on crickets, lizards, wild onions, and
three prairie dove eggs. He had not seen a human being for the entire time, and
"no one dreamed that he could still be living."[35]

Many of the free blacks along the trail were men of substantial accomplishments.
Wagonwright Hiram Young purchased his freedom in 1847 and was building wagons
at Independence by 1850. "People who had to deal with Hiram Young, a tall, dark
skin colored man, found him to be a good businessman. He had a large plant and
gave employment to all white and black," recalled James Thomas, a fellow freeman.
"Wagons of his make could be seen on the plains from Kansas City to San Francisco."
Young's quality craftsmanship made him one of the town's wealthiest entrepreneurs.
By 1860 he employed twenty-five men at his wagon and yoke factory with an annual
production of about three hundred wagons and six thousand yokes.[36]

The frontier was a violent place, and blacks experienced more than their share
of brutality. Rumor said that a Mr. Hoppe (probably Jacob D. Hoppe) had a special reason for not camping with the rest of the party. "It was noised about that
he had killed a Negro slave in Missouri and had hurriedly crossed the state border
in order to escape possible punishment," Heinrich Lienhard wrote.[37] While living at a hunting camp in northern California in 1842, Nancy Kelsey watched as
"Salvador Vallejo and his men chased a runaway Negro nearly into our camp and
shot him four times and then ran their swords through him. They said they ran
their swords through his body to bring them good luck."[38]

---

[31] Bancroft, *History of California*, 4:394n30.
[32] Kelly and Morgan, *Old Greenwood*, 124–26.
[33] Ford, The Pioneer Road Makers, Bancroft Library, 21.
[34] Bryant, *What I Saw in California*, 5 May 1846, 20.
[35] Parkman, *The California and Oregon Trail*, 184–85.
[36] Gardner, *Wagons for the Santa Fe Trade*, 34–35.
[37] Lienhard, *From St. Louis to Sutter's Fort*, 14.
[38] Kelsey, Nancy Kelsey's Own Story, NFTC Manuscripts, Mattes Library, 6.

One of the most remarkable Americans who ever came west was George Bush, who had worked for the Hudson's Bay Company, later grew rich farming in Missouri, and returned to the Northwest in 1844. "George Bush doubtless left Missouri because of the virulent prejudice against his race in the community where he lived," his friend Ezra Meeker recalled. Meeker claimed Bush carried one hundred pounds of silver to Oregon, but on arriving found "the very first effort in establishing an American government in Oregon outlawed the negro or whoever had negro blood in his veins." The provisional government of Oregon passed several Exclusion Laws that made slavery illegal and required free blacks to leave the territory. Bush moved north of the Columbia, where Meeker met him in 1853. The massive emigration of 1852 created near-famine prices for food, Meeker recalled. "And yet this man divided out nearly his whole crop to new settlers who come with or without money—'pay me in kind next year,' he would say to those in need, and to those who had money, he would say 'don't take too much—just enough to do you.'" Bush gave Meeker milk for his child and "divided his large crop and became a benefactor to the whole community."

"George Bush was an outlaw but not a criminal; he was a true American and yet was without a country; he owned allegiance to the flag and yet the flag would not own him," Meeker wrote years later, paying tribute to his old friend and benefactor in one of the most eloquent nineteenth-century denunciations of racism. "He was firmly held to obey the law and yet the law would not protect him; he could not hold landed property; his oaths would not be taken in the courts of law—in a word, an outlaw and yet not a criminal," all because "he had some Negro blood in his veins."[39]

Defying Wind, Rain, and Indians:
Fort Laramie, Fort Bridger, and Trade on the Early Trails

Opportunities to restock and make repairs on the trail in 1841 were not merely limited: they were practically nonexistent. Until the founding of Fort Kearny in 1848, there were no military posts west of Fort Leavenworth and only a handful of trading stations. These included Fort John on the Laramie River (and nearby Fort Platte, at least until 1845), Fort Bridger near the Uinta Mountains, the Hudson's Bay Company's Forts Hall and Boise on the Snake River and Fort Walla Walla on the Columbia. As the only posts along the trail that survived the demise of the fur trade, they remained resolutely committed to their primary function,

---

[39] Meeker, A Biographical Sketch of George Bush, Allen Library, 2–4, 14–15, 29, 32. Oregon's provisional legislature in 1849 passed "an act, to prevent Negroes and Mulattos from coming to, or residing in Oregon," Meeker recalled, but it "became a dead letter and was never enforced."

the Indian trade. They bartered furs and buffalo robes for powder and lead, tools, weapons, trinkets, and frontier luxuries such as coffee and sugar with Natives and free trappers but maintained only an erratic supply of staples and so failed to exploit the new market wagon trains offered. The posts generally provided black-smithing services and sometimes had a few animals to trade, but they seldom had provisions available—and when they did, such goods could only be had at exorbitant prices. Even the most famous trading stations were often disappointing and always outrageously expensive. "Prices are most extortionate," Francis Parkman wrote at Fort Laramie, noting that 5-cent tobacco cost $1.50 and sugar sold for $2.00 per cup. The American Fur Company was "exceedingly disliked in this country—it suppresses all opposition, and keep[s] up these enormous prices."[40]

Since independent operators were hard pressed, emigrants had no reliable resupply point between the Missouri River and the Pacific until the Mormons settled in the Great Basin. Ironically, Indians proved to be a better source of provisions than trading posts. Benjamin S. Lippincott met a band of Shoshones "returning from the Buffalo country loaded with meat, for which we traded & gave in return beads, knives, etc."[41] The Snake River's Salmon Falls became an important food source for travelers: Ralph Geer recalled, "we laid in such a supply of salmon that we had to throw away two-thirds of it before we traveled far."[42] A great many of Clarborne Walker's companions ran out of provisions before reaching The Dalles in 1845, but "on arriving at the Umittila River they obtained potatoes and peas of the Indians, having to pay high prices in clothes," he reported.[43] The Indians on the Columbia in 1845 "appeared quite friendly and would bring quantities of fish and fowls to trade," Samuel Hancock found.[44] The tribes, however, were as unreliable a source of food as the trading posts. "The Indians were great traders, but their stock in trade was usually something made of buckskin and beads," Georgia Hughes recalled. "Sometimes they had salmon, both dried and fresh, and sometimes huckleberries which they exchanged for whatever we had, usually clothing or bread. Money they did not want. They did not even know what it was."[45]

Founding Fort Laramie, the most famous frontier outpost in American history, was no easy task. "You have never built a fort? Then pray Heaven you never may; for of all the trouble and annoyance I have ever experienced, that gives the most," fur trader Robert Campbell wrote to his brother from the post he dubbed

---

[40] Parkman, *The Journals of Francis Parkman,* 2:440.

[41] Lippincott to John L. Stephens, 6 February 1847, Bancroft Library.

[42] Geer, "Occasional Address for the Year 1847," 36.

[43] Walker to "Dear Brother, Sister and Friends," 1845, Purvine Family Records. The Cayuses "trade in shirts altogether," Walker wrote.

[44] Hancock, *The Narrative of Samuel Hancock,* 37.

[45] Hughes, Recollections, Oregon Historical Society, 3.

Fort William at the mouth of the Yellowstone River in 1833.[46] Six months later, Campbell's partner, William Sublette, and William Marshall Anderson undertook the same troublesome and annoying job, building another Fort William at the confluence of the Laramie and North Platte rivers. It was a favorite rendezvous spot, where the Arapahos had killed a mysterious Canadian free trapper named J. LaRamee or Loremy in 1821.[47] The traders "laid the foundation *log* of a fort, on Laramee's fork" on 31 May 1834, Anderson noted, and by August the stockade enclosed ten thousand square feet and stood "defying wind, rain & Indians."[48]

Sublette and Campbell sold Fort William to Jim Bridger, Thomas Fitzpatrick, and Milton Sublette in 1835, but within a year they transferred the cottonwood stockade to the American Fur Company. Much about Fort William, including its location, remains a mystery. As one expert observed, "No one seems to really know exactly how big the stockade was." Besides Anderson's statement that "there is enclosed one hundred feet," eyewitnesses such as Alfred Jacob Miller and Frederick Wislizenus provide both larger and smaller estimates. A 1998 archeological survey examined possible sites for the fort, including a spot west of "Old Bedlam" and an area east of Fort John at the south end of the military post's parade ground. "No evidence of Fort William's stockade wall was found in either site." The current working hypothesis is that Fort John was built around Fort William, which was then demolished.[49]

Lancaster P. Lupton founded Fort Platte nearby in 1839, and the competition responded in 1841 by building the adobe fort they called Fort John about a mile upstream from Fort Platte. After Lupton abandoned Fort Platte about 1844, Joseph Bissonette moved the post's stock downriver to a small station he called Fort Bernard, "a small building rudely constructed of logs," six miles southeast of Fort John.[50] That winter John Baptiste Richard occupied the outpost and competed successfully with the American Fur Company, undercutting the firm's prices by as much as 30 or 40 percent. But Astor's agents proved to be tough competitors: after Richard departed for New Mexico to pick up a new supply of his main stock-in-trade, Taos Lightning, the fort mysteriously burned to the ground. P. D. Papin became Fort John's factor in 1845, but James Bordeaux, known to his Lakota in-laws as the Bear, essentially managed the fort until the company sold it to the government in 1849.[51]

---

[46] Campbell to "Dear Brother," 16 November 1833, *The Rocky Mountain Letters of Robert Campbell*, 14.

[47] Hafen, *The Mountain Men*, 6:223. Despite his obscurity, LaRamee gave his name to a city, mountain, and plain in present-day Wyoming.

[48] Anderson, *The Rocky Mountain Journals*, 34–35.

[49] Walker, *Searching for Fort William*, 144–45.

[50] Bryant, *What I Saw in California*, 23 June 1846, 106.

[51] McDermott, "James Bordeaux," in Hafen, *The Mountain Men*, 5:65–80; and "John Baptiste Richard," ibid., 2:294–95. John Richard ("Reshaw") was a French-American whose family apparently had been in the Mississippi Valley since 1738. For the next six years, he ran several small trading operations along the Platte and even took up farming for a short time before entering the ferrying and bridge-building business.

Despite its official name, Fort John, everyone knew it as Fort Laramie. The new establishment impressed John C. Frémont, who visited in July 1842 and complimented the "large post, having more the air of military construction than the fort at the mouth of the river. It is on the left bank, on a rising ground some twenty-five feet above the water; and its lofty walls, whitewashed and picketed, with the large bastions at the angles, gave it quite an imposing appearance in the uncertain light of evening." A wooden palisade surmounted the fifteen-foot high mud walls, he reported, enclosing a yard about 130 feet square.[52]

Fort John was "built of bricks dried in the sun, and externally is of an oblong form, with bastions of clay, in the form of ordinary blockhouses, at two of the corners," Francis Parkman wrote after his visit in 1846. The fort had two ingeniously constructed gates separated by an arched passageway. A small square window set high above the ground opened into the passage so that traders could communicate with those outside when the inner gate was closed and do business with suspicious characters they wanted to keep out of the fort. The company had such good relations with the local tribes, especially the Lakota, that Parkman thought they seldom used the window. The interior of the fort was divided into two sections: a square lined with storerooms, offices, and apartments; and a narrow corral surrounded by high walls, where the post's horses and mules were crowded for safekeeping.[53]

Edwin Bryant estimated the distance between Independence and Fort Laramie at 672 miles, guessed the fort covered between one-half and three-quarters of an acre, and noted that two brass swivel cannons defended the gate. The staff raised large numbers of horses, cattle, and poultry, made butter, and had "an abundance of milk for their own consumption."[54] When A. H. Garrison visited in 1846, the fort stood on a beautiful plain, commanding a fine view of snowcapped mountains: the surrounding country was so level "that you can see evry thing that goes on for miles around." When someone asked the post's manager why the fort was built far above the stream, he said so it would not be so liable to surprise by the Indians.[55]

A settlement so remote from civilization offered protection "in the midst of this wild country," Samuel Hancock wrote in 1845. He "found the occupants clever people who seemed pleased to see us, while we were equally glad to meet with them."[56] Jacob Wright Harlan found large numbers of Lakotas camped around

[52] Spence and Jackson, *The Expeditions of John Charles Frémont*, 1:211, 218.

[53] Parkman, *The California and Oregon Trail*, 126.

[54] Bryant, *What I Saw in California*, 23 June 1846, 109.

[55] Garrison, "Reminiscences of Abraham Henry Garrison," 16.

[56] Hancock, *The Narrative of Samuel Hancock*, 19.

the fort, including some five hundred warriors who had just returned from a fight in which they had killed about one hundred and fifty Pawnees, captured a great many ponies, and lost about eighty of their own warriors. "They were all in war paint, and danced around a big fire, with the Pawnee scalps in their hands. The one who had taken the most scalps received greatest honor. They were hideous to behold," Harlan remembered.[57] Edwin Bryant arrived at the fort at the end of "a grand war-dance," but he reported it was held for an attack being organized against the Shoshones and Crows. Bryant claimed he found three thousand Sioux camped in about six hundred lodges, but the less colorful Virgil Pringle counted only two hundred lodges.[58]

Like all the other outposts on the Oregon Trail, "the object of the establishment" at Fort John was trade with the surrounding tribes. The post enabled the American Fur Company, Parkman noted, to "well-nigh monopolize the Indian trade of this whole region."[59] The fort played host to small-time traders, John C. Frémont observed, who stocked Indian trade goods, including "blankets, calicoes, guns, powder, and lead, with such cheap ornaments as glass beads, looking-glasses, rings, vermilion for painting, tobacco, and principally, in spite of the prohibition, of spirits, brought into the country in the form of alcohol, and diluted with water before sold."[60] Despite a distinct shift in their business, fur-company posts like Fort John never really adapted to the emigrant trade.

In contrast to the corporate managers of the fur trade, one of the West's living legends was quite interested in the emigrant trade. "I have established a small store with a Black Smith Shop, and a supply of iron in the road of the Emigrants, on Black's Fork, Green River, which promises fairly," James Bridger informed Pierre Choteau in December 1843. Bridger said his prospective customers "were generally well supplied with money, but by the time they get there, are in want of all kinds of supplies. Horses Provisions, Smith work, &c." In addition to the "considerable business" he expected to do with the emigrants, Bridger said he planned to trade with the Shoshones, who had "mostly a good number of Beaver among them."[61]

The small store Bridger described in 1843 was actually his third attempt to establish a trading station. By summer 1841, he and Henry Fraeb had built a post on Green River, three and one-half miles below the mouth of the Big Sandy River, at the spot where the Oregon Trail later turned west.[62] The Bidwell-Bar-

[57] Harlan, *California '46 to '88*, 39–40.

[58] Bryant, *What I Saw in California*, 107; and Pringle, "Diary of Virgil Pringle," 22 June 1846.

[59] Parkman, *The California and Oregon Trail*, 126.

[60] Spence and Jackson, *The Expeditions of John Charles Frémont*, 1:219.

[61] Alter, *Jim Bridger*, 209–10. Choteau apparently declined to provide Bridger with supplies. See ibid., 212.

[62] Bryant, *What I Saw in California*, 15 July 1846, 139. Bryant saw "the ruins of several log cabins" at the spot.

tleson party may have visited that summer, or at least they ran into Fraeb and his "wicked, swearing company" on a hunting expedition.[63] Jim Baker, who came west with Bidwell and went on to become a noted frontiersman, joined them. He remembered fighting a pitched battle on the Little Snake River with a large party of Sioux, Cheyennes, and Arapahos. They left Fraeb's corpse braced against a stump, "the ugliest looking dead man I ever saw," Baker recalled.[64]

Fraeb's demise probably inspired Bridger to move fifty-four miles to the west. Here Bridger and his new partner, Louis Vasquez, erected several cabins "built of logs, plastered with mud" atop a bluff overlooking Blacks Fork. By summer 1843, this post was also deserted and dismantled.[65] Both men initially used Blacks Fork as a base rather than a home: during the early 1840s neither spent much time at the outpost. Bridger and Vasquez departed for Saint Louis about June 1842 and returned in August with a brigade of some forty men to trap near the Three Forks of the Missouri. The partners came back to Blacks Fork in November, where they apparently spent the winter with their Indian families. The next spring, Bridger led a brigade north to hunt beaver, while Vasquez headed east, "loaded with furs and skins, which they were taking to the Forts on the Platte, where they supply themselves."[66]

Bridger had been in the mountains since 1822. By the time he founded his trading post, the veterans of the fur trade affectionately called him "Old Gabe," even though he was not yet forty. He was already renowned as "the most celebrated trapper of the Rocky mts," Theodore Talbot noted in 1845. "Bridger was tall—fully six feet high—erect, thin, wiry, and suburnt almost to the complexion of an Indian—a light olive—with a face noble and expressive of generosity, dark brown hair and liquid hazel eyes, bright almost to blackness," H. J. Clayton recalled years later. "In form he was straight as an arrow, wore moccasins, and, as an Indian, turned his toes as he walked slightly inward, so strikingly did his manners conform to those of the wild denizens of the forests."[67] Not everyone remembered the old mountaineer so favorably. Judge William Carter, who in the 1860s ruled Fort Bridger like a feudal lord, knew him well but considered Bridger "densely ignorant" and believed "he had lived so long with the Indians that he had absorbed all their cunning and duplicity."[68]

[63] Williams, *Narrative of a Tour*, 23 July 1841, 30–31.

[64] Hafen, *The Mountain Men*, 3:137–38.

[65] Talbot, *The Journals*, 30 August 1843, 41. Richard Grant wrote, "fearing the Shyans and Sewes Indians, [Bridger] removed to Blacks fork a couple days riding from Green River." See Grant to Simpson, 15 March 1844, D.5/10, HBC Archives, 426.

[66] Alter, *Jim Bridger*, 205; and Anderson, *The Rocky Mountain Journals*, 266–68.

[67] Ibid., 265, 267.

[68] Carter, "Fort Bridger Days," 86.

Louis Vasquez, who joined forces with Bridger determined "to make money or die," was every bit as colorful a character as his partner. Travelers often identified him as a Frenchman or Mexican, but Vasquez was born in Saint Louis in 1798, the son of a Spanish official and a French-Canadian mother. He joined the fur trade in his early twenties. During the 1830s he partnered with Andrew Sublette to run Fort Vasquez, a station on the South Platte. Handsome and gregarious, Vasquez was "a great favorite of the mountaineers," and when he reappeared in 1834 after being given up for dead, one old trapper said, "Thank God he lives, and I shall hear his merry laugh again." Vasquez and Bridger could be "relied on for doing business honorably and fairly," James Frazier Reed wrote in 1846, but others blamed them for promoting the Hastings Cutoff more out of self-interest than good faith. Vasquez traveled from Fort Laramie to Blacks Fork with Elizabeth Dixon Smith's wagon train in 1847 and impressed her as "a good and inteligent man." She commented on his "white wife," the widow Narcissa Land Ashcraft. During the gold rush, Vasquez "put on a great deal of style, and used to ride about the country in a coach and four."[69]

It is not clear when the partners moved their fort down from the bluff to an island in Blacks Fork, where they built two double-log cabins surrounded by a stockade. But when the 1843 emigration arrived at Bridgers Fort in August, the proprietors were gone. The sojourners originally intended to stay ten or fifteen days to make meat, John Boardman wrote, but they learned "the Sioux and Cheyennes had been here, run off all the buffalo, killed 3 Snake Indians, and stolen 60 horses."[70] When Bridger reported to Chouteau in December, he said he planned to make a spring hunt in 1844, and after he received his trade goods would "make an expedition into the California," which he did at the end of August. Vasquez, meanwhile, had been "drinking and frolicking at the Platte, [where] he neglected his business."[71]

The opening of the Sublette Cutoff in 1844 diverted much of the fort's traffic, leaving it located on a "zigzag road." James Clyman described it as a "temporary concern calculated for trade with the Shoshonees and Eutaws which trade is not very valuable."[72] Nonetheless, the longer trail to Bridgers Fort was much easier on livestock than the new cutoff and still attracted customers. Emigrants were irresistibly drawn to the opportunity to trade or simply to see something resembling civilization, though what they found almost always disappointed them. The

---

[69] Anderson, *The Rocky Mountain Journals,* 375–76; Smith, "The Diary," 9 August 1847, 128; and Hafen, *The Mountain Men,* 2:321–38.

[70] Boardman, "The Journal," 13 August 1843, 107. Trail expert Paul Henderson told Gregory Franzwa that construction of a reservoir on an elevation just north of today's town destroyed the site of the first post on Blacks Fork, which was only active for a few weeks.

[71] Alter, *Jim Bridger,* 210–11.

[72] Clyman, *James Clyman, Frontiersman,* 99–100.

fort was "built of poles and daubed with mud; it is a shabby concern," Joel Palmer wrote in July 1845. The post offered flour, pork, powder, lead, blankets, butcher knives, spirits, hats, readymade clothes, coffee, and sugar to its clients, most of whom were white trappers with Indian wives.[73] The leading attraction, however, was grass. "The excellent grazing at no great distance, with pure mountain water, made it a little paradise in contrast with most of the country over which we had passed," recalled David Shaw.[74] William Findley camped a mile from Fort Bridger in August 1845 and praised the fine grass and water. He found forty Indians and trappers at the post, and their two hundred horses and livestock "equal to any in the states." He saw goats, sheep, and poultry. "Last night it snowed," he noted, "so that the mountains are white and have a wintery appearance."[75]

"Fort Bridger consisted of two blockhouses, surrounded by palisades about ten feet tall," observed Heinrich Lienhard in 1846. "It could hardly be defended for long against a determined attack."[76] Edwin Bryant found only "two or three miserable log-cabins, rudely constructed, and bearing but a faint resemblance to habitable houses." He estimated some five hundred Shoshones were camped nearby when he visited, along with traders from Taos, who had brought "dressed buckskins, buckskin shirts, pantaloons, and moccasins, to trade with the emigrants. The emigrant trade is a very important one to the mountain merchants and trappers." The countenance and bearing of these frontier businessmen was "generally expressive of a cool, cautious, but determined intrepidity." Bryant thought they had no consciences as businessmen, "but in a matter of hospitality or generosity they are open-handed—ready, many of them, to divide with the needy what they possess."[77]

The Mormons who arrived at the post in 1847 were even less excited about its appearance than previous visitors. "Bridger's Fort is composed of two double log houses about forty feet long each and joined by a pen for horses about ten feet high constructed by placing poles upright in the ground close together, which is all the appearance of a fort in sight," William Clayton wrote. Orson Pratt estimated "the number of men, squaws, and half-breed children, in these houses and lodges, may be about 50 or 60." Bridger impressed his new neighbors even less than his fort did. "From his appearance and conversation, I should not take him to be a man of truth," a sour Howard Egan observed—and relations between Bridger and the Mormons would quickly get worse.[78]

[73] Palmer, *Journal of Travels*, 25 July 1845, 74.

[74] Shaw, *Eldorado*, 62.

[75] Findley, Overland Journey to Oregon and a Return Trip, 12 August 1845, Beinecke Library.

[76] Lienhard, *From St. Louis to Sutter's Fort*, 95.

[77] Bryant, *What I Saw in California*, 17 July 1846, 142–43.

[78] Clayton, *An Intimate Chronicle*, 285; Pratt, *The Orson Pratt Journals*, 7 July 1847, 440; and Egan, *Pioneering the West*, 87.

THE SNAKE COUNTRY:
FORT HALL, FORT BOISE, AND THE HUDSON'S BAY COMPANY

Nathaniel Wyeth established Fort Hall, "which was a stockade 80 Fort square built of Cotton wood trees," in 1834 to dispose of the goods he could not sell at the rendezvous. "On the 4th of August the Fort was completed," Osborne Russell recorded. "And on the 5th, the 'Stars and Stripes' were unfurled to the breeze at Sunrise, in the center of a savage and uncivilized country over an American Trading Post." It did not remain so long: Wyeth sold the station to the Hudson's Bay Company in 1837, and within two years they replaced the stockade with an adobe fort of the same dimensions.[79] For the next fifteen years, the Company would be a formidable presence in what it called the Snake Country, which encompassed today's Idaho and vast stretches of the surrounding region.

Located about twelve miles north of present-day Pocatello, Idaho, on the floodplain of the Snake near the mouth of the Portneuf River, Fort Hall was the southernmost Hudson's Bay station and the northernmost spot on the long detour the Oregon Trail took around the Great Salt Lake. "The fort was situated on the south bank of Snake River, in a wide, fertile valley, covered with luxuriant grass, and watered by numerous springs and small streams," Peter Burnett recalled. He found buffalo skulls scattered everywhere, but now "the Company had bands of horses and herds of cattle grazing on these rich bottom-lands."[80] Francis Ermatinger managed the station when members of the Bidwell-Bartleson party visited, but next year he was replaced by Chief Trader Richard Grant, "a Scotchman, from Canada, a fine looking portly old man, and quite courteous, for an old mountaineer."[81]

Many travelers considered Grant exceedingly kind and sociable, but the veteran frontiersman got mixed reviews from emigrants. He was "very hospitable old fellow, but rough as a grizzly bear," Dr. John Prichet reported. "He treated us with much more kindness and attention than they did at either of the other Forts we passed."[82] Grant dressed cleanly enough, Zilphia E. Rigdon noted, "but he looked *slomicky* for all that."[83] When Theodore Talbot visited in September 1843, he thought the place was "a small and rather ill constructed Fort, built of 'Dobies.'" Grant was a good-looking gentleman who considered the country British and treated the Indians as serfs of the Hudson's Bay Company, Talbot wrote. He admired Grant's large cattle herd and fine horses but not his diverse

[79] Russell, *Journal of a Trapper,* 5, 156n17.
[80] Burnett, *Recollections and Opinions of an Old Pioneer,* 116.
[81] Bruff, *Gold Rush,* 1:103.
[82] Prichet, "A Letter from California," 17 January 1850, Mattes Library.
[83] Rigdon to Perkins, 1 February 1900, in Bristow Papers, University of Oregon Library, 7.

workforce: "The employees of the Fort are a motley group. English, Scotch, Orkney men, Canadians, Spaniards, Americans, Owyhees, Chenooks, Neepercees, Kaiwahs, &c. There are several lodges of French free trappers under one 'Bonaparte' camped at the gate of the fort. They are here to overawe the emigrants, and protect Capt. Grant, at whose expense they are living."[84] The Bannocks, Grant observed, "do not overlove the Americans in general" and served as his "life guards." The Shoshones were the fort's main customers, but the post also became a favorite rendezvous for the Nez Perces, Flatheads, and even the "set called diggers or chochoukos." Through independent agents known as freemen, Grant traded with the Crows and Blackfeet, and he periodically visited the "Youtaw Indians"—the Utes—to barter for beaver pelts.[85]

Perhaps no other place on the trail played host to so many different peoples from such an astonishing number of homelands as Fort Hall.[86] Travelers from Britain, Germany, France, Belgium, Italy, Switzerland, and Austria visited the post, as did Indian nations from throughout the West. When David Campbell arrived in 1846, he "found about 500 Indians of the Flathead tribe who had come in to trade. They had buffalo hides and deer skins and would pay any price for beads and tobacco."[87] Forty-niner James M. Daigh reported there were about twenty-five white men trading with the Indians at the fort, plus three white women, one of whom was the wife of a "half-Indian Negro."[88]

Another 275 miles on the road to Oregon brought travelers to the Hudson's Bay Company's second station in the Snake Country, Fort Boise. Thomas McKay built the stockade known as Snake Fort eight or ten miles above the mouth of the Boise River in 1834 to make sure the Company did not lose the Nez Perce trade to Nathaniel Wyeth's Fort Hall. After François Payette, "a merry fat old gentleman of fifty," began managing the post in 1835, he moved it a mile below the mouth of Boise River and closer to the Snake, where he built a neatly constructed adobe citadel. Payette had "undergone many hardships, in consideration of which and his valuable services, he has been placed in charge of this post," Theodore Talbot wrote. He found Payette "exceedingly polite, courteous and hospitable."[89]

When Medorem Crawford reached "Fort Boyzea" in September 1842, he thought it was "a new Establishment. It has been a short time in operation and is not yet completed. We saw but one white man who is French." The fort raised

---

[84] Talbot, *The Journals of Theodore Talbot,* 47–48.

[85] Grant to Simpson, 15 March 1844, D.5/10, HBC Archives, 424, 426; 2 January 1846, D.5/16, HBC Archives, 224; and 1 April 1847, D.5/19, HBC Archives, 443.

[86] Boag, "Idaho's Fort Hall as a Western Crossroads," 20–26.

[87] Campbell, "Pioneer of 1846," *Porterville Recorder,* 11, 12, and 13 August 1910.

[88] Daigh, *"Nuggets from '49,"* 29.

[89] Talbot, *The Journals,* 14 October 1843, 59.

corn and a few other vegetables in small quantities, and even muskmelon, Crawford noted, "but of a very indifferent quality."[90] The outpost offered salt, coffee, and sugar for fifty cents a pint, but not much a traveler needed. "Fort Boise is built of mud and situated in a valley near the mouth of 2 rivers. Has a little timber 1 or 2 miles off, and good grass up Boise River," John Boardman wrote after visiting with Joseph Chiles's half-starved band in 1843.[91]

Payette managed the fort until 1844, and the post's fortunes and appearance declined sharply after he retired. The next year, Joel Palmer reported the fort had a quantity of flour brought from Oregon City on sale for $20 per hundredweight, in cash.[92] James Field described it as "a small, mean-looking fort" and found the Indians very poor, "many of them nearly naked and living on fish and roots."[93] Subsequent impressions were no more favorable. "Reached Fort Boise after driving 4 miles over a very dusty road. Fort Boise is situated on the north bank of Snake River, 1 miles below the mouth of Boise River," John Wesley Yeargain wrote in 1852. "It is rather a hard looking place, most of the emigrants are sadly disappointed on reaching the place, expecting to recruit their stock of provisions but there was very little for sale and that at an unreasonable price."[94]

"Here we are at fort Boise the long looked for place," wrote Mary Stone Smith. She saw only "a few miserable Indians huts swarming with naked and half naked Indians and an enclosure looking as though there was about half an acre of ground in it situated on the east side of Snake river."[95] Others found the Natives at the fort impressive. In 1849 William Watson saw "hundreds of Indians, fat and sleek, and the best made Indians I ever saw; stout, and robust; large arms and full chests."[96] The Snake River flooded and destroyed the old trading fort in 1854, and two years later the Company shut it down. The original site has vanished, but a marker on the riverbank points to its location. A replica stands nearby in Parma, Idaho.[97]

Independent traders, ranging from the obscure to the infamous, soon challenged the virtual monopoly the fur companies had on trail trade during the 1840s. By 1848, men such as the Robidoux brothers, John Richard, Thomas "Peg-leg" Smith, and James Bordeaux had established trading posts from Scotts Bluff to the Bear River. The mountain traders and trappers were always willing to divide

---

[90] Crawford, "Journal," 3 September 1842, 17.

[91] Boardman, "The Journal," 30 September, 1 October 1843, 113–14.

[92] Palmer, *Journal of Travels,* 2 September 1845, 99.

[93] Field, Crossing the Plains, 24 August 1845, Oregon Historical Society.

[94] Yeargain, Oregon Trail Diary, 1852, Oregon-California Papers, Missouri Historical Society.

[95] Smith, Diary, 14 August 1852, Western Historical Manuscript Collection.

[96] Watson, *Journal of an Overland Journey to Oregon,* 9 August 1849, 36.

[97] Franzwa, *The Oregon Trail Revisited,* 338–42. Boise, Idaho, which is fifty miles upriver from the old post, began life as Fort Boise during the Civil War.

whatever they possessed with their guests, but in a trade, "they are as keen as the shrewdest Yankee that ever peddled clocks or wooden nutmegs," Edwin Bryant observed. Whether they came from New Mexico and or the United States, the traders were always happy to "extort money from the emigrants."[98]

NOT LIKE GRANDMA'S INDIANS:
EMIGRANTS, INDIANS, AND VIOLENCE

Overland travelers and their heirs believed they were making "a journey through two thousand miles of unexplored wilderness, inhabited only by wild animals and savage men," but the Indian cultures they encountered were as complex and dynamic as their own.[99] The introduction of horses to the Great Plains following the Pueblo Revolt in 1680 transformed many tribes from sedentary agricultural societies into mounted equestrian bands perfectly equipped to dominate the bison. Well before 1840, the availability of horses and firearms dramatically altered the balance of power among all the nations between the Missouri River and the Great Basin, conjuring up entirely new patterns of competition and warfare. Rather than the ageless and changeless bands of savages white sojourners anticipated meeting, they encountered cultures undergoing a process of continual transformation that made the plains "a different realm of imagined possibility."[100]

Nineteenth-century Americans brought their own traditions with them. Their journals in the 1840s characterized Indians as merciless, hostile, roving, benighted, and vicious savages. Emigrants should never forget that Indians were "as treacherous as tigers," J. Quinn Thornton warned.[101] "Our foreparents had been pioneers of Virginia and Kentucky and were Indian fighters," Oregon pioneer Martha Gay Masterson recalled, and most of those who took the trails to the West came from families that had been fighting indigenous Americans for generations.[102]

Americans today prefer to recall the West's last colorful and dramatic Indian wars, but the long campaign to push Native peoples out of the eastern states was more bitter, brutal, and terrifying. "One of my main concerns was encountering Indians, the very thought of which frightened me no end," wrote Virginia Reed Murphy. "But right here let me say that we suffered vastly more from fear of the Indians before starting than we did on the plains." Reed had grown up listening

---

[98] Bryant, *What I Saw in California*, 25 June 1846.
[99] Bidwell, *Addresses, Reminiscences, etc. of General John Bidwell*, 59.
[100] West, *Contested Plains*, 55.
[101] Thornton, *Oregon and California in 1848*, 16 June 1846, 82.
[102] Masterson, *One Woman's West*, 25.

to her grandmother's stories about an aunt whom the Shawnees had held prisoner for nearly five years during the Revolution. The first tribe her family met on the trail were Kanzas running a ferry. "I watched them closely, hardly daring to draw my breath," Murphy remembered, "and was very thankful when I found they were not like Grandma's Indians."[103]

"Grandma's Indians" had a long history. Hundreds if not thousands of captivity narratives survive, the oldest examples predating John Smith's encounter with Pocahontas. Such tales had been bestsellers since colonial times and, along with the novels of James Fenimore Cooper, created among overlanders an anticipation of violence that had little connection to reality.[104] A few westbound emigrants were veterans of the last, bitter Indian conflicts east of the Mississippi, such as the Black Hawk War and the Seminole Wars, but most of them knew of Indians only through dark family traditions that cast Native peoples as barbarous savages. This generated fear, fear spawned hatred, and overlanders imagined they would have to fight their way across the prairies.

Raids on livestock were a constant reality throughout trail times, and relations between whites and Indians deteriorated dramatically as tensions mounted, but fearful fantasies found little justification during the first decade of overland travel. "The evidence is that the Indians were universally feared, but only sporadically hostile during the most important years of emigration, and more or less continually the guides and purveyors of vital services to the emigrants," observed historian Lillian Schlissel. Until the 1860s, the level of violence on the road west was surprisingly low. In her random sample of 103 women's overland accounts, Schlissel found that only 7 percent of these narratives recorded Indian attacks, "and these account for the deaths of two men, one woman, and two families."[105] Glenda Riley's survey of 150 trail diaries identified 15 that recorded significant conflicts, 22 reported minor problems—and 113 noted no Indian trouble whatsoever.[106]

Long traditions of hospitality and a desire to trade obliged most tribes to treat strangers well, so their initial encounters with Indians posed little danger to emigrants. The Lakotas prized their good relations with the whites, while the Cheyennes "boasted that they had never shed the blood of the white man," Peter Burnett recalled.[107] "Crows never kill a white man, and if they find him in want they will give him food," wrote William Chandless, noting that they

---

[103] Murphy, "Across the Plains in the Donner Party," 409.

[104] Derounian-Stodola and Levernier, *The Indian Captivity Narratives;* and VanDerBeets, *The Indian Captivity Narrative.*

[105] Schlissel, *Women's Diaries of the Westward Journey,* 12, 154.

[106] Riley, *Women and Indians on the Frontier,* 155, cited in Tate, "From Cooperation to Conflict," 18. Michael L. Tate's excellent *Indians and Emigrants* is the first comprehensive study of the subject.

[107] Burnett, *Recollections and Opinions of an Old Pioneer,* 113.

would "strip him of all superfluities" if they could, but they would never launch a mass attack.[108] John Wilson, the first Indian agent sent to the Eastern Shoshones, praised the tribe's reputation as "an honest and sober people, decidedly friendly to the whites." The Crows and the Nez Perces, he heard, boasted that they had never killed a white man.[109]

Like all humans, Indians were inherently curious, and the novelty of their encounters with whites initially defused conflicts. In addition, Natives had a keen desire to acquire European technology, and encounters with wagon trains provided excellent opportunities for trade. "I can emphatically say their treatment of us was of the most friendly kind. They seemed to welcome us, and I think regarded us as curiosities. Anything we possessed was of value to them," Washington Smith Gilliam wrote, recalling his experiences with the Shoshones in 1844. "For a pin or a rag we could buy a large salmon."[110]

The cultural expectations emigrants brought with them led to any number of complications. "When we came in contact with Indians our people were so easily excited that if we had not had with us an old mountaineer the result would certainly have been disastrous," John Bidwell recalled.[111] In our own times, historian Robert L. Munkres observed, Hollywood created the impression that wagon trains had to fight their way through hostile Indians almost every mile between the Missouri and the Pacific.[112] Despite such stereotypes, the reality was different. The Lakotas were famous for the warm welcome they extended the first wagon trains, and they provided overlanders with food and a variety of services, including swimming their stock across rivers and carrying mail back to trading posts. The Indians' skill at rounding up lost livestock often proved invaluable (although some cynics believed many such helpers had taken the animals in the first place).[113] The Cayuse leader Stickus repeatedly guided wagon trains across the Blue Mountains during the 1840s, and Chief Truckee of the Northern Paiutes led emigrants up the river they named after him in 1844, essentially defining the California Trail's classic route. Sarah Winnemucca recalled that the Paiutes would have helped the Donner party, "only my people were afraid of them."[114]

"We had no war with the Indians," Peter Burnett wrote of his 1843 experience, "and no stock stolen by them." He also identified the primary cause of trouble between emigrants and Indians: young males. At Fort Laramie, he watched

---

[108] Chandless, *A Visit to Salt Lake*, 101.
[109] Morgan, "Washakie and the Shoshoni," 1:149.
[110] Gilliam, "Reminiscences," 206.
[111] Bidwell, in Nunis, *The Bidwell-Bartleson Party*, 105.
[112] Munkres, "The Plains Indian Threat on the Oregon Trail before 1860," 193.
[113] Unruh, *The Plains Across*, 156, 159, 160.
[114] Hopkins, *Life among the Piutes*, 12–13.

an impressive Cheyenne chief encounter a rash young emigrant who "wantonly insulted" him: "I saw from the expression of his countenance that the chief was most indignant, though perfectly cool and brave." The Cheyenne walked away slowly, but stopped some twenty feet from the hothead who had insulted him "and solemnly and slowly shook the forefinger of his right hand at the young man several times, as much as to say, 'I will attend to your case.'" Burnett saw trouble brewing and using earnest gestures made him understand that this young man was considered a half-witted fool by all, "and that we never paid attention to what he said, as we hardly considered him responsible for his language." The chief understood and departed, apparently satisfied. "He was a clear-headed man; and, though unlettered, he understood human nature," Burnett concluded.[115] Unfortunately, many young and inexperienced men from both cultures lacked such attributes.

Emigrant expectations that American Indians would act as warlike savages led to many close encounters and caused much unnecessary violence. As "General" McCarver approached Fort Boise in 1843, his men spotted Indians waving what they considered a red battle flag. The general formed his men for battle and marched toward the Indians, Nineveh Ford recalled. "When he got near enough he discovered that the red flag was a salmon split open and spread out as a sign to the packers that they had salmon for sale. So they marched up and bought some salmon." His men, Ford wrote, "had a good deal of fun with McCarver."[116]

Virtually every initial encounter between Indians and emigrants was positive, and serious resistance only began after they had endured years of provocation. Long contact between such different cultures and increasing competition for resources created friction, and it got worse over time. The tribes were very conscious that the bison were disappearing with "extraordinary rapidity" as early as 1846, and "Indians considered the grass, trees, and wild game their property and expected to be compensated for its use, and their ways of extracting payment continually aggravated emigrants," J. Quinn Thornton observed. The Sioux and Cheyennes were growing "each year more and more hostile to, and jealous of the whites." Nothing but a realistic dread of American military force restrained them "from making an open war upon the emigrants, as they pass through their country, on their way to Oregon," he noted.[117]

Indian perspectives on the trail are hard to come by, but Lakota scholar Joseph Marshall III heard his tribal elders speak about the *Wasicu Tacunhu kin*—the White

---

[115] Burnett, *Recollections and Opinions of an Old Pioneer,* 113.

[116] Ford, The Pioneer Road Makers, 21–22. The Missouri Republican published a letter written at "Larmie's fork" from "M. M'Carver . . . late a citizen of Burlington" on 21 November 1843. Morton M. McCarver was a partner of Peter Burnett and a member of the California Constitutional Convention of 1849. He founded Tacoma, Washington, in 1868. See Flora, "Emigrants to Oregon in 1843," retrieved 20 May 2009 from http://www.oregonpioneers.com/1843.htm.

[117] Thornton, *Oregon and California in 1848,* 28 June 1846, 1:114.

Man's Road or the Holy Road—in "odd, hushed voices, if they spoke of it at all."
The stories Marshall heard did not celebrate military victories or successful raids
but described helping emigrant women and children. In an incident Marshall
dates to 1854, after watching wagons pass up the North Platte from a ridgeline,
several young warriors found a small boy whimpering under some bushes. That
night they fed him and gave him a place to sleep, and the next day the warriors
followed the wagons, careful to keep out of sight until the train made camp. Two
warriors took the boy, crept close to the wagons, and then let him go back to his
people. Elders later debated whether such aid was appropriate and concluded that
it was, but the Lakota memory ran deeper. "We should not forget the Holy Road,"
elders warned Marshall, "and we should not let it happen again."[118]

As noted, livestock raiding was the main cause of conflict between emigrants
and Indians. It usually involved a covert operation: most trains did not learn of
their losses until dawn—and Indians did not steal all lost animals. Violence generated by botched trading sessions, misinterpreted intentions, or simply by bad
actors on both sides occurred all along the road and sometimes had fatal results,
but during the 1840s, no known wagon train ever came under a sustained attack.
Even in the Great Basin, where most Indian-emigrant violence took place, virtually every fight began over livestock, yet early travelers found that the Indians
posed little threat to them or their animals.

There is one possible exception. While hunting antelope "far up" the Humboldt with Levi Scott in 1846, Lindsay Applegate recalled they "came upon wagon
tracks, leading away from the river towards a gulch among the hills, two or three
miles distant. Several wagons seem to have been in this train, and on either side
of the plain tracks made by the wagon wheels in the loose sand were numerous
bare-foot tracks." At the mouth of the gulch, the men found several burned wagons, "only the rims being left among the ashes." They saw no human remains, but
Applegate concluded that a small train "had been taken here not a great while
before, and that they had perished at the hands of their blood-thirsty captors, not
one having escaped to recite the awful tale of horror."[119] Jacob Snyder's journal
suggests Applegate's story was not as fantastic as it might sound. "At this place
some years ago the Indians massacred & burnt 8 white persons. Their bones are
yet to be seen." Snyder dated the event to several years before 1845, but this may
have been an unidentified company attacked sometime during the previous two
years or even the three families with five wagons that Jesse Harritt saw leave Fort
Hall at the end of July, far in advance of the other 1845 companies.[120]

---

[118] Marshall, *On Behalf of the Wolf and the First Peoples,* 79, 84, 86.
[119] Applegate, "Notes and Reminiscences," 16.
[120] Kelly and Morgan, *Old Greenwood,* 143; and Harritt, "Diary of Jesse Harritt," 30 July 1845, 517.

The Indians he met in 1844 "seemed very friendly and every night hundreds of them visited the camp," Moses Schallenberger recalled. "This they continued to do during the entire journey down the Humboldt." His train kept a vigilant guard and only lost one pony. The Natives David Hudson saw the next year "appeared to be very much afraid of us," but they frequently filled his party's animals with arrows. Jacob Snyder's diary confirms this in part. Between leaving Goose Creek on 21 August and 4 September 1845, when his train passed west of the Big Bend of the Humboldt, Snyder mentions shooting at Indians once and being visited by friendly, or at least peaceful, Indians three times. His party saw no Indians for five days, which he attributed to intertribal warfare between the "Snakes" and the "Diggers." After the Natives began peppering livestock with arrows and John Greenwood wantonly shot an Indian, the violence rapidly escalated: it continued to intensify over the next three decades.[121]

Although conflicts between Indians and emigrants during the 1840s were the exception rather than the rule, many overland emigrants witnessed the devastating results of intertribal violence. "Several Kansas Indians came to our camp; they were well armed with bows and arrows, and some had guns," wrote John Bidwell. "They were daily expecting an attack by the Pawnees, whom they but a short time ago had made inroads upon, and had massacred at one of their villages a large number of old men, women and children, while the warriors were hunting buffalo."[122]

The Kanzas "told me that the Pawnees were a bad nation, and that they had a battle with them," Joseph Williams wrote on his way to overtake Bidwell. "They had their women and children hid in a thicket, whom they (the Pawnees) slaughtered in a barbarous manner."[123] The Pawnees themselves would soon be victims of the same indiscriminate violence when the Lakota raided their villages on the Loup and Platte. Peter Burnett met a Kanza and Osage war party of almost a hundred men in 1843. "They were all mounted on horses, had their faces painted red, and had with them one Pawnee scalp, with the ears to it, and with the wampum in them."[124] The Indians "are always fighting with each other not battles of equal numbers for then they do not fight," wrote Richard Rowland. "[They] may skirmish a little at a distance too far off to do any damage. But when hundreds meet tens the hundreds are very brave. Seldom many lives are taken because they will not risk much. They are more adept in stealing horses."[125]

Indian assistance impressed most emigrants, especially given their grim expectations. When Washington Gilliam's train came to the deep, dangerous, and

---

[121] Kelly and Morgan, *Old Greenwood*, 117, 153, 161–64.

[122] Bidwell, 19 May 1841, in Nunis, *The Bidwell-Bartleson Party*, 29.

[123] Williams, *Narrative of a Tour*, 21 August 1841, 24.

[124] Burnett, *Recollections and Opinions of an Old Pioneer*, 103.

[125] Rowland to Mary Ann Rowland, 9 January 1844, in Western Travel Collection, Missouri Historical Society.

swift first crossing of the Snake River at Three Island Crossing, Shoshones volunteered to help negotiate the narrow bar. "A man had been drowned the previous season by getting off into deep water," he remembered. An Indian rode ahead of his train's lead team, directing the wagons to the shallowest water, while others steadied each team "to prevent them from being beaten down by the strong current into the deep water." The Shoshones, Gilliam recalled, "performed their task faithfully, and took us over safely, for which we felt very grateful." But Gilliam's story had a grim epilogue: a party of gamblers behind them believed they had lost a horse to the Indians and "followed them up, overtook them and killed one of them, and ever after that they were hostile."[126]

Since they offered such splendid opportunities for trade, wagon trains acted as magnets for widely dispersed Shoshone bands, and some travelers reported seeing thousands of Indians gathered along the Green River. Like the Lakotas, the Shoshones impressed American travelers. "I never have seen any cleaner better looking and finer shaped Indians th[a]n these," army veteran Theodore Boos recalled, "and I have seen a great many different tribes."[127] "Many of the men we saw were finely formed for strength and agility, with countenances expressive of courage and humanity," Edwin Bryant wrote.[128] The amity they showed travelers helped the relationship, for ever since their encounter with the Lewis and Clark expedition, the Shoshone people had been firm friends of the Americans. One morning a large band visited James Field's train to deliver a mare belonging to an emigrant, "receiving a few presents as a reward for their honesty," he noted. "Contrast this with the conduct of the owner of the mare, who is reported to have robbed a Sioux grave a little this side of Larimie of several buffalo robes and other articles which it is their custom to deposit with their dead."[129]

Although many Shoshone bands crossed the Rockies to hunt bison in summer, they ruled a land that was rich in food sources such as camas roots, pine nuts, deer, and fish, particularly salmon and trout. Trekking up the clear and salmon-filled Boise River in 1845, Field met "Indians of all sizes, sexes and conditions coming out to the roadside and standing in motley groups to see us pass, some of them holding up fish and crying out 'swap!' 'swap!' There were squaws with pappooses slung to their backs, young chaps 14 or 15 years old standing in the primitive simplicity of Father Adam, and some full-grown men making a very near approach to it. Some few old men whose hair was nearly white with age holding up their hands and saying 'How do?'"[130]

---

[126] Gilliam, "Reminiscences," 206–207.
[127] Boos, My Life in the Army, Beinecke Library.
[128] Bryant, *What I Saw in California*, 138.
[129] Field, Crossing the Plains, 9 August 1845, Oregon Historical Society.
[130] Ibid., 21 August 1845.

The great Washakie was the generally acknowledged leader of the first Sho-shone bands overland travelers encountered. During the more than sixty years he led his people, one early settler recalled, he was "trusted alike by red and white men." Washakie was said by many to resemble Henry Ward Beecher, the most famous preacher of the era.[131]

In contrast to the generally favorable experiences emigrants had along most of the trail, violence quickly engulfed the Great Basin tribes. Contempt for their lifeways and fear of their night attacks led emigrants to engage in the wholesale slaughter of the bands they met on the Humboldt River. Jacob Harlan recalled a brutal-but-typical encounter with Northern Paiutes, whom he said were "hostile and very troublesome, killing the emigrants, and stealing their stock whenever they could get a chance." Harlan's party had no trouble until it reached the Sink of the Humboldt, where Indians shot arrows at an emigrant. Investigating, Har-lan and a companion "brought down two of them." That night, Harlan's mule awakened him. "The night was clear and bright, and we could plainly see a party of Indians a short distance off. There were thirty or forty of them, and they had no brush or other means of hiding or lying in ambush." Harlan and another man decided to "advance toward the savages and fire upon them. We did so, and shot two more of them . . . and they all ran off in a general stampede." Shortly after breaking camp, Harlan found a board warning that the Indians were hostile and dangerous. It said this party had a "severe fight" the previous day that killed one man and badly wounded another: in response, the company killed about forty Indians they believed planned to steal stock and murder emigrants.[132]

A few Great Basin travelers recognized the ingenuity and hard work required to wring life from the desert. William W. Wood found a large encampment at Humboldt Lake, where Paiute Indians were making "a kind of Sugar out of a Species of Cane that grows here." The Paiutes cut and dried the cane in the sun, producing a gummy substance. The tribe's old and young folks beat the stalks and then fanned or sifted the chaff. "It looks like Sugar and has the taste of honey," Wood reported.[133] Abner Blackburn traded with a fisherman on the Humboldt in 1847 who had landed a fine lot of fish using "a long stick forked [that] had barbes on the end." He noticed sagebrush pulled up about every ten yards, with the roots pointed skyward. "We supposed it was something about catching rabbits and let it go at that." In the Ruby Mountains, Blackburn saw "a high fence made of brush and small pines. Well, this bothered us again: who made the fence? It looked like it was made for deer and we let it goe at that."[134]

---

[131] Stone, "A Washakie Anecdote," 356–57.

[132] Harlan, *California '46 to '88*, 45–47.

[133] Wood, Journal of an Overland Trip from Ohio to California, 30 August 1850, Beinecke Library.

[134] Blackburn, *Frontiersman*, 114.

The frontier could indeed be a vicious and dangerous place, but popular culture has exaggerated the general level of violence on the trails. Historian John Unruh famously calculated that between 1840 and 1860, Indians killed only 362 emigrants, whereas overlanders killed 426 Indians—and before 1849, emigrants killed only 34 Indians, whereas Indians killed 26 whites. Significantly, 90 percent of the murders took place west of South Pass.[135] "I have never witnessed the shedding of one drop of human blood," Pierre-Jean De Smet wrote in 1846, and the same good fortune persisted throughout his remarkable career in the West, which ended with the passing of the golden age of wagon roads.[136] Many emigrants never saw an actual Indian on the trail, and others imagined many more than actually existed, as one 1847 overlander observed. "My wife saw more Bloody Indians this day, or thought she did," groused Loren B. Hastings, "than she ever saw before or ever will see."[137]

A Sort of Magic Mirror: Was It Worth the Trip?

"I am much better pleased with Oregon than I expected to be," Charles Saxton wrote after reaching the Columbia in 1844. Many, if not most, overlanders shared his positive perspective.[138] "It is as beautiful a country as I have ever seen . . . They sow wheat here from October until June, and the best wheat I ever saw and plenty of it," wrote Mariah King in spring 1846. "There are thousands of strawberries, gooseberries, blackberries, whortleberries, currents and other wild fruits." Oregon was unlike any other new country where you had to pay for a farm, she said, because the free land was "already paid for when you get here." Even though King had been opposed to leaving the States, she was delighted with her new home, where grass grew all winter and free-ranging cattle were as fat as if they had been stall-fed year round. "It is an easy place to make a living," she told the folks back home.[139]

More than a few overlanders waxed ecstatic about their new homes: "Suffice it to say," John E. Lose wrote after reaching the Willamette Valley, "that we have taller trees, better soil, prettier land, larger turnips, sweeter fish, clearer water, a purer atmosphere; and more Indians, than can be scared up on the eastern side of the long white back-bone of the western hemisphere, 'any how.'"[140] Oregon was "the best portion of God's land that I know anything about," I. Franklin wrote home. "I find that a man cannot take hold of any kind of business without making money."[141]

---

[135] Unruh, *The Plains Across,* 184–85. How Unruh arrived at these numbers is unclear.

[136] De Smet, *Life, Letters and Travels,* 113.

[137] Hastings, Overland Journey from Illinois, Beinecke Library, 20 June 1847, 9.

[138] Saxton to the Editor, 14 April 1845, in Clyman, *James Clyman, Frontiersman,* 325.

[139] Mariah King to "Dear Mother, Brother, and Sisters," 1 April 1846, Oregon Historical Society.

[140] Lose, "From Oregon," undated letter, ca. early 1847, *Defiance* [Ohio] *Democrat,* 25 November 1847, 1/6. Courtesy of Kristin Johnson.

[141] Franklin to Morritz Langsdorf, 26 August 1852, Oregon Historical Society.

Since they had risked so much, it is hardly surprising that new arrivals cast as favorable an eye on the West as they could manage. But as they considered the trials of their journey and their lives in the new lands from the perspective of great age, veteran pioneers came to different conclusions about whether they had found the better life they all sought. "The trip is a sort of magic mirror, and exposes every man's qualities of heart connected with it, vicious or amiable," Edwin Bryant observed.[142] For some, like Tolbert Carter, the trek was a costly experiment. "Such a journey has a tendency to destroy in [human] nature much of its benevolence and sympathy for distress of all kinds," he wrote, recalling the ordeals of the southern route to Oregon in 1846, "until we are almost devoid of those essential humane characteristics."[143]

For many settlers, the trek was only the beginning of the challenges their new lives presented. Most overlanders arrived at the end of the trail in desperate condition, often starving, broke, and exhausted. Oregon's rainy season greeted most trains, and their impoverished people had to find food and shelter quickly. John McLoughlin provided John Boardman and his companions "plenty of salmon and potatoes, furnished us house room, and wood free of charge, and was very anxious that all should get through safe."[144] Prices were high, and if it had not been for McLoughlin's generosity, many Americans would have suffered even greater privations than they did, Peter Burnett remembered. "The Company furnished many of our immigrants with provisions, clothing, seed, and other necessaries on credit"—and the credit of many emigrants was doubtful at best. Burnett admitted many of his compatriots "were unworthy of the favors they received, and only returned abuse for generosity."[145]

The first Americans to go to Mexican California faced more difficult challenges than those who went to Oregon. They were illegal aliens in a foreign country, where "the government is tyrannical, the weather unseasonable, poor crops, and the necessaries of life not to be had except at the most extortioned prices, and frequently not then," William Todd complained.[146] Like their countrymen in Oregon, many new California residents were dependent on the benevolence of established traders like John Sutter.

More than a few found the West Coast so alien and life there so arduous that they returned to their familiar homes as quickly as possible. Ralph C. Geer met a man named Grant (perhaps 1844 emigrant David Grant) at the last crossing of the

---

[142] Bryant, *What I Saw in California*, 1 June 1846, 68.

[143] Carter, "Pioneer Days," 79.

[144] Boardman, "The Journal," 3 November 1843, 118.

[145] Burnett, *Recollections and Opinions of an Old Pioneer*, 142.

[146] Todd, "Interesting from California," 17 April 1846.

Sweetwater: he was taking his entire family back to Missouri. When Geer asked why he was leaving Oregon, Grant said: "In the first place they have no bees there; and in the second place, they can't raise corn, and whar they can't raise corn they can't raise hogs, and whar they can't raise hogs they can't have bacon, and I'm going back to old Missouri where I can have corn bread, bacon and honey."[147]

Others did not like the climate: Charles C. Smith complained that Oregon had only two seasons, "*rust & dry.*"[148] After the hard winter of 1846–47 killed most of his livestock, A. H. Garrison's father felt that the country had been badly misrepresented and wrote an open letter to a Missouri newspaper stating "in plain language what he thought of the winters of Oregon, and of those who had written so pleasingly of the country. He told his old neighbors back there not to believe the lies that had been written about this coast. He told them of the hard winter, and that if he had the means, they would see his wagon come rolling back to Old Missouri." But Oregon quickly won the elder Garrison over, and by the next spring, he could not speak highly enough of Oregon "as a grand country to live in, and the mildness and healthfulness of its climate."[149]

Some learned their dreams had been mere illusions. But most expressed satisfaction with their new homes and considered the sacrifices they had made on the trek worth its rewards. "The curiosities that are to be seen upon the plains, are enough to compensate me for all my trouble," Daniel Toole wrote from Fort Hall in 1846. "This is a long and tedious trip, and requires great patience—but, I have not for a moment regretted the undertaking—for it has been of great benefit to my health, and I find health better than friends."[150] The mild climate of the Pacific delighted most new arrivals. "This winter has appeared more like spring to one than winter," Clarborne Walker wrote from the Willamette Valley. He found Oregon's advantages over the Midwest were too numerous to mention.[151] "Notwithstanding we had experienced some disagreeable adventures on this expedition, we could but feel a great admiration for this part of Oregon," Samuel Hancock wrote after surveying his new home in 1845, "and satisfaction that we had abandoned our old homes, for one here."[152]

---

[147] Geer, "Occasional Address for the Year 1847," 35–36.

[148] Whitney, Journal, 30 June 1847, LDS Archives.

[149] Garrison, Reminiscences of A. H. Garrison, Oregon Historical Society.

[150] Toole to "Dear Brother," 2 August 1846, *Liberty Tribune,* 19 December 1846.

[151] Walker to "Dear Brother, Sister and Friends," 1845, Purvine Family Records.

[152] Hancock, *The Narrative of Samuel Hancock,* 48.

CHAPTER 10

Tragedy in Oregon,
Gold in California, and
a City at the Great Salt Lake,
1847 and 1848

War in California reduced emigration to the conquered province in 1847 by two-thirds, but the peaceful resolution of the Oregon question opened the floodgates to settlement of the Pacific Northwest: some four thousand Americans crossed the plains to the Columbia River in 1847. As thousands of families headed to Oregon, the War with Mexico transformed the California Trail. The Latter-day Saints, whose move west was largely financed by enlisting five hundred of their men in the U.S. Army, founded Great Salt Lake City, creating a vital way station for overland travelers. Under Lieutenant Colonel Philip St. George Cooke, the Mormon Battalion built a wagon road from Santa Fe to Los Angeles in 1846. After their discharge in July 1847, many of the unit's veterans headed east to reunite with their families and soon opened critical new elements of the trail. Emigration would ebb and flow during the hostilities, but by the end of 1848 emigrants, soldiers, and discharged veterans had worked out most of the major alternate trails and cutoffs to Oregon and California.

America made peace with Mexico early in 1848: the Treaty of Guadalupe Hidalgo made California an American possession. Now the nation began to wrestle with the knotty question of whether the nation's newly conquered dominion should be slave or free, as Congress failed to organize a single territorial government anywhere in the nation's vast acquisitions. Yet by the end of 1848, more than fourteen thousand people had traveled the Oregon and California trails to new homes in the West.[1] As the pioneering epoch of the road across the plains drew

---

[1] Unruh, *The Plains Across*, 119.

to a close, several thousand Mormons were settled midway between the Missouri and the Pacific, a brutal murder in Oregon had marred relations between its newest and oldest residents—and a melancholy carpenter from New Jersey had plucked a stone from the American River that would change the world.

A Travelling Mob: The Oregon Emigration of 1847

"In the spring of 1847, my Father and Grandfather and Uncle John Grim had a chronic case of Oregon fever," Calvin Geer recalled in 1925, "and the only cure was a trip across the plains to that far off country."[2] Geer's family joined the large company trail-veteran Joel Palmer assembled at Saint Joseph, part of some four or five thousand people who made up the largest influx yet of newcomers to Oregon—and almost ten times the number of Americans who went to California that year.

Some who took their wagons across Iowa and Missouri met Mormon refugees who had fled Illinois and survived a brutal winter at their rude camps on both sides of the Missouri River—but everyone heard fantastic rumors about them. Again, their presence north of the Platte deterred others from departing from Council Bluffs. "There is a great deel said about the Mormons. They say they have gone and joined three tribes of Indians and are going to cut us all off," Phoebe Stanton wrote in early May. "We are asked a great many times if we are Mormons. When we tell them no they say I know you are but you wont own it [but] your wagons look like it." Rumor said the Mormon road was "marked with stolen property and all manner of wickedness," Stanton observed, but she knew many crimes were simply done "on their credit."[3]

The Latter-day Saints began their migration to the Great Basin in 1847, but only a small advance party under Brigham Young departed early enough to interact occasionally with trains bound for Oregon and California. The poverty of the Mormons appalled even those who had little sympathy for their cause. At one of their camps in Iowa, Rev. James Rayner observed, "An appearance of wretchedness seemed to hang over this town." He confirmed that emigrants tended to blame the refugees for any of their losses. One April morning his party was missing a mare and naturally suspected the thieving Mormons, "which caused some unpleasant feeling in camp." A hunter soon found the animal.[4]

The emigration was a colorful spectacle—Joseph Henry Brown recalled one company was called the Blue Wagon Train "for the reason that their wagon covers were

[2] Geer, "My Trip to Oregon."

[3] Stanton, Letter, 9 May 1847, Oregon Historical Society. Published as "On the Plains," 622–23.

[4] Rayner, Journal of a Tour to Oregon, April 1847, Oregon Historical Society, 2.

made of blue colored material."[5] Most notable of all the 1847 travelers was Henderson Luelling (or Lewelling), a Quaker determined to transport an entire nursery from Iowa to Oregon. None of his company could be called wealthy, William A. Hockett recalled, but Luelling had two wagons and teams, John Fisher one wagon and team, and the men fitted out a wagon in partnership "which was loaded with nursery stock, seeds, picks and such tools as they thought they would need in the nursery business, as they intended to make that their business when they got to Oregon." Another Iowan, William Meek, also hauled fruit trees to Oregon in 1847.[6]

Roman legions used odometers, but Benjamin Franklin is credited with inventing the device during his term as deputy postmaster general of British North America between 1754 and 1774. Luelling was among the first to attach such a device to an overland wagon wheel.[7] The Fisher-Luelling "traveling nursery" filled an entire wagon bed with some seven hundred trees and shrubs planted in twelve inches of compost made of charcoal and soil. Eliza Luelling complained that her father was almost more concerned about his plants than his family. Luelling traveled with Stephen Bonser's party of twenty wagons and arrived at The Dalles about 1 October, where Bonser's fine stock of cattle vastly improved the herds along the Columbia. The cargo of apple, pear, plum, cherry, and quince trees; grape and berry vines; and flowers "was the mother of all our early nurseries and orchards," Ralph Geer remembered. "That load of living trees and shrubs brought more wealth to Oregon than any ship that ever entered the Columbia river."[8]

"Nurseries of fruit trees were carried through safe," Robert Caufield wrote at the end of his "long, tedious, and perilous journey" in 1847, "& there being no honey bees in the country, a man came very near getting in a hive safe but failed."[9] Caufield may have referred to a Mr. Wood, who had taken a hive of bees safely over the southern route until reaching Canyon Creek in 1846, where "the wagon conveying them upset in the creek, broke the hive to pieces, and the bees all drowned." The bees had cost Wood "a great deal of trouble," Tolbert Carter recalled, "as he had to feed and water them during the long journey." Wood also lost the $500 he had been offered if he got the bees through safely.[10]

---

[5] Brown, Recollection of 1847, Bancroft Library.

[6] Hockett, Recollections, 1914, Oregon Historical Society, 2. John Fisher died shortly after his party reached the Platte River.

[7] Bowen, *The Most Dangerous Man in America*, 240–42. The mileage figures used on his map suggest cartographer T. H. Jefferson had an odometer attached to his wagon in 1846.

[8] Tadlock, "The Migrating Orchard," 23; Morgan, "The Mormon Ferry on the North Platte," 162; and Unruh, *The Plains Across*, 391. According to Gregory Franzwa, some of these trees still bear fruit.

[9] Robert Caufield to John Caufield, Letter, 1 April 1848, Oregon Historical Society.

[10] Carter, "Pioneer Days," 79. Lucy Ann Henderson Deady recalled that in Cow Creek Canyon, "One man had brought two hives of bees clear across the plains and hated to give them up, but the men of the train decided he could get along without them; so they were left." See Deady, "Crossing the Plains to Oregon," 57–59. Thanks to Nick Bennett of the Oregon Trail Foundation.

Word spread that a thousand prairie schooners set out for Oregon that spring: Irish emigrant Robert Caufield calculated that about 1,117 started but only eight hundred of them reached the Willamette Valley.[11] Independence and St. Joseph were "the two great starting points to Oregon" in 1847. There was at least a week's wait to ferry the Missouri at Saint Joseph, so William Hockett's father went to Independence and joined "about 200 wagons, and two or three companies had already started on the trail."[12] Once they reached the plains, the emigrants had serious trouble with the Pawnees. One train invited some of them into their camp and fed them breakfast. "They then went out on the prairie and tried to steal our horses," Loren B. Hastings complained. After raiding another company, the Indians found two hunters and "robbed them of their rifles & all of their clothing & sent them into camp naked." Three nights later, raiders crept into camp and rode off on two horses. "The Pawnee Indians are the greatest thieves I ever saw—the best way I think to civilize them is with powder & lead, & this is the way we shall do hereafter," Hastings concluded.[13]

The Lakotas camped at Fort Laramie had a less dangerous way than their Pawnee enemies to profit from emigrants: they simply charged a toll for the use of their lands. Approaching the fort in late June, Hastings's company met a very friendly band bearing an American flag. "The old Chief made a speech wishing us to give them some powder & lead & something to eat. We gave them some & went to the fort," where "old Sue Chief" Whirlwind assessed another toll.[14] "At Fort Laramie the old Chief told us we had to pay him for passing through his country," was the way James and Nancy Coon recorded the same encounter. "The commander at the Post told us it was customary to give him something. He spread down his blanket and each man put on his pay, some flour, some meat, coffee, beans, peas, dried fruit, etc. He was well pleased."[15] These payments, however, did little to reduce raids on emigrant livestock.

Several trains celebrated the Fourth of July at Independence Rock, which Robert Caufield thought appeared "heavy enough one would think to weigh the globe down."[16] The Democrats of Knox County, Tennessee, had given Ralph Geer a small cannon weighing only sixteen pounds dubbed the "Young Democrat," and Geer hauled it to Oregon. "It was a real screamer to talk—it could be heard 15

---

[11] Robert Caufield to John Caufield, Letter, 1 April 1848, Oregon Historical Society.

[12] Hockett, Recollections, 1914, Oregon Historical Society, 2–3.

[13] Hastings, Overland Journey from Illinois, Beinecke Library, 2, 6, 7. For an apparent recollection of this event, see Cosgrove, "Reminiscences of Hugh Cosgrove," 259–60. Cosgrove recalled the men were "notorious boasters" who "from the first had been declaring that they would shoot, first or last, one Indian a piece before they got to Oregon."

[14] Hastings, Overland Journey from Illinois, 28 June 1847, Beinecke Library, 10.

[15] Coon and Coon, Diary, 27 June 1847.

[16] Robert Caufield to John Caufield, Letter, 1 April 1848, Oregon Historical Society.

or 20 miles," he wrote. Old mountaineers said that if he fired the gun every night after he camped, Indians would give him no trouble. "And I think it was true," he recalled, "for we adopted that plan and no stealing only when we neglected to let her bark." Geer's son recalled his company planted the stars and stripes on Independence Rock on the Fourth of July "& carried up a little cannon to the top of it & fired her off in honour of the day."[17]

When Loren Hastings arrived at Fort Bridger at the end of July, the proprietor met his train a mile from his fort and "treated us like a gentleman." Here Bridger and Vasquez employed some fifteen or twenty men, mostly French-Canadians, and Bridger and many of the others had Indian wives. "At night having a fiddle & fiddler, we went up with our wives to the Fort & danced until 2 o'clock. I showed Bridger's wife & other squaws how to dance U.S. dances," Hastings wrote. "There was some wild romance in this."[18]

By the end of July, 337 wagons had passed Fort Hall bound for Oregon. Richard Grant counted 901 wagons on their way to Oregon or California as they streamed past Fort Hall from 11 July to 2 September. Peter Ogden called them a "travelling mob," but typically, Grant contrived "to get them quietly off his hands." Ogden reported Grant sold $620 worth of goods from the paltry supply at the fort, but on his own hook Grant had traded horses and wagons for items he later resold and managed to pick up nearly $2,000. The post's small profits reflected the Hudson's Bay Company's failure to provide Fort Hall with appropriate goods. A stock of stout packhorses and a well-assorted shop "would in my opinion gather up a good few Dollars in the year," Grant pointed out. If the Company did not assist and satisfy the emigrants, he warned, it would "expose the HBC to the hatred and censure of the Public in the States, and prove injurious to us in the end."[19]

Disease and mortality stalked the 1847 migration. By the time James N. Harty's train reached the Platte River, they had already passed eight new graves. After his company buried a child on the Platte, Lester Hulin described one of the emigration's many encounters with death, "the king of terror." William Hockett lost both his mother and father on the trail. "If any person ever died of a broken heart," he recalled in 1914, "it was my mother." Nathan Hockett apparently died on the Sublette Cutoff and his wife died five days later. "How my sister escaped a nervous collapse is more than I have ever been able to understand," William recalled. She was left "out in the wilds" with three little boys and an infant. By the time he reached Cascade Falls,

---

[17] Geer, "Occasional Address for the Year 1847," 33; and Geer, "My Trip to Oregon."

[18] Hastings, Overland Journey from Illinois, Beinecke Library, 16–17.

[19] "From Fort Hall," *California Star,* 4 September 1847; Grant to Simpson, 31 December 1847, D.5/20, HBC Archives, 715; and Ogden and Douglas to Simpson, 1 September 1847, Anne Morton transcription, HBC Archives, D.5/20, 185–185d.

Hockett's hips and backbone had worn through the skin. "We heard of a great deal of sickness in other companies," Hockett wrote: an entire family reportedly died in the Burnt River Mountains. He could never read his father's trail letters "without feeling a horror of what my parents, sister and uncle must have endured, and their sufferings were no worse than the sufferings of hundreds of others of the emigrants in 1847, as that has passed into history as the sickly season on the plains."[20]

A few emigrants had reached the mission station at Waiilatpu by the second week of August, and "parties of single men preceding the great body of American emigrants" began to arrive at Fort Vancouver by 1 September.[21] Sickness, death, and stampedes plagued the 1847 Oregon companies, but their real suffering began after they arrived at the barren, rocky Snake River country with its "great scarcity of water." In the Blue Mountains, "the wolves howled so that we could not hear ourselves talk," Joseph Brown recalled.[22] Having survived that ordeal, the weary sojourners still had to cross two hundred miles of deserts and mountains to reach "the rolling roaring foaming dashing splashing rumbling tumbling smooth gentle Columbia," as Isaac Pettijohn called it, and the trail's final and greatest challenge.[23] "The 'Blue' and 'Caskade' range of mountains are worse to cross than the Rocky mountains," Robert Caufield wrote.[24] The Cascades, emigrants soon learned, were much worse.

SIMPLY A RAVINE: THE BARLOW ROAD

At The Dalles in 1847, travelers could choose to pay the Barlow Road toll and cross the Cascades or raft down the treacherous river to Fort Vancouver. "The reports from the Barlow road through the mountains had pronounced it impassable," Loren Hastings heard on 20 October. His party built a boat large enough to take their families and wagons and joined the majority of the emigration that braved the whitewater journey down the Columbia, which was as arduous and dangerous as ever. Ominously, Hastings wrote, "many of our children had the measles."[25]

In addition to the difficult terrain it crossed, the Barlow Road's key problem was a lack of feed for exhausted livestock, and the scarcity became worse with use. Paul Darst, one of the first to cross the mountains in 1847, "campt on a small creek at the tolegate at the foot of the cascades" on 1 September and reported passing Nathaniel Bowman's train, "the foremost company on the road," two days

---

[20] Harty to "Dear Father," 29 June 1847; Hockett, Recollections, 1914, Introduction, 4, 9, 11, both Oregon Historical Society; and Hulin, Day Book or Journal, 19 June 1847, Lane County Pioneer Museum.

[21] Drury, *Marcus and Narcissa Whitman,* 2:192–93.

[22] Brown, Recollection of 1847, Bancroft Library.

[23] Pettijohn, Diary, 27 August 1847, Bancroft Library.

[24] Robert Caufield to John Caufield, Letter, 1 April 1848, Oregon Historical Society.

[25] Hastings, Overland Journey from Illinois, 20 October 1847, Beinecke Library, 31. The emigrants contracted measles *after* arriving in Oregon.

later. His party camped within a mile of Oregon City on 7 September without noting any difficulties.[26] At Barlows Gate on 30 September, James and Nancy Coon paid the five-dollar toll. Three days later—two of them with no grass— they crossed the summit. "We packed our plunder all up the hill," James Coon wrote. "It stunk with dead cattle. Here we lost five oxen. I buried an anvil and some log chains to the left of the road at the foot of the summit." Over the next six rainy days, the Coons spent four nights with no grass (they cut maple branches for browse at the foot of Laurel Hill) and two nights with little grass. After ten days on the toll road, the family upset their wagon again in a massive mud hole where the road made a sharp turn around a log. "We spilled all we had, even our sack of gold and silver in all amounting to five dollars. All said, we had a muddy fingering getting it all together again." On 10 October they passed Philip Foster's farm—the "first house in oregon!!!"—and camped at last with ample grass.[27]

"The rainy season had set in and the emigration ahead of us had cut the roads up until our wagons would go down to the hubs," recalled Calvin Geer after his family lost all their cows. "The roads were awful with mud."[28] Joseph Henry Brown was especially critical of the route, which "was simply a ravine—nothing more—cut through a tremendous forest, very narrow, stumps so high that wagons could scarcely pass over them, while the swamps and creeks if bridged at all, were loose poles that would slide about." Even the weather was awful—"cold insinuating rain and continuous sleet." Brown saw an incredible amount of dead livestock, and his party's worn-out animals died rapidly. The travelers "looked in dismay and the cattle seemed to moan in distress" at the yawning abyss and sharp descent at Laurel Hill. "Of all the hills or mountains that we had heretofore encountered and surmounted, this was the most appalling," Brown wrote.[29] Isaac Pettijohn "had it rough and tumble" climbing "over stumps stones rocks logs roots and evry thing immagineable."[30] A year later the road made a lasting and more favorable impression on Zilphia E. Rigdon. "Two days of climbing the slippery hills found us at Philip Fosters," she recalled fifty-one years later, "which was considered a haven of rest, to the weary emigrants."[31]

The Barlow Road never made money during its long life, but it had a romantic payoff for the Barlow family. Brothers William and James K. Barlow met sisters Rachel Ann and Rebecca Larkin at the end of their family's hard journey to Oregon in 1847. William married Rachel Ann, and James married Rebecca.[32]

---

[26] Darst, Diary, University of Oregon Library, 6.

[27] Coon and Coon, Diary, 10 October 1847. The location is now the Philip Foster Farm National Historic Site.

[28] Geer, "Occasional Address for the Year 1847," 33; and Geer, "My Trip to Oregon."

[29] Brown, Recollection of 1847, Bancroft Library.

[30] Pettijohn, Diary, 6 September 1847, Bancroft Library.

[31] Rigdon to Perkins, 1 February 1900, in Bristow Papers, University of Oregon Library, 10.

[32] Thanks to James M. Tompkins for alerting me to this story.

TROUBLE WITH THE CAYUSE INDIANS

Early in May 1847, Southern Road Commissioner Levi Scott led a party of east-bound travelers south through the Willamette Valley. They were "about 35 in number," Isaac Pettijohn recorded, "besides three small children."[33] After Scott arrived at Fort Hall in mid-June, about seventy wagons followed him west: they benefited immensely from the suffering and sacrifices of the emigrants who had built the road in 1846. Their first train reached the site of what is now Eugene in early November, while the last wagons of 1847 arrived by month's end.[34]

But it was not easy. "Toiling over these horrible roads," Lester Hulin complained, produced upsets, breakdowns, and other losses. He called them the worst roads he had ever traveled. Indians proved to be the trail's primary challenge: they constantly raided the emigrants' stock and sometimes attacked the travelers directly. "These prowling indians are as hard to find as the deer," Hulin groused. When one set of raiders found the stock too closely guarded, Hulin charged they vented their spite on fourteen-year-old Hannah Ann Davis, who had been baking by the fire. "They shot 3 arrows at her. Two of them hit her. One passed through the calf of her leg and the other through her arm into her side."[35] The wounded girl fell into the fire but survived to give birth to ten children.[36]

On the main road to Oregon in 1847, an eerie sight greeted travelers at the end of the trail. "There has been two emptyings of this mountain since we came here," wrote Robert Caufield, describing the volcanic eruptions that were percolating from Mount Saint Helens. "The report we could hear distinctly, & the reflections seen in the sky at night."[37] Even more ominous omens marked the end of the trail that year. Blood began flowing at The Dalles when the first ten men arrived on 23 August. "Several Americans had a fatal affray with the Indians," Hudson's Bay Company officers reported, and the Walla Wallas killed a traveler and badly wounded two others. The emigrants abandoned all their property to the Indians, who lost a principal chief in the affair. The Americans would warmly resent this, the officers predicted, "and the consequences will be disastrous to the wretched Indians."[38]

---

[33] Pettijohn, Diary, 1 May 1847, Bancroft Library.

[34] Davis, *The Oskaloosa Company*, 46, 47.

[35] Hulin, Day Book or Journal, 23, 25 October 1847, Lane County Pioneer Museum.

[36] Davis, *The Oskaloosa Company*, 117–18.

[37] Robert Caufield to John Caufield, Letter, 1 April 1848, Oregon Historical Society. Both Frémont and Wilkes reported volcanic activity at Mount Saint Helens that continued well into the 1850s. "Contemporary sketches and paintings by Paul Kane suggest the mountain was probably erupting at a point halfway down the north slope before or during 1847. The vent was apparently the Goat Rocks dome, which was removed by the 1980 eruption. On the basis of these and other observations, scientists think eruptive activity may have continued intermittently until 1857." See Pringle, *Roadside Geology of Mount St. Helens*, 14.

[38] Ogden and Douglas to Simpson, 1 September 1847, D.5/20, HBC Archives, 185–185d.

The flood of newcomers reported a dramatic increase in rumors of violence and actual conflict with Oregon's Indians. At the foot of the Blue Mountains, Joseph Henry Brown recalled, "we began to hear vague rumors of trouble with the Cayuse Indians, that they had robbed some trains etc., which was confirmed the next day by a letter written by a victim."[39] Loren Hastings "learned that the Walla Walla Indians had robbed several wagons and killed a white man & the whites had killed their chief, so we intend to take Whitman's near road."[40] West of the Umatilla River, John E. Ross found the site of one attack covered with scattered books and destroyed beds. Near the John Day River, he discovered four families hiding in a canyon. While the men were searching for stolen cattle, Walla Wallas stole a wagon, goods, money, and clothing, leaving six naked women and their children wrapped in a bolt of muslin. One of the women, a Mrs. Rodgers, defended her wagon with an ax.[41] Perhaps reporting the same incident, Loren Hastings "found three wagons that had been robbed by the Indians & 12 head of Oxen driven off. Tears stood in the eyes of the women & children & the men were down in the mouth."[42]

Native Oregonians were only reacting to the obvious. "Our cattle and hogs destroy the grapes and roots upon which the Indians, and their horses in part subsist. Their fisheries are also disturbed," Columbia Lancaster wrote from the Willamette Valley that December. He and his neighbors had expected that government agents would have paid the tribes for their lands, but the Indians "had been promised this and had often been deceiv'd." Seeing the swelling tide of emigration, the more remote bands were "assured that the day is at hand when they too must retire and surrender their lands without consideration."[43] The tribes had been pushed to the wall.

Those emigrants who went to the Waiilatpu Mission learned of the faster, drier cutoff Marcus Whitman had shown emigrants in 1844, although Frémont had first used it the previous fall. Whitman guided emigrants over his trace in 1847 and returned to improve it. "I found it necessary to look out a new road to avoid the hills along the shore of the Columbia & the Crossing of the John Days River," he wrote after traversing the wretched road down the Columbia to The Dalles. Whitman explored a new route back to his mission and opened "a much shorter & better" trail between the Umatilla and The Dalles. "By following a small stream & then a dry ravine I was able to avoid most of the hills & heavy obstacles of the old wagon road," he said. It bypassed most Indians, and for travelers headed for

[39] Brown, Recollection of 1847, Bancroft Library.

[40] Hastings, Overland Journey from Illinois, 10 October 1847, Beinecke Library, 29.

[41] Bancroft, *History of Oregon,* 1:645.

[42] Hastings, Overland Journey from Illinois, Beinecke Library, 30.

[43] Lancaster, "A Columbia Lancaster Letter about Oregon in 1847," 43.

the Barlow Road, the new route road did not strike the Columbia at all. Now wagons could head west along the south bank of the Umatilla River from the base of the Blue Mountains to the ford at present-day Pendleton, recross the river at Echo (Fort Henrietta in 1848), and take a better trail. Over the next two years, emigrants who followed the old guidebooks down the Columbia met wagons coming at them on the same road in the opposite direction, generating surprise and confusion when parties learned they were both bound for Oregon.[44]

Peter W. Crawford recalled Whitman's "mission of benevolence, conveying and escorting a company of immigrants over a new and much improved road to the Dalles." The cutoff shortened the route "and gave us good grass and water all the way," he noted. On 18 October 1847, Whitman proudly described his much shorter and better route in a letter, claiming his new road avoided "many bad hills as well as the sands of the Columbia and what is still more desirable, they have grass in abundance."[45]

It was the last known letter Marcus Whitman ever wrote.

FEW CARED TO COME TO CALIFORNIA: 1847

The entire 1847 overland emigration to California, Chester Ingersoll reported, consisted of "only about 60 or seventy wagons," but it probably numbered ninety wagons and as many as 450 emigrants.[46] This was less than half the 1846 total, since "few cared to come to California on account of the Mexican War."[47] Ironically, several hundred Americans used the trail to leave California, including two large military contingents, the first under the command of General Kearny (who had the mutinous Frémont in tow), and the second led by Commodore "Fighting Bob" Stockton, who in March ordered Archibald Gillespie to determine how many men and mules were necessary "to take us home comfortably and with the proper dignity as conquerors of the country."[48]

General Kearny's Mormon bodyguard buried the bodies they could find at the "Cannibal Camp" at Donner Lake.[49] William Trubody recalled meeting the command at the Big Sandy. Since it was the year after the Donner disaster, Trubody wrote, Frémont particularly cautioned the emigrants "to avoid delays but to keep

---

[44] Whitman to Greene, 18 October 1847, in Hulbert and Hulbert, *Marcus Whitman, Crusader,* 3:243.

[45] Ibid.; and Bancroft, *History of Oregon,* 1:647.

[46] Ingersoll, *Overland to California in 1847,* 36; and Unruh, *The Plains Across,* 119.

[47] Camp, "William Alexander Trubody and the Overland Pioneers of 1847," 125.

[48] Stockton to Gillespie, 11 March 1847, Gillespie Papers, UCLA. Stockton signed two receipts in Gillespie's collection: an advance on 27 June of $5,324.57 to buy animals and cover expenses and an additional $7,000 receipt on 27 October 1847 for the overland expedition.

[49] Jones, "The Journal of Nathaniel V. Jones," 22 June 1847, 19.

moving along, but not to crowd the teams lest they give out." At the mouth of the Raft River, Trubody remembered, "many persons standing at the forks of the road bidding good bye to each other and saying if you ever come my way come & see us."[50] Bidwell-Bartleson party veteran Charles Hopper led the largest California-bound party of some one hundred men, women, and children into the Great Basin. "At one place on the Humboldt River, the Indians had placed large stones in the road, and we caught them engaged in that business with the design of impeding the trains that came along," James Findla recalled.[51] Hooper's company crossed the Sierra and arrived in detachments at Johnsons Ranch in the first weeks of October.

Chester Ingersoll was with a second company of twenty wagons that met Stockton's escort on 19 August on the road to "Hot Spring valley," today Thousand Springs Valley in Nevada. Farther down the trail Ingersoll encountered almost naked Indians he called the Shawshawnees. "This tribe will steal and kill your cattle—they will come as friends, but you must treat them as enemies, and keep them out of your camp," he warned. His party treated them as friends until they stole four oxen, a cow, and a horse. The emigrants then followed the raiders twenty miles and found a dead ox but nothing else. "After that we shot at every Indian we saw—this soon cleared the way, so that we did not see any Indians for 200 miles." Ingersoll's train arrived at Johnsons Ranch on 2 October.[52]

"The last companies arrived at the first settlements before the middle of October," reported the *California Star*. "It is not deemed safe to be on the mountains later than the last of that month."[53] Fears grew that another disaster had overtaken the emigration, for it seemed the last trains had vanished. Sixteen wagons under the command of a Mr. Gordon met Stockton's escort, who advised them to take the new southern route to Oregon until they reached the Sacramento River, "and by descending it they would avoid the Sierra Nevada." The new South Road to Oregon did not cross the Sacramento, but this advice may have come from Stockton's guide, Samuel Hensley, who had not seen the route but had descended the Sacramento with Joseph Chiles in 1843. "But after laying by one week at the [Lost River] examining the country they concluded it would be safer to follow the road to Oregon." Eleven Oregon-bound wagons passed Gordon's party and it followed them to the Willamette Valley, arriving in late October.[54]

---

[50] Camp, "William Alexander Trubody and the Overland Pioneers of 1847," 125–26.

[51] Findla, Statement, 1878, Bancroft Library. Findla says his party killed two Indians "at Caw Village" in today's Kansas and implies they killed four others on the Humboldt.

[52] Ingersoll, *Overland to California in 1847,* 37–39, 43.

[53] "The Old Road," *California Star,* 1 April 1848, 4/4.

[54] *Oregon Spectator,* 25 November 1847. For Hensley's previously unrecognized status as captain—or, more probably, guide—for Stockton, see Gillespie, autograph certificate "showing that Captain Hensley was Captain of the party which escorted Stockton across the Rocky Mountains from California," Gillespie Papers, UCLA.

A second party under William Wiggins set out for the Humboldt River with eighteen wagons and about eighty people. Upon reaching the Black Rock Desert, he decided to follow the "new route across the country to the head waters of the Sacramento." Someone heading east gave him a waybill to California, and Wiggins surely had a copy of the 1845 Frémont-Preuss map that confused the Lost River with the "Headwaters of the main Branch of the Sacramento," a mistake repeated in the waybill Scott drafted and Jesse Applegate sent to the *Oregon Spectator* in April 1848. The *California Star* hoped the fate of the Donner party would persuade way-worn travelers not to try "*short cuts*," but even this example was "not sufficient to deter Mr. Wiggins." With no tidings from his party, the *Star* was "constrained to fear" that the weather or treacherous and ferocious Indians had wiped them out.[55] Such fears were groundless, for Wiggins, like Gordon, wisely pointed his wagons toward Oregon. His company followed the South Road into the settlements, arriving in early November. Fearing a repeat of the Donner disaster, Californians dispatched two parties to search for the lost wagons, but Wiggins finally put such concerns to rest when he sailed into San Francisco in April 1848.[56]

A ROAD FOR THE HOUSE OF ISRAEL: DESERET

In his notes describing the Oregon Trail in 1844, fur-trade veteran James Clyman thought establishing "a resting place" in the Salt Lake Valley "would verry much assist Emigrants and others passing to and from the states to all parts of the Pacific Country."[57] Such a task had no appeal for most Americans, who felt the trails crossed a vast and barbaric wilderness that was fatally inhospitable for a civilized people. So the task of building a city on the road west fell to the religious movement whose members called themselves Latter-day Saints but who were known to the world as the Mormons.

Founded by twenty-four-year-old visionary Joseph Smith in 1830, this singular American religion created controversy and conflict wherever its adherents tried to build a gathering place to await the return of Jesus Christ. After being driven out of Missouri in 1838, Smith's political ambitions and revolutionary religious doctrines on statecraft, economics, and marriage contributed to his murder in 1844. His most talented successor, Brigham Young, led the Mormons out of Illinois in 1846, determined to find a refuge where they could build the Kingdom of God and rule themselves.

[55] Jesse Applegate to George Abernethy, 20 March 1848, Oregon Historical Society; and "The Old Road," *California Star,* 1 April 1848, 4/4.

[56] Stewart, *California Trail,* 189–92.

[57] Clyman, *James Clyman, Frontiersman,* 127.

War and poverty prevented the Saints, as they identified themselves, from moving to Alta California as quickly as they had hoped, but in April 1847 Young began his modern exodus, leading a small party west from Council Bluffs to pioneer "a road for the House of Israel to travel in for many years to come."[58] Other caravans totaling four or five hundred wagons and (according to Captain Henry Turner's tally near Fort Laramie) 3,106 people followed two months behind "the Pioneer Camp."[59] By fall 1847 more than three thousand Latter-day Saints had settled around Great Salt Lake City, the settlement Brigham Young founded that summer.[60]

Even the Mormons were not convinced they could survive in the harsh environment of the Great Basin, but with much hard work they built a string of settlements along the fertile natural oasis of the Wasatch Mountains. The community tried to enter the Union in 1849 as the State of Deseret, a word from their scriptures meaning honeybee. They almost achieved statehood in 1850, when Zachary Taylor proposed creating one big state out of most of the conquered Mexican territory, but the Compromise of 1850 instead created Utah Territory. Utah would never become a state while the Mormons practiced their doctrine of "Celestial Marriage"—polygamy.[61]

This deeply religious society, whose devout members gave their complete political, economic, and spiritual loyalty to their church, developed interdependent relations with the annual emigration. Overlanders sought the supplies, rest, and restored animals the Mormons could provide, and the travelers brought clothing, manufactured goods, and money desperately needed in Utah. Travelers also abandoned immense piles of property "stacked like cordwood" along the trail that the Mormons systematically recovered—stoves, plows, furniture, books, clothes, medicine, and bacon.

Many visitors wrote very positive accounts of meeting the Mormons, whose dreadful popular image hardly matched the reality of the orderly and polite people they found in Utah. Salt Lakers quickly earned the reputation of being religious eccentrics and sharp but fair traders. Whether they were harmless or dangerous was a matter of intense debate. The Mormons, however, had long and hard memories of the wrongs they had endured in the states, and many of them had a deep-seated desire to even the score with the unbelieving "Gentiles" from Illinois

---

[58] Woodruff, *Journal*, 27 May 1847.

[59] "Interesting from the Emigration," *California Star*, 18 September, 2/1; and Turner, *The Original Journals*, 133–34. The usual estimate of the size of the main Mormon 1847 emigration is two thousand, but in addition to 1,550 adults, Turner's census counted "1,556 [of] both sexes under 16 years of age."

[60] Great Salt Lake City remained the city's official name until 1868, when local officials removed "Great."

[61] The best history of Utah Territory is Bigler, *Forgotten Kingdom*.

in general and Missouri in particular. Territorial Governor Brigham Young's ill-concealed resentment of the American government contributed to this natural hostility; the territorial legislature passed a series of laws aimed at "fleecing the Gentiles" with punitive grazing laws and criminalizing swearing on a territorial road. Local courts consistently convicted travelers of ridiculous offenses and refused to rule against Mormons. Such abuses led to a host of complaints—and the more time sojourners spent in the territory and learned about the workings of Mormon theocracy, the more bitter their objections.[62]

Nonetheless, however heated and colorful the rhetoric that entertained and appalled visitors to the Mormons' brush tabernacle on Temple Square, the hospitality of the people and the good order and industriousness of their neat communities won them many friends. Even those who came away appalled at their oddly puritanical form of polygamy were amazed at the towns and villages they had created with astonishing speed in the midst of the wilderness. And even the most violent anti-Mormons quickly realized how valuable it was to have a self-sustaining way station on the roads to Oregon and California, where exhausted sojourners could find respite from the hardships of the trail or take refuge from the quick approach of winter. The Oregon and California trails would never be the same.

SOME KIND OF METTLE: THE GREAT RUSH BEGINS, 1848

According to legend, Francisco Lopez first discovered gold in California on his fortieth birthday, 9 March 1842, when he pulled up some wild onions and saw the glittering metal clinging to the roots. By the end of the year Lopez and his compatriots had extracted some 125 pounds of gold from Placeritas Canyon, but recent research indicates that Spanish miners had found gold in southern California as early as 1820. Still, even though these discoveries drew varying amounts of attention, they aroused little interest in the remote province.[63]

The golden wealth scattered along the slopes of the Sierra Nevada had not entirely escaped the notice of American pioneers. Elisha Stephens, a veteran of the gold mines of Georgia, told John Townsend he started across the plains for the express purpose of finding gold. "We are in a gold country," he allegedly said somewhere in the Rocky Mountains, and upon washing some gravel, Stephens "got the color of gold." He spent much of spring 1845 retrieving the wagons his party had abandoned at Truckee Lake, but he saw "no signs of gold where subsequently the whole country was found to contain it."

---

[62] David L. Bigler studied this phenomenon in Goodell, *A Winter with the Mormons.*
[63] Worden, "New Study Will Nag scv Historians," *Santa Clarita Valley Signal,* 14 August 1996.

John Bidwell, later dubbed the "Prince of California Pioneers," recalled that Pablo Gutierrez told him in 1844 that he had made an important discovery while searching for his Native wife. "There surely is gold on Bear River in the mountains," he said. Bidwell followed Gutierrez five or six miles into the mountains on the Bear River, but Gutierrez said he could not find the gold without a *batea,* which Bidwell thought must be a complicated machine, but which was in fact a simple wooden bowl. Bidwell meant to investigate further, but his plans were interrupted, and Gutierrez was taken prisoner while carrying rebel dispatches during the insurrection against the oppressive regime of Governor Manuel Micheltorena and "hanged to a tree."[64]

A veteran of the Donner party recalled finding at least a half ounce of gold about fifty miles west of the Great Salt Lake, but "this was lost in our further troubles," he wrote. "And while my wife and children were pent up in their cabin in the snow, John Denton, a cutler, whose knowledge of gold was undisputed, collected out of the gravel rock used as back and sides of the fire place, a spoonful of gold," James Frazier Reed remembered three years later. Denton intended to bring it to California but died in the mountains. Reed said his little boy Tom called one of these rocks "his gold mine." Reed later asked his wife why did she not save the gold. Margaret Reed replied that "gold was least in her thoughts;—something to eat for herself and children was to her of more value than all [the] gold in the world."[65]

Despite these stories, for all practical purposes this vast mineral wealth was undetected until John Augustus Sutter decided to build a sawmill on the South Fork of the American River to support his burgeoning frontier empire. To do the job, Sutter formed a partnership with James Marshall, a skilled carpenter who had trekked to Oregon in 1844, and hired Mormon Battalion veterans who had applied for work at his fort. On the morning of 24 January 1848, Marshall inspected the mill's tailrace. That night, Henry W. Bigler wrote, "this day some kind of mettle was found in the tail race that looks like goald." He later inserted in darker ink, "first discovered by James Martial, the Boss of the Mill." Another worker, Azariah Smith, recorded that the metal was "found in the raceway in small pieces; some have been found that would weigh five dollars."

"Boys," Marshall told his workers the next morning, "by G—d I believe I have found a gold mine."[66] Marshall and Sutter tried to keep the discovery secret, but within four months gold fever had swept the region, and two thousand copies of the *California Star* were carrying the news to the East Coast.

---

[64] Bidwell, "Life in California Before the Gold Discovery," 173, 177–79.

[65] Reed to "Dear Brother," 11 August 1848, "From California. A Letter from James F. Reed," *Illinois Daily Journal,* 29 June 1849, 2.

[66] Paul, *The California Gold Discovery,* 62; Smith, *The Gold Discovery Journal,* 108; and Bigler, *Bigler's Chronicle of the West,* 89.

On 2 February 1848, less than two weeks after Marshall's discovery, Mexico ceded the territory that now comprises the states of Utah, Nevada, California, and New Mexico, plus large parts of Arizona, Wyoming, and Colorado, to the United States for fifteen million dollars. The Treaty of Guadalupe Hidalgo made James K. Polk's vision of a continental nation a reality, but the lightly populated region the United States first conquered and then purchased posed its own challenges—and put the issue of the future of slavery squarely before the young republic.

Peace with Mexico did not enhance emigration to the West Coast in 1848. As Indian Agent Thomas Fitzpatrick traveled east that spring, he met the vanguard of the migration at the forks of the Platte, "and between that point and West Port met 364 wagons moving along quietly in small parties of from 12 to 30 wagons." Fitzpatrick estimated that 1,700 emigrants were bound for Oregon and only about 150 for California, but several hundred travelers would change their destination.[67] More importantly, the discovery of gold would soon produce the largest voluntary migration in history. As if in anticipation, the California Trail expanded as men and one very determined woman worked out new routes around the Great Salt Lake and over the Sierra Nevada.

THE GREAT OREGON ROAD: 1848

"I crossed the river Missouri at St. Joseph," William Anderson wrote on 27 April 1848, "and with the emigration I steered my course across the plains for Oregon."[68] On the Independence Road, Edward Smith camped at Elm Grove, which was now reduced to "a lone tree with the top cut off and a few goose berry bushes." Smith indicated that year's emigration divided into Oregon and California companies not long after setting out on "the great Oregon road."[69]

The westbound trains boasted an impressive roster of trail veterans, including Peter Lassen. Joseph Chiles and Samuel Hensley had each made four trips across the plains, and James Clyman had made even more. Clyman's party, under "Camp Master" W. N. Wambaugh, left the frontier in late April and soon had a month's lead on the other trains.[70] Years later, Thomas S. Bayley recalled that his father agreed to carry "about 500 letters for Oregon" from Independence. "I do not

---

[67] Fitzpatrick to Harvey, 24 June 1848, in Mattes, *Platte River Road Narratives*, 115. In all about 1,700 Americans went overland to the Pacific in 1848, with 1,300 going to Oregon and 400 to California, only about a third of the previous year's migration. Unruh probably underestimated the size of the California emigration. See Unruh, *The Plains Across*, 119; and Clyman, *James Clyman, Frontiersman*, 292.

[68] Anderson, "The Diary and Memoirs," 1.

[69] Smith, "A Journal of Scenes and Incidents," 29 April, 1 and 7 May 1848.

[70] Clyman, *James Clyman, Frontiersman*, 283.

know, but think that was the first and last regular mail that was ever dispatched in the United States by ox teams." The Bayleys wound up following Joseph Chiles to California, where they charged two dollars a letter for their services. It took "just four days short of six months" for the mail to reach Placerville, Bayley said, but "There was not a man that ever made any complaint about the price."[71]

The traveling parties coalesced into four large trains and several smaller ones, plus Hensley's mounted party of a dozen men, which had originally been organized to escort Lieutenant Archibald Gillespie back to California.[72] Upon reaching the Platte, Chiles's company consisted of 112 souls, including 37 men, but by the time it arrived at the forks of the Platte, the train had grown to forty-seven wagons "and near 80 men quite a formidable force," Richard Martin May reported.[73] Wilson Blain's Oregon outfit consisted of twenty-five wagons, 35 able-bodied men, and 95 total members, indicating that a majority of Blain's companions were women and children. Despite this, Blain reported, "From the number of the guns, pistols, bowie knives, &c., which abound, we might be mistaken for a band of banditti."[74]

After a dry winter that produced a poor crop of grass on the plains, hard weather greeted the emigrants. "It rained all day," Richard May complained on 22 May near the junction of the Saint Joseph Road, "and in the evening it fell in Torrents." The storms at least provided a distraction from a constant of overland travel: boredom. "The dull Monotony of a Prarie Journey is quite Tiresome it being so uniform that the variety which we Seek is no where to be found," May wrote. "The Crack of the whip the clanking of Chains and the Still more disagreeable Schreek of Wagons" accompanied the routine and hard work.[75]

At the head of Grand Island the rearguard of the emigration found the Oregon Battalion of Mounted Volunteers laying the foundations of Fort Childs, at year's end renamed Fort Kearny and known as new Fort Kearny to distinguish it from an abandoned post of the same name on the Missouri River. The fort was formally established in May 1848: by early June, the battalion was laying off the grounds and the "tented field in the open Prarie had quite an imposing appearance."[76] This no-frills stronghold, the first U.S. military station designed explicitly to protect overland wagon travel, quickly became a trail milepost.

---

[71] Bayley, The First Overland Mail Bag to California, Bancroft Library.

[72] Gillespie to Captain Hensley, 13 May 1848, giving Hensley command at Weston, Missouri, of the party for California, Gillespie Papers, UCLA. The ten men apparently were part of Stockton's escort and were returning to California at government expense.

[73] May, The Schreek of Wagons, 21–22, 30.

[74] Blain to Kerr, The Preacher, 22 August 1849, 130, Oregon Historical Society.

[75] May, The Schreek of Wagons, 15, 22.

[76] Settle, The March of the Mounted Riflemen, 14; and May, The Schreek of Wagons, 3 June 1848, 25. The fort was named after Gen. Stephen Watts Kearny, but the town built across the river adopted the spelling "Kearney," resulting in generations of confusion.

Most companies had the usual encounters with the Pawnees and Lakotas, but it appears the entire emigration experienced no fatalities. The Pawnees "are the scourge and terror of the plains, and with good reason are much dreaded by the emigrants," noted Wilson Blain, reporting a typical reaction. In contrast, he found the "children of nature," the Sioux, "just like the rest of mankind; some of them are rude, ignorant, and almost in a state of nudity, while others are as aristocratic and dressy as nabobs."[77]

Other travelers saw few Indians. "I have lived to See one Pawnee Indian," wrote Richard May at Fort Kearny. "He came into camp." May estimated there were about 150 lodges of Indians camped around Fort Laramie, where the sojourn-ers traded off lame cattle and repaired their wagons. Traveling leisurely, Joseph Chiles caught up with the last of the wagons on 25 June. The night before, James Bordeaux, the post's proprietor, had provided "an entertainment." May com-mented, "Several young Ladies and Gentlemen from the Train partook of his generosity. Dancing was the Civil Mirth resorted to on this occasion."[78] Edward Smith was not entertained: "last night they had a real fandango at Fort John and to their shame be it said some young ladies belonging to [the] emigrants went to it where some of the gentlemen got gloriously drunk."[79]

At the end of July the last wagons arrived on Thomas Fork of Bear River. After experiencing "the most severe winter and dreadful storms that I have known since my residence in this country, which is twenty-four years," Thomas L. Smith had received a starving band of messengers from Oregon led by his old friend, Joe Meek, who had "suffered extremely" to reach Bear River in early April 1848. "I wish to inform the public in the states, that I am building a trading post at Big Timber, on Bear River for the purpose of supplying the Oregon emigration with all sorts of Vegetables, and will give a liberal price for their broken down cattle," Pegleg announced in a letter he sent east with Meek, who was carrying urgent messages to Washington, D.C. "I shall soon have a large farm in opera-tion."[80] Clearly, competition for the emigrant trade was opening up. Edward Smith complained about the millions of mosquitoes and green-headed horse flies that attacked him some two miles below Smith's principal trading post. On the last day of July, his train "had a select party at old Pegleg's" and the quality of the camp had to attend "to take comfort among their equals the half breeds and the drunken mountaineers."[81]

---

[77] Blain to Kerr, June 1848, in Blain, Letters, 1848–57, Oregon Historical Society, 14.

[78] May, *The Schreek of Wagons,* 26, 41–42.

[79] Smith, "A Journal of Scenes and Incidents," California State Library, 129.

[80] Smith to Mr. Editor, 3 April 1848, in *St. Joseph Adventurer,* 19 May 1848, 183–84.

[81] Smith, "A Journal of Scenes and Incidents," 31 July 1848.

Returning from Oregon with about twenty mounted companions, Isaac Petti-john kept a detailed count of the oncoming emigration. He met a single wagon that led the way at Pacific Springs on 24 June and over the next eight days encountered a total of 343 wagons.[82] West of South Pass, Chiles led his train over Greenwoods Cutoff and camped the next day at Green River, where Edward Smith reported they did "some trading with the trappers & Mormons & repairing of wagons." At noon on 26 July, Smith met Joseph Walker, who may have spent the previous winter at Browns Hole. The celebrated mountaineer now "conducted us by a new Route to Hams fork of The Green River to avoid a very bad mountain," Smith reported. Chiles sold "much liquor" to the throng of trappers and Indians camped nearby, Smith complained. Many of them, naturally, "got beastly drunk."[83]

Wilson Blain reported Walker's adventures before the trapper fell in with the Chiles party. Blain's company crossed South Pass on 10 July and found a group of Mormons running a ferry at Green River. The ferrymen "attempted to appropri-ate eight of our cattle to their own use by driving them to Salt Lake. But we were so fortunate as to discover their trail and also to secure the services of Joseph Walker, the celebrated mountaineer," Blain wrote. Walker's posse pursued the thieves almost seventy-five miles and recaptured the cattle. Blain's company did not get a satisfactory report about the fate of the rustlers, but his companions "generally believed that Walker shot them." The Reverend Blain then made an ominous prediction: "If emigration to this Territory continues across the coun-try, the Mormons will be found to be a greater annoyance than the Indians. They station themselves at favorable points all along the road, and rob, and steal regularly as opportunity occurs of doing so with impunity. And being in constant communication with the Indians they possess a power which might be exerted with fearful effect." Many overlanders who later had positive experiences with the Latter-day Saints would dispute Blain's analysis of "this very usual exhibi-tion of Mormon character," but such charges would persist for as long as wagons crossed the trail.[84]

The emigrants of 1848 knew about the grisly fate of the Donner party, and reports of Indian trouble on the Oregon Trail did not stop the vast majority of them from going to the Northwest rather than California. Two companies stopped at Fort Hall to wait "for reinforcements having been told at the fort that they must go strong handed through the cayuse country as they were then at war with the oregon settlers [and] it was thought to be very dangerous traveling through their country." Edward Smith found "Indians Half Breeds Mexicans &ct." trading at the

---

[82] Clyman, *James Clyman, Frontiersman,* 292.

[83] Carter, *Our Pioneer Heritage,* 17:101–102; and Smith, "A Journal of Scenes and Incidents," 134.

[84] Blain to Kerr, *The Preacher,* 22 August 1849, 130, Oregon Historical Society.

TWO WORLDS COLLIDE.
Artist Nick Eggenhofer captured the tension
overland emigrants felt when they first encountered
American Indians. From Oren Arnold's *Thunder in the Southwest:
Echoes from the Wild Frontier.* Courtesy Evelyn E. Herman.

fort, along with two Mormon families making good-quality butter and cheese; corn, peas, and fine potatoes were growing in the post's garden.[85] (If he could not get the Hudson's Bay Company to outfit his post to trade with emigrants, Richard Grant apparently decided he could at least open a restaurant.)

Here the last of the "Californians of the season formed a single outfit," William Anderson reported, while those bound for Oregon organized into two parties he called the Gates and Jackson companies, which subsequently jockeyed for the lead position. "From Fort Hall the journey becomes more and more laborious and harassing," Blain wrote. "The pasturage is miserable, and the dust excessively annoying." The rumored Indian threat proved unfounded. William Anderson met several Cayuses in the Blue Mountains who showed no sign of hostility. Two days later he met volunteers from Oregon who told him the Indian war was over, for "they had all the hostile ones run back into the mountains." At the foot of the Umatilla Mountains, his party found the ruins of a Cayuse village and large bands of horses running wild.[86]

---

[85] Smith, "A Journal of Scenes and Incidents," 136.
[86] Anderson, "The Diary and Memoirs," 42–43, 60–62, 64, 65; and Blain to Kerr, *The Preacher,* 22 August 1849, 130, Oregon Historical Society.

Those who chose to follow the old trail to Oregon generally had hard but uneventful trips. "The Blue Mountains presented more high, steep hills to climb than any other part of the road," Wilson Blain recalled, "but we surmounted them without much difficulty." Anderson arrived at "what is called Barlows gate" in early September. Barlow charged his five-dollar toll to "pay him for working the road through the Cascade mountains." Some paid the toll, Anderson noted, some gave notes, "and others drove right along without doing either."[87]

Despite the Barlow Road, the Cascades were still "the most difficult and dangerous piece of road in the whole route," Blain wrote. "It is only some sixty-five miles through them, but it is the hardest week's work for both man and beast in the entire journey." Blain reached Oregon City in early October, "almost worn out with the tedious journey." He marveled, "Take it altogether, the road in its entire length is one of the wonders of the world."[88] But the Barlow Road had a key failing, and General Persifer Smith pointed out the road's major problem: its steep descents on the western slopes of the Cascade Range meant the only road to the Willamette Valley was "made to get into it, but not to go out of it."[89]

[87] Ibid., 24; and Anderson, "The Diary and Memoirs," 73–74.
[88] Blain to Kerr, October 1848, in Blain, Letters, 1848–57, Oregon Historical Society, 24.
[89] Bancroft, *History of Oregon,* 2:64n47, citing Smith's 1849 report to the Secretary of War.

WHERE A WAGON HAD NEVER BEEN BEFORE:
HENSLEY'S SALT LAKE CUTOFF

Not surprisingly, James Clyman's party led the first of three or four trains headed to California in 1848. Two Mormon dissenters, Hazen Kimball and James Pollock, joined Clyman's train. Later that fall, Kimball proudly boasted he had opened a new road to Fort Hall "where a wagon had never been before without a guide." He left Fort Hall on 15 August and turned south at Raft River four days later.[90] Twenty-six-year-old Pierre Barlow Cornwall led about twenty-five wagons only a day or so behind Clyman, perhaps simply the slower part of Clyman's train. Peter Lassen apparently followed about ten days later with ten wagons, meeting Mormon Battalion veterans west of Gravelly Ford, near what is now Beowawe, Nevada.[91] According to Samuel Rogers, Lassen's wagons "came by way of Salt Lake," and they had a Mormon bishop named Levi E. Riter with them.[92]

Traveling with the last of the California companies, Edward Smith left the Oregon Trail on 12 August and began climbing the Raft River Valley with Joseph R. Walker and Joseph Chiles, whose carriage broke down two days later on the rough road. "We encamped in a dell surrounded by rocks the roughest and most romantic that eyes ever beheld or fancy could imagine," Smith reported. "Broad and lofty domes tall and slender minarets towering spires &c. which I shall call the city of rocks."[93] Around noon the next day, "Capt. Hensley of the army with a pack of mules overtook us [on the road to Goose Creek]. They had left us at Rock Independence went to Salt Lake and got lost and nearly starved."[94]

In detouring to Salt Lake to take the Hastings Cutoff, Samuel J. Hensley had inadvertently opened the Salt Lake Cutoff, one of the last major components of the California Trail. Richard May described the disaster that turned Hensley into a trailblazer, although he initially intended only "to pass to Fort Bridger & Thence South of Salt lake." The packers ran into trouble on the Great Salt Desert when a heavy rainfall caught them on the thin crust of salt covering the snow-white playa. Unfortunately for Hensley and his ten men, the rain "So weakened the incrustation that they were verry near perishing in the mire." They had to abandon their packs to save their animals and lost most of their provisions and

---

[90] Clyman, *James Clyman, Frontiersman*, 286–87.

[91] Bigler, *Bigler's Chronicle of the West*, 122; and Smith, *The Gold Discovery Journal*, 139.

[92] Rogers, *The 1848 Trail Journal of Samuel Hollister Rogers*, 26 August 1848. Rogers's intriguing entry raises the possibility that it was Lassen and his wagons, not Samuel Hensley, who opened the Salt Lake Cutoff. Rogers was probably mistaken about Lassen's route.

[93] Smith, "A Journal of Scenes and Incidents," 16 August 1848, California State Library. This is the first use of the site's modern name I have found.

[94] Ibid., 12–17 August 1848, 137–38. Hensley was an officer in Frémont's California Battalion but never served in the regular army.

part of their clothing. The party went "48 hours without food or water and hard at work most of the time to Save the Property. They then retraced their Steps to the Mormon City and there replenished their Larder."[95]

Except for Hensley's unsuccessful foray into the Great Salt Desert, there is no record of any westbound emigrants using the Hastings Cutoff in 1847 or 1848, but mountaineer Miles Goodyear used the route both years to drive California horses to the Missouri frontier. In early November 1848, Goodyear told William Ridenbaugh that he had "learned after he left the valley of the Salt Lake, that a part of the Mexican trading expedition, who were on their return to Santa Fe had come into the Mormon camp for assistance and protection against the Utah Indians, and that some had gone back to California by the northern route rather than pass through the Utah country." Mormon apostle Parley P. Pratt noted that this "Mexican Caravan" helped to break "upon the monotony of our busy and peaceful life" in Great Salt Lake City. So it seems a band of New Mexican traders also joined the companies going west on the Humboldt Road.[96]

Not long after Hensley resupplied in Great Salt Lake City and left, the leaders at the new settlement reported his party had "tried the Hastings route, but the desert was so miry from heavy rains that they have returned and gone on by way of Fort Hall."[97] Instead of following Hazen Kimball's wagon tracks, after fording Bear River Hensley turned northwest across the Blue Springs Hills, heading directly for the Silent City of Rocks and the California Trail. In finding a relatively safe and easy way to get from the Salt Lake Valley to the California road, Hensley opened a trail that became a key connection in the gold-rush trail system.[98]

Hensley's pack train reached the California road on the morning of 17 August and overtook the Walker-Chiles company. Both groups soon had violent confrontations with the local tribes. "Mr. Peirson found a paper stating that Capt. S. J. Hensley's Co. of mules had shot three Digger Indians in this canion on the 29 of August," Edward Smith reported. The emigrants "encamped in a nest of Digger Indians" near present-day Winnemucca, Nevada, on 10 September. Next morning Joseph Chiles found four arrows in his bull and four other wounded animals. In revenge a member of the party shot an Indian.

At noon on 25 August, Chiles's train met twenty Mormons who had left Sutters Fort with pack mules in late July. As his wagon struggled westward over the next month, Edward Smith met two more pack trains and two wagon trains bound for

---

[95] May, *The Schreek of Wagons,* 86.

[96] Ridenbaugh, "From California and the Mountains," *St. Joseph Gazette,* 3 November 1848; and Journal History, 5 September 1848.

[97] Pratt to Young, Journal History, 9 August 1848.

[98] Hensley's route crossed several low mountain ranges to reach the Curlew Valley at present-day Snowville, Utah. Ironically, his memory is inaccurately preserved in the names of the Hansel Mountains and the Hansel Valley.

Salt Lake. The Mormons brought remarkable news: some of them had witnessed the discovery of gold the previous January, and they had opened a "new road to California" over the Sierra Nevada.[99] They had on average each extracted two ounces of gold per day," and "one particular Man made 700 dollars in one day," Richard May wrote.[100] Clyman's company heard the news at the Humboldt Sink. "They were all much elated at hearing about and seeing the California gold," wrote Mormon diarist Addison Pratt. Legend tells of an aged man who "sprang to his feet, threw his old wool hat upon the ground, and jumped upon it with both feet, then kicked it high in the air and exclaimed, 'Glory, hallalujah, thank God, I shall die a rich man yet!'"[101]

Word of the gold discovery was also making its way east over the trail along other paths. Zilphia E. Rigdon recalled that while her Oregon-bound party was camped on Bear River "that we first heard of the discovery of Gold in California" from Pegleg Smith. "It was a stunner to the men."[102]

A New Road to California: Carson Pass

On their two-thousand-mile march across the Southwest in 1846 and 1847, the Mormon Battalion hauled the first wagons to reach California from New Mexico. The process also transformed these mostly midwestern farm boys into skilled frontiersmen. After their discharge in Los Angeles in July 1847, more than two hundred of the veterans began a long march north to return to their families. Near the Donner camps in the Sierra, they received word from Brigham Young that those with no supplies should stay in California and work through the winter. More than half of them pressed on to Salt Lake, and a few went all the way back to the Missouri to find their kinfolk, but about eighty men returned to Sutters Fort, where many of them found work. As witnesses to Marshall's discovery, the Mormons became California's first prospectors and were able to extract small fortunes in gold from placer mines using their pocketknives and Indian baskets. Despite the wealth that would soon beckon the rest of the world to the new El Dorado, by June 1848 most of these men packed up and left.

Having seen the hard road over Truckee Pass, one veteran recalled, "We had become accustomed to pioneer life [and] thought we could find a better route."[103] A heavy snowpack turned back their first scouting party and delayed their departure until July. Despite the disappearance of the next three scouts sent into the

[99] Smith, "A Journal of Scenes and Incidents," 138–44. Ephraim Green, *A Road from El Dorado*, 30 August 1848, 32, reported the Walker-Chiles train had thirty-six wagons when they camped with the Mormons at Gravelly Ford.

[100] May, *The Schreek of Wagons*, 93.

[101] Pratt, *The Journals of Addison Pratt*, 350; Tyler, *A Concise History of the Mormon Battalion*, 340.

[102] Rigdon to Lilly Perkins, 1 February 1900, University of Oregon.

[103] Brown, *Life of a Pioneer*, 107.

Sierra to find a pass, the Mormons who assembled in a valley near today's Placerville were eager to start. Forty-five men and one woman, Melissa Burton Coray, a former army laundress, set out on 15 July 1848 to open a wagon road over the pass Kit Carson had crossed with Frémont in winter 1843. They discovered their murdered scouts and buried them near what is still known as Tragedy Spring. Wilford Hudson cut a blaze and carved an inscription on a nearby fir tree: "To the Memory of Daniel Browett, Ezrah H. Allen, Henderson Cox, Who was supposed to have Been Murdered and Buried by Indians On the Night of the 27th of June 1848."[104] Browett had been the party's chosen leader, and to replace him the men elected Samuel Thompson as their captain and Jonathan Holmes as their spiritual leader.

In a notable feat of pioneer road engineering, during the next two weeks the Thompson-Holmes party hauled eighteen wagons over West Mountain and Carson Pass. The veterans used fire and water to demolish the boulders that blocked their way through the narrows of West Carson Canyon, where the river at last escaped into the Carson Valley. They followed the Carson River some eighty miles to the edge of the Forty-mile Desert, where they turned northwest and traveled twenty-five miles to strike the Truckee River and the California Trail near what is now Wadsworth, Nevada.[105]

A second company of twelve wagons under Ebenezer Brown followed in August and improved the road.[106] Brown's party included two former employees of José Castro, who led the revolt against Governor Micheltorena and became commanding general of California. While waiting in Pleasant Valley, Jane Tompkins Hunter recalled, a man named Pedro and a woman who had been Castro's cook joined them, "and we took them to Salt Lake with us, where later the girl died, but Pedro remained with us, a faithful servant, and came back to California with us."[107] The terms of the Treaty of Guadalupe Hidalgo meant the couple would be the first known Mexican-American citizens to live in Utah. When Richard May met Brown's party on 11 September, the Mormons told him about their "New route over the Mountains," praising it as "Much better than the old road." They also told "glowing Stories about the gold mines."[108] "The road is very good," agreed Hazen Kimball, "much better than the old one, it is said by those who have travelled both."[109]

James Clyman and Joseph B. Chiles led their trains over the new route, blazing a direct path from the Humboldt Sink to the Carson River. No detailed accounts

[104] Green, *A Road from El Dorado*, 20, 51n49. The blaze became a famous trail landmark and is now preserved at the Marshall Gold Discovery Historic State Park at Coloma.

[105] Smith, *The Gold Discovery Journal*, 136n36.

[106] Green, *A Road from El Dorado*, 11.

[107] Hunter, "From the Record of Jane E. Hunter," LDS Archives.

[108] May, *The Schreek of Wagons*, 100.

[109] Clyman, *James Clyman, Frontiersman*, 287.

are known from Clyman's party, but May and Smith report that the Chiles company battled Indians all the way through Carson Valley and then fell to bickering among themselves. Edward Smith was especially unhappy that Chiles had exacted a wagon and team from one party member as payment for hauling about six hundred pounds of possessions to the settlements. "These were the only conditions or he might perish in the mountains," Smith observed. The man was obliged to accept this hard bargain.[110] "We have experienced a great many hard ships," May wrote, and he then made one of the first uses of a phrase that would become an enduring aphorism among overland travelers: "Let me tell you I have Seen the Elephant."[111] Richard May felt he had seen about everything there was to see.

Despite the ordeal, these parties proved the new road over the Sierra Nevada was passable by westbound wagons. As Kimball noted, men who had also been over the Truckee route considered the new road to be far better than the old. Samuel Hensley repaid the Mormons for their favor when he met the Thompson-Holmes party on 27 August and gave them what Henry Bigler called "a way bill of our Road from here to salt lake" by a route that "waggons have never went." In mid-September, the Mormons found Hensley's trail at City of Rocks and "made a waggon road" from there to Salt Lake. Hensley's Salt Lake Cutoff allowed Forty-niners who visited the new Latter-day Saint settlements to return directly to the California Trail, and during the gold rush the road the Mormon veterans blazed over Carson Pass became the most popular gateway to the new El Dorado.[112]

He Always Got Lost:
Lassen's Cutoff and Burnett's Road to Oregon

Peter Lassen was born in 1800 near Farum, Denmark, and immigrated to the United States in 1829. Ten years later he traveled to Oregon. By 1840 he had made his way to California, where he worked for John Sutter and acquired a Mexican land grant of 22,000 acres on the Sacramento River about ninety miles north of Sutters Fort. His Rancho Bosquero prospered as he developed his talents as a millwright and cattleman.[113] "Peter was a singular man, very industrious, very ingenious, and very fond of pioneering—in fact, of the latter stubbornly so," John Bidwell said of his Danish neighbor. "He had great confidence in his own power as a woodsman, but, strangely enough, he always got lost."[114]

[110] Smith, "A Journal of Scenes and Incidents," 145–46.

[111] May, *The Schreek of Wagons*, 110–11.

[112] Korns and Morgan, *West from Fort Bridger*, 283.

[113] Details on Lassen's adventures are from Hammond, "Peter Lassen and His Trail," 33–41.

[114] Bidwell, "Earliest Explorations of Colusa County," in Rogers, *Colusa County*, 47.

Lassen appreciated the benefits Sutter enjoyed because his fort was located at the end of the California Trail, and he may have hoped to put his own ranch in a similarly advantageous position. Lassen had guided Lieutenant Gillespie and his black servant, Ben, through northern California to Frémont's camp on Klamath Lake, perhaps along the route he intended for his new trail.[115] Lassen left California for Missouri on 19 July 1847 with Commodore Stockton and returned to his old hometown at Keytesville, where the local paper reported he had brought "a young Indian chief with him to show the sights and will take him back next spring." Lassen recruited a wagon party to follow him west in 1848, and among its members were a Master Mason, Saschal Woods, who carried a Masonic charter issued by the Grand Lodge of Missouri on 10 May 1848 for Western Star Lodge No. 98 that listed Peter Lassen as junior warden.[116]

At a meadow near what is now Rye Patch Reservoir in central Nevada, the Danish trailblazer turned his train of about ten wagons northwest onto the Applegate Trail. This oasis at the edge of the Black Rock Desert was soon known as Lassens Meadow (or, more often, Lawsons). After Lassen left the road to Oregon and headed south at Goose Lake, it quickly became apparent that the trailblazer was lost. To his exhausted and discouraged followers' good fortune, a company of Oregonians under Peter Burnett were heading for the gold mines and had followed Lassen's tracks.

With forty-six wagons and about 150 men, Burnett had left Oregon City "well provided with provisions, and means of every kind necessary to enable us to accomplish the trip." The worst part of the trek was not in California but in the notorious canyon in the Umpqua Mountains that had brought so much grief to the 1846 emigrants. Burnett's men "followed Applegate's Southern route" to Tule Lake, where they turned southeast. After blazing forty miles of wagon road to reach Pitt River and the drainage of the Sacramento, "we came across a wagon trail made by a party of Immigrants from the United States, and conducted by Cap. Lawson as pilot." The Oregonians found the rancher and his desperate followers "lost in the mountains and half-starved." Ten or fifteen of Burnett's men "cut out the road in one day as far as the timber extended—say fifteen miles—and did it as fast as the wagons could follow."[117] Lassen's people had converted their wagons into carts, and with the help of Burnett's party they reached the Sacramento Valley at the end of October.

---

[115] Bancroft, *History of California*, 5:24.

[116] Anonymous, "Tidings from the West," 29. Bancroft doubted that Lassen returned to Missouri in 1847 and thought he left his ranch the next spring to explore his new trail. Wendell Huffman discovered a Missouri newspaper that proves otherwise: "Lawson, Myers and their company left here last Friday for California. Some seven teams in all will go from Chariton and Carroll counties." Notice, *The Brunswicker*, Brunswick, Missouri, 4 May and 4 November 1848.

[117] Burnett to "Mr. Editor," *California Star & Californian*, 8 November 1848.

Like most inspired shortcuts, Lassen's "cutoff" was actually many miles longer than the established trail. The road attracted enormous traffic over the next few years but quickly developed an unenviable reputation, earning a variety of derogatory nicknames, such as Lassens Horn and the Death Route.[118] Lassen never gave up, despite losing his land and fortune in the gold rush. He served as a guide for the Pacific Wagon Road Survey in 1857 before he was murdered on his trail while prospecting for silver in Black Rock Canyon in 1859. A monument at Susanville, California, commemorates the affable but inept Dane, and his memory lives on in the name of a national forest, a national park, a county, and Lassen Peak, an active volcano.[119]

Burnett bravely touted his new wagon road to Oregon in standard trailblazer terms. "We found the whole route very well supplied with grass and water," he wrote, claiming there were only three waterless drives of thirty, twenty, and eighteen miles. "We found the pass through the mountains one of the finest natural passes in the world. The ascent and descent are very gradual and with a little labor an excellent road could be made," he noted. "The route for wagons is now open, and the approaching year will witness the passage of many wagons from Oregon to California," he said. "This route must prove of great benefit to parties of emigrants from Oregon and from the United States," Burnett prophesied.[120]

He was half right.

A Central Southern Route:
The Salt Lake to Los Angeles Wagon Road

Mule trains from New Mexico had been packing wool and silver over the Rocky Mountains, across Green River, around the San Rafael Swell, over the Awapa Plateau, and into the Little Salt Lake Valley since 1830. From there the packers crossed the rim of the Great Basin, the Mojave Desert, and southern flank of the Sierra Nevada via Cajon Pass to reach Pueblo de Los Angeles, the City of the Angels. Known as the Old Spanish Trail or simply Spanish Trail, it was neither old nor Spanish, and though its eastern passage was clearly impractical for wagons, the route from the Little Salt Lake held promise for wheeled vehicles.[121]

The trail was not only familiar to New Mexicans but was a favored route of the Ute Indians and their mountaineer allies to the winter pastures of California. Along

---

[118] See, for example, The Diary and Letters of Dr. Joseph Middleton, Beinecke Library.

[119] Hammond, "Peter Lassen and His Trail," 33, 39, 40; and Bishop, Itinerary of Route, Henderson Oregon Trail Collection.

[120] Burnett to "Mr. Editor," *California Star & Californian,* 8 November 1848.

[121] See Madsen and Crampton, *In Search of the Spanish Trail,* for a description of the trail; and Hafen and Hafen, *Old Spanish Trail,* for source documents.

with the legendary war chief Wakara, mountain men such as Pegleg Smith and James P. Beckwourth long used the trail to raid the ranches of southern California for horses.[122] An "Old Spanyard" at Los Angeles who "had traviled much in the mountains" informed Mormon Battalion member Charles B. Hancock in 1847 that at Utah Lake and "further north as the trail led to Oregon there was a large lake vary Salt watter," indicating that a Mexican trade route connected the Spanish Trail with the road to Oregon. It might, the Mormons thought, be passable by wagons.[123]

For overlanders arriving in the Great Basin too late to risk crossing the Sierra Nevada, a southern route to Los Angeles would offer an attractive alternative to wintering in the Mormon settlements, although no one tried it until after 1848. There was not a single non-Indian habitation between Utah Valley and the Lugo Ranch at San Bernardino before 1851, but Solomon Sublette had returned to Bridgers Fort in 1846 from California via Los Angeles. In fall 1847 former Mormon Battalion Captain Jefferson Hunt led a mounted party to southern California, and in an almost forgotten feat of trailblazing, the next spring Battalion veteran Captain Daniel Davis and his wife took a wagon from Los Angeles to Salt Lake, opening a snow-free alternative to the Humboldt route—and a wagon road that would witness some of the most dramatic events of 1849.[124]

As Smooth As a Barn Floor:
The Physical Transformation of the Trails

The Wild West in 1840 was not wild: it was a controlled natural system. For more than a century, equestrian tribes on the Great Plains had harvested native plants, raised crops, and used fire to encourage the growth of grass. Scattered stands of cottonwood and ash trees along the great river valleys of the Arkansas, Kansas, Republican, Blue, Platte, Yellowstone, and Powder rivers provided refuges and forage for the Plains Indians. They dispersed into small bands that camped together during the harsh winters, whose blizzards kept the size of their prolific horse herds in check. During their summer rut the great bison herds swept the prairies bare, but the grass revived with the fall rains.

The cumulative impact of such use was relatively light. When Colonel Henry Dodge marched his dragoons to the South Platte in 1835, they found sufficient wood for fuel below the forks, "and occasionally a solitary tree standing in bold relief against a clear blue sky."[125] Thick groves of cottonwoods were scattered

---

[122] See Van Hoak, "Waccara's Utes," 309–30, for a current perspective on the Utes.

[123] Bigler and Bagley, *Army of Israel,* 207–208.

[124] Morgan, *Overland in 1846,* 62; and Bigler and Bagley, *Army of Israel,* 395–400, which contains all the known source documents on Davis's feat.

[125] Kingsbury, "Journal of the March of a Detachment of Dragoons," 6 July 1835.

along the valleys of the Platte's forks, timber grew in its side canyons, and there were still ash trees in Ash Hollow. The impact of the white man's wagons and livestock was soon glaringly obvious. Ten years later James Field found that the North Fork of the Platte below Fort Laramie appeared "to have been lately quite well timbered, but it is now nearly all destroyed by fire, the dead and dry wood strewing the bottom." By 1849 the trees had either vanished entirely or were quickly disappearing.[126]

A surprising number of random environmental factors favored early efforts to cross the West by wagon, not the least of which was climate. Beginning about 1825, extraordinarily abundant rainfall blessed the Great Plains, which doubled its human population over the next quarter century—and most importantly for overland emigrants, produced bountiful crops of grass along the Platte River throughout the 1840s. As the decade ended, however, a profound change was becoming evident.[127] The huge bison herds and the Indians' burning of the dead grass each spring accounted for the barren, treeless state of the plains between Grand Island and the Forks of the Platte, but the prairie was resilient. The vast grassland had always recovered from periodic droughts and overgrazing, but along the Platte River, the Oregon-California Trail changed all that. When Pierre-Jean De Smet came to the "noble highway" along the North Platte in 1851, it was "as smooth as a barn floor swept by the winds": not a blade of grass could sprout on it due to the continual passing of wagons and livestock.[128]

The poor pasturage was partly the result of the wear and tear some twelve thousand people, one hundred thousand head of livestock, and thousands of wagons had inflicted on the central Plains in less than a decade. As early as 1845 emigrants and soldiers competed for grass as they marched up the Platte. "The grass near the Mountains is not so good as usual," eastbound travelers reported, "and the cattle were suffering."[129] The advance companies, James Field complained, had "fired the prairie in many places, as they passed along, destroying so much pasture it will be difficult for the companies behind us to get good camps."[130] The grass was backward and scanty, one dragoon captain complained, and the soldiers feared the emigrants and their cattle would be harder on forage than the clouds of locusts they had seen near the Blue River, which "would make a clean sweep of the grass near all the spots where it is necessary to encamp for water." The dragoons often had to search hard to find enough feed for their horses, and it

---

[126] Field, Crossing the Plains, 19 June 1845, Oregon Historical Society; and West, Contested Plains, 230.
[127] Ibid., 31, 67, 231.
[128] De Smet, Life, Letters and Travels, 671–72.
[129] "From the Mountains," St. Joseph Gazette, 15 August 1845, 2/1.
[130] Field, Crossing the Plains, 16 June 1845, Oregon Historical Society.

got worse when they reached the Platte and found the grass had been "swept off by ten thousands buffaloes."[131] The grasslands' remarkable ability to recover from overgrazing would be sorely tested over the next twenty years.

"Grass is not as good this season as it commonly is," William Porter wrote while waiting to cross the North Platte in 1848. A party returning from Oregon warned that "grass is very scarce on the route from this [point] on, and it will be very difficult getting there."[132] That year's "very dry season, the scarcity of grass, the heavy dragging, dusty roads and inhaling so much of the alkali" was killing Mormon livestock, Brigham Young complained at the last crossing of the Sweet-water.[133] The scarcity of grass signaled an especially dry year, and although ample rainfall blessed the Platte River Valley over the next few years, the aridity of 1848 was a harbinger of decades of drought to follow.

The loss of several "Lone Trees" along the trail is a classic example of the affect Americans heading west had on the natural world. The solitary and beloved Lone Pine on Oregon's Powder River did not last long enough for Frémont to see it in 1843; a Forty-niner found that the Lone Elm, one day's travel from Independence, was the only tree for miles around. It was an object of curiosity with its "beautiful Spreading top, the limbs of which however have been cut off within the last few years by Emigrants for camp fires & it is now on the decline."[134] The Lone Elm's decline would not be gradual, nor would the trail's impact on the natural world moderate as emigration ebbed and flowed over two more decades.

BRAVE AND ENTERPRISING PEOPLE: OREGON'S INDIANS

If the first eight years of overland emigration had been a triumph for Oregon's settlers, they were a disaster for its Native peoples. During all that time, the country's Natives had been essential to the success of wagon travel, providing salmon to sustain travelers on the Snake River and guides to help them get over the Blue Mountains. Oregon's Indians sold Americans meat, potatoes, and other vegetables, tracked down lost animals, and helped them ford streams and ferry down the Columbia. Near the river in 1847, James Coon "lost two of my oxen, Jack and Jerry. A few Indians standing around offered to hunt them down for

---

[131] Cooke, *Scenes and Adventures*, 26 May and 2 June 1845, 285, 297.

[132] Porter to "Dear Father, Mother, Brothers and Sisters," 24 June 1848.

[133] Young and Kimball to Elders Hyde, Smith and Benson, Journal History, 28 August 1848.

[134] Burgert and Rudy, "The Rough Road West," 30 April 1849, Mattes Library Collection, NFTC, 6. The Lone Elm, first known as Round Grove, is often confused with Elm Grove, a campground two and one-half miles to the northwest on the Westport Road. Both campgrounds were on Cedar Creek, only a few miles from the separation of the Oregon and Santa Fe trails. Local historian Craig Crease straightened out the confusion in "The Lone Elm and Elm Grove Case," 24–31. Apparently, neither the Lone Elm nor Elm Grove survived the gold rush.

two shirts." Coon searched himself until he was exhausted. "Then I accepted
their offer, whereupon they mounted their ponies. Presently they returned with
the oxen and I finished the bargain by giving them two shirts."[135] In a pattern that
soon developed a haunting familiarity, this initially favorable relationship deteriorated and ultimately collapsed as migration and its impact on the region's Native
peoples increased dramatically.

Many Indians tried to adapt to the changing world by mastering white ways. The
Cayuses, Walla Wallas, and Nez Perces had incorporated horses into their cultures
and successfully integrated elements of Christianity into their own vigorous reli-
gions even before the arrival of the first overlanders. "Dr. Whitman and his wife
had been there with the Indians for several years and had them civilized," recalled
Martha Williams Reed. "We could hear them say their prayers at night and morning and singing. They had learned them to do all kinds of work, the same as the
white people."[136] Their distance from the ruthless competition between American and British traders caused remote tribes less social disruption and resulted
in better relations with the Hudson's Bay Company, which taught them how to
profit from their dealings with other whites.[137] "It is hardly possible to conceive
of a greater change than Dr. Whitman had worked in the life of the Cayuses,"
Catherine Sager Pringle recalled. "They had now growing fields, could have good
homes, a mill to grind their meal, and they were taught things of the greatest use."
Such long contact had prepared them to benefit from the work of Protestant missionaries, but this relationship proved to be a double-edged sword.[138]

Oregon's Native peoples impressed many Americans, and the Indians were
remarkably kind to the new settlers who often arrived in desperate straits. At
the Grande Ronde, missionary Abigail Smith found an Indian who agreed to take
her party to the Whitman mission, and they followed "our Indian Pilot" to Waiilatpu.[139] Methodist missionary Henry Perkins called the Cayuses "the elite of
the country. They are few in number but exert a very great influence. They are
a brave, & enterprising people, & command a great deal of respect from the surrounding tribes."[140] The plantations of the Walla Wallas produced corn, potatoes,
peas, camas root, and cherries, which spoke well for their advancement in agriculture and civilization, Indian Agent Elijah White reported. He lavished praise

[135] Coon and Coon, Diary, 18 September 1847.

[136] Reed, "Old California Pioneer Passes Away," retrieved 8 April 2009 from http://www.oregonpioneers.com/williams.htm.

[137] Boyd, The Coming of the Spirit of Pestilence, 70–71, 117, 241–44. Boyd's groundbreaking study provides a detailed analysis of population decline among the coastal tribes of the Pacific Northwest.

[138] Pringle, Across the Plains in 1844, Oregon Historical Society.

[139] Smith to "Brother and Sister Kirby," 18 September 1840, Mattes Library.

[140] Perkins, "Journal," 4 December 1843, 293, cited in Boyd, People of the Dalles, 70.

on the Cayuses, who had "made most commendable advancement in agriculture, science, arts, morals and religion—many of the latter reading their own language fluently and writing well, and in the regularity of their family devotions, and observance of the Sabbath, it is believed few equal them."[141]

"The Indians of Oregon are very different from those east of the mountains," Clarborne Walker observed in 1845. The "Skyanys"—Cayuses—were generally Christians: he considered them "the most civilized of any Indians on the route." The Cayuses and Nez Perces were "getting all the cattle they can. They traded for goodly numbers from our immigrants, trading their horses." He recommended bringing American mares, which were extremely popular with the tribes, to Oregon.[142] At the Lapwai mission Joel Palmer found "a quiet, civil people, but proud and haughty." The Nez Perces had already adapted the Roman alphabet as their written language and were "quite cleanly, and are an industrious people," Palmer wrote: they had large droves of horses and were quickly learning to cultivate the soil, "and many of them are raising large herds of cattle."[143]

Although they easily and enthusiastically adopted the material aspects of white culture, Indians were baffled when American authorities began imposing laws, sanctions, and punishments on the tribes. Not long after Marcus Whitman returned to the United States in 1842, Indians burned the Waiilatpu Mission's gristmill and threshing mill. Agent Elijah White introduced a "law code" at Lapwai that decreed flogging and fines for various infractions and hanging for any Indian who willfully took a life or burned a dwelling. White's code directed that chiefs would inflict punishment on tribal members, while he would administer justice to "white men," meaning Americans. White also attempted to limit dog ownership to those "who travel or live among the game." Practically, the agent had no authority over Native peoples or British subjects, and not much more over his countrymen.[144]

The Nez Perces adopted White's code and selected a high chief at the agent's insistence, but the Cayuse refused to endorse the plan and put off deciding the issue until spring. They already suspected the Americans were plotting to seize their lands. White's policy, one historian concluded, was doomed to failure due to the great gulf separating white and Native cultures, along with the fact that no courts, no police, and no jails existed east of the Willamette Valley to enforce the code's sanctions. Even worse, Marcus Whitman's departure for the states

---

[141] White, "Overland Mail from Oregon," 17 November 1845, 1,045.

[142] Walker to "Dear Brother, Sister and Friends," 1845, Purvine Family Records.

[143] Palmer, *Journal of Travels,* 235–36.

[144] Boyd, *People of The Dalles,* 159–62. As his order to kill all the dogs in his 1842 wagon train indicated, White had "a thing" about canines.

made the Cayuses intensely suspicious: Narcissa Whitman told her husband they thought he was "coming back next fall with fifty men to fight them." Archibald McKinlay, the Hudson's Bay Company agent at Fort Walla Walla, heard that the Cayuses believed Dr. White would return in the spring "with an armed force to take away their lands."[145]

Despite many positive experiences with their Indian neighbors, white settlers could not shake the distrust they brought with them from the states. "The Indians are very much exasperated against the whites in consequence of so many of [them] coming into their country, to destroy their game, and take away their lands," Henry Perkins wrote to Sub-agent White about 1843. Perkins claimed the Nez Perces had sent one of their chiefs on snowshoes the previous winter to encourage the Indians east of Fort Hall "to cut off the party that [it] is expected Dr. Whitman will bring back with him." He charged that the Indians were trying to form a coalition to destroy all the "Boston people"—Americans—for "it is not good to kill a part of them, and leave the rest, but that every one of them must be destroyed."[146] Whitman was able to smooth over his relations with the Indians, but the continuing hostilities and growing fear led many settlers to arrive at similar conclusions.

A War Whose End We Cannot Foresee:
Murder at Waiilatpu

As Keturah Belknap's family prepared to eat supper one spring evening in 1848, "Joe Meek and his posse of men road into camp. They were going to Washington, D.C., to get the government to send soldiers to protect the settlers in Oregon and they told us all about the Indian Massacre at Walla Walla called the 'Whitman Massacre.'"[147] Meek reached Washington on 28 May 1848, where he met with his cousin, First Lady Sarah Polk, and the president. Spurred on by Meek's dramatic story and his exalted status as "Minister Extraplenipotentary of the Republic of Oregon," Congress finally created Oregon Territory in August 1848. Polk ordered the army's Oregon Volunteers to force-march to the new territory to replace the ragtag militia. He appointed Meek territorial marshal, selected Joseph Lane as governor, and Meek escorted Lane back to Oregon.[148]

---

[145] Drury, *Marcus and Narcissa Whitman*, 2:20–25.

[146] Stern, *Chiefs and Change in the Oregon Country*, 164.

[147] Belknap, "The Commentaries," in Holmes, *Covered Wagon Women*, 1:225. Belknap recalled meeting Meek at Ash Hollow, but George Ebbert reported that the men did not encounter wagon trains until after they reached the Little Blue River. See Ebbert, Reminiscences, in "Joe Meek Trip to Washington," 266–67.

[148] Thrapp, *Encyclopedia of Frontier Biography*, 967; and James M. Tompkins's commentary.

The emigration of 1848 marked the close of the pioneer epoch of overland wagon roads. But the culminating event of the era took place with the murder of Marcus and Narcissa Whitman in Oregon the previous fall. For both the Indians and whites who lost their lives in the affair and its aftermath, it was a brutal and bloody tragedy—and it foreshadowed the ultimate impact the trails had on America's Indians and those who came to make new homes in the West.

The mission station at Waiilatpu prospered after Marcus Whitman returned to Oregon in 1843, but the lives of the missionaries did not get easier. The next spring, Pierre-Jean De Smet arrived at Walla Walla to discuss opening a Catholic mission, a possibility the Cayuses welcomed since it would, as an anxious Whitman noted, "create competition." Twelve emigrant families consisting of more than fifty-five souls stayed at the station during the winter of 1844–45, bringing its total white population to about seventy. Narcissa Whitman now fed twenty to twenty-five people at every meal. While this "work is very good & humane," the mission board noted, the Whitmans' task was "the work of guiding men to Christ," not feeding indigent emigrants. Waiilatpu, they feared, would be seen as a moneymaking venture and paint their mission with the money-grubbing brush that had blackened the Methodists. Meanwhile, Whitman built a sawmill "for ourselves, the Indians, and perhaps a settlement."[149]

Dr. Whitman stoutly resisted the mission board's heartless economics. "If we are not legally, religiously nor morally bound to relieve the passing Immigrant we are necessarily: for the sick & hungry cannot be sent away however penyless," he argued.[150] In addition to the lack of support from back home, corrosive jealousy burned among the missionaries in Oregon. On his way east in 1845 Elijah White advised emigrants to avoid the detour to Waiilatpu and buy supplies at The Dalles. This dramatically cut Whitman's income, and he charged that White had caused much suffering, since the scarcity of food at The Dalles added to the deaths induced by Stephen Meek's "wild attempt at a southern route from Boise to the Dall[e]s."[151]

Narcissa Whitman was a devoted Christian and a brave woman, but she was ill suited for the hardships of frontier life. Although she grew stronger as she faced the trials of her years in Oregon, it was impossible for her to comprehend Indian culture on its own terms. She had little sympathy for or understanding of the Cayuses and ultimately came to feel an ill-disguised contempt for her Native neighbors. The drowning of her two-year-old daughter Alice Clarissa in 1839

---

[149] Drury, *Marcus and Narcissa Whitman*, 2:122–125, 133.

[150] Whitman to Greene, 1 April 1847, in Hulbert and Hulbert, *Marcus Whitman, Crusader*, 3:216.

[151] Drury, *Marcus and Narcissa Whitman*, 2:132, 139.

threw her into a profound depression. Taking in the daughters of Jim Bridger and Joe Meek and adopting the Sager children helped restore her naturally cheerful disposition, but the Whitmans' clash with Indian culture grew deeper every year. Despite their precarious situation, she and her husband refused to appreciate its reality. "We had rather die in the battle than retreat," Narcissa wrote.[152]

The failure of the Cayuses to respond to their New England brand of Protestantism gradually led the Whitmans to abandon their religious mission. After 1843, Marcus Whitman increasingly turned his energies to what he saw as his "greatest work"—to "aid the white settlement of this country." Writing to a fellow missionary in 1844, Whitman speculated that no country on the globe surpassed Oregon, and he thought its interior would soon be its most sought-after region. An American population to secure the commerce of the Pacific was of the "greatest value" to the nation's interests—but not necessarily to its existing inhabitants, who would have to be content with the offer of eternal salvation. "I do not know how long we will be called to operate for the benefit of the Indians," he wrote. "But be it longer or shorter it will not diminish the importance of our situation. For if the Indians are to pass away we want to do what can be done in order to give them the offer of life & then be ready to aid as indeed we have done & are doing to found & sustain institutions of learning & religion in the Country."[153]

Early in 1847, Whitman tentatively asked the mission board to discharge him, and whether the Indians or the board dismissed him, he hoped to "locate a claim for land in this lower Country to be ready in case of retirement."[154] Narcissa Whitman wrote to fellow missionary Abigail Smith about the "discouragements and hindrances" of their work, bravely saying that they felt their influence for good with the Indians was never greater, but she conceded that "when our hands are not employed for the Indians directly as is frequently the case," the Lord filled them with other work "for souls of such as have come from our dear native land."[155]

Despite her brave front, relations with the Cayuses only got worse. Rumors spread that Whitman had used his talents as a *tewat,* or shaman, to kill a young man who had died of apoplexy. Whitman knew it was the tribe's custom to kill unsuccessful medicine men: he feared for his life, he told Dr. McLoughlin when he visited Fort Vancouver in June 1845. After Tomahas attacked Whitman and Young Chief accused him of conniving with the whites to kill the Indians "with poison and infection" to steal their land and horses, Whitman threatened to move to the Willamette

---

[152] Jeffrey, *Frontier Women,* 149, 182.

[153] Whitman to Rev. A. B. Smith, 31 May 1844, in Smith, Oregon Mission Letters, Beinecke Library, 1–2, 3, 4. See also Drury, *Marcus and Narcissa Whitman,* 2:111.

[154] Whitman to Greene, 1 April 1847, in Hulbert and Hulbert, *Marcus Whitman, Crusader,* 3:220.

[155] Whitman to "My Dear Mrs. Smith," 8 February 1847, in ibid., 3:214–15.

Valley in the spring. By February 1846, however, he felt that the "kindness, confidence, good will & affection" of the Indians was better than ever.[156] The good feeling Whitman perceived was an illusion. Catherine Sager recalled that the bitter winter of 1846–47 was very cold, "the coldest ever known in the country and the Indians charged the whites with bringing the cold weather upon them."[157]

"The poor Indians are amazed at the overwhelming numbers of Americans coming into this country," Narcissa Whitman wrote late that summer, in her last surviving letter. "They seem not to know what to make of it." Many Cayuses did in fact recognize what this swelling tide of land-hungry Americans meant. As thousands of emigrants flooded into their lands that fall, they struck back, running off livestock and looting isolated wagons, sometimes both robbing and humiliating their victims.[158]

Disaster struck when Yellow Serpent and his band brought the measles back from Sutters Fort. "Great Sickness and disease among the Indian tribes, and a great number of them were dying," John Sutter had reported in mid-June, and in addition to measles, dysentery swept through the Oregon tribes, which had no immunity to Old World diseases. Some Indians thought the emigration brought the epidemic with them, and so did Martha Williams Reed, who recalled "some emigrants came through who had the measles and the Indians caught it from them."[159] A few trail veterans later claimed measles cases had actually broken out earlier in the trip, but in fact the disease reached the Columbia in late July, before the first overland companies arrived.[160]

Paul Kane, an artist staying at Fort Walla Walla, told of the arrival of one of Yellow Serpent's sons on 23 July "bringing the most disastrous tidings, not only of the total failure of the expedition, but also of their suffering and detention by sickness." As the son reported each death, "a terrific howl ensued" and "signs of intense grief followed the mention of each name." Over three hours, the young man "named upwards of thirty" of the dead. The tribe dispatched messengers in every direction to warn their neighbors, and the couriers carried the virus with them. When the emigrants arrived, they conveyed the disease down the river.[161] But to the Indians of Oregon, it appeared they were the victims of bad magic.

As this particularly virulent form of measles swept through Waiilatpu station, the Cayuses concluded the Americans had brought death with them. At least one

---

[156] Drury, *Marcus and Narcissa Whitman*, 2:132–33, 135, 151–53, 155, 157.

[157] Pringle, Across the Plains in 1844, Oregon Historical Society.

[158] Drury, *First White Women over the Rockies*, 1:160.

[159] Reed, "Old California Pioneer Passes Away."

[160] For recollections that measles struck overland companies on the trail, see Angel, Memoir of 1847, Mattes Library, 2; and Shaw, "Reminiscence of 1844," *Oregon Statesman*, 12 June 1885.

[161] Boyd, *The Coming of the Spirit of Pestilence*, 146–48.

white child, Salvijane Osborne, died, but most recovered—yet the Indians were dying by the dozens: "I have seen from five to six buried daily," Catherine Sager recalled. One survivor told a Catholic missionary that 197 Cayuse died after the emigration arrived, perhaps more than half of the band. Since most of the white victims survived and virtually all of Whitman's Indian patients died, some Cayuse believed the doctor's medicine murdered them.[162] The bad Indians planned to kill him, Stickus warned Whitman. "Yes, the situation looks pretty dark," he told a settler, "but I think I shall be able to quell any trouble."[163]

Congregationalist Marcus Whitman at last arrived at the same conclusion Methodist Jason Lee reached about the prospect of bringing salvation to Native peoples: it was hopeless, but Oregon was a land of opportunity. "The Indians along the Columbia from here to Waskopam are a low, pilfering race," Whitman wrote in August 1847. As he toured their villages that fall he recovered whatever stolen property he could and warned that "the innocent can only escape by pointing out the guilty."[164] Still obsessed with saving Oregon from "the Papists," he devoted his time to encouraging Americans to come to Oregon and keep the Columbia Basin out of the hands of the "the half breed & French population from the Willamette." In October 1847 he proposed creating a string of outposts along the Oregon Trail, but he was now ready to abandon his old flock for a new one: Central Oregon was probably unrivaled by any country in the world for raising grazing animals, Whitman informed the mission board, "of which sheep are the best."[165]

Tensions at Waiilatpu exploded on 29 November 1847. "In a fit of desperation," Hudson's Bay officials Ogden and Douglas reported, a few renegade criminals and part of one band of the Cayuse had attacked the American mission and brutally murdered the Whitmans and twelve others.[166] John and Frank Sager were among the dead, and the Indians took fifty-three women and children hostage. Louise Sager and Helen Mar Meek died of measles during their captivity. Within a month, Peter Skene Ogden of the Hudson's Bay Company paid a ransom of some $500 in trade goods and secured the hostages' release. The negotiations demanded all of Ogden's considerable skill, since the Indians wanted to keep the hostages to protect themselves.

News of the murders outraged the settlements. "We look upon this outbreak by the Kyuse Indians as a declaration of war against the Americans," cried Loren

---

[162] Drury, *Marcus and Narcissa Whitman*, 2:206–209.

[163] Jeffrey, *Frontier Women*, 216.

[164] Whitman to Greene, 3 August 1847 and 18 October 1847, in Hulbert and Hulbert, *Marcus Whitman, Crusader*, 3:230, 244.

[165] Whitman to the Secretary of War, 16 October 1847; and Whitman to Greene, 18 October 1847, in ibid., 3:238, 245.

[166] Drury, *Marcus and Narcissa Whitman*, 2:209.

Hastings on 27 November.[167] "This tragical scene moved the inhabitants of the Willamette Valley to raise a mob of three to four hundred men to avenge the murders," Bishop Augustin Blanchet reported from Walla Walla, "and here we are in the middle of a war whose end we cannot foresee." As the Catholic prelate noted, only a few of the Cayuses were involved in the murders, and "afterwards the chiefs seemed to regret it sincerely." They sent a note "in which they described the motives of the murderers and their desire to avoid a war with the Americans."[168] It was no use. The settlers quickly organized a militia and fought Oregon's first Indian war to exact vengeance for the martyred Whitmans.

The Cayuse War was a farmer's war that lasted two years and occasionally degenerated into a comedy of errors, for the farmers were much better at organizing than strategizing and more skilled at collecting munitions than using them. The volunteers chased rumors of Indian sightings across the countryside, but the war was merely a series of indecisive engagements that did little damage to either side. At Well Spring on the Oregon Trail, the Cayuses let the Oregon artillerymen see them, waited for the commander to drop his arm (which they knew meant a volley was on its way), and moved to a new spot to watch the shot land harmlessly at their previous location. The farmers and their ammunition were soon exhausted, with no cost to the Indians. To their credit, the volunteers from the Willamette Valley did prevent other tribes, such as the Palouses, from joining the Cayuses. As with many frontier Indian wars, the conflict came to an abrupt halt in 1849 with the arrival of U.S. Army regulars from Fort Leavenworth. The only major casualty of the war was the man elected to be field commander, Colonel Cornelius Gilliam—the bombastic veteran of the Seminole War, the 1838 Missouri Mormon War, and the 1844 emigration. Gilliam was mortally wounded at Well Spring when he pulled a rope out of a wagon and accidentally shot himself in the gut.

"The Oregon war appears to me to be all wind & bombast on the part of the Americans in the Oregon papers," Richard Grant wrote from Fort Hall. The war's purpose, he felt, was to make prizes of the Indians' cattle and horses. The settlers cared "very little for the murderers who I believe are now peaceable in their own Country. For my part I never anticipated any danger from the Indians to our people." The Fort Hall outfit the next spring met most of the murderers near the Powder River: the Cayuses could have cut them off but did not.[169]

When Governor Joseph Lane arrived in March 1849, he demanded that the Cayuses surrender the five men—Telokite, Tomahas, Clokomas, Isiaasheluckas, and

---

[167] Hastings, Overland Journey from Illinois, Beinecke Library, 37.
[168] Blanchet to Kendrick, 30 March 1848, General Archives of the Society of Jesus.
[169] Grant to Simpson, 4 January 1849, D.5/24, HBC Archives, 229.

Kiamasumkin—he believed had been involved in the Whitman murders. The more levelheaded Cayuse leaders were eager to rid their lands of white soldiers and get on with their seasonal rounds and surrendered the five to Governor Lane and Marshal Meek at The Dalles. The trial of the Cayuses at Oregon City in May 1850 was a travesty of justice. "Suave, sleek, swollen with self-esteem, incurably covetous," Judge Orville C. Pratt impressed historian Malcolm Clark as "slippery as a greased eel," and simply wanted the trial over.[170] Governor Lane was anxious to resign and head to California's gold fields. Only the murder of Marcus Whitman was tried and the defense had only one hot afternoon to call two witnesses, John McLoughlin and Stickus. To save time Pratt instructed the jury to sentence the Indians as soon as they found them guilty. The five were convicted of the murder of Dr. Whitman and condemned to hang. Lane headed south, leaving his resignation on his desk.

Upon Lane's resignation, the governor's office and the power to pardon the Indians fell to Territorial Secretary Kintzing Pritchette, who had defended the Cayuse leaders. Before Pritchette was able to commute the sentence, Marshal Meek carried out their executions on 3 June 1850. Meek's rationale was that Lane had left instructions not to pardon the five men, no one knew if he had actually left the territory—and Joe Meek was not going to allow the death of his daughter Helen go unavenged.[171]

The tragedy at Waiilatpu established a pattern Americans and Indians would repeat along the overland trail for the next two decades. The trickle of emigration swelled into a flood that had a devastating impact on Indian food sources. Conflict and hostility increased, eventually leading to bloodshed, often gratuitously initiated and inflicted by whites. To the Indians it was increasingly apparent they could not survive the onslaught, and in desperation they turned to violence. Settlers like the Whitmans suffered the consequences of this grim cycle, but the suffering and starvation of Indian peoples throughout the West proved to be a tragedy of far greater magnitude.

Writing to Narcissa Whitman's sister two years after the murders, Reverend Henry Perkins candidly summarized the reasons he felt led to her death. Although the Cayuses "*feared* the Doctor, they did not *love* him," Perkins wrote. Whitman's personality dictated that he would never get along with Oregon's Indians, and the mission station was the last place he should have been sent. Whitman never had Indian interests as his paramount concern, and he regarded them "as an inferior race & doomed at no distant date to give place to a settlement of enterprising Americans." Perkins believed the doctor devoted his sympathies and ultimately

---

[170] Clark, *Eden Seekers*, 228.

[171] Oregon historian James M. Tompkins provided much of the description of the first Cayuse War and the Whitman trial. Helen Mar Meek died of measles while a captive.

all his energies to the pioneers and their interests. "He wanted to see the country settled," he said. His wife was even more out of place. "Mrs. Whitman was not adapted to savage but *civilized* life." She loved company, society, and excitement. "It was her *misfortune,* but not her *fault.* She was adapted to a different destiny," Perkins observed. "She was not a *missionary* but a *woman,* an American highly gifted, polished American lady. And such she died."[172]

Marcus Whitman's last letters indicate Perkins's assessment was correct, for the idealistic dreams that brought Whitman to Oregon died when they collided with the harsh realities of the frontier. Yet it would be unjust not to acknowledge the service, sacrifice, and suffering that marked Narcissa Whitman's hard life. It would be unfair not to recognize the courage required to be one of the first two American women to cross the Rocky Mountains or appreciate her singularly lively record of her adventures. "She was overwhelmed by the independent, demanding, and threatening converts who left her exhausted, demoralized, aggravated, and frightened. Yet she never shirked her responsibility to them or to the countless needy emigrants and orphans who came to her for help," noted archaeologist Lee Kreutzer. "She worked like a horse. She lost her only child. She was far from her family and increasingly in danger. Her husband did little to comfort and support her, and the American Board of Commissioners for Foreign Missions, who had sent her to do an impossible task, essentially abandoned her. By any standard, she had been pushed to the edge, and the fact that she kept herself together and never failed those who depended upon her suggests an impressive strength of character."[173]

Her tragic death ensured Narcissa Whitman's enduring place in her country's history, but it is impossible not to wish her life had been marked by a far greater measure of happiness and more by joy than by celebrity. The tragedy of the Whitman Massacre would eventually encompass far more than the cruel and terrifying deaths at Waiilatpu, because the martyrdom of the Whitmans provided justification for a series of increasingly ruthless Cayuse Wars, and the martyrs would help vindicate the calculated and brutal devastation of the West's American Indians as an act of righteous necessity.

LAWLESS AND UNBRIDLED: A NEW AGE BEGINS

Although often overlooked in the chronicles of the California Trail, the events of 1848 spurred tremendous development of the road across the plains. By the time the floodtide of a massive population transfer began to build in the eastern United States that fall, adventurous trailblazers had opened a new wagon road over the

---

[172] Perkins to Jane Prentiss, 19 October 1849, in Drury, *Marcus and Narcissa Whitman,* 2:392–94.

[173] Lee Kreutzer to Will Bagley, 9 April 2003, copy in author's possession.

Sierra Nevada at Carson Pass, a wagon trace between Great Salt Lake City and the California Trail, and a trail that connected Oregon and California. Far to the south, Capt. Daniel Davis, his wife, Susan Davis, and veterans of the Mormon Volunteers had brought a single wagon from Los Angeles to Salt Lake, proving it could be done. The Oregon-California Trail would continue to evolve throughout its existence, but all its basic elements were now in place.

The trail was now a road, and the great pioneering era was over. By the end of the 1840s, pioneers had forged a complex network of wagon trails across the American West: over the next two decades, their creation took on a life of its own, expanding and evolving like an organic creature. The discovery of gold and its subsequent promotion quickly transformed the very nature of overland wagon travel. President Polk's annual message may have hoped to entice a few Americans to go west and settle the newly conquered provinces, but when the War Department displayed a tea caddy of California gold that December, it sewed the whirlwind. What had been a slowly evolving trail soon became in a national highway for the greatest voluntary migration in history.

Ordinary American men and women had accomplished all this pretty much on their own hook. Edwin Bryant met Jesse Applegate and his surveying crew "engaged in exploring a new and more feasible wagon-route to Oregon" in August 1846. The encounter led him to reflect on the public spirit and enterprise of this small band of men. The United States government, Bryant observed, had long wanted to open the best possible routes to the Pacific and had even appropriated large sums of money for the task, but whatever had been accomplished in the way of exploration was due to "the indomitable energy, the bold daring, and the unconquerable enterprise, in opposition to every discouragement, privation, and danger, of our hardy frontier men and pioneers, unaided directly or remotely by the patronage or even the approving smiles and commendations of the government." These frontier folk, Bryant observed, had discovered the original wagon routes to Oregon and California, and they had made all the valuable refinements and cutoffs along the way. "To them we are indebted for a good, well-beaten, and plain trail to the Pacific ocean, on the shores of which, in the face of almost insurmountable difficulties, unsupported, they have founded an empire," Bryant rhapsodized. "Let us honor those to whom honor is due."[174]

As word of the gold discovery spread, even Californians greeted it with skepticism. After the territory's two newspapers mentioned the strike in March 1848, few people seemed to pay attention, even when the *California Star* reported, "So great a quantity of gold taken from the mine recently found at New Helvetia, that

---

[174] Bryant, *What I Saw in California,* 9 August 1846, 196–98.

it is become an article of traffic in that vicinity." That changed on 10 May, when promoter Sam Brannan, waving a bottle of gold dust in one hand and swinging his hat with the other, ran up San Francisco's Montgomery Street shouting, "Gold! Gold! Gold from the American River!" In less than a month, the town was deserted and Californians were rushing to the gold fields. "The Gold Mines in the North will gather together as wild a class of unchristianized fellows as ever escaped the thraldom of honest law and broke loose upon barbarism," the *Star* announced before ceasing publication.[175]

"I found California in another revolution," M. T. McClellan told Zenas Leonard, "not of blood, but of gold." His family had reached Weavers Creek after five months and five days of "a toilsome, tedious, and perilous journey" to find a world where gold was "nothing more thought of than dirt." Flour that had cost $2 a hundredweight in Missouri commanded $100 in Sacramento, and the mines swarmed with "all kinds of men and monsters." His daughter could make $25 a day washing gold in pans, but it took $250 to hire an average man for month—a phenomenal sum at the time, and one worth $5,333.88 in 2005 dollars. He did not like the country and intended to become independently wealthy and "spend the balance of my days in peace and quietness" in Missouri, a hope shared by thousands who followed him. "Mr. Z.," McClellan told his friend, "I always believed I was born a child of destiny."[176]

In June 1848, former confidential agent Thomas Larkin assured the secretary of state that the fifteen million dollars the United States had paid Mexico in "consideration" of the concession of its vast holdings in today's American Southwest was a bargain. If the president could see what was happening in California, Larkin wrote, he would think that a few thousand people working one hundred square miles of the Sacramento Valley would "turn out of this river the whole price our country pays for the acquired territory" in a single year. "Should this news reach the emigration of California and Oregon, now on the road," Larkin wrote, California should have a large addition to its population, especially when overlanders learned about the Indian wars tearing Oregon apart. "And should the richness of the gold region continue, our emigrants in 1849 will be many thousand, and in 1850 still more."[177]

---

[175] Bancroft, *History of California*, 6:54, 56; and *California Star*, 25 March and 3 June 1848. *The Californian* of San Francisco made the first announcement of the gold discovery on 15 March 1848: "GOLD MINE FOUND.—In the newly made raceway of the Saw Mill recently erected by Captain Sutter, gold has been found in considerable quantities. One person brought thirty dollars worth to New Helvetia, gathered there in a short time. California, no doubt, is rich in mineral wealth; great chances here for scientific capitalists. Gold has been found in almost every part of the country."

[176] McClellan to Leonard, 28 October 1848, in Clyman, *James Clyman, Frontiersman*, 294–96.

[177] Larkin to Buchanan, 28 June 1848, in Larkin, *The Larkin Papers*, 7:303.

Larkin could not have been more right.

One man who had traveled with the first wagons bound for California remained a perceptive observer of the pioneering epoch as it drew to a close. After his adventures with the Bidwell-Bartleson party in 1841, Father Pierre-Jean De Smet established the Saint Mary's Mission in the Bitterroot Valley and then visited Europe to raise allies and money to support his work. He returned west in 1844 via Cape Horn with eleven additional missionaries (including six Sisters of Notre Dame de Namur) and spent the next two years roaming the Pacific Northwest, founding the Saint Ignatius Mission on Clarks Fork of the Columbia River. In late summer 1846 he attempted to make peace between the Blackfeet and Flathead nations in the Judith Basin, and that fall he returned via Fort Benton and the Missouri River to Saint Louis.

On 18 November 1846, Father De Smet stopped at "the vast and beautiful plain" near present-day Omaha where the Mormons had built their Winter Quarters. "There are more than 10,000 of them here," he noted. He was introduced to their new leader, Brigham Young, "an affable and very polite gentleman," who earnestly pressed the Jesuit priest to remain a few days and share his extensive knowledge of the West. Time prevented De Smet from obliging, but the priest highly recommended the Salt Lake Valley as a potential settlement site. When he returned to Saint Louis after three years and six months, he was given a desk job and his missionary career came to an end. But in the four years between 1843 and 1846, Father De Smet's travels had taken him over 44,277 miles.

From Saint Louis in April 1849, the new procurator of the Missouri Province of the Society of Jesus watched as some forty thousand souls rushed to the frontier to prepare to go overland to California. Every day men came to seek his advice, and he had "succeeded in curing some of them of the gold fever." But a vast horde could not be deterred from joining the "thousands of adventurers of all countries, deserters, sailors, robbers, murderers, the Scum of the States, of Mexico, Peru, Chile, the Sandwich Islands (with some good honest men among them, no doubt, all living lawless and unbridled)" already plundering the immense riches of El Dorado. "The news of the abundance of gold," observed Pierre-Jean De Smet, "seems to have shaken the United States to the foundation."

During the previous decade, the charming Jesuit had seen as much of the Great American Desert as any man alive and learned of "its wild inhabitants, of its animals, its flowers and trees, its rivers and lakes, its wastes, its mountains and plains." In the wake of America's acquisition of its immense new territories, like many of his fellow countrymen De Smet—a U.S. citizen since 1833—was intoxicated with the nation's prospects. "Show me a spectacle more glorious, more encouraging than this, in all the pages of history," he wrote. "What a breadth of latitude and longitude, and that too in the fairest part of North America! What a variety of climate, and then, what a variety of production!" he rhapsodized. "What an immense national domain, unsurveyed, of extinguished and unextinguished Indian tribes, within the States and Territories," and there were still 760 million acres without any organized government.[178] Here were the makings of a new world.

This new world meant the end of the old. De Smet outlined certain facts about the condition of the Indians in the Rocky Mountains and the "melancholy future which at no very remote epoch awaits these nations." Game was decreasing at an alarming rate, and "the buffalo is disappearing and diminishing each successive year on the prairies of the upper Missouri." Bison had already vanished entirely from the homeland of the Shoshones, and like the Poncas they were forced "to scour the country in every direction" and confront traditional enemies on their way to hunt bison. The Pawnees and Omahas were near absolute destitution, and everywhere Indian populations were in decline. "In the plains, war and famine lend their aid; on the frontier of civilization, liquors, vices and maladies carry them off by the thousands."

De Smet was working with an honorable government agent, Thomas Fitzpatrick, to do what he could to stop the trade in ardent spirits, that "deadly scourge of the Indians"; to end "the cruel wars which decimate these nations"; and to send them missionaries "with no object but the happiness of the poor souls entrusted to their care." The shopworn notion that nomadic Indians could be transformed into yeoman farmers was a chimera, he thought, but he could offer no alternative and hoped the tribes would "become more and more attached to the soil" and quit their internecine wars to live a "more peaceable and domestic life." In his heart, the good father must have known his hopes were illusions, and the sad foreboding born of his long experience envisioned a grim future for "these forsaken children of the forest."[179]

Nine years had passed since De Smet traveled to the wilds of the Oregon Country with the first overland party seeking to find "the great road leading from the Rocky Mountains to California."[180] During that time trekkers on the trail had grown from a handful of people to thousands, and now tens of thousands would follow it to the West. Every inch of land on the route between the Missouri River and the Pacific Ocean had belonged to Indian nations in 1830, but now a

---

178 De Smet, *Life, Letters and Travels*, 611, 1421–23, 1427.
179 De Smet to "Gentlemen," 10 June 1849, ibid., 1186–92.
180 De Smet, *Travels in the Great Desert in 1851*, series 2, letter 1, 30 June 1853.

burgeoning settlement stood in the valley of the Great Salt Lake, and its determined inhabitants were already spreading to the north and south. The U.S. Army
had built its first outpost on the Platte River, and soon the river valley would be
too denuded to support the winter camps of the tribes. Fur traders, farmers,
preachers, adventurers and ne'er-do-wells, craftsmen, fugitives from marriage
or justice, soldiers, lawyers, hunters on safari, doctors, single women seeking
husbands or simply plying their trade, schoolteachers, stockmen, millwrights,
lumbermen, blacksmiths, and now even lawyers and politicians all followed the
trail west, seeking a better life or merely an escape from the past. The discovery
of gold in the American River would transform these wagon traces to the Pacific
into broad and busy highways.[181]

The era of pioneer trails was over, but an age of gold had just begun.

---

[181] Unruh, *The Plains Across,* 385.

ACKNOWLEDGMENTS

M ore than thirty years ago historian Merrill J. Mattes pointed out that any attempt to add to the vast literature on the Oregon-California Trails "must justify itself by exploring new territory or by at least providing new interpretations or fresh syntheses of old data."[1] In this spirit, this study builds on the scholarly foundation laid by historians such as Dale L. Morgan, Robert G. Athearn, Louise Barry, Stephen Dow Beckham, Charles Camp, John Cumming, Aubrey Haines, Kenneth L. Holmes, W. Turrentine Jackson, Walter Jacobs, Charles Kelly, David Lavender, Earl Pomeroy, and George Stewart. I have been blessed by the advice, friendship, and inspiration of scholars and friends who have investigated this story for decades: David L. Bigler, Gregory Franzwa, Richard H. Dillon, J. S. Holliday, Larry Jones, Howard B. Lamar, Brigham D. Madsen, Robert Munkres, Doyce B. Nunis, Jr., Floyd A. O'Neil, John Phillip Reid, Martin Ridge, Robert M. Utley, Jeanne Watson, and Merle Wells.

This work incorporates the insights and perspectives of my contemporaries, the "New" western historians, who like me are now looking more like old historians: Peter Boag, Tom Chaffin, William Cronon, Brian W. Dippie, John Mack Faragher, Rosemary Gardner, Albert L. Hurtado, Julie Roy Jeffrey, Kristin Johnson, Patricia Nelson Limerick, Sandra L. Myres, Walter Nugent, Kenneth N. Owens, Charles E. Rankin, James Ronda, Richard L. Rieck, Glenda Riley, Lillian Schlissel, Sherry L. Smith, and Michael L. Tate. I am especially indebted to Elliott West and Richard White, whose engaging perspective on western history has helped us all tell, as Elliott put it, a "longer, grimmer, but more interesting story."

Over the course of this project I was privileged to visit many of the leading archives of western Americana. These include the American Heritage Center, University of Wyoming, Laramie, Wyoming; Special Collections, Harold B. Lee Library, Brigham Young University, Provo, Utah; the California Room, California State Library,

---

[1] Mattes, *The Great Platte River Road*, vi.

Sacramento; Clackamas County Historical Society, Oregon City; Denver Public Library and Colorado State Historical Society; Idaho State Historical Society, Boise, Idaho; Henry E. Huntington Library, San Marino, California; Jesuit Oregon Province Archives, Special Collections, Gonzaga University, Spokane, Washington; Family and Church History Department Archives, The Church of Jesus Christ of Latter-day Saints, Salt Lake City, Utah; Merrill J. Mattes Library, National Frontier Trails Center, Independence, Missouri; Missouri Historical Society, Saint Louis; Nevada Historical Society, Reno; Oregon State Historical Society, Portland; Polk County Historical Museum, Rickreall, Oregon; Sacramento Room, Sacramento Public Library; Special Collections, Marriott Library, University of Utah, Salt Lake City; Special Collections, University of Oregon, Eugene; Sutter's Fort Museum Services Collection Management Warehouse, Sacramento; University of Washington Special Collections, Seattle; Utah State Historical Society, Salt Lake City; Washington Room, Washington State Library, Olympia; Washington State Historical Society Research Center and the Washington State Museum, Tacoma; Western Historical Manuscript Collection, Ellis Library, University of Missouri–Columbia; and the Harry S. Truman Presidential Library, Independence, Missouri. I am deeply indebted to the staffs of these fine institutions and am especially grateful for a research grant from the Yale Collection of Western Americana, Beinecke Library, Yale University.

The staffs of the Delaware County Historical Society, Delaware, Ohio; the Fort Saint Joseph Museum, Niles, Michigan; the Indiana Historical Society, Indianapolis, Indiana; the Newbury Library, Chicago, Illinois; and the Bentley Historical Library, University of Michigan, Ann Arbor, have substantially assisted this project through correspondence.

Assembling an appropriate, and hopefully fresh, set of illustrations would not have been possible without the generosity of those who shared their portraits of youthful pioneers, of W. L. Rusho and Roy D. Tea for their landscapes, and especially of Evelyn Eggenhofer Herman, who granted permission to use her father's unmatched illustrations.

Synthesizing this material into a comprehensive narrative history became more challenging as the number of primary sources seemed to increase exponentially. I regret that I cannot credit each of the many hundreds of people who have assisted me over the past nine years, but I must thank several historians, buffs, and archivists who have made invaluable contributions to this study: Todd I. Berens, Randy Brown, Mike Brown, Don Buck, Robert A. Clark, Terry Del Bene, Andy and Joanne Hammond, Arlie Holt, Ken and Arleta Martin, Morris Werner, Jack and Patricia Fletcher, John Mark Lambertson, George Miles, Ross A. Smith, Roy D. Tea, Michael N. Landon, and Susan Badger Doyle and Roger P.

Blair, M.D. Special thanks must go to James M. Tompkins and Stafford Hazelett, whose contributions to this study are beyond measure, and to Lesley Wischmann and the late Bob Wier for all their work applying the latest technology to the understanding of western trails. Susan Boyle helped put the trails' social history in perspective. Teresa Bichard, Lee Kreutzer, Kay Threlkeld, and Jere Krakow of the National Park Service made this project possible. Finally, the support and immense contribution of my wife and collaborator, Laura Bayer, made this work immeasurably better.

Selected Bibliography

This bibliography consists of abbreviated entries for every work cited in this study, with separate listings for primary sources; secondary sources including books, articles, theses, dissertations, government reports; and finally maps. Footnotes provide complete citations to newspaper articles. Complete citations for more than 3,200 sources will be available on the National Park Service Long Distance Trails Office website in a comprehensive "Oregon-California Trail Bibliography." The site includes links to hundreds of online resources. See http://www.nps.gov/cali/ and http://www.nps.gov/oreg/.

Abbreviations

Allen Library	Special Collections, Allen Library, University of Washington
Beinecke Library	Yale Collection of Western Americana, Beinecke Rare Book and Manuscript Library, Yale University
BYU Library	Special Collections, Harold B. Lee Library, Brigham Young University
Huntington Library	Henry E. Huntington Library, San Marino, California
Journal History	Journal History of The Church of Jesus Christ of Latter-day Saints
LDS Archives	Church History Department, The Church of Jesus Christ of Latter-day Saints, Salt Lake City, Utah
Missouri Historical Society	Missouri Historical Society Library and Archives, Saint Louis
Mattes Library	Merrill J. Mattes Research Library, National Frontier Trails Center, Independence, Missouri
Oregon Historical Society	Oregon Historical Society Research Library
UCLA	Special Collections, University of California at Los Angeles Library
Western Historical Manuscripts	Western Historical Manuscript Collection, Ellis Library, University of Missouri–Columbia

Primary Sources

Abbey, James. California. *A Trip across the Plains, in the Spring of 1850, Being a Daily Record of Incidents of the Trip.* New Albany, Ind.: Kent and Norman, and J. R. Nunemacher, 1850.

Abert Family Papers, Missouri Historical Society.

Ackley, Mary E. [Medley]. *Crossing the Plains and Early Days in California.* San Francisco: by the author, 1928, 13–34.

"An Act to Establish Certain Post Routes," *Acts of the Twenty-Ninth Congress,* 3 March 1847, 132.

Anderson, William Marshall. *The Rocky Mountain Journals of William Marshall Anderson: The West in 1834.* Edited by Dale L. Morgan and Eleanor Towles Harris. San Marino, Calif.: The Huntington Library, 1967. Reprint, Lincoln: University of Nebraska Press, 1987.

Anderson, William Wright. "The Diary and Memoirs of William Wright Anderson, Oregon Pioneer [1848] and Forty-niner." Edited by F. Michael Williams. Ph.D. diss., Ball State University, 1984.

Angel, James Newton. Memoir of 1847, told to Edward H. Davis, 1933. Life of James Newton Angel, 1841–1933, Edward Harvey Davis Papers, MS Collection 75 and 920 ANG, San Diego Historical Society. Janie Angel Pollock Typescript, NFTC Manuscripts, Mattes Library.

Anonymous. Overland Diary, 1849. In John T. Mason Diaries, Box 2, fd 11. WA MSS S-2173, Beinecke Library.

Applegate, Jesse, to George Abernethy, 20 March 1848. Oregon Historical Society. Courtesy Stafford Hazelett.

———. "A Day with the Cow Column in 1843." *Overland Monthly* 1, no. 2 (August 1868): 127–33.

Applegate, Jesse A. "Recollections of My Boyhood." In Martin Ridge, ed., *Westward Journeys: Memoirs of Jesse A. Applegate and Lavinia Honeyman Porter Who Traveled the Overland Trail,* 11–182. Chicago: The Lakeside Press, R. R. Donnelley and Company, 1989.

Applegate, Lindsay. "Notes and Reminiscences of Laying Out and Establishing the Old Emigrant Road into Southern Oregon in the Year 1846." *Oregon Historical Quarterly* 22, no. 1 (March 1921): 12–45. Edited and reprinted Ella May Young, Andy Hammond, and Joanne Hammond. *Overland Journal* 11, no. 1 (Spring 1993): 2–23.

Aram, Joseph. "Across the Continent in a Caravan [1846]," *Journal of American History* 1 (Fourth Quarter 1907): 617–632. Reprint, Fairfield, Wash.: Ye Galleon Press, 1988.

Arthur, David. "Arthur's Prairie First Furrow Plowed in Clackamas County [Across the Plains in 1843]." Undated item, *Sunday Oregonian,* 1889.

Atkinson, Lydia B., to Anna Knox, 15 October 1852. Typescript, NFTC Manuscripts, Mattes Library.

Ball, John. *Autobiography of John Ball.* Grand Rapids, Mich.: The Dean-Hicks Company, 1925.

Barlow, William. "Reminiscences of Seventy Years." *Quarterly of the Oregon Historical Society* 13, no. 3 (September 1912): 240–79.

Batchelder, Amos. Journal of a Tour across the Continent of North America from Boston, via Independence, Missouri, the Rocky Mountains, to San Francisco, by the author in 1849. Batchelder-Nelson Family Papers, MSS C-B 614, Bancroft Library. Charles Kelly Typescript, MSS A 14, Utah State Historical Society.

Bayley, Betsey, to Lucy P. Griffith, 20 September 1849. Mss 1508, Oregon State Historical Society. "Across the Plains in 1845." In Holmes, ed., *Covered Wagon Women,* 1:35–38.

Bayley, Thomas S. The First Overland Mail Bag to California, in Five Chapters in Pioneer His-

tory. Recollections of California during the Gold Rush, (ca. 1900), Bancroft Library, C-D
      5011:1.

Beaver, Herbert. "Indian Conditions in 1836–38." Edited by Nellie B. Pipes. *Oregon Historical
      Quarterly* 32, no. 4 (December 1931): 330–42. See also *Reports and Letters of Herbert Beaver,
      1836–1838*. Edited by Thomas E. Jessett. Portland, Oreg.: Champoeg Press, 1959.

Belknap, Keturah. "The Commentaries of Keturah Belknap." In Holmes, ed., *Covered Wagon
      Women*, 1:189–229.

Benton, Thomas Hart. *Thirty Years' View; or, A History of the Working of the American Government for
      Thirty Years, from 1820 to 1850*, 2 vols. New York: D. Appleton and Company, 1854.

Bidwell, John. "The First Emigrant Train to California." *Century Magazine* 41 (November 1890):
      106–29.

———. "Life in California before the Gold Discovery," *Century Magazine* 41 (December 1890):
      163–83.

———. "Fremont in the Conquest of California." *Century Magazine* 41 (February 1891): 518–
      25.

———. "Earliest Explorations of Colusa County." In Justus H. Rogers, ed., *Colusa County: Its
      History Traced from a State of Nature*, 37–54. Orland, Calif.: n.p., 1891.

———. *Addresses, Reminiscences, etc. of General John Bidwell*. Edited by C. C. Royce. Chico, Calif.:
      n.p., 1906.

Bigler, Henry W. *Bigler's Chronicle of the West: The Conquest of California, Discovery of Gold, and Mor-
      mon Settlement*. Edited by Erwin G. Gudde. Berkeley and Los Angeles: University of California
      Press, 1962.

Bishop, Francis A. Itinerary of Route, June–October 1857, from Placerville to City of Rocks.
      Typescript, Box 4, Henderson Collection.

Blanchet, Augustin Magloire, to Peter R. Kendrick, 30 March 1848. General Archives of the
      Society of Jesus, Rome, Italy. Copies at Jesuit Oregon Province Archives, Special Collections,
      Gonzaga University.

Blain, Wilson. Letters, 1848–57. Mss 1035, Oregon Historical Society.

Blackburn, Abner. *Frontiersman: Abner Blackburn's Narrative*. Edited by Will Bagley. Salt Lake City:
      University of Utah Press, 1992.

Boardman, John. "The Journal of John Boardman: An Overland Journey from Kansas to Oregon
      in 1843." *Utah Historical Quarterly* 2, no. 4 (October 1929): 99–121.

Bogart, Nancy M. (Hembree) Snow. Reminiscences of a Journey across the Plains in 1843. Lock-
      ley Collection, Huntington Library.

Boggs, Lilburn, "Route to the Pacific." *St. Louis Weekly Reveille*, 22 May 1848. Typescript in Ore-
      gon-California Papers, 1804–1876, Missouri Historical Society.

Bonniwell, George. The Gold Rush Diary of George Bonniwell, 1850. Manuscript in the posses-
      sion of Barbara Sumner. J. R. Tompkins transcription.

Boos, Theodore. My Life in the Army. WA MSS S-2275 B644, Beinecke Library.

Boylan, Robert J. Gold Rush Letters, 1850–1853. Manuscript SMCII, Box 12, Folder 3, Califor-
      nia State Library.

Boyle, Charles E. Diary, 1849. Serialized in the *Columbus* [Ohio] *Dispatch*, 2–28 October 1849,
      and 2 October–11 November 1949.

Brannan, Samuel. Fragmentary remarks re: his expedition to California with the Mormons [circa
      1878], Brannan Collection, HM 4089, Huntington Library.

————. *Scoundrel's Tale: The Samuel Brannan Papers*. Edited by Will Bagley. Spokane, Wash.: Arthur H. Clark, 1999.

Brown, Delia Thompson. Diary Kept by Delia Thompson Brown, 1860–1869. Typescript. Print /NC 79/1/1, Nevada Historical Society.

Brown, James S. *Life of a Pioneer: Being the Autobiography of James S. Brown*. Salt Lake City, G. Q. Cannon, 1900. Reprint, New York: AMS Press, 1971.

Brown, John Henry. *Reminiscences and Incidents of Early Days of San Francisco (1845–50) by John Henry Brown*. Edited by Douglas S. Watson. San Francisco: The Grabhorn Press, 1933.

Brown, Joseph Henry. Recollection of 1847 Trip to Oregon. In Autobiography and Related Materials, 1878–1888, MSS P-A 8, Bancroft Collection, Bancroft Library. Copy in OCTA Manuscripts, Mattes Library.

Brown, Tabitha. 1854 Letter. *Oregon Historical Quarterly* 5 (June 1904): 199–205. "A Brimfield Heroine, Tabitha Brown." In Holmes, ed., *Covered Wagon Women*, 1:47–63.

Bruff, J. Goldsborough. *Gold Rush: The Journals, Drawings, and Other Papers of J. Goldsborough Bruff, Captain, Washington City and California Mining Association, April 2, 1849–July 20, 1851*. 2 vols. Edited by Georgia Willis Read and Ruth Gaines. New York: Columbia University Press, 1944.

Bryant, Edwin. *What I Saw in California*. New York: D. Appleton & Co., 1848. Reprint, Palo Alto, Calif.: Lewis Osborne, 1967.

Buckingham, Harriet Talcott. "Crossing the Plains in 1851." In Holmes, ed., *Covered Wagon Women*, 3:15–52.

Budd, Daniel H. Journal, Potosi, Wisconsin to California, 1852, Harvard University. Typescript, Mattes Library.

Burgert, Daniel, and Manlius Stone Rudy. "The Rough Road West: 120-Year-Old Diary Reveals Hardships of Party of Ohioans in '49 Gold Rush." Edited by David R. Rudy. *The Columbia Dispatch Magazine* (8 June 1969): 46–53.

Burnett, Lucy Jane Hall. "Reminiscences of a Trip across the Plains in '45." In Mary Osborn Douthit, ed., *Souvenir of Western Women*, 27–28. Portland, Oreg.: Anderson and Dunway, 1905.

Burnett, Peter H. *Recollections and Opinions of an Old Pioneer*. New York: D. Appleton and Company, 1880. Reprinted as Burnett, *An Old California Pioneer*. Oakland, Calif.: Biobooks, 1946.

————. "Letters of Peter Burnett." *Quarterly of the Oregon Historical Society* 3, no. 4 (December 1902): 398–426.

Burrell, Mary. "Council Bluffs to California, 1854." In Holmes, ed., *Covered Wagon Women*, 6:225–55.

Burrows, Rufus Gustavus. "Crossing the Plains with R. G. Burrows." *Colusa County Historical Society Wagon Wheels 1964* 13, no. 1 (May 1964): 6–34.

Campbell, David. "Pioneer of 1846: Sketch of Hardships Endured by Those Who Crossed the Plains in '46." *Porterville Recorder*, 11, 12, and 13 August 1910.

Campbell, Robert. *The Rocky Mountain Letters of Robert Campbell*. Introduction by Charles Eberstadt. New Haven, Conn.: Printing Office of the Yale University Press for Frederick W. Beinecke, 1955.

Carleton, James H. *The Prairie Logbooks: Dragoon Campaigns to the Pawnee Villages in 1844, and to the Rocky Mountains in 1845*. Edited by Louis Pelzer. Lincoln: University of Nebraska Press, 1983.

Carpenter, Helen. "A Trip across the Plains in an Ox Wagon." In Sandra L. Myres, ed., *Ho for*

California! Women's Overland Diaries from the Huntington Library, 92–188. San Marino, Calif.: Huntington Library, 1980.

Carson, Christopher. *Kit Carson's Own Story of His Life, as Dictated to Col. and Mrs. D. C. Peters about 1856–57, and Never Before Published.* Edited by Blanche C. Grant. Taos, N.M.: n.p., 1926. Reprint, Taos: Kit Carson Memorial Foundation, 1955.

Carter, Tolbert [or Talbert]. "Pioneer Days." *Transactions of the Oregon Pioneer Association* (1906): 65–168.

Case, William. "Reminiscences of William Case." Edited by H. S. Lyman. *The Quarterly of the Oregon Historical Society* 1, no. 3 (September 1900): 269–95.

Cason, Mary Marsh. The Whitman Massacre as Recalled by Mary Marsh Cason. Typescript, Oregon State Archives.

Caufield, Robert, to John Caufield, 1 April 1848. Mss 1508, Oregon Historical Society.

Cauthorn, James D. Diary, 1865. A17, Special Collections, University of Oregon Library.

Chambers, Andrew Jackson. *Recollections: Crossing the Plains in 1845.* Fairfield, Wash.: Ye Galleon Press, 1975.

Chandless, William. *A Visit to Salt Lake; Being a Journey across the Plains.* London: Smith, Elder, and Co., 1857. Reprint, New York: AMS Press, 1971.

Christy, Thomas. *Thomas Christy's Road across the Plains.* Edited by Robert H. Becker. Denver: Fred A. Rosenstock, Old West Publishing, 1969.

Clark, John Hawkins. "Overland to the Gold Fields of California in 1852: The Journal of John Hawkins Clark, Expanded and Revised from Notes Made During the Journey." Edited by Louise Barry. *Kansas Historical Quarterly,* 11, no. 3 (August 1942): 227–96.

Clayton, William. *An Intimate Chronicle: The Journals of William Clayton.* Edited by George D. Smith. Salt Lake City: Signature Books, 1991.

Clyman, James. *James Clyman, Frontiersman.* Edited by Charles L. Camp. San Francisco: California Historical Society, 1928. Second edition, Portland, Oreg.: The Champoeg Press, 1960.

Cole, Gilbert L. *In the Early Days along the Overland Trail in Nebraska Territory, in 1852.* Compiled by Mrs. A. Hardy. Kansas City, Mo.: Franklin Hudson Publishing Company, 1905.

Cooke, Lucy Rutledge. *Crossing the Plains in 1852: Narrative of a Trip from Iowa to "The Land of Gold," as Told in Letters Written During the Journey.* Modesto, Calif.: Frank W. Cooke, 1923. Republished as "Letters on the Way to California." In Holmes, ed., *Covered Wagon Women,* 4:209–95.

Cooke, Philip St. George. *Scenes and Adventures in the Army; or, Romance of Military Life.* Philadelphia: Lindsay and Blakiston, 1857.

Coon, James Madison, and Nancy Coon. The Diary of James Madison Coon and Nancy Iness (Miller) Coon on the Oregon Trail from Mercer County, Illinois to Clackamas County, Oregon in 1847. Edited by Robert Lewis. Copy in possession of author.

Coon, Polly. "Journal of a Journey over the Rocky Mountains." In Holmes, ed., *Covered Wagon Women,* 5:173–206.

Cooper, Andrew, to "Mr. and Mrs. Hieronymous and Molly," 12 June 1864. Mattes Library.

Cornwall, J. A. "The Cornwall Family Coming to the Oregon Country." *Oregon Statesman,* 12 July 1941. Typescript. MS File/Print File, Nevada Historical Society.

Cornwall, Bruce. *Life Sketch of Pierre Barlow Cornwall, by Bruce Cornwall, His Son.* San Francisco: A. M. Robertson, 1906.

Cosgrove, Hugh. "Reminiscences of Hugh Cosgrove." Edited by H. S. Lyman. *The Quarterly of the Oregon Historical Society* 1, no. 3 (September 1900): 252–69.

Cramer, Thomas. Overland Journey from Kansas to California by Thomas J. B. Cramer, 1859. WA MSS 115, Beinecke Library.

Crawford, Medorem. "Journal of Medorem Crawford: An Account of His Trip across the Plains with the Oregon Pioneers of 1842." Edited by F. G. Young. *Sources of the History of Oregon* 1, 1 (1897): 5–28.

———. "To Emigrants." Broadside, 1863. Clackamas County Historical Society, Oregon City, Oregon.

Creel, Virginia Fackler. Diary, 1864. Microfilm C995, V. 9, #280, Western Historical Manuscript Collection.

Crews, Angeline. Recollection of 1846. William Smith Family Papers. Mss 1188, Oregon Historical Society.

Crockett, Samuel B., to "Dear Friends," 16 February 1845. Mss 1500, Typescript, Oregon Historical Society.

———. "Diary of Samuel Black Crockett, 1844." Edited by Vernon Cartenson. In *Building a State, Washington State Historical Society Publications* 3 (1940): 594–607.

Crooks, Ramsey. "Who Discovered the South Pass?" Letter of 28 June 1856 to *The Detroit Free Press. The Quarterly of the Oregon Historical Society* 17, no. 1 (March 1916), 50–51.

Cummings, Charles J. Diary, 1859. WA MSS 118, Beinecke Library.

Currier, Elizabeth B. Foster. Crossing the Plains in 1846, Interview, 1914. Typescript, NFTC Manuscripts, Mattes Library.

Curry, George B. "Occasional Address." *Transactions of the Oregon Pioneer Association* (1887): 32–47.

Daigh, James M. *"Nuggets from '49": An Account of Pike County Men in the Gold Rush Condensed from the Diary of James M. Daigh by Owen Hannant.* Fairfield, Wash.: Ye Galleon Press, 1985.

Darst, Paul. Diary: Crossing Plains in 1847 from Fort Laremy to Oregon City. Typescript, A 26, Special Collections, University of Oregon Library.

Davis, Dr. George W., to Walter Watkins, 6 December 1850. MSS S-694, Beinecke Library.

Day, Alphonse B. Journal of the Trip to California, 1849. Vault MSS 658, BYU Library.

Deady, Lucy Ann Henderson. "Crossing the Plains to Oregon." Edited by Fred Lockley. *Transactions of the Oregon Pioneer Association* (1928): 57–59.

Decker, Peter. *The Diaries of Peter Decker—Overland to California in 1849 and Life in the Mines, 1850–1851.* Edited by Helen S. Griffen. Georgetown, Calif.: The Talisman Press, 1966.

Delano, Alonzo. *Life on the Plains and among the Diggings.* New York: Miller, Orton and Co., 1857.

De Smet, Pierre-Jean. *Life, Letters and Travels of Father Pierre-Jean de Smet, S.J., 1801–1873. Missionary Labors and Adventures among the Wild Tribes of the North American Indians.* 4 vols. Edited by Hiram Martin Chittenden and Alfred Talbot Richardson. New York: F. P. Harper, 1905. Reprint, New York: Kraus Reprint Co., 1969.

Downey, Joseph T. *The Cruise of the Portsmouth, 1845–1847: A Sailor's View of the Naval Conquest of California by Joseph T. Downey, Ordinary Seaman.* Edited by Howard R. Lamar. New Haven, Conn.: Yale University Library, 1958.

Ebbert, George Wood. Reminiscences. In "Joe Meek's Trip to Washington, 1847–8." *The Quarterly of the Oregon Historical Society* 19, no. 3 (September 1918): 262–67.

Edwards, Philip Leget. *Sketch of the Oregon territory; or, emigrants' guide, by P. L. Edwards.* Liberty, Mo.: Printed at the "Herald" Office, 1842.

Egan, Howard R. *Pioneering the West, 1846 to 1878: Major Howard Egan's Diary.* Edited by Howard Ransom Egan. Richmond, Utah: Howard R. Egan Estate, 1917.

Elgin, James Henry. "To the Oregonian: Over the Plains 50 Years Ago." James H. Elgin, II, transcription. Copy in possession of author.

E. M. "Road to Oregon." *Oregon Spectator,* 9 January 1851. In Holmes, ed., *Covered Wagon Women,* 1:155.

Estes, Mary Elizabeth Munkers. Crossing the Plains in 1846 as Told by Mrs. Mary Elizabeth Munkers Estes While Sitting by Her Fireside Christmas Eve 1916. Digital copy in possession of author.

Farnham, Thomas. *Travels in the Great Western Prairies and Rocky Mountains and in the Oregon Territory.* Poughkeepsie, New York: Killy and Lossing, 1841.

Ferris, Warren Angus. *Life in the Rocky Mountains.* Edited by LeRoy Hafen and Paul C. Phillips. Revised edition, Denver: Fred A Rosenstock, the Old West Publishing Company, 1983.

Field, James, Jr. Crossing the Plains, Diary, 1845. Oregon Historical Society, Typescript, Mss 520. Originally published 18 April–1 August 1879 in the *Willamette Farmer.*

Field, Matthew C. *Prairie and Mountain Sketches.* Edited by Kate L. Gregg and John Francis McDermott. Norman: University of Oklahoma Press, 1957.

Findla, James. Statement, 1878. California Biographical Manuscripts, C–D 79, Bancroft Library.

Findley, William. Overland Journey to Oregon and a Return Trip. WA MSS S-33, Beinecke Library.

Fish, Mary C. Diary 1860. California State Library. Typescript, OCTA Manuscripts, Mattes Library.

Ford, Nathaniel. "Letter from Oregon," 6 April 1845, in Clyman, *James Clyman,* 270–71.

Ford, Nineveh. The Pioneer Road Makers: A Narrative of 1843. 1878, MSS P-A 32, Bancroft Library.

Fosdick, Lucy H. Across the Plains in '61. WA MSS S-1410 F786, Beinecke Library.

Fosdick, Sarah. "Going to California." *Davenport Gazette,* 10 February 1848, 1/5–6. Courtesy Kristin Johnson.

Franklin, I. to Morritz Langsdorf. Letters, 1852–1853. Mss 184, Oregon Historical Society.

Frink, Margaret A. *Journal of the Adventures of a Party of California Gold-Seekers Under the Guidance of Mr. Ledyard Frink During a Journey across the Plains from Martinsville, Indiana, to Sacramento, California, from March 30, 1850, to September 7, 1850. From the Original Diary of the Trip Kept by Mrs. Margaret A. Frink.* Oakland, Calif.: For the Author, 1897. Reprinted in Holmes, ed., *Covered Wagon Women.* 2:55–167.

Galbraith, Thomas. Journal of Mess Number Twenty-seven of the Pittsburg and California Enterprise Company. Typescript, OCTA Manuscripts, Mattes Library.

Garrison, A. H. Reminiscences of A. H. Garrison His Early Life, Across the Plains and of Oregon from 1846 to 1903. Mss 1508, Oregon Historical Society. Published as "Reminiscences of Abraham Henry Garrison—Over the Oregon Trail in 1846." Edited by James M. Tompkins. *Overland Journal* 11, no. 2 (Summer 1993): 10–31.

Gates, Jacob. Journal, 1847. LDS Archives.

Geer, Calvin. "My Trip To Oregon By Calvin Geer." Ed. by Ralph C. Geer, Jr., 1925. Retrieved 23 January 2006 from http://www.theragens.com/history/Geer%20-%20My%20Trip%20 To%20Oregon.htm.

Geer, Ralph C. "Occasional Address for the Year 1847." *Transactions of the Ninth Annual Re-union of the Oregon Pioneer Association for 1879.* Salem, Oreg.: E. M. Waite, Steam Printer and Bookbinder, 32–42.

Geer, T. T. *Fifty Years in Oregon: Experiences, Observations, and Commentaries upon Men, Measures, and Customs in Pioneer Days and Later Times.* New York: The Neale Publishing Company, 1916.

Gillespie, Archibald H. Personal Papers of Archibald H. Gillespie, 1847–1860. Collection 133, UCLA.

Gilliam, Washington Smith. "Reminiscences." *Transactions of the Oregon Pioneer Association* (1903): 202–22.

Gilmore, [Samuel Mathison]. Letter attributed to S. H. Gilmore, Fort Vancouver, 11 November 1843. In *Western Journal.* Reprinted in *The Quarterly of the Oregon Historical Society* 4, no. 3 (September 1903): 280–84.

Goode, James Madison, to "Catherine McRae Goode," 24 September 1912. Letter, Manuscript SMCII Box 12 Folder 2, California State Library.

Goodell, Jotham. *A Winter with the Mormons: The 1852 Letters of Jotham Goodell.* Edited by David L. Bigler. Utah, the Mormons, and the West, vol. 15. Salt Lake City: Tanner Trust Fund, 2001.

Graham, J. M. Diary of John Melvin Graham, Brownville, Nebraska Territory to Denver City 1860. Mattes Library.

Grant, John Francis. *Very Close to Trouble: The Johnny Grant Memoir.* Edited by Lyndel Meikle. Pullman: Washington State University Press, 1996.

Grant, Richard. Correspondence, in George Simpson. Incoming Correspondence, R3C 1T5, Hudson's Bay Company Archives, Provincial Archives of Manitoba, Winnipeg, Manitoba, Canada.

Gray, William H. *A History of Oregon, 1792–1849; Drawn from Personal Observations and Authentic Information.* Portland, Oreg.: Harris and Holman, 1870.

Green, Ephraim. *A Road from El Dorado: The 1848 Trail Journal of Ephraim Green.* Edited by Will Bagley. Salt Lake City: The Prairie Dog Press, 1991.

Gregson, James, and Eliza Gregson, "The Gregson Memoirs. Mrs. Gregson's 'Memory' and the Statement of James Gregson [1845]." *California Historical Society Quarterly* 19, vol. 2 (June 1940): 113–43.

Gunnison, John W. *The Mormons, or, Latter-day Saints, in the Valley of the Great Salt Lake.* Philadelphia: Lippincott, Grambo and Co., 1852. Second edition, 1860. Reprint, Brookline, Mass.: Paradigm Publications, 1993.

Hadley, Amelia E. "Journal of Travails to Oregon," in Holmes, ed., *Covered Wagon Women,* 3:53–96.

Hale, Israel F. "Diary of a Trip to California in 1849." *Quarterly of the Society of California Pioneers* 2, no. 2 (June 1925): 61–130.

Hamelin, Joseph P., Jr. Journals, 1849 and 1856. WA MSS 239, Beinecke Library.

Hamilton, Ezra M. Reminiscences. Ezra M. Hamilton Collection, Box 213, California State Library.

Hammer, Jacob. *This Emigrating Company: The 1844 Oregon Trail Journal of Jacob Hammer.* Edited by Thomas A. Rumer. Spokane, Wash.: Arthur H. Clark., 1990.

Hancock, Samuel. *The Narrative of Samuel Hancock, 1845–1860: With an Introduction by Arthur D. Howden Smith and a Map of the Oregon Trail.* New York: R. M. McBride, 1927.

Hanna, Esther Belle McMillan. Diary of a Journey from Pittsburgh to Oregon City. MSS P-A 313, Bancroft Library. Published with editor's insertions as *Canvas Caravans: Based on the Journal of Esther Belle McMillan Hanna, Who with Her Husband, Rev. Joseph A. Hanna, Brought the Presbyterian Colony to Oregon in 1852.* Edited by Eleanor Allen. Portland, Oreg.: Binfords and Mort, 1946. Kay Threlkeld transcription.

Harlan, Jacob Wright. *California '46 to '88.* San Francisco: The Bancroft Company, 1888.

Harritt, Jesse. "Diary of Jesse Harritt, 1845." *Transactions of the 38th Annual Reunion of the Oregon Pioneer Association* (1910): 206–26.

Harrow, Edward C. *The Gold Rush Overland Journal of Edward C. Harrow, 1849.* Austin, Tex.: Michael Vinson, 1993.

Harty, James N. Letters, 29 June and 9 July 1847. Mss 1508, Oregon Historical Society.

Hastings, Lansford W. *The Emigrants' Guide, to Oregon and California; Containing Scenes and Incidents of a Party of Oregon Emigrants; a Description of Oregon; Scenes and Incidents of a Party of California Emigrants; and a Description of California; with a Description of the Different Routes to those Countries; and All Necessary Information Relative to the Equipment, Supplies, and the Method of Traveling.* Cincinnati: George Conclin, 1845.

———, to John C. Calhoun, 20 May 1844. *Annual Report of the American Historical Association* (1929): 234–35.

Hastings, Loren B. Overland Journey from Illinois. WA MSS 248, Beinecke Library. Published in *Transactions of the Oregon Pioneer Association* (1923): 12–26.

Hecox, Margaret M. "The Story of Margaret M. Hecox." Edited by Marie Valhasky. *Overland Monthly and Out West Magazine* 19, no. 113 (May 1892): 535–47.

Hewitt, Randall Henry. *Notes by the Way: Memoranda of a Journey across the Plains, from Dundee, Ill., to Olympia, W.T. May 7, to November 3, 1862.* Olympia, Wash.: Printed at the Office of the Washington Standard, 1863. Revised edition, *Across the Plains and Over the Divide: A Mule Train Journey East to West in 1862, and Incidents Connected Therewith, with Map and Illustrations, by Randall H. Hewitt.* New York: Broadway Publishing, 1906.

Hill, John Berry. *A Gold Hunter: Memoirs of John Berry Hill, 1827–1917.* Edited by Kristin Delaplane. Vacaville, Calif.: Masterpiece Memoirs, 1997.

Hockett, William A. Recollections, 1914. Typescript, Mss 1036, Oregon Historical Society.

Hopkins, Sarah Winnemucca. *Life among the Piutes: Their Wrongs and Claims.* Edited by Mrs. Horace [Mary] Mann. Boston: Cupples, Upham and Co., and the author, 1883.

Horn, Hosea B. *Hosea B. Horn's Overland Guide, from the U.S. Indian Sub-Agency, Council Bluffs, on the Missouri River, to the City of Sacramento, in California.* New York: J. H. Colton, 1852.

Houghton, Eliza P. Donner. *The Expedition of the Donner Party and Its Tragic Fate.* Chicago: A. C. McClurg and Co., 1911. Republished with an introduction by Kristin Johnson, Lincoln: University of Nebraska Press, 1997.

Hudgins, John. California in 1849. Typescript C2189, Western Historical Manuscript Collection.

Hudson's Bay Company Archives, Provincial Archives of Manitoba, Winnipeg, Manitoba, Canada.

Hughes, Georgia. Recollections of 1850 Trip to Oregon, 1910. Typescript, Mss 2999, Oregon Historical Society.

Hulin, Lester. Day Book or Journal of Lester Hulin, Oregon Trail and Applegate Route 1847. Typescript, Lane County Pioneer Museum, Eugene, Oregon, 1959.

Hunt, Nancy A. "By Ox-Team to California: Personal Narrative." *Overland Monthly* 67 (April 1916): 317–26.

Hunter, Jane Elizabeth Tompkins. "From the Record of Jane E. Hunter, Born in Steuben County, N.Y. Jan. 11, 1843." A lost pamphlet copied into the Manuscript History of the California Mission, CR 1316, vol. 1, LDS Archives.

Ingersoll, Chester. *Overland to California in 1847.* Edited by Douglas C. McMurtrie. Chicago: Black Cat Press, 1937.

Isham, Giles S. *Guide to California and the Mines.* New York: A. T. Mouel, Printer, 1850. Reprint, Fairfield, Wash.: Ye Galleon Press. 1972.

Jackson, Alonzo C. "The Conquest of California." *The Westerners New York Posse Brand Book* 5, no. 3 (1958): 49, 51–57.

Jackson, Andrew. *Message from the President of the United States, In Answer to a Resolution of the Senate Relative to the British Establishments on the Columbia, and the State of the Fur Trade, etc.,* 26 January 1831. Sen. Doc. 39 (21:2), Serial 203. Washington, D.C., 1831.

Jackson, Edward. Journal of Edward Jackson on His Route from Fort Independence to California in 1849. MSS SC 2493, BYU Library.

James, Edwin. *Account of an Expedition from Pittsburgh to the Rocky Mountains, Performed in the Years 1819, 1820,* 2 vols. Philadelphia: H. C. Carey and I. Lea, 1822–23.

James Family Papers. Letters and Overland Diary, 1851. Accession Number 3575–5, Box 1, Folder 11, Manuscripts, Allen Library.

Jefferson, T. H. *Map of the Emigrant Road from Independence, Mo., to St. Francisco California by T. H. Jefferson.* Edited by George R. Stewart. San Francisco: California Historical Society, 1945.

Johnston, William G. *Experiences of a Forty-niner.* Pittsburgh, Pa.: By the author, 1892. Republished with a foreword by Joseph A. Sullivan, *Overland to California.* Oakland, Calif.: Biobooks, 1948.

Jones, Mary Annie Smith. Recollections of Mary Ann Jones: Alamo, Contra Costa County, ca. 1915. Typescript, MSS C-D 509, Linnie Marsh Wolfe, Papers relating to California Pioneers and to California History, Folder 15, MSS C-R 91, Bancroft Library.

Jones, Nathanial V. "The Journal of Nathaniel V. Jones with the Mormon Battalion (Extracted)." Edited by Cecil Alter. *Utah Historical Quarterly.* 4, no. 1 (January 1931): 6–23.

Kearny, Stephen W. "Report of a Summer Campaign to the Rocky Mountains, &c." House Exec. Doc. 2 (29:1), Serial 480, 210–13.

Kelly, William. *An Excursion to California over the Prairie, Rocky Mountains, and Great Sierra Nevada. With a Stroll through the Diggings and Ranches of that Country.* 2 vols. London: Chapman and Hall, 1851.

Kelsey, Nancy. "Nancy (Roberts) Kelsey's Own Story of Her Life." *Pomo Bulletin* (February 1983), Lake Country Historical Society, Lakeport, Calif. Notes by Roy M. Sylar. Typescript, NFTC Manuscripts, Mattes Library.

Kenderdine, Thaddeus S. *A California Tramp.* Newton, Pa.: Globe Printing House, 1888.

Kern, Edward M. "Journal of Mr. Edward M. Kern of an Exploration of Mary's or Humboldt River, Carson Lake, and Owens River and Lake, In 1845." Appendix Q, in J. H. Simpson, *Report of Explorations across the Great Basin,* 475–86.

———. Fort Sutter Collection, 1845–1862. CSHV00-A56, Huntington Library.

Kilgore, Daniel. Danl Kilgore to Myron Bradley, Packson Co., 28 February 1859. Pioneer Letter File, California State Library.

King, Henry, to "Dear Parents," 30 March 1846, in "Appendix: Copy of Henry King's Letter from California," *Congressional Globe,* 2 February 1847, vol. 16 and Appendix (29:2), 137–38.

King, Mariah [and Stephen King], to "Dear Mother, Brother, and Sisters," 1 April 1846. Typescript, Mss 1508, Oregon Historical Society.

Kingsbury, Lt. Gaines P. "Journal of the March of a Detachment of Dragoons, Under the Command of Colonel Henry Dodge, During the Summer of 1835." House Doc. 138 (24:1), Serial 21.

Kip, Lawrence. *The Indian Council in the Valley of the Walla-Walla, 1855.* San Francisco: Whitton, Towne and Co., Printers, 1855.

Knight, Amelia. "Iowa to the Columbia River." In Holmes, ed., *Covered Wagon Women,* 6:33–75.

Lancaster, Columbia. "A Columbia Lancaster Letter about Oregon in 1847." Edited by Mentor L. Williams. *Oregon Historical Quarterly* 50, no. 1 (March 1949): 40–44.

Lander, Frederick W., and U.S. Dept. of the Interior. *Maps and Reports of the Fort Kearney, South Pass, and Honey Lake Wagon Road.* House Exec. Doc. 64 36:2. Washington: The House, 1861. Serial 1100.

Larkin, Thomas O. *The Larkin Papers: Personal, Business, and Official Correspondence of Thomas Oliver Larkin, Merchant and United States Consul in California.* 10 vols. Edited by George P. Hammond. Berkeley: University of California Press, 1951–68.

Leonard, Zenas. *Narrative of the Adventures of Zenas Leonard, a Native of Clearfield county, Pa., Who Spent Five Years in Trapping for Furs, Trading with the Indians, &c., &c., of the Rocky Mountains; Written by Himself.* Clearfield, Pa: D. W. Moore, 1839. Republished as *Adventures of Zenas Leonard, Fur Trader.* John C. Ewers, ed. Norman: University of Oklahoma Press, 1959.

Lewis, Fielding, to "Dear Cosin," 8 May 1852. Typescript, NFTC Manuscripts, Mattes Library.

Lienhard, John Heinrich. *A Pioneer at Sutter's Fort, 1846–1850: The Adventures of Heinrich Lienhard.* Edited and translated by Marguerite Eyer Wilbur. Los Angeles: The Calafia Society, 1941.

————. *From St. Louis to Sutter's Fort, 1846.* Edited by Erwin G. Gudde and Elisabeth K. Gudde. Norman: University of Oklahoma Press, 1961. See also Dale L. Morgan's superior translation in "The Lienhard Journal." In Korns and Morgan, ed., *West from Fort Bridger,* 113–84.

Lieuallen, William. The Journal of William Lieuallen, Emigrant of 1864. End of the Oregon Trail Interpretive Center, Oregon City, Oregon.

Lippincott, Benjamin S. Letters, 1847–1851. MSS 95/15 c, Bancroft Library and Madera Method Foundation Library, Sierra Vista School, Madera, California. Published as *Frontiersman to States-man: Memories of Benjamin S. Lippincott.* Edited by John Osborne and the Lippincott Historians of Sisk School. Preface by Irving Stone. Madera, Calif.: Classroom Chronicles Press, 1994.

Longmire, James. "James Longmire, Pioneer: Interesting Story of His Experience." *Tacoma Sunday Ledger,* 21 August 1892, 9–10.

Loomis, Leander V. *Journal of the Birmingham Emigrating Company of 1850 by Leander V. Loomis, Together with Five Early Itineraries Covered in Part by this Company, with Supplementary Data Compiled from Historical Sources and Notes and Photographs taken along the Line of Travel.* Edited by Edgar M. Ledyard. Salt Lake City: By the editor, 1928.

Looney, Jesse, to John C. Bond, 27 October 1843, Waiilatpu, Oregon Ter. Manuscript letter, Mss 2263, Oregon Historical Society. Typescript letter, Folder 30, T-177, Overland Journeys, Washington State Historical Society.

Lose, John. "From Oregon," *Defiance* [Ohio] *Democrat,* 25 November 1847, 1/6. Courtesy of Kristin Johnson.

Lovejoy, Asa. "Lovejoy's Pioneer Narrative, 1842–48." Edited by Henry E. Reed. *Oregon Historical Quarterly* 31, no. 3 (September 1930): 236–60.

Lowe, Thomas. Private Journal kept at Fort Vancouver, 1843–1850. Typescript E B L95A, British Columbia Archives and Records Service, Victoria, British Columbia.

Manlove, Jonathan [attributed to Mark D. Manlove]. An Overland Trip to the California Gold Fields. Typescript, Manuscript SMCII Box 17, Folder 13, California State Library.

Marcy, Randolph B. *The Prairie Traveler. A Handbook for Overland Expeditions, with Maps, Illustrations, and Itineraries of the Principle Routes between the Mississippi and the Pacific.* New York: Harper and Brothers, 1859.

Masterson, Martha Gay. *One Woman's West: Recollections of the Oregon Trail and Settling of the Northwest Country.* Edited by Lois Barton. Eugene, Oreg.: Spencer Butte Press, 1986.

Mathews, Dr. Samuel. "By Wagon Train to California, 1849: A Narrative." *The Mathews Family in America.* Edited by Dean C. Mathews. Rio Verde, Ariz.: Alondra Publishing, 1996.

May, Richard Martin. *The Schreek of Wagons: 1848 Diary of Richard M. May.* Edited by Devere Helfrich and Trudy Ackerman. Hopkinton, Mass.: Rigel Publications, 1993.

McBride, John R. "Pioneer Days in the Mountains." *Tullidge's Quarterly Magazine* 3, no. 3 (July 1884): 311–20.

———. "Dr. James McBride—Uncle Jim—Circuit Riding Oregon Preacher." Retrieved 16 January 2007 from Pioneer History, Churches of Christ and Christian Churches in the Pacific Northwest, http://ncbible.org/nwh/ProMcBrideJ.html.

———. Recollections, ca. 1900. Typescript, 105 pages, Mss 458, Oregon Historical Society. Summarized in Morgan, ed., *Overland in 1846,* 90–100.

McClenny, B. T.[?], to "Dear Sister and Brother," Diamond Ranch, Calif., 12 February 1859, in W. S. Bryan Papers, Missouri Historical Society.

McLoughlin, John. *The Letters of John McLoughlin from Fort Vancouver to the Governor and Committee, First series, 1825–38; Second Series, 1839–44; Third Series, 1844–46.* Edited by E. E. Rich. London: Hudson's Bay Record Society, 1941, 1943, 1944.

———. *John McLoughlin's Business Correspondence, 1847–48.* Seattle: University of Washington Press, 1973.

Meek, Stephen H. L. "A Sketch of the Life of the First Pioneer." *The Golden Era* (April 1885). Retrieved 2 May 2009 from http://www.xmission.com/~drudy/mtman/html/smeek.html.

Meeker, Ezra. *Ox-team Days on the Oregon Trail.* Revised and edited by Howard R. Driggs; illustrated by F. N. Wilson. Yonkers-on-Hudson, N.Y.: World Book Company, 1922.

———. A Biographical Sketch of George Bush. Acc. 4814–001, Allen Library.

Meyers, William H. *Naval Sketches of the War in California: Reproducing Twenty-Eight Drawings Made in 1846–47.* Descriptive text by Capt. Dudley W. Knox. Introduction by Franklin D. Roosevelt. New York: Random House, 1939.

Middleton, Joseph. The Diary and Letters of Dr. Joseph Middleton: Embracing his Trip Across the Plains via the Lassen or "Death Route" Cutoff through the Desert and over the Sierra Nevada to California in 1849. Joseph Middleton Papers. MSS S-39, Beinecke Library. Richard L. Rieck transcription.

Minges, Abram. Journal, 8 May to 15 September 1849. 85320 AA Vault, Bentley Historical Library, University of Michigan.

Minto, John. "Reminiscences of Experiences on the Oregon Trail in 1844." Edited by H. S. Lyman. *The Quarterly of the Oregon Historical Society* 2, nos. 2–3 (June, September 1901): 119–67, 209–30.

Minto, Martha Ann Morrison. Female Pioneering in Oregon. 1878 interview, Hubert Howe Bancroft Collection, MSS P-A 51, Bancroft Library.

Morgan, Amasa. Diary, 2 April to 28 July 1849. MSS 2001/111 cz, Bancroft Library.

Munger, Asahel. *Diary of Asahel Munger and Wife: Travel to the Marcus Whitman Mission, May 4, 1839 to September 3, 1839.* Fairfield, Wash.: Ye Galleon Press, 1992. Reprinted from *The Quarterly of the Oregon Historical Society* 8, no. 4 (December 1907).

Murphy, Andrew Lopp. Diary 1849. Typescript C2723, Western Historical Manuscript Collection.

Murphy, Virginia Reed. "Across the Plains in the Donner Party: A Personal Narrative of the Overland Trip to California." *Century Illustrated Magazine* 4, no. 3 (July 1891): 409–26. Reprinted in Kristin Johnson, ed., *Unfortunate Emigrants,* 265–86.

Nichols, B. F. "Across the Plains in 1844." *Laidlaw Chronicle,* weekly serial beginning 16 November 1906. Copy at Western Historical Manuscript Collection.

Nesmith, James Willis. "Diary of the Emigration of 1843." *The Quarterly of the Oregon Historical Society* 7, no. 4 (December 1906): 329–59.

———. "The Occasional Address." *Transactions of the Oregon Pioneer Association* (1875): 42–62.

———. *Two Addresses.* Fairfield, Wash.: Ye Galleon Press, 1978.

Newell, Robert. *Memoranda: Travles in the Teritory of Missourie; Travle to the Kayuse War; Together with a Report on the Indians South of the Columbia River.* Edited by Dorothy O. Johansen. Portland, Oreg.: Champoeg Press, 1959. See also Hafen, ed., *The Mountain Men and the Fur Trade of the Far West,* 8:253–74.

Nixon, Alexander B. Diary of an Overland Journey from Cincinnati, Ohio, to California starting March 10, 1849. CF 865 N5 A3, 2 vols. California State Library.

Ogden, Peter Skene. *Peter Skene Ogden's Snake Country Journals, 1827–1828 and 1828–1829.* Edited by Glyndwr Williams, with an introduction and notes by David E. Miller and David H. Miller. London: Hudson's Bay Record Society, London, 1971.

Orton, Joseph. History of Joseph Orton. BX 8670.1.Or8, BYU Library.

Owen, Benjamin Franklin. My Trip across the Plains, March 31, 1853–October 28, 1853. Typescript, Lane County Historical Society Collection.

Palmer, Harriet Scott. *Crossing Over the Great Plains by Ox-Wagon.* Pamphlet in Oregon Historical Society. Typescript, Library of Congress.

Palmer, Joel. *Journal of Travels over the Rocky Mountains to the Mouth of the Columbia River, Made during the Years 1845 to 1846, Containing Minute Descriptions of the Valleys of Williamette, Umpqua, and Clamet.* Cincinnati: J. A. and U. P. James Publisher, 1847. Reprinted as *Journal of Travels: Over the Oregon Trail in 1845,* Portland: Oregon Historical Society Press, 1993.

Parker, Samuel. *Journal of an Exploring Tour beyond the Rocky Mountains.* Ithaca, N.Y.: By the author, 1838. Reprint, Minneapolis, Minn.: Ross and Haines, 1967. Republished Santa Barbara, Calif.: The Narrative Press, 2001.

———. Diary of Samuel Parker, 1845. MSS 1508, Oregon Historical Society.

Parkman, Francis, Jr. *The California and Oregon Trail: Being Sketches of Prairie and Rocky Mountain Life.* New York: George P. Putnam, 1849.

———. *The Journals of Francis Parkman.* 2 vols. Edited by Mason Wade. New York: Harper, 1947.

———. *Letters of Francis Parkman.* Edited by Wilbur R. Jacobs. Norman: University of Oklahoma Press, 1960.

Patterson, Edwin H. N. Diary and Letters in *Oquawka Spectator,* 1850. OCTA Manuscripts, Mattes Library.

Perkins, Elisha Douglas. *Gold Rush Diary: Being the Journal of Elisha Douglass Perkins on the Overland Trail in the Spring and Summer of 1849.* Edited by Thomas D. Clark. Lexington: University of Kentucky Press, 1967.

Pettijohn, Isaac. Diary, 1847 and 1848. MSS P-A 336 A, Bancroft Library. Richard L. Rieck transcription.

Pickett, Belinda Cooley. Covered Wagon Days from the Original Journal Written by Belinda

Cooley Pickett to her Parents . . . on her Journey across the Plains from Iowa to California in 1853. Verlee Chambers Dauma typescript, copy in OCTA Manuscripts, Mattes Library.

Platt, P. L., and Nelson Slater. *The Travelers' Guide across the Plains, upon the Overland Route to California Showing Distances from Point to Point, Accurately Measured by Roadometer.* Chicago: The Daily Journal Office, 1852. Second edition. Edited by Dale L. Morgan. San Francisco: John Howell Books, 1963.

Polk, James K. Papers. Manuscript Division, Library of Congress.

Poor, R. S. Ft. Kearney, South Pass and Honey Lake W[agon] R[oad] Co. Journal 1857. American Heritage Center.

Porter, William, to "Dear Father, Mother, Brothers and Sisters," 24 June 1848. Retrieved 15 May 2006 from http://www.oregonpioneers.com/porter2.htm.

————. Oregon Trail Diary, 1848. Property of granddaughter Maude Porter. Retrieved 4 June 2009 from http://www.oregonpioneers.com/porter.htm.

Pratt, Addison. *The Journals of Addison Pratt.* Edited by S. George Ellsworth. Salt Lake City: University of Utah Press, 1990.

Pratt, Orson. *The Orson Pratt Journals.* Edited by Elden J. Watson. Salt Lake City: E. J. Watson, 1975, 375–457.

Preuss, Charles. *Exploring with Frémont: The Private Diaries of Charles Preuss, Cartographer for John C. Fremont on his First, Second, and Fourth expeditions to the Far West.* Edited and translated by Erwin G. and Elisabeth K. Gudde. Norman: University of Oklahoma Press, 1958.

Pringle, Catherine Sager. Recollections, ca. 1860. Mss 1194–1, Typescript, Pringle/Sager Family Collection, Oregon Historical Society. Published as *Across the Plains in 1844.* Fairfield, Wash.: Ye Galleon Press, 1989.

Pringle, Virgil. "Diary of Virgil Pringle." In Morgan, ed., *Overland in 1846, Diaries and Letters of the California–Oregon Trail,* 1:159–88.

Prichet, John. "A Letter from California," 17 January 1850. *Richmond Palladium,* 3 April 1850. Typescript, OCTA Manuscripts, Mattes Library.

Rabbeson, Antonio B. Growth of Towns. Bancroft MS PB-17. Bancroft Library. Published as Kristin Johnson, ed., "An Overland Emigrant of 1846: Antonio B. Rabbeson's Account," *Crossroads* 7, nos. 2–3 (Spring/Summer 1996): 16–17.

Rayner, James O. Journal of a Tour to Oregon, April 1847. Typescript, Mss 1508, Oregon Historical Society.

Reading, Pierson B. Diary of P. B. Reading, 1843. California State Library. Published as "Journal of Pierson B. Reading." Edited by Philip B. Bekeart. *Quarterly of the Society of California Pioneers* 7, no. 3 (September 1930): 134–98.

Reed, Martha Williams. "Old California Pioneer Passes Away at Fallbrook. Martha Williams Reed, Age 87, Crosses the Plaines by Ox-Team in the Early Gold Excitement of California." *The Fallbrook Enterprise,* 12 January 1917.

————. "Fallbrook's Prima Donna." *The Fallbrook Enterprise,* 26 September 1913. Typescript, Fallbrook Museum, Fallbrook, California.

Rees, Willard H., to "Mother," Oregon City, 20 March 1846. NFTC Manuscripts, Mattes Library. See also Letters to H. H. Bancroft, 18 September and 23 October 1879. MSS P-A 115, Bancroft Library.

Rhoads, Amanda. Amanda Esrey (Mrs. Daniel) Rhoads to "Dear Parents," Fort Laramie, 15

June 1846. In Rhoads Family Papers, 1846–1856. Photocopy. BANC MSS 71/38 c, Bancroft Library.

Rhoads, Daniel, to "Dear Parents," 1847. *Quarterly Bulletin of California Pioneers of Santa Clara County* 5, no. 1 (March 1965): 4–8.

Rigdon, Zilpha E. Recollection of 1848 in letter to Lillian Perkins, 1 February 1900. Bristow Family Papers. SFM 115, Special Collections, University of Oregon Library.

Riley, James Francis. *Recollections*. Independence, Mo.: John R. James, 1959.

Robinson, Thomas Maury. A Brief Review of the Life of Isaac Constant, 1852, As Told in Part by His Daughter Lavinia Jane (Constant) Robinson to Her Son. Used by permission of Kevin R. Biersdorff.

Rockefellow, Alice. The Story of My Life. Southern Oregon Historical Society.

Rogers, Samuel Hollister. Journal, 1848. LDS Archives, MS 883. Published as *The 1848 Trail Journal of Samuel Hollister Rogers*. Edited by Will Bagley. Salt Lake City: The Prairie Dog Press, 1991.

Rowland, Richard, to Mary Ann Rowland, 9 January 1844. Western Travel Collection, 1622–1968. Missouri Historical Society.

Ross, Alexander. *Adventures of the First Settlers on the Oregon or Columbia River, 1810–1813*. London: Smith, Elder and Co., 1849. Republished Lincoln: University of Nebraska Press, 1986.

————. *The Fur Hunters of the Far West: A Narrative of Adventures in the Oregon and Rocky Mountains*. London: Smith, Elder and Co., 1855.

Rothwell, William Renfro. Notes of a Journey to California in the Spring and Summer of 1850. In Papers, WA MSS 409, Beinecke Library.

Russell, Osborne. *Journal of a Trapper, Or Nine Tears Residence among the Rocky Mountains between the Years of 1834 and 1843*. Edited by Aubrey L. Haines. Portland: Oregon Historical Society, 1955. Reprint, Lincoln: Bison Books, University of Nebraska Press, 1965.

Schmölder, Bruno. *Neuer praktischer Wegweiser für Auswanderer nach Nord-Amerika: in drei Abtheilungen mit Karten, Plänen und Ansichten* [Newest and Most Practical Guide for Emigrants to North America: In Three Parts with Maps, Plans and Views]. Mainz: Le Roux'sche Hofbuchhandlung, 1848. Translated selections, HM2271, Huntington Library. Taken from later German edition, *Der Führer für Auswanderer nach Californien*. Leipzig und Gera: I.M.C., 1849.

Sharp, James Meikle. *Brief Account of the Experiences of James Meikle Sharp*. N.p.: By the author, 1931, 18–37.

Shaw, David Augustus. *Eldorado; or, California As Seen by a Pioneer, 1850–1900. By Hon. D.A. Shaw.* Los Angeles: B. R. Baumgardt and Co., 1900.

Shaw, Thomas C. "Reminiscence of 1844." *Oregon Statesman*, 22 May and 12 June 1885.

Shelton, David. Autobiographical Sketch of 1847. Holograph, Accession Number 4025, Manuscripts, Allen Library.

Sherman, James E., and Edward F. Ronstadt. "Wagon Making in Southern Arizona." *The Smoke Signal*. No. 23. The Tucson Corral of Westerners (Spring 1971). Retrieved 2 May 2009 from http://www.library.arizona.edu/images/ronstadt/jan/ss31/ss31pt1.html#1.

Shively, John M. *The Road to Oregon and California across the Rocky Mountains: Route and Distance to Oregon and California*. Washington, D.C.: Wm. Greer, Printer, 1846. Reprinted as "The Shively Guide." In Morgan, ed., *Overland in 1846*, 734–42.

Simons, N. Letter, ca. 28 June 1854. MSS SC 2421 1854, Special Collections, BYU Library.

Simpson, George. Incoming Correspondence. R3C 1T5, Hudson's Bay Company Archives, Provincial Archives of Manitoba, Winnipeg, Manitoba, Canada.

————. *Overland Journey Round the World during the Years 1841 and 1842. Selections: California, its History, Population, Climate, Soil, Productions, and Harbors.* Cincinnati: J. A. and U. P. James, 1848. Reprint, Fairfield, Wash.: Ye Galleon Press, 1988.

————. *Fur Trade and Empire: George Simpson's Journal. Remarks Connected with the Fur Trade in the Course of a Voyage from York Factory to Fort George and back to York Factory 1824–25; Together with Accompanying Documents.* Edited by Frederick Merk. Cambridge, Mass.: Harvard University Press; London: H. Milford, Oxford University, 1931. Reprint, Cambridge, Mass.: Belknap Press of Harvard University Press, 1968.

————. *Part of Dispatch from George Simpson, Esqr., Governor of Ruperts Land, to the Governor and Committee of the Hudson's Bay Company, London, March 1, 1829; Continued and Completed March 24 and June 5, 1829.* Edited by E. E. Rich, Introduction by W. Stewart Wallace. Toronto: Champlain Society, for the Hudson's Bay Record Society, 1947.

Simpson, J. H. *Report of Explorations Across the Great Basin of the Territory of Utah for a Direct Wagon-Route from Camp Floyd, to Genoa, in Carson Valley, in 1859.* Washington: Government Printing Office, 1876. Reprint, Reno: University of Nevada Press, 1983.

Smith, Abigail, to "Brother and Sister Kirby," Walla Walla, 18 September 1840, Mattes Library.

Smith, Asa Bowen. Oregon Mission Letters. WA MSS S-624, Beinecke Library.

Smith, Azariah. *The Gold Discovery Journal of Azariah Smith.* Edited by David L. Bigler. Salt Lake City: University of Utah Press, 1990.

Smith, Edward. A Journal of Scenes and Incidents on a Journey from Missouri to California in 1848. Typescript in California DAR, *Genealogical Records Committee Report.* Series 2, Volume 4, Miscellaneous Records of Several States and Counties. Copy at CS 68 C 34 v. 4, California State Library.

Smith, Elizabeth Dixon, to Pauline Foster and Cynthia Ames La Porte, 25 May 1848. Published as "Diary of Elizabeth Dixon Smith." *Transactions of the Oregon Pioneer Association* (1907): 153–179. Republished as "The Diary of Elizabeth Dixon Smith." In Holmes, ed., *Covered Wagon Women,* 1:111–55.

Smith, Ellen Skidmore. A Brief Sketch and History of an Oregen [sic] Pioneer. 1846 Original at Huntington Library. Copy in Mattes Library, NFTC.

Smith, G. A. Journal 1852. Western Travel Collection, 1622–1968, Missouri Historical Society Library.

Smith, Ignatius M. A Trip across the Plains, 1859. Typescript, QCB S 6491, California State Library.

Smith, Jedediah. *The Southwest Expedition of Jedediah S. Smith: His Personal Account of the Journey to California, 1826–1827.* Edited by George R. Brooks. Glendale, Calif.: Arthur H. Clark, 1977. Reprint, Lincoln: University of Nebraska Press, 1989.

Smith, Mary Ann Harlan. "Recollection of a Pioneer Mother." *The Grizzly Bear* (March 1923): 4, 28–29.

Snyder, Jacob. "Diary While Crossing the Plains." *Quarterly of the Society of California Pioneers* 8, no. 4 (December 1931): 224–60.

Spalding, Henry H. "A Letter by Henry H. Spalding from the Rocky Mountains," 11 to 16 July 1836. *The New York Evangelist,* 22 October 1836. Reprinted *Oregon Historical Quarterly* 51 (1950): 127–33.

Stabæk, Tosten Kittelsen. "An Account of a Journey to California in 1852." Translated by Einar J. Haugen. *Norwegian-American Studies* 4 (1929): 99–124.

Standley, William, Copies of Letters Written by Dr. William Standley, 1852, in Papers, 1852–1853. Typescript C2717, Western Historical Manuscript Collection.

Stansbury, Howard. *Exploration and Survey of the Valley of the Great Salt Lake. Including a Description of its Geography, Natural history, and Minerals, and an Analysis of Its Waters; with an Authentic Account of the Mormon Settlement.* Philadelphia: Lippincott, Grambo and Co., 1852.

Stanton, Phoebe. "On the Plains: Letter from Mrs. Alfred Stanton, a Well Known Pioneer of Marion County, Oregon," 9 May 1847. *Transactions of the Oregon Pioneer Association* (1912): 622–24.

Stevens, Benjamin? Trip of Capt. Archibald Sampson RoBards and his son John Lewis RoBards, their negro slave Green and Company of Citizens of Hannibal . . . to the Gold Mines of California, 1849. In John Lewis RoBards, Papers, 1832–1922, folders 11, 12. C3609, Western Historical Manuscript Collection.

Stewart, Agnes. Diary, 1853. Mss 1508, Oregon Historical Society.

Stockton, John K. The Trail of the Covered Wagon. Copied by Lillian Raymond, 1929. Edited by Nancy Wanita Stockton Bernhardt and John P. Kirkpatrick. Retrieved 29 August 2006 from http://www.jpkirkpatrick.com/kirkbooks/covered-wagon.htm.

Stoughton, John A. "Passing of an Immigrant of 1843." Edited by J. Orin Oliphant. *Washington Historical Quarterly* 15, no. 2 (July 1924): 205–10.

Sublette, William. "A Fragmentary Journal of William Sublette." Edited by Harrison Dale. *Mississippi Valley Historical Review* 6, no. 1 (June 1919): 99–110.

Sutter, John A. "The Discovery of Gold in California." *Hutchings' California Magazine* (November 1857): 193–98.

Talbot, Theodore. *The Journals of Theodore Talbot, 1843 and 1849–52: With the Fremont Expedition of 1843 and the First Military Company in Oregon Territory, 1849–1852.* Edited by Charles H. Carey. Portland, Oreg.: Metropolitan Press, Publishers, 1931.

Thornton, Jessy Quinn. *Oregon and California in 1848.* 2 vols. New York: Harper and Bros., 1849.

———. "Occasional Address." *Transactions of the Oregon Pioneer Association* (1878): 29–71.

Threlkeld, Kay. Trail Journal: California National Historic Trail Wagon Train, April 26–September 1, 1999. Copy in possession of author.

Tiffany, Pardon Dexter. Journals and Letters, 1849. Typescript, Mattes Library. Originals in Tiffany Family Papers, 1779–1967, AMC94–001159, Missouri Historical Society. Kay Threlkeld transcription.

Todd, William L. "Interesting from California." *Sangamo Journal,* 13 August 1846. Reprinted in Kelly and Morgan, *Old Greenwood,* 176–77.

Toole, Daniel, to "Dear Brother," 2 August 1846. Western Travel Collection, 1622–1968, Missouri Historical Society. Typescript of letter in *Liberty Tribune,* 19 December 1846.

Townsend, John Kirk. *Narrative of a Journey across the Rocky Mountains to the Columbia River* [1834]. Philadelphia: H. Perkins, 1839. Reprinted as *Across the Rockies to the Columbia.* Introduction by Donald Jackson. Lincoln: University of Nebraska Press, 1978.

Tuller, Miriam A. Robinson Thompson. "Crossing the Plains in 1845." *Transactions of the Oregon Pioneer Association* (1895): 87–90.

Turner, Henry Smith. *The Original Journals of Henry Smith Turner: With Stephen Watts Kearny to New Mexico and California, 1846–1847.* Edited by Dwight L. Clarke. Norman: University of Oklahoma Press, 1966.

Tustin, William. "California and Oregon: Letter from Wm. T. Tustan [sic]." 1 May 1846, *Illinois Gazette,* 26 February 1848.

Van Dorn, Thomas J. Diary of T. J. Van Dorn [1849]. WA MSS S-1319, Beinecke Library.

Wadsworth, William. *National Wagon Road Guide, from St. Joseph and Council Bluffs, on the Missouri River, Via South Pass of the Rocky Mountains, to California, with a Map of the Route, including the Salt Lake Country.* San Francisco: Whitton, Towne and Co., Printers and Publishers, 1858.

Walker, Clarborne Campbell, to "Dear Brother, Sister and Friends," 1845, Purvine Family Records, Kathy Sedler transcription with corrected spelling and punctuation in author's possession.

Walker, Joel Pickens. Narrative of Adventures through Alabama, Florida, New Mexico, Oregon, California &c. MSS C-D 170, Bancroft Library, 1878. Published as *A Pioneer of Pioneers; Narrative of Adventures thro' Alabama, Florida, New Mexico, Oregon, California, &c.* Los Angeles: Glen Dawson, 1953.

Ware, Joseph E. *Emigrants' Guide to California.* St. Louis: J. Halsall, 1849. Edited by John Walton Caughey. Princeton, N.J.: Princeton University Press, 1932.

Waters, Lydia Milner. "Account of a Trip across the Plains in 1855." *Quarterly of the Society of California Pioneers* 6, no. 2 (June 1929): 58–79.

Watson, William J. *Journal of an Overland Journey to Oregon Made in the Year 1849: With a Full and Accurate Account of the Route, Its Distances, Scenery, Plains, Mountains.* Jacksonville: E. R. Roe, 1851. Reprint, Fairfield, Wash.: Ye Galleon Press, 1985.

Webster, Daniel. *The Papers of Daniel Webster: Correspondence, Volume 5, 1840–1843.* Edited by Harold D. Moser. Hanover, N.H: The University Press of New England, 1982.

Webster, Kimball. *The Gold Seekers of '49; a Personal Narrative of the Overland Trail and Adventures in California and Oregon from 1849 to 1854.* Manchester, N.H: Standard Book Company, 1917.

Wells, William. Letters to Wife, 1849. Typescript, Missouri Historical Society.

Wertz, Henry M. California Letters, 1850–1854. WA MSS S-734 W499, Beinecke Library.

White, Elijah. "Overland Mail from Oregon." *Independence Express,* 17 November 1845. Reprint, "From the West," Nauvoo, Illinois *Times and Seasons,* 1 December 1845, 1,046–50.

Whitman, Narcissa. *My Journal, 1836, by Narcissa Prentiss Whitman.* Fairfield, Wash.: Ye Galleon Press, 2000.

Whitney, Horace Kimball. 1847 Journal, LDS Archives.

Whitney, Lois. Interview with Gene Kaplan, Peg Kaplan, and Will Bagley, 9 January 2002, in Elko, Nevada. From shorthand notes by Peg Kaplan.

Williams, Joseph. *Narrative of a Tour from the State of Indiana to the Oregon Territory in the Years 1841–2.* Cincinnati: J. B. Wilson for the author, 1843. Reprinted in LeRoy R. and Ann W. Hafen, eds., *To the Rockies and Oregon, 1839–1842.* Glendale, Calif.: Arthur H. Clark, 1955.

Williams, Lucia Loraine, to "Dear Mother," 16 September 1851. "A Letter to My Mother." In Holmes, ed., *Covered Wagon Women.* 3:127–159.

Wilson, Luzena S. *Luzena Stanley Wilson, '49er; Memories Recalled Years Later for Her Daughter Correnah Wilson Wright.* Introduction by Francis P. Farquhar. Mills College, Calif.: The Eucalyptus Press, 1937.

Winter, William, and Overton Johnson. *Route across the Rocky Mountains with a Description of Oregon and California.* Lafayette, Ind.: John B. Semans, Printer, 1846.

Wislizenus, Frederick Adolph. *A Journey to the Rocky Mountains in the year 1839, by F. A. Wislizenus, M. D. Tr. from the German, with a sketch of the author's life, by Frederick A. Wislizenus, esq.* Saint Louis: Missouri Historical Society, 1912. Reprint, Fairfield, Wash.: Ye Galleon Press, 1992.

Wood, Julia Newton. Diary of Mrs. Julia Newton Wood, 1853. Manuscripts, Mattes Library.

Wood, Tallmadge B. "Tallmadge B. Wood Letter." *The Quarterly of the Oregon Historical Society* 3, no. 4 (December 1902): 394–98.

Wood, William W. Journal of an Overland Trip from Ohio to California, 1850. WA MSS S-1440 W85, Beinecke Library.

Woodruff, Wilford. *Wilford Woodruff's Journal,* 10 vols. Edited by Scott G. Kenney. Midvale, Utah: Signature Books, 1983. 1847 Overland Account, 3:146–289.

Woodworth, Selim. "Letter from an Officer of the Navy," 14 May 1846, *The Home Journal* (New York City), 13 June 1846, 2; "Letter from Oregon," 15 June 1846, *The Home Journal* (New York City), 8 August 1846, 2; "Letter from California," 6 February 1847, *The Home Journal* (New York City), 31 July 1847, 2–3. Transcribed by Kristin Johnson.

Wyeth, John B. *Oregon; or, A Short History of a Long Journey from the Atlantic Ocean to the Region of the Pacific by Land.* Cambridge, Mass.: Printed for J. B. Wyeth, 1833.

Wyeth, Nathaniel Jarvis. *The Correspondence and Journals of Captain Nathaniel J. Wyeth, 1831–6.* Eugene: Oregon University Press, 1899. Reprinted as *The Journals of Captain Nathaniel J. Wyeth's Expeditions to the Oregon Country, 1831–1836.* Edited by Don Johnson. Fairfield, Wash.: Ye Galleon Press, 1984, 1997.

Yeargain, John Wesley. Oregon Trail Diary, 1852. Typescript, Oregon-California Papers, 1804–1876, Missouri Historical Society.

Young, Brigham. Collection. LDS Archives.

Zieber, Eugenia. "Journal of Our Journey to Oregon, 1851." In Holmes, ed., *Covered Wagon Women,* 3:179–202.

SECONDARY SOURCES: BOOKS, ARTICLES, THESES AND DISSERTATIONS

Adams, Hank, et al. *Report on Trust Responsibilities and the Federal Indian Relationship; Including Treaty Review, Task Force One, Final Report to the American Indian Policy Review Commission.* Washington, D.C.: General Printing Office, 1976.

Albright, Zella Rae. *One Man's Family: The Life of Hiram Vasquez, 1843–1939.* N.p.: By the author, 1984.

Alter, J. Cecil. *Jim Bridger.* Norman: University of Oklahoma Press, 1962.

Andrews, Thomas F. "The Controversial Hastings Overland Guide: A Reassessment." *Pacific Historical Review* 36 (February 1968): 21–34.

Anonymous. "Tidings from the West." *The Builder: A Journal for the Masonic Student* 3 (January 1917): 29.

Ault, Phillip H. "Pioneer Nancy Kelsey: 'Where My Husband Goes, I Go'." *The Californians* 9, no. 5 (March–April 1992): 32–41.

Bancroft, Hubert Howe. *History of California,* 7 vols. San Francisco: The History Company, 1886–1890.

———. *History of Oregon,* 2 vols. San Francisco: The History Company, 1886, 1888.

Barnett, William A. "The First Overland Letter to California." *Overland Journal* 11, no. 3 (1993): 21–33.

Barry, Louise. *The Beginning of the West: Annals of the Kansas Gateway to the American West, 1540–1854.* Forward by Dale L. Morgan. Topeka: Kansas State Historical Society, 1972.

Bayard, Samuel John. *A Sketch of the Life of Com. Robert F. Stockton.* New York: Derby and Jackson, 1856.

Beall, Thomas J. "Recollections of Wm. Craig: He Came to the Lewiston Country in 1829—Craig Mountain Named in His Honor." *Lewiston Morning Tribune,* 3 March 1918, 8.

Beckham, Stephen Dow, Carolyn M. Buan, and Richard Lewis, eds. *The First Oregonians.* Portland: Oregon Council for the Humanities, 1991.

Bennett, Richard E. *We'll Find the Place: The Mormon Exodus, 1846–1848.* Salt Lake City: Deseret Book, 1997.

Bigler, David L. *Forgotten Kingdom: The Mormon Theocracy in the American West, 1847–1896.* Spokane, Wash.: Arthur H. Clark, 1998.

Bigler, David L., and Will Bagley, eds. *Army of Israel: Mormon Battalion Narratives.* Spokane, Wash.: Arthur H. Clark, 2000.

Bird, S. Elizabeth. *Dressing in Feathers: The Construction of the Indian in American Popular Culture.* Boulder, Colo.: Westview Press, 1996.

Blackhawk, Ned. *Violence over the Land: Indians and Empires in the Early American West.* Cambridge, Mass.: Harvard University Press, 2006.

Boag, Peter. "Idaho's Fort Hall as a Western Crossroads." *Overland Journal,* 16, no. 1 (Spring 1998): 20–26.

Bommersbach, Jana. "Hitching Your Wagon to a Star." *True West* 51, no. 4 (May 2004): 41.

Bonebright-Closz, Harriet. *Founding of Newcastle Now Webster City, Iowa or Remembrances of Newcastle: Narrated by Sarah Brewer-Bonebright, Written by her Daughter, Harriet Bonebright-Closz.* Des Moines: Historical Department of Iowa, 1921.

Boorstin, Daniel J. *The Americans: The National Experience.* New York: Random House, 1965. Reprint, New York: Vintage Books, 1967.

Bowen, Catherine Drinker. *The Most Dangerous Man in America: Scenes from the Life of Benjamin Franklin.* Boston: Little, Brown and Company, 1974.

Boyd, Robert. *People of The Dalles: The Indians of Wascopam Mission.* Lincoln: University of Nebraska Press and the American Indian Studies Research Institute, 1996.

———. *The Coming of the Spirit of Pestilence: Introduced Disease and Population Decline among Northwest Coast Indians, 1774–1874.* Vancouver and Seattle: UBC Press and University of Washington Press, 1999.

Camp, Charles L. "Colonel Philip Leget Edwards and His Influence upon Early Immigration to the Far West." *California Historical Quarterly* 3, no. 1 (1924): 72–83.

———. "William Alexander Trubody and the Overland Pioneers of 1847." *California Historical Society Quarterly* 16, no. 2 (June 1937): 122–43.

Camp, Charles L., ed. *George C. Yount and His Chronicles of the West, Comprising Extracts from his "Memoirs" and from the Orange Clark "Narrative."* Denver: Fred A. Rosenstock, the Old West Publishing Company, 1966.

Campbell, John V. "The Sinclair Party: An Emigration Overland along the Old Hudson's Bay Company Route from Manitoba to the Spokane Country—1854." *Washington Historical Quarterly* (1916): 187–201.

Capps, Michael A. "Wheels in the West: The Overland Wagon." *Overland Journal* 8, no. 4 (Winter 1990): 2–11.

Carey, Charles H., ed. *The Emigrants' Guide, to Oregon and California by Lansford W. Hastings.* Princeton, N.J.: Princeton University Press, 1932.

Carriker, Robert C. *Father John Peter De Smet: Jesuit in the West.* Norman: University of Oklahoma Press, 1995.

Carter, Edgar N. "Fort Bridger Days." In *The Westerners Brand Book 1947,* 83–88. Los Angeles: Los Angeles Corral of Westerners International, 1947.

Carter, Kate B., ed. *Our Pioneer Heritage.* 20 vols. Salt Lake City: Daughters of Utah Pioneers, 1958–77.

Chaffin, Tom. "How the West Was Lost." *Harper's Magazine* (June 2000): 137–40.

———. *Pathfinder: John Charles Frémont and the Course of American Empire.* New York: Farrar, Straus and Giroux; Hill and Wang, 2002.

Chittenden, Hiram Martin. *The American Fur Trade in the Far West,* 2 vols. New York: Press of the Pioneers, 1935. Reprinted with a foreword by James P. Ronda; Introduction and notes by Stallo Vinton. Lincoln: University of Nebraska Press, 1986.

Churchill, Charles B. *Adventurers and Prophets: American Autobiographers in Mexican California, 1827–1847.* Spokane, Wash.: Arthur H. Clark, 1995.

Clark, Keith, and Lowell Tiller, *Terrible Trail: The Meek Cutoff, 1845.* Caldwell, Idaho: Caxton Printers, 1967. Reprint, Bend, Oreg.: Maverick Publications, 1993.

Clark, Malcolm, Jr. *Eden Seekers: The Settlement of Oregon, 1818–1862.* Boston: Houghton Mifflin, 1981.

Clark, Robert Carlton. "Hawaiians in Early Oregon." *Oregon Historical Quarterly* 35 (March 1934): 22–31.

Clarke, Charles G. *The Men of the Lewis and Clark Expedition: A Biographical Roster of the Fifty-One Members and a Composite Diary of their Activities from all Known Sources.* Glendale: Arthur H. Clark, 1970. Reprint, 2002.

Conroy, Drew, and Dwight Barney. *The Oxen Handbook.* LaPorte, Colo.: Butler Publishing, 1986.

Crapol, Edward P. "John Tyler and the Pursuit of National Destiny." *Journal of the Early American Republic* 17, no. 3 (October 1997): 467–91.

Crease, Craig. "The Lone Elm and Elm Grove Case: A Study in Mistaken Identity." *Overland Journal* 11, no. 1 (Spring 1993): 24–31.

Crum, Beverly, and Richard Hart, Winona Holmes, Larry Piffero, June Tom, et al. *Newe: A Western Shoshone History.* Reno: Inter-Tribal Council of Nevada, 1976.

Cumming, John. "Lansford Hastings' Michigan Connection." *Overland Journal* 16, no. 3 (Fall 1998): 17–28.

Davis, Charles George. *The Oskaloosa Company: Last Wagon Train to Skinners in 1847.* Portland, Oreg.: Frontier Publishing, 1996.

Davis, Richard M. "Where Have All the Wagons Gone? Gone, Gone Long Ago, or Very Nearly So." Part 1, *Overland Journal* 15, no. 3 (Autumn 1997): 16–39. Part 2, *Overland Journal* 16, no. 2 (Summer 1998): 24–42.

Dawson, Glen. "The Only Known Copies of Emigrant Guides." *The Westerners Brand Book Number 7,* 164–171. Los Angeles: Los Angeles Corral of Westerners International, 1957.

Derounian-Stodola, Kathryn Z., and James A. Levernier. *The Indian Captivity Narrative, 1550–1900.* New York: Maxwell Macmillan International, 1993.

DeVoto, Bernard. *The Year of Decision, 1846.* New York: Houghton-Mifflin, 1943.

Dillon, Richard H. *Fool's Gold: The Decline and Fall of Captain John Sutter of California.* New York: Coward McCann, 1967. Reprint, Santa Cruz: Western Tanager, 1981.

———. "Stephen Long's Great American Desert." *Proceedings of the American Philosophical Society* 111, no. 2 (14 April 1967): 93–108.

Downs, James. *The Two Worlds of the Washo: An Indian Tribe of California and Nevada.* New York: Holt, Rinehart and Winston, 1966.

Drury, Clifford M. *Marcus and Narcissa Whitman and the Opening of Old Oregon,* 2 vols. Glendale, Calif.: Arthur H. Clark, 1973. Reprint, Seattle: Northwest Interpretive Association, 1994.

————, ed. *First White Women over the Rockies: Diaries, Letters, and Biographical Sketches of the Six Women of the Oregon Mission Who Made the Overland Journey in 1836 and 1838,* 3 vols. Vol. 1: Narcissa Prentiss Whitman, Eliza Hart Spaulding, Mary Augusta Dix Gray, and Sarah White Smith; Vol. 2: Mary Richardson Walker and Myra Fairbanks Eells; Vol. 3: Diary of Sarah White Smith, Letters of Asa B. Smith and Other Documents relating to the 1838 Reenforcement to the Oregon Mission. Glendale, Calif.: Arthur H. Clark, 1963, 1966.

Duffin, Reg. P. "The Grave of Joel Hembree." *Overland Journal* 3 ,no. 2 (Spring 1985): 6–16.

Duncan, Janice K. *Minority without a Champion: Kanakas on the Pacific Coast, 1788–1850.* Portland: Oregon Historical Society, 1972.

Eggenhofer, Nick. *Wagons, Mules and Men.* Mamaroneck, N.Y.: Hastings House, 1961.

Eells, Myron. *Marcus Whitman, Pathfinder and Patriot.* Seattle: Alice Harriman, 1909.

Evans, Elwood, et al. *History of the Pacific Northwest: Oregon and Washington,* 2 vols. Portland, Oreg.: North Pacific History Company, 1889.

Faragher, John Mack. *Women and Men on the Overland Trail.* New Haven, Conn.: Yale University Press, 1979.

Fey, Marshall, R. Joe King, and Jack Lepisto. *Emigrant Shadows: A History and Guide to the California Trail.* Edited by Stanley W. Paher. Virginia City, Nev.: Western Trails Research Association, 2002.

Ficken, Robert E. "The 'Real' Oregon Trail." *Columbia: The Magazine of Northwest History* 8, no. 3 (Fall 1994): 3–5.

Franzwa, Gregory M. *The Oregon Trail Revisited.* Saint Louis: Patrice Press, 1972. Fifth edition, Tucson: Patrice Press, 1997.

Galbraith, John Semple. "Early History of the Puget's Sound Agricultural Company." *Oregon Historical Quarterly* 55 (September 1954): 234–59.

Gardner, Mark L. *Wagons for the Santa Fe Trade: Wheeled Vehicles and Their Makers, 1822–1880.* Albuquerque: University of New Mexico Press, 2000.

Gaston, Joseph. *The Centennial History of Oregon, 1811–1912.* Chicago: S. J. Clarke, 1912.

Gibson, James R. *The Lifeline of the Oregon Country: The Fraser-Columbia Brigade System, 1811–47.* Vancouver: University of British Columbia Press, 1997.

Gillis, Michael J., and Michael F. Magliari. *John Bidwell and California: The Life and Writings of a Pioneer, 1841–1900.* Spokane, Wash.: Arthur H. Clark, 2003.

Goddard, Ives, and Thomas Love. "Oregon, the Beautiful." *Oregon Historical Society Quarterly* 105, no. 2 (Summer 2004): 238–59. Retrieved 5 November 2008 from http://www.historycooperative.org/journals/ohq/105.2/goddard.html.

Goetzmann, William H. *Army Exploration in the American West, 1803–1863.* New Haven, Conn.: Yale University Press, 1959.

Goetzmann, William H., and William N. Goetzmann. *The West of the Imagination.* New York: Norton, 1986.

Gowans, Fred R., and Eugene E. Campbell. *Fort Bridger: Island in the Wilderness.* Provo, Utah: Brigham Young University Press, 1975.

Graebner, Norman A. *Empire on the Pacific: A Study in American Continental Expansion.* New York: Ronald Press, 1955.

Graebner, Norman A., ed. *Manifest Destiny.* Indianapolis: Bobbs-Merrill, 1968.

Graydon, Charles K. *Trail of the First Wagons over the Sierra.* Saint Louis: The Patrice Press, 1986.

Guenther, Todd. "Pioneers Extraordinaire: A Most Unusual Wagon Train." *Overland Journal* 18, no. 4 (Winter 2000/2001): 2–17.

Hafen, Leroy, and Ann Hafen, eds., *Old Spanish Trail: Santa Fé to Los Angeles.* Glendale, Calif.: Arthur H. Clark, 1954.

Hafen, LeRoy R. *The Overland Mail, 1849–1869: Promoter of Railroads, Precursor of Settlement.* Cleveland: Arthur H. Clark, 1926.

Hafen, LeRoy R., ed. *The Mountain Men and the Fur Trade of the Far West* 10 vols. Glendale, Calif.: Arthur H. Clark, 1965–1972.

Hague, Harlan. *The Road to California: The Search for a Southern Overland Route.* Glendale, Calif.: Arthur H. Clark, 1978.

Hammond, Andy. "Peter Lassen and His Trail." *Overland Journal* 4, no. 1 (Winter 1986): 33–41.

Harlow, Neal. *California Conquered: War and Peace on the Pacific 1846–1850.* Berkeley: University of California Press, 1982.

Hassrick, Royal B. *The Sioux: Life and Customs of a Warrior Society.* Norman: University of Oklahoma Press, 1964.

Hawgood, John A. *First and Last Consul: Thomas Oliver Larkin and the Americanization of California.* Palo Alto, Calif.: Pacific Books, 1970.

Hebard, Grace Raymond. *Washakie: An Account of Indian Resistance of the Covered Wagon and Union Pacific Railroad Invasions of Their Territory.* Cleveland: Arthur H. Clark, 1930. Reprinted as *Washakie, Chief of the Shoshones.* Introduction by Richard O. Clemmer. Lincoln: University of Nebraska Press, 1995.

Heitman, Francis B. *Historical Register and Dictionary of the United States Army, From Its Organization, September 29, 1789, to March 2, 1903,* 2 vols. Washington, D.C.: Government Printing Office, 1903. Reprint, Urbana: University of Illinois Press, 1965.

Heizer, Robert Fleming. "Walla Walla Indian Expeditions to the Sacramento Valley, 1844–1847." *California Historical Society Quarterly* 21, no. 1 (March 1942): 1–7.

Holder, Preston. *The Hoe and the Horse on the Plains: A Study of Cultural Development among North American Indians.* Lincoln: University of Nebraska Press, 1970.

Holliday, J. S. *Rush for Riches: Gold Fever and the Making of California.* Oakland and Berkeley: Oakland Museum of California and University of California Press, 1999.

Holmes, Kenneth L., ed. *Covered Wagon Women: Diaries and Letters from the Western Trails, 1840–1890.* 11 vols. Glendale, Calif., and Spokane, Wash.: Arthur H. Clark, 1983–93.

Hopkins, Sarah Winnemucca. *Life among the Piutes: Their Wrongs and Claims.* Edited by Mrs. Horace [Mary] Mann. Boston: Cupples, Upham and Co., 1883.

Hudson, Linda. *The Mistress of Manifest Destiny: Jane McManus Storm Cazneau.* Austin: The Texas State Historical Association, 2001.

Hunsaker, Joyce Badgley. *Seeing the Elephant: The Many Voices of the Oregon Trail.* Lubbock: Texas Tech University Press, 2003.

Hulbert, Archer Butler, and Dorothy Printup Hulbert, eds. *Marcus Whitman, Crusader.* 3 vols. Colorado Springs and Denver: The Stewart Commission of Colorado College and the Denver Public Library, 1936, 1938, 1941.

Hurtado, Albert L. *John Sutter: A Life on the North American Frontier.* Norman: University of Oklahoma Press, 2006.

Hussey, John Adam. "The Origin of the Gillespie Mission." *Calif. Hist. Soc. Quarterly* 19 (March 1940): 43–58.

————. *Fort Vancouver Historic Structures Report,* 2 vols. Denver: National Park Service, 1972, 1976.

Hussey, John Adam, and George Walcott Ames, Jr. "California Preparations to Meet the Walla Walla Invasion, 1846." *California Historical Society Quarterly* 21, no. 1 (March 1942): 9–21.

Illustrated History of Plumas, Lassen and Sierra Counties with California from 1513 to 1850. San Francisco: Farris and Smith, 1882.

Inter-Tribal Council of Nevada. *Numa: A Northern Paiute History.* Reno: Inter-Tribal Council of Nevada, 1976.

Irving, Washington. *Astoria, or Anecdotes of an Enterprise beyond the Rocky Mountains.* Philadelphia: Carey, Lea, and Blanchard, 1836.

————. *The Rocky Mountains: or Scenes, Incidents, and Adventures in the Far West; Digested from the Journal of Capt. B. L. E. Bonneville, of the Army of the United States, and Illustrated from Various Sources.* 2 vols. Philadelphia: Carey, Lea, and Blanchard, 1837. Reprinted as *The Adventures of Captain Bonneville, U.S.A.* Edited by Edgeley W. Todd. Norman: University of Oklahoma Press, 1961.

Jeffrey, Julie Roy. *Frontier Women: The Trans-Mississippi West, 1840–1880.* New York: Hill and Wang, 1979.

Jessett, Thomas E. *Chief Spokan Garry, 1811–1892: Christian, Statesman, Friend of the White Man.* Minneapolis, Minn.: T. S. Denison and Company, 1960.

Johnson, Kristin, ed. *"Unfortunate Emigrants": Narratives of the Donner Party.* Logan: Utah State University Press, 1996.

Johnson, Kristin. "1879: Virginia Reed Tells It Like It Was." *Donner Party Bulletin* 2 (November/December 1997): 1–3.

Kelly, Charles, and Dale L. Morgan. *Old Greenwood: The Story of Caleb Greenwood, Trapper, Pathfinder, and Early Pioneer.* Georgetown, Calif.: The Talisman Press, 1965.

————. Charles Kelly Collections, Utah State Historical Society and Special Collections, J. Willard Marriott Library, University of Utah.

Killoren, John J., S.J. *"Come, Blackrobe": De Smet and the Indian Tragedy.* Norman: University of Oklahoma Press, 1994.

Kimball, Stanley B. *Heber C. Kimball: Mormon Patriarch and Pioneer.* Urbana: University of Illinois Press, 1981.

Koppel, Tom. *Kanaka: The Untold Story of Hawaiian Pioneers in British Columbia and the Pacific Northwest.* Vancouver: Whitecap Books, 1995.

Korns, Roderic, and Dale L. Morgan, eds. *West from Fort Bridger: The Pioneering of Immigrant Trails across Utah, 1846–1850.* Salt Lake City: Utah State Historical Society, 1951. Revised and updated by Will Bagley and Harold Schindler. Logan: Utah State University Press, 1994.

Kroeber, Alfred Louis. *Handbook of the Indians of California.* Washington, D.C.: Government Printing Office, 1925. Reprinted New York: Dover, 1976.

LaLande, Jeff. *First over the Siskiyous: Peter Skeen Ogden's Journey through the Oregon-California Borderlands.* Portland: Oregon Historical Society Press, 1987.

Lamar, Howard R., ed. *The New Encyclopedia of the American West.* New Haven, Conn.: Yale University Press, 1998.

Lavender, David. *Westward Vision: The Story of the Oregon Trail.* New York: McGraw Hill Book Company, 1963.

Levy, Jo Ann. *They Saw the Elephant: Women in the California Gold Rush.* Hamden, Conn.: Archon Books, 1990.

Lewin, Jacqueline, and Marilyn S. Taylor. *The St. Joe Road, Emigration Mid-1800s: A Traveler's Guide from the Missouri River to the Junction of the St. Joe and Independence Roads.* Saint Joseph: Saint Joseph Museum, 1992.

Lewin, Jacqueline, Marilyn S. Taylor, and Bonnie Watkins. "St. Joseph, Missouri: Early Impressions." *Overland Journal* 6, no. 1 (1988): 2–7.

Lecompte, Janet. *French Fur Traders and Voyageurs in the American West: Twenty-five Biographical Sketches.* Edited by LeRoy R. Hafen. Spokane: Arthur H. Clark, 1993 and 1995.

Lent, E. Geneva. *West of the Mountains: James Sinclair and the Hudson's Bay Company.* Seattle: University of Washington Press, 1963.

Lupo, Karen D. "The Historical Occurrence and Demise of Bison in Northern Utah." *Utah Historical Quarterly* 64, no. 2 (Spring 1996): 168–80.

MacKay, Douglas. *The Honourable Company: A History of the Hudson's Bay Company.* Indianapolis: Bobbs-Merrill, 1936.

Madsen, Brigham D. *The Bannock of Idaho.* Caldwell, Idaho: The Caxton Printers, 1958.

Madsen, Brigham D, ed. *Exploring the Great Salt Lake: The Stansbury Expedition of 1849–50.* Salt Lake City: University of Utah Press, 1989.

Madsen, Steven K., and C. Gregory Crampton. *In Search of the Spanish Trail: Santa Fe to Los Angeles 1829–1848.* Salt Lake City: Gibbs Smith, Publisher, 1994.

Marshall, Joseph, III. *On Behalf of the Wolf and the First Peoples.* Santa Fe, N.M.: Red Crane Books, 1995.

Marshall, William I. *Acquisition of Oregon and the Long Suppressed Evidence about Marcus Whitman.* Seattle: Lowman and Hanford, 1911.

Martin, Charles W., and Dorothy Devereux. "The Omaha–Council Bluffs Area and the Westward Trails." *Overland Journal* 7, no. 4 (Winter 1989): 2–11.

Mattes, Merrill J. *The Great Platte River Road.* Lincoln: Nebraska State Historical Society, 1969. Second edition, Lincoln, Nebr.: Bison Books, 1978.

———. "Potholes in the Great Platte River Road: Misconceptions in Need of Repair." *Wyoming Annals* 65, no. 2/3 (Summer/Fall 1993): 6–14.

———. *Platte River Road Narratives.* Urbana: University of Illinois Press, 1988.

May, Christina Rae. *Pioneer Clothing on the Oregon Trail.* Pendleton, Oreg.: Drigh Sighed Publications, 1998.

McGlashan, C. F. *History of the Donner Party.* Truckee, Calif.: Crowley and McGlashan, 1879.

McKnight, W. J. *Pioneer Outline History of Northwestern Pennsylvania.* Philadelphia: J. B. Lippincott, 1905.

Meldahl, Keith H. *Hard Road West: History and Geology along the Gold Rush Trail.* Chicago: University of Chicago Press, 2007.

Menefee, Leah Collins, Donald F. Menefee, and Lowell Tiller. "Cutoff Fever." *Oregon Historical Quarterly* 77, no. 4 (December 1976): 309–40. Part 2: "Cutoff Fever: Planning a Free Emigrant Road." *Oregon Historical Quarterly* 77, no. 5 (March 1977): 41–72. Part 3: "Cutoff Fever: The Migration for the West Forms, 1853." *Oregon Historical Quarterly* 77, no. 6 (June 1977): 121–57. Part 4: "Cutoff Fever: To Harney Valley." *Oregon Historical Quarterly* 77, no. 7 (September 1977):207–50. Part 5: "Into the Cascades—Visions of Bread and Butter." *Oregon*

Historical Quarterly 77, no. 8 (December 1977): 293–331. Part 6: "Commissioners Versus Alexander." *Oregon Historical Quarterly* 77, no. 9 (March 1978): 5–50.

Merk, Frederick. *Manifest Destiny and Mission in American History: A Reinterpretation.* New York: Knopf, 1963.

———. *The Oregon Question: Essays in Anglo-American Diplomacy and Politics.* Cambridge, Mass.: The Belknap Press of Harvard University Press, 1967.

Miles, Edwin A. "'Fifty-four Forty or Fight': An American Political Legend." *The Mississippi Valley Historical Review* 44 ,no. 2 (September 1957),:291–309.

Moquin, Wayne, and Charles van Doren, eds. *Great Documents in American Indian History.* New York: Praeger, 1973.

Morgan, Dale L. "The Ferries of the Forty-niners." Part 1, *Annals of Wyoming* 31, no. 1 (April 1959): 4–31. Part 2, *Annals of Wyoming* 31, no. 2 (October 1959): 144–89. Part 3, section 1, "Green River Ferries." *Annals of Wyoming* 32, no. 1 (April 1960): 50–69. Part 3, section 2, "The Ferries on the Sublette Cutoff." *Annals of Wyoming* 32, no. 2 (October 1960): 167–201.

———. "The Mormon Ferry on the North Platte: The Journal of William A. Empey." *Annals of Wyoming* 2–3, no. 21 (July–October 1949): 110–167.

———. "The Significance and Value of the Overland Journal." Toole et al., eds., *Probing the American West,* 26–34.

———. *In Pursuit of the Golden Dream: Reminiscences of San Francisco and the Northern and Southern Mines, 1849–1857 by Howard C. Gardiner.* Stoughton, Mass.: Western Hemisphere, 1970.

———. *Jedediah Smith and the Opening of the West.* Indianapolis: Bobbs-Merrill Company, 1953.

———. *Overland in 1846: Diaries and Letters of the California-Oregon Trail,* 2 vols. Georgetown, Calif.: The Talisman Press, 1963. Reprint, Lincoln: University of Nebraska Press, 1993.

———. Papers. Bancroft Library. Microfilm copies in Special Collections, J. Willard Marriott Library, University of Utah.

———. Papers. Utah State Historical Society.

———. *The Humboldt: Highroad of the West.* New York: Farrar and Rinehardt, 1943.

———. "Washakie and the Shoshoni." *Annals of Wyoming* 25–28. part 1, 1849–1852, 25:2 (July 1953), 141–89; part 2, 1852, 26:1 (January 1954), 65–80; part 3, 1852–1857, 25:2 (July 1954), 141–90; part 4, 1857–1859, 27:1 (April 1955), 61–88; part 5, 1860–1862, 27:2 (October 1955), 198–220; part 6, 1862–1863, 28:1 (April 1956), 80–93; part 7, 1862–1863, 28:2 (October 1956), 193–207; part 8, 1863–1864, 29:1 (April 1957), 86–102; part 9, 1864–1866, 29:2 (October 1957), 194–227; conclusion, 1867–1869, 30:1 (April 1958), 53–89. Reprint, Dale L. Morgan, *Shoshonean Peoples and the Overland Trail: Frontiers of the Utah Superintendency of Indian Affairs, 1849–1869.* Edited by Richard L. Saunders, with an ethnohistorical essay by Gregory E. Smoak. Logan: Utah State University Press, 2007.

———. *The West of William Ashley: The International Struggle for the Fur Trade of the Missouri, the Rocky Mountains, and the Columbia, with Explorations beyond the Continental Divide, Recorded in the Diaries and Letters of William H. Ashley and His Contemporaries, 1822–1838.* Denver: Fred A. Rosenstock, the Old West Publishing Company, 1964.

Mormon Pioneer Overland Travel, 1847–1868. LDS Church Library and Archives website at http://www.lds.org/churchhistory/library/pioneercompanysearch/.

Mortensen, A. R. "A Pioneer Paper Mirrors the Breakup of Isolation in the Great Basin." *Utah Historical Quarterly* 20 (January 1952): 77–92.

Mullen, Frank, Jr., *The Donner Party Chronicles: A Day-by-Day Account of a Doomed Wagon Train,*

1846–1847. Photographs by Marilyn Newton. Foreword by Will Bagley. Preface by Rollan Melton. Reno: Nevada Humanities Council, 1997.

Munkres, Robert L. "The Plains Indian Threat on the Oregon Trail before 1860." *Annals of Wyoming* 40 (October 1968): 193–221.

Myres, Sandra L. *Westering Women and the Frontier Experience, 1800–1915*. Albuquerque: University of New Mexico Press, 1982.

Nasatir, A. P. "The French Consulate in California, 1843–56." *California Historical Society Quarterly,* 11, nos. 3–4 (September–December 1932): 195–223, 339–57.

Nevers, Jo Ann. *Wa She Shu: A Washo Tribal History*. Reno: Inter-Tribal Council of Nevada, 1976.

Nixon, Oliver W. *How Marcus Whitman Saved Oregon: A True Romance of Patriotic Heroism, Christian Devotion and Final Martyrdom, with Sketches of Life on the Plains and Mountains in Pioneer Days*. Introduction by Frank W. Gunsaulus. Chicago: Star Publishing, 1895.

Nunis, Doyce B., Jr., ed. *The Bidwell-Bartleson Party, 1841 California Emigrant Adventure: Documents and Memoirs of the Overland Pioneers*. Santa Cruz, Calif.: Western Tanager Press, 1991.

O'Donnell, Terence. *An Arrow in the Earth: General Joel Palmer and the Indians of Oregon*. Portland: Oregon Historical Society Press, 1991.

Owens, Kenneth N., ed. *John Sutter and a Wider West*. Lincoln: University of Nebraska Press, 1994.

———. "The Mormon-Carson Emigrant Trail in Western History." *Montana: The Magazine of Western History,* 42, no. 4 (Winter 1992): 14–27.

———. "Frontiersman for the Tsar: Timofei Tarakanov and the Expansion of Russian America." *Montana: The Magazine of Western History,* 53, no. 3 (Autumn 2006): 3–21.

Paul, Rodman Wilson, ed. *The California Gold Discovery: Sources, Documents, Accounts and Memoirs Relating to the Discovery of Gold at Sutter's Mill*. Georgetown, Calif.: The Talisman Press, 1966.

Pipes, Nellie B. "Indian Conditions in 1836–38." *Oregon Historical Quarterly* 32, no. 4 (December 1931): 332–42.

Powell, Allen Kent, ed. *Utah History Encyclopedia*. Salt Lake City: University of Utah Press, 1994.

Price, Glenn W. *Origins of the War with Mexico: The Polk-Stockton Intrigue*. Austin: University of Texas Press, 1967.

Pringle, Patrick T. *Roadside Geology of Mount St. Helens National Volcanic Monument and Vicinity*. Washington State Department of Natural Resources Information Circular 88. Olympia: Washington State Department of Natural Resources, 1993.

Ramsey, Jarold, ed. *Coyote Was Going There: Indian Literature in the Oregon Country*. Seattle: University of Washington Press, 1977.

Richardson, James D., ed. *A Compilation of the Messages and Papers of the Presidents,* 20 vols. New York: Bureau of National Literature, 1897–1914.

Riley, Glenda. *Women and Indians on the Frontier, 1825–1915*. Albuquerque: University of New Mexico Press, 1984.

Roberts, Brigham H., ed. *History of the Church*. 7 vols. Salt Lake City: Deseret News, 1932.

Roberts, David. *A Newer World: John C. Frémont, Kit Carson and the Claiming of the American West*. New York: Simon and Schuster, 2000.

Rogers, Justus H., ed., *Colusa County: Its History Traced from a State of Nature*. Orland, Calif.: s.n., 1891.

Rolle, Andrew F. *John Charles Frémont: Character as Destiny*. Norman: University of Oklahoma Press, 1991.

Ronda, James P. *Astoria and Empire*. Lincoln: University of Nebraska Press, 1990.

Rowland, Donald E. *John Rowland and William Workman: Southern California Pioneers of 1841.* Spokane, Wash.: Arthur H. Clark; Los Angeles: Historical Society of Southern California, 1999.

Royce, Josiah. *California from the Conquest in 1846 to the Second Vigilance Committee in San Francisco: A Study of American Character.* New York: Houghton, Mifflin and Company, 1886. Reprint, Santa Barbara, Calif.: Peregrine, 1970.

Ruby, Robert H., and John A. Brown. *The Spokane Indians: Children of the Sun.* Foreword by Clifford M. Drury. Norman: University of Oklahoma Press, 1970.

————. *The Cayuse Indians: Imperial Tribesmen of Old Oregon.* Foreword by Clifford M. Drury. Norman: University of Oklahoma Press, 1972.

Rumer, Thomas A. *The Wagon Trains of '44: A Comparative View of the Individual Caravans in the Emigration of 1844 to Oregon.* Spokane, Wash.: Arthur H. Clark, 1990.

Schlissel, Lillian, ed. *Women's Diaries of the Westward Journey.* New York: Schocken Books, 1982.

Schoolcraft, Henry Rowe. *History of the Indian Tribes of the United States: Their Present Condition and Prospects, and a Sketch of Their Ancient Status.* Philadelphia: J. B. Lippincott and Co., 1857.

Scott, Lalla. *Karnee: A Paiute Narrative.* Notes by Charles R. Craig. Reno: University of Nevada Press, 1966.

Seale, Doris, and Beverly Slapin, eds. *A Broken Flute: The Native Experience in Books for Children.* Walnut Creek and Berkeley, Calif.: AltaMira Press and Oyate, 2005.

Sellers, Charles. *James K. Polk, Continentalist, 1843–46.* Princeton, N.J.: Princeton University Press, 1966.

Settle, Raymond W., ed. *The March of the Mounted Riflemen: First United States Military Expedition to Travel the Full Length of the Oregon Trail from Fort Leavenworth to Fort Vancouver, May to October, 1849, as Recorded in the Journals of Major Osborne Cross and George Gibbs and the Official Report of Colonel Loring.* Glendale, Calif.: Arthur H. Clark, 1940. Reprint, Lincoln: University of Nebraska Press, 1989.

Sheldon, Addison Erwin. *Nebraska, Old and New: History, Stories, Folklore.* Chicago: The University Publishing Co., 1937.

Smith, Ross A. "The Southern Route Revisited." *Oregon Historical Quarterly* 105, no. 2 (Summer 2004): 292–307.

Spedden, Rush. "Who Was T. H. Jefferson?" *Overland Journal* 8, no. 3 (Fall 1990): 2–8.

Spence, Mary Lee, and Donald Jackson, eds. *The Expeditions of John Charles Frémont,* 4 vols. Chicago: University of Illinois Press, 1970–1984.

Spicer, Edward. *A Short History of the Indians of the United States.* New York: Van Nostrand Reinhold, 1969.

Staab, Rodney. "Sutter in Westport: Prelude for a Pioneer." Part 1, *Overland Journal* 21, no. 2 (Summer 2003): 42–67. Part 2, *Overland Journal* 21, no. 3 (Fall 2003): 94–107.

Steed, Jack. *The Donner Party Rescue Site: Johnson's Ranch on Bear River.* Fresno, Calif.: Pioneer Publishing, 1988. With research by Richard Steed. Third edition, 1993.

Stenhouse, T. B. H. *The Rocky Mountain Saints: A Full and Complete History of the Mormons.* New York: D. Appleton and Company, 1873.

Stern, Theodore. *Chiefs and Change in the Oregon Country: Indian Relations at Fort Nez Percés, 1818–1855.* Corvallis: Oregon State University Press, 1996.

Stewart, George R., Jr. *The California Trail: An Epic with Many Heroes.* New York: McGraw-Hill, 1962.

————. "The Prairie Schooner Got Them There." *American Heritage Magazine* 13, no. 2 (February 1962): 7–16.

————. *Ordeal by Hunger: The Story of the Donner Party*. Boston: Houghton Mifflin, 1960.

Stone, Elizabeth Arnold. "A Washakie Anecdote." *Utah Historical Quarterly* 3, no. 2 (April 1930): 356–57.

Sullivan, Maurice S. *The Travels of Jedediah Smith*. Santa Ana, Calif.: The Fine Arts Press, 1934.

Swagerty, William R. "'The Leviathan of the North': American Perceptions of the Hudson's Bay Company, 1816–1846. *Oregon Historical Quarterly* 104, no. 4 (Winter 2003): 478–518.

Tadlock, Nancy. "The Migrating Orchard." *Overland Journal* 3, no. 3 (Summer 1985): 22–27.

Tate, Michael L. *Indians and Emigrants: Encounters on the Overland Trail*. Norman: University of Okalahoma Press, 2006.

————. "Civilization's Guardian: Army Aid to Emigrants on the Platte River Road, 1846–1869." *Annals of Wyoming* 69, no. 1 (Winter 1997): 2–16.

————. "From Cooperation to Conflict: Sioux Relations with the Overland Emigrants, 1845–1865." *Overland Journal* 18, no. 4 (Winter 2000/2001): 18–31.

Thompson, Erwin N. *Whitman Mission National Historic Site*. National Park Service Historical Handbook No. 37. Washington, D.C.: Government Printing Office, 1964.

————. *Shallow Grave at Waiilatpu: The Sagers' West*. Portland: Oregon Historical Society Press, 1973.

Thrapp, Dan L. *Encyclopedia of Frontier Biography,* 4 vols. Glendale, Calif., and Spokane, Wash.: Arthur H. Clark, 1988, 1994.

Tinker, George E. *Missionary Conquest: The Gospel and Native American Cultural Genocide*. Minneapolis, Minn.: Fortress Press, 1993.

Tobie, Harvey E. *No Man like Joe: The Life and Times of Joseph L. Meek*. Portland: Binfords and Mort, for the Oregon Historical Society, 1949.

Tompkins, James M. *Discovering Laurel Hill and the Barlow Road: A Self-Guided Tour of Sites along the Western-Most Branch of the Oregon Trail*. Oregon City: Oregon Trail Foundation, 1996. Second edition, 1997.

————. "The Law of the Land: What the Emigrants Knew That Historians Need To Know about Claiming Land at the End of the Oregon Trail." *Overland Journal* 19, no. 3 (Fall 2001): 82–112.

————. "Political Development in Oregon: The Provisional Government 1843–1849." M.A. thesis, Portland State University, 1976.

Toole, K. Ross, John Alexander Carroll, A. R. Mortensen, and Robert M. Utley, eds. *Probing the American West: Nineteen Papers from the Santa Fe Conference*. Introduction by Ray A. Billington. Santa Fe: Museum of New Mexico Press, 1962.

Townley, John M. *The Trail West: A Bibliographic-Index to Western Trails, 1841–1869*. Reno, NV: Jamison Station Press, 1988.

Tullidge, Edward W. *Life of Brigham Young; or, Utah and Her Founders*. New York: Tullidge and Crandall, 1876.

Tyler, Daniel. *A Concise History of the Mormon Battalion in the Mexican War, 1846–1847*. Glorieta, N.M.: Rio Grande Press, [1969].

Tyson, Carl N. *The Pawnee People*. Phoenix, Ariz.: The Indian Tribal Series, 1976.

Unrau, William E. *The Kaw People*. Phoenix, Ariz.: The Indian Tribal Series, 1975.

Unruh, John D., Jr. *The Plains Across: The Overland Emigrants and the Trans-Mississippi West, 1840–1860*. Urbana: University of Illinois Press, 1979.

U.S. Senate. "Report to the Committee on Naval Affairs." 3 March 1851, Senate Report 319 (31-2).

U.S. House. "Letter from the Secretary of the Navy," 3 March 1845, House Report 161 (28-2).

Utley, Robert M. *A Life Wild and Perilous: Mountain Men and the Paths to the Pacific.* New York: Henry Holt, 1997.

Van Hoak, Stephen. "Waccara's Utes: Native American Equestrian Adaptations in the Eastern Great Basin, 1776–1876." *Utah Historical Quarterly* 67, no. 4 (Fall 1999): 309–30.

Van Kirk, Sylvia. *Many Tender Ties: Women in Fur Trade Society in Western Canada, 1670–1870.* Norman: University of Oklahoma Press, 1980.

VanDerBeets, Richard. *The Indian Captivity Narrative: An American Genre.* Lanham, Md.: University Press of America, 1984.

Vattel, Emmerich de. *The Law of Nations; or, Principles of the Law of Nature, Applied to the Conduct and Affairs of Nations and Sovereigns.* Northampton, Mass.: Simeon Butler, 1820.

Victor, Frances Fuller. *The River of the West: Life and Adventure in the Rocky Mountains and Oregon.* Hartford, Conn.: R. W. Bliss and Co., 1870. Reprinted as *The River of the West: The Adventures of Joe Meek.* Edited by Win Blevins. 2 vols. Missoula, Mont.: Mountain Press, 1984.

Volpe, Vernon L. "The Origins of the Fremont Expeditions: John J. Abert and the Scientific Exploration of the Trans-Mississippi West." *Historian* (Winter 2000): 245–63.

Vrooman, Nicholas C. P. "The Métis Red River Cart." *Journal of the West* 42, no. 2 (Spring 2003): 8–20.

Wagner, Henry R., and Charles L. Camp. *The Plains and the Rockies: A Bibliography of Original Narratives of Travel and Adventure, 1800–1865.* Third edition. Columbus, Ohio: Long's College Book Company, 1953.

Walker, Danny N., ed. *Searching for Fort William: An 1834 Trading Post at Fort Laramie National Historic Site, Wyoming.* Laramie: Wyoming State Archaeologist Office and the Department of Anthropology, University of Wyoming, 2004.

Walker, Margaret F. "'All the Fantastic Costumes': Rags on the Way to Riches (And No Skirting Around the Issue of Who Really Wore the Pants!)." *Overland Journal* 15, no. 4 (Winter 1997–1998): 12–18.

Watkins, Albert. "Notes of the Early History of the Nebraska Country [Extracts from the *Missouri Republican* and Other Newspapers, 1807–1860]." *Publications of the Nebraska State Historical Society* 20 (1922): 1–379.

West, Elliott. *The Way to the West: Essays on the Central Plains.* Albuquerque: University of New Mexico Press, 1995.

———. *The Contested Plains: Indians, Goldseekers and the Rush to Colorado.* Lawrence: University of Kansas Press, 1998.

———. "American Pathways: An Exploration of Trails and the American Imagination." *Montana: The Magazine of Western History* 51, no. 3 (Autumn 2001): 20–31.

White, David A., ed. *News of the Plains and the Rockies, 1803–1865,* 8 vols. Spokane, Wash.: Arthur H. Clark, 1996–2001.

———. *Plains and Rockies, 1800–1865: One Hundred Twenty Proposed Additions to the Wagner-Camp and Becker Bibliography of Travel and Adventure in the American West, With 33 Selected Reprints.* Spokane, Wash.: Arthur H. Clark, 2001.

White, Richard. *It's Your Misfortune and None of My Own: A New History of the American West.* Norman: University of Oklahoma Press, 1991.

Whiteley, Lee. "The Trappers Trail: 'The Road to Fort Laramie's Back Door." *Overland Journal,* 16, no. 4 (Winter 1998–99): 2–16.

Wilkes, Charles. *Narrative of the United States Exploring Expedition during the Years 1838, 1839, 1840, 1841, 1842.* Philadelphia: Lea and Blanchard, 1845. Reprinted as *Life in Oregon Country before the Emigration by Charles Wilkes.* Edited by Richard E. Moore. Ashland: Oregon Book Society, 1974–1975.

Williams, Jacqueline B. *Wagon Wheel Kitchens: Food on the Oregon Trail.* Lawrence: University Press of Kansas, 1993.

Worsham, James. "Jefferson Looks Westward: President Secretly Sought Funds from Congress to Explore Louisiana Territory, Develop Trade." *Prologue* 34, no. 4 (Winter 2002): 254–59.

Zollinger, James Peter. *Sutter: The Man and His Empire.* New York: Oxford University Press, 1939.

Maps

Berry, Robert, ed., and James A. Bier, cartographer. "Western Emigrant Trails, 1830–1870." Second edition. Independence: Oregon-California Trails Association, 1993.

Carroll, Allen, Chief Cartographer, National Geographic Society. "Western Migration: Dreams of Gold and a Better Life Drive Mass Movement, 1841–1869." Washington, D.C.: National Geographic Society, September 2000.

Franzwa, Gregory M. *Maps of the Oregon Trail.* Saint Louis: Patrice Press, 1982. Third edition, 1990.

———. *Maps of the Santa Fe Trail.* Saint Louis: Patrice Press, 1989.

———. "Covered Wagon Roads to the American West." Tucson, Ariz.: Patrice Press, 1998.

———. *Maps of the California Trail.* Tucson, Ariz.: Patrice Press, 1999.

Spence, Mary Lee, and Donald Jackson, eds. Map Portfolio, for *The Expeditions of John Charles Frémont.* Chicago: University of Illinois Press, 1970.

Wheat, Carl I. *Mapping the Transmississippi West,* 5 vols. San Francisco: The Grabhorn Press [vol. 1], and The Institute of Historical Cartography, 1957–1963.

INDEX

References to illustrations are in italic type.

Abbey, James, 153, 285

Aberdeen, George Gordon, 288, 290

Abert, John J., 118, 197, 226

Absaroka Indians (Crows), 3, 18, 28, 29, 32, 51, 91, 96, 224, 340, 345, 348, 349

Ackley, Mary Medley, 153

African Americans, 17, 172, 193, 225, 314, 333–36, 345, 385

Alaska, 17, 68, 70, 114, 206, 217, 288

Alcohol, 19–21, 52, 130, 264, 340

Alcove Springs, Kans., 129, 272

Alder Creek, 320

Allen, Ezra H., 383

Alta California, 43, 68, 69, 100, 180, 204, 208, 227, 245, 253, 292, 316, 371

Alvarado, Juan Bautista, 207

American Board of Commissioners for Foreign Missions (ABCFM), 61, 62, 187, 399

American Falls, 13, 103, 150, 332

American Fur Company, 10, 48, 79, 82, 83n17, 94, 145, 185, 216n2, 281n124, 337–38

American Indians. *See* Indian peoples

American River, 53n24, 207, 225, 248, 360, 373, 401, 404

American Southwest, 122n12, 275, 287, 382, 401

Anderson, Alex, 127

Anderson, Kirk, 150

Anderson, William, 374, 378–79

Anderson, William Marshall, 338

Angel, James Newton, 121, 149, 260

Animal doctoring, 273–74

Antelope, 8, 31, 34, 35, 91, 177, 240, 271, 298, 351

Antelope Spring, 298

Appalachian Mountains, 24, 45, 70, 120, 121

Applegate, Charles, 194

Applegate, Jesse, 193–95, 197, 201, 257, 262, 271, 295–99, 301–304, 309, 319, 370, 400

Applegate, Jesse A., 177

Applegate, Lindsay, 194, 296, 298, 351

Applegate, O. C., 297n15

Applegate Trail, 296, 303, 304n51, 385

Aram, Joseph, 40n74, 308

Arapaho Indians, 18, 29, 31, 91, 199, 338, 341

Archambault, Auguste, 73

Arkansas, 25, 128, 172, 268, 293

Arkansas River, 6, 9, 30, 47, 175, 190, 227, 245, 388

Arthur, David, 126

Ash Hollow, Neb., 9, 92, 93, 276, 388, 392n147

Ashley, William, 50–53, 103

Assiniboine River, 113

Astor, John Jacob, 48, 73, 332, 338

Astoria, Ore., 19, 48, 50, 73, 275; Astorians, 49, 224, 332, 333

Atkinson, Henry M., 174–75

Atkinson, Lydia B., 330

Avenue of Rocks. *See* Devils Backbone

Ayres, Miles, and daughters, 212

Ayres Natural Bridge, 10

Bacon, J. M., 237

Baker, James, 340

Baldridge, William, 205

Ball, John, 9, 29, 54, 58, 72, 81, 93, 262n30, 333

Bancroft, George, 217, 227, 253, 255, 289